A WORLD HISTORY OF RAILWAY CULTURES, 1830–1930

A WORLD HISTORY OF RAILWAY CULTURES, 1830–1930

Edited by
Matthew Esposito

Volume II
The British Empire

Routledge
Taylor & Francis Group

LONDON AND NEW YORK

First published 2020
by Routledge
2 Park Square, Milton Park, Abingdon, Oxon OX14 4RN

and by Routledge
52 Vanderbilt Avenue, New York, NY 10017

Routledge is an imprint of the Taylor & Francis Group, an informa business

British Library Cataloguing-in-Publication Data
A catalogue record for this book is available from the British Library

Library of Congress Cataloging-in-Publication Data
A catalog record for this book has been requested

ISBN: 978-0-8153-7722-1 (set)
eISBN: 978-1-351-21184-0 (set)
ISBN: 978-0-8153-7752-8 (Volume II)
eISBN: 978-1-351-21176-5 (Volume II)

Typeset in Times New Roman
by Apex CoVantage, LLC

Publisher's Note
References within each chapter are as they appear in the original complete work

CONTENTS

VOLUME II   The British Empire   **1**

   All the world is India; India is a world apart   3

PART 1
Mobility and mutability   **53**

1 Amelia Cary, *Chow-Chow*, 2 vols. (London: Hurst and
  Blackett, 1857), I, pp. 46–50   55

2 Robert Bowne Minturn, *From New York to Delhi*,
  Second ed. (New York: D. Appleton, 1858), pp. 6,
  122–126   57

3 Bholanauth Chunder, *The Travels of a Hindoo to Various
  Parts of Bengal and Upper India* (London: N. Trubner,
  1869), I, pp. 139–141, 149–150, 162–173, 326–327,
  332–333, 348, 433 II: 130–131   61

4 'Modes of Travelling in India', *Illustrated London News*,
  September 19, 1863, 284   72

5 Sidney Laman Blanchard, *The Ganges and the Seine*, 2
  vols. (London: Chapman and Gall, 1862), II, pp. 6–13   73

6 William Howard Russell, *My Diary in India in the Year
  1858–1859*, 2 vols. (London: Routledge, 1860), I,
  pp. 154–162, II, pp. 407–409   77

7 G. O. Trevelyan, *The Competition Wallah*, Second ed.
  (London: Macmillan, 1866), pp. 21–30   81

CONTENTS

8 Mary Carpenter, *Six Months in India*, 2 vols. (London: Longmans, Green, 1868), I, pp. 27–31, 227–228, 234–235, 238–239 86

9 John Matheson, *England to Delhi: A Narrative of Indian Travel* (London: Longmans, Green, and Co., 1870), pp. 278–286, 347–348, 509–510 91

PART 2
Modernity and the masses **97**

10 Jules Verne, *Around the World in Eighty Days*, trans. George M. Towle (Philadelphia: Porter & Coates, 1873), pp. 55–56, 60–62, 70–78 99

11 C. F. Gordon Cumming, *In the Himalayas and on the Indian Plains* (London: Chatto & Windus, 1884), pp. 44–47, 76, 266–268, 274–277, 593–594 105

12 James Hingston, *The Australian Abroad: Branches from the Main Routes Round the World*, 2 vols. (London: S. Low, Marston, Searle, and Rivington, 1879), pp. 98–101, 163–164, 200–203, 209–210 114

13 W. S. Caine, *A Trip Round the World in 1887–8* (London: G. Routledge & Sons, 1888), pp. 264–269, 273–276 120

14 Annie Brassey, *The Last Voyage: 1887* (London: Longmans, Green, 1889), pp. 99–102, 104–105 124

15 Mrs. Brassey, *Around the World in the Yacht "Sunbeam": Our Home on the Ocean for Eleven Months* (New York: H. Holt, 1889), pp. 398–399 127

16 C. F. Gordon Cumming, *Two Happy Years in Ceylon*, 2 vols. (London: Blackwood and Sons, 1892), I, pp. 155–159, 1716, II, pp. 27–29, 184–186, 238–239 129

17 Flora Annie Steel, 'In the Permanent Way', *In the Permanent Way and Other Stories* (London: William Heinemann, 1898), pp. 27–42 135

PART 3
Kipling's railway kingdom   **145**

18 Rudyard Kipling, 'An Escape Northwards', in *Out of
    India: Things I Saw and Failed to See in Certain Days
    and Nights at Jeypore and Elsewhere* (New York: G. W.
    Dillingham, 1895), pp. 116–119   147

19 Rudyard Kipling, 'Namgay Doola', from *Mine Own
    People*, in *Works*, 15 vols. (New York: Lovell, n.d.),
    I, pp. 31–37   150

20 Rudyard Kipling, 'The Man Who Would Be King', in
    Works, 15 vols. (New York: Lovell, 1899), V, pp. 92–99   153

21 Rudyard Kipling, 'Letters of Marque', in *Works*, 15 vols.
    (New York: Lovell, 1899), XII, pp. 5–9   157

22 Rudyard Kipling, 'Among the Railway Folk', in *Works*,
    15 vols. (New York: Lovell, 1899), VII, pp. 65–93   160

PART 4
Anglo-Indian junctions   **173**

23 Rabindranath Tagore, 'A Journey with My Father', in
    My Reminiscences (London: Macmillan, 1917),
    pp. 77–81, 86–87   175

24 Fanny Bullock Workman and William Hunter Workman,
    *Through Town and Jungle: Fourteen Thousand Miles
    A-Wheel among the Temples and People of the Indian
    Plain* (London: T. F. Unwin, 1904), pp. 6, 48, 63–64, 66,
    102, 204–207, 226   178

25 Walter Del Mar, *The Romantic East: Burma, Assam, &
    Kashmir* (London: A. and C. Black, 1906), pp. 106–110   186

26 Robert Maitland Brereton, *Reminiscences of an Old
    English Civil Engineer, 1858–1908* (Portland, Ore.:
    Irwin-Hodson, 1908), pp. 11–16   188

27 C. O. Burge, *The Adventures of a Civil Engineer: Fifty
    Years on Five Continents* (London: Alston Rivers, 1909),
    pp. 73–74, 98–101   193

28 Frank A. Swettenham, *The Real Malay: Pen Pictures*,
Second ed. (London: John Lane, 1907), pp. 37–42   196

29 Malcolm Watson, *The Prevention of Malaria in the
Federated Malay States*, Preface by Ronald Ross
(Liverpool: Liverpool School of Tropical Medicine, 1911),
pp. 111, 121, 134   199

**PART 5
Colonial railways: third-class passengers, famine,
and the drain**   **203**

30 John L. Stoddard, *Lectures*, Ten vols. (Boston: Balch,
1899), IV, India, pp. 23–24   205

31 Mahatma Gandhi, *Third-Class in Indian Railways*
(Lahore: Gandhi Publications League, 1917), pp. 3–7   207

32 'Third-Class Passenger Complaints and Indian Pilgrims',
from East India Railway Committee, 1920–21. *Report
of the Committee Appointed by the Secretary of State for
India to Enquire into the Administration and Working of
Indian Railways*. Vol. I. (London: His Majesty's Stationary
Office for the India Office, n. d.), pp. 54–55   210

33 M. Gandhi, 'The Question of Real Convenience', *Young
India* 2, 8, February 25, 1920, pp. 1–2   213

34 'Treatment of Indians Abroad', *Young India* 2, 44,
November 3, 1920, 7   215

35 M. Gandhi, 'Carping Criticism', *Young India* 3, 19, May
11, 1921, 146   218

36 Sir Richard Temple, 'The Bengal Famine (1874)', in *The
Story of My Life*, 2 vols. (London: Cassell, 1896), I,
pp. 229–248   219

37 Vaughan Nash, *The Great Famine and Its Causes* (London:
Longmans, Green, 1900), pp. 12–13, 102–104, 110–114,
144–152, 163–165, 175–182, 229   228

38 Romesh Chunder Dutt, *Open Letters to Lord Curzon on
Famine and Land Assessments in India* (London: K. Paul,
Trench, Trübner, 1900), pp. 124–125, 305, 314–315   238

39 Dadabhai Naoroji, *Poverty and Un-British Rule in India*
    (London: S. Sonnenschein & Co., 1901), pp. 193–196,
    227–229   241

PART 6
Railways and the spread of epidemic disease   **247**

40 R. Senior White, 'Studies in Malaria as it Affects
    Railways', Railway Board Technical Paper 258 (Part
    I), (Reprint), *Indian Medical Gazette*, LXII (Calcutta:
    Government of India, 1928), 55–59   249

41 J. A. Sinton, 'The Effects of Malaria on Railways',
    Records of the Malaria Survey of India 5, 4 (December
    1935), 471–476   257

42 R. Nathan, *The Plague in India, 1896, 1897*, 4 vols.
    (Simla: Government Central Printing Office, 1898), I,
    pp. 291–297   262

43 James Knighton Condon, 'Railway Inspection', *The
    Bombay Plague, Being a History of the Progress of Plague
    in the Bombay Presidency from September 1896 to June
    1899* (Bombay: Education Society, 1900), pp. 141–146   268

PART 7
Railways and crime   **273**

44 L. F. Morshead, *Report on the Police Administration in
    the Bengal Presidency* (Calcutta: Bengal Secretariat Book
    Depot, 1907), pp. 36–38   275

45 S. T. Hollins, *The Criminal Tribes of the United Provinces*
    (Allahabad: Government Press, 1914), pp. 2–5, 90–94,
    109–110, 115–117   279

46 M. Pauparao Naidu, *The History of Railway Thieves with
    Illustrations & Hints on Detection*, Fourth ed. (Madras:
    Higginbothams, 1915), pp. 4–19   288

47 *Report of the Railway Police Committee, 1921* (Simla:
    Government Monotype Press, 1921), pp. 2–5   296

48 *Abstract of Evidence Recorded by the Railway Police Committee, 1921* (Calcutta: Superintendent Government Printing, 1921), pp. i–iv, 1–8 301

PART 8
The railway as oasis: Egypt, the Near East, and the Middle East
321

49 Isabella F. Romer, *A Pilgrimage to the Temples and Tombs of Egypt, Nubia, and Palestine in 1845–6*, 2 vols. (London: R. Bentley, 1846), pp. 98 100 323

50 James Hingston, *The Australian Abroad on Branches from the Main Routes Round the World* (Melbourne: W. Inglis, 1885), p. 348 325

51 C. F. Gordon Cumming, *Via Cornwall to Egypt* (London: Chatto & Windus, 1885), pp. 102–104 327

52 Hadji Khan (Gazanfar Ali), Armin Vamberry and Wilfrid Sparroy, *With the Pilgrims to Mecca* (London: J. Lane, 1905), pp. 83–84, 87 329

53 Norma Lorimer, *By the Waters of Egypt* (London: Methuen, 1909), pp. 1–3, 425–427 331

54 E. L. Butcher, *Egypt as We Know It* (London: Mills & Bonn, 1911), pp. 6–16, 22–23, 153–155 335

55 E. L. Butcher, *Things Seen in Egypt* (London: Seeley, Service and Co., 1914), pp. 177–178. 341

56 Francis E. Clark and Harriet E. Clark, *Our Journey around the World* (Hartford, Conn.: A. D. Worthington, 1896), pp. 377–380, 383–389 342

57 Louisa Jebb Wilkins, *By Desert Ways to Baghdad* (London: T. Nelson & Sons, [1912]), pp. 55–87 348

PART 9
Railways and the re-partitioning of British Africa
361

58 Thomas Joseph Willans, *The Abyssinian Railway* (London: 1870), pp. 163–176 363

59 Rudyard Kipling, *The Light that Failed*, in *Works*, 15 vols.
    (New York: Lovell, 1899), III, pp. 296–303   376

60 Annie Brassey, *The Last Voyage: 1887* (London:
    Longmans, Green, 1889), pp. 435–437   380

61 Frank Vincent, *Actual Africa; or, The Coming Continent*
    (New York: D. Appleton & Co., 1895), pp. 208–210,
    295–296, 298–306, 312–314, 376–379, 414–415, 419–428   382

62 Henry M. Stanley, *Through South Africa* (London:
    Sampson Low, Marston, 1898), pp. 4–19, 22–23, 76–79   405

63 Joseph Conrad, 'Heart of Darkness', in *Youth, and Two
    Other Stories* (New York: McClure, Phillips & Co., 1903),
    pp. 71–80. Originally published in *Blackwoods Magazine*
    165, 1,000–1,002 (February, March, and April 1899),
    193–220, 479–502, 634–657   414

64 'Lions', *The Spectator*, March 3, 1900, pp. 307–308   420

65 J. H. Patterson, *The Man-Eaters of Tsavo and Other East
    African Adventures* (London: Macmillan and Co., 1910),
    pp. 61–74   424

66 C. O. Burge, *The Adventures of a Civil Engineer: Fifty
    Years on Five Continents* (London: Alston Rivers, 1909),
    pp. 154–155   429

67 Charlotte Mansfield, *Via Rhodesia: A Journey through
    Southern Africa* (London: S. Paul, 1911), pp. 161–168   430

68 John R. Raphael, *Through Unknown Nigeria* (London:
    T. W. Laurie, 1914), pp. 43–53, 130–138   433

PART 10
Australiana and Aborigines: possession and dispossession

                                                             443

69 Samuel Calvert, Engraving, 'Skipton Jacky Jacky and His
    Tribe at the Opening of the Beaufort Railway', September
    7, 1874   445

70 *Eastern Excursionists. The Early Morning Train at
    Spencer Street Station* (Melbourne, Victoria), May 4, 1881   446

CONTENTS

71 James Hingston, *The Australian Abroad on Branches from the Main Routes Round the World* (Melbourne: W. Inglis, 1885), pp. viii–ix, 151–153 ... 447

72 Hume Nisbet, *A Colonial Tramp: Travels and Adventures in Australia and New Zealand*, 2 vols. (London: Ward & Downey, 1891), pp. 166–172, 233–234, 274–276 ... 453

73 May Vivienne, *Sunny South Australia* (Adelaide, Australia: Husse & Gillingham, 1908), pp. 299, 301, 303, 305–312, 314, 316–318 ... 458

74 May Vivienne, *Travels in Western Australia*, Second ed. (London: W. Heinemann, 1902), pp. 325–326, 329–330 ... 464

75 Robert Watson, *Queensland Transcontinental Railway. Field Notes and Reports* (Melbourne: W. H. Williams, 1883), pp. 85–86 ... 467

76 Mark Twain, *More Tramps Abroad*, Third ed. (London: Chatto & Windus, 1898), pp. 201–206 ... 470

77 Annie Brassey, *The Last Voyage: 1887* (London: Longmans, Green, 1889), pp. 233–239 ... 475

78 Julius M. Price, *The Land of Gold* (London: S. Low, Marston & Company, 1896), pp. 15–21, 23–24 ... 479

79 Albert Frederick Calvert, *My Fourth Tour in Western Australia* (London: W. Heinemann, 1897), pp. 4, 6, 8 ... 483

80 Daisy Bates, *The Passing of the Aborigines: A Lifetime Spent among the Natives of Australia* (London: John Murray, 1938), pp. 163–164, 168–171, 190–192, 194–195, 207–208 ... 486

81 Anthony Trollope, *Australia and New Zealand* (Leipzig: B. Tauchnitz, 1873), pp. 210–213, 222–224 ... 493

Volume II

THE BRITISH EMPIRE

ALL THE WORLD IS INDIA; INDIA IS A WORLD APART

> There are railways everywhere, through prairies, beneath moun-
> tains, over chasms, across seas, under rivers, and in strange lands
> that seemed very unlikely a few years ago to be dominated by steel
> rail and locomotive. The Chinaman runs, with his pigtail flying, to
> catch the train; the Maori, who once fought the English settler in
> New Zealand defile, now puts his knobstick peacefully under his
> arm, and takes a third-class ticket like a Christian. The American
> Indian does not go so frequently on the trail after scalps. He finds
> it easier to journey by train, and scarcely misses the savagery and
> poetry of his old life, with its hideous yell and crash of tomahawk,
> with its howl of wild beast, and rustle of grass, and whisper of wind
> in the forest. The Sepoy has become a railway passenger; so has
> the Kaffir; and in a few years the strange tribes in Central Africa
> may be clamouring for thicker sun-shades to their railway carriage
> windows, and grumbling at the fines for smoking in non-smoking
> compartments or at the heavy railway rates for the transit of goods
> to and from Mombasa, or along other lines in the interior.
>
> John Pendleton, *Our Railways* (1894), 99–100.

John Pendleton stereotyped non-western peoples by focusing on the detailed physical characteristics (pig-tails), practices (scalping), and artifacts (knobsticks, tomahawks) that orientalized them, rendering them backward, savage, and exotic. Pendleton spared the Sepoys, Kaffirs, and Central Africans from similar caricatures to clarify his main assertion that British railways had begun the process of civilizing the brutish masses in India and Africa. Like so many Europeans and Americans of his day, Pendleton believed that railways universalized the world's cultures, but they were wrong. Like mirrors, railways directly reflected the diverse cultures they served.[1]

India proved the rule, not the exception. From 1853 to 1930, British India experimented with ten different methods to build and manage its railways, reflecting every approach ever tried worldwide, not just in Great Britain. Nalinaksha

Sanyal distinguished these models by ownership and management style in *The Development of Indian Railways* (1930). Railway historian Ian J. Kerr classified Sanyal's categories as: 1) state-owned lines worked by private companies; 2) state-owned and state-worked lines; 3) lines owned and worked by private companies guaranteed under old contracts; 4) lines owned and worked by private companies guaranteed under new contracts; 5) district board lines; 6) assisted companies lines; 7) native state lines worked by private companies but owned by the native state; 8) native state lines worked by state railway agency; 9) lines owned and worked by native states; and, 10) lines in French or Portuguese India. In 1902 alone, no less than thirty-three administrations (twenty-four private companies, four government agencies, and five princely states) operated railways in the Indian subcontinent.[2] Despite this variety, what started as a colonial railway system has been consolidated into the single largest national network in the world under one manager, the government-operated Indian Railways, which today oversees 38,000 route miles.

The rationale for undertaking the largest colonial infrastructure project in world history changed over the course of the nineteenth century.[3] From 1785–1850, British canal and roadbuilding projects improved communications along the major rivers. Warren Hastings' rehabilitation of the Grand Trunk Road, 30,000 miles of newly constructed roads, and massive canal excavations complemented the riverine subcontinent.[4] Lancashire merchants, who expressed unease with their reliance on cotton production in the slave south of the United States, viewed India as a limitless resource of raw cotton and cheap labor. After the growth of steamship lines, they asserted that the new railway from Bombay to the cotton districts of the Deccan were mere extensions of the L&M Railway. In the decade following the worldwide cotton shortage in 1846, Manchester and Glasgow textile producers pressured the East India Company, Parliament, and the Secretary of State for India to construct a rail system.[5] The subcontinent captivated other investors who sought to profit from the unequal exchange of India's natural resources for British manufactured goods. British merchants asserted their comparative advantage over Indian manufacturing and advocated for India's conversion into an agricultural producer of cash crops for the world market. Cheap machine-made British textiles soon displaced small handicraft producers in the Indian textile market. Virtually every agricultural and pre-industrial good underwent the same process. Wool, silk, hides, dyes, rice, wheat, sugar, oil seeds, tea, opium, and jute all left Calcutta, Bombay, Karachi, and Madras for English ports in exchange for cheaply produced industrial products. The Government of India (GOI or *Raj*) either deindustrialized native sectors or never supported them in the first place. Railway expansion greatly impacted traditional modes of transport and altered the relationships among village artisans, old cart routes, and traditional trade marts. After the 1857 Mutiny, the primary motive for building an efficient railway system shifted to the rapid movement of soldiers from cantonments and capitals to areas of rebel activity. Famine relief was a predominant concern of the 1870s and 1880s, as subsistence crises exposed deficiencies in transportation networks. Although the main justification for rapid railway development changed over time, freight receipts rarely surpassed revenue derived from the massive number of tickets sold to railway passengers in India.[6]

The finance and construction of India's railways were both exemplary of global developments and a world apart from them. One way they differed was that the GOI guaranteed private companies 5 percent interest on total capital spent to build eight main railways: the Great Indian Peninsula; East Indian; Madras; Bombay, Baroda and Central India; Sind, Punjab, and Delhi; South India; Eastern Bengal; and Oudh and Rohilkand. Since only the East Indian Railway (EIR) earned enough revenue to pay dividends annually, the "guarantee" obligated the colonial government to pay off deficits and issue 5 percent guarantees to the remaining companies. Economic historian Daniel Thorner estimated that Indian taxpayers absorbed £50 million in guaranteed interest in the first thirty years of railway construction.[7] Although the overall costs of India's network amounted to a reasonable £14,000–£18,000 per track mile, British firms overspent on broad-gauge lines, and parliamentary committees later accused them of wasteful spending with very little regulatory oversight. The Governor of Madras Sir Charles Trevelyan famously called railways a "gift of an elephant . . . eating us out of house and home."[8] The Government Director of Indian Railways Juland Danvers and first secretary of the India Office William Thornton testified about the lack of economy in construction and poor service record, especially for Indians. Leland Jenks reported that railways only benefited "those in a position to manipulate the new machinery of commerce."[9] The system was built faster than those in Great Britain and France but without Indian building materials or intensive development of native industry. Sanyal claimed that the influx of foreign goods drove the village artisan out of work with no alternative but to work the land.[10] This point was reinforced with telling data; the British Empire shipped 2.76 million tons of railroad building materials valued at over £15 million on 3,571 ships by 1863.[11] By the same year, British manufacturers had shipped the parts for 12,000 engines, carriages, and trucks on India's largest four lines.[12] About 91 percent of India's broad-gauge and 77 percent of its meter-gauge trains were manufactured in Great Britain. Notable individuals from vastly different backgrounds, such as Arthur Cotton, Florence Nightingale, and Vaughan Nash, even doubted that Indian railways protected against famine.[13] To get out from under the guarantee system, the colonial government tried building railways (1869–1880), but the slow pace of construction combined with the famine of 1878–1879 forced the industry back into private hands. During the second wave of construction, private companies ended the practice of telescoping the permanent way in one direction in favor of the departmental system of building multiple parts of the railways simultaneously. India built almost 25,000 route miles by 1900, which made it the fourth largest network in the world. Still, the colony paid an estimated 8.4 billion rupees or £630 million for its railway system by 1933,[14] which far exceeded the British investment of £150 to £200 million. India paid handsomely for its railway network. Indeed, it took fifty years for the railways to turn a profit.

When pioneer of India railways Rowland Macdonald Stephenson first drew up a visionary plan to cover India with iron bands, Calcutta was not only the capital, seat of government, and leading port, but the gateway to the Ganges Valley, which concentrated India's largest population.[15] Irrigation canals and trunk roads in India had always been worked by massive numbers of unskilled workers called *coolies*. Many of these unheralded laborers in India were supervised by British personnel and managers, sometimes even by British navvies themselves. Stephenson's "Report upon the Practicability and Advantages of the Introduction of Railways in British India" stated that labor was plentiful and cheap in India. From 1853 to 1900, approximately eight million South Asians participated in railway construction. Of the £14 million budgeted for the EIR's construction of 900 track miles from Calcutta to Delhi, less than £2 million went toward labor.[16] British railway companies used low labor costs as justification for not importing expensive steam shovels. Easing the burden of arduous working conditions for coolies was unimportant compared to providing them with menial, low-paying jobs. Indians needed work, so they sold their labor, and even their wives and children pitched in. They shunned tools like the wheelbarrow because it took the place of a laborer who was in need of wages.

Marx wrote that railways were the "products of human industry . . . *created by the human hand*" and "the power of knowledge, objectified." To Marx, railways represented fixed capital and the "degree to which general social knowledge has become a direct force of production."[17] European, American, and Japanese railways were all socially constituted and socially constitutive of ruling elites and permanent underclasses. Railways required enormous capitalization that necessitated alliances among power-wielders in the state and private sectors. These partnerships galvanized hegemonic ruling classes on one hand and mobile labor forces on the other to extend railway networks and other communications technologies alongside the expansion of global capital. Since governments sold or permitted railway companies land rights up to twenty-five miles on each side of the road bed or "permanent way," surveyors and construction crews were bound to encroach on the lands of rural agrarians. Traditional rural underclasses resisted the onset of railways, primarily because of the land question. Despite the use of various legal mechanisms to acquire land, governments and railway companies violated property rights, voided ancestral claims to lands, and interfered with customary access to fields and waters. Farmers and peasants objected less to the technology itself than to how railways altered the relationship between their land use and local markets. They also took exception to railways depositing navvies, coolies, soldiers, convicts, law enforcement officers, and settlers on their doorsteps. Railways that spanned great distances and conquered geographical barriers threatened rural communities that valued isolation, autonomy, and traditional lifestyles far away from cities and mainstream society. For agrarian peoples, locomotives symbolized dispossession of land, political subjugation, economic subordination, and foreign military conquest. In the end, hegemonic elites, imperial governments, and colonial bureaucracies created the conditions of what is described variously as imperialism, informal empire, indirect rule, and neocolonialism in world regions controlled by European and American capital. Whether in Asia, Africa, Latin America, or Australia railways were generally built in direct lines from commercial treaty ports to the interior, extracting raw material resources for shipment to industrial nations and delivering industrially manufactured goods inland. Private railways enriched the few, not the many.

The "railway invasions" of the nineteenth century never went uncontested. Modifying the nineteenth-century construct of "railway invasion" to the twentieth-century concept of "railway imperialism" acknowledged that incursions were always give-and-take processes resulting in successes and failures on both sides of the divide. In recent years, scholars have dispelled the myth of the tranquil countryside. Landowners, peasants, indigenous groups, and aboriginal peoples worldwide reacted to forces of historical change in countless ways hardly suggestive of rural inertia, immobility, and powerlessness. If anything, peasants living under conditions of subjugation projected still waters of tranquility, while violent undercurrents eroded structures of domination with quotidian acts of resistance. This masked equanimity accomplished with less risk what armed insurrection could not. In peripheral regions of the British Empire, peasants, indigenous groups, and farmers developed adversarial attitudes toward railways and undermined invaders with three self-defense strategies: negotiated resistance, veiled resistance, and armed insurgency.[18] Through much of this insubordination, traditional underclasses developed worldviews that equated railways with political oppression, foreign domination, and colonialism.

The great variety of the railway experience in South Asia reflected the incredible cultural diversity of the subcontinent. Railways surely shaped modern India, but nineteenth-century records show Indians reshaping railways. The peoples of pre-partition India (including Pakistan), Bangladesh, Ceylon, and Malaya expressed much the same expectations and reservations about railways as did early-nineteenth-century Britons. Once the railways were in place, however, South Asians and Southeast Asians pioneered new railway cultures based on their daily interaction with the mode of transport. The down trains of India left main terminals to new destinations, and the up trains returned richer and more distinctive than they were when they left.[19] For cultural and literary studies scholar Marian Aguiar, railways signified the contradictions in India that arose out of the uneven process of modernization: "As a product of British colonialism, the railway was inextricably linked to the history of the empire; as a tool for the anti-colonial struggle and state-sponsored space, the railway also symbolised the new national sovereignty."[20] Passengers on railways in the British colonies of Africa, the protectorates of the Middle East, and the settler colonies of Australia and New Zealand faced similar departures, but the return trips often differed. The railways of British India provide the starting point for transcultural comparisons with the United Kingdom of Volume I and the rest of the British Empire in Volume II.

Inception

Among the major themes in Indian history is the dominant role that third-class passenger railways played in unifying an independent nation. The English firms that built Indian railways in the 1850s replicated the insularity of first-class carriage space in the UK to protect upper-class passengers from the masses. The Board of Directors of the EIR predicted that poor peasants in scattered villages would never afford railway transport.[21] British authorities in India disregarded their own nation's railway history when they predicted wrongly that the poor would shun railways or that higher-caste Indians would never ride in the same carriages as the lower castes. Such caste-based discrimination originated with Hindu beliefs that individuals who committed offenses in one lifetime were reincarnated into the lower castes.[22] Caste distinctions prohibited Brahmins, for example, from eating with "untouchables," and lower-caste food preparation was considered ritually defiling to the upper castes. At first, the Hindu *rais* (gentry) indeed requested separate carriages and refreshment rooms to protect their status against the taboos of physical contact. In the late 1870s, the Australian traveler, James Hingston reported elder Brahmins building luggage barricades between themselves and the lower castes in third-class cars.[23] But they soon rode with the lower castes when only one class of carriage was available.[24] Within weeks of the railway's introduction, Indians boarded together, and caste barriers began to break down in affordable third-class trains. Inveterate travelers from the start, Bengali merchants and villagers from the *moffussil* alike adapted their customs to the new railway and vice versa. The railway journey became so habitual that parents no longer hesitated to marry their children at distant places because they could always visit by train.[25] In its first full year of service (1855), the EIR carried 790,281 passengers on the short Calcutta to Ranegungee line, yielding £25,000 in net revenue. Freight in goods and coal totaled only £14,241. From 1858–1859, the number of EIR passengers increased from over 1.1 million to nearly 1.4 million. By 1869, the EIR served sixteen million passengers and moved twelve million tons in freight.[26] This pattern repeated itself on many of India's main trunk lines. By 1903, travelers rode an average of 40.8 miles per year on trains. From 1880–1921, the annual number of passengers exploded from eighty million to 500 million, as 96 percent of all passengers rode third-class.[27]

Indian metonyms reveal processes of cultural adaptation to railways in various forms. In *Producing India*, Manu Goswami asserted that the railway itself was a conspicuous symbol of the colonial modernizing project in India. British railway companies mobilized thousands of Indian workers from Bengal, Madras, and Bombay to construct the first lines. Few flocked more enthusiastically to railway inaugurations. River boats full of prospective railway passengers from Calcutta crossed the Hooghly to Howrah, where they boarded trains destined for each new EIR station along the Ganges. They walked miles along the Great Trunk Road, crossed rivers and bridges, and even shuffled over a bridge made of boats across the Jumna to reach the railway station at Delhi.[28] In *Tracking Modernity*, Marian

Aguiar argued that the Raj envisioned railways as sites of assimilation, education, and social reform, but the compartmentalized utopia was actually porous, as writers Rudyard Kipling and Flora Annie Steele suggested. These and other literary writers used their fictional and personal narratives to negotiate colonial relationships with Indians. Colonial technologies were supposed to secularize India and transform wage laborers into capitalist subjects who followed precise train timetables like Englishmen. The ideal colonial subjects never fully materialized, but neither did Indian narratives seriously challenge British rule.[29] The nationalist economist Mahadev Ranade believed railways were an ephemeral influence on Indians compared to the fixed impact of steam-powered mills and factories.[30] The noise, stress, and chaos of modern railway stations astonished Indian travelers. The author of a Christian tract entitled "Advice to Travelers" (Yatri Vigyapan, 1876) likened the hardships of railway travel to the ordeal experienced by those who followed the path to Christ.[31]

Passengers in British India used railways in counterhegemonic ways in compensation for unrelenting colonial taxation. In utter disregard of the wishes of the modernizing and secularizing government, Hindus rode the rails on *tirthayatra*, pilgrimages to sacred sites to uphold their religious beliefs. The journeys themselves, as expressed by the poet-travel writer Bharatendra Harischandra, not only fulfilled spiritual needs but signified annual renewals of faith in the ongoing search for national identity.[32] Train carriages were never the rationalized public spaces British travelers in India expected. Women prayed, performed rituals, and otherwise considered locomotive carriages as sacred private spaces in which to demonstrate their religiosity. British travelers who described women passengers with "pots, pans, and other chattels" failed to understand that the burden was incidental to the Indian view that the train was both vehicle and the road.[33] Hence, the pots and pans fulfilled women's need to cook and feed their family in transit and carry out compulsory cultural and religious traditions on the pilgrim's road. Few foreigners appreciated the religious tenacity of Hindu women who, in essence, constructed their own space in third-class carriages without the amenities of the first- and second-class cars. What were these first-class luxury cars other than mobile Victorian living rooms pre-fitted with the bourgeois material artifice that abolished personal hardship or sacrifice? Hindi writers valued the train as vehicles to reach the shrines of the divine. In their letters to the editors of Hindi journals, they described in detailed vernacular the surrounding natural landscapes and temples of pan-Indian pilgrimage sites such as Hardwar.[34] Whereas the railways may have served as contact zones for Anglo-Indian homogenization under the colonial order, the regional Mela festivals continued to represent religious traditions that took place in national spaces. Railways played the contradictory role of preserving Indian cultural traditions in the face of the modernizing European colonial state.

From a global perspective, the complaints of British travel writers about Indian abuses and misuses of railways appear classist, as much as racist, especially when considering the invectives directed against those in the transatlantic world who should have known better. Travel writers were an irritable bunch, and some even claimed that their readers expected them to maintain airs of superiority toward their lessors. The Irish, French, and Americans were easy targets of English ridicule. Henry James despised railway travel, but he probably hated railway passengers more, especially the younger purveyors of incoherent babble in Savannah.[35] Thackeray and Isabella Bird were of like mind. George Otto Trevelyan lambasted the *sahibs* as aggressively as the Indians in *The Competition Wallah*. The behaviors he described read like subaltern hidden transcripts.[36] Trevelyan's observation that Indians haggled inappropriately for better prices on the railways is less persuasive as the complaint of a racially insensitive author than as evidence of the cultural persistence of Indians, who compelled railway companies to lower rates one bartering attempt at a time. Ultimately, this proves the mutability not of natives but of railway companies and their pricing.[37] It appears also that the hagglers considered the railway station as their bazaar and the railway authorities as persons of equal standing in terms of fair market exchange. Likewise, when Trevelyan registers his displeasure with native men "in high exhilaration, stripped to the waist, clattering, smoking hubble-bubbles, chewing betel-nut,"[38] he places the Indian within the whirlpool of western railway cultures of mostly young adult males exhibiting deviant behavior attributable to American beer and tobacco, Italian wine and cigarettes, or Russian vodka and cedar nuts.[39] Stations, platforms, and trains were often more crowded in India than anywhere else, which testified to the inadequacies of unprofitable railway companies, not Indians. Focusing on the behavior of native passengers as reported in travel writing, which police reports and annual railway reports corroborated, yields significant conclusions. The abuses of fare-dodgers, fakirs, con-men, and passengers sleeping with their feet outside windows can be interpreted as the ethnocentric rantings of travel writers, but they also come to represent assertions of local autonomy and efforts of the dispossessed to capitalize on the illicit opportunities that railways furnished.[40] John Mitchell expressed the enormous difficulties of ticket checking on the Bengal-Nagpur Railway where Indian families who spoke Bengali, Oriya, Hindi, and Telegu got separated into different overcrowded railway carriages, while a single individual representing a traveling party held all the tickets.[41] The Raj upheld the discriminatory and segregationist policies and structures of the railway companies – in essence, the British government in India promoted apartheid. This racist model was replicated in the U.S., South Africa, and elsewhere.

Beyond pilgrims, working-class Indians and peasants rode third-class for their own purposes. Millions of unskilled workers on tea estates, and even railway coolies, used the network to increase their labor mobility, find better opportunities for employment, and secure higher-paying jobs than those offered by local *zamindars* and *sahibs*.[42] *Ryots* (also *raiyat*, peasants) who lived within ten or twenty miles of a railway or canal dealt with the endless alterations to their fields' water supplies in familiar ways. They altered embankments, pilfered construction yards for building materials, and filed grievances with the district against the damming or bunding of rivers. Poaching goods at railway depots, what the French called *braconnage*, was widespread and undetectable. Individuals and merchants complained about systemic pilferage of commercial merchandise on Indian trains. These alleged "inside jobs" of railway theft is reminiscent of longstanding practices in England. At railway stations, English railway officers pilfered goods from freight cars in exactly the same way that canal bargemen did in the UK.[43] Local coal merchants complained that engine drivers in transit on the Manchester, Sheffield, and Lincolnshire Railway, for example, stole coal from the merchant's trackside wagons before its delivery without the company paying for it. The manager of the railway Edward Watkin dismissed the allegations as preposterous until one day his train happened to approach a siding where a driver was transferring huge lumps from a coal wagon to his tender. Watkin exclaimed to his crewmen, "The d—d fool, *in broad daylight!*"[44]

Pilfering followed British-built railways all over the world. In India, special commissioners that heard complaints from all parties reported on customary "abstractions" of coal and other goods on the East India Railway into the twentieth century.[45] According to Ambalal S. Desai, President of the Third Indian Industrial Conference, one stationmaster plainly admitted that all goods transshipped by his railway were subjected to his toll.[46] Railway thieves also stole whatever they could get their hands on. Clever pilferers approached grain cars, poked holes in burlap sacks, and used hollow bamboo poles to siphon grain into their containers. They deployed the same technique with different tools to siphon kerosene oil from barrels.[47] "Railway criminal tribes" organized themselves as foils against the Foucauldian disciplinary nightmare of omnipresent railway police.[48] The diffusion of state surveillance was met body for body with an ever-growing brigand population engaged in underground acts of larceny. Higher-placed railway officials also "blackmailed" merchants into paying bribes for use of extra freight cars during high times and holidays. Railway employees in perfectly good standing sought promotions to these highly coveted jobs for the "extra benefits."[49] Women and children boarded trains with heavy goods on their person, refusing to pay extra freight or baggage charges. Elderly men traveled as fake 'sadhu' holy men. Indian men defied railway stationmasters by mounting and riding on carriage roofs and dangling their feet out the windows, while women travelers performed purification rituals on the train. Local merchants complained of high rates and slow service, applying pressure to the system to lower costs. Rapid acculturation to a colonial regime ultimately produced popular benefits, because Indians developed local knowledge and modern strategies to operate within unjust systems and unfair structures. In 1921, mass protests focused on the inequities perpetuated by the railways. By the time private railways were turned over to the state, the most profitable lines had already acclimated themselves to the new realities of Indian railway cultures that had emerged from lived experiences.

Thus, British projections about the immutability and immobility of India were uniformly wrong. Predictions that conservative Indians would shun the railways for their cost and speed proved incorrect. Rates fell to three-eighths pence per mile in third-class carriages and, by 1906, the railway superintendent of the EIR

George Huddleston supported trial runs of third-class express trains: "The native of India likes to travel as fast as he can be carried."[50] British contractors and their gangers planned for labor shortages due to the mobile laborers who performed seasonal work on tea estates. They also anticipated shortfalls due to the prevalence of epidemics. Engineers even ordered one-third more materials from England to accommodate the "local pilfering tax." Aguiar discussed the strange example of alterity when the railway companies performed an about-face from the Raj's assault on Indian religion and began promoting pilgrim travel.[51] In perhaps the greatest reversal of all, the colonial industry that rarely hired Indians to top jobs employed over 1.75 million in the year 2000, making Indian Railways the largest single employer in the world. Railways once deemed "memorials of British rule" now belong to the Indian people.[52]

Egyptian railways evolved from basic iron camels to luxurious moving oases in just a half-century. They were originally very slow, always sandy, and carried few passengers and little freight. Travelers after 1900 commented on the cosmopolitanism of Egyptian railway traffic and noted unexpected scenes: "I saw a stately Arab spread out his prayer-mat close to the wall of the stationmaster's office, the one spot free from luggage, and commence his evening prayer." To Norma Lorimer it was as if he stood calmly before a mosque. "The engine shrieked," she continued, "the European passengers lost their manners and their seats in their noisy nervousness about their luggage, but that unmindful Moslem prayed on. . . . I was lost in admiration."[53] As the train began to pull away, he calmly gathered his things and boarded it effortlessly.

Railway history in British Africa suggests that Europeans did not partition Africa precisely enough to end European rivalries and native resistance. The first railway in South Africa harmlessly extended from Durban to its harbor in 1860. A trunk line out of Cape Town north to Paarland and Karoo formed the first segment of a Cape to Cairo Railway projected to run through Northern Rhodesia, the Sudan, and Egypt. Despite the African, Indian, and Chinese workforces that suffered in 120 degree heat building railways, African lines predominantly served European military and commercial interests from 1860 to 1930. *The Abyssinian Railway* (1870) by Lieutenant Thomas Joseph Willans proved this point. Willans described the international labor pool that laid tracks from the shoreline of the Red Sea into the Sudan in 1867 and 1868. Royal Engineers used a pier at Annesley Bay to unload cargo holds full of materials and coolies from India and China. A local African tribe of Shohoes leveled the ground and transported sleepers and rails to the construction site. Willans commended the Punjab Pioneer Regiment (23rd) for their auger and boring techniques, as well as the Chinese for their carrying strength and fishplating. The international workforce completed the Hadas Bridge and Zoulla station. The fall of Magdala in April sped their pace. Despite ongoing water shortages, they completed the railway to Koomyleh and the Sooroo Pass a distance of 11.25 miles in seven and a half months.

Railways in Africa caused more conflicts than prevented them. In Cape Colony, building schedules for private railways stagnated until an Act of Parliament

(1872) ceded the lines to the government, which then authorized £5 million in construction. Natal's own government line commenced four years later in 1876, linking Durban and Pietermaritzburg. The discoveries of the Kimberley diamond fields and later gold in the Transvaal boosted both British settlement and railway activity in the mid-1880s. In Dutch South Africa, British encroachment provoked the Orange Free State to forge an alliance with the South African Republic (1896) so trains could transship war material from Lourenço Marquez (Delagoa Bay) to the Transvaal. The nearly 4,300 miles of track in South Africa played integral roles in the military strategies and tactics of the Second Boer War (1899–1902). British Field Marshall Lord Roberts faced enormous difficulties moving troops and materials over the single-track narrow-gauge lines from Cape Town to the interior. Pretoria was 1,000 miles away. British soldiers suffered from crippling delays of provisions. Poor railway operations and the shortage of rolling stock delayed the outcome of the war.[54] Rehabilitated railway systems survived the war and assisted the unification of Cape Colony, the Orange Free States, Transvaal, and Natal into one South Africa (1910). In East Central Africa, the Uganda Railway spanned the 600 miles between Mombasa and Kilindini and Kavirondo Gulf on the northeastern shore of the Victoria Nyanza.[55]

British colonies in Australia generally outperformed their resources in railway construction and operation. The issue of quicker overland transportation was a huge source of frustration for colonial and Federation officials who wanted to integrate eastern and western Australia by rail only to see parochial interests prevail. Regardless of competing visions, Australian leaders rarely awaited actual settlement to expand railway systems from the coasts to the interior. Dirt roads from the eastern seashores of New South Wales were so worn that one commissioner recommended leaving standing timber in narrow highways and tearing down roadside fences to force horse-drawn drays to carve new paths instead of deepening existing ruts. In heavy rains these ruts turned into channels of running water, slowing transport and driving up the price of goods.[56] Everyday people with rising expectations demanded relief from endlessly winding cart roads, dangerous carriages, and primordial floods that threatened starvation by isolation and desolation.[57] At Berrima just eighty miles outside of Sydney, travelers on a mail coach encountered life-threatening river floods that washed away bridges, submerged carriages, horses, and drivers, and stranded the starving townsfolk. Once waters ebbed, logs were seen lying atop telegraph wires twenty-four feet in the air.[58] Railways played a definitive role in speeding Australia's transition from a loose collection of pastoral colonies to a highly urbanized and productive industrial nation. As each of the main colonies developed independently of one another, gauges, construction methods, locomotive sizes, and styles all varied, depending on factors as wide-ranging as availability of coastal and river transportation, natural terrain, demographics, freight needs, and colonial budgets. The colonies avoided wasteful spending on parallel and redundant lines, and governments rarely overbuilt railways.

13

Reception

Prior to the 1850s, British finance capital reached southeastern Australia, but the colonies yielded little profit. Australians earned speedier returns in land, mining, and the commodities trade than in long-term speculative investments in railways.[59] Steam locomotives first appeared in Melbourne as early as 1854, Sydney in 1855, and Adelaide in 1856. However, the Australian gold rush, merino wool boom, and capitalization of transoceanic shipping lines all predated railway expansion. When the imperial government disallowed the Australian colonies from granting railway companies public lands, contractors concluded that railways would not pay. Henceforth, Australia's railways were completed not by private firms but by colonial governments with English finance capital, British and Australian engineers, English and Irish navvies, and Aussie day laborers. In 1867, the two largest colonies of New South Wales (NSW) and Victoria together had fewer track miles (400) than Wisconsin or Cuba.[60]

The railway history of Victoria vividly illustrates these themes. One of Robert Stephenson's locomotives ran on the Melbourne & Hobson's Bay Railway to and from Sandridge (Port Melbourne) as early as 1854, but Victorians built most of their own trains for the rest of the century. In Victoria, the government concentrated capital on networks extending from Melbourne while centralizing skilled labor at railway yards in Newport and Braybrook Junction (Sunshine). Once built, Victoria's railways helped curb Australian brigandage, called bushranging, symbolized by the 1880 capture and public execution of thief, kidnapper, and murderer Ned Kelly.[61] Victorian Railways also started excursions to tourist destinations such as the St. Kilda baths, Ferntree Gully, and Queenscliff.[62] Patsy Adam-Smith's classic autobiography *Hear the Train Blow* described the "railway family" connected to one another despite the remoteness of rural Victoria. Her father's employment as a platelayer and fettler on the Victorian Railway blessed her with countless memories and even an adopted sister, Mick.[63] Her childhood experiences could well have taken place in Eastern Pennsylvania or Alberta.

New South Wales was the first colonial government to manage a state-owned railway within the British Empire. In 1850, city fathers briefly succumbed to the same false argument of private capitalists that railways created their own business in freight and passenger traffic. Charles Cowper formed the Sydney Railway Company to raise capital and build the first line from Sydney to Parramatta. But at a cost of £40,000 per mile, the first fourteen-mile section cost £500,000, and the line to Goulburn was projected to exceed £2.5 million. The railway turned a small profit but ran out of money to expand.[64] When the NSW government took over operations, the Governor Sir William Denison and the Public Works Department sensibly balanced the lofty aspirations of spreading rails throughout the colony with the pragmatism of its new engineer-in-chief John Whitton. The influential capitalist Sir Moreton Peto had recommended Whitton after his years of service on the Oxford, Worcester, and Wolverhampton Railway in England. In Sydney, Whitton argued against cheap horse-trams on wooden rails, advocated double lines for two-way traffic, and brought steam-locomotive railways to Goulburn and Bathurst. In addition, Whitton was among the first to condemn inhumane treatment of animals in carting heavy loads at fast rates in hot weather: "it is an act of the greatest possible cruelty to work horses at ten miles an hour in such a climate as this."[65] Tracks began to fan in every direction from Sydney, but public officials also kept Whitton's ambitions in check, overriding his preference for the broader Irish gauge (used by neighboring Victoria) in favor of cost-effective standard-gauge railways.[66] The colonial government proved responsive to its constituents, insisting that Whitton hire idle gold diggers to relieve unemployment and look the other way when locals stole railway ties for firewood. Residents along the lines complained that the sparks of passing trains set fire to their grass paddocks. Commissioner John Rae responded by ordering the fireboxes of locomotives retrofitted with wire screens to prevent flying cinders.[67] In the 1860s, navvies and store owners petitioned Parliament to investigate the NSW Railway's Tommy Shops, Sly Grog Shops, contractors, and agents for allegedly extorting railway worker earnings with expensive liquor and basic staples.[68] Tourists traversing the Blue Mountains to reach Mount Victoria complained about high prices in the shops but also marveled at Whitton's transmontane viaducts: the picturesque Zig-Zag railways at Lapstone Hill and the Lithgow Valley.

Competition for wool traffic in the southwestern Riverina accelerated railroad development in NSW. As early as 1862, the Victorian Railway had reached Echuca on the Murray River, where merchants in Melbourne and Adelaide (South Australia) diverted the NSW wool traffic through a combination of river steamer and overland transport. NSW had twice the number of sheep as Victoria, but the port at Melbourne was closer to London. Sydney capitalists and railway commissioners built railways to protect their financial interests from their Melbourne counterparts. One traveler in the region described how dozens of double-tiered railway cars were loaded with sheep from end to end in just twenty minutes.[69] Under Commissioners Rae and Charles A. Goodchap, NSW Railways rapidly galvanized into three main lines: the Great Northern, the Great Western, and the Great Southern. The former connected the Sydney network to the coal traffic of Newcastle, the middle reached Bourke on the Darling River, and the latter ran along the Murrumbidgee and linked up with Victoria and the Murray at Albury. The Southern and South-western railways diminished Victoria's leadership in the wool market and granted Sydney concerns larger shares.[70] By 1888, railway earnings constituted 38 percent of NSW revenue. In fact, railroads were the greatest source of revenue among all three eastern Australian colonies. Promotional literature at the World's Columbian Exposition in Chicago (1893), written by Australian boosters who sought European immigration and investment capital, emphasized the profitability of Australian railways.[71] The railways of NSW cost almost twice as much per track mile as those in the U.S., but they also produced twice the net earnings per mile largely due to robust goods traffic.[72] At the close of the nineteenth century, the total track miles of NSW was just 2,776.[73] The *Annual Reports of the Railway Commissioners* note incremental growth of passenger and freight tonnage on NSW lines. The number of passengers increased from 16 million (1888–1889) to 47.5 million (1908) and then 96.7 million (1917); freight tonnage, excluding livestock, rose from 3.5 million (1888–1889) to 9.7 million (1908) and then 11 million (1917).[74] Entrepreneurs in towns that railways passed through, such as Goulburn, Wagga Wagga, Orange, and Grafton, lost business to companies with greater capital in Sydney.[75]

Challenged by sparse populations and scarce capital, the other three colonies – South Australia, Queensland, and Western Australia – nevertheless took pride in their rail systems. South Australia used an efficient rail system that ran along the coasts and the Murray to export massive quantities of wheat and wool. One of its narrow-gauge lines extended over 800 miles to Oodnadetta. In 1889, engineers completed a bridge over the Hawkshury Rivor to connect Adelaide and Brisbane.[76] Since Brisbane and Ipswich were already served by river steamers, Queensland's first locomotive, the *Faugh-a-Ballagh* ("clear the road"), chugged its way from "a shallow river port to a minor village."[77] After 1865, Queenslanders relied on inexpensive "pony" railways with small steam engines and light rolling stock to satisfy the freight needs of farming communities. The Southern and Western Railway built fences to keep frightened horses and other livestock off the rails, but the fences also cut off local residents from their footpaths even when trains were not running. Railways that operated on the Sabbath "in violation of the fourth commandment" always risked the ire of Presbyterian Clergyman Charles Ogg.[78] The British company of Peto, Brassey, and Betts built Queensland's narrow-gauge lines one expensive section at a time to Bigge's Camp (Granchester) and Toowoomba. By 1871, when the 188-mile line approached £1.9 million, the pioneering chief engineer Abraham Fitzgibbons had more to worry about than fences and Sabbatarian protests. Cost overruns guaranteed latter-day economizing by Government Railway Department engineers H. T. Plews and Henry Charles Stanley. Plews offered Barry, Rourke, and Munro the Great Northern contract from Rockhampton to Westwood. To escape the worst summer temperatures, navvies toiled from dawn to mid-morning, cooled off at midday, and resumed work at 4 pm until dusk. Their sacrifices are the real legacy of this unprofitable early line. Stanley, the fiscal conservative par excellence, upheld Queensland's distinction as the only Australian colony to hire private companies to build railways. Robert Ballard extended the Great Northern to Blackwater and Emerald (called the Central Railway after 1879) with a mobile workforce that had access to cheap public housing and a moveable schoolhouse.[79] Western Australia proved the exception to private railway companies receiving public land grants. Private capitalists extended trunk lines out of Perth to Albany and Geraldton to stimulate economic development in a small colony of 30,000. Tasmania had one of the longest stretches of private railways in Australia.

Rapid expansion of the railway industry transformed Victoria, NSW, and South Australia from sheep ranches to proto-nations, while Queensland and Western Australia cobbled together permanent ways with sales of their great assets in land. Overall, Australian railways were the fastest growing industrial sector from 1861–1889, and rural expansion boosted local mining and manufacturing, as well as beef, mutton, and wheat exports. During the same period, Australia's gross domestic product (GDP) rose 390 percent from £53 million to £203 million (adjusted for inflation). The trend coincided with a healthy 3.5 percent growth rate of Australia's population from 1,156,000 to 3,022,000 (1861–1891). Intermittent recessions slowed the influx of capital, but high wool prices carried the colonies through the 1870s. From 1883–1886, Australia's four main colonies together invested more than £6 million per year in railways, and total track miles exceeded 10,500 miles by 1900.[80] By 1904, only 4.5 percent of Australian railways – 640 of 14,000 miles – were owned by private companies.[81] The picture of railways modernizing Australia could not be clearer.

Incursion

India was such a vast place that millions of people remained untouched by railways. The travel writer William Digby criticized the Raj for creating two Indias, a favored and prosperous "Anglostan" along the rails and a neglected "Hindustan" everywhere else fifty miles beyond the railway lines.[82] Ian Kerr relates a case in 1873–1874, in which a famine relief collector bemoaned that a low-caste Mushir of the Monghyr district (Bengal) lived within a few hundred paces of the railway but never profited from it.[83] In Tagore's short story *Aparachita*, a relative of the eponymous heroine never traveled by railway because he was deathly afraid of crossing the bridge. Even as late as 1930, India had one track mile for every forty-five square miles, whereas England had one for every 4.4 miles.[84]

Famines often exposed the shortcomings of India's railway networks rather than demonstrate the technological prowess to relieve them. During famines, people starved not only because of the failure of the monsoon and scarcity of food, but also as a result of the soaring prices of grain. The availability of railway transport drove up wages and food prices, but the former could never catch up with the latter.[85] Prices also rose because of the high demand for wheat exports to Great Britain. Exceptionally high costs for grain during famines hurt local ryots who no longer found cheap *rabi* (spring crops such as millet) available, because planters had all switched to more profitable wheat for export. In acute crises, grain from other provinces had to be imported into the United Provinces, Bihar, and Orissa (1878–1879). The Collector of Patna predicted that outrageous prices would remain high due to the extension of railways and canal shipping to international markets.[86] Usurious sellers took advantage of famines to inflate foodgrain prices. During the 1896–1897 famine, the Collector of Gaya (Bihar) reported that rich peasants and small landlords gambled with their stocks of foodgrain, hoarding it or otherwise withholding it from the market when prices dipped and selling surpluses in famines. If supplies dwindled or their harvests failed, they used the profits gained from famine rates to purchase grain.[87]

Railway officials in India often accused third-class passengers of riding the trains without paying for tickets. Railway reports and Indian editorials admitted to freeloading but also explained that the great impediments to ticket purchases were rushed timetables, overcrowded trains, and long ticket lines. Passengers without tickets to the next down or up train sped from platform to platform, and faced closed booking offices, impossible queues, and railway agents in no hurry to expedite sales for third-class customers who paid the lowest prices for tickets.[88] At the turn of the twentieth century, Special Commissioner for Indian Railways Thomas Robertson learned of a "very extensive system of levying unauthorized charges" among railway employees and native police on the East India Railway. For example, the police and station staff allowed ticket sales only to those who included a gratuity (bribe) while others waited indefinitely.[89] In 1921 alone, forty-five million Hindu and Muslim passengers packed train stations throughout India. In Ahmedabad, as elsewhere, third-class passengers risked being caught without a ticket just so they could join the rush to board trains before they departed.[90]

The Robertson report itemized the complaints expressed by third-class passengers all over India in 1902–1903. Primary among grievances was dangerous overcrowding of carriages, which pointed to an insufficient number of both carriages and trains. The clearest evidence of overcrowding were the hundreds of passengers who rode prostrate on luggage racks, stood in the crush of doorway platforms hanging precariously halfway outside the cars, and squatted on the steps leading up to the cars. Many young men felt perfectly comfortable riding on the roofs of carriages, but this practice was outlawed to prevent accidental deaths. More than this, travel conditions within the cars ranged from uncomfortable to abominable. Awad Harischandra directed his criticism against the companies:

> It seems that the railway company is a great enemy of Nature because anything that is connected to it, such as eating, drinking and sleeping, going to the loo and so on is a great inconvenience on the train. Perhaps it is for this reason that there is now so much disease in Hindustan.[91]

Railway administrations often deployed cattle trucks and goods wagons for pilgrims on holy days, and neither type of car had latrines, water closets, drinking water stations, or food service. When cars did have sanitary facilities they were filthy and contributed to the spread of communicable diseases like cholera and typhus.[92] In 1867, 132 passengers were found dead or dying on trains throughout British India, mostly from cholera and heat stroke.[93] British officials believed that cholera originated in India, specifically at Puri on the Bay of Bengal, caused during the pilgrimages of Rath Jatra to the temple of Jagannath.[94] In addition, railway stations lacked waiting rooms and adequate ticket offices. Passengers complained about harassment at every point of interaction with railway staff. Bribery eased the ticketing and baggage handling processes, but such exactions were illegal. In Burma, women who rode in overheated trains with their backs to the windows and arms dangling outside were systematically robbed by thieves outside along the rails who slashed at the women's arms to dislodge bracelets and other jewelry.[95] The public accused railway officials of discriminating against native Indian goods and favoring imported merchandise and exported raw materials. No progress had been made in Indianizing top-paid positions in the railway workforce.[96] Almost 20 years later, the Acworth Committee of 1920–1921 found that the railways had achieved no significant improvements since the Robertson report.[97]

A preliminary study of railway workshops tells the familiar story of colonial growth without development. The Indian Commission of 1916–1918 reported that the seventy or more working complexes that date back to the 1850s and 1860s were "the most important development of mechanical engineering in India."[98] Each employed up to 11,000 workers, primarily of Anglo-Indian and Indian descent. Indian workers generally manufactured carriages, wagons, and the components of both, as well as performed repairs on locomotives at complexes such as Jamalpur for the EIR and Lahore for the North Western Railway. The disparity between colony and seat of empire follows. Between 1865 and 1941, Indian workshops built just 700 steam locomotives, while the British produced and shipped 12,000 engines for India's rail system.[99] Arguments against the guarantee system, the "drain" of food grains, natural resources, and labor from India, and British-controlled railways by liberal economists Naoroji and Dutt seeped into the national consciousness and found an even greater critic in Mahatma Gandhi. His simple but sincere formula that the British used railways in "evil" ways to exploit India and to tighten its hold on the subcontinent resonated in the first half of the twentieth century.[100]

Racism pervaded Indian railway history. In two published essays, *Indian Home Rule* and *Third Class in Indian Railways*, Gandhi elaborated their evils based on arguments handed down from late-nineteenth-century protonationalists, such as Dadabhai Naoroji and Romesh Dutt.[101] Gandhi generated the second of these two writings from actual railway experiences while serving as an attorney in South Africa. Racial hierarchies in India persisted throughout the era of railway construction. Like the military cantonments in India, the colonies of European bungalows, gardens, and chapels set up by British railway companies relied on segregationist policies to distance European staff from the squalid villages and makeshift camps of low-paid line workers and coolies.[102] Railway trains and stations were segregated by class and caste; trains were divided into three classes, and rules prohibited Indians from standing on platforms or using sanitary facilities reserved for whites.[103] During operations, the pay structure, promotional trends, and persistence of a British and Anglo-Indian "squirearchy" all favored Europeans over native workers. David Edgerton writes:

> On the vast Indian railway network, the great majority of its senior engineers were white British. In the interwar years whites born in India became more important, as did, at lower levels, mixed-race "Anglo-Indians" or "Eurasians," of whom there were over 100,000. Into the 1930s there were still many British-born locomotive drivers among the large number of Anglo-Indian train drivers.[104]

The numerous railway strikes from 1917–1922 and 1928–1930 called attention to European and Eurasian control of high-paid supervisory positions, which appeared remarkably similar to the discriminatory caste distinctions that the railways purported to break down. When racial conflict intensified between European foremen and Indian workers, railway management and government officials interpreted the laws of industrial violence, sabotage, and personal assault broadly and ambiguously so that the colonial state could wield the instruments of state power to limit workers' rights to strike.[105] David Arnold examined the colonial government's case against workers in the sensitive political moment of the South India Railway strike of 1928. After a decade of general strikes, the Government of India classified the 1928 railway strike as one of many "unlawful and violent movements," which coincided with local political agitation and deployed the Auxiliary Force against strikers.[106] The Raj directed the district magistrates of the Madras Presidency to take precautions against inflammatory speeches or other incitements to violence. Rajnarayan Chandavarkar explained that the very definitions of "sabotage" and "physical force" were remarkably similar to what happened during work stoppages, picketing, and strikes, no longer meaning the "physical destruction of machinery," but any intent to impede or appear to intimidate the workforce. Police who perceived workers as "rough" members of the lower orders could construe any disorderly behavior as "industrial violence."[107] Railway strikes were especially egregious offenses because both the Raj and its Indian subjects regarded railways as a public utility upon which many depended. Railway workers on strikes "violated" laws that were deliberate ideological and political constructions of a colonial regime that wanted to control the workers of a caste-based railway industry.[108] During periods of social action, workers were brought up on criminal charges or suffered imprisonment without having committed any actual violence or property destruction. Hence, for railways in British India, the period under review ends with metonyms of racial discrimination (third-class railways), an apartheid-like regime of segregation that affected the railway workforce through discriminatory legal practices that infringed on the rights of Indian workers to unionize, collective bargain, and strike.

European naming traditions in white settler colonies such as the U.S., Canada, and Australia both erased and honored the indigenous cultures they pushed aside, symbolizing the physical marginalization of living native populations while memorializing dead ones. Railway planners appropriated aboriginal names for railway boom towns, stations, and geographical features to the continental interior. On September 12, 1854, *The Argus* of Melbourne inaugurated Australia's railway age with powerful sarcasm about England's willingness to steal land from Aborigines:

> There comes *Christian* England, to absorb your hunting grounds; destroy your game, inoculate you with her vices, and shew her christian spirit by dooming you to "extirpation." . . . Rejoice, you dark-skinned savage, at the advent of your kind, magnanimous, and *most Christian brother.*[109]

Aborigines joined exploration and survey teams. Records of their initial participation in the construction of railway lines remain unclear, even though "half-breeds" or "half-castes" were regularly involved in railway building. Turn-of-the-century writers insisted that Aborigines they met harbored no personal ill will against them. The Conservative journalist Richard Twopeny referred to Aborigines as educable "black fellows," instead cautioning the world against the "larrikins," a bastardized term for the rough white men "larking" the streets of Melbourne in gangs, threatening women, Chinamen, and civil society in general.[110] Another travel writer recorded his conversation with an "old native" to suggest times had changed since Pinjarrah:

> I like white fellow; he take all my land, but he make my house, and my big railway, grow big corn, big potatoes; black fellow do nothing, white fellow know everything, so white fellow do what he like – you give me sixpence?[111]

Other railway passengers throughout Australia described destitute "blacks" dressed in tattered clothing and begging at railway stations. Distant from the major cities, railway stations became oases for survival and drew desperate wayfarers of all races as the readiest source of food, water, shade, and rest. A combination of ignorance, arrogance, and repulsion blinded white observers to any shared humanity with Aborigines largely due to persistent reports of cannibalism, incest, polygamy, tribal violence, and cosmetic mutilation such as blood-letting that led to near-universal ophthalmia. In travel narratives and autobiographies, Aborigines were often depicted as beasts of nature with behavioral characteristics ranging from innocent children to scavenging dingoes.[112] In 1886, West Australia placed Aborigines under the guardianship of the government to end white settler abuses.

Despite the ragged appearance of Aborigines, many white Australians described them in positive terms and lamented the diminished status of an ancient culture rent asunder by modern society. The arrival of *waijela*, the Aborigines' pronunciation of "white fellow," forced natives into lives of prostitution, alcoholism, panhandling, and disease. Daisy Bates, the Irish-born journalist from London who worked with W. T. Stead on *Review of Reviews*, investigated the living standards of Aborigines for the *Times* (London). Bates reached Perth in 1899, lived in Western Australia and South Australia for the next thirty-six years, and spent her final sixteen years in a small white tent one mile from the Transcontinental Railway. She retired to England in 1936 at age 76 and died in 1951 at the age of 90. During her lifetime, Australian Aborigines regarded her as their *Kabbarli*, or ancestral "grandmother" from the spiritual world. She adapted to their nomadic lifestyles, studied their totems, and learned how to hunt for lizards and extract rabbits from holes in the blazing desert sands. She mothered and nursed her blind, diseased, and starving charges, providing them with sanctuary, food, and medicine. Bates wrote editorials that defended their rights in the Nullarbor Plain and Ooldea, and decried the "massive crime" perpetrated by men engaged in the railway gangs.[113]

Bates has been unfairly characterized as an anti-aboriginal racist (an obstruction-ist) and a liar.[114] Bates was nothing of the kind. Like many of her contemporaries, she undertook fieldwork as a self-trained ethnographer, and as such bestowed her records as gifts to humanity. As it turns out, her amateur empiricism, more valu-able for the Western Australian tribes than her South Australian work, contributed to the field.[115] In contrast to Christian missionizing, she used professional activism to confront the abhorrent practices of both white settlers and aboriginal tribes. She had every reason to believe the Aborigines were a dying race; this was the Australia of epidemic diseases, the Myall Creek Massacre, and the Black War of Van Dieman's Land.[116] Tasmanian Aborigines, once 20,000 strong in 1802, faced extinction by 1825, when there were just 320 left. Those that remained died at Oyster Cove in the 1860s, and the last woman, Truganina, passed in 1876. Estimates of the aboriginal population on the mainland stood at 300,000 in 1788; that figure declined to one-fifth or 60,000 in 1930. The population is still recover-ing, with 200,000 counted in 1985.[117] Bates's opinions on miscegenation and her hatred of "half-castes" offend readers today, but they reflected the prejudices of social Darwinists in the late-Victorian and Edwardian eras. Despite miscalcula-tions of the extent of aboriginal cannibalism, she aimed to administer to the health and welfare of the Australian Aborigines.[118] Her closest contemporaries were the indomitable professional nurses Florence Nightingale, Edith Cavell, and Agnes Elizabeth ("Aggie") Weston, none of whom experienced such sustained hardship, misery, and deprivation as Bates did. The "Great White Queen of the Never-Never Lands" left an unexpected legacy: her ethnographic data about aboriginal lands in Murchison and Kimberly have supported Native Title claims long after her death.[119]

Despite her reputation as an unabashed British imperialist, Bates's ambivalence toward Australian railways appears throughout *The Passing of the Aborigines*, an autobiographical account once described as "an unwitting monument to human courage and endeavor."[120] The highly respected anthropologist Isobel White cred-ited Bates for her pioneering approach:

> She adopted methods not common in anthropological research for many years to come, by going to live with the people themselves, setting up her tent amidst their huts and makeshift shelters, sitting on the ground and sharing her food with them, observing their behaviour and listen-ing to their accounts. Her successful research amongst the Southwestern Aborigines depended on her seemingly inexhaustible patience in listen-ing to the recollections of a few intelligent old people.[121]

Bates attached her own "goat car" to railways in Western Australia. Trains brought her to and from Sandstone and Perth, and transported *Bibbulmun* tribesmen she knew to the Perth carnival where, in a typical example of colonial exhibitionism, they demonstrated skills with their boomerangs and spears before appreciative audiences. The 1919 railway strike that brought supply train service to a halt caused her and her native charges awful privations, which she contrasted with the favored and pampered class of fettlers.[122] As a Justice of the Peace for South Australia, Bates persuaded a hostile tribe to suspend their rebellion and help her prepare for an official reception at Cook Siding for the Prince of Wales' tour of the transcontinental railway (July 1920). She reasoned with them that the railways would bring tobacco, food, and blankets from the English and assured those who trusted her that better days lie ahead. What ensued was pure cultural hegemony manifested in colonial performance: exhibitions of song and dance, weaving, flint-chipping, seed-grinding, spear-throwing, and wielding the bull-roarer in full corroboree paint and feathers in exchange for royal gifts and a feast. Through sandstorms and drought, the continuing service of supply trains sustained Bates's desert operations and enhanced the safe mobility of her charges. But Bates also deplored that the Perth Railway Station displaced natives from their hunting and gathering grounds and reported that a train struck and killed the blind Aborigine Woolburr. She also related stories of Fanny Balbuk, a fierce aboriginal woman, whose transgressions included walking the railway tracks just to break the fences of houses that blocked her old walkabout paths. The transcontinental railway's insatiable need for water (70,000 gallons per week) drained ancestral lands of this life sustenance, exacerbating an eight-year drought that ravaged Aborigines. She concluded that the railway accelerated the passing of the Aborigines, insisting that civilization destroyed in one century Australian natives who had survived droughts and thirst, floods and starvation for millennia.[123] Bates claimed to have spoken 185 aboriginal dialects, but her painful words in plain English echo through the centuries:

> As I dream, the red glow of those fires of fancy grows hard and cold and yellow, regular as the street-lights of a city, and the ranges beyond them are lost in the shadow – even as the last of their people.[124]

Like the Raj in India, the Australian colonies struggled to accommodate growing armies of unskilled workers. Railroad cuttings, tunneling, and embankment work employed thousands of locals and immigrants, and many shifted their attention to and from gold mines, farm labor, and line construction. In stark contrast to the major cities, there were only 310 Europeans in the Northern Territory in 1888. The following year 6,000 Chinese and Tamils began laying metal sleepers manufactured by Krupp of Germany on the railway south from Darwin (Palmerston), spanning 341 rivers and streams in just 316 miles of "Never-Never Land."[125] Many Chinese stayed after their service and formed a nascent community in Darwin, even while anti-Chinese sentiment swept through the colonies. New South Welshmen and Victorians accused coolies of immoral behavior that included gambling, thieving, and, of all things, profligate waste of water.[126] The Anglo-Indian traveler C. R. Sail described Chinese he saw in white settler colonies including Australia as "the pig-tailed heathen . . . looking unnatural and preternaturally ugly in his European clothes."[127] Elsewhere, the fluid nature of labor made for a concentrated but highly mobile white workforce that eventually professionalized and settled.

Railways played an important part in the urbanization of Australia. By 1891, two-thirds of Australia's population lived in cities and towns, prompting historian N. G. Butlin to assert: "The process of urbanisation is the central feature of Australian history, overshadowing rural economic development and creating a fundamental contrast with the economic development of other 'new' countries."[128] The inauguration of the Commonwealth brought a surge in national railway development. In 1901, two-thirds of all Australians lived in New South Wales and Victoria, with relatively small populations in Queensland (503,000), South Australia (360,000), and Western Australia (184,000).[129] During the pre-war years 1911–1914, Australia attracted 200,000 immigrants per year from Great Britain, Ireland, Germany, Italy, Greece, and Russia.

Travelers uniformly praised the working staffs of Australian railways. When a worldwide depression abruptly ended Australia's economic expansion in 1889, colonial railways proved resourceful. Rank-and-file railroad workers in NSW formed the Amalgamated Railway and Transit Service Association (ARTSA). Of 9,600 railway employees, fully 4,543 were active members of 24 branches. While unionism faltered with the Great Strike of 1890 and one of four Australians was out of work, ARTSA rebounded under the leadership of J. H. Catts. By 1914 membership stood at 16,000, representing one-third of all rail and tram workers in NSW. The largest Australian union of any kind, ARTSA resolved disputes and negotiated the introduction of Taylorism during the Great War. After an eighty-two-day general strike in 1917, union workers called "lilywhites" held out longer while "early birds" returned to work. "Loyalists" were rewarded with top positions, and strikers who once occupied senior positions either worked for them or lost their jobs. Such workplace tensions in NSW were repaired only with the formation of the Australian Railways Union.[130] Prior to 1930, the voting public generally sided with the government against striking railway workers.[131]

Not long after Federation on January 1, 1901, Australians overcame stark regionalism and linked the railway systems of southeastern and western Australia via transcontinental railway. From the earliest explorations to the squatter settlements of the late nineteenth century, Australian bushmen and explorers had probed the interior and dreamt of an overland highway across the harsh continent. Planning for expeditions through the Great Victorian Desert, explorers imported camels and their drivers from Karachi, India, in 1865. Two decades later, in the *Sydney Quarterly Magazine* (1883), Charles Davis published a description and map of a proposed diagonal railway from Sydney to Collier Bay.[132] One survey from 1901 estimated that the transcontinental railway would cost £4.4 million and result in a net loss after just five years of operation.[133]

The nation ultimately completed the "trans" through the inhospitable desert of Nullarbor (Latin for "no trees") in just five years (1912–1917). Bolstered by surplus labor from European immigration and farmers in drought-stricken South Australia, Henry Deane organized an ornate tendering process from Port Augusta.

Australia's Transcontinental Railway, or TAR (Trans-Australian Railway), connected Port Augusta and Kalgoorlie. It spanned 1,050 miles and required 3,000 men to move five million cubic yards of earth and lay 2.5 million sleepers and 140,000 tons of rail. Historian David Burke described the TAR as a "steel road through a wilderness of sandstorm, sweat, sunstroke, and strike."[134] Attacked by blowflies on a waterless limestone plateau, workers built the longest run of straight track in the world – 297 miles without a curve. The living conditions of navvies on the TAR were a step above Paleolithic. The lifestyle of "a day's work for a day's pay" was so transient that only one ganger on record, Jack Wollard, worked for the duration of its four-year construction.[135] Navvies lived in tents with no access to running water, dining areas, or sanitary facilities. They bathed once a week, and even then improvised a "half-and-half" bath with water out of a kerosene tin. They ate heartily but unhealthily – large quantities of easily attainable boiled meats, potatoes, and cabbages but rarely any fresh vegetables or fruits. The 117-degree desert heat otherwise ruined bread and meat within hours. When stocks ran low, they cooked dampers and wild turkeys in the kerosene tins. At night, when supply trains lost visibility of the work camps, they blew their whistles and entire families with hurricane lamps emerged from the dust and darkness. Crews on the supply trains claimed that they could smell the notoriously filthy 125-mile camp from miles away. Typhoid fever broke out in 1916. Neither stench nor fever kept the men from gambling away their wages on two-up in a tent hut made of bags. Traveling ministers like the Pentecostal Mission tried to teach the gospel to the men of the hessian camps.[136] Although engineers relied on intensive pick and shovel work instead of steam shovels, and depended on imported camels and native horses as much as on working trains, the TAR actually cost £6.7 million, 50 percent more than projected. The Nullarbor Plain was so devoid of water and vegetation that the Commonwealth supplied fodder for 750 horses and camels. At places like Woocalla, site of a huge ballast pit, authorities set up a state primary school for the thirty-seven children of railroad workers. Bakers, butchers, and grocers set up shop at railheads, in special coaches on sidings, and on moving trains. When supplies ran low, workers asked: "Where's the bloody tea and sugar?" And the "Tea and Sugar" supply train was born.[137] The east-west meeting point between Watson and Ooldea was so distant from civilization that only workers and their supervisors celebrated the union. Trains that left from Port Augusta or Kalgoorlie still had to travel three days and nights to cross a Western Australia as large as Europe.

Invasion

Peasants and natives associated railways with aggressive outsiders who usurped lands, conscripted laborers, prospected for minerals, worshiped different gods, and carried diseases. In South Africa, diamond and gold discoveries in the Transvaal heightened tensions between Dutch farmers and British settlers, with Africans caught in between. Even before land survey companies arrived, maps gave clues to colonial intentions. German cartographer and Boer bureaucrat Friedrich Jeppe began altering his maps from geographical surveys of the Transvaal to visual expressions of its geological riches. His six-sheet "Map of the Transvaal or S.A. Republic and Surrounding Territories," published in 1899, tempted investors and colonists by objectifying a modern landscape embedded with gold. It showed uniform delineation of lots proposed as settler farms with ready access to nearby goldfields. The maps also showed African tribal groups concentrated on reserves to the far corners.[138] Jeppe's maps played a role as significant as European guns in the systematic effort to appropriate land, mining leases, and precious minerals.[139] Plans for a railway from Delagoa Bay in Portuguese territory gained ground when Jeppe's maps plotted the Praetoria, Heidelberg, Kaap, Witwatersrand, and Zoutpansberg Goldfields. Boer President Kruger soon faced encirclement of his colony and railway competition from the British, especially Cecil Rhodes. The first and second Boer Wars were fought in part over Rhodes' plans for a Cape to Cairo railway. Natives transformed from potential miners to porters of war material overnight.

If not precious minerals, the promise of commercial agriculture brought railways and European colonists to previously isolated valleys. If native peoples already inhabited those lands, then Europeans simply converted them into plantation laborers, ranch hands, landless peasants, or even deported or exterminated them. Prior to Captain James Cook's contact with the indigenous Maori of New Zealand in 1769, populations were on the rise to an estimated 115,000–119,000. Smallpox, measles, tuberculosis, influenza, and venereal diseases ravaged native villages as old world organisms propagated by the billions and attacked the immunologically virgin society. In 1840, the year of the treaty of Waitangi, indigenous New Zealand Maoris declined to 70,000–90,000 range and British colonists increased to 2,000. In the mid-to-late 1850s, Maoris plummeted to 56,000 while whites increased to 32,000.[140] The Maori population declined to 50,000 souls when the New Zealand Settlements Act of 1863 and Native Lands Act of 1865 permitted British settlers to lease or purchase Maori lands. White settlers, who used the same derogatory word for New Zealand natives as for blacks, aborigines, and Hindis elsewhere, resented Maoris for occupying lands with commercial potential. White colonists used a Native Land Court and British regiments from the Crimea to break up Maori resistance in the Waikato War. The British confiscated newly conquered territories, and the defeated Maori adopted a strategy to refuse lease or sale of native lands to *pakeha*, their term for white settlers. The strategy of passive resistance under Te Whiti slowed the pace of land usurpation, but the pakeha New Zealander population exploded to 250,000 by 1870. Good lands were overrun by 9 million sheep, 80,000 horses, and 400,000 cattle.[141]

With the domesticated herds of the pakeha overrunning their lands, Maori leaders sought legal protections. In the late 1880s, the leading Ngati Maniapolo Chiefs Rewi and Wahanui invited the main trunk railway into the King Country as a means to put their lands before the court and define tribal boundaries. In the Rohepotae case (1888), the court found that the tribe had no claim to the land. The ruling destroyed the Maori King's anti-land-selling leagues and paved the way for railway construction. Faced with the legal decision, the Maori leased one-fifth of their holdings because they predicted the lands would be confiscated anyway. In the next decade, Maori reported the pakeha taking advantage of indebted, drunk, and inexperienced tribal members to purchase land. In 1884, the Superintendent of Wellington Province told author Walter Buller: "The Maoris are dying out and nothing can save them. Our plain duty as good compassionate colonists is to smooth their dying pillow. Then history will have nothing to reproach us with."[142] The Maori population bottomed out at 40,000 in 1890, prompting a number of observers to predict their extinction.[143] Maoris who survived to adulthood in the 1910s and 1920s felt differently than the elders about their native status. In 1924, a young man told George Pitt-Rivers:

> We have now finished with the past, there is no going back, we accepted Christianity because our old gods failed us. Henceforth we must copy the European and acquire his learning and knowledge. . . . The only thing is to learn to make things like the Pakeha.[144]

Railway invasions were primary or secondary causes of the Second Boer War, Boxer Rebellion, Manitoba rebellion, and Russo-Japanese War, all of which occurred from 1890–1910. Manifest destiny, European and Japanese imperialism, and grand plans of domination drove the Great Powers to expand their influence to the farthest reaches of the planet. The U.S. built the transcontinental railroad; Great Britain began the Cape to Cairo African railway; Germany envisioned a Berlin to Baghdad railway; Japan started its imperial railway ventures in Taiwan (Formosa), Korea, and Manchuria; and French capital financed a trans-Saharan railway and Russia's trans-Siberian line to the Pacific, solidifying the Entente. Railways helped partition Africa, China, and the Ottoman Empire. Nationalists and other colonials perceived trains as the harbingers of unavoidable conflict. When modernizing empires and nation-states were not actively depriving peasants of the advantages of railways, they used them to crush rural rebellions. In South Africa, the Boers under Commander Christian de Wet captured long stretches of British railways, planted mines that detonated trains, and dynamited track, bridges, and siding equipment to delay British regiments. Boer tactics so infuriated British leaders that they retaliated with a scorched-earth policy against Boer civilians and transported Boer women and children by train to some of the world's first concentration camps. Over 100,000 were interned, and 26,000 of them died in the horrid conditions of the camps.[145] The British also shipped Boer soldiers to prison camps in Ceylon (Sri Lanka).

Railways split British colonial societies in two but ultimately unified rather than divided the British Empire. One million people of India attended the Calcutta Exhibition in 1883, largely because the railways brought exhibitors and fairgoers from all parts of the subcontinent. The numbers included at least 50,000 women who visited the commercial bazaar of the fairgrounds. Over 2,500 exhibitors displayed 100,000 articles to "attract the attention of foreign countries to the great natural wealth of India and the opportunities for profitable trade which the country presents."[146] The exhibition's Australian organizer Jules Joubert enlisted British and Anglo-Indian publicists to ask Indian princes to subsidize railway travel for South Asian artisans willing to present their wares. Editors of the *Statesman and Friend of India* and other Bengal newspapers thought that the Calcutta event would influence the Indian masses the same way that the Crystal Palace Exhibition of 1851 positively affected the English working class:

> The native artisan of India who shall see it, will be from that hour another man. It is the subject of common remark that a native of India who has once travelled by the railway, is no longer the same man; and a railway journey to Calcutta to this Exhibition as its consummation, will revolutionise the ideas of the masses of the native workmen, who are able to come and see it.[147]

The restoration of India and China as powerful emerging economies in a multipolar world was understood by post-war economists in 1950.[148] British-financed railways had helped create a native commercial business class but one that flocked toward the nationalist movement. Railways encouraged national imaginings but not the kind intended by British imperial authorities. The history of Indian railways, however, is predominantly one of cultural adaptation and acceptance, not active resistance. India's greatest poet, Rabindranath Tagore, understood the vast influence of railways in modern India. Known to Bengalis as Rabindranath ("Lord of the Sun") and acclaimed by the rest of the world as Tagore, the poet, philosopher, and composer wrote the national anthems of India and Bangladesh as well as the poetry collection *Gitanwali* (Song Offerings) that earned him the Nobel Prize for Literature in 1913. His grandfather, the Bengali merchant Dwarkanath Tagore, had once co-founded a firm to raise capital for a prospective railway from Calcutta to Burdwan.[149] Rabindranath chose a different path, remained apolitical and ambivalent toward Indian nationalism for most of his life, and published poems, songs, and novels that won him international recognition and a knighthood from George V in 1914. Edward John Thompson, father of the eminent historian E. P. Thompson and a guest of Tagore's at the time he received notification, related the poet's initial reaction as one of sadness, for he predicted that he would never know peace again.[150] That statement proved prophetic. The Jallianwalla Bagh Massacre at Amritsar in 1919 provoked Tagore to renounce his knighthood in protest. For his part, Gandhi regarded Tagore as India's "Great Sentinel," but the utopian poet envisioned a Greater, pan-Asian, and internationalist India.[151] Tagore possessed the same spiritual and intellectual restlessness that the world's great innovators used to advance human creativity and knowledge.[152] Among Tagore's poems, "Railway Station" stands out for its explication of how a foreign institution presents itself as an organic feature of the city's landscape to serve the transcultural needs of a meaningful social space. Here, one of the world's greatest poets provided the vivid imagery of hegemony at work along the highway to modernity. Jawaharlal Nehru considered the railways to be India's lifeline and greatest national asset.[153]

The diaspora of thirty million contract workers from British India and Ceylon, many of whom accumulated experience building railways, illustrates the extent to which capitalism had achieved global hegemony alongside the growth of the British Empire. The mere existence of this labor regime in the Indian Ocean system proved India's underdevelopment as a British colony for almost a century. The Raj could not provide enough employment opportunities for the expanding population. Underemployed indentured coolies left ports at Bombay, Madras, and Calcutta in steamers destined for Ceylon, Malaya, Mauritius, the British Caribbean (Trinidad, Guyana, Jamaica), and Fiji in the Pacific. In the Federated Malay States of Selangor, Perak, and Negri Sambilan, two divisions of Ceylon pioneers – comprised of Tamils and Sinhalese alike – completed the railways from Taiping to Port Weld and Kuala Lumpur to Klang and Port Swettenham by 1889. By 1906, Malaya's meter-gauge trunks reached nearly 500 track miles with ninety-three stations, linking Kuala Lumpur with both Singapore and Malacca. The station and workshops at Kuala Lumpur ran on electricity. Daily mail trains between Kuala Lumpur and Penang took eleven hours, and an overnight mail train from Penang reached Malacca sixteen hours later. The Johore State Railway added another 120-mile branch from Penang to Singapore. Twelve or thirteen ocean steamers brought British goods to Port Swettenham every year and left with Malay exports that included in descending order of volume rice, tin, kerosene, pigs, coffee, poultry, and firewood.[154] After 1870, Indian workers were affordable replacements for emancipated slaves in the Americas. In East Africa, Indians worked on railways and plantations, as well as in mines.[155] Geography was never the primary reason why Indian contract labors migrated outside of South Asia. Since work on railways were pull-factors for the mass emigration of contract laborers, railways came to represent the global mobility of the most extensive unfree labor system since the legal death of slavery.

British Africa also advanced ahead with railways. The prolific travel diarist Frederick William Hugh Migeod, a former Colonial Civil Service officer in the Gold Coast, spent much of the early 1920s crisscrossing North and Central Africa. His books on British East and West Africa, French Equatorial Africa, and the Belgian Congo described every form of pre-modern transportation known on the continent – foremost among them travel by dugout canoes and pedestrian modes supported by porters.[156] Migeod endured an exhausting twenty-mile-per-day average for treks on foot, registering disappointment whenever circumstances hindered him from covering that distance. He left the relative safety of the coasts to explore village life in the interior. His diary entries for Dar es Salaam (Sudan), Mombasa (Kenya), West Africa (Sierra Leone), and Matadi (Congo) contained some important data, but his adventures off the beaten path in French Equatorial Africa (Gabon), parts of Nigeria, and British Cameroon impressed for their rich detail. In his earliest work, railways appeared as passing glimpses to reflect the unfinished projects of Africa: "At one place we saw a wrecked train on its side, and at another the train had fallen off the bridge down a deep ravine."[157] Even in East Africa, where Kitchener and British soldiers owned plantations along the railways, train service to the country was limited to once weekly on Sundays. Migeod grumbled that Indians overcrowded the railways in Dar es Salaam and that sparks from the engines threatened to set his bedding on fire. At Albertville Station, local women he identified as Baluba or Basonge tied their hair in tiny plaits that circled up the crown of their heads. The station rest houses at Albertville and Kabalo consisted of rooms partitioned with cardboard and topped with a great grass roof.[158] In the former German colony of Cameroon, Migeod walked and rode trains from Victoria to Yola, returned to Calabar, and later advanced up the Niger and Benue rivers to Bornu, Lake Chad, and eventually the railhead at Kano. His books read like loosely edited travel guides, for he took care to mark the transitions between footpaths, cart roads, and the routes served by modern steamers, trains, motor cars, and lorries. But Migeod meant for them to serve as travel studies that combined ethnology, philology, geography, natural history, and tribal history. He described the flora and fauna of regions, as well as the physical characteristics, languages, dialects, housing, and lifestyles of hundreds of distinct tribes. His ethnographies reveal instances of objectivity, empathy, and humanity, but they are also tainted with the racial determinism of the day, especially as they pertained to the "superior" culture of the white race over the "primitive" and "savage" black man. His painstaking records exemplified the European traveler as semi-professional anthropologist of the "dark continent." Skepticism toward modern transport vehicles eventually subsided in Africa. Indeed, a British Commander of the Carrier Corps during WWI was astonished at how quickly Africans adapted to twentieth-century technology:

> Men of tribes which had never advanced so far in civilization as to use wheeled transport, who a few years ago would have run shrieking from the sight of a train, had been steadied till they learned to pull great motor lorries out of the mud, to plod patiently along hardly stepping to one side while convoy after convoy of oxcarts, mule carts and motor vehicles grazed by them, till they hardly turned their heads at the whirr of passing aircraft.[159]

Part 1: mobility and mutability

The first section on railway cultures in the British Empire follows several wayside travelers in India. The Englishwoman Amelia Cary rode the first branch of the Great Indian Peninsular Railway (GIPR) from Byculla outside Bombay to Tannah. Cary's comments to readers epitomized several tropes on mobility and mutability. She noted the juxtaposition of the recently constructed railway station and a "handsome new Hindu temple," which she called "the work of the rulers and the ruled." Like the Viceroys of India, she predicted that science would triumph over superstition and the railway would break down caste divisions. American merchant Robert Browne Minturn journeyed aboard the East India Railway from Howrah to Raneegunge at the foothills of the Rajmahal hills. In 1856, Minturn crossed the Hooghly and completed his travels to Delhi the year before the Mutiny. He wrote about the "Guarantee" and the British regret of not completing the line prior to the rebellion. Minturn also traveled by *dak*, a horse-drawn *garhee* or wagon that writer John Matheson called a "moving couch." Along the Grand Trunk Road, Minturn complemented both the dak bungalow system and Indian cooking. The Bengali travel writer Bholanauth Chunder produced the best Indian narrative of overland travels during several excursions from 1845–1866. At the time, the people of India had adopted multiple forms of transportation, as represented in the full-page graphic composition, "Modes of Travelling in India," from *Illustrated London News* (1862). Chunder regarded the rail as the "great leveler" that broke down the walls dividing peoples of the continent. His two-volume account chronicles travel along the Ganges and Hooghly Rivers, as well as trips on the East India Railway. After the unexpected death of Lord Elgin, the Viceroy of India in 1863, Chunder attended the grand Durbar at Agra for the incoming Governor-General Sir John Lawrence, amidst thirty square miles of men, elephants, horses, camels, bullocks, and carts. He used vivid language to expound upon the positive influence of railways in India, which was the prevailing view among residents of Calcutta. National discourse like Chunder's has prompted scholars, such as Manu Goswami, to trace nationalist yearnings back past the Indian National Congress (1885) to the 1860s.

By the time Sidney Layman Blanchard boarded trains in Bengal in 1860, the EIR had stretched for hundreds of miles and implemented many improvements that added comfort for first-class passengers. The traveler mentioned a hotel, the first signs of competition for the government-run dak bungalows, and related tales of a scantily clad, hookah-smoking *baboo* who offended an English gentleman in first class. In addition, Blanchard described the transshipment from dak to train of the personal effects and baggage of an Indian passenger. The extensive inventory of household items elucidates the continuities of Indian modes of travel despite the novelty of British-built locomotives. Importantly, Blanchard stated on his way to Chandernagore that the EIR was primarily supported by third-class passengers. Much of the narrative consists of useful advice for the novice traveler; after the Mutiny, he reported that English dak passengers carried Colt revolvers, soda water, corkscrews for brandy and sherry bottles, a box of 500 Manillas, and stores of biscuits in dutiful preparation for any long sieges. Diary entries of the *Times* reporter William Howard Russell from 1858 and 1859 briefly related the events of the Mutiny at Allahabad. The Irish correspondent had spent almost two years in the Crimea, where he reported on the events of the battle of Alma, siege of Sebastopol (where he famously coined the phrase "thin red line" to describe the cordon of red uniforms worn by the British), and most famously the Charge of the Light Brigade. He criticized British India for lacking railways that may have bolstered

31

the war effort and testified about the casual violence and abuse of Indian coolies in the aftermath of Lucknow.

The sardonic and waggish narratives of William Douglas and G. O. Trevelyan contain several important hidden truths about the interactions between the popular classes and British railways. To use travel narratives as historical sources requires disciplined interpretive readings past the obvious biases of the travel authors. George Trevelyan's laconic tone suggested a self-awareness of his outsider pretensions as colonial insider in much the same way Thackeray did for Irish, English, and French railway cultures. Foreign writer Mary Carpenter left Marseilles for Egypt in September 1866 and traveled through the Suez Canal, Red Sea, and Arabian Sea on her way to Bombay and Calcutta. She claimed locals viewed the railway crossing of the Nerbudda River as sacrilege and countenanced the response of English railway engineers of halting the train halfway across the bridge, without weighing the possibility that they were ridiculing those superstitions. Instead, she interpreted the engineer's act as a necessary ritual to disabuse Indians of the notion that their gods disfavored railways. To Carpenter, the railway acted as agent of change. Her narrative yields information about the Anglo and Indian divide and underlines the hypocrisy of a missionizing imperialist who evoked Christian teachings that upheld Indians as children of the same Heavenly Father but saw no contradiction in characterizing those children as inferior, ignorant, and ragged. John Matheson wrote a more traditional account of "railway glimpses" along the EIR. These included the requisite references to the "babel of sound and confusion" at railway stations, the omnipresent "cooking pans, clothes, and bedding" carried by passengers, Indian frugality, and the picturesque scenes of rustic figures, wooded forests, and tiny dwellings visible from carriage windows. He remarked that the trip to the collieries at Raneegunge now took only five hours by train and described the railway's displacement of natives who once transported coal on barges called *dhandies*. Matheson's narrative contains hegemonic turns of phrase to mask the reality of European control of higher-paying positions: "As regards the visible staff of Indian railways it is of course mainly composed of native officials, the European element being represented only by the guard, engine-driver, and station-master." As examined earlier, this language of fictitious inclusivity of the Indian masses diverted attention from the disparities in pay and discriminatory hiring practices.

Part 2: modernity and the masses

One cannot but wonder if Jules Verne's fictional account *Around the World in Eighty Days* would have been more interesting if Phileas Fogg and Passepartout spent the remainder of their days in India: "Mosques, minarets, temples, fakirs, pagodas, tigers, snakes, elephants! I hope you will have ample time to see the sights." The novel stands as an insightful fictional travel narrative. The Frenchman Verne paid homage to the European presence in South Asia with ample references to the benign British influence over Thuggee stranglers, the French town of Chandernagore, and a Victorian time consciousness (e.g. Greenwich meridian, London time, train timetables, steamer departures, watches, haste, etc.) that could only preoccupy the white man in timeless India. Unfortunately, the traveling party abruptly ran out of railway track at the hamlet of Kholby, fifty miles from Allahabad, a circumstance mildly reminiscent of the railway's shortcomings during the Mutiny, but what better plot device to engage the services of an elephant? Animals abound in C. F. Gordon Cumming's account of the menageries of India. Among other compendiums, Gordon Cumming provides a table that compiled the numbers of persons and cattle killed by wild beasts in India as well as the numbers of wild animals killed by humans from 1875–1881. Her comprehensive travel account *In the Himalayas and on the Indian Plains* plunged readers into immersive experiences, but not without the overbearing presence of the guide's own cannonball splashes. She advised travelers to bring bedding with them wherever they went since hotels only provided rudimentary bedsteads called *charpoy* to sleep on. She noted the "incongruity" between the shabby physical appearances of pilgrims to holy shrines and the "business-like trains" they rode. To prevent missing the morning trains, families arrived at railway stations the night before, smoked tobacco, gargled "hubble bubbles," and wrapped themselves in heavy blankets to sleep on outdoor platforms and walkways. To Cumming the rows of bodies looked like "chrysalides" that stirred, shook, and came to life in the cold mornings. During the beastly summer months, stations kept coffins for passengers who died of heat exhaustion on the trains. The London-born Australian writer James Hingston contributed some of his best travel writing to the *Argus* of Melbourne. He was at his best in Asian countries where the lack of communication with natives granted him long periods of travel time to write down his impressions. *A Trip Round the World in 1887–8* was the title of W. S. Caine's popular account of travels through Great Britain's Crown Colony of Ceylon. Written at a time when Europeans disregarded trains as unfortunate infrastructural appendages of society, Caine's account nonetheless weighs their impact among the Singhalese. Reminiscent of Humboldt's writings, Caine depicts a botanical paradise – travelers aboard steamers smelled cinnamon and other spices in the air when approaching the island. Caine later intimated that the slow and uncomfortable trains spoiled the effects of paradise. Renowned author Annie Brassey detailed her travel experiences in Ceylon in more conventional form. In order to reach majestic Rambukkana and Peradeniya, her party had first to traverse the "Valley of Death" which cost so many railway workers their lives. Brassey's descriptions in *The Last Voyage* of the home-like architecture of an Indian railway carriage drew comparisons to the domestic households of Indian women.

Railways receded into the background of travel accounts from the 1890s, which focused more attention on human socioeconomic activity. Gordon Cumming revisited South Asia for a two-year residency stay in Ceylon, during which the incisive and often biting criticism of previous writings mellowed into cultural understanding. Indeed, she turned her negative comments about natives toward "disgusting" water buffaloes and honored the sacrifices of railway coolies and engineers who survived malaria, extreme environments, and brutal climates to complete the railway. She wrote, "At each [station], pretty Singhalese children offer for sale baskets of tempting fruit, and cool and refreshing young cocoa-nuts which they cut open, and hand all ready to the thirsty traveller." She mastered the railways and visited the remote stations of Trincomalee, Nuwara Elia, Uva, and Kalutara. She described the Muslim use of trains during pilgrimages to Alutgama Mosque at Bentota. Her invaluable 600-page travel narrative was a testament to the lifelong learning and wisdom that comes with longer stays in-country and endures as a useful source of information for Ceylon in the 1890s. Flora Annie Steel's poignant and sad short story about the costs of modernity, "In the Permanent Way," graces this section.

Part 3: Kipling's railway kingdom

Passages from five of Kipling's celebrated works comprise this section. Born in Bombay in 1865, Rudyard Kipling spent most of his lifetime writing poetry and novels informed by his incredible powers of observation. Like Dickens, he started in journalism for seven years before traveling and committing his thoughts to paper in various forms of expression. He is universally known for his children's books *The Jungle Book* and *Kim*, but his poetry and his famous phrase "White Man's Burden" continue to inspire and haunt incisive world readers. Even though most of his major works had been completed by 1900, Kipling won the Nobel Prize for Literature in 1907. The machined road recurred throughout his works on nineteenth-century Indian culture. It is difficult to decode his many simple railway references as those of an unabashed British imperialist and propagandist during the Great War. In the following passages, however, his characters despise, poke fun at, or patronize the Native States of India. In his short story "An Escape Northwards," Kipling adopts the voice of a travel guide in his explanation that passengers were to be sociable in order to survive the slog through the desert. Local slang aboard the English train confused those with the best intentions: "What are you for?" and "What house do you represent?" were the icebreakers heard in stations. Women in Jodhpur served as baggage carriers. Dak bungalows were intentionally made uncomfortable. Other incongruities unravel the modernity of India: crooning camels converged at railway stations, a few paces from which the pedestrian sinks ankle deep into the sand and risked sunstroke and wild pigs. The railway liberated travelers – from comfort and safety. Namgay Doola, from the short story "Mine Own People," was the red-haired subject of a ruler in one of Kipling's imaginary kingdoms. Kipling described the king's patrimony as more impressive vertically than horizontally, as it measured four square miles but held towering stands of deodar trees that he sold to the railways to earn £400 a year. The king had a prime minister, secretary of education, five-man army, a lone "elephant of state," and some gifts of sheep. But his troublesome subject, the best logger in the land, named Namgay Doola, defied the king by evading taxes. Kipling's famous novel *The Man Who Would Be King* begins on a railway train in

Central India destined for Ajmir in Rajasthan. The term "Intermediate" class was a euphemism for third-class coach, judging by Kipling's references. The writer explored the theme of long train rides as a test of one's grace, the customary sociability of experienced sojourners making the best of the situation without committing the heinous sins of silent snobbery or disdainful arrogance. The wayfaring of wandering vagabonds on the train is reminiscent of the transience of loafers, hoboes, out-of-work day laborers, railway navvies, and coolies in other world contexts. All roads led to Marwar Junction for those alienated from the world of production. In *Letters of Marque*, a tourist rode the rails to see the Taj Mahal. He left on the journey with an air of cynicism about the so-called mystique of the Taj, images of its architecture appearing everywhere, most recently at the Fine Arts Exhibition at Simla. When his carriage pivoted at just the right angle, he became completely undone by the spectacle: "It was the Ivory Gate through which dreams come . . . . the mists wrought the witchery." Appropriately for this collection, Kipling's "Among the Railway Folk" moved beyond the narrow experiences of a few Anglo-Indian travelers to examine the "English Village" in Jamalpur and the railway settlement's workshops and forge. Kipling moved from top to bottom in social class, from the 200 European families that make up Jamulpur to the 3,500 mechanics laboring in the shops and Vulcan's Forge. The ratio of British to Indian in the shops was three to eight or nine, with natives living far down the East India Railway line.

Part 4: Anglo-Indian junctions

In the period from 1900 to 1920, the British Empire united not only in the war effort against Germany and its allies but also in other efforts to solve seemingly intractable problems. This Edwardian trend encompassed the *belle époque* in Europe and Latin America, as well as the City Beautiful movement and Progressive Era in America. The positive tidings of the new century was reflected in printed materials. Rabindranath Tagore's *Aparachita* and *My Reminiscences*, while not free of conflict, illustrated the newfound confidence of Indian daughters and fathers defending themselves on railways. Tourists Fanny and William Workman mounted their bikes for a ride through an India that possessed railways but did not yet embrace the bicycle craze. The Workmans proudly admitted that the railway stations, especially those with a buffet, served as their lifelines whenever a dak bungalow was not available. In this, they imitated mobile Indians who used railway stations, waiting rooms, platforms, and lavatories in similar fashion. They stayed overnight at places like Jalarpet Junction and Salem Junction: "usually rest is disturbed by the snores of other occupants, the screeching of locomotive whistles, the rumble of trains, the harsh and discordant shouting of natives on the platform and the incoming of passengers." Their Indian servant, a Christian named Jacob, went missing for three days until they encountered him at the Tiptur railway station in Mysore "possessed of the Devil of intemperance."

The selection from Walter Del Mar, a knowledgeable railway man, centers on the problems of the Assam-Bengal Railway from Chittagong to the Brahmaputra Valley, which historically transported thousands of workers to and from tea estates. Two civil engineers provide equally insightful memoirs. Robert Maitland Brereton looked back on his fifty-year career, mostly as chief engineer of the North-Eastern division of the Great Indian Peninsular Railway. The secret to his success in remaining ahead of the construction schedule was adoption of the American system of using temporary lines to build permanent ones. Cholera epidemics and famine killed hundreds of his workers, but Brereton claimed his medical and surgical kit helped him gain their respect. The Viceroy and Duke of Edinburgh inaugurated the section Brereton built to connect Bombay and Calcutta on March 8, 1870. The subtitle of C. O. Burge's *Adventures of a Civil Engineer* says it all: *Fifty Years on Five Continents*. Burge worked for the Madras Railway company, and he recalled the hardworking native men and women excavators who worked for him. An anti-Semitic analogy detracts from the greater point that he admired Indian techniques in carpentry. The alliterative device of bullocks, bamboo, and buckets described the local method of extracting water from wells. Burge explains why Madras natives called locomotives *Ballaster Bandy* and told of a cruel practical joke his employees played on native workers.

Two British white-collar professionals, Frank Swettenham and Malcolm Watson, greatly influenced the infrastructural development of the Federated Malay States around the turn of the twentieth century. With little support from the British government or European banks, Swettenham played a critical role in establishing commercial ports and promoting railways in Klang. The behavioral characteristics that he ascribed to the different races and ethnic groups in Malaya epitomized British attitudes of white superiority over Asians. Watson was one of the five greatest Anglo physician-scientists in the Indian Medical Service and British Medical Service to identify and combat malaria prior to 1930. The other four, Ronald Ross – who discovered the cause of malaria and identified the mosquito vector – and parasitologists Gordon Covell, J. D. Bailey, J. A. Sinton, and R. Senior White all incriminated railways for producing the standing water in which mosquitos bred. This theme is pursued more rigorously in Section 6.

Part 5: colonial railways: third-class passengers, famine, and the drain

Without third-class passenger trains, the railway system in British India would have been defunct by 1900. Freight and first-class traffic alone never constituted enough business. In fact, railways did not pay for themselves, much less earn a profit, until well into the twentieth century. In this context, the poem "A Wail from India's Coral Strand" by John L. Stoddard sheds important light on western attitudes toward Indian infrastructure that the West built. In a moment of despair, Stoddard wrote the poem about Kalighat at the turn of the century: "My bones are racked by traveling/ In India's jerky way: Far better weeks in Pullman cars/

Than one night in Cathay!" In other stanzas, Stoddard reviled the Indian masses for their loincloths and naked skins, their filthy, knavish priests, the unwashed millions. He yearned for a society in which commoners wore pants and socks. The sight of human misery and wretchedness wore him down. The land's fertility seemingly had done nothing for those who lived in mud and straw huts, toiled and died. He despised their cosmetic practices and the way they raised their children. Hotel rooms were more dreadful than prison cells. Servants swarmed but performed no helpful work. He wanted to pitch his pith hat, Buddha myths, and whining beggars into the nearest trash bin. His only source of solace was the arrival of the outgoing steamer.

Gandhi believed that railways represented British dominion, and he excoriated railway administrations and employees in South Africa and India for their physical brutality, enforcing segregation and racial violence against Indian populations. In Transvaal and Pretoria, he personally suffered physical assaults at the hands of railway guards when he refused to switch carriages or move out of the way. His views appeared in several publications, including *Third-Class in Indian Railways* (1917), "Pietermaritzburg Railway Station" from his *Autobiography*, and Bengali journals such as *Young India* and *Modern Review*. The most important single essay was the former, which anticipated a decade-long struggle to improve traveling conditions for more than 95 percent of all passengers in India. Gandhi subjected himself to the very hardships he criticized, not only to gain firsthand experience of the miseries of travel but also to proscribe to "leading men" of India to do the same, complain to the officials, and advocate for change. Importantly, he also advised travelers to educate their unknowing companions about careless dirty habits as a means to improve conditions. The Secretary of State for India formed a committee on railways to investigate persistent complaints of third-class passengers, which produced the "Robertson Report," a list of grievances from the past two decades that India's railway companies never seriously addressed. Worst among the problems was the lack of safety due to overcrowded cars, which confirmed time and again that a hegemonic alliance between the Raj and railway boards of directors fatefully refused to accord railways the status of a public utility. As a "colonial" railway with "colonial" passengers, the Indian system had counterparts in the most underdeveloped areas of Asia and Africa. The issue of third-class travelers never left the pages of *Young India*, a paper Gandhi edited, and his staff continued to publish provocative news about the ongoing abuses of the railways at the expense of their loyal customers.

Famines preceded the Raj in India, but scholars have proven that their effects intensified during British rule. Failures of the monsoon led to drought and subsistence crises in Orissa (today's Odisha) in 1865–1866, Bihar (Bengal) in 1873–1874, and elsewhere such as the Deccan in 1876–1878. Orissa had no railway infrastructure to boost relief efforts. However, railways that paralleled the Ganges and dissected the arid Deccan plateau should have relieved the peoples of central and western India, who protested untimely new taxation in between famines during the riots of 1875. During the Bihar Famine of

1873–1874, Bengal lieutenant governor Sir Richard Temple averted short-term disaster by importing rice from Burma. Temple was a career bureaucrat who governed "Two Indias" for four decades. In *India in 1880*, he pointed out that British railway companies had created colonies within the colony – of English neighborhoods, churches, hospitals, schools, recreation grounds, and gardens. Notwithstanding these advances, most Indians were a drought away from perishing in famine. Temple's autobiography *The Story of My Life* chronicles the heroic efforts of a life well-lived. Featured here is the eleventh chapter entitled "The Bengal Famine," in which he detailed his "promotion" from Finance Minister to "Famine Minister," by temporarily accepting the lieutenant governorship of Bengal. Temple used military metaphors to describe an all-out offensive on the famine of 1874. He proved the effectiveness of railways in three ways: first, he transported grain, especially rice, from other provinces over existing lines to provide immediate relief for acute starvation. Second, he built a provisional railway from the Ganges north toward the Himalayas to hasten shipments to villages of people who had already confined themselves to their homes, accepting their fate. His relief staff used the improvised rails and riverboats to go from house to house in Bihar, restoring peasants to seated position, feeding them, and, if necessary, treating them for smallpox and cholera. Third, he employed peoples from stricken areas on relief works and on railway lines to help them afford the high prices of food during months of scarcity. This involved deploying famine immigrants from Bengal to perform the earthwork for Burma's Irrawaddy Valley State Railway. Vaughan Nash's influential study *The Great Famine and Its Causes* praised government relief efforts but took issue with the argument that railways prevented the worst depredations of famine. He witnessed the much larger mortality events of the 1890s in the Punjab, North-West Provinces, Central Provinces, and the smaller princely states such as Rajputana. Vaughan criticized the government and railways for discontinuing fodder shipments to cattle regions like Gujarat: "The railways remained deaf and obdurate." Two Indian nationalists who wrote extensive studies at the beginning of the twentieth century also challenge assertions about the railways' impact on India's economic development. Romesh Chunder Dutt and Dadabhai Naoroji belonged to a school of Bengali economists who argued that the Guarantee, taxation, and railway expansion hastened "The Drain" of India's natural resources and national wealth to British capitalists.

Part 6: railways and the spread of epidemic disease

Railway malaria was a severe problem in the late nineteenth and early twentieth centuries. In malarial regions throughout the globe, doctors examined the spleens of children who lived in close proximity to railways to determine if the parasite was active in their bodies. Swollen spleens were the telltale sign of sickness, and spleen rates allowed physicians to determine the severity of epidemics. Large-scale excavations of any kind, such as canal works, port works, and railway "borrow pits," where crews transferred dirt to build embankments, always filled with standing water during rains. Female anophelines, the vector of the malaria parasite, bred in this fresh and, in some cases, brackish water. The only missing element of a kingdom populated by millions of mosquitos, their larvae, and malarial microorganisms, were humans, until the arrival of railway gangs. Once mosquitos discovered all the blood meals they needed, they bit the railway workers, nursed the malarial parasite in their guts for a few cycles, and reinjected the evolved germ called plasmodium back into the human carrier. Within the human body, the most lethal species of the organism – falciparum malaria – attacked the liver, spleen, and other internal organs. Patients died of fever within days.

Patrick Manson, Ronald Ross, Malcolm Watson, and a cadre of British physicians in India, as well as Italian scientists in Rome, pieced together the life cycle of the anopheline. Mosquitos thrived along railways because so many coolies and peasant villagers aggregated there. Since malaria killed millions every decade, these medical health officers in the Indian Medical Service (IMS) and British Medical Service (BMS) investigated the disease in endemic areas of India. They discovered that natural, flowing rivers were not the ideal habitat for anopheline larvae. Instead, the species bred in human-made holdings of very clean water, which quickly spawned algae that was the food for mosquito larvae. This almost always implicated recent construction, and malariologists left their laboratories to devise means to eradicate the species. The first two readings from the *Indian Medical Gazette* and the Records of the Malaria Survey of India detail their efforts along railways.

R. Nathan and James Knighton Condon discussed the role that railways played in transporting plague-carrying rats and fleas from Bombay port to the virgin soil of an India that had never been exposed to the bubonic plague. Grain cars especially harbored the vermin that bore fleas to infected places as close as Poona and as far as Punjab. When Bombay residents fled the city by train, many physicians feared that they could carry the disease with them. The plague epidemics of 1896–1899 were so deadly that the Government of India (GOI) administered a vaccine created by the brilliant Armenian bacteriologist Waldemar Haffkine. What became clear after 1896 was the speed with which a global pandemic had spread from Hong Kong (1894) to Bombay (1896), to Cape Town (1900) and Nairobi (1902). Disease transmission was undeniably tied to new forms of steam transport, which attained its most devastating effects in the influenza pandemic of 1918–1919.

Part 7: railways and crime

Trains and railway stations were conspicuous targets for petty thieves and organized gangs of robbers alike. Police reports and early texts on the latest branch of study, criminology, contain significant information for research in cultural history. These reports typically compiled data from several District Commissioners. In Lower Bengal, for example, Inspector General of Police Monro amassed information from the massive region of Burdwan, the Presidency division, Rajshahye,

Dacca, Chittagong, Patna, Bhagulpore, Orissa, and Chota Nagpore. Rural district police called *chowkidars* kept the peace. The number of inspectors, sub-inspectors, constables, and staff in Lower Bengal alone totaled 17,432. Monro's report from 1878 classified criminal offenses by the degree of severity. Class I and II activity included riots, murders by dacoits, robbers, and poisoners. Class III and IV crimes involved robbery on trains and stations, burglary of station houses, trespassing, serious mischief, and wrongful restraint. Everything else was categorized as minor offenses against property, vagrancy, pickpocketing, obstruction, spike theft, excise cases, and opium smuggling in Class V and VI. Smuggling salt to avoid the Salt Tax was criminalized in India, and enforcement along a 2,500-mile thorn fence required upwards of 12,000 patrol agents. Gandhi later urged the British government to abolish the salt tax. Historians can tell by the way criminal offenses were defined and categorized that the GOI was most concerned about infractions along the railways. Railway crimes and their punishments appear in this collection. Reports also addressed the activity of "criminal tribes" and other "professional offenders." In 1883, organized criminal tribe activity increased, especially during regional fairs. Later data shows downturns in many crimes, except the theft of railway spikes. The Morshead report for 1907 and the Railway Committee Report in 1921 saw increases in cognizable and non-cognizable railway crimes. The 1921 publication lists a number of grievances from individuals, businesses, and Chambers of Commerce. The Mysore Chamber claimed that itinerant women carried off in their baskets 50 percent of their freight in coal. Complainants attributed goods pilferage and railway theft to the very employees charged with their protection.

S. T. Hollins and M. Pauparao Naidu both wrote on the subject of "criminal tribes" after their years of service patrolling the passenger traffic on trains in the United Provinces (UP) and Madras. In the UP, Hollins alphabetized criminal tribes and singled out different ethnic groups such as the Aherias, Badhaks, Barwars, and Bhars as main offenders: "Children learn to steal at an early age, and by the time they are 15 or 16, they are expert enough to join expeditions." Gangs of ten to twenty men left their homes for several months and plundered enough to get them through the year. Hollins remarked that the Aherias moved from well-traveled cart paths to railways, snatching purses from train windows and boarding goods cars and throwing merchandise toward trackside telegraph poles while the locomotives sped down the track. Accomplices picked up the goods at the poles. The number of Aherias convicted of crimes (1,600) probably represented both prosecution and persecution. Hollins maintained that different tribes specialized in different crimes. The Badhaks posed as *fakirs*, with the women committing petty theft. Barwars used railways to pilfer, elevated their leaders to the status of *zemindars*, and executed well-organized heists like professionals, and distributed money by remissions (money orders). The Bhars once dominated their region but fell on hard times and turned to stealing from other peoples' fields. Naidu's history on the railway thieves examined the "peculiar manners and customs" of seven railway tribes of Madras, Central

Provinces, and UP. As a Railway Police Investigator, he encountered some of the same tribes as Hollins: the Barwars (Bharwars) of Gonda and Lallatapur and Aherias (Ahiryas) of the UP, for example. But his investigations into the Bhamptas, who operated on night trains, revealed that their scions were worth tens of thousands, and their professional operations spread over multiple provinces like the railways themselves.

Part 8: the railway as oasis: Egypt, the Near East, and the Middle East

To mid-nineteenth-century travelers, British-built railways were among the least impressive features of the Egyptian landscape, and with good reason. Isabella Romer toured the land of Alexandria, Cairo, the Nile, pyramids, the Sphinx, and the holy shrines of the Near East in 1845 and 1846 before railways debuted. Her thoughts were with Indian visitors of England who returned to India under terrible duress. She explained the ordeal they endured each time they left Southampton, England by steamship to Alexandria, followed by another thirty-six-hour trip by Nile steamer to Cairo. Once at the crossroads to the East, overland "vans" took them to Suez, where they boarded the Red Sea steamer to a port destination in India. To return to England involved the reverse trip from one of India's ports: Calcutta, Bombay, Karachi, or Madras, and what Romer observed was true until the opening of the Suez Canal (1869): Indians in an invalid state were suspended in a sedan chair between a pair of donkeys at Suez and unceremoniously trotted off to Cairo. Thus, the progressive peoples of Egypt and India shared Romer's dream of a Cairo to Suez rail to replace the donkey ride with a three-hour train ride. But even in the 1880s, Egyptian trains could not compete with the spectacular Nile, dainty villages, nor even the flocks of fowl and sheep. The train that Australian journalist James Hingston rode out of Cairo broke down just long enough for him to see the mud huts and hives of the Egyptian peasantry, recount what he learned about the Mahmoodieh canal project of the slave-driving Mehemet Ali, and pontificate about England's burden to uplift the masses. Unbeknownst to Hingston, the estimated deaths of Ali's canal (38,000) were nearly matched by British India's "death a sleeper" railway construction in the Bhore Ghat and Thal Ghat. In her travel account *From Cornwall to Cairo*, C. F. Gordon Cumming was back at it again with tales of "Eastern" mothers who kept their children in filth to keep the evil spirits away. Until her life-changing experience in Ceylon, Gordon Cumming routinely portrayed non-western mothers as the evil spirits – neglectful and unwitting purveyors of sicknesses from fever to ophthalmia. To the flippant travel writer, soap was the remedy. More importantly, she justified the hiring of only European railway signalman based on the poor eyesight of Egyptian men and their inability to tell a green signal from a red one at one hundred yards. Hadji Khan was the penname of Gazanfar Ali, a writer who followed pilgrims to Mecca with fellow travelers Armin Vamberry and Wilfred Sparroy in 1904. The three-hour railway journey from Port Said to Ismailia and four-hour leg to the Suez ended with reports of a cholera outbreak in Arabia, an almost annual occurrence in the high nineties and first decades of the twentieth century. In 1883, the German chemist Robert Koch had isolated the cholera vibrio in both Egypt and India, and announced that India was the original home of the disease. Steam transport on land and seas quickly spread the germ, which appeared in food contaminated by fecal matter from the filthy lavatories of overcrowded third-class pilgrim trains and steam vessels. Tens of thousands died annually in epidemics associated with pilgrimages.

In late 1907, Norma Lorimer described the new Egyptian railways in terms suggestive of a new metonym. The *Oasis* Railway with *wagon lits* carriages and *train-de-luxe* service was aptly named for its luxuriousness. Lorimer established that the journey from Cairo to the Western Oasis in Gurgah once took five or six days by camel before the railway reduced it to twenty-four hours. E. L. Butcher wrote about life as an English lord in Egypt. His kin traveled only by special train with accommodation for eight harem. Passengers looking out the carriage windows saw vast desert, telegraph poles, and plantations, but followed the green fringe that marked the course of the Nile. Butcher reported on several thousand "wild-looking" agrarian workers called *fellahs* who made up a corvée that dragged baskets of nutrient-rich wet mud from the riverbanks to the fields. Supervisors clad in white robes and bearing sticks drove them on. When sand storms caused Butcher's locomotive to jump the tracks between Boulak da Krur and Tel el-Baroud, he waited at a nearby desert station until four specials were dispatched to rescue him. In his later account *Things Seen in Egypt*, Butcher recorded the chants of Suez railway workers, helped a servant find his English master, and elaborated on a few surprising trends associated with Muslim pilgrimages to Jeddah. Francis and Harriet Clark alternately admired and denigrated the Egyptians but carried forth the oasis metaphor: "one moment the train is in the arid purgatory of the desert, the next it is in the smiling paradise of the oasis." The boys with donkeys who helped transport their luggage from the port of Ismailia to the train station competed for the Americans' business by claiming their donkeys were named "Yankee Doodle," "Washington," or "Washy Washington." The Clarks interpreted other street cries, but when it came to explaining Egyptian poverty, they never overcome their ethnocentric partiality for victim blaming. Louisa Jebb Wilkins viewed the colorful costumes and poor neighborhoods along the German-built Anatolian Railway as picturesque and the fancy trousers from Manchester and modern homes near the railway station as shoddy and grotesque. She published her exceptional travel account *By Desert Ways to Baghdad* in 1912. In her second chapter "The Dawn of the Baghdad Railway" she depicted the railway as a "Monster." She loathed its effects. Cheap trinkets from England appeared in bazaars. The price of wheat doubled while the plains of Turkey exported nothing that could be eaten (opium, hides, wool, mohair), except salt. And a photograph of the German Kaiser at a Turkish harem in Eskishehr "hit one terribly in the eye." As she surmised, "One shuttered here at the effect of prosperity unaccompanied by civilising influences."

Part 9: railways and the re-partitioning of British Africa

As previously explored, British Africa's railways represented dominion over an overextended patrimony the UK fought to hold. As such, the metonyms of railways tended to focus on the singular shortcomings of individual colonies and their evolution to grand mirages of structures built on sand. Egypt's transition from the utilitarian iron camel to the luxurious desert oasis was a prime example. This section on British Africa explores several other chimeras. Lieutenant Thomas Joseph Willans' *The Abyssinian Railway* (1870) meticulously reported on the British Army's effort to build a railway to assist the return of Kitchener's army from the siege of Magdala. Willans' account is a familiar one to railway historians: the pace of 400 feet a day in frightfully hot temperatures in the driest season was crippled by the scarcity of water. A well was finally sunk by the Madras Sappers and Miners in late March, ending the need for mules, water ships, and condensers. The multinational workforce triumphed with the line's completion but not without water rationing and speculating whether Kitchener's army might be better served by a water works than a 12-mile light railway to the coast. For Kipling's *The Light that Failed*, an armored night train traversed the desert and came under enemy fire. The "fuzzies" fired pot shots and the "children of the night" piled obstructions on the track – just another night on British railways in the Sudan. It was always as dark as night within the armored train. Annie Brassey's "Appendix" in *The Last Voyage* (1889) presents her perspective on Anglo-Boer relations after the discovery of the Transvaal gold fields. The Englishwoman distinguished between the white race with railways and the Boer settlements without them. To Brassey, railways symbolized English superiority over all races. African natives pined for jobs on British-owned railways, farms, and mines. Brassey asserts: "They are content to live under the rule of a superior race."

Sources on British Africa show that the empire used railways to unite the distant territories of many Africas but continue to divide the two races: white and black. In *Actual Africa* (1895), Frank Vincent reported on conditions in Wadi Halfa, Nubia, Mozambique, Lorenzo Marquez, and Natal. Railways linked these smaller southwestern colonies controlled by Great Britain and Portugal. Since the outbreak of war in Sudan, British officers commanded 4,000 Egyptian soldiers at Wadi Halfa, where Mahdists tore up railway track and threw it into the river. Vincent claimed the Mahdists used ties (sleepers) for their cooking fires and telegraph wires for their spurs. A dozen troops accompanied Vincent's tour group on a train named the "Gorgon," the fierce, terrifying, and repulsive mythological creatures best exemplified by Medusa. The train extended to the contested outpost of Sarras, 1,000 miles from the Mediterranean. Vincent's painstaking references to railways and steamers that carried Hotchkiss and Nordenfeldt guns, as well as soldiers who wielded repeating guns and Martini-Henry rifles, underlined ongoing hostilities in occupied Africa. Vincent passed infantry battalions, cavalry companies, camel corps, fortresses, garrisons, and citadels. In contrast, journeys through established coastal colonies in Southwestern and Southeastern Africa, such as Komati Poort outside Lorenzo Marquez and Durban, Addington, and Berea in Natal, reinforced the role of trains and tramways as civilian people-movers through Europeanized enclaves. Trains in Natal left people off at botanical gardens, theaters, museums, and public libraries, while Amatonga and Swazi natives at Komati Poort stood "like animals" in fourth-class railway wagons. Native policemen wore the uniforms of their London counterparts except the short breeches that showed their "chocolate-colored calves." The metalled road bed, stone bridges, brick stations, and restaurant bars of the partially completed line from Natal to Johannesburg, through Maritzburg, Newcastle, Charlestown, suggested the permanence of the British presence in South Africa. Vincent later rode a stagecoach through the Veldt and Witwatersrand of the Transvaal, which he likened to the steppes of Central Asia, as the narrative reads like a trip back in time. His railway journey from Johannesburg to Cape Town, via the Orange Free State, Cape Colony, and British Bechuanaland, covered 1,013 miles of track in fifty-six hours. This was the closest Vincent came to the American, Indian, or Russian railway experience in terms of contiguous distances traveled. Instead of California, Delhi, or the Urals, he arrived at the Kimberley diamond mines. Tropical railways brought Vincent through Portuguese and Dutch settlements to Benguela's palm and coconut plantations. He reported on the African contract workers who committed to five years of labor on the coffee and cacao plantations of Prince and St. Thomas Islands. In the Belgian Congo, the Pan-African traveler visited the first thirty miles of the Matadi to Stanley Pool branch of the Leopold Railway. Welsh-born British American explorer Henry Morton Stanley picked up where Vincent left off, covering the inauguration of the Bechuanaland Railway at Bulawayo. Stanley attempted to affirm the works in British Africa by drawing comparisons from other railways around the globe. In a series of short vignettes, the British civil engineer C. O. Burge remembered a story about his Zulu workforce. Foreign traveler Charlotte Mansfield visited Northern Rhodesia at a time when the Kafue River flooded and railway employees had to pull the train through waist-high water. John R. Raphael wrote a travel guide to Nigerian railways between Lagos and Minna, which included the Bauchi Light Railway and Baro-Karo Railway.

In yet other parts of British Africa, railways brought death. Building railways took more lives than the infamous man-eating lions of Tsavo. Reading about the deaths of railway coolies by the "prehistoric revival" of man versus beast in *The Spectator* and J. H. Patterson's *The Man-Eaters of Tsavo and Other East African Adventures* leaves cynical readers wondering if the lions symbolized the railway's casualties. Joseph Conrad depicted the deadly slave-like labor regimes in the Congo in a three-part series in *Blackwood's Magazine* (1899), later collected as the novel *Heart of Darkness* (1902). In the selection below, the protagonist, Marlow, disembarked from a steamship to the deafening sound of blasting rock and the sight of half-clad black laborers dying of disease, both of which signaled work on a nearby railway line. Near the station, other black men were hauled away in chains: "I could see every rib, the joints of their limbs were like knots in a rope; each had an iron collar on his neck, and all were connected together with a chain."

Part 10: Australiana and Aborigines:
possession and dispossession

Samuel Calvert's engraving, "Skipton Jacky Jacky and His Tribe at the Opening of the Beaufort Railway" (1874) introduces the Australia section. The name refers to a fictional aboriginal tribesman who observes the inauguration of the new Victorian Railway. Calvert depicted the native Australians in their "natural state" not unlike the manner in which artists presented indigenous peoples on other continents. Skipton Jacky Jacky appears at center, showing the other men what he has already seen. His western-styled overcoat and hat signify his leadership through slight adaptations to modern European culture. The barefoot men otherwise wear loose-fitting rags for pants, traditional cloaks, and headbands. Apprehensive, they adopt a defensive repose and bear the stereotypical spears, walking sticks, boomerangs, waddies, knobsticks, and pipes. The women calmly hold children, their seated postures and facial expressions revealing their subordinate status, curiosity, and attentiveness as one points to the train and another reaches for an ill-defined object on the ground. Sheltered by the safe distance of a tree, the observers stare at the passing train while passengers, engineer, and fireman stare back. It is the Aborigines, not the truncated train, that dominates three-fourths of the composition. The darker hues and anatomical details of the natives and dogs in the foreground overshadow the truncated train and roughly sketched landscape in the background. From this perspective, the artist demonstrates sympathy for his primary subjects, despite rendering natives in caricatured forms recognized by white audiences. Calvert honors aboriginal peoples in the only way conscientious nineteenth-century painters knew, as noble savages, and decries their subjugation to western civilization without realizing the irony of colonializing the very subjects he captured through reproductive art.

Source materials dating since the mid-1850s, when railway service began, illustrate the rich experiences of middle-class Australians who interacted daily with the railways. No single engraving quite captures their railway experience like *Easter Excursionists*, showing a scene from Melbourne's Spencer Street Station in *Illustrated Australian News* (May 4, 1881). Recalling William Powell Frith's *Paddington Station* (1862), the composition focuses on the hustle and bustle of a compact crowd during high-Victorian holiday travel. In this painting appears the formally attired doting mother sitting atop her luggage readying her daughter for travel. Next to them the rifle-toting father in a frock coat provides a protective physical barrier against other men hurrying along with their hunting rifles, outerwear, gear, and dogs. The school-aged child is picture perfect as *haute bourgeoisie* in full bonnet, bowtie, hooded puffy coat, skirt, stockings, and a toy flying saucer. Everyone carries a folded or rolled blanket in preparation for a long journey, recreation, and a picnic. One railway porter pushes a hand-truck in an attempt to navigate the thickly packed crowd. Smoking is prohibited, but a defiant huntsman enters the picture with his pipe, insisting on the holiday's suspension of rules. At center, doffing his hat and overlooking the father's shoulder is perhaps a self-portrait of the anonymous artist amidst the pandemonium. The railway themes of most white settler colonies dominated the Australian sources: the transition from freight to passenger traffic, the growth of tourism and sightseeing, and high probabilities of encounters with the aboriginal "other." On these motifs expounded writers of variable reknown – Mark Twain, Anthony Trollope, Annie Brassey, James Hingston, May Vivienne, and Daisy Bates – as well as relative unknowns Hume Nisbet, Robert Watson, Julius Price, and Albert Frederick Calvert.

Notes

1 See Edward Said, *Orientalism* (London: Routledge and Kegan Paul, 1978), Said, *Culture and Imperialism* (New York: Alfred A. Knopf, 1993).

2 *The Development of Indian Railways* (Calcutta: University of Calcutta, 1930); Kerr, ed., *Railways in Modern India* (New York: Oxford University Press, 2001), 27. See also the article of John Hurd II in the same volume, 149.

3 Ian Derbyshire, "Private and State Enterprise: Financing and Managing the Railways of Colonial North India, 1859–1914," in Ian J. Kerr, ed., *27 Down: New Departures in Indian Railway Studies* (Delhi: Orient Longman, 2007), 277–278.

4 Sanyal, 3.

5 *Investment in Empire: British Railway and Steam Shipping Enterprise in India, 1825–1849* (Philadelphia: University of Pennsylvania, 1950), 1–3, 96; Damien Bailey and John McGuire, "Railways, Exchange Banks, and the World Economy: Capitalist Development in India, 1850–1873," in Kerr, ed., *Railways in Modern India*, 107–112.

6 Thorner, *Investment in Empire*, 3–10, 96; Mahadev Ranade, *Essays on Indian Economics*, Third ed. (Madras: G. A. Natesan, 1920), 85; Derbyshire, 277.

7 Thorner, *Investment in Empire*, 392. On the origins of the guarantee system, see *Investment in Empire, passim*, and for its effects, see Thorner's essay "The Pattern in Railway Development in India," in Kerr, ed., *Railways in Modern India*, 84–85.

8 See Jenks, *The Migration of British Capital to 1875* (London: reprinted edition, 1963), 222; Ian J. Kerr, *Building the Railways of the Raj, 1850–1900* (London: Oxford University Press, 1995), 18–19, 29.

9 Jenks, 227–230.

10 Sanyal, 61.

11 *The Engineer*, 19 August 1864, 120; Kerr, *Building the Railways of the Raj*, 19–22.

12 *The Engineer*, 19 August 1864, 120.

13 Hugh Hughes, *Indian Locomotives, Part 1-Broad Gauge, 1851–1940* (Harrow: The Continental Railway Circle, 1990), and *Part 2- Metre Gauge, 1872–1940* (Harrow: The Continental Railway Circle, 1992); Fritz Lehmann, "Great Britain and the Supply of Railway Locomotives of India: A Case Study of "Economic Imperialism," *Indian Economic and Social History Review* 2:4 (October 1965); Kerr, ed., *Railways in Modern India*, 6; Romesh C. Dutt, *The Economic History of India in the Victorian Age: From the Accession of Queen Victoria in 1837 to the Commencement of the Twentieth Century* (London: Routledge & Kegan Paul, 1956), 353–359, 366.

14 Kerr, *Building the Railways of the Raj*, 24, 43, 53–54, 82–83, 179–181; Daniel R. Headrick, *The Tools of Empire: Technology and European Imperialism in the Nineteenth Century* (New York: Oxford University Press, 1981), 181; Kerr, ed., *Railways in Modern India*, 3. In 1933, one rupee exchanged for .075 pounds sterling.

15 Thorner, *Investment in Empire*, 45.

16 *Ibid.*, 61; Kerr, *Building the Railways of the Raj*, 5–6, 211–226, Appendix II, Tables 1–14; Kerr, *Railways in Modern India*, 25.

17 *Grundrisse: Foundations of the Critique of Political Economy*, Trans. Martin Nico-
   laus (London: Penguin, 1973), 706. Italics in original.
18 Ranajit Guha, *Elementary Aspects of Peasant Insurgency in Colonial India* (Delhi:
   Oxford University Press, 1983), 11–12; James C. Scott, *Weapons of the Weak:
   Everyday Forms of Peasant Resistance* (New Haven: Yale University Press, 1985);
   Scott, *Domination and the Arts of Resistance: Hidden Transcripts* (New Haven: Yale
   University Press, 1990); Jan de Vos, "Las rebeliones de los indios de Chiapas en la
   memoria de sus descendientes," in Jane-Dale Lloyd and Laura Perez Rosales, eds.,
   Paisajes rebeldes: Una larga noche de resistencia indigena (Mexico City: Univer-
   sidad Iberoamericana, 1995), 239–240; Allen Wells and Gilbert M. Joseph, *Summer
   of Discontent, Seasons of Upheaval: Elite Politics and Rural Insurgency in Yucatán,
   1876–1915* (Stanford: Stanford University Press, 1996), 167; Adolfo Gilly, "Chiapas
   and the Rebellion of the Enchanted World," in *Rural Revolt in Mexico: U.S. Intervention and the Domain of Subaltern Politics*, edited by Daniel Nugent (Durham: Duke
   University Press, 1998), 272–273.
19 Ian J. Kerr, ed. *27 Down*, xxii.
20 Marian Aguiar, "Railway Space in Partition Literature," in Kerr, ed., *27 Down*, 40.
21 Sanyal, 8, 43.
22 Paul Brians, *Modern South Asian Literature in English* (Westport, Conn.: Greenwood
   Press, 2003), 12.
23 *The Australian Abroad: Branches from the Main Routes Round the World*, 2 vols.
   (London: S. Low, Marston, Searle, and Rivington, 1879), 201.
24 Harriet Bury, "Novel Spaces, Transitional Moments: Negotiating Text and Territory in
   Nineteenth-Century Hindi Travel Accounts," in Kerr, ed., *27 Down*, 8–9.
25 Sanyal, 61.
26 George Huddleston, *History of the East Indian Railway* (Calcutta: Thacker, 1906),
   17–18, 27; Sanyal, 43–45.
27 Kerr, ed., *Railways in Modern India*, 3; Manu Goswami, *Producing India: From
   Colonial Economy to National Space* (Chicago: University of Chicago Press, 2004),
   108; John W. Mitchell, *The Wheels of Ind* (London: Thornton Butterworth, 1934), 54.
28 Manu Goswami, *Producing India*, 104, 108–109.
29 Marian Aguiar, *Tracking Modernity: India's Railway and the Culture of Mobility*
   (Minneapolis: University of Minnesota Press, 2011), 26–27, 43–47.
30 Mahadev Ranade, *Essays on Indian Economics*, Third ed. (Madras: G. A. Natesan,
   1920), 83–84.
31 Ian J. Kerr, *Engines of Change: The Railroads that Made India* (Westport, Conn.:
   Praeger, 2007), 107–108.
32 Harriet Bury, 16–17.
33 Aguiar, *Tracking Modernity*, 28, 30; Mitchell, 21.
34 Harriet Bury, 16–17.
35 James, *The American Scene* (London: Chapman and Hall, 1907), 433.
36 Scott, *Domination and the Arts of Resistance*, xii.
37 Trevelyan, *The Competition Wallah*, 24; Aguiar, 30.
38 Trevelyan, 28; Aguiar, *Tracking Modernity*, 30.
39 Samuel Turner, *Siberia: A Record of Travel, Climbing and Exploration*. London:
   Unwin, 1905), 89.
40 Mitchell, 50; Aguiar, *Tracking Modernity*, 30.
41 Mitchell, 55.
42 Ian J. Kerr, "The Railway Workshops and Their Labour: Entering the Black Hole," in
   idem., ed., *27 Down*, 234.
43 William T. Jackman, *The Development of Transportation in Modern England*, 2 vols.
   (Cambridge: The University Press, 1916), I: 440–441. According to Jackman, the
   English bargemen "would extract wine and put in water, withdraw salt and make up

its weight in water, and add to their income by taking groceries, provisions, etc., from the cargo entrusted to their care." And it happened also in the U.S.

44 Joseph Tatlow, *Fifty Years of Railway Life in England, Scotland and Ireland* (London: Railway Gazette, 1920), 76–77. Italics and exclamatory abbreviation in original.

45 Robertson, *Report*, 75.

46 "Railway Transport in India," *The Modern Review* 3: 1 (Jan. 1908), 244; Robertson report, 61.

47 Mitchell, 76.

48 Goswami, 127.

49 *Ibid.*, Robertson report, 61; Mitchell, 69–70, 76.

50 Huddleston, 16.

51 Aguiar, *Tracking Modernity*, 35.

52 Kerr, *Railways in Modern India*, 3; Goswami, 47, 130.

53 *By the Waters of Egypt* (London: Methuen, 1909), 2.

54 S. M. Phillip, "The Use of Our Railways in the Event of Invasion or a European War," *Railway Magazine*, May 1, 1901, 426; Edwin A. Pratt, "Railways in the Boer War," in *The Rise of Rail-Power in War and Conquest* (Philadelphia: J.B. Lippincott, 1916), 232; "Railways and the War," Chapter C in *The Times History of the War* 6 (1915), 162–164.

55 Sir Harry Hamilton Johnston, *A History of the Colonization of Africa* (London: Cambridge University Press, 1913), 148–149, 272, 279, 387.

56 N. G. Butlin, *Investment in Australian Economic Development, 1861–1900* (Cambridge: Cambridge University Press, 1964), 318.

57 See John Gunn, *Along Parallel Lines: A History of the Railways of New South Wales* (Melbourne: Melbourne University Press, 1989), 2. Gunn shares the tragic instance when NSW Governor Sir Charles Augustus Fitzroy drove recklessly and his wife was thrown from the carriage and killed at Parramatta in 1847.

58 *Old Times: An Illustrated History of the Early Days* (Sydney: Commercial Pub. Co., 1903), I: no. 1 (April 1903), 49–50.

59 Butlin, *Investment in Australian Economic Development*, 33, 303; Victor S. Clark, "Australian Economic Problems I. Railways," *The Quarterly Journal of Economics* 22: 3 (May 1908), 403.

60 Clark, 402–403, 413–414; Dunn, 32, 35; John Kerr, *Triumph of Narrow Gauge: A History of Queensland Railways* (Brisbane: Boolarong Publications, 1990), 6.

61 Robert Lee, *The Railways of Victoria, 1854–2004* (Carlton, Victoria: Melbourne University Publishing, 2007), 14–15, 111–113.

62 Lee, 114–115.

63 Patsy Adam-Smith, *Hear the Train Blow* (Melbourne: Thomas Nelson, 1981), 8–15.

64 *Old Times*, I: 3 (June 1903), 193; Lee, 12–14, 28–29, 32; Dunn, 46–47.

65 Cited in Dunn, 67.

66 Gunn, 60–62, 67.

67 J. K. Arthur, *Kangaroo and Kauri: Sketches and Anecdotes of Australia and New Zealand* (London: Sampson Low, Marston & Company, 1894), 38; John Rae, *Railways of New South Wales: Report on Their Construction and Working, from 1872–1875 Inclusive* (Sydney: Thomas Richards, 1876), 14.

68 See John Rae, *Report of Commissioner for Railways*, 30 September 1865, 33, fn. 32, cited in *Ibid.*, 46, See also 61, 68–69; John Rae, *Thirty-Five Years on the New South Wales Railway*.

69 Arthur, 15.

70 Dunn, 171.

71 Edward Dowling, *Australia and America in 1892: A Contrast* (Sydney: Charles Potter, 1893), 82–89.

72 Rae, *Railways of New South Wales: Report* (1872–1875), 24, 35.
73 Dunn, 236.
74 New South Wales Government and Tramways: Annual Report of the Railway Commissioners (Sydney C. Patton, 1890–1931): (1888–1889), 19, Appendix 10; (1907–1908), 3, 8; (1916–1917), 2, 18.
75 Lee, 145, 171–172; Butlin, 346.
76 Clark, 414, 416.
77 John Kerr, 11–12.
78 *Ibid.*, 6, 11, 13. For Sabbatarianism in Victoria, see Lee, 113.
79 *Ibid.*, 22–26, 32–34.
80 Butlin, 9–10, 12–13, 35, 322 (Table 69), 324 (Table 70).
81 Clark, 400.
82 *"Prosperous" British India: A Revelation from Official Records* (London: T. Fisher Unwin, 1901), 292. See also Kerr, *Railways in Modern India*, 13.
83 Kerr, *Railways in Modern India*, 15. Kerr cites proceedings of the Lieutenant Governor of Bengal in the Oriental and India Office Collections of the British Library. See also Gyan Prakash, *Bonded Histories: Genealogies of Labor Servitude in Colonial India* (Cambridge: Cambridge University Press, 1990), 218.
84 Mitchell, 31–32.
85 Sanyal, 60.
86 Elizabeth Whitcombe, *Agrarian Conditions in Northern India* (Berkeley: University of California Press, 1972), 70–71, 81–82, 87, 93, 273–275; Whitcombe, "Indo-Gangetic River Systems, Monsoons, and Malaria," Philosophical Transactions of the Royal Society A (2012) 370: 2217; Gyan Prakash, *Bonded Histories: Genealogies of Labor Servitude in Colonial India* (Cambridge: Cambridge University Press, 1990), 116.
87 Prakash, 126.
88 *Young India* 4: 17 (April 27, 1922), 216.
89 Thomas Robertson, *East India (Railways) Report on the Administration and Working of Indian Railways* (London: Darling & Son, 1903), 60–62.
90 *Young India* 4: 17 (April 27, 1922), 216.
91 Quoted in Kerr, *Engines of Change*, 108.
92 Radhika Ramasubban, "Imperial Health in British India, 1857–1900," in Roy MacLeod and Milton Lewis, *Disease, Medicine, and Empire: Perspective on Western Medicine and the Experience of European Expansion* (London and New York: Routledge, 1988), 38–41, 48, 53.
93 Sanyal, 57.
94 *Report of the Pilgrim Committee, Bihar and Orissa*, 1913 (Simla: Govt. Central Branch Press, 1915), 52–53.
95 Mitchell, 51.
96 Robertson, *Report*, 60–62; N. Sanyal, 296–299.
97 East India (Railway Committee, 1920–21), [Acworth Committee], *Report of the Committee Appointed by the Secretary of State for India to Enquire into the Administration and Working of Indian Railways*, 4 vols. (London: His Majesty's Stationary Office, 1921), I: 53–55; Sanyal, 299. See also the reports of Government of India Sanitary Commissioners and Pilgrim Committees.
98 Kerr, "The Railway Workshops," 234.
99 *Ibid.*, 235–236, 254.
100 Kerr, ed., *Railways in Modern India*, 8.
101 M. K. Gandhi, *Indian Home Rule*, Fifth ed. (Madras: Ganesh, 1922; M. K. Gandhi, *Third Class in Indian Railways* (Lahore: Gandhi Publications League, 1917), 3–7.
102 Rajnarayan Chandavarkar, *Imperial Power and Popular Politics: Class, Resistance and the State in India, c. 1850–1950* (New York: Cambridge University Press, 1998), 307.

103 Goswami, 117; Aguiar, Tracking Modernity 31, 34.
104 David Edgerton, *The Shock of the Old: Technology and Global History Since 1900* (New York: Oxford University Press, 2007), 135.
105 Chandavarkar, 75, 97, 151. Raymond Williams discussed this hegemonic process in *Keywords: A Vocabulary of Culture and Society* (New York: Oxford University Press, 1976), 278–279.
106 David Arnold, "Industrial Violence in Colonial India," *Comparative Studies in Society and History* 22: 2 (1980), 253–254.
107 Chandavarkar, 152.
108 *Ibid.*, 75, 97, 152.
109 *The Argus*, September 12, 1854. Quoted in Lee, 14–15.
110 R. E. N. Twopeny, *Town Life in Australia*, Facsimile edition with Introduction by John M. Ward (Sydney: Sydney University Press, 1973), 2, 98–99, 126.
111 May Vivienne, *Travels in Western Australia* (Second ed. London: W. Heinemann, 1902), 98.
112 Bates, 76.
113 David Burke, *Road through the Wilderness: The Story of the Transcontinental Railway, the First Great Work of Australia's Federation* (Kensington, Australia: New South Wales Press, 1991), 222–223.
114 This drivel is dismissed by the historian and biographer Bob Reece in *Daisy Bates: Grand Dame of the Desert* (Canberra: National Library of Australia, 2007), 7–12.
115 Isobel White, "Daisy Bates: Legend and Reality," in Julie Marcus, ed., *First in their Field: Women and Australian Anthropology* (Melbourne: Melbourne University Press, 1993), 47–66, especially 47, 58–65.
116 R. W. H. Reece, *Aborigines and Colonists: Aborigines and Colonial Society in New South Wales in the 1830s and 1840s* (Sydney: Sydney University Press, 1974), 40–42; David Davies, *The Last of the Tasmanians* (London: Frederick Muller, 1973), 33–36, 71–101.
117 *New York Times*, June 12, 1869, 4; Davies, 234, Appendix II: 273–274; Samuel Clyde McCulloch, Review of Davies, *The Last of the Tasmanians*, in *American Historical Review* 81: 4 (Oct. 1976), 948–949; Isobel White, "Introduction," in Daisy Bates, *The Native Tribes of Western Australia, ed. Isobel White* (Canberra: National Library of Australia, 1985), 17.
118 Isobel White, "Introduction," in Daisy Bates, *The Native Tribes of Western Australia*, ed. Isobel White (Canberra: National Library of Australia, 1985), 16–18; Bob Reece, *Daisy Bates: Grand Dame of the Desert* (Canberra: National Library of Australia, 2007), 4.
119 Reece, *Daisy Bates*, 10.
120 K. O. L. Burridge, Review in *The Geographical Journal* 132: 4 (Dec. 1966), 549.
121 White, "Introduction," 18–19.
122 Patsy Adam-Smith, *The Desert Railway* (Adelaide: Rigby, 1974), 116–118, 121, 126.
123 Bates, *The Passing of the Aborigines* (London: John Murray, 1938 or 1966), 67, 70–71, 73, 90–92, 181–186, 191–194, 211.
124 Bates, xviii. In 1933, at the age of 74, Bates received the Order of Commander of the British Empire, formalizing her title as "Grand Dame of the Desert." Three years later, she gave the National Library of Australia almost 100 folios of her anthropological research, correspondence, and photographs.
125 Patsy Adam-Smith, *When We Rode the Rails* (Sydney: Lansdowne, 1983), 133.
126 Dunn, *Along Parallel Lines*, 44.
127 *Farthest East, and South and West: Notes of a Journey through Japan, Australasia, and America by an Anglo-Indian Globetrotter* (London: W.H. Allen & Co., 1892), 204.

128 Butlin, 6.
129 Robert A. Lee, "Fractious Federation: Patterns in Australian Railway Historiography, *Mobilities in History* 4 (2013), 149–158. See also Gunn, *Along Parallel Lines*.
130 Mark Hearn, *Working Lives: A History of the Australian Railways Union* (NSW Branch) (Sydney: Hale and Iremonger, 1990), 17–45, especially 20–32; Robert Lee, *The Greatest Public Work: The New South Wales Railways, 1848 to 1889* (Sydney: Hale & Iremonger, 1988), 148.
131 Clark, 450.
132 Charles Davis, *Sydney Quarterly Magazine* (October 1883), 29–32.
133 Burke, 54.
134 *Ibid.*, xxii–xxiii, 28, 85–86, 151–152. Quote on xx.
135 Adam-Smith, *The Desert Railway*, 81.
136 *Ibid.*, 83–87, 90.
137 Burke, xxiii, 14, 84, 202, 242, 244. Quote on p. 202; Adam-Smith, *The Desert Railway*, 84.
138 Jane Carruthers, "Cartographical Rivalries: Friedrich Jeppe and the Transvaal," in Norman Etherington, ed., *Mapping Colonial Conquest: Australia and Southern Africa* (Crawley, Western Australia: University of Western Australia Press, 2007), 119–121.
139 Miles Harvey, *The Island of Lost Maps*, 297.
140 D. Ian Pool, *The Maori Population of New Zealand, 1769–1971* (Auckland: Auckland University Press, 1977), *passim*; Pool, *Te Iwi Maori: Population Past, Preset and Projected* (Auckland, NZ: Auckland University Press, 1991), 35–36, 40–43, 54–55, 57; Crosby, 253–257, 265, 268. The ranges provided combine data from the two authors. Crosby's numbers are based on Pool's earlier study, but Pool's more recent studies offer greater precision.
141 Harold Miller, *Race Conflict in New Zealand, 1814–1865* (Auckland: Blackwood and Janet Paul, 1966), 107–125; Crosby, 265, 268.
142 Quoted in Pool, *Te Iwi Maori*, 28.
143 M. P. K. Sorrenson, "Maori and Pakeha," Chapter 7 in W. H. Oliver, ed., *The Oxford History of New Zealand* (Wellington, N.Z.: Oxford University Press, 1981, 179, 186–187.
144 "A Visit to a Maori Village," *The Journal of the Polynesian Society* 33: 1 (March 1, 1924), 53.
145 Christian Wolmar, *Engines of War: How Wars Were Won and Lost on the Railways* (New York: Public Affairs, 2010), 102–109.
146 Peter H. Hoffenberg, *An Empire on Display: English, Indian, and Australian Exhibitions from the Crystal Palace to the Great War* (Berkeley: University of California Press, 2001), 2, 11, 17–19, 21. Quote is on p. 2.
147 *Ibid.*, 214.
148 Thorner, *Investment in Empire*, vii.
149 Thorner, "The Pattern of Railway Development in India," 81.
150 Thompson, *Rabindranath Tagore: His Life and Work* (London: Oxford University Press, 1921), 44.
151 William Radice, "Introduction," in *Rabindranath Tagore: Selected Poems*, Trans. William Radice (London: Penguin, 2005), 27, 29.
152 *Ibid.*, 20–21, 23.
153 Aguiar, *Tracking Modernity*, 43; "Railways in Partition Literature," 41.
154 Frank Swettenham, *British Malaya: An Account of the Origin and Progress of British Influence in Malaya* (London: J. Lane, 1907), 239–240, 278–282; Arnold Wright, *Twentieth Century Impressions of British Malaya* (London: Lloyd's Great Britain, 1908), 304, 306, 308–309.
155 Goswami, 60.

156 F. W. H. Migeod, *Across Equatorial Africa* (London: Heath Cranton, 1923); *Through Nigeria to Lake Chad* (London: Heath, Cranton, 1924); *Through British Cameroons* (London: Heath, Cranton, 1925); *A View of Sierra Leone* (London: K. Paul, Trench, Trubner, 1926).

157 Migeod, *Across Equatorial Africa*, 347.

158 *Ibid.*, 278, 291, 297.

159 Carl G. Rosberg, Jr. and John Nottingham, *The Myth of "Mau Mau:" Nationalism in Kenya* (New York: Praeger, 1966), 28.

Part 1

MOBILITY AND MUTABILITY

1

AMELIA CARY, *CHOW-CHOW*, 2 VOLS. (LONDON: HURST AND BLACKETT, 1857), I, PP. 46–50

SHORTLY before we left India, the railroad at Bombay was completed to a short distance beyond Tannah.

This was the first railroad opened in India. It can well be imagined what astonishment and excitement it caused among the natives, as well as what surprise it occasioned to many Europeans; for there were Anglo-Indians at Bombay, who had not been in Europe for many years, and who, therefore, had not seen a railroad. The station from whence we started on a kind of experimental trip, is at Byculla, about three miles from the fort of Bombay.

A very handsome new temple had been commenced before the railroad was contemplated, actually contiguous to the station, and was on the verge of completion when the latter was opened.

A railway station, and a Hindoo temple in juxta position—the work of the rulers and the ruled. Could one possibly imagine buildings more opposite in their purposes, or more indicative of the character of the races? the last triumphs of science side by side with the superstitions of thousands of years ago.

We made the journey from the commencement to the end of the line, as far as it was finished.

All the country was familiar to me; but, as we approached Tannah, there are the ruins to the left of a Portuguese church, where St. Francis Xavier is said to have performed a great miracle, that of converting a number of Pagans to Christianity at one time.

When we reached Tannah, a place near the railroad was shown us where a few months ago a tiger was shot. This reminds me of a drawing (I think it was in 'Punch') in which a tiger is represented carrying away a stoker, or a porter on an Indian railroad. However, I do not think this will ever happen, as the steam-engines will speedily drive away all the tigers and jackals from the islands of Bombay and Salsette.

A few miles from Tannah, we stopped to look at the scenery, which is very beautiful. We were protected from the sun by a very high hill about seven hundred feet high. On it had lived in peaceful retirement, a few months previously, numerous monkeys. They had been frightened away, and had sought some more secluded spot.

55

When I had last travelled on a railroad, (going to Southampton, *en route* to India), what different objects had presented themselves to those that I saw this afternoon. Here and there a religious mendicant standing with his eyes wide open, staring at the puffing, blowing engine, thinking it might be another avatar of Crishna!—a bullock gharee creeping on at about two miles an hour!—or a bridal-party on foot, the bride walking behind the bridegroom, the progress of the procession being momentarily arrested by the novelty of the sight. The scene was altogether curious, and very interesting.

The introduction of railways into India, must, in time, destroy the influence of caste; the natives will be obliged to mix more with each other, and, by degrees, such distinctions will disappear. It is to be hoped so; for, so long as caste exists, it is to be feared, that even education will do but little to introduce Christianity in India. All those who become Christians are considered outcasts by those who still remain heathens; and are deserted even by relations; therefore, unless the individual be protected by those who have been instrumental in his conversion, he is without any means of getting a livelihood.

Not long ago, a wealthy Hindoo at Bombay wishing to go to Tannah by the rail-road, expressed a desire that he might not be in the same carriage with natives of another caste from himself. He was told this could not be the case; he must travel with other passengers of the same class; he was obliged, of course, to submit.

As we rushed along, on our return to Parell, on the occasion of the excursion, of which I have spoken, the palms appeared more majestic than usual, and to look down upon us with contempt and disgust, while the monster of an engine sent forth an unearthly, protracted yell, as it tore over the flats of Bombay, where, after sunset, the jackals had for so long held undisputed sway.

2

ROBERT BOWNE MINTURN, *FROM NEW YORK TO DELHI*, SECOND ED. (NEW YORK: D. APPLETON, 1858), PP. 6, 122–126

I LEFT Calcutta on the evening of the first of November, 1856. Crossing the Hoogly to Howrah, I took the railway to Raneegunj, a distance of 120 miles, which we accomplished in nine and a half hours. It was dark when we started, and before morning, we had passed the limits of lower Bengal. I have since regretted not taking a train by day, as the country which this road traverses is one of the few parts of India where much cultivation or natural luxuriance of vegetation is to be seen. The carriages were very comfortable, and divided into compartments, on the European plan. I enjoyed a comfortable night's rest, the seats being arranged to draw out, and form a bed.

This railway is to extend to Delhi, and probably in time, to some place on the Indus, as Mooltan. It is to connect at Agra with a proposed road to Bombay, and is one of a great net-work of railways projected to connect all the important points in India. The road had been in construction twelve years, when I was there, and only these 120 miles were completed. Another section was nearly finished, but has been since that time much injured by the mutineers. In the Presidencies of Bombay and Madras, not 200 miles of road altogether had been completed. It is now seen that it was a great error of Government, not to have pushed forward more rapidly the completion of these great highways, since the facility of transporting troops on them would have done much for the prevention or suppression of the recent mutiny. Independently of the use of the railways in a military point of view, they would no doubt have been eminently successful financially, as the navigation of the Ganges is very dangerous, and precarious as regards time; and the transportation of merchandize on camels or ox-carts by the Grand Trunk Road, could never compete with a railway in time or expense. These railroads were the first great public work that the Government of India intrusted to private enterprize, and it was supposed that the advantages presented by the scheme were so great, that private capital would be readily furnished for their completion, especially as Government guaranteed the stockholders a dividend of five per cent. It was found, however, that the rich natives, from whom much of the money was expected, were very backward in contributing to an enterprize of a kind in which they had previously had no experience, and from which any immediate return beyond the five per cent. guaranteed, was doubtful. The idea of any great public work being accomplished by private capital, is something quite opposed to a native's habits of thought—if he has any spare money, he hesitates about investing it permanently in land, or any other way, preferring to retain it in his own hands, and loan it to individuals on short time, and at a high rate of interest. In India, twelve per cent. a year can always be obtained, with the best security, and where the money is loaned to the poor ryuts by the month, at compound interest, and in sums of a few rupees, as is generally the practice of native bankers, the rate amounts to six or seven per cent. a month.

Raneegunj, the present terminus of the railway, is situated at the foot of the Rajmahal hills, a low, irregular range, bounding lower Bengal on the west. It has but few European residents, and they are all connected with the railway, *dâk* companies, or coal mines. The coal obtained is of excellent quality, it is said, and if so, will supply a great want, as the Labuan coal is far from good.

I had engaged at Calcutta my passage to Futtehghur, by the "North Western Dâk Company," one of the three staging companies, (*dâk* being Hindoostanee for "staging,") which conveyed persons and light parcels up-country, along the line of the Grand Trunk Road. As soon as I arrived at Raneegunj, I went to see the vehicle in which I was to proceed to Bĕnarĕs. I found it a square-built, roughly-finished, but strong *gárrhee*, with patent axles, sliding doors, and a row of windows on both sides, shaded by Venetian awnings. The *well*, where, in an ordinary carriage, we put our feet, was covered over, and appropriated to small parcels; and a mattrass extended the whole length of the vehicle. This is a most admirable arrangement for travelling a long time in a carriage, as lying down is, no doubt, the position which can be continued the longest time with the least fatigue; and the convenience for sleeping is a matter of importance, where, as in India, it is customary to travel night and day, and in the hot weather, principally, if not solely, by night.

The Grand Trunk Road is at present the great line of communication between all Northern, and North-Western India, and the coast. It is a broad, macadamized road, as well kept up as any in Europe, stretching in an unbroken line from Calcutta to Peshawur, at least 1,500 miles. The operations of these dâk companies extend along the line of the Trunk Road and its branches, as far to the north-west as Umbala, (the first Punjab station,) beyond which point the bridges are not completed. The branches of the Grand Trunk Road go to Lucknow, Futtehghur, and Moozuffurnuggur, beyond Meeruth. The construction of this great road is entirely the work of the English Government, the Ganges having been previously the only line of communication with the interior.

The dâk companies do not run their gárrhees at any fixed time, but whenever they are engaged. The usual practice is, for one traveller to occupy a gárrhee alone, but the expense and comfort are occasionally shared by two persons, who must be in rather close quarters when they lie down, as the interior of the carriage is not more than four feet wide, if so much. Each gárrhee has a native coachman, who accompanies it for about sixty miles, and a *sáees* or groom, who is changed with the horse, every six miles.

I had heard a great deal about the dâk-horses, but the reality far exceeded my expectations. They are the most vicious and untamed set of brutes that it is possible to conceive as being made in any respect useful. The first specimen which I saw, made his appearance with eight or ten sáeeses, tugging at a rope made fast to one of his fore legs; the object of this was to move his leg forward, upon which, he, of his own accord, brought his body up to it. This mode of progression is, as may be imagined, slow, although sure. It took about twenty minutes to get him into the shafts, and when made fast, he planted his fore-legs firmly apart, and again refused to move. The sáeeses renewed their efforts, first trying mild measures, and calling the stubborn beast by every endearing name, among which were the sweet titles of "father," and "mother." As the brute, however, showed himself utterly insensible and unmollified by the attributed honours of paternity; and moreover, seemed determined at least to assume the parental privilege of chastisement by biting and kicking his swarthy and supposititious offspring, the original plan of dragging his foot forward was again resorted to, accompanied and aided by the united efforts of a dozen or more black fellows who pushed the gárrhee behind. These efforts being persisted in for half a mile, and the coachman vigourously applying the *chabook* (whip), our gallant steed at length was wearied with resistance, and, determining to free himself from his persecutors, and give up an unavailing struggle for the rights of horses, rushed off at a ten mile pace, which he kept up the whole stage. The next horse was quieter, but lame. Natives, however, have very little of that quality which "is not strained," and the lame horse did his five or six miles in less time than his predecessor. The above performances, and practical lessons in the art of horse-breaking, are generally repeated at every third or fourth stage. The only variety in the exercises is when you have a particularly pig-headed animal who *lies down*—the remedy for which amiable peculiarity is to light a straw fire under him. These performances are at first amusing, but "familiarity breeds contempt," and their oft repetition causes them to pall. When one is in a hurry, they are particularly annoying, and I have often felt very like shooting some of these beasts, after an hour or so spent in endeavouring, by every gentle and violent means, to terminate an obstinate *baulk*.

It was nine o'clock before I left Raneegunj. Two officers left at the same time in another gárrhee, but as their horse had lamed himself the night before, by falling into a ditch when chased by a leopard, I soon left them behind. India is so thinly populated a country, that there is an enormous number of wild animals, even close to settlements. Everywhere, the jackals make night hideous with their dreary wolf-like howl; and in many parts of the road, even in the day-time, every one you meet, on foot or on horseback, is armed with a sabre, spear or halbert— whether against man or beast, I could not precisely make out, but probably a little for both, and a great deal "děkne kee wastee," *i. e.*, "for show"—a phrase that explains more than one thing in India.

The country, after leaving Raneegunj, was an undulating common, but little cultivated or inhabited, and with but few trees. We arrived at two o'clock at Gyra dâk-bungalow, where I stopped for dinner. These dâk-bungalows are buildings for the accommodation of travellers, erected by the liberality of Government, at fixed distances, on all the great roads in India. On the Grand Trunk Road, they are generally ten or twelve miles apart, but on the less frequented routes, the interval between one bungalow and another is often twenty or thirty miles. All dâk-bungalows are of one build, and the size varies but little. They are generally about forty feet square, with walls ten or twelve feet high, a verandah running all around, and covered by a steep thatch or tile roof, the edges of which rest on the verandah wall, the ridge being twenty-five feet or more from the ground. There are in each, two suites of apartments, consisting of a parlour, dressing room and bath room—the latter a great advantage in a hot climate. Each bungalow has about a dozen servants, of whom only two or three are paid by Government—the others being dependent upon the traveller's generosity. Every traveller has a right to occupy one suite of rooms for 24 hours, and as much longer as they are unclaimed by a new arrival. These bungalows are not only a great convenience, but almost a necessity for a dâk traveller in India, where there are no hotels except in the largest stations, and where caste forbids the native to allow a Christian's food to be cooked in his house, or even to give him a drink of water from his cup.

On arriving at the bungalow I was received with low saláms by Khansáhma*n*, Khitmutgrá, and Béras, (*Anglice*, steward, waiter and valets,) and the Khansáhma*n* asked what my honour would be pleased to order. I asked what could be had; and was answered "anything!" On further inquiry, however, I discovered that the only choice was between fowl and duck, of which I preferred the former. A scampering and screaming of the feathered bipeds outside soon told me that my wishes were being carried out, and I made a good meal off curry and rice, and grilled-fowl (commonly called "sudden death"). If there is any one thing that a native can do well, it is cooking; they all seem to be born with a natural talent for the culinary art—a talent practically developed in most cases by the rules of caste, which oblige each man to cook for himself, unless he is rich enough to hire a Brahmun to do so for him. The servants in the dâk-bungalows, except the bearers, are all Moosulmans, as no Hindoo will cook, or have anything to do with the eating of beef or fowls. The bungalow furniture consists of a native cotton floor-cover, a table, bed (with no mattrass), three chairs and a punkah, to each suite of rooms. The bath-room is about ten feet square, with a cement floor, and a ridge to prevent the water flowing into the next room. There is no regular *bath*, but instead, five or six earthen *gurras* of water, each holding about a gallon, which the traveller empties over his head.

3

BHOLANAUTH CHUNDER, *THE TRAVELS OF A HINDOO TO VARIOUS PARTS OF BENGAL AND UPPER INDIA* (LONDON: N. TRUBNER, 1869), I, PP. 139–141, 149–150, 162–173, 326–327, 332–333, 348, 433 II: 130–131

Chapter III

THE tale of our journey opens with all the pomp and circumstance of an Eastern romance. Our party was composed of four,—dear reader. But, instead of the prince, the minister, the commander, and the merchant, you must be content with the less conspicuous characters of the doctor, the lawyer, the scholar, and the tradesman. All the charm of a resemblance lies only in the beginning. The story then professes to be something more serious than the tale of an Indian nursery, which induces the very opposite of what is aimed at here—to help the reader to keep awake to the interest of the scenes and sights about him.

Friday, the 19th of October, 1860, was the day appointed for our departure. Crossing over to Howrah, we engaged passage for Burdwan. The train started at 10 A.M., and we fairly proceeded on our journey. Surely, our ancient Bhagiruth, who brought the Ganges from heaven, is not more entitled to the grateful remembrance of posterity, than is the author of the Railway in India.

Travelling by the Rail very much resembles migrating in one vast colony, or setting out together in a whole moving town or caravan. Nothing under this enormous load is ever tagged to the back of a locomotive, and yet we were no sooner in motion than Calcutta, and the Hooghly, and Howrah, all began to recede away like the scenes in a Dissolving View.

The first sight of a steamer no less amazed than alarmed the Burmese, who had a tradition that the capital of their empire would be safe, until a vessel should advance up the Irrawady without *oars* and *sails!* Similarly does the Hindoo look upon the Railway as a marvel and miracle—a novel incarnation for the regeneration of Bharat-versh.

The fondness of the Bengalee for an in-door life is proverbial. He out-Johnsons Johnson in cockneyism. The Calcutta Baboo sees in the Chitpoor Road the same

61

'best highway in the world,' as did the great English Lexicographer in the Strand of London. But the long vista, that is opening from one end of the empire to the other, will, in a few years, tempt him out-of-doors to move in a more extended orbit, to enlarge the circle of his terrene acquaintance, to see variety in human nature, and to divert his attention from the species Calcutta-wallah to the genus man. The fact has become patent, that which was achieved in months and days is now accomplished in hours and minutes, and celerity is as much the order of the day as security and saving.

The iron-horse of the 19th century may be said to have realized the Pegasus of the Greeks, or the Pukaraj of the Hindoos. It has given tangibility and a type to an airy nothing, and has reduced fancy to a matter-of-fact. The introduction of this great novelty has silenced Burke's reproach, 'that if the English were to quit India, they would leave behind them no memorial of art or science worthy of a great and enlightened nation.'

From Howrah to Bally the journey now-a-days is one of five minutes. In twice that time one reaches to Serampore. The next station is Chandernagore—thence to Chinsurah, and then on to Hooghly and Muggra. The Danes, the Dutch, the French, the Portuguese, and the English, all settling at these places in each other's neighbourhood, once presented the microcosm of Europe on the banks of the Hooghly.

All along the road the villages still turn out to see the progress of the train, and gaze in ignorant admiration at the little world borne upon its back.

Six miles interior to the right of the station-house at *Batka* is Davipoor. The Kali, to whom the village is indebted for its name, is a fierce Amazonian statue, seven feet high, and quite terror-striking to the beholder. The opulent family of the Singhees have adorned their native village with a lofty pagoda, which is much to the credit of the rural masons. From the Rail the crest of this temple is faintly descried near the horizon. Personally to us the place shall always be memorable for a cobra eating up a whole big cat.

The locomotive quickens in its pace by the turn of a peg similarly to the horse of the Indian in Scheherzade's tale; and it goes on and on quite 'like a pawing steed.' Passed *Mamaree*,—a pretty village with many brick buildings, and a fine *nuboruttun*, or nine-pinnacled Hindoo temple. The beautiful country, the invigorating air, the rich prospect of cultivation for miles, the rapid succession of villages, the innumerable tanks and fish-ponds, the swarming population, and the numerous monuments of art and industry peculiar to Indian society, tell the traveller that he has entered the district of Burdwan—the district which for salubrity, fertility, populousness, wealth, and civilization, is the most reputed in Bengal. Burdwan, Bishenpoor, and Beerbhoom, were the three great Hindoo Rajdoms in the tract popularly known under the name of Raur. That of Burdwan has alone survived, and is contemplated with a far deeper interest than the other two. Though sacked and pillaged many a time, the industry, intelligence, and number of its people, have as often covered the face of the land with wealth. Nowhere in our province is ancient capital so much hoarded. Out of the wealth annually created by its population, Burdwan pays the largest revenue of all the zillahs in Bengal. The Banka, winding in serpentine meanders, adds that 'babbling brook' to 'the pomp of groves' and 'the garniture of fields,' which completes the charming variety of this well-known tract. The grand Railway viaduct, half a mile long, is an architectural wonder in the valley of the Damoodur. It is a bridle curbing that river notorious for its impetuosity.

October 20th.—LEFT Burdwan for Raneegunge. The train goes on careering upon the terra-firma as merrily as does a ship upon the sea. In it, a Hindoo is apt to feel the prophecies of the sage verified in the Rail—riding upon which has arrived the Kulkee Avatar of his Shasters, for the regeneration of the world.

Little or no change as yet in the scenery about us. The same vegetation, the same paddy-fields, the same sugar-cane plantations, the same topes of bamboos and mangoes, and the same dark bushy villages fringing the horizon, meet the eye in all directions. The botany of Burdwan hardly exhibits any difference from the botany of Hooghly or Calcutta. But the atmosphere at once tells as bracing, and cool, and free from damp. The soil, too, shows a partial change—the soft alluvium has begun to cease, and in its place occurs the gravelly *kunkur*. The country is no more a dead flat, it has begun to rise, and the surface is broken in those slight undulations that indicate the first and farthest commencement of the far-off hills.

The track of our progress then lay skirting the edge of the district of Beerbhoom—the *mullo bhoomee* of the ancient Hindoos. Mankur is yet an insignificant town, and Paneeghur still more poor-looking. Lying thus far in the interior, these places were once 'out of humanity's reach.' This was, when a journey to these far away, and almostt hermetically-sealed, regions, exposed the traveller to 'disastrous chances' and 'moving accidents'—to the perils of the Charybdis of wild beasts, or to the Scylla of thugs and marauders. Way-faring was then inevitable from way-laying. Highwaymen in squads infested the roads, and had their appointed haunts to lie in wait, spring upon a stray and benighted pedestrian, and fling his warm corpse into a neighbouring tank or roadside jungle. The very men of the police, in those days, laid aside their duties after dark, and acted as banditti. But, under the auspices of the Rail, towns and cities are springing up amidst the desert and upon the rock,—and security of life and property is pervading the length and breadth of the land. Less danger now befalls a man on the road than what threatened him within his own doors in the early part of the century. Hercules of old turned only the course of a river. The Rail turns the courses of men, merchandise, and mind, all into new channels. 'Of all inventions,' says Macaulay, 'the alphabet and the printing press alone excepted, those inventions which abridge distance have done most for the civilization of our species. Every improvement of the means of loco-motion benefits mankind morally and intellectually, as well as materially, and not only facilitates the interchange of the various productions of nature and art, but tends to remove national and provincial antipathies, and to bind together all the branches of the great human family.'

Beyond Paneeghur, the district begins to savour of the jungle. The traveller here enters upon a new order of things, and meets with a new regime in nature.

First from the damp, and then from the dry, he has now attained a region which is decidedly sterile. No luxuriant vegetation to denote a soft locality—no other tree of an alluvial soil than a few straggling palms. The magnificent banyan, and the graceful cocoa, have long bidden their adieu, and now lag far—far behind. The transition is great from fertility to aridity. The soil, hard and kunkerry, and of a reddish tinge, denoting the presence of iron, is covered chiefly with low jungles and thin stunted copsewood. The ground is broken into deeper undulations than before—appearing billowy with enormous earthy waves, here leaving a hollow, and there forming a swell with a magnificent sweep.

To carry on the road in a level, they have cut through one of these swells or elevations, to the depth of thirty-six feet, and a mile in length. It is a stupendous work. On the right of this cutting is a gloomy tract of jungles extending to the Rajmahal Hills. In the heart of this desolate region is a romantic spot, wherein the Shivite Brahmins have planted the *linga* of Byjnath—dogging in the steps of the Buddhists to oust them from even their mountain-fastnesses. The god was being brought from Cailasa by Ravana on his shoulders, to act as the guardian deity of Lunka. But he assumed an immoveable ponderosity by coming in contact with the earth when laid down by Ravana to relieve himself from the hands of Varuna, who had entered his stomach to excite the action of his kidneys, that he may be necessitated to drop the god, and disappointed of his promised deliverance. Thus put up, Byjnath has become a famous pilgrimage. His present shrine is three hundred years old, and a mile in circumference. The god must be content only with our distant salutations.

Out of the cut, the eye meets towards the horizon a faint blue wavy streak, which is a perfect novelty to a *Ditcher*. Soon the dim and indistinct outline assumes the tangible form of detached spurs, and the towering Chutna and Beharinath clearly stand out in view—a welcome sight to him 'who long hath been in populous cities pent.' The land here is 360 feet higher than the level of the sea, and the two spurs are thrown off, like two out-scouts, to announce the beginning of the hills. From Khyrasole commence those coal-beds, which, say the Hindoos, are vestiges of their Marut Rajah's Yugya. By far more rational than this, is the version of the African Barotsees, in whose opinion coals are 'stones that burn.' Near Singarim, the phenomenon of a petrified forest reads a more valuable lecture upon the formation of our planet, than all the cosmogony of Menu. *Raneegunge* is then announced;—and as one stands with his head projected out of the train, the infant town bursts on the sight from out an open and extensive plain, with its white-sheening edifices, the towering chimneys of its collieries, and the clustering huts of its bazar—looking like a garden in a wilderness, and throwing a lustre over the lonely valley of the Damooder.

From the neighbourhood of the sea, the Rail has transported a whole town of men and merchandise, and set it down at the foot of the hills. The iron-horse also snorts as it goes, and slackens its pace in sight of the terminus of its journey. On arrival, it is unsaddled from its fetters, washed and groomed, and then led away to rest for fresh work on the morrow.

No comfortable lodgings are yet procurable at Raneegunge. The project of a staging caravanserai here might be a profitable speculation, considering the large tide of men that pass through this gateway of Bengal. To an untravelled Calcutta Baboo, this want of accommodation is a serious stumbling-block in the path of his journey. True, there is the Railway Hotel. But a native may read Bacon and Shakespeare, get over his religious prejudices, form political associations, and aspire to a seat in the legislature—he may do all these and many things more, but he cannot make up his mind to board at an English Hotel, or take up a house at Chowringhi. By his nature, a Hindoo is disposed to be in slippers. He feels, therefore, upon stilts before aliens. Ethnologically, he is the same with an English-man—both being of the Aryan-house. Morally and intellectually, he can easily Anglicize himself. Politically, he may, sooner or later, be raised to an equality. But socially, in thought, habit, action, feelings, and views of life, he must long measure the distance that exists geographically between him and the Englishman. If not travelling *en grand Seigneur*, a Hindoo gentleman would rather choose to put up in a small shed pervious to the cold drafts of the night wind and the rays of the moon, than be restrained from indulging in the tenor of his habits in a for-eign element. It was a lucky thing for us to have picked up the acquaintance of a fellow-Ditcher on the way, who offered us an asylum in his lodge.

Raneegunge is on the confines of a civilized world—beyond commence the inhospitable jungles and the domains of barbarism. Few spots can surpass this in charming scenery and picturesque beauty. On the left tower those spurs which give the first glimpse of the classic Vindhoo-giris. To the right, spread forests ter-minating as far off as where the Ganges rolls down its mighty stream. Before, is the realm of the hill and dale—wood and jungle. The sky over-head is bright as a mirror. No dust or exhalation bedims the prospect. Through the smokeless atmo-sphere, the eye kens objects in the far distance. The town itself has a busy and bustling look with its shops, warehouses, and collieries. But it is yet too early to possess any feature of grandeur or opulence. As a new town, Raneegunge should not have been allowed to be built in defiance of those sanitary rules and laws of hygiene, which lengthen the term of human life. The Indians need lessons in town-building, as much as they do in ship-building. The streets here are as nar-row, crooked, and dirty, as in all native towns. The shops are unsightly hovels, crowded together in higgledy-piggledy. Buildings deserving of the name there are none—excepting those of the Railway Company. The population consists of petty shopkeepers, coolies, and other labourers. No decent folk lives here—no permanent settler. The wives and daughters of the Santhals are seen hither from the neighbouring villages to buy salt, clothing, and trinkets. The rural dealers open a bazar under the trees. But after all, the change has been immense from a jungly-waste—from the haunt of bears and leopards into a flourishing seat of trade, yielding annually a quarter of a million. Raneegunge, making rapid advances under the auspices of the Railway, is destined in its progress to rival, if not outstrip, Newcastle. At present it is the only town in India which supplies the nation with mineral wealth—which sends out coals that propel steamers on the Ganges and on the Indian Ocean. Many such towns will rise hereafter to adorn the face of the country, and throw a lustre of opulence over the land. True, agriculture is India's legitimate source of wealth. But her vast mineral resources, once brought to notice, are not likely to be again neglected. Our forefathers were at one time not only the first agricultural, but also the first manufacturing and commercial nation in the world. In the same manner that Manchester now clothes the modern nations, did India clothe the ancient nations with its silks, muslin, and chintz—exciting the alarm of the Roman politicians to drain their empire of its wealth. Steel is mentioned in the Periplus to have been an article of Indian export. But scarcely is any iron now smelted in the country, and our very nails, and fishing-hooks, and padlocks are imported from England. Ten miles to the north-west of Burdwan, the village of Bonepass was long famous for its excellent cutlery. But the families of its blacksmiths have either died off, or emigrated, or merged into husbandmen. This passing off of the manufactures of our country into foreign hands, is the natural result of unsuccessful competition with superior intelligence and economy. India was the garden and granary of the world, when three-fourths of the globe were a waste and jungle, unutilized as is the interior of Africa. Her relative position has considerably altered, since vast continents have been discovered rivalling her in fertility, and forests have disappeared and gardens spread in every part of the two hemispheres. The nations of the world have abated in their demand for her produce, when America is producing better cotton, Mauritius and Brazil growing cheaper sugar, Russia supplying richer oil-seeds and stronger fibres, Italy and France producing finer silks, Persia growing opium, and Scotland attempting the manufacture of artificial saltpetre. How great is the contrast between the times, when sugar could be procured in England only for medicine, and when her supplies of that article from various ports are now so vast, that she can do without a single pound from India. There was a time, when a pair of silk-stockings, now so commonly used by all classes, constituted a rarity in the dress of King Henry VIII. Not two hundred years ago did a member of the House of Commons remark, that 'the high wages paid in this country made it impossible for the English textures to maintain a competition with the produce of the Indian looms.' How in the interval has the state of things been reversed, and the Indian weavers have been thrown out of the market. Day by day is the dominion of mind extending over matter, and the secrets of nature are brought to light to evolve the powers of the soil, and make nations depend upon their own resources. The present native cannot but choose to dress himself in Manchester calico, and use Birmingham hardware. But it is to be hoped that our sons and grandsons will emulate our ancestors to have every *dhooty*, every shirt, and every *pugree* made from the fabrics of Indian cotton manufactured by Indian mill-owners. The present Hindoo is a mere tiller of the soil, because he has no more capital, and no more intelligence, than to grow paddy, oil seeds, and jute. But the increased knowledge, energy, and wealth of the Indians of the twentieth or twenty-first century, would enable them to follow both agriculture and manufactures, to develop the subterranean resources, to open mines and set up mills, to launch ships upon the ocean, and carry goods to the doors of the consumers in England and America.

The collieries at Raneegunge afford quite a novel sight-seeing. The Hindoos of old knew of a great many things in heaven and earth,—but they had never dreamt of any such thing as geology in their philosophy. The science has not even a name in the great tome and encyclopædia of their shasters. The tree of knowledge had not then grown to a majestic size. Now it has put forth a thousand branches, and daughter stems have grown about the parent trunk. More than sixteen hundred people work at the Raneegunge coal-mines. These have been excavated to a depth of one hundred and thirty feet—nearly double the height of the Ochterlony monument. The mines extend under the bed of the Damooder, and a traveller can proceed three miles, by torch-light, through them. The coal beds are 300 feet in thickness.

The idea haunting the public mind about the Damooder, is that it is a stream of gigantic velocity, which throws down embankments, inundates regions for several miles, and carries away hundreds of towns and villages in the teeth of its current,—for all which it is distinguished as a Nud or masculine river, and justifies its name of the Insatiate Devourer. But up here at Raneegunge it is stripped of all such terrors, and flows a quiet and gentle stream—a 'babbling brook,' with scarcely audible murmurs, awakening a train of the softest associations, as one takes a walk along its lonely and steepy banks.

Made inquiries in vain for two carriages from the dawk-wallahs to depart on the morrow, so many folks were out this season on a holiday tour like ourselves. There are altogether four companies of them,—two European, one Hindoostanee, and one Bengalee, all of whom keep more gharries than horses. To ensure ourselves against disappointment and delay, it was arranged to have a gharry each from two of the companies. The dawk-wallahs should make hay while the sun shines,—their game is near its end. From post-runners first started by the Persian monarch Darius, to the post-riders introduced by the Mussulman emperors of India, it was a great step to improvement. The same step was made from travelling 'in horrible boxes yeleped palkees,' to that by horse-dawk conveyances. In its day, people talked of this species of locomotion as a 'decided improvement.' But before long, the days of all 'slow coaches' are to be numbered in the past. Two or three years hence, the tide of men, now flowing through this channel, will have to be diverted to the grand pathway that is forming to connect the ends of the empire. The annual exodus of the Calcutta Baboos would then increase to a hundred-fold degree. People would be pouring in streams from all parts of the realm, to seek for a pleasant break to the monotony of their lives, and for a rational use of the holiday. All debasing amusements would then give way to the yearning for the lands memorable in history and song, and the indulgence in religious mummeries would be superseded by the pleasures of revelling in scenes and sights of nature—the Railway acting no less than the part of the Messiah.

October 21*st*.—By nine o'clock this morning the gharries were ready at our doors. Made haste to pack up and start. This is emphatically the age of Progress.

From the Railway, the next forward step should have been to sail careering through the regions of air,—'to paw the light winds, and gallop upon the storm.' But far from all that, we had to step into a dawk-gharry of the preceding generation, and our fall was like Lucifer's fall from heaven,—a headlong plunge from the heights of civilization to the abyss of low Andamanese life. By travelling over a hundred and twenty miles in six hours, the feelings are wrought up to a high pitch. It is difficult afterwards to screw down the tone of the mind, and prepare it for a less speedy rate of travelling. The exchange of the iron horse for one of flesh and blood, soon made itself apparent. The foretaste of luxury made the change a bitter sequel—which well nigh disposed us to believe in the philosophers who maintain the doctrine of the alternate progression and retrogression of mankind. But endurance got the better of disagreeableness, and we began gradually to be reconciled to our now mode of travelling, and to the tardiness of our progress.

The Grand Trunk Road—the *smooth bowling-green* of Sir Charles Wood—the royal road of India, that is soon to be counted among by-gones—the great thoroughfare, which being metalled with *kunker*, earned to Lord Wm Bentinck the singularly inappropriate *soubriquet* of William the Conqueror—now lay extended before us in all its interminable length. In coming up by the train, often did it burst upon and retire from the sight—as 'if bashful, yet impatient to be seen,' and to rival the rail in the race it runs. Dr Russel compares this road to 'a great white riband straight before us.' But more aptly it is to be fancied as a sacerdotal thread on the neck of India, which runs so slanting across the breadth of our peninsula.

The upward train from Allahabad starts at four in the afternoon,—so the whole day is left to us to spend it in exploring the town. In many parts it still has a desolate, poverty-stricken appearance, and consists of thatched huts, with a few brick-houses at intervals. The *Duria-ghaut* on the Jumna is a sacred spot. They say that Rama, with his wife and brother Luchmun, crossed here at this ghaut, on their way from Ajoodhya to go over to the land of their exile. He passed by this place to give a visit to his friend Goohuk Chandal. But it was a long time after Rama, that the Chundail kings of Chunar made their appearance in India, and held Allahabad under their sway. There is properly no ghaut with a flight of steps at the spot to do justice to the memory of Rama. The concourse of people, however, bathing there in this holy month presents a lively scene—with groups of Hindoostanee women performing their matin rites, and returning home in processions clothed in drapery of the gayest colours. The Rajah of Benares has a fine villa in the neighbourhood of this ghaut.

Not far below the Duria-ghaut they were busy at the site of the intended Railway bridge over the Jumna. In two years, they have sunk about twenty shafts. The pits, more than forty feet deep, are awful. They lie side by side of each, and have extremely narrow brinks to walk from one to the other. Three or four lives have been lost in sinking the shafts, and it is difficult to get men for the work. The diver has to remain below for half the day. One man had just been taken up as we arrived. He was below forty feet of water for six hours together. But on taking off his waterproof coat, his body was found to have been untouched by a single drop of water—only the hands were dripping and shrivelled. The face also showed a little paleness on removal of the diving-helmet. But he came to himself again after a few minutes in the open air. The shafts have collected a little *chur* about them— and this is to be the foundation for a bridge to ride triumphantly across the Jumna.

There is a question on the tapis to make Allahabad the seat of the North-Western Presidency. Hereafter, the excellent geographical position, the strength of the natural boundaries, the fine climate, and the great resources of the neighbouring provinces, may point the place out for the seat of the Viceroy himself. Two years ago, here was uttered the dirge over the funeral of the late East India Company,— here was inaugurated the era of the Sovereignty of the Queen, with royal promises of pardon, forgiveness, justice, religious toleration, and non-annexation,—and here was Lord Canning installed as the first Viceroy of India.

Once more to move on by rail to Cawnpore. The station at Allahabad is not half so large as that at Howrah. But it is very picturesque to look at the up-country train with its vari-coloured turbaned Hindoostanee passengers. They use here wood instead of coal, and the great evil of it is, that you are liable to catch fire from the sparks—sometimes pieces of red-hot charcoal—from the engine. 'The other day, as a detachment of Sikh soldiers were going up-country, one of them had his clothes set on fire by the embers. All his comrades were dressed in cotton-quilted tunics, with their pouches full of ammunition; and in their alarm they adopted the notable device of pitching the man out of the window, in order to get rid of the danger to which they were exposed.'

There now lay before us the prospect of the extensive, beautiful, and historic valley of the Doab—the *Anterved* of the ancient Hindoos. From the narrow point in which it has terminated, the valley broadens as it stretches away towards the west, embracing a greater and greater area between the Ganges and Jumna, that form the highways of nature,—while the rail laid across between them forms the rival highway of man. The whole of its immense superficies forms a vast, populous, and busy hive, enriched by human industry, and embellished by human taste. On the map, no country is so thickly dotted with great townships and cities,—and under the sun, no country makes up such a highly interesting prospect of green fields, orchards, and gardens, in a continuous succession. In this fair *savanah* man has had his abode from a remote antiquity, to reap rich harvests, and live amidst plenty. Here were the cities of the pre-Vedic *Dasyas*. Here rose the first cities of the *Aryas*. In the plains of the Doab, the Rajahs of Hastinapoor, of Indraprasthra, and of Kanouge, exhibited the highest power and splendour of Hindoo sovereignty. The rich districts watered by the Ganges and Jumna have always tempted the avarice of the foreign conqueror. To these regions did Alexander point as the utmost goal of his ambition. Here was the residence of the most famous Hindoo sages. From this birth-place of arts and civilization has wisdom travelled to the West. The Doab is the battle-ground of the Pandoo against the Kuru—of the Ghiznivide and Ghorian against the Hindoo—of the Mogul against the Patan—of the Mahratta against the Mogul—and of the English against the Mahratta.

But before many years, when agricultural produce shall pour hither by rail, river, and road—from a large part of the surrounding country, and from the rich districts of Oude and Rohilcund—for transit to the port of shipping, a succession of warehouses and sheds will extend to the Railway station. By the speculative Up-country wallahs, the place may be raised to the importance of the first cotton market in Hindoostan; and in time, Hindoostanee enterprise, calculating on the profits of reviving the defunct manufactures of their country, may emulate Manchester, and start projects for turning Cawnpore into a rival town. The cessation of its military importance would then be more than compensated by the enhancement of its commercial importance.

Carpet-making is observed in many of the shops. The produce of these far-away districts can never compete with the produce grown near the ports of shipment. The ancient wealth of the city is still helping the inhabitants, as are also the emoluments of the various offices under the present régime. But the position of Agra makes it the most eligible outlet and inlet for the traffic of Rajpootana; and when the Rail shall have removed the disabilities under which its trade labours, and goods shall come up from the sea in twice the time that the earth travels round its axis, the place will rapidly advance in wealth and prosperity.

But how the charms of illusion fade away before stern truth, that recalls us from our reveries to the realities of the scene before us. Our journey drawing to a close, the train discharged such numbers of all classes of people, travellers, merchants, shopkeepers, gentlemen of elegant leisure, invalids, and speculators, as will have a sensible effect upon the manners and customs of the men in these places. The road beneath the platform was thronged by a dense crowd of coolies, sweetmeat vendors, and hooka-burdars, running and hawking about in all directions. Carriages of various description, but all included under the common name of 'buggies,' lay waiting to be engaged by the passengers. The dust, loosened by the tread of steps, was flying about to make big folks turn up their aristocratic noses. The 'flies of Delhi' lagged not behind to give a sample of their welcome to the stranger, by attacking his ears, eyes, nose, and mouth most inhospitably. Our patience would have given way under the strain put to it, were there not faces to peep from behind the *purdahs* of *ekkas*—faces of females whom the rash innovator, Rail, had drawn out from the seclusion of their zenanas, to throw them upon the rude gaze of the public. The *hookah*, too, came to our relief after six long, long hours,—the poor *hookah*, or cheroot, or pipe, that is in such awful unpopularity with the Railway authorities, and threatened by their highest penal denouncements. Hiring a gharry, and taking in it all our luggage and baggage, that made us feel about as comfortable as one is in stocks, we proceeded,—pulling at, and puffing away from, a *hubble-bubble* to keep off the unceremonious flies—to make our entry into the city of the Great Mogul in a right earnest Mogul style. Before us intervened the Jumna, spanned by a bridge of boats, similar to which there existed one in the days of the Timurean princes. The beautiful railway bridge through which the train is to ride hereafter direct into the city, is nearly complete for being thrown open for traffic. Forsooth, that iron-bridge is as it were the reality of Xerxes' chain and rod thrown over the proud Jumna. Oh! ye shades of Judisthira, Bheema, and Arjoona, with what pious horror must you look down from your blest abodes, upon the impious bridge that binds and lashes the waves of that classic stream.—But poetry has had its reign, and science now must hold her sway for the comfort of wayfaring men. It was not our blessed fortune to be able to go across through that bridge, though it might have been profaning the memory of our ancestors by hurrying at once most unclassically right into the heart of their city. Greatly to our disappointment, our gharry had to go rumbling over the bridge of boats 'towards the grand donjon of a giant keep that frowns over the flood.'

4

'MODES OF TRAVELLING IN INDIA', *ILLUSTRATED LONDON NEWS*, SEPTEMBER 19, 1863, 284

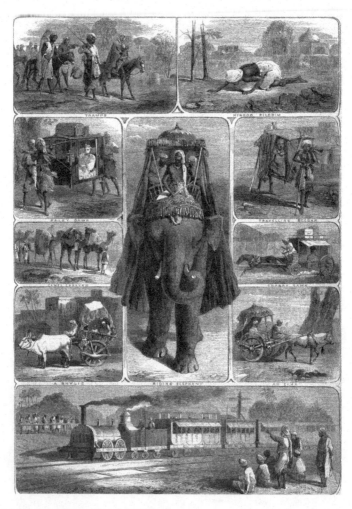

Figure 4.1 Modes of Travelling in India

5

SIDNEY LAMAN BLANCHARD, *THE GANGES AND THE SEINE*, 2 VOLS. (LONDON: CHAPMAN AND GALL, 1862), II, PP. 6–13

The railway station at Howrah had a small hotel when I knew it, but now I believe has a large one. In all essential features it is as like an English station as need be. The engines and engineers are British to a fault; the carriages are perhaps an improvement: they seem larger and more lofty, but are built strictly upon the home model. One difference the traveller will not fail to note when he arrives with his traps: instead of the porters who wheel off his luggage upon their trucks and get them labelled out of hand, he will find nobody available for the purpose but a crowd of native coolies, clad, or rather unclad, in their usual light and airy manner—a few inches of cloth round the middle being considered a liberal arrangement. Two or three would be amply sufficient for the work required; but the service is a competition one, and there are generally about twenty of them, pushing, squeezing, and howling at once for the appointment. If you do not take care and have traps enough, the whole twenty will each seize an article and run with it in a different direction. I know less embarrassing positions in which to be placed than this, especially if time is short, the train likely to be punctual, and you have yet to get your ticket. But a judicious traveller will anticipate the onslaught, and defend his baggage tooth and nail until two or three of the "competition wallahs" have selected themselves from the rest and taken possession of the post of looking after it. You have then nothing to do but to get out of the dispute, which you are sure to have with these on the subject of their *baksheesh*, as well as you can, and to see your baggage safely labelled and stowed away. This is supposing that you take any baggage at all, which of course you will not do if you are only on an excursion for the day.

If you travel first class, you are not likely to meet with any but European fellow passengers. Natives are not prohibited from travelling by that class; but there appears to be a tacit understanding that they should prefer to go by the others. This, be it observed, is not on account of any exclusive spirit on the part of our countrymen, but is rather the fault of the natives themselves. The English are very often blamed for not mingling more freely with them, but more often than not it is the natives who make the mingling impossible by their unwillingness to conform to European ideas. It may be said, why do European ideas not conform to those of the native? I believe they do in most matters which admit of the concession; but in some cases the concession is simply impossible. Take that of railway travelling for instance: the difficulty was experienced immediately on the opening of the line from Calcutta to Raneegunj. It happened that an English traveller, a merchant, entered a first-class carriage in company with two ladies. To them came a fat *baboo*, who took his seat opposite one of the latter. The day was warm, nevertheless, I need scarcely remark that the merchant and his friends were decently clothed. The baboo, however, though born in the country, could not endure the discomfort of such restrictions; and he had no sooner taken his seat than he proceeded to remove the only covering—which was light enough, being of thin muslin—that he wore above his waist; and, exposed in this manner, he tranquilly betook himself to his hookah to enjoy himself for the journey. Now I think the most liberal-minded reader must admit that a fat baboo, in a semi state of nudity, is not a very pleasant person with whom to be shut up in a railway carriage on a hot day in Bengal, more especially when the baboo smokes a hookah, and addicts himself at intervals to *pân*, the eating of which is attended with rather more unpleasantness to the eye than the mastication of tobacco. In the presence of ladies, moreover, the whole proceeding amounted to a wanton insult; and even supposing that it was meant as a mark of respect, surely no man could expect a lady so to accept it. Accordingly, our chivalrous merchant requested the baboo to put on his vest, and I rather think to put out his pipe, but am not quite sure as to the latter. But the baboo only grinned, and when the Englishman reinforced his request by observing that he was dressed more like a coolie (native labourer) than a gentleman; the baboo responded by saying, "*Tum coolie hai*," (you are a coolie) the form of expression (through the use of the second instead of the third person) being as offensive as its meaning. Upon this the Englishman seized the astonished baboo and turned him forcibly out of the carriage. The baboo charged him before a magistrate for the assault, and the offence was visited with a tolerably heavy fine. So strong was public opinion upon the subject, however, that the fine was at once paid by subscription, and a large additional sum collected *for the expenses of the next prosecution*. This significant determination seems to have had its effect; for I have not heard of another rencontre of the kind occurring; and the natives, as a general rule, avoid the first class, except in the case of a great man, who takes a carriage to himself when he does not happen to want the entire train.

"The Great Shoe Question," which arose at the same time, involved a less important consideration; but it illustrates the difficulty which exists in assimilating European with Asiatic manners, except to the degradation of the former. Orientals remove their slippers before entering a room, as we remove our hats. The courtesy in either case has precisely the same value and signification. Certain natives who were received at the levées of the Governor-General, appeared in their slippers, for the reason, as they alleged, that the British appeared in their boots. It was intimated to them that if they desired to conform to European usages

they could retain their slippers, but they must doff their turbans. As the latter proceeding would involve disgrace, they declined to comply, and the pros and cons of
"the Great Shoe Question" were hotly discussed all over the country. Ultimately it
was settled, by a sufficiently liberal concession on the part of the local authorities,
that any native gentleman choosing to wear his slippers at the levées must doff
them at the door, according to Oriental custom; but that any who might choose to
wear European boots might retain them if he so pleased. That he would so please
may be easily imagined, as the British boot usually requires certain ingenious
machinery to enable the wearer to get it on or take it off; and he would not be very
likely to find boothooks and bootjacks in the verandah to assist him in a struggle
with that article of costume upon arrival and departure. The order appears to have
satisfied all parties, and we heard nothing more of the Great Shoe Question, until
it was revived the other day in Bombay, to be settled again, it is to be hoped, as
amicably as before. A great many of the natives in Calcutta—principally belonging to the class of "Young Bengal," who eat beef, drink champagne, and read
Shakspeare and Milton—now wear the British boot, and are as proud of the privilege of stamping about in it at Government House as the Spanish grandees of
wearing their hats in the presence of the sovereign, or the solitary nobleman may
be who enjoys the same privilege in England.

It would be well if a great many of the obstacles to intercourse between natives
and Europeans in India could be as easily overcome; but in the majority of cases it
is the native who opposes the impassable bar. No man can become very intimate
with another whose domestic relations are on so different a footing, who will not
eat with him, and who in many cases considers that his dinner would be defiled by
the shadow of a Christian passing over it.

But I am detaining the reader all this time at the station.

One of the most characteristic sights which the traveller is likely to meet with
while waiting for his train, is the arrival of another traveller from the North-West,
with all his bags and baggage. Having been journeying downwards by dâk, for a
long distance it may be, he is very unlikely to be as clean and neat in his appearance as if just starting from Calcutta. If I said that he is very likely to be quite
unfit to be seen, I should not perhaps be exaggerating. Some persons do the dâk
journey in decorous costume enough, but there are many who reduce themselves
to a *toilette de nuit*, and as they lie at full length in the carriage, and bring sheets
and blankets and pillows with them, the whole proceeding is as much like "going
to bed" as can well be. I do not mean to say that they appear at the railway station
precisely in the costume indicated above, but their toilette is of a very hurried
character, and is decidedly more picturesque than polite. However, it is scarcely
wonderful that people should not care much about their appearance when there
is nobody to see them. What is more worthy of remark is the amount of baggage
that they carry, and the extraordinary variety of articles of which it consists. Half
of these are not packed up, having been disposed loosely in the dâk gharry, an
arrangement which, as the traveller has the gharry all to himself, is as convenient
as any other. I have seen a gharry unpacked at the railway station, from which the

contents have been extracted in the course of three quarters of an hour, in something like the following manner:—

First, five coolies come toiling in with a little portmanteau that one could carry with ease. They are followed by two coolies staggering under the weight of a large trunk which would be a fair load for double their number. Then come half a dozen coolies bringing two or three *pittarahs*, (native boxes made of tin, secured in a wooden framework,) which they carry as they can between them. They are followed by a single coolie, dragging after him an immense portmanteau which he cannot manage to lift at all. These, it may be, include all the heavy baggage which has been piled on the top of the carriage; and the miscellaneous articles have next to be dealt with. One man brings a hamper which has held soda water, &c., and may hold it still. Another follows with a box of cheroots. A third comes laden with the responsibility of a corkscrew. A fourth succeeds him, bending, not under the weight but under the bulk, of a huge *rezai*, a warm covering stuffed with cotton, not quite so thick as a featherbed. A fifth comes bearing an English railway rug, blankets perhaps, and pillows, forming the rest of the bed. A sixth brings a stray pair of boots which have been left loose for contingencies. A seventh succeeds with three or four stray coats, also kept loose in case of being wanted. An eighth accommodates himself to the burthen of a box of Reading biscuits, or one or two ditto of potted meats. A ninth solemnly inducts a volume of Railway Library appearance, with a blue and yellow picture outside. A tenth carries the oak case of a Colt's revolver, the weapon being probably at the traveller's waist. In the same manner half a hundred other more or less considered trifles are brought into the station, and piled up in a heap on the ground; after which the traveller himself follows, bearing, perhaps, a sword in its leather case, and most certainly some fifty or sixty walking sticks, of every possible variety, bound together with a strap. These articles being contributed to the heap, he has nothing to do but to have his "row" with the coolies on a subject to which I need not more particularly allude, which diversion is sure to occupy him until the arrival of his train. If a lady be the occupant of the carriage, of course the confusion of traps is doubled at least. Workbaskets and such matters increase the miscellaneous character of the collection; bandboxes are inevitable; two or three birdcages are more than possible; with very likely a parrot on a perch, and may be a monkey. Among the inanimate portion of a lady's luggage which there had apparently been no time to pack up, I once saw a mysterious thing shaped like a figure of eight, which I was informed was a crinoline in a state of collapse. Travellers truly see strange sights!

But away to Chandernagore. The train does not take one very quickly; at least the pace is not so fast as in England, though a tearing one for the languid East. The second and third classes are filled with natives, who take to this mode of conveyance with an avidity never expected from them; for it was supposed that they would stand upon their *antiquas viâs* even though condemned to traverse them by the bullock train. As the event has proved, however, the natives are the main support of the line, and even the poorest among them are so anxious to avail themselves of its advantages that not long ago they were clamouring for the establishment of a *fourth* class.

6

WILLIAM HOWARD RUSSELL, *MY DIARY IN INDIA IN THE YEAR 1858–1859*, 2 VOLS. (LONDON: ROUTLEDGE, 1860), I, PP. 154–162, II, PP. 407–409

After a long conversation, of which I have said quite enough, I went into one of the tents to present a letter of introduction to one of his Lordship's suite. A young slight active officer was sitting in a chair at a table, covered of course with papers, when I entered. That cheery genial voice, that bright look, full of intelligence and life, struck me at once. "L—— is not in just now; but I am a friend of his," quoth he; "and if I can be of any service, pray command me." When he knew my name and errand, he at once proposed to show me over the fort. I could not have had a more intelligent guide, and so we sauntered about the old lines of Akbar's engineers, and observed where his work was dovetailed into ours, and censured defects, and praised good points as long as we could stand the sun. As Stewart— for it was he—heard he was to accompany me to Cawnpore, we made arrangements for starting ere we parted. The rail, which once more makes a spasmodic effort to establish itself in India, here goes about halfway to Cawnpore. One is weary of thinking how much blood, disgrace, misery, and horror had been saved to us if the rail had been but a little longer here, had been at all there, had been completed at another place. It has been a heavy mileage of neglect for which we have already paid dearly. But the bill is not yet settled in full.

February 11*th*.—Up early, preparing for our start, though the train does not go till 9·30. Met Lord Mark Kerr, who is in command of Her Majesty's 13th Regiment here, at the railway side, for there is no station, and had a slight inspection of the regiment, which marched past, with band playing, as a little mark of attention, I conceive, towards Sir Robert Garrett.

At last the train was ready, filled with soldiers, officers and their servants, and no passengers; for the Government has monopolized the train: and only those who get tickets on service are permitted to go by it at present. The carriages were old second-class invalids of English lines: but they were luxurious enough after the long journey in dust and sun. Stewart was ready to his time, and duly superintended by Captain Maxwell, the quartermaster-general, who acted as station-master, we started not more than one hour behind our time, which was not of any consequence, as there was no fear of collisions. How many of my fellow-passengers are gone to their account, or are disfigured by wounds, or enfeebled by the fevers and sicknesses, which in India leave their mark on a man for his lifetime! There is one, I see, before me now—a tall deep-chested fine young fellow—blue-eyed, tawny-maned—the old Scandinavian type, full of energy, "dying to see service," hurrying up now to the front, with a wound, received in the first encounter he had with the enemy, not yet quite healed. Poor Clarke! The last time I saw him he was one of the most dreadful objects I ever beheld—burnt, black, and covered with blistered skin from head to foot, blown up by that horrid explosion of powder at Lucknow. But he was at peace, poor fellow! for ever; and great as his agony must have been, he carried none of it out of this world; for his face bore, at the moment of his death, as I was assured, a calm and peaceful expression. It is sad, indeed, to look back now in one's mind, and to remember the conversation and the plans of those fellow-passengers who have since then gone on their long journey.

For some distance outside the station we passed through deserted villages, through lines of bungalows devastated by fire; then we entered on a plain, burnt and dry, covered with bushes growing out of sand, the favourite resort of nylghy (blue cow), deer, and antelopes. Here and there were villages abandoned, and never very desirable. The stations, such as they were, seemed crude and incomplete. The bright hot sun lent no joyousness or pleasant life to those arboriferous wastes; and I was glad to arrive at the terminus of the line, which consisted of a cessation of the rails in the sand, at a place called Khaga, about sixty-five miles from Allahabad, at two o'clock. Under a grove of trees, filled with green parrots, and vultures, and buzzards, were pitched a few tents, which represented the station. The clerk and station-master was in one, sick with fever; the others were occupied by travellers waiting for dâks, all of them connected with the public service. Those who were going towards Calcutta were invalids, some of them with their families. In griffin-hood I admired the proportions of their establishments; but I could safely say, "*Haud equidem invideo, miror magis.*" A luxurious little baby was carried forth for a walk under the shade of the trees; it was borne in the arms of a fat ayah, beside whom walked a man, whose sole business it was gently to whisk away the flies which might venture to disturb baby's slumbers. Another man wheeled a small carriage, in which lay another little lord of the Indian creation, asleep, likewise with his human flapper by his side, whilst two ayahs followed the procession in rear; through the open door of the tent could be seen the lady-mother reading for her husband; a native servant fanned her with a hand-punkah; two little terriers, chained to a tree, were under the care of a separate domestic. A cook was busy superintending several pots set upon fires in the open air, a second prepared the curry-paste, a third was busy with plates, knives, and forks. In the rear of the servants' tents, which were two in number—making, with the master's, four—were two small tents for the syces, grass-cutters, and camel-men, or doodwallahs, behind which were picketed three horses, three camels, and a pair of bullocks, and ere we left, another servant drove in a few goats, which were used for milking. I was curious to know who this millionnaire could be, and was astonished to learn that it was only Captain Smith, of the Mekawattee Irregulars, who was travelling down country, with the usual train of domestics and animals required under the circumstances. The whole of this little camp did not contain more than eight or nine tents; but there were at least 150 domestics and a menagerie of animals connected with them. The tope was exceeding rich; the trees swarming with the common noisy green parroquet, and with the ever-active squeaking squirrel.

On our return we found gharrys waiting for us, and the whole of the party which had started from Allahabad set out for Cawnpore at five o'clock at night. As there was no advantage to be gained by arriving at the Cawnpore cantonments in the middle of the night, we halted on the road after half-an-hour's drive, and in the shade proceeded to make our dinner. Sir Robert Garrett had a preserved tongue in a tin case, like a huge red sugar-loaf, and a strong wish was expressed to investigate the interior, which would, it was supposed, form an agreeable addition to the resources of our banquet; but we had no means of opening it. It turned all the edges of our knives, broke all their points, set forks and hunting-knives at defiance; at last, in a rage, we put it up on end against a tree, and I fired my revolver through the angle of the case, so as to make a hole in the tin. Having first made this lodgement in the salient, the rest of the work was easy, and the tongue almost answered our ardent expectations.

About seven we halted again at the bungalow, in a very decayed straggling old town, called Futtehpore. There were many sheds well-thatched, and substantial enough, in the court-yard, which had been erected for the soldiers on their march along the trunk-road; and again one read the old stereotyped inscriptions on the walls, which almost made me regret that writing was included in the branches of education taught to the soldier. Near us was encamped a small force—some infantry and guns. Sir Robert with Dallas set out to visit the camp, in order to see his old friend Colonel David Wood, who was in command, whilst Oxenden, Stewart, and myself managed to extricate a supper out of the Khansamah's very limited *repertoire*. At night the gharrys came round, and we rumbled along in peaceful sleep over the trunk-road by which Neill and Havelock had advanced to attack the Butcher of Cawnpore—a road, by the way, of which many of the trees had been hung with natives' bodies as the column under Neill and Renaud marched to open the way from Allahabad. I hear many stories, the truth of which I would doubt if I could. Our first spring was terrible; I fear our claws were indiscriminating.

On my way back from this visit, I had occasion to go to the railway office to give instructions for forwarding my baggage—which had not yet arrived from Lucknow—if I were obliged to start ere it reached Cawnpore; and I am obliged to confess the fears which are expressed—that the sense of new-sprung power, operating on vulgar, half-educated men, aided by the servility of those around them, may produce results most prejudicial to our influence among the natives—are not destitute of foundation, if I may take the manners of the person whom I found at the chief engineer's house, as a fair specimen of the behaviour of his class towards gentlemen. As I was returning to the hotel, I saw another exemplification of the mischiefs which are to be dreaded from a large infusion of Europeans into India, in positions where they are really irresponsible, unless to their own good feelings. The Company foresaw the danger, which, however, arose very much from the system of legal administration and police which they founded, or were forced to accept. If Europeans are not restrained by education and humanity from giving vent to their angry passions, there is little chance of their being punished for anything short of murder—and of murder it has been oftentimes difficult to procure the conviction of Europeans at the hands of their countrymen. This is what happened. There were a number of coolies sitting idly under the shadow of a wall: suddenly there came upon them, with a bound and a roar, a great British lion—his eyes flashing fire, a tawny mane of long locks floating from under his pith helmet, and a huge stick in his fist—a veritable Thor in his anger. He rushed among the coolies, and they went down like grass, maimed and bleeding. I shouted out of the gharry, "Good Heavens, stop! Why, you'll kill those men!" (One of them was holding up his arm as if it were broken.) A furious growl, "What the——business have you to interfere? It's no affair of yours." "Oh, yes, sir; but it is. I am not going to be accessory to murder. See how you have maimed that man! You know they dared not raise a finger against you." "Well; but these lazy scoundrels are engaged to do our work, and they sneak off whenever they can, and how can I look after them!"

Now I believe, from what I heard, these cases occur up-country frequently; in one place there has been a sort of mutiny and murder among railway labourers; and in fact, the authorities have issued injunctions to the railway subordinates to be cautious how they commit excesses and violence among their labourers, and warn them they will be punished. A ganger, or head navvy, accustomed to see around him immense results, produced by great physical energy and untiring strength, is placed over hundreds of men, remote from supervision or control; he sees the work is not done—"a good-for-nothing set of idlers;" and so he takes to stick and fist for it. Going home, I called on Major Tombs, Paymaster, of Cawnpore, and brother of Colonel Tombs of the Bengal Artillery; and on Dr. Elliot, an old friend in the Crimea, now stationed at Cawnpore. All paymasters are in distress about their "balances" in wartimes. How they and the Commissariat, and the doctors, and the brigade officers, rejoiced when the gale of the 14th November, before Sebastopol, blew all their papers into the sea! In India, paymasters handle enormous sums; and the "balance" will sometimes, in such times as these, amount to seven or eight lacs—that is, 70,000l. or 80,000l.

7

G. O. TREVELYAN, *THE COMPETITION WALLAH*, SECOND ED. (LONDON: MACMILLAN, 1866), PP. 21–30

On the evening of the 31st I left Calcutta by train, with the intention of living a week at Patna with Major Ratcliffe, who is on special duty there, and then passing the rest of my leave with my cousin, Tom Goddard, at Mofussilpore. Ratcliffe is a Bengal Club acquaintance, who gave me first a general, and then a most particular invitation to stay with him up country. There is something stupendous in the hospitality of India. It appears to be the ordinary thing, five minutes after a first introduction, for people to ask you to come and spend a month with them. And yet there is a general complaint that the old good-fellowship is going out fast; that there are so many Europeans about of questionable position and most unquestionable breeding, that it is necessary to know something of a man besides the colour of his skin before admitting him into the bosom of a family.

There is something very interesting in a first railway journey in Bengal. Never was I so impressed with the triumphs of progress, the march of mind. In fact, all the usual common-places genuinely filled my soul. Those two thin strips of iron, representing as they do the mightiest and the most fruitful conquest of science, stretch hundreds and hundreds of miles across the boundless Eastern plains—rich, indeed, in material products, but tilled by a race far below the most barbarous of Europeans in all the qualities that give good hope for the future of a nation— through the wild hills of Rajmahal, swarming with savage beasts, and men more savage than they; past Mussulman shrines and Hindoo temples; along the bank of the great river that cannot be bridged, whose crocodiles fatten on the corpses which superstition still supplies to them by hundreds daily. Keep to the line, and you see everywhere the unmistakable signs of England's handiwork. There are the colossal viaducts, spanning wide tracts of pool and sandbank, which the first rains will convert into vast torrents. There are the long rows of iron sheds, with huge engines running in and out of them with that indefiniteness of purpose which seems to characterise locomotives all over the world. There is the true British stationmaster, grand but civil on ordinary occasions, but bursting into excitement and ferocity when things go wrong, or when his will is disputed; who fears nothing human or divine, except the daily press. There is the refreshment-room, with its half-crown dinner that practically always costs five and ninepence. Stroll a hundred yards from the embankment, and all symptoms of civilization have vanished. You find yourself in the midst of scenes that Arrian might have witnessed; among manners unchanged by thousands of years—unchangeable, perhaps, by thousands more. The gay bullock-litter bearing to her wedding the bride of four years old; the train of pilgrims, their turbans and cummerbunds stained with pink, carrying back the water of the sacred stream to their distant homes; the filthy, debauched beggar, whom all the neighbourhood pamper like a bacon-hog, and revere as a Saint Simeon—these are sights which have very little in common with Didcot or Crewe Junction.

A station on an Indian line affords much that is amusing to a curious observer. Long before the hour at which the train is expected, a dense crowd of natives collects outside the glass-doors, dressed in their brightest colours, and in a wild state of excitement. The Hindoos have taken most kindly to railway-travelling. It is a species of locomotion which pre-eminently suits their lazy habits; and it likewise appeals to their love of turning a penny. To them every journey is a petty speculation. If they can sell their goods at a distance for a price which will cover the double fare, and leave a few pice over, they infinitely prefer sitting still in a truck to earning a much larger sum by genuine labour. A less estimable class of men of business, who are said to make great use of the railway, are the dacoits, who travel often sixty or seventy miles to commit their villanies, in order to escape the observation of the police in their own district. Every native carries a parcel of some sort or kind; and it often happens that a man brings a bundle so large that it cannot be got in at the door.

At length the barrier is opened, and the passengers are admitted in small parties by a policeman, who treats them with almost as little courtesy as is shown to Cook's tourists by a Scotch railway official. When his turn comes to buy a ticket, your true Hindoo generally attempts to make a bargain with the clerk, but is very summarily snubbed by that gentleman; and, after an unsuccessful effort to conceal a copper coin, he is shoved by a second policeman on to the platform, where he and his companions discuss the whole proceeding at great length and with extraordinary warmth.

Natives almost invariably travel third-class. At one time a train used to run consisting entirely of first and third-class carriages. Every first-class passenger was entitled to take two servants at third-class prices. It was no uncommon thing for well-to-do natives to entreat an English traveller to let them call themselves his servants for the sake of the difference in the fares. The most wealthy Hindoos would probably go first-class if it were not for a well-founded fear of the Sahibs; and therefore they share the second-class with our poorer countrymen. In fact, in spite of the fraternity and equality which exist in theory between the subjects of our beloved Queen, the incompatibility of manners is such that English ladies could not use the railway at all if native gentlemen were in the constant habit of travelling in the same compartment. If you ask how our countrymen manage to appropriate to themselves the first-class carriages without a special regulation to that effect, I ask you in return, How is it that there are no tradesmen's sons at Eton or Harrow? There is no law, written or unwritten, which excludes them from those schools, and yet the boys take good care that if one comes he shall not stay there very long.

To return to the scene at our station. Suddenly, in the rear of the crowd, without the gates, there arises a great hubbub, amidst which, from time to time, may be distinguished an imperious, sharp-cut voice, the owner of which appears to show the most lordly indifference to the remarks and answers made around him. A few moments more, after some quarrelling and shoving about, the throng divides, and down the lane thus formed stalks the Sahib of the period, in all the glory of an old flannel shirt and trousers, a dirty alpaca coat, no collar, no waistcoat, white canvas shoes, and a vast pith helmet. Behind him comes his chief bearer, with a cash-box, a loading-rod, two copies of the *Saturday Review* of six months back, and three bottles of sodawater. Then follows a long team of coolies, carrying on their heads a huge quantity of shabby and nondescript luggage, including at least one gun-case and a vast shapeless parcel of bedding. On the portmanteau you may still read, in very faint white letters, "Calcutta. Cabin." The Sahib, with the freedom and easy insolence of a member of the Imperial race, walks straight into the sacred inclosure of the clerk's office, and takes a ticket, at five times the price paid by his native brethren. Meanwhile, his bearer disposes the luggage in a heap, rewards the coolies on a scale which seems to give them profound discontent, and receives a third-class ticket from his master's hand with every mark of the most heartfelt gratitude. If there happen to be another Sahib on the platform, the two fall to talking on the extreme badness of the road in the district made by the Supreme Government, as opposed to those constructed by the local authorities. If he is alone, our Sahib contemplates the statement of offences committed against the railway rules and regulations, and the penalties inflicted, and sees with satisfaction that his own countrymen enjoy the privilege of being placed at the head of the list, which generally runs somewhat thus:—

"John Spinks, formerly private in the —th Foot, was charged before the mag-
"istrate of Howrah, with being drunk and disorderly on the Company's premises,
"in which state he desired the station-master to run a special train for him, and on
"this being refused, he assaulted that official, and grievously wounded three native
"policemen. On conviction, he was sentenced to three months' imprisonment."

"David Wilkins, who described himself as a professional man, was charged
"with being drunk and disorderly, and with refusing to leave a railway carriage
"when requested to do so. He was reprimanded and discharged."

Then comes a long series of native misdemeanours, chiefly consisting in riding with intent to defraud.

At length the train arrives. As the traffic is very large, and there is only a single line (though the bridges and viaducts have been built for a double line), the trains are necessarily composed of a great number of trucks. First, perhaps, come eight or ten second-class carriages, full of pale panting English soldiers, in their shirt-sleeves. Then one first-class, of which the *coupé* is occupied by a young couple going to an appointment up-country. They have become acquainted during the balls and tiffins of the cold season at Calcutta, and were married at the end of it. Perhaps they may never see it again until the bridegroom, who seems a likely young fellow, is brought down from the Mofussil to be put into the Secretariat. They have got a happy time before them. India is a delightful country for the first few years of married life. Lovers are left very much to themselves, and are able to enjoy to the full that charmingly selfish concentration of affection which is sometimes a little out of place in general society. When the eldest child must positively go home before the next hot season, and ought to have gone home before the last—when aunts, and grandmothers, and schoolmistresses at Brighton, and agents in London have to be corresponded with—then troubles begin to come thick. The next compartment is filled by a family party—a languid, bilious, mother; a sickly, kindly, indefatigable nurse; and three little ones sprawling on the cushions in different stages of undress. In the netting overhead are plentiful stores of bottles of milk, bread and butter, and toys. Poor things! What an age a journey from Calcutta to Benares must seem at four years old! In the third compartment are two Sahibs smoking, who have filled every corner of the carriage with their bags and trunks, the charge for luggage in the van being preposterously high out here. Our Sahib, who is too good-natured to disturb the lovers, and who has no great fancy for children as fellow-travellers, through the dust and glare of a journey in India, determines to take up his quarters with the last-mentioned party. The two gentlemen object very strongly to being crowded, although there is full room for eight passengers; but our Sahib is a determined man, and he soon establishes himself, with all his belongings, as comfortably as circumstances will admit, and before very long the trio have fraternized over Manilla cheroots and the Indigo question. Behind the first-class carriage come an interminable row of third-class, packed to overflowing with natives in high exhilaration, stripped to the waist, chattering, smoking hubble-bubbles, chewing betel-nut, and endeavouring to curry favour with the guard—for your true native never loses an opportunity of conciliating a man in authority. Though there does not appear to be an inch of room available, the crowd of new comers are pushed and heaved in by the station-master and his subordinates, and left to settle down by the force of gravity. In an incredibly short space of time the platform is cleared; the guard bawls out something that might once have borne a dim resemblance to "all right behind," the whistle sounds, and the train moves on at the rate of twenty-five miles an hour, including stoppages.

If one of the pleasures of travel be to find a preconceived notion entirely contradicted by the reality, that pleasure I enjoyed to the full at Patna. A city of nearly three hundred thousand inhabitants, the capital of an immense province, one of the earliest seats of Batavian commerce, connected with the history of our race by the most melancholy and glorious associations;—I expected to pass through a succession of lofty streets, of temples rich with fretwork, of bazaars blazing with the gorgeous fabrics of the Eastern loom; in fact, through such a scene as you described in your unsuccessful prize poem upon "Delhi." Somewhere in the centre of this mass of wealth and magnificence I depicted to myself a square or crescent of architecture less florid than elsewhere, but more nearly approaching to European ideas of comfort. This was to be the quarter appropriated to the English residents. Here were to be their shops and factories, their courts, their offices, and the churches of their various persuasions. Such was the picture which I had composed in about equal proportions from the "Arabian Nights" and Macaulay's Essay on Lord Clive. Now for the original.

We were due at Patna at 2 P.M., and, punctual to the time, the engine slackened its pace. There were no signs of a town to be seen; nothing but a large collection of mud huts standing in small untidy gardens, and shaded by a great number of trees. We arrived at the station, and I alighted, and collected my things—a course of conduct which appeared to excite some surprise among the English passengers, none of whom left the carriages. The natives got out in herds, and the platform was instantly covered with a noisy multitude, who surged round my baggage, which I had placed in front of me as a species of breakwater. After some minutes the train moved off, and the station-master came up and demanded my ticket. I asked him whether I could get a conveyance to take me to Major Ratcliffe's. "No. There were no conveyances at the station." Would he send some one to the nearest hotel to order me a fly? "Quite impossible. The nearest hotel was at Dinapore, twelve miles off." At length, the awful truth began to dawn upon my bewildered intellect. Patna was the native town; Bankipore, the civil station, was six miles farther on; and Dinapore, the military station, six miles again beyond that. The railway people were very civil, and procured a couple of bullock-carts for my luggage. As it was so early in the day, there was nothing for it but to wait at least three hours before the sun was low enough to allow me to venture on a six-mile walk; and an Indian waiting-room is a perfect black-hole of dulness.

8

MARY CARPENTER, *SIX MONTHS IN INDIA*, 2 VOLS. (LONDON: LONGMANS, GREEN, 1868), I, PP. 27–31, 227–228, 234–235, 238–239

Some woody mountains at no great distance bounded our view on the right, and formed a striking object. We had good opportunities for observing the lower classes of the population, since the stations were frequent, and as the arrival of the train appeared to be the great event of the day in these regions, numbers of natives crowded round, every time we stopped; their unregulated manners, loud discordant jabbering, and insufficient clothing, did not impress the mind with a favourable idea of the peasantry of the country, but we felt that it would be unfair to select such a concourse as a type of the people. As the railways are under the control of English companies, we did feel a right to complain of the neglectful conduct of the railway officials, whose attention we found it very difficult to obtain; and the stations themselves were so roughly built, that it was seldom possible for a lady to alight there, or to obtain any refreshment.

At length, after passing over several smaller rivers, we came to the beautiful Nerbudda, whose wide sandy banks indicate that during the rains it must be of considerable width. The bridge which crosses it is long, and it had been recently repaired after some damage from the rains. This stream is held sacred by the superstitious natives, and considerable indignation was felt at the idea of its being crossed, in defiance of the goddess of the river, by the sacrilegious machinery. On the appointed day, therefore, when all was prepared for the opening of the railway, immense multitudes of the natives assembled on the banks of the sacred stream, expecting to see its titular divinity execute vengeance on the perpetrators of this impious outrage. The train arrived and began to cross the bridge, when, in the very middle of its course, there was a sudden stoppage! The power of the goddess was now manifest to the assembled multitudes; she was about to be avenged. Hideous shrieks and yells arose with the most tremendous excitement. But in a few moments there was another shout such as is never heard from Hindoos—a true British hurrah from the triumphant officials mounted on the train, who set on the steam again, and gloriously crossed the river. Then the astonished natives changed their minds, and said it was a god! Cocoanuts and other votive offerings were showered in profusion; and even now at times such presents are made, to gain the favour of so powerful an agency.

The railway must indeed appear something supernatural to these ignorant inhabitants of districts which before had seldom been disturbed by the inroads of civilisation. The real effects on the population are more wonderful than fiction would dare to represent; in a variety of ways the railroad is probably producing a greater change in the population than any other single agency. The mere fact of connecting by an easy and agreeable day's travelling, places which formerly could be reached only by tiresome and expensive journeys of weeks, is of incalculable importance in breaking down the narrow ignorance which characterises most parts of India, and in promoting friendly intercourse between different parts of the country, as well as in facilitating commerce, &c. The railway carriages are also extremely useful, indirectly, in leading the most exclusive natives to disregard the regulations of caste. A Brahmin has frequently been known to draw back on entering a carriage, when perceiving it filled with persons of other castes, with whom contact would, in his opinion, be pollution. He retreats to seek another, but all are equally infected; he appeals for protection to the railway official, who coolly informs him that his remedy is easy; he may take a first-class ticket, and enjoy solitary state in a carriage to himself. But this greatly-increased outlay is not at all to his mind, and as his business is pressing he swallows the indignity, and steps into the carriage with the other passengers. An amusing story was told us of a proud Brahmin thus being unexpectedly shut in with a number of persons of the most despised class, on whom he had been accustomed to heap every species of insult. Finding him now in their power, they returned to him some of the contemptuous treatment which he had lavished on them, and he was obliged to bear it from his fellow-passengers until the train stopped. Christianity had not taught him that we are all children of the same Heavenly Father, nor them that we are to forgive injuries and to overcome evil with good; the railway was giving this arrogant man a lesson that he had better in future restrain himself in his treatment of his humbler fellow-beings. My friend Mr. G. saw some persons of different castes drinking together in a railway carriage; on his pointing out to them their impropriety, they excused themselves on the ground that the current of air which passed through the carriage when in motion removed contamination from them! Habits of punctuality and attention to duty are also taught, both directly and indirectly, by the railway. At first, passengers were constantly too late, or arrived just as the train was starting, and being thus unable to take their tickets, had the mortification of seeing it go off without them. Persons of consequence were at first very indignant on the occasion, but soon learnt that they, too, must submit to the inexorable law of railroads, which, like time and tide, wait for no man. The railway officials, who are chiefly natives, are here obtaining unconsciously an excellent training, of more value to them than any pecuniary recompense. While, then, we were frequently annoyed by many inconveniences and discomforts on this journey, we could not but feel that under the circumstances the Indian railways are very wonderful, and show the possibility of improving even the inferior portions of the native races, under judicious government and proper training. Our English fellow-passenger, whose duties in the Civil Service gave him much opportunity of forming a judgment on these subjects, fully corroborated my opinion. He spoke much of the importance of cotton cultivation in this district. By his extensive knowledge of the country, and the friendly manner in which he conversed in the vernacular with the native gentleman, and spoke of the natives generally, he gave us a very favourable impression of the tone of feeling existing in this province between the English and the natives. Having heard much of the unhealthy effect of the Indian climate on our countrymen, I was astonished to learn from him that he had been more than twenty years in the country, since his florid appearance indicated the healthy condition of an English country gentleman. This he attributed to regular active exercise, and to having his mind fully occupied by his work. A similar testimony I received from many in various parts of the country. The native gentleman could speak a little English, and showed us with much pride likenesses of the Queen and Royal Family in lockets appended to his handsome gold watch-chain. He politely asked us to occupy his villa on our return.

At length we reached Surat, where we were rejoiced to meet our friend Mr. Tagore, who had come from Ahmedabad that morning to meet us. Though we had sent him a telegram announcing our journey on the morning preceding, he had not received it until the middle of the night, and had kindly started at once to make every possible arrangement for our comfort. We had been informed that we could pass the night at the railway station; all the accommodation provided there, however, for passengers, consisted of cane sofas in very uncomfortable-looking ladies' waiting-rooms, with miserable dirty dressing-rooms. There seemed to be nothing like an hotel in the place, and Mr. Tagore had therefore telegraphed to a native gentleman who had borrowed from a friend a beautiful villa or 'garden house' in the neighbourhood, where a dinner in English style was kindly provided for us. We afterwards learnt that, had the time of our coming been known, many of the English families resident in or near Surat would have shown us hospitality; having, however, no introductions to this city, I had not calculated on any such courtesy.

Howrah

We paid a visit to Howrah on our way back to the city, and there saw a school which presented a striking contrast to that which we had just visited. This was a large Government school, in fine buildings, with abundant room and excellent masters, all in perfect order. The school seemed much valued, as it was well frequented. Howrah is situated on the west bank of the River Hooghly, opposite Calcutta, and contains a vast heathen population, which may be fairly estimated at 70,000 souls, within three miles of the church. Here is situated the Calcutta terminus of the great East Indian Railway, which is now open for traffic to the distance of nearly 1,000 miles, and reaches almost to Delhi. Here are found nearly all the docks, in which the numerous ships in the port are received and repaired; and here, too, are several other large industrial establishments—such as ironfoundries, flourmills, rope manufactories, distilleries, cotton screws, coal depôts, and salt warehouses, in addition to the extensive workshops for the erection of railway locomotive engines and carriages—which all give employment to an immense number of native artisans and workmen. Howrah has risen to importance through the traffic brought by the railway. The families of the officials employed in it are not neglected, and there is an excellent school for the children, which I visited with the Inspector. It was striking to observe that the girls in this school appeared of a superior grade to those whose parents would be of the same rank in England. They were being well taught, and had an air of refinement.

Serampore

This is a very celebrated spot in the history of missionary enterprise. The name of Dr. Carey, one of the founders of the Baptist College in that place, will ever be remembered in that part of the world, not only for his piety and zeal, but for his scientific attainments. It was then with much pleasure that I accepted a kind invitation from the editor of the 'Friend of India,' and his lady, to pay them a visit. A railway ride of about an hour ought to have brought us to our journey's end; but an accident (not a very unusual occurrence in these parts) detained us so long on the road, that our arrival by this train was nearly given up. Serampore is not more than a village, beside the English residences and the college. There are some rich zemindars in the neighbourhood, but, these not being enterprising or friendly to progress, the buildings around are generally in a dilapidated condition: the country then does not lose the charms of wild nature by being traversed by well-made roads, or divided into fields by well-trimmed hedgerows. As our time was not limited, a ride through it in a somewhat primitive style was very pleasant. A little girls' school in an open bungalow is under my hostess's kind supervision; many of the girls looked intelligent, but it was sad to observe the significant red spot on the foreheads of the little creatures six or seven years old, and to know that the poor children were considered as married, and would shortly be removed from their homes, and placed in the zenana of their husbands' family! We saw another little girls' school under the patronage of a rich zemindar, but he did not honour us with his presence on the occasion. Probably, as he was far from being of the party of progress, he did not wish to encounter those who might be in favour of innovations which he did not desire. Serampore is indeed situated in the midst of a very unenlightened population. We used to suppose that the car of Juggernaut was a thing of the past. Here, however, I actually beheld it in all its native clumsy hideousness—a dreadful reality! On certain festivals the idol is conveyed in this car to visit his sister, in the midst of the greatest excitement of all the surrounding population; not many years ago, a man, wearied of life, actually threw himself under the ponderous wheels, and was crushed to death! Such an example is very contagious among these people, and it is found necessary to set the police on guard, at these festivals, in order to prevent similar catastrophes. It was a marvellous contrast to visit a little country church in the neighbourhood, very sacred from many old associations, and in a quiet rural spot.

My return to Government House was not quite as easy and agreeable as might have been expected. I have heard, in some distant countries, of a railway accident being common on alternate days; I therefore thought that it was fair to expect none to-day, as we had had an accident on the preceding morning. I was, however, too sanguine. Being now quite alone, one of my native friends accompanied me to the station, to see me safely off. No train had arrived—it had broken down at a considerable distance. At these stations there is rarely any accommodation for ladies, and I was obliged to sit under a shed as a protection from the sun for about two hours, waiting for the arrival of another train. It was a strange feeling to be thus isolated; but I was beginning to feel quite at home with the natives, though I could not speak their language.

It was a matter of regret to me to learn that I had been expected that day at Rishrat, a village two miles from Serampore, and that considerable disappointment had been felt at my non-appearance by the managing commitee of the girls' school there. This was inevitable, as I had received no invitation, and was not aware of the existence of the place! It is, however, an interesting fact, that so many schools are springing up for the instruction of young girls, and that native gentlemen are taking so much interest in their management. 'This school,' the secretary writes, 'is of little more than three years' standing, during which period some of the girls were taught as far as Sanscrit, and double rule-of-three in arithmetic.' This is remarkable progress.

9

JOHN MATHESON, *ENGLAND TO DELHI: A NARRATIVE OF INDIAN TRAVEL* (LONDON: LONGMANS, GREEN, AND CO., 1870), PP. 278–286, 347–348, 509–510

It was naturally, then, with a pleasant feeling of anticipation that we took our way 'up-country.' We started from the Howrah terminus of the East Indian Railway, then open to Raneegunge, a distance of 120 miles; and it may be premised that the characteristic features, according to the example here furnished, of a 'railway station' in India, would afford Mr. Frith, who has immortalized the subject in England, a fresh and lively theme for his pencil. The native mind does not take matters easy while travelling, and the presence of a leisurely person on the platform is quite a phenomenon. The place is therefore a Babel of sound and confusion, in which the varied tones of manhood mingle with the shrill call of women and children, more or less lost to one another in the crowd. Dark eyes flash, dishevelled turbans stream, and white togas flow, in the impatient rush for places, as if such hot haste afforded the only chance of securing them, while the staff of railway porters, called *chokydars* or police, stylishly attired at Howrah in black cloth edged with yellow (exchanged for a white cotton dress in the hot season), red turban, and leathern belt adorned with a large brass buckle, glide among the throng directing the more bewildered passengers, or swelling the tumult by rapping with official canes the knuckles of the unmanageable and refractory.

Exclusive men of caste complicate the *mêlée* in their eager, but generally vain, search for a carriage where they may chiefly, if not altogether, consort with their peculiar order; and the confusion is further enhanced by the presence of such articles as cooking-pans, clothes, and bedding, which the owner desires to carry about with him, and beseeches for permission to introduce into the crowded carriage. The passenger urges his suit, the *chokydar* shouts his refusal, while the picturesque bone of contention is alternately seized and recaptured by either disputant.

Anon ensues a fresh bustle of official preparation, and a clearing of the way, enlivened by an occasional sharp cry, as the *jemmidar's* (foreman's) cane is applied to the poor spindle-shanks of some idle coolie who happens to block the passage. The signal for this movement may be the arrival of a great English *sahib*, or native nobleman, with attendant suite and profuse display of railway comforts; or some 'light of the harem' closely encased in a palanquin, which the bearers fairly thrust into the compartment ere the lady emerges, the better to conceal her charms from the prying gaze of man.

Strange in itself, and fraught with important results, is the fact that the Indian public have elected to travel almost exclusively in third class carriages; first and even second class passengers constituting a mere fraction of the whole number, as the official details to be afterwards quoted will show.

The first class representative of so distinguished a minority reclines comfortably in a cushioned compartment, provided with a double roofing and Venetian blinds to shield him at once from the heat and the glare of the day. But no padded interiors or shaded windows await the eager crowd of ticket-holders, who are simply provided with standing room in covered waggons half open at the sides, into which they are content to flock like sheep into a pen. Content too, not in all cases from necessity, for such is the force of Indian frugality that it prompts the aspiring baboo and the high caste dignitary to huddle thus together with their poorer fellows, the attractions of cheap travelling being paramount and irresistible. What a contrast to the exclusive habits of ante-railway days is afforded by this spectacle!

As regards the visible staff of Indian railways it is of course mainly composed of native officials, the European element being generally represented only by the guard, engine-driver, and station-master. The cost of traffic is as yet somewhat higher for goods than the average European rate; but the passenger fares although greater in the first class, are lower in the third than those of the West. Meanwhile, it is satisfactory to know from the public returns that, in giving a guarantee for these splendid schemes, the Government had rightly calculated on their prospective success.

Before starting we were glad to observe that a few other white faces besides our own mingled with the calico-clad crowd around us, and specially welcome were those of our friends and fellow-travellers, a Rev. Doctor and his wife, to whom we had had the good fortune of being introduced in Calcutta. They were bound to their home in the far North, and what between their knowledge (through former experience) of the way, and their truly delightful society, were indeed serviceable friends to us, smoothing all the asperities of the journey until we bade them farewell in Delhi. Although the country through which we passed between Calcutta and Raneegunge possessed no such favourite attractions as 'mountain, cataract, and glen,' yet, as strangers, we found in the total absence of these the negative advantage of a change, while, on a soft couch under a pleasant awning, we enjoyed the novel luxury of sweeping at railway speed through the sunny plains of Bengal. The route was diversified with picturesque glimpses of dense little woods and forests on either side of the way, peopled with rustic figures almost entirely luxuriating in beauty unadorned, and apparently in thorough enjoyment of the *dolce far niente*; brick works were in operation at intervals among the rank foliage; and tiny dwellings, constructed of earth or reed-work, nestled beneath the shade of palm and banyan trees, with ebony children whom scarf, *saree*, or other habiliment had never yet encircled, staring or gambolling in the foreground. Here, and during our further progress northward we had peeps of villages where life seemed to stagnate through excess of heat, and in which the Mussulman was visible at prayer in his mosque, or the Hindoo in his temple. Bordering the line tanks great and small came successively into view, wherein, according to custom, men, women, and children were assembled, holding a Bengal conversazione in refreshing conclave; or, net in hand, engaged together with an equally assiduous throng of ducks and geese in grubbing for something of which the natural element was mud. The rice-fields, to which the lines of irrigation crossing each other gave the appearance of a colossal chessboard, had recently been shorn of their crops, and were only diversified here and there by farmhouses shrouded in clumps of trees, and stark human forms far out in the sunshine, bending over the renewed work of cultivation. The wide level plains, apparently devoid of knoll or mound, stretched away until they melted into the horizon; their only verdure, the dense-leaved trees by which they were studded; their only life, the herds of cattle visible at intervals around.

A run of about five hours brought us to Raneegunge, a place having a more English aspect than the scenes of wood and jungle we had just traversed. Here was a more open country, a harder soil, and the familiar spectacle of coal mounds and colliery shafts, intermingled with trim white chimney stacks emitting clouds of smoke in the glowing atmosphere.

This is, I believe, the largest of the twenty-seven known coal fields of India, which are chiefly situated in the districts between Calcutta and Bombay. It is described in the recent 'Memoirs of the Geological Survey of India,' as covering an area of about 500 square miles, and containing an available supply of more than 14,000,000,000 tons.

According to a statement in the 'Calcutta Englishman,' the total production of Raneegunge in 1868 amounted to 1,34,50,829 *maunds*—a quantity which, taking the *maund* at 80 lbs. 2 oz., amounts to 493,608 tons. The out-turn of the five principal mining concerns was estimated at 1,19,21,065 *maunds* (about 437,061 tons), that of the Bengal Coal Company, which is said to employ 3,000 hands, alone amounting to 61,39,105 *maunds* or 225,077 tons. Next to the Bengal Company in order of extent come the Sirsole mines belonging to an enterprising Bengalee.

It is to be remarked, however, that although extensive coal fields thus exist in British India, the quality is much inferior to that of our home supply, yielding, as I have been told, more than five times the quantity of ash, and a deficiency of carbon or heat-giving power to the extent of about one-third.

Till recently some difficulty was experienced in procuring a sufficient supply of labour for the deeper mines, the Hindoos having, naturally enough, had a strong objection to descend into the bowels of the earth; but these scruples were gradually overcome, as the people became familiar with the situation.

With very few exceptions the construction and routine of Indian coal mines are still of a rude primitive order. Many of them are entered by means of steps cut in the solid rock, and thence by ladders to the mine galleries. Below ground the hewn coal is carried to the bottom of the shaft, chiefly by women and children in baskets sustained on the head. It is then raised to the surface through the instrumentality of a 'gin' or windlass, which is worked by from thirty to thirty-six women. Neverthe-less, it appears that the number of steam engines at work among the Raneegunge coal fields had increased from twenty-eight with 490 horse-power in 1860, to sixty-one, aggregating 867 horse-power, in 1868.

The railway has for the present entirely superseded the original method of for-warding coals to Calcutta, the great sphere of consumption; and although the rate of carriage is dear, namely, four and a half rupees per ton, or nearly a penny per mile, this change is by no means surprising in view of the former system of con-veyance in boats by a long winding course, first down the river Damoodah, and thence by the Hooghly to the place of destination. The great obstacle presented by the Damoodah itself, which is not always in a navigable condition, was aggravated by the dilatory habits of the *dhandies*, or rowers. In this, as in other departments of labour in Bengal, the baneful system of money advances prevailed, and the *dhan-dies* were frequently in no hurry to complete their voyage, so tedious at the best, preferring to idle over, and sometimes entirely to shirk a task, for which little or no remuneration remained to be claimed. Then hope deferred sickened the heart and soured the temper of disappointed employers in the capital, and it became neces-sary to scour the hot banks of the Damoodah in search of the recalcitrant bargers. A long-expected crew might be found to have abandoned their craft in some soli-tary creek of the river after carousing with their friends for weeks together in the villages by the way. Such was one of the 'troubles' incidental to the Bengal coal trade. Not less vexatious to those concerned were the freaks of the colliers proper of Raneegunge, who, when such was their pleasure, simply declined to work by the very effectual plan of absenting themselves. For the furtherance of their views, no complicated machinery, such as strikes or trades' unions, was requisite. The fund on which each man fell back in any access of idleness, was the supply of rice in the cupboard; and, if that was enough to admit of a few days' vacation, he felt himself sufficiently independent to go into hiding, leaving the *chokydar*, who would inevitably be despatched for the purpose of ferreting him out, to succeed according to his diligence and ability. This Indian game of hide and seek was or, I may say still, *is* by no means confined to the area of the coal fields, but extends to other spheres of labour. A salutary change, however, which all the *chokydars* in the land could not accomplish, is being gradually brought about by British capital and industry; still if it be true, as some aver, that colliers, even in civilized Europe, are a somewhat troublesome order of 'blacks,' it need scarcely excite our surprise, if the remark should yet apply in a measure to the fast-coloured fraternity of Raneegunge.

Not, however, that the railway ought to or will have the traffic of such districts to itself, for we now learn that the Indian Government has given its sanction to the immediate formation of a canal leading from the Damoodah river at Raneegunge to a point on the Hooghly just below Calcutta. Such a mode of conveyance, by reason of its greater economy, will undoubtedly again divert not only the coal of

Raneegunge but much cereal produce to the boat, although of the fugitive *dhand-ies* it may safely be predicated that their race is run.

To wind up these 'railway glimpses,' one terrible glance remains. In the roasting months of June and July, when the noonday heat in carriages rolling between Cawnpore and Calcutta, packed with a dense crowd, sometimes approaches 120 degrees Fahrenheit, there are passengers who become faint and prostrate in the course of the run. On these occasions the guard in going his rounds rouses dormant figures, in order to ascertain if they are possessed of consciousness; and European travellers, as I have also heard from their own lips, have been fain to call the *bheestie* engaged in watering the platform of any station by the way, and, presenting their steaming heads, beseech him for a gush of water from his *mussack!*

More incidents of the way

FROM this point the railway was open as far as Shekoabad, a distance of 264 miles. Cawnpore lies between, and in a few hours we slid into the shadow of its handsome and commodious station. Here a mixed crowd of ticket-holders, who, after being locked in a waiting-room pending the arrival of the train, had been just set loose, were streaming over the platform in great excitement. Threading the maze of moving forms walked the inevitable railway *chokydar*, glorious with spruce official cap and bright belted uniform, and remarkably active with the little cane which he was privileged to carry. It was thus only natural that shouting, and rushing, and knuckle rapping should be going on as we arrived at Cawnpore. The platform seemed familiar ground; nor less familiar the brass-mounted locomotive, emitting its wonted hiss, and driven by an English engineer. Yet there were features in the scene truly oriental, for the place, heavily roofed to shut out the sun, looked like some great twilight tunnel beneath a field of vivid light; and the engine, as it moved with a shriek from this grateful shelter, sped away with its burden, not through fresh green valleys and across flowing rivers, but through a hot glowing landscape, in which tracts of jungle alternated with dry watercourses and parched brown plains.

On this day, however, it so happened that the heavens were propitious, and we witnessed what had become even to us a delightful novelty. A more agreeable temperature seemed suddenly to pervade the air; the strong light had waned sensibly; and looking forth from the carriage window, we perceived a sky over which dark clouds were diffusing the folds in which they had already shrouded the sun. A few minutes more and down on the thirsty soil fell the precious rain torrent with a fine, plashing music—Nature's prelude to man's harvest hymn.

But this unlooked-for deluge in such a place was in another sense destructive, sweeping unsuspecting pilgrims and pedestrians from the highway into every possible place of protection, and making soaking havoc of the loose, bright colours and tinsel decorations of the eastern wardrobe. In a very short time the fields on either hand were streaked with watery trenches, while groups of travellers might be seen crouching under hastily constructed awnings. The transformation was as complete as that upon a mimic stage; for, indeed, the spectacle of improvised tents erected beside the flood, with draggled, half-clad figures cowering for shelter within them, was more suggestive of a shipwreck than an incident of the scorching plain.

Such is the sphere of action within which the Government of India prosecutes its onerous and responsible work. Above the clamour of editorial voices is heard that of the Administration, conciliatory though firm, enforcing its authority not solely on approved principles of British law, but with due regard to the complications of existing Hindoo and Mahommedan codes, as well as to the dogmas of ancient usage.

The incongruous mass of land schemes, the muddle of municipal measures, the insecurity of the citizen, the indefinite position of the ryot—all that legacy of confusion bequeathed by Mahommedan rule—is gradually assuming an aspect of form and order. Only twelve years have elapsed since the country was smitten with social anarchy and an impoverished exchequer. Now it is blessed with peace throughout its bounds, and, speaking in a general way, with an income of fifty millions sterling to pay a debt of only twice that amount. Refreshing signs of material progress begin to relieve the stagnation of former times, while the work of moral regeneration proceeds with a rapidity and precision unknown in the record of empires.

Annexed is a copy of the last official map of Indian railways, completed, in progress, and projected. The first group, as was indicated in a previous portion of this volume, embraces 4,096 miles; the second comprises about 1,820 miles, and includes the great trans-peninsula line (now said to be just on the point of completion), which will connect Calcutta with Bombay; while the 'projected' routes consist of about 10,000 miles, which, if they advance at the computed rate of 300 miles per annum, will be finished, perhaps, in thirty-three years hence.

I have already alluded to the significant fact that nearly the whole of the people of India, yielding hereditary prejudices to considerations of economy, have chosen to travel together in third class carriages. The figures relating to this point, as now given in the report of the 'Government Director of the Indian Railway Companies,' are as follow:—

'Total number of passengers conveyed, 15,066,530; being an increase of more than a million per annum during the last two years.

'Of the 15,000,000 carried last year, only 130,000, or less than one per cent., were first class; and 535,000, or about three and a half per cent., were second class.'

Here is presented to the moral reformer a circumstance seemingly insignificant, which involves a portentous consequence. A practical benefit, offered impartially to all, is breaking down in effect the evil it rebukes in principle. Men of high caste are induced to associate with those whom their vanity had ever taught them to shun; the Brahmin rubs shoulders with the Pariah. And so the power of caste, that ancient social monstrosity which no ethical or religious arguments could subdue, is yielding to those influences which follow in the steps of human progress through the intercourse of nations.

Part 2

MODERNITY AND THE MASSES

10

JULES VERNE, *AROUND THE WORLD IN EIGHTY DAYS*, TRANS. GEORGE M. TOWLE (PHILADELPHIA: PORTER & COATES, 1873), PP. 55–56, 60–62, 70–78

"If I am not mistaken," said he, approaching this person with his most amiable smile, "you are the gentleman who so kindly volunteered to guide me at Suez?"

"Ah! I quite recognize you. You are the servant of the strange Englishman—"

"Just so, Monsieur—"

"Fix."

"Monsieur Fix," resumed Passepartout, "I'm charmed to find you on board. Where are you bound?"

"Like you, to Bombay."

"That's capital! Have you made this trip before?"

"Several times. I am one of the agents of the Peninsula Company."

"Then you know India?"

"Why—yes," replied Fix, who spoke cautiously.

"A curious place, this India?"

"Oh, very curious. Mosques, minarets, temples, fakirs, pagodas, tigers, snakes, elephants! I hope you will have ample time to see the sights."

"I hope so, Monsieur Fix. You see, a man of sound sense ought not to spend his life jumping from a steamer upon a railway train, and from a railway train upon a steamer again, pretending to make the tour of the world in eighty days! No; all these gymnastics, you may be sure, will cease at Bombay."

"And Mr. Fogg is getting on well?" asked Fix, in the most natural tone in the world.

"Quite well, and I too. I eat like a famished ogre; it's the sea air."

"But I never see your master on deck."

"Never; he hasn't the least curiosity."

"Do you know, Mr. Passepartout, that this pretended tour in eighty days may conceal some secret errand—perhaps a diplomatic mission?"

"Faith, Monsieur Fix, I assure you I know nothing about it, nor would I give half-a-crown to find out."

EVERYBODY knows that the great reversed triangle of land, with its base in the north and its apex in the south, which is called India, embraces fourteen hundred thousand square miles, upon which is spread unequally a population of one hundred and eighty millions of souls. The British Crown exercises a real and despotic dominion over the larger portion of this vast country, and has a governor-general stationed at Calcutta, governors at Madras, Bombay, and in Bengal, and a lieutenant-governor at Agra.

But British India, properly so called, only embraces seven hundred thousand square miles, and a population of from one hundred to one hundred and ten millions of inhabitants. A considerable portion of India is still free from British authority; and there are certain ferocious rajahs in the interior who are absolutely independent. The celebrated East India Company was all-powerful from 1756, when the English first gained a foothold on the spot where now stands the city of Madras, down to the time of the great Sepoy insurrection. It gradually annexed province after province, purchasing them of the native chiefs, whom it seldom paid, and appointed the governor-general and his subordinates, civil and military. But the East India Company has now passed away, leaving the British possessions in India directly under the control of the Crown. The aspect of the country, as well as the manners and distinctions of race, is daily changing.

Formerly one was obliged to travel in India by the old cumbrous methods of going on foot or on horseback, in palanquins or unwieldy coaches; now, fast steamboats ply on the Indus and the Ganges, and a great railway, with branch lines joining the main line at many points on its route, traverses the peninsula from Bombay to Calcutta in three days. This railway does not run in a direct line across India. The distance between Bombay and Calcutta, as the bird flies, is only from one thousand to eleven hundred miles; but the deflections of the road increase this distance by more than a third.

The general route of the Great Indian Peninsula Railway is as follows:— Leaving Bombay, it passes through Salcette, crossing to the continent opposite Tannah, goes over the chain of the Western Ghauts, runs thence northeast as far as Burhampoor, skirts the nearly independent territory of Bundelcund, ascends to Allahabad, turns thence eastwardly, meeting the Ganges at Benares, then departs from the river a little, and, descending south-eastward by Burdivan and the French town of Chandernagor, has its terminus at Calcutta.

The passengers of the "Mongolia" went ashore at half-past four p.m.; at exactly eight the train would start for Calcutta.

Mr. Fogg, after bidding good-bye to his whist partners, left the steamer, gave his servant several errands to do, urged it upon him to be at the station promptly at eight, and, with his regular step, which beat to the second, like an astronomical clock, directed his steps to the passport office. As for the wonders of Bombay—its famous city hall, its splendid library, its forts and docks, its bazaars, mosques, synagogues, its Armenian churches, and the noble pagoda on Malebar Hill with its two polygonal towers—he cared not a straw to see them. He would not deign to examine even the masterpieces of Elephanta, or the mysterious hypogea, concealed south-east from the docks, or those fine remains of Buddhist architecture, the Kanherian grottoes of the island of Salcette.

Having transacted his business at the passport office, Phileas Fogg repaired quietly to the railway station, where he ordered dinner.

During the night the train left the mountains behind, and passed Nassik, and the next day proceeded over the flat, well-cultivated country of the Khandeish, with its straggling villages, above which rose the minarets of the pagodas. This fertile territory is watered by numerous small rivers and limpid streams, mostly tributaries of the Godavery.

Passepartout, on waking and looking out, could not realize that he was actually crossing India in a railway train. The locomotive, guided by an English engineer and fed with English coal, threw out its smoke upon cotton, coffee, nutmeg, clove, and pepper plantations, while the steam curled in spirals around groups of palm-trees, in the midst of which were seen picturesque bungalows, viharis (a sort of abandoned monasteries), and marvellous temples enriched by the exhaustless ornamentation of Indian architecture. Then they came upon vast tracts extending to the horizon, with jungles inhabited by snakes and tigers, which fled at the noise of the train; succeeded by forests penetrated by the railway, and still haunted by elephants which, with pensive eyes, gazed at the train as it passed. The travellers crossed, beyond Malligaum, the fatal country so often stained with blood by the sectaries of the goddess Kali. Not far off rose Ellora, with its graceful pagodas, and the famous Aurungabad, capital of the ferocious Aureng-Zeb, now the chief town of one of the detached provinces of the kingdom of the Nizam. It was thereabouts that Feringhea, the Thuggee chief, king of the stranglers, held his sway. These ruffians, united by a secret bond, strangled victims of every age in honour of the goddess Death, without ever shedding blood; there was a period when this part of the country could scarcely be travelled over without corpses being found in every direction. The English Government has succeeded in greatly diminishing these murders, though the Thuggees still exist, and pursue the exercise of their horrible rites.

At half-past twelve the train stopped at Burhampoor, where Passepartout was able to purchase some Indian slippers, ornamented with false pearls, in which, with evident vanity, he proceeded to incase his feet. The travellers made a hasty breakfast, and started off for Assurghur, after skirting for a little the banks of the small river Tapty, which empties into the Gulf of Cambray, near Surat.

Passepartout was now plunged into absorbing reverie. Up to his arrival at Bombay, he had entertained hopes that their journey would end there; but now that they were plainly whirling across India at full speed, a sudden change had come over the spirit of his dreams. His old vagabond nature returned to him; the fantastic ideas of his youth once more took possession of him. He came to regard his master's project as intended in good earnest, believed in the reality of the bet, and therefore in the tour of the world, and the necessity of making it without fail within the designated period. Already he began to worry about possible delays, and accidents which might happen on the way. He recognized himself as being personally interested in the wager, and trembled at the thought that he might have been the means of losing it by his unpardonable folly of the night before. Being much less cool-headed than Mr. Fogg, he was much more restless, counting and recounting the days passed over, uttering maledictions when the train stopped, and accusing it of sluggishness, and mentally blaming Mr. Fogg for not having bribed the engineer. The worthy fellow was ignorant that, while it was possible by such means to hasten the rate of a steamer, it could not be done on the railway.

The train entered the defiles of the Sutpour Mountains, which separate the Khandeish from Bundelcund, towards evening. The next day Sir Francis Cromarty asked Passepartout what time it was; to which, on consulting his watch, he replied that it was three in the morning. This famous timepiece, always regulated on the Greenwich meridian, which was now some seventy-seven degrees westward, was at least four hours slow. Sir Francis corrected Passepartout's time, whereupon the latter made the same remark that he had done to Fix; and upon the general insisting that the watch should be regulated in each new meridian, since he was constantly going eastward, that is in the face of the sun, and therefore the days were shorter by four minutes for each degree gone over, Passepartout obstinately refused to alter his watch, which he kept at London time. It was an innocent delusion which could harm no one.

The train stopped, at eight o'clock, in the midst of a glade some fifteen miles beyond Rothal, where there were several bungalows and workmen's cabins. The conductor, passing along the carriages, shouted, "Passengers will get out here!"

Phileas Fogg looked at Sir Francis Cromarty for an explanation; but the general could not tell what meant a halt in the midst of this forest of dates and acacias.

Passepartout, not less surprised, rushed out and speedily returned, crying, "Monsieur, no more railway!"

"What do you mean?" asked Sir Francis.

"I mean to say that the train isn't going on."

The general at once stepped out, while Phileas Fogg calmly followed him, and they proceeded together to the conductor.

"Where are we?" asked Sir Francis.

"At the hamlet of Kholby."

"Do we stop here?"

"Certainly. The railway isn't finished."

"What! not finished?"

"No. There's still a matter of fifty miles to be laid from here to Allahabad, where the line begins again."

"But the papers announced the opening of the railway throughout."

"What would you have, officer? The papers were mistaken."

"Yet you sell tickets from Bombay to Calcutta," retorted Sir Francis, who was growing warm.

"No doubt," replied the conductor; "but the passengers know that they must provide means of transportation for themselves from Kholby to Allahabad."

Sir Francis was furious. Passepartout would willingly have knocked the conductor down, and did not dare to look at his master.

"Sir Francis," said Mr. Fogg, quietly, "we will, if you please, look about for some means of conveyance to Allahabad."

"Mr. Fogg, this is a delay greatly to your disadvantage."

"No, Sir Francis; it was foreseen."

"What! You knew that the way—"

"Not at all; but I knew that some obstacle or other would sooner or later arise on my route. Nothing, therefore, is lost. I have two days which I have already gained to sacrifice. A steamer leaves Calcutta for Hong Kong at noon, on the 25th. This is the 22nd, and we shall reach Calcutta in time."

There was nothing to say to so confident a response.

It was but too true that the railway came to a termination at this point. The papers were like some watches, which have a way of getting too fast, and had been premature in their announcement of the completion of the line. The greater part of the travellers were aware of this interruption, and leaving the train, they began to engage such vehicles as the village could provide—four-wheeled palkigharis, waggons drawn by zebus, carriages that looked like perambulating pagodas, palanquins, ponies, and what not.

Mr. Fogg and Sir Francis Cromarty, after searching the village from end to end, came back without having found anything.

"I shall go afoot," said Phileas Fogg.

Passepartout, who had now rejoined his master, made a wry grimace, as he thought of his magnificent, but too frail Indian shoes. Happily he too had been looking about him, and, after a moment's hesitation, said, "Monsieur, I think I have found a means of conveyance."

"What?"

"An elephant! An elephant that belongs to an Indian who lives but a hundred steps from here."

"Let's go and see the elephant," replied Mr. Fogg.

They soon reached a small hut, near which, enclosed within some high palings, was the animal in question. An Indian came out of the hut, and, at their request, conducted them within the enclosure. The elephant, which its owner had reared, not for a beast of burden, but for warlike purposes, was half domesticated. The Indian had begun already, by often irritating him, and feeding him every three months on sugar and butter, to impart to him a ferocity not in his nature, this method being often employed by those who train the Indian elephants for battle. Happily, however, for Mr. Fogg, the animal's instruction in this direction had not gone far, and the elephant still preserved his natural gentleness. Kiouni—this was the name of the beast—could doubtless travel rapidly for a long time, and, in default of any other means of conveyance, Mr. Fogg resolved to hire him. But elephants are far from cheap in India, where they are becoming scarce; the males, which alone are suitable for circus shows, are much sought, especially as but few of them are domesticated. When, therefore, Mr. Fogg proposed to the Indian to hire Kiouni, he refused point-blank. Mr. Fogg persisted, offering the excessive sum of ten pounds an hour for the loan of the beast to Allahabad. Refused. Twenty pounds? Refused also. Forty pounds? Still refused. Passepartout jumped at each advance; but the Indian declined to be tempted. Yet the offer was an alluring one, for, supposing it took the elephant fifteen hours to reach Allahabad, his owner would receive no less than six hundred pounds sterling.

Phileas Fogg, without getting in the least flurried, then proposed to purchase the animal outright, and at first offered a thousand pounds for him. The Indian, perhaps thinking he was going to make a great bargain, still refused.

Sir Francis Cromarty took Mr. Fogg aside, and begged him to reflect before he went any further; to which that gentleman replied that he was not in the habit of acting rashly, that a bet of twenty thousand pounds was at stake, that the elephant was absolutely necessary to him, and that he would secure him if he had to pay twenty times his value. Returning to the Indian, whose small, sharp eyes, glistening with avarice, betrayed that with him it was only a question of how great a price he could obtain, Mr. Fogg offered first twelve hundred, then fifteen hundred, eighteen hundred, two thousand pounds. Passepartout, usually so rubicund, was fairly white with suspense.

At two thousand pounds the Indian yielded.

"What a price, good heaven!" cried Passepartout, "for an elephant!"

It only remained now to find a guide, which was comparatively easy. A young Parsee, with an intelligent face, offered his services, which Mr. Fogg accepted, promising so generous a reward as to materially stimulate his zeal, The elephant was led out and equipped. The Parsee, who was an accomplished elephant driver, covered his back with a sort of saddle-cloth, and attached to each of his flanks some curiously uncomfortable howdahs.

Phileas Fogg paid the Indian with some bank-notes which he extracted from the famous carpet-bag, a proceeding that seemed to deprive poor Passepartout of his vitals. Then he offered to carry Sir Francis to Allahabad, which the brigadier gratefully accepted, as one traveller the more would not be likely to fatigue the gigantic beast. Provisions were purchased at Kholby, and while Sir Francis and Mr. Fogg took the howdahs on either side, Passepartout got astride the saddle-cloth between them. The Parsee perched himself on the elephant's neck, and at nine o'clock they set out from the village, the animal marching off through the dense forest of palms by the shortest cut.

11

C. F. GORDON CUMMING, *IN THE HIMALAYAS AND ON THE INDIAN PLAINS* (LONDON: CHATTO & WINDUS, 1884), PP. 44–47, 76, 266–268, 274–277, 593–594

Crossing the river by steamboat one early morning, we made our first acquaintance with an Indian railway-station thronged with natives, some starting on pilgrimage, others on divers business. For the facilities of modern travel have developed a curiously locomotive tendency in the Hindoo. Their old proverb that "No one is so happy as he who never owed a debt, nor undertook a journey" is quite out of date, and now whole families start from one end of the country to the other, on the smallest pretext, carrying with them their poor stock of worldly goods, tied up in a little bundle, to which are added their cooking pots, and brazen drinking-cups, as no man could ever borrow the use of such articles from a neighbour, for fear of ceremonial defilement.

The incongruity between the appearance of these pilgrims to holy shrines (for such were most of my fellow passengers), and the solid business-like train, reminded me vividly of my brother's description of the sensation produced among the hill tribes of Bombay, when first a solitary engine came up the newly made railway, rushing madly onward, and yet stopping obediently at the bidding of the white man. The excitement was increased tenfold, when at night the terrible creature with red wrathful eyes flew over the ground, bellowing and snorting, in fire and fury.

What wonder was it that they believed it to be in truth a familiar spirit tamed by the white man; and that these worshippers of all evil powers came straightway crowding to "make pooja" and bring offerings to the tame devil? They brought garlands of fragrant flowers to hang around him, and pots of the red paint with which they smear their gods, and prayed to be allowed to daub the whole engine. They had to be content, however, with painting the buffers, which gratified them exceedingly, more especially as they declared they heard the familiar spirit roaring inside, and that (when the stokers stirred him up) they saw his great wheel-like limbs move. (The wheel, you know, is a sacred symbol wherever Sun-worship has prevailed.) So, as he undoubtedly was a devil, they sought to propitiate him with their accustomed offerings of little bowls of honey and ghee and sugar, and

105

garlands of flowers; then stood by in reverential postures, while he went roaring on his resistless way.

Nor did their wonder lessen when trains commenced running, and they beheld this tamed and mighty demon rushing to and fro dragging along strings of enormous gharrys, which a hundred bullocks could not have moved.

Now the novelty is forgotten, the railroad and telegraph rank high among Britain's best gifts to India, and the crowd of travelling Hindoos equals that of a British excursion train.

So amazed are these easy-going Orientals by the punctuality of the trains, that, in dread of being late, they generally assemble at the station some hours before the time for starting—often overnight. Of course they carry their bedding with them, and as it consists merely of a wadded blanket-cloak of gaily coloured calico (or in the case of the very poor, only of a piece of coarse canvas) one realises how easy of fulfilment was the injunction once spoken in Judea, "Take up thy bed and walk!" So the early arrivals just lie down on the pavement, wrapping their cloak or canvas), tightly over head and body, and look like rows of corpses laid out in order. In due time these chrysalides begin to stir, and then shake themselves up, each revealing a long pair of lean black legs, surmounted by a bundle of raiment, out of which gleam two glittering black eyes. As long as their heads and shoulders are warm, they seem to care little for any chill about the lower extremities. Then they solace themselves, and try to counteract the chill of the night air by a few whiffs of tobacco, and the gurgling of many "hubble-bubbles" resounds on every side.

The carriages are ticketed off, for natives, native women, and Europeans. Some of the upper class natives still find themselves sorely perplexed how to combine railway travelling with the seclusion of women. Of this I had an amusing illustration, as we were no sooner comfortably ensconced in a carriage set apart for ladies, than a gorgeously apparelled merchant brought his wife and her ayah, both closely veiled, and shut them in with us. The former was richly dressed and loaded with jewels, and I hoped at last to get a glimpse of a real native lady. The jealous husband stood at the door, till the train was actually in motion, when he stepped in, chuckling at having got into a carriage where no other man dare follow. The officials were, however, on the watch, and, stopping the train, desired him to get out, as the carriage was reserved for ladies only. In vain he battled and raged, and finally, sooner than leave his wife in my dangerous society, he made her and her attendant get out with all their bundles, and go with him into another carriage.

As journeys to the far north may involve travelling without a break night and day for sixty hours or more, night travelling has of course to be provided for; so, long before American luxury devised Pullman's sleeping cars, these Indian carriages were built with a special view to the accommodation of sleepers, not being divided into seats, but left so that one person can lie down comfortably, while the padded back of each carriage is in fact the mattrass of an upper berth, which at night is raised, and fastened to the ceiling with strong straps, so that each carriage affords good sleeping quarters for four persons. Then the bundle of bedding comes into play, though not till the invariable basket of provisions has done its part.

All the windows have projecting shades to keep off the burning sun, and each carriage has a double roof of white for the same purpose. Some are provided with tanks of cold water, not merely for the comfort of washing (though that is very great, and it is well to secure a carriage with a dressing-room) but as a measure of safety in the fearful heat, when the constant application of wet cloths to the head is one of the best safeguards for such as are compelled to travel. Of the risk involved, one gains some impression by hearing of the number of persons, who, in the stifling summer months, are lifted from the train, stricken with heat apoplexy. In fact the possibility of death from this cause is such a well-recognised danger, that while we—the pleasure-seekers—were revelling in the temperate climate on the great hills, we knew that the railway authorities found it necessary to keep coffins ready at every station, to receive such travellers as thus, too quickly, reached their journey's end.

For the first few hours after leaving Calcutta, our route lay through rich vegetation and fertile land, made more beautiful by the early lights and the clear golden sunrise, and the balmy morning air was still deliciously fresh and cool. New and full of interest to our eyes were the clumps of waving bamboos, the tamarind and neeme trees, the spreading banyans and slender palms with crown of feathery fronds, and even the hedges of aloes and tall sirkee grass which surround the little mud villages. These are almost invariably marked by the tall pyramidal dome, or the three low rounded domes which respectively denote the Hindoo or Mohammedan shrine. The cottages are half hidden by large-leaved gourds which trail all over them, heavy with golden fruit, and overshadowed by the gigantic glossy leaves of the plantain (the very ideal of tropic foliage), beneath which played groups of odd-looking little brown children, carrying babies as big as themselves.

So effectually are these cottage homes veiled by the rich foliage, that the casual traveller forms no notion of their multitude—still less does it occur to him that those brown babies form one of the most perplexing questions which harass Indian statesmen. For, thanks to the security of life under British rule (and the removal of many causes of death, which in past generations have checked a too rapid increase of the people), *the population of Bengal has actually trebled in the last century*, and the land which in A.D. 1780 amply sufficed to feed twenty-one million persons, now yields scant sustenance for sixty-three millions, and still (as very early marriage is a religious obligation, binding on every Hindoo, quite irrespective of means of supporting a family) the evil goes on progressively, and the population of India increases at the rate of two and a half millions per annum, so that ten years hence there will be considerably more than twenty-five million hungry extra mouths to feed.

Here we were also shown a budding tree, supposed to be of extraordinary antiquity; a fiction by no means shaken, though the Brahmans frequently substitute a new tree. So holy is this temple that when, at one time, all natives were excluded from the fort one rich Hindoo pilgrim arrived and offered twenty thousand rupees for permission to worship here. The commandant, however, had no authority to admit any one, so was compelled to refuse his prayer, in spite of so tempting a bait. It was with a feeling of thankful relief that we emerged from that noxious and oppressive darkness into the balmy air and blessed sunlight.

We spent some pleasant hours in one of the balconies overhanging the river, while in the cool room within fair women with musical voices accompanied themselves on the piano, in Akbar's old quarters; and so we idled away the heat of the day till the red sun sank into the water, behind the great dark railway bridge—a bridge which the Brahmans declared the gods would never tolerate on so sacred a river as the Jumna, but which nevertheless spans the stream in perfect security. It was a vast undertaking, as, owing to the great extent of country subject to inundation during the rains, it was necessary to construct a bridge well-nigh two miles in length. The Indian railway has certainly necessitated an amazing amount of work, on a scale so vast as to test engineering skill to the uttermost, and in no respect more strikingly than in the construction of these monster bridges, one of which, across the Soane, is about a mile and a quarter in length, while that on the Sutlej, between Jellunder and Loodiana, is about two miles and a half, being probably the longest bridge in the world.

On the sandbanks just below the fort, huge mud-turtles lay basking, and the gentlemen amused themselves by taking long shots at them from the balconies, whereupon the creatures arose and waddled into the water with a sudden flop. These sandbanks are favourite haunts of crocodiles—*muggers*, as they are called—which, however, declined to show on this occasion.

A grand Durbar

THE journey from Meerut to Umballa which cost the cavalry and artillery ten days under canvas, and ten morning marches before sunrise, was accomplished by the rest of the world in an afternoon by rain. The line was still so new as to be liable to considerable irregularity. On the present occasion we waited three hours before our train appeared. Happily, being a cheery set, we cared little; and the railway officials had the more time to master the intricacies of our baggage. I listened with much amusement to my sister's explanation: "You see I have tickets for four horses and two dogs. Two of the horses are cows, and one of the dogs is a goat, and the other is a cat!" I bethought me of *Punch's* picture of an old lady whose menagerie had been thus classified—all, save her pet tortoise, which, "being an insect," did not require a ticket. She looked as much disgusted as did one of my friends on being told that her lovely green frogs and pet salamander were "vermin!"

Late in the afternoon we passed Seharanpore, where we had already spent some pleasant days. It is one of the headquarters of the Government Stud Department, which has immense stables here; whence, at the periodical sales of rejected horses, wide-awake individuals recruit their private stables greatly to their own advantage. Seharanpore is famed for its gardens, whence all India is supplied with plants and seeds. Here an old well, of the sort called Persian Wheel, struck me as extremely picturesque. The water is drawn from an immense depth by an endless chain of great red earthen jars, fastened between two ropes, and passing over a wheel, which is in connection with another wheel, turned by bullocks, and driven by brown men in white turbans, the whole overshadowed by fine old trees. One of the ropes, being new, was adorned with a large bunch of flowers as a votive offering to the Spirit of the Well.

Before us stretched a wide hill-range, bounding the intervening plain. It did not seem to us very grand; very much like the Ochils from some points near Stirling. Only we knew that these were indeed the low spurs of that mighty range we had come so far to see, and that those little patches and peaks of glittering white were our first glimpse of the eternal snows of the Himalayas. One mountain in particular, the Chor, we were afterwards taught to look up to with reverence, but I cannot say that was our first impulse.

It was late and dark when we reached Umballa. Our luggage-ticket was mislaid in the confusion, and there was no end of tantalising trouble, and going to and fro, before we were allowed to rescue one atom of our property, which lay piled before our eyes. We forcibly carried off one box of nursery goods, and the authorities, after wearisome delays, allowed the rest to follow us. Tired and hungry, we at last found ourselves safe in a large empty bungalow, of which a friend had kindly allowed us the use. The house was literally empty, so we had commissioned a furniture agent to supply such things as were actually necessary. The sudden influx of strangers made all such supplies meagre in the extreme; and you can imagine nothing more dreary than a large, empty Indian bungalow, where the uncarpeted floors and bare whitewashed walls make every voice and footstep resound; every room acting as a passage to its neighbours, and no curtains to veil the ill-fitting doors.

However, when morning returned, with its flood of warm sunshine, we no longer thought it dreary, but turning plaids into table-cloths, and filling every native bowl and hubble-bubble vase, on which we could lay hands, with loads of roses and jessamine, we soon made our quarters cosy enough. Afterwards, when we saw how every nook and cranny of the town was crowded with strangers, we felt thankful indeed for our large cool rooms and shady garden, where orange and pomegranate-shrubs (those "busy plants," as old George Herbert calls them) mingled their white or scarlet blossoms with their own ripening fruit, and where, more beautiful than all, the tall beauhinia or camel's foot (so called from the shape of its leaf) showered down exquisite blossoms like large white geraniums, with lilac markings.

Here we often lingered in the cool evening watching the vivid sheets of lightning, while crashing peals of thunder made the night solemn, and harmonised the various camp-sounds on every side, bands playing, bugles calling, voices of men and of camels. One native regiment quartered near us seemed to be for ever marching to the sound of a very musical little French horn. In short, we soon made *aural* acquaintance with our many neighbours.

On one side stretched the great Maidan, a fine, wide plain, affording scope for all manner of military evolutions. The troops were camped all round the edge of this plain; and the mass of white canvas cutting against the background of dark foliage, the Himalayas lying blue in the distance, and the brilliant foreground of native figures gorgeously attired, combined to make a very fine picture. At the farther end of the great plain lay the Governor-General's camp, a white city of tents, all ready for his reception; and a little farther was that of the Commander-in-Chief, both overshadowed by the Union Jack.

Perhaps the most curious of all the quaint varieties of equipage in the great gathering at Umballa was an English open phaeton drawn by a pair of dromedaries; and I heard of a similar carriage and four! Anything more utterly incongruous you cannot imagine. Of course, it was an object of special aversion to all other carriages, as no horse can endure meeting either camels or elephants, for which reason both are generally prohibited from appearing on the Mall.

But as to the native vehicles, they are always picturesque. Scores of queer little *ekkas*, with their curtained hoods, and high shafts, balancing two wheels, were for ever tearing along as fast as one fat pony could gallop; while the more stately family coach, with its double pyramidal hood (a small hood in front and a large one at the back), all closely draped with scarlet and gold, is drawn by beautiful white oxen very richly caparisoned, and stepping as proudly as though they knew how precious a burden of "lights of the harem," "coral lips," "heart's desires," "delight of the eyes," "morning stars," and other dainty dames, were hidden from the vulgar gaze by that envious drapery. Sometimes a little jewelled hand would cautiously draw back a corner of the curtain, and a pair of beautiful bright eyes would peep forth, and even favour us with a smile; then all too quickly retreat again, and leave us to the contemplation of the casket only, wherein were concealed so many dazzling gems.

As to the turbaned crowd on foot, each ingredient was a picture in itself, and there were thousands upon thousands of such picturesque mortals, each gaily attired, and all turbaned, and perpetually forming new combinations of bright colour in the clear sunlight. There were much the same figures as we had already seen at various holy fairs. Women attired in jackets and in the very tightest of silk trousers, worn on the leanest of legs; their veils of finest muslin, gold-spangled or plain, as the case may be. Others were more draped. All alike were adorned with every jewel they could muster, including small looking-glasses set in silver and worn as thumb-rings. For the most part they carried a child astride on the hip. Sometimes on the other shoulder sat a still younger child, its head resting on its mother's. Perhaps the whole family were present, in which case the father probably carried a bamboo across his shoulder from which two large baskets were suspended by long cords. Probably one basket contained a little brown boy, in robes of rich satin or silk, really valuable jewels, and a gay silken cap embroidered with gold; the other represented the luggage of all the party, food and cooking-pot included.

Even the varied methods of driving divers animals was not without interest. The bullocks being driven by a rope through the nose, and by a twist of the tail;

drawing, as I before said, only by pressure of a wooden yoke against the hump. The camel's bridle is attached to a piece of wood with small bits of cork, also passing through the nostril. The elephant is generally obedient to his driver's voice; but if obstinate, a little gentle suasion is applied with a spiked iron prod, horrible to behold.

Wednesday morning came, and with it should have arrived our Afghan guests. Every one was waiting at the station, at dawn of day, anxiously expecting the train. Crowds of Europeans and brilliantly dressed natives, and a large cavalry escort, waited till they were weary, when tidings were brought that His Highness Shere Ali Khan, Ameer of Afghanistan, had unfortunately eaten a whole bottle of pickles and drunk the vinegar, and would certainly be unable to come till the afternoon. So in the afternoon we returned. Again there was a great gathering of Europeans, as well as of gorgeous natives; the road was lined with native cavalry and other troops; an escort of Hussars awaited our guests, and altogether the scene was as brilliant as heart could wish.

The poor Ameer looked decidedly ill, and it must be confessed that he seemed as horribly frightened as you or I might have done, when twenty-one fog-signals successively exploded under the engine as it came in, preparatory to a grand artillery salute! You must recollect that the railway was in itself a startling novelty to him, and to one trained from his cradle in the villanous treacheries sanctioned in all Asiatic policy, such a step as venturing unarmed, and with but a handful of followers, into the heart of the British Empire, might well be accompanied by some qualms, which, however well concealed in general, were likely to be fairly roused by the first fog-signal! Of the treacheries so freely sanctioned in the politics of Asia, few better examples can be offered than the career of Shere Ali's father, Dost Mohammed, who may be said to have founded the Afghan kingdom by the assassination of one after another of the leading chiefs, till all power was vested in his own hands. He appointed Shere Ali, his third son, as his successor, a decision naturally objected to by his elder brothers, and one which led to five years' civil war ere his position was established, and he himself recognised by the British Government and accepted as an ally.

Next morning all the troops turned out at daybreak for a grand review, but His Highness, not having quite got over the pickles, deferred it till the afternoon—rather to the disgust of all concerned, as the morning was exquisite. Happily the evening proved just as fine, so we magnanimously forgave him. It was a beautiful field. The mixture of native troops in turbans, the 79th Highlanders, with their tall feather bonnets defying the sun; the European cavalry and artillery with white helmets; the picturesque corps of native horse; and the brilliant native foreground, with camels, bullocks, elephants, and horses, without number, each with trappings and housing more brilliant than its neighbour. In the background lay the city of white tents and dark trees; and far beyond all, bathed in the soft evening light, lay the snow-capped Himalayas, aim and end of our wanderings.

Several times when we returned from the river in the evenings, the kind old Rajah came to see us, and, leaving his gold-wrought slippers at the door, would sit chatting quite happily for a good while. Of course, I could not understand him, but a little interpreting made the conversation general; and it was pleasant to watch the benevolent expression of a face that always reminded me of some saintly bishop. I confess it was a great shock to my feelings, on going to return his visit, to see that dear old face painted with streaks and caste marks, received that morning at his temple. He received us with all ceremony in a large handsome house, took us to the roof to see the view, adorned us with large silver *harrs* (necklaces of silver ribbon, plaited), and offering us *pân* (betel-nuts and cardamoms, chatted on all manner of subjects, while his confidential servants, our trusty guides and guardians, looked on with evident interest, very anxious that we should be duly impressed by everything. They were men of just the same stamp as the faithful, trusty Highland retainers of olden days—such men as we still happily find from time to time—attached old servants.

I did not venture to ask for "the house," meaning the women-kind, as I could not have talked to them; so when we had said our say, Sir Deo himself escorted us back to his own carriage, his servants looking on admiringly. The good old man was as anxious to ensure our church-going on Sunday, as all other *ploys* of the week. He knew the exact hours of morning and evening service, and insisted on sending us there in the usual state, though we ventured to plead that for so short a distance we might surely walk. So from first to last there was no end to his kindness, the remembrance of which ranks very high amongst happy memories of India.

Amongst my many pleasant reminiscences of Benares was a chance railway acquaintance with a very charming Englishwoman—one of the ladies of the Zenana Mission—whose life-work it is to fraternise with as many of her Hindoo sisters as care to welcome her to their homes (and these are legion), and then try to impart to them some of the commoner branches of civilised education. It is only of late years that such a thing has become possible, as hitherto learning of any sort has been forbidden to all women of good character, and a knowledge of reading, writing, singing, or dancing, has marked those damsels only who were essentially "fast." Thus, anything more dreary than the home-life of a Hindoo matron could scarcely be devised. She may cook for her husband, but may not eat in his presence; nor may she even speak to him in presence of his mother or sisters, who rule the house, in which she is but a cipher. Very few even know how to sew.

Now a new era seems dawning on these dull lives. Multitudes are gladly learning to read and write, and the "Zenana ladies" receive a cordial welcome wherever they go, and are often invited to extend their visits to new houses, of rich merchants and great men. Some, even of the influential Rajahs, have formally admitted them to visit "their house" (as they say, in order to avoid even a distant allusion to their feminine relations), and seem well pleased that their women-folk should now begin to cultivate their minds after the manner of their white sisters. Hitherto, when any one ventured to suggest such a possibility as that of allowing dark women the same freedom as white ones, the men would scout the idea, declaring that they would be utterly incapable of using it. Now little by little they seem to be admitting the thin end of the wedge, and allowing the first glimmer of light to enter into those Zenanas, in which their sons and daughters are being reared. Who can tell how this may act on the next generation?

As regards the intellect of the women of India, there have already been a sufficient number of notable examples among such as have from time to time dared to escape from the trammels of their early training, and to assert their own powers of thought and action. Some of the most beautiful hymns in the Rig Veda are ascribed to women—the Miriams of the Aryan host! The writings of Avyar, a female philosopher of the ninth century, are to this day taught in the Tamul schools, and are classed among the standard works of the land.

Moreover, as I have already had occasion to remark, there seems no reason to doubt that the most intellectual of all games, which even to this day is deemed worthy exercise for the brains of our wisest men—I mean chess—was invented by an Indian.

12

JAMES HINGSTON, *THE AUSTRALIAN ABROAD: BRANCHES FROM THE MAIN ROUTES ROUND THE WORLD*, 2 VOLS. (LONDON: S. LOW, MARSTON, SEARLE, AND RIVINGTON, 1879), PP. 98–101, 163–164, 200–203, 209–210

The palace-city of India

I AM kindly advised, before starting on my overland journey through India, of the wants I shall find by the way. In addition to the railway ticket, I have to purchase a pillow, a towel, and some soap; the pillow is to go as a head-rest, at the end of the stuffed leathern carriage seat which will be my sleeping sofa for the night; the soap and towel are for use in the little closet adjoining the carriage. The pace of the train is slow, and the country is flat, and looks hot and uninteresting to those who have only eyes for scenery. Among the indigo and the poppies are now and again seen the heads of the natives, and here and there an occasional hill breaks the dead level of the far-stretching plain. The villages on the line of road are merely collections of mud-hovels, but one degree better than those seen on the banks of the Nile. The labourers are, I fear, but little better off, to judge by the wretched appearance of their dwellings. Those who in Egypt are called "fellahs," are here "ryots."

The opium-fields are mostly white when the poppies are in flower. Of those grown for this produce, the white is the favourite, though red and purple patches are to be seen about. Fifty years or so ago, opium was heard of and used mostly as a medicine. The use as a stimulant has steadily increased since, and here in India is the greatest field for its manufacture. The poppy, that we know of only in the wheat-fields and in the druggists' shops, takes here the place that potatoes do in Ireland, and tobacco in the Southern States of America. This district through which I come, from Calcutta, is about the largest in which it is cultivated and is a plain of 600 miles by 200 or thereabouts broad. It was ceded to England less than a century ago. One end of it runs to Patna, and the other is taken charge of as a district of Benares. The whole plain is divided thus into two districts, of which the cities named are the head-quarters. Patna had a name once for rice, which she has not maintained in the market, finding opium-growing more profitable. The heads of the poppies are, when on the stem, probed in the early morning, and then left for the juice to trickle out during the day. It is next morning scraped off in a gummy state and deposited in a jar, carried by the labourer. By him it is then transferred to other jars, and in that state collected from his hands by the officials of his district. So many jars make a chest, and the value of a chest is 150*l.*

When it is added that eight or a hundred thousand chests are a year's product for India, it will be seen by heads not much given to cyphering what a source of revenue opium is to India! When it is further considered that one-half of this produce is forced upon the Chinese market by the British, it will be perceived how little creditable opium-growing is to Great Britain. There are spots in the sun, and this opium-producing business is, from beginning to end, a dark spot on the lustre of England's commerce and means of wealth. The opium is grown by little better than slave labour, and its great profit is only realized from those Chinese, who have to take it, or a war is the penalty of their refusal. Let a spade be called a spade; and this opium business is but little less disgraceful than was the slave-trade of old!

The world, though large, is, in one sense, small. It is difficult for those who wish to get away altogether from a recognition to find the seclusion they seek. I think of that when finding, as a station-master at one of the out-of-the-way stations on this line, an old Australian acquaintance. He tells me that he is not so happy as when in that land from which he was one morning suddenly missed, and in which he now much wished himself back. The heat here made life, he said, unbearable, and he could well understand why the devisers of punishments to come had made extra heat the chief one awaiting the sinner. He hoped, for himself, that he was here doing a semi-purgatorial course, that might be carried to his credit when he, like the rest of us, should have to answer hereafter to the great "roll-call."

It is on this journey, and this evening, my first effort at getting a night's rest in a railway train. Like most first attempts, it is a failure. I must get accustomed to it, however, as I have, in the far distance before me, long rides upon the rail to do, over other continents. Sleeping over the screw, in the after part of a steamer, is not learnt at once. I thought at one time that I should never get used to the thumping noise, until at last I found sleep difficult to get without that monotonous lullaby. The rattle of the wheels in a railway-carriage tell in the same way in time, and even the shrill steam-whistle does not, at last awaken me. We are more adaptable to circumstances than we think for. Somebody said, "We are wiser than we know," and, perhaps, that is equally true, and we are not all the fools that we look.

The railway from Benares to Lucknow is called the Oude and Rohilcund line, and is about the worst to be found in India. To make up for the discomforts of dirty old carriages, and other objectionable things that are noticeable on long journeys, I happen upon good company. There is a silver lining to every cloud, and such here appears in the form of three Americans, who are travelling with no better reason for doing so than I have. In the long journey from Calcutta to Benares I had but Hindoos for company, and conversation therefore rather flagged; that is a mild way of saying that I could not understand a word that I heard said by those around me. I once met with a man of defective articulation, but exceedingly given to talking. He never expected any reply or remark to be made to him, and that fortunately, as scarcely a word of his long utterances was understood by any one. The like of him could have travelled comfortably for a day among these Hindoos, and have talked all the time, or for such part of the time as passengers could have been got to stay in the carriage with him.

This Lucknow, that was so grand-looking but awhile ago, is the capital of the kingdom of Oude, and is in the very garden of Hindoostan. Hence its troubles! The late East India Company set their eyes upon it, and then followed their acquisitive hands. Such occurred as lately only as 1856. It was the last of the "annexations" made during their reign, and the "hottest" in its results. Following the deposition of Wadi Ali Shah, the late King of Oude, came that mutiny of 1857—events which those with whom I talked in India looked upon as cause and effect. The native soldiery at Lucknow, Cawnpore, Benares, Delhi, and other places, were by some means, only to be guessed, instigated to mutiny and to the massacre of the British. Though the promoters have never been fully discovered, the organization was complete, and terribly effective for a time.

The visitor sees in Lucknow, in addition to its many palaces, some of the finest mosques to be seen in Hindoostan; for Lucknow, like Delhi, was of Mohammedan faith.

With the thugs

BETWEEN two and three hundred miles from Allahabad I get tired of the train, and stop at Jubbulpore. It is, perhaps, the grand-looking station that tempts me to do so; or maybe it is the changed character of the scenery, which has become most picturesque during the last hour or so now that I am come into the valley of the Nerbudda—a noble river of this land of India.

Jubbulpore has an admirably made railway to it. The Indian railways have been constructed by the help of British capitalists, to whom a certain percentage in the shape of dividend is guaranteed by the Government. I never saw such natty stations anywhere as there are on this line. At all those I have been lately passing there is printed the station's name, in pretty flowers, in their well-kept gardens, fronting the line of rails. I withstand all their fascinations, however, until I reach the handsome Jubbulpore terminus, and here I come to a dead stop. There may be better things ahead, but the attractions about here are very satisfactory.

Jubbulpore is under the Sautpore Hills or North Ghauts, which means a high table-land. It is a thousand feet above the level of Allahabad, to which the railway toils through cuttings, and the scenery is all the better for it. It is a city of some 60,000 folks, not reckoning the nine Thugs, the last of their race, who are here in gaol. There is something painfully interesting in the last of a race. How the "Last of the Mohicans" interests one for that reason! In Hobart Town I was shown the last of the Tasmanians—a poor old lubra, that looked as wretched as the last apteryx, a New Zealand wingless bird, believed to be extinct, that I saw exhibiting once in Melbourne, and which interested me as much as does Campbell's "Last Man."

The feeling of the traveller throughout India is, that he is in a foreign land—the land of other people, and liable at any time to be kicked out of it. All the crowds of people that he meets with speak in unknown tongues, and in tongues not always understood by each other, for of different languages India has no less than fifteen. They have all of them the most un-English costumes, ways, and manners. All the buildings that one sees, other than railway stations and barracks, are such as are not seen elsewhere. The birds and beasts are new to one, and so are the trees and field produce. The feeling creeps over the right-minded traveller who thinks of what he sees, that he is in somebody's grounds which have lately been the subject of an ejectment suit, and that the decision of the court may yet be appealed against and reversed. Other claimants will then come about, and the feeling of insecurity be greatly increased to the British traveller. If England cannot, for climatic reasons, colonize India, what chance has she of permanently holding it? Even the Monguls that conquered it and did colonize it, and that largely, lost, like the Persians, their power in it. Than Akbar, better king, better warrior, and wiser ruler, never lived. Did he still live, India would be his land only. But he left descendants from whom his power passed away. What has been will be. England may not always keep half her army in India, and the mutiny of 1857 showed her that she cannot always rely upon the sepoys and native soldiers. What Colonel Cory tells us is well known to the nations of the world, and such a many-times transferred country as India is will be certainly looked upon as fair prey for any Power at variance at any time with England.

British power has nothing to fear from those that are now in India. The Hindoos cannot combine. Their different religions and terrible slavery to "caste" keep them in isolated bands and abject subjection. I never thoroughly understood what religious training could do for men until I came to Hindoostan. None of my guides through Ceylon and India would eat or drink with me; they would equally have refused a seat at the table of the Governor-General himself. They would lose "caste" by doing so, and losing caste is losing heaven to them. The Brahmins must attend to duties clerical only. The Kshatriyas reserve themselves for military service, the Varsyas for agricultural and herdsmen employ only, the Sudras for artisan and mechanical labour, and the sons of each must follow the caste or occupation of their fathers. If he loses caste by any of the many ways of doing so, the Hindoo feels much in the position of a man just out of gaol, and forced to go about, hanging his head, among his friends and former acquaintances.

In the crowded railway carriages I often noticed, throughout Hindoostan, old Brahmins trying to secure themselves by barricades of baggage from hateful contact with those of lower caste. It was painful to witness their efforts in that way. Surrounded by bundles and packages, they would sit content to perspire and suffocate, rather than touch or be touched by unholy ones. They shrink from and scowl at intruders in a manner that used at first to frighten me—thinking I had got locked up with a lunatic. The time came at last, however, when no nonsense could be further endured. The demand for room necessitated the entrance of the guard, who came like a hawk upon a pigeon. The baggage is taken from around the holy man, and pushed away under the seats, or thrust into the rack above, and some dreadful lower-caste folks jostle, shoulder to shoulder, with the exclusive one.

What penance is necessary to wash away the stain of such contact I never learnt. It must be something as bad as a day spent with unboiled peas in his shoes, to judge by the expression I see upon this good man's features. At another station, in the small hours of the morning, the train draws up, and a Brahmin, who had been waiting for it, ran along looking in vain for an empty carriage. In his unquiet state of mind he rushed back again, as if doubting his eyes, but could see no seat fit for himself to take. The bell began ringing, and the guard, who understood such matters, called him to a carriage, to which he ran, and was at once pushed in, where he felt, probably as unhappy as Ignorance must have felt when pushed in at the door by the hill-side of which Bunyan tells us. The question of dealing with caste—by smashing through its forms and breaking down its barriers—is thus being settled on the railway. It is with such folks as this Brahmin that the guard deals, as the toper did with the various liquors of his night's drinking bout—"I take them all, and in any quantity, and then leave them to fight it out amongst themselves." A people so divided by creeds and castes as are the natives of India are easy, indeed, to govern. Could they combine, they would then withstand the whole world in arms.

Caste is a tree of great toughness, ancient growth, and wide-spreading roots and branches. Yet it is marked for falling at some distant date. In addition to what the railways do in bringing all castes together as fellow-passengers, the school system, a strictly secular one, does more. The structure of caste is thus being sapped and shaken, and also in its restrictions on marriage and social intercourse, and on freedom of choice in occupations. They are gradually found to be the hindrances that they really are to the native population competing with the European for advancement in social political life. Caste has bred nothing but a false pride in its strict observers, and led to such anomalies as a rich man of low degree having to bow to his poor but proud servant of higher caste.

A high caste Hindoo—a Koolin Brahmin—fallen to low financial condition, had better die, unless he can live on his pride and descent and intense self-respect. His blue blood gets thin on such nourishment, and yet he cannot work, and is debarred from begging. Caste, by forcing the continuance of the child in the trade of the father, put no doubt a number of square pegs into round holes, and many a Pegasus into harness, but it developed the greatest skill in handicrafts, and made the most proficient of workmen. A little of that I had seen in the wonderful superiority of the jugglers who had from childhood watched their fathers' doings, and learnt all of the art of *diablerie* before they had learnt much else.

There is less regret at leaving India after a hurried visit, as it is seen that a stay of months only is useless. It would take years to see this great country, and a long lifetime well to understand the meaning of all that should be seen—the glory and the shame, the splendour and the decay, the grandeur and the ruin, of this gorgeous Eastern land! The further time that I could give to it is forbidden by its climate. Go I must, uttering that "Il faut quitter tout cela" which Mazarin muttered on looking at the world of treasures that he knew he would soon have to leave.

Panorama-like will be for the future what the mind's eye will focus of all that the past months have shown me. The towers, temples, palaces, and tombs; the wretched huts, bespattered with discs of dung, drying for fuel; the men with tortoise-shell combs for head-dress and table-covers for leg-wraps; the women and children with ringed noses and toes, and white metal anklets; the shaven-headed men in yellow gaberdines; the nearly naked forms of humanity which have been to one like a study of "subjects" in the dead-house of a hospital; the blood-red mouths of the chewers of betel and areca; the distended goatskins of the water-carriers—looking like the swelled body of the animal itself pulled out of a pond after a month's immersion; the palkis and their heavily-freighted bearers; the confectionery sellers and the everlasting rice; the eternal curries and those aromatic, breath-sweetening, Bombay ducks, with that "chota-hazra" of tea and toast at six a.m.; the coin-decorated foreheads, and those sidewalk exhibitions of domestic life, in which the presumed phrenological examination of the head is so prominent, and that tongue-scraping so needlessly obvious; the street money-changers; the endless beggars; the cocoanut-anointed skins; the long-haired men; the never-shaven men; the half-shaved ones and the no-haired men; the endless styles of turban head-dress; the shoeless feet and the sandalled feet; the half-shoe with the up-curled toes; the night scenes of street-strewn sleepers; the public tank washings; the perpendicular and horizontal caste-marks; the white-marked, the red-marked ones; the red and white dotted noses; the squatting cloth-vendors with their bales; and the itinerant merchants, with shawl-tied packages.

13

W. S. CAINE, *A TRIP ROUND THE WORLD IN 1887–8* (LONDON: G. ROUTLEDGE & SONS, 1888), PP. 264–269, 273–276

At two o'clock we drove to the station and took our seats in the train for Kandy, with a 75-mile journey before us. The Ceylon railways are a Government monopoly, and there are 185 miles open for traffic. The carriages are horribly uncomfortable, the first-class being no better than the third-class on an English trunk line. I had to pay heavy excess on our luggage. The journey lasted five hours, an average speed of 15 miles an hour. For some miles out of Colombo the train runs through a flat country chiefly under rice cultivation, or in grass for cattle. The whole area is one vast swamp, every crop being profusely irrigated, the cattle, all black buffaloes, feeding knee deep in water. Wherever there is a knoll, or a bit of rising ground, a beautiful tropical picture forms itself; a clump of quaint cottages and barns, surrounded by palms, jack-fruit trees, bananas, and vegetable gardens, the dark red tiles of the buildings, the bright yellow and crimson dresses of the peasants, and the brown skins of the naked children relieving the intense and somewhat monotonous tropical green. Presently the Kelani-Ganga River, the greatest stream of water in the island, is crossed by a very fine iron bridge, and on the other side a branch line turns off to the quarries from which were got the stones for building the breakwater at Colombo. Fifty miles from Colombo the railway begins the great climb of 6,000 feet to Nuwera Eliya. It creeps up the flank of a magnificent mountain, Allagalla, whose high peak, crowning a sheer precipice, dominates the whole valley. From the summit of Allagalla, the old Kandyan kings used to hurl those whom they suspected of treason. On the opposite side of the great green valley of Dekanda are the Camel Mountain, so called from its resemblance to that animal, and the Bible Mountain, with a chain of connecting peaks 4,000 to 5,000 feet above the sea. In the valley are seen terraced fields of pale green rice, the flower-like branches of the Kekuna trees, magnificent forest trees covered with purple and pink blossoms, palms of all kinds, with here and there noble specimens of the great talipot palm, and patches of luxuriant tropical jungle, bright with a score of different brilliant flowers or creepers which throw themselves from one tree-top to the other, as they tower above the tangled undergrowth. Beautiful waterfalls are seen up the glens, as the train climbs slowly by, while others rush under us as we cross them on bridges, to leap into mid-air, and lose themselves in clouds of mist and spray, in which the sun dances in all the colours of the rainbow. Every now and then we get a glimpse beneath us of the fine road constructed long since by the English Government, to enable them to take and keep possession of the ancient capital, which had been wrested from the Portuguese and Dutch by the valiant old Kandyan kings; this road is now superseded by the railway. A few miles from Kandy the train, after passing through several tunnels, runs over what is called "Sensation Rock," skirting the edge of the cliff so closely that the sight drops a thousand feet before it rests on anything on which a blade of grass or a tropical creeper can lay hold. Just beyond this exciting scene we cross the dividing ridge of two water-sheds, and in a very short time reach the lovely valley of Kandy, run into the station, and by seven o'clock find ourselves comfortably settled at the Queen's Hotel.

Ceylon is an island of villages, and Kandy, though the ancient capital, is not much more than a group of two or three villages, containing in all a population of 22,000. It has little of general interest, the only buildings of any importance being the gaol, the barracks, three or four churches and chapels, the Government office, and the world-renowned Temple of the Sacred Tooth of Buddha; this latter being an insignificant little shrine of no great antiquity or architectural beauty, its only interest lying in its peculiarly sacred character, rendering it the heart from which all Buddhist sentiment ebbs and flows.

The temple is a small building with a good-sized courtyard surrounding it, the outer walls of which are decorated with hideous ill-executed frescoes of the various punishments inflicted in the Buddhist Hell, differing very little in character from those one so often sees depicted in Roman Catholic churches in Italy. The deepest and hottest hell, with the most gruesome fiends to poke the fire, is reserved for those who rob a Buddhist priest, or plunder a Buddhist temple. The great relic, which is two inches long and one inch thick (what a tooth to ache!) is preserved in a gold and jewelled shrine, covered by a large silver bell, in the centre of an octagonal tower with pointed roof. It is only exposed to view once a year, but I was privately informed that five rupees would open the door for me. I preferred my five rupees.

In the porch of the temple were groups of horrible beggars, who display their various wounds and defects of nature with much liberality.

In the afternoon we drove out to the Government Botanical Gardens at Peradenia, whose distinguished director, Dr. Triman, I had become acquainted with in the train, and who showed us much kindness and hospitality. The entrance to the garden is through a fine avenue of tall india-rubber trees, towering into the air a hundred feet, spreading out into enormous leafy crowns fifty or sixty feet in diameter, their huge roots, longer than the tree is high, creeping over the surface of the ground like great snakes, sometimes growing straight up in the air till they attach themselves to the lower branches, thus forming stout props to support the weight of heavy foliage, and enable it to resist storm and tempest.

The next day we left Kandy in company with Dr. Triman to visit the great health resort of the English residents in Ceylon Nuwera Eliya, 6,200 feet above the sea level. In the advertisements of one of the hotels here the attraction is held out that it is "so cold as to make it possible to burn open English fires all the year round." The great desire of a European who has been baked for eight or ten months in the oven of Colombo is to feel cold, to wear a great coat and comforter, to sleep without mosquito nets, and with half a dozen blankets over him. So he goes to the most detestable place on the whole island, where the rain-clouds of a radius of 1,000 miles love to dwell; where the climate is cold and damp; where the thermometer is at freezing point at six in the morning and eighty in the shade at noon; where the rainfall is 150 inches and the sun shines only sixty days in the year. Here the Anglo-Cingalese love to play at "being in England." They build themselves feeble imitations of English cottages; despising the fine flora of the country, they fill their gardens with pallid pinks, roses, and other English flowers, which look as miserable as a Hindoo beggar in a November London fog. They grow wilted specimens of English vegetables, and on rare occasions really clever gardeners have been known to ripen a strawberry; then a solemn dinner party is given to intimate and valued friends, and that strawberry is reverently divided and eaten in solemn silence. It is the dream of their lives to grow a cherry, and the man who succeeds will have a monument. They have cherry trees, but they all turn into weeping willows, and blossom feebly all the year round. These cottage gardens gave me a nightmare, and I dreamt that Nuwera Eliya was a bit of England, dying of a bad cold in the head. The only English plant that has acclimatised itself with any vigour is gorse, which was all about the hedges in odorous profusion.

Dr. Triman took us to see his hill garden at Hakgala, six miles from Nuwera Eliya, where his clever deputy, Mr. Nock, grows with some little success various English plants and flowers, and with distinguished success a wonderful variety of semi-tropical flora; he also experiments on possibilities for the advantage of Ceylon planters. Here we saw the magnificent New Zealand tree ferns, the huge shield fern, splendid rhododendron trees as big as oaks, with trunks 2 feet thick, beautiful ground orchids, lobelias, large gentians, balsams, an endless variety of ferns and lycopods, and a brace of magnificent jungle cocks, which flew out of a tree as we passed by, resplendent in their gold and crimson plumage.

Nuwera Eliya is a great plateau, on which is a fine lake about two miles long, which has recently been stocked with English trout. One was caught with the artificial fly the other day, and the intelligence was immediately cabled to the English press. They are said to be thriving, but Dr. Triman fears that as soon as the natives find out they are there they will manage to clear the lake out somehow or other. Fish have a poor chance in this Buddhist country. A Cingalese won't take life, so he never tastes butcher's meat; he has, however, no scruple to help a fish on to dry land and let him die if he can't get back to his native element, and by this amiable quibble he is able to add fish to his mess of rice without any breach of conscience. Your Buddhist is a true Pharisee. The highest peak in the island, Peduru Galla, rises just behind our hotel, and is a favourite excursion, but as we were not fortunate enough to get one of the rare sunny days, we did not ascend it. Peduru, and all the peaks round Nuwera Eliya, are forest-clad to the summit, and are the chosen home of the wild elephant, which still exists in considerable numbers in Ceylon. There were five or six of these huge beasts in the jungle, within half a mile of Hakgala gardens, and every now and then they had a tramp through them, to the sore dismay of poor Mr. Nock. There are also leopards, cheetahs, tiger-cats, jackals, elk, wild boar, monkeys, and a fine crested eagle, all plentiful in the ancient and sombre forests which clothe these lofty mountains.

Instead of returning to Kandy by the railway we determined to drive from Nuwera Eliya through a fine mountain pass to Gampola, a distance of forty miles, taking the train thence back to Kandy. It was very curious, in our descent of nearly five thousand feet, to watch the gradual change from temperate vegetation to all the luxuriance of the tropics. Half-way down we stopped at the Government Rest House at Ramboda to bait our wretched pair of ponies, and get some refreshment for ourselves.

These Government rest houses are placed at intervals of fifteen miles along all the roads in Ceylon. They contain a good guest room and five or six bedrooms, rudely furnished, but tolerably clean and comfortable. The charges are moderate. For the use of the house, 9*d.*; for a bed, 1*s.*; for sheets and blankets, 1*s.*; a lamp, 4*d.*; breakfast of tea or coffee, toast, eggs, and meat, 2*s.* 3*d.*; dinner of three courses, 2*s.* 6*d.* There is also accommodation for poor people at reduced rates, and for horses and cattle.

Ramboda is situated in a wide amphitheatre of mountains, and has a dozen fine waterfalls within a few hundred yards of each other, the amphitheatre indeed being one great spring of water. From Ramboda to Gampola we passed through a succession of coffee, tea, cocoa, and chinchona plantations, of which I shall have something to say in my next chapter, when I shall refer to the natural resources of this rich and fertile colony, and we finally arrived at the station in a deluge of tropical rain.

We spent a quiet Sunday at Kandy, visiting some of the missionary stations and native churches. Next day we came down to Colombo to spend two or three days previous to sailing for Calcutta and Madras.

14

ANNIE BRASSEY, *THE LAST VOYAGE: 1887* (LONDON: LONGMANS, GREEN, 1889), PP. 99–102, 104–105

The beauty of the journey by rail up to Kandy in the cool air of the early morning quite compensated us for the inconvenience of so early a start. A comfortable saloon carriage, with luxurious armchairs, had been attached to the train for our use, besides a well-arranged refreshment car, in which civil waiters served an excellently prepared meal.

After leaving Colombo we passed through vast fields of paddy, some covered with the stubble of the recently cut rice, while others were being prepared for a new crop by such profuse irrigation that the buffaloes seemed to be ploughing knee-deep through the thick, oozy soil. It was easy to understand how unhealthy must be the task of cultivating a rice-field, and what swampy and pestiferous odours must arise from the brilliant vegetation. 'Green as grass' is a feeble expression to those familiar with the dazzling verdure of a paddy-field. Grain cultivation in Ceylon does not, however, appear to be a very profitable occupation, and seems to be pursued by the natives for sentimental rather than for practical reasons. Sir C. P. Layard, who was for many years Governor of the Western Province, has stated that 'the cultivation of paddy is the least profitable pursuit to which a native can apply himself. It is persevered in from habit, and because the value of time and labour never enters into his calculation. Besides this, agriculture is, in the opinion of a Cingalese, the most honourable of callings.' All the grain grown in Ceylon is consumed in the island, and the supply has to be largely supplemented by imports from India and elsewhere.

After our train had ascended, almost imperceptibly, to a considerable height, we came to the Valley of Death, so called because of the enormous mortality among the workmen employed upon this portion of the railway. Thence we passed through scenes of wondrous beauty to Rambukkana, where the train really begins to climb, and has to be drawn and pushed by two engines—one in front and one behind. It would be wearisome even to name the various types of tropical vegetation which we passed; but we thought ourselves fortunate in seeing a talipot palm in full bloom, with its magnificent spike of yellowish flowers rising some twenty feet above a noble crown of dark green fan-shaped leaves. This sight is uncommon, for the trees never bloom till they are seventy or eighty years old, and then die directly.

Just before arriving at Peradeniya, the new line branches off to Nanu-oya, 128 miles from Colombo, and 5,300 feet above the sea-level. Nuwarra-Ellia is reached in about four hours from this, the line passing through some of the richest and best of the tea-and quinine-growing estates—formerly covered with coffee plantations. The horrid coffee-leaf fungus, *Hemileia vastatrix*—the local equivalent of the phylloxera, or of the Colorado beetle—has ruined half the planters in Ceylon, although there seems to be a fair prospect of a good crop this year, not only of coffee but of everything else.

There are over six hundred thousand acres of ground under rice cultivation in Ceylon, as compared with 130,000 acres of coffee, 175,000 acres of tea, 650,000 acres of palms, and 35,000 acres of cinchona. Cinnamon and other spices, besides tobacco, cacao, and other trees and plants, are also more or less extensively grown. Sugar-cultivation has proved a failure, probably owing to the too great dampness of the climate.

The Satinwood Bridge at Peradeniya, across the Mahaweliganga, seemed quite a familiar friend; though the old Englishman who for so many years washed the sand of the river in search of gems is dead and gone.

March 7th.—The morning broke misty, foggy, and decidedly cold for our early start back to Colombo. We found this change rather trying after the heat through which we have been voyaging. We left at eight, relying upon breakfast in the train; but in this hope we were disappointed, and had to content ourselves with biscuits and some rather unripe fruit; for the breakfast-car is only attached to upward trains, to suit travellers from Colombo who want to make the trip to Nuwarra-Ellia or to Kandy and back in one day. The scenery was so lovely, however, that there was plenty to occupy and distract our minds, and we were able to do all the more justice to our good lunch when we reached the comfortable Galle Face Hotel.

There was a great deal of business still to be done at Colombo, including the engagement of a new under-cook, the purchase of additional cool clothing for the crew, and the laying in of fresh stores and provisions. It was therefore not until the evening that we were able to start upon a little expedition, I in a jinrikisha, Tom on foot, followed by another jinrikisha, into which, to the great amusement of the group of lookers-on, he insisted on putting our interpreter, or 'English-speak-man,' as he calls himself.

There is always, to my mind, something supremely ludicrous in the sight of a half-naked individual trudging gaily along under an umbrella in pouring rain. His clothes cannot be spoiled, for he wears none; and one would think that his body must long ago have been acclimatised to every degree of moisture. The natives of Ceylon get over the difficulty very well by gathering one of the many beautifully spotted large caladium leaves which abound in the roadside ditches. For a time it serves its purpose, combining utility with elegance, and when the shower is over it is thrown away. I have also seen these leaves used as sunshades, but they do not answer so well in this capacity, for they wither directly and become limp and drooping. We had a pleasant stroll through the town and outskirts, exploring some lovely little nooks and corners full of tropical foliage. Colombo seems to be progressing, and to have benefited greatly by the railway.

We went to the station to meet the train from Nuwarra-Ellia, by which the children were expected to arrive, but, as the time-tables have just been altered, we found ourselves too early. The interval was pleasantly filled, however, by an instructive and interesting little chat with the traffic-manager. At last the train appeared, and with it the children, who expressed great delight at the procession of six real Japanese jinrikishas which we had organised to convey them and the rest of the party from the station to the hotel.

15

MRS. BRASSEY, *AROUND THE WORLD IN THE YACHT "SUNBEAM": OUR HOME ON THE OCEAN FOR ELEVEN MONTHS* (NEW YORK: H. HOLT, 1889), PP. 398–399

The heat was intense, though there was a pleasant breeze under the awning on deck; we therefore amused ourselves by looking over the side and bargaining with the natives, until our letters, which we had sent for, arrived. About one o'clock we went ashore, encountering on our way some exceedingly dreadful smells, wafted from ships laden with guano, bones, and other odoriferous cargoes. The inner harbor is unsavory and unwholesome to the last degree, and is just now crowded with many natives of various castes from the South of India.

Colombo is rather a European-looking town, with fine buildings and many open green spaces, where there were actually soldiers playing cricket, with great energy, under the fierce rays of the midday sun. We went at once to a hotel and rested; loitering after tiffin in the veranda, which was as usual crowded with sellers of all sorts of Indian things. Most of the day was spent in driving about, and having made our arrangements for an early start to-morrow, we then walked down to the harbor, getting drenched on our way by a tremendous thunderstorm.

Saturday, March 31st.—Up early, and after rather a scramble we went ashore at seven o'clock, just in time to start by the first train to Kandy. There was not much time to spare, and we therefore had to pay sovereigns for our tickets instead of changing them for rupees, thereby receiving only ten instead of eleven and a half, the current rate of exchange that day. It seemed rather sharp practice on the part of the railway company (*alias* the Government) to take sovereigns in at the window at ten rupees, and sell them at the door for eleven and a half, to speculators waiting ready and eager to clutch and sell them again at an infinitesimally small profit.

The line to Kandy is always described as one of the most beautiful railways in the world, and it certainly deserves the character. The first part of the journey is across jungle and through plains; then one goes climbing up and up, looking down on all the beauties of tropical vegetation, to distant mountains shimmering in the glare and haze of the burning sun. The carriages were well ventilated and provided with double roofs, and were really tolerably cool.

About nine o'clock we reached Ambepussa, and the scenery increased in beauty from this point. A couple of hours later we reached Peradeniya, the junction for Gampola. Here most of the passengers got out, bound for Neuera-ellia, the sanitarium of Ceylon, 7,000 feet above the sea. Soon after leaving the station, we passed the Satinwood Bridge. Here we had a glimpse of the botanical garden at Kandy, and soon afterwards reached the station. We were at once rushed at by two telegraph boys, each with a telegram of hospitable invitation, whilst a third friend met us with his carriage, and asked us to go at once to his house, a few miles out of Kandy. We hesitated to avail ourselves of his kind offer, as we were such a large party; but he insisted, and at once set off to make things ready for us, whilst we went to breakfast and rest at a noisy, dirty, and uncomfortable hotel. It was too hot to do anything except to sit in the veranda and watch planter after planter come in for an iced drink at the bar. The town is quite full for Easter, partly for the amusements and partly for the Church services; for on many of the coffee estates there is no church within a reasonable distance.

About four o'clock the carriage came round for us, and having dispatched the luggage in a gharry, we drove round the lovely lake, and so out to Peradeniya, where our friend lives, close to the Botanic Gardens. Many of the huts and cottages by the roadside have 'small-pox' written upon them in large letters, in three languages, English, Sanskrit, and Cingalese, a very sensible precaution, for the natives are seldom vaccinated, and this terrible disease is a real scourge among them.

16

C. F. GORDON CUMMING, *TWO HAPPY YEARS IN CEYLON*, 2 VOLS. (LONDON: BLACKWOOD AND SONS, 1892), I, PP. 155–159, 1716, II, PP. 27–29, 184–186, 238–239

Leaving the level plain, we gradually ascended—upward, still upward, all the way, wending round sharp curves and by many zigzags, so that we could sometimes see both the last carriage of the train and the engines! The carriages are provided with broad white roofs and venetian shutters as some protection against the sun. The engines are all of the most powerful construction, as well they may be, see-that for upwards of twelve miles, while rounding the flank of Allagalla, a grand craggy mountain, the uniform gradient is 1 in 45. By the time we reached the summit of Kadugannawa Pass, about sixty miles from Colombo, we had ascended 1700 feet. In front of each engine is a "cowcatcher," intended to sweep off any inquisitive animals which may rashly wander on to the line. Unfortunately even this is not always effectual, and the carelessness of owners of cattle in allowing their animals to stray upon the railway is incredible. The railway report for 1890 shows that 129 bullocks and cows were run over by trains during the year, besides occasional buffaloes. Last May a herd of these were run into near Polgahawela station, and though some were swept aside, one was run over, causing the wheels to run off the rails. Fortunately the train was stopped ere grave damage was done.

It is a single broad-gauge line, and in truth, when we see what frightful engineering difficulties had to be overcome in its construction, the succession of tunnels (one of which, through Moragalla, is 365 feet in length), and the skirting of precipitous crags, we can understand something of the causes which limited its width.

Worse even than the stubborn rocks of the mountains in the central province, was the awful malaria, which in those days was so prevalent in some of the low-lying inland districts, that it was almost certain death to sleep in them. The coolies who worked on the line died by hundreds; and in the tract lying between Mirigama and the Dekanda valley, so many perished that at last there literally was not found room for their burial within easy distance of the line. As the only possibility of keeping them alive, it was found necessary to take them all back to Colombo every night, a distance of about fifty miles. Of the Europeans in charge of the works, one after another succumbed, and had to be shipped off from Ceylon with health shattered by the deadly fever.

Now, doubtless owing to improved drainings, and to the wholesale cleaning of the jungle to make room for divers forms of cultivation, the pestilential malaria is a story of the past; and of the dense impenetrable forest which fifty years ago clothed the steep Kadugannawa Pass only a few trees remain, and there is nothing whatever to suggest to the luxurious traveller what pains and perils were endured, and how many lives were sacrificed, ere this splendid line was opened even thus far. Indeed, on one's first journey, there is no time for any impressions save those of wonder and admiration at the rapidly changing panorama of most beautiful scenery.

Even when gliding along the face of sheer crags, looking down on the valley a thousand feet below, one scarcely realises the situation. For myself, frequently passing and repassing up and down this line, and living for happy weeks in its neighbourhood, always pencil in hand, I learnt to realise something of what must have been the dangers involved in constructing such portions as "The Bear's Mouth," "Sensation Rock," and the half-tunnel gallery along the face of the Mee-angalla precipice.

And yet all these are said to be plain sailing as compared with the difficulties which are now being successfully overcome by the engineers of the extension to Haputale, which is opening up much of the grandest scenery in the Isle; so that almost ere these pages are published, the most easygoing tourist will be able, without the smallest exertion, to see whole districts which hitherto have been inaccessible even to old residents. And not in this direction only, but north, south, east, and west, the necessity of railway extension is being recognised; and in a very few years, so far as any difficulty is concerned, travelling to any corner of Ceylon will be as matter-of-fact as a journey from London to Edinburgh!

The railway system in Ceylon is entirely in the hands of Government, and it is urged by those who plead for extension, that opening up the country will certainly lead to great increase of traffic and consequent revenue. With the exception of that between Kandy and Matala, the lines hitherto constructed are said to be about the best paying in the world. As to the stations, so much care is bestowed on their gardens that each is a thing of beauty, embowered in luxuriant climbing plants, and all manner of fragrant and brilliant flowers. All names are written up in English, Tamil, and Singhalese, in their respective characters, so that all travellers may read, every man in his own tongue, unperplexed by the hateful advertisements which disfigure our British stations.

At each, pretty Singhalese children offer for sale baskets of tempting fruit, and cool refreshing young cocoa-nuts which they cut open, and hand all ready to the thirsty traveller. Fortunately for sight-seers, the rate of travel is not excessive, twenty-eight miles an hour being the utmost speed on the very best bit of level, while on the steep incline twelve miles an hour is the regulation limit, and at one point rather less.

There is so much to see on either side, that eyes and mind must be constantly on duty, whether looking right up to the mountains overhead, or down to the grand valley outspread far far below, all clothed with richest vegetation, every variety of palm mingling with endless varieties of hardwood, while the little terraced rice-fields on the slopes of the hills, and those on the flat expanse below, either present sheets of the most dazzling green or seem like a mosaic of innumerable tiny lakes. And on every side of this great valley rise hills of every variety of form—a billowy sea of mountain-ranges, all glorified by ever-changing effects of light and shadow, veiling mist or sweeping storm, followed by that "clear shining after rain" which daily reveals new beauties in mountain regions.

To me that scene recalls endless pleasant memories of happy days and weeks spent in exploring many a lovely corner in that vast panorama—memories of the cordial hospitality which gave me welcome to nest-like homes on many a hill and valley, and of one in particular, to which I was welcomed again and again, perched at the base of the mighty crag which crowns Allagalla Peak—which is a beautiful isolated mountain, 3394 feet in height—from the summit of which, it is said, the Kandyan monarchs were wont to precipitate persons accused of high treason.

That home was in a sheltered nook embosomed in fruit-trees, and overlooking such a magnificent view as we may sometimes obtain for a few moments by climbing some mighty Alp, but which few homes can claim as their perpetual outlook.

Thence far below us, and yet far above the valley, we could discern two narrow lines, and we knew that the lower one was the cart-road and the upper one the railroad, and suddenly a double puff of steam would rise, and there, darting from a tunnel, was a long train with an engine at either end, labouring on its tortuous uphill course, winding round the steep hillside. It was so far below us that it seemed like a fairy's toy, and yet it gave us a sense of touch with our fellow-creatures, which in so isolated an eyrie was rather pleasant.

To travellers and other folk to whom time is precious, the railway seems so vast an improvement on "the old carriage-road," that it is difficult to realise the amazing change which was effected by its creation only about sixty years ago (A.D. 1822). Prior to that time there were only two roads even in the Maritime Provinces, and those so bad as scarcely to be worthy of the name. Along these, travellers were carried in palanquins, with a retinue of heavily laden baggage coolies. As to the Central Province, it was altogether inaccessible to any but hill-climbers.

Kandy itself, the mountain capital, to which the railway now carries us from Colombo in four hours of luxurious travel (by a route which is one of the great triumphs of railway engineering), could then only be approached with infinite toil by steep, rugged, narrow jungle-paths, in many places dangerous for riders, and quite impossible for vehicles of any description.

We left Haldummulla and all the warm-hearted friends there with much regret, and mounted the steep ascent (all by admirable roads, both as regards engineering and upkeep) till we reached the famous Haputale Pass, 4550 feet above the sea, where a small roadside village offered rest and shelter to weary wayfarers, and a halting-place for the tired bullocks which had dragged up heavily laden waggons.

Never has any place undergone more rapid change than has been wrought here within the last two years. For the long-desired railway, which is to open up the province of Uva and bring it into direct communication with Colombo, is to cross the dividing range at Patipola, which is just above Haputale, at a height of 6223 feet above the sea, thence descending to the south-western plains.

Hitherto the railway terminus has been at Nanuoya, five miles from Nuwara Eliya, and the difficulties of making a railway over the twenty-five miles of mountain and crag which separate Nanuoya from Haputale seemed well-nigh insurmountable. Now, however, all difficulties are being conquered by skilful engineers and the patient toil of an army of five thousand workers, chiefly Tamil coolies, but including many Singhalese and Moormen—all, of course, under European direction. And for all this great body of men daily rice and all other necessaries must be provided, and the once quiet village of Haputale is now a centre of busy life, and also unfortunately of a nest of too tempting arrack, beer, and gin shops, to say nothing of an opium den, all of which are responsible for a grave amount of crime and lawlessness.

The railway work is divided into two sections—one from Nanuoya to Summit, passing below the Elk Plains, and crossing comparatively tame grassy hills and patenas, but involving a rise of about 1000 feet, the other from Haputale to Summit, rising 1673 feet over a rocky chaos of shattered cliffs and ravines. At the actual summit there is a level of about three miles, and at a point not far from there, in the direction of Nanuoya, will be the station for the Horton Plains, the grand sanatorium of the future, which lies only about three miles off the line of railway; so that the weakest women and children will be able without any conscious effort to breakfast at Colombo and sleep on these breezy plains, where already a comfortable rest-house and most lovely garden await their coming.

Little will travellers over the completed line dream what tremendous difficulties have been overcome in preparing the way for their easy journey over a region which can only be described as a chaos of huge crags, break-neck precipices, dangerous and impassable gorges, necessitating a continuous series of heavy cuttings, viaducts, embankments, and long tunnels through solid rock. In the course of a single mile seven tunnels follow in such rapid succession that travellers will be sorely tantalised by too rapid glimpses of the magnificent scenery all around— mountains seamed with rocky ravines, clear sparkling streams glancing among huge boulders or dashing in foaming cataracts over sheer precipices to the cultivated lands far below; tea and coffee estates all sprinkled over with enormous rocks, each as large as a cottage, and then the vast panorama of the sunny lowlands of Uva, its vast expanses of grass-land and rice stretching far, far away to the ocean.

But whatever they see can convey no idea of the toil and danger faced by those who traced this road and commenced its construction—of their hair-breadth escapes as they crept along rock ledges of crumbling quartz or gneiss, with a wall of mountain above, and a sheer precipice below from 300 to 500 feet in depth, or zigzagged by giddy tracks down the face of crags where goats could scarcely climb for pleasure.

Still less will they realise how pitiless rains disheartened the coolies and sodarned the earth, occasioning terrible landslips, in one of which seven poor fellows were buried alive, while another brought down a thousand cubic yards of boulders, earth, and gravel. Awful gales likewise, for days together, have positively endangered the lives of the workers, and proved a powerful argument in favour of adhering to the heavier carriages of a "broad gauge" line, rather than yield to the temptation of constructing a cheaper "narrow gauge" as was urged by some economists, and most vigorously and ceaselessly opposed by the veteran Editor of the 'Ceylon Observer.'

It is said that "a turn begun is half ended," and great was the joy of the isolated planters on this side of the island when the long-desired railway was actually commenced; and energetically has it been pushed on by all concerned.

So my recollection of Haputale as a lonely mountain village will seem as a dream of a remote past to those who now anticipate the time when it will rank as a busy town.

It is a sore subject that, whereas Hindoo, Mahommedan, and Buddhist conquerors have ever abstained from deriving any revenue from the intoxicating spirits which are forbidden by each of these religions, a Christian Government should so ruthlessly place temptation at every corner both in Ceylon and in India, where, as has been publicly stated by an Archdeacon of Bombay, the British Government has created a hundred drunkards for each convert won by Christian missionaries.

The toddy is converted into arrack in small local distilleries with copper stills capable of containing from 150 to 200 gallons, which is about the daily produce from a thousand trees, to which a small quantity of sugar and about one-third of rice is generally added. When distilled, a liquor is produced which is called pol-wakara. A second distillation produces talwakara, a spirit about twenty degrees below proof. When the process has been repeated a third time, arrack of the desired strength is obtained, at first very crude in flavour, but after having been stored in wood for several years it mellows, and even finds favour with Europeans. It is exported from Ceylon to Madras and served to the native troops as a daily ration.

The arrack trade is entirely under control of the Ceylon Government, which derives a considerable revenue from the sale of licenses to distillers (each of whom pays a yearly fee of one hundred rupees), and from the annual sale by auction of the right to farm arrack taverns in all parts of the Isle, a privilege which, being annually sold to the highest bidder, of course makes it to his interest to push the odious trade and establish fresh centres of temptation wherever he can possibly do so. Never was the old proverb that *l'occasion fait le larron* better exemplified, and many a planter has good cause to complain of the temptation thus brought to the very door of his coolies, who now too often barter the very food provided for them, in order to obtain fiery liquor.

Nor is this true only of the intoxicants natural to the country. Government holds a monopoly of the whole liquor traffic of the Isle, and has therefore a direct interest in pushing the sale of drink. Hence railway refreshment-cars and refreshment-rooms at railway stations are exempt from paying license, and the stations themselves (which are Government property) are placarded with advertisements of the whisky which, as has been so truly said, has dug more British graves in Ceylon than malaria, sunstroke, and cholera put together, and there is no doubt that these widely scattered "suggestions" are largely responsible for the practice of dram-drinking, which is said to be so much on the increase.

As regards the natives, who are always so largely influenced by any indication of the will of the ruling power, the mere fact that drinking-places are sanctioned by Government gives them a measure of respectability altogether contrary to unbiassed native opinion.

It is much to be feared that future travellers will miss much of the enjoyment of this lovely drive to Colombo, for the railway is now open as far as Bentota, with a station at the mouth of the Alutgama River—a beautiful line of railway, skirting still lagoons and generally running close along the shore, where the mighty waves break with a crash louder than the roar of the rushing train. But railway travel allows small leisure to realise all the beauties of the panorama so rapidly revealed, and in an Oriental land, where each moment we whirl past something of interest, it is the worst form of the aggravation of *tableaux vivants*, for at best we catch an unsatisfying glimpse of scenes which in the twinkling of an eye have vanished from our gaze.

Nothing is more remarkable in the history of all Oriental railways than the rapidity with which pilgrims of various faiths avail themselves of this mode of lightening the toil of their pilgrimage. The extension to Bentota proved no exception, for very soon after it was opened crowds of Mahommedans poured down from Colombo and elsewhere to worship at the Alutgama mosque.

Here, as elsewhere, the old life and the new flow side by side, sometimes in strange contrast. Thus while the railway from Kalutara to Bentota was in process of completion, three persons, including a native headman, were tried before the District Court for having subjected several persons to the torture known as the "ordeal by boiling oil," in order to extract a confession of the theft of some plumbago.

The accused, who did not attempt to deny the offence, were very much aggrieved that British law should interfere, and even punish them for an act sanctioned by ancient custom, and which, it appears, is still commonly practised in out-of-the-way parts of the Isle.

17

FLORA ANNIE STEEL, 'IN THE PERMANENT WAY', *IN THE PERMANENT WAY AND OTHER STORIES* (LONDON: WILLIAM HEINEMANN, 1898), PP. 27–42

I HEARD this story in a rail-trolly on the Pind-Dadur line, so I always think of it with a running accompaniment; a rhythmic whir of wheels in which, despite its steadiness, you feel the propelling impulse of the unseen coolies behind, then the swift skimming as they set their feet on the trolly for the brief rest which merges at the first hint of lessened speed into the old racing measure. Whir and slide, racing and resting!—while the wheels spin like bobbins and the brick rubble in the permanent way slips under your feet giddily, until you could almost fancy yourself sitting on a stationary engine, engaged in winding up an endless red ribbon. A ribbon edged, as if with tinsel, by steel rails stretching away in ever narrowing lines to the level horizon. Stretching straight as a die across a sandy desert, rippled and waved by wrinkled sand-hills into the semblance of a sandy sea.

And that, from its size, must be a seventh wave. I was just thinking this when the buzz of the brake jarred me through to the marrow of my bones.

'What's up? A train?' I asked of my companion who was giving me a lift across his section of the desert.

'No!' he replied laconically. 'Now, then! hurry up, men.'

Nothing in the wide world comes to pieces in the hand like a trolly. It was dismembered and off the line in a moment; only however, much to my surprise, to be replaced upon the rails some half a dozen yards further along them. I was opening my lips for one question when something I saw at my feet among the brick rubble made me change it for another.

'Hullo! what the dickens is that?'

To the carnal eye it was two small squares of smooth stucco, the one with an oval black stone set in it perpendicularly, the other with a round purplish one—curiously ringed with darker circles—set in it horizontally. On the stucco of one were a few dried *tulsi*[1] leaves and grains of rice; on the other suspicious-looking splashes of dark red.

'What's what?' echoed my friend, climbing up to his seat again.

'Why, man, that thing!—that thing in the permanent way!' I replied, nettled at his manner.

He gave an odd little laugh, just audible above the first whir of the wheels as we started again.

'That's about it. In the permanent way—considerably.' He paused, and I thought he was going to relapse into the silence for which he was famous; but he suddenly seemed to change his mind.

'Look here,' he said, 'it's a fifteen-mile run to the first curve, and no trains due, so if you like I'll tell you why we left the track.'

And he did.

.   .   .   .

When they were aligning this section I was put on to it—preliminary survey work under an R.E. man who wore boiled shirts in the wilderness, and was great on 'Departmental Discipline.' He is in Simla now, of course. Well, we were driving a straight line through the whole solar system and planting it out with little red flags, when one afternoon, just behind that big wave of a sand-hill, we came upon something in the way. It was a man. For further description I should say it was a thin man. There is nothing more to be said. He may have been old, he may have been young, he may have been tall, he may have been short, he may have been halt and maimed, he may have been blind, deaf, or dumb, or any or all of these. The only thing I know for *certain* is that he was thin. The *kalassies*[2] said he was some kind of a Hindu saint, and they fell at his feet promptly. I shall never forget the R.E.'s face as he stood trying to classify the creature according to Wilson's *Hindu Sects*, or his indignation at the *kalassies'* ignorant worship of a man who, for all they knew, might be a follower of Shiva, while they were bound to Vishnu, or *vice versâ*. He was very learned over the *Vaishnavas* and the *Saivas*; and all the time that bronze image with its hands on its knees squatted in the sand staring into space perfectly unmoved. Perhaps the man saw us, perhaps he didn't. I don't know; as I said before, he was thin.

So after a time we stuck a little red flag in the ground close to the small of his back, and went on our way rejoicing until we came to our camp, a mile further on. It doesn't look like it, but there is a brackish well and a sort of a village away there to the right, and of course we always took advantage of water when we could.

It must have been a week later, just as we came to the edge of the sand-hills, and could see a landmark or two, that I noticed the R.E. come up from his prismatic compass looking rather pale. Then he fussed over to me at the plane table.

'We're out,' he said, 'there is a want of Departmental Discipline in this party, and we are out.' I forget how many fractions he said, but some infinitesimal curve would have been required to bring us plumb on the next station, and as that would have ruined the R.E.'s professional reputation, we harked back to rectify the error. We found the bronze image still sitting on the sand with its hands on its knees; but apparently it had shifted its position some three feet or so to the right, for the flag was fully that distance to the left of it. That night the R.E. came to my tent with his hands full of maps and his mind of suspicions.

'It seems incredible,' he said, 'but I am almost convinced that *byragi* or *jogi*, or *gosain* or *sunyasi*, whichever he may be, has had the unparalleled effrontery to move my flag. I can't be sure, but if I were, I would have him arrested on the spot.'

I suggested he was that already; but it is sometimes difficult to make an R.E. see a Cooper's Hill joke, especially when he is your superior officer. So we did that bit over again. As it happened, my chief was laid up with sun fever when we came to the bronze image, and I had charge of the party. I don't know why, exactly, but it seemed to me rough on the thin man to stick a red flag at the small of his back, as a threat that we meant to annex the only atom of things earthly to which he still clung; time enough for that when the line was actually under construction. So I told the *kalassies* to let him do duty as a survey mark; for, from what I had heard, I knew that once a man of that sort fixes on a place in which to gain immortality by penance, he sticks to it till the mortality, at any rate, comes to an end. And this one, I found out from the villagers, had been there for ten years. Of course they said he never ate, nor drank, nor moved, but that, equally of course, was absurd.

A year after this I came along again in charge of a construction party, with an overseer called Craddock, a big yellow-headed Saxon who couldn't keep off the drink, and who had in consequence been going down steadily in one department or another for years. As good a fellow as ever stepped when he was sober. Well, we came right on the thin one again, plump in the very middle of the permanent way. We dug round him and levelled up to him for some time, and then one day Craddock gave a nod at me and walked over to where that image squatted staring into space. I can see the two now, Craddock in his navvy's dress, his blue eyes keen yet kind in the red face shaded by the dirty pith hat, and the thin man without a rag of any sort to hide his bronze anatomy.

'Look here, sonny,' said Craddock, stooping over the other, 'you're in the way—in the permanent way.'

Then he just lifted him right up, gently, as if he had been a child, and set him down about four feet to the left. It was to be a metre gauge, so that was enough for safety. There he sat after we had propped him up again with his *byraga* or cleft stick under the left arm, as if he were quite satisfied with the change. But next day he was in the old place. It was no use arguing with him. The only thing to be done was to move him out of the way when we wanted it. Of course when the earthwork was finished there was the plate-laying and ballasting and what not to be done, so it came to be part of the big Saxon's regular business to say in his Oxfordshire drawl—

'Sonny, yo're in the waiy—in the permanent waiy.'

Craddock, it must be mentioned, was in a peculiarly sober, virtuous mood, owing, no doubt, to the desolation of the desert; in which, by the way, I found him quite a godsend as a companion, for when he was on the talk the quaintness of his ideas was infinitely amusing, and his knowledge of the natives, picked up as a loafer in many a bazaar and *serai*, was surprisingly wide, if appallingly inaccurate.

'There is something, savin' yo're presence, sir, blamed wrong in the whole blamed business,' he said to me, with a mild remonstrance in his blue eyes, one evening after he had removed the obstruction to progress. 'That pore fellar, sir, 'e's a meditatin' on the word *Hom—Hommipuddenhome*[3] it is, sir, I've bin told— an' doin' 'is little level to make the spiritooal man subdoo 'is fleshly hinstinckts. And I, Nathaniel James Craddock, so called in Holy Baptism, I do assure you, a-eatin' and a-drinkin' 'earty, catches 'im right up like a babby, and sets 'im on one side, as if I was born to it. And so I will—an' willin', too—so as to keep 'im from 'arm's way; for 'eathin or Christian, sir, 'e's an eggsample to the spiritooal part of me which, savin' your presence, sir, is most ways drink.'

Poor Craddock! He went on the spree hopelessly the day after we returned to civilisation, and it was with the greatest difficulty that I succeeded in getting him a trial as driver to the material train which commenced running up and down the section. The first time I went with it on business I had an inspection carriage tacked on behind the truck-loads of coolies and ballast, so that I could not make out why on earth we let loose a danger whistle and slowed down to full stop in the very middle of the desert until I jumped down and ran forward. Even then I was only in time to see Craddock coming back to his engine with a redder face than ever.

'It's only old Meditations, sir,' he said apologetically, as I climbed in beside him. 'It don't take a minute; no longer nor a cow, and them's in the reg'lations. You see, sir, I wouldn't 'ave 'arm come to the pore soul afore 'is spiritooal nater 'ad the straight tip hoäm. Neither would none of us, sir, coolie nor driver, sir, on the section. We all likes old *Hommipuddenhome*; 'e sticks to it so stiddy, that's where it is.'

'Do you mean to say that you always have to get out and lift him off the line?' I asked, wondering rather at the patience required for the task.

'That's so, sir,' he replied slowly, in the same apologetic tones. 'It don't take no time you see, sir, that's where it is. P'r'aps you may 'ave thought, like as I did first time, that 'e'd save 'is bacon when the engine come along. Lordy! the cold sweat broke out on me that time. I brought 'er up, sir, with the buffers at the back of 'is 'ed like them things the photographers jiminy you straight with. But 'e ain't that sort, ain't Meditations.' Here Craddock asked leave to light his pipe, and in the interval I looked ahead along the narrowing red ribbon with its tinsel edge, think-ing how odd it must have been to see it barred by that bronze image.

'No! that ain't his sort,' continued Craddock meditatively, 'though wot 'is sort may be, sir, is not my part to say. I've arst, and arst, and arst them pundits, but there ain't one of them can really tell, sir, 'cos he ain't got any marks about him. You see, sir, it's by their marks, like cattle, as you tell 'em. Some says he wor-ships bloody *Shivers*[4]—'im 'oos wife you know, sir, they calls *Martha Davy*[5]—a Christian sort o' name, ain't it, sir, for a 'eathin idol?—and some says 'e worships *Wishnyou Lucksmi*[6] an' that lot, an' *Holy*[7] too, though, savin' your presence, sir, it ain't much holiness I see at them times, but mostly drink. It makes me feel quite 'omesick, I do assure you, sir, more as if they was humans like me, likewise.'

'And which belief do you incline to?' I asked, for the sake of prolonging the conversation.

He drew his rough hand over his corn-coloured beard, and quite a grave look came to the blue eyes. 'I inclines to *Shiver*,' he said decisively, 'and I'll tell you why, sir. *Shiver*'s bloody; but 'e's dead on death. They calls 'im the Destroyer. 'E don't care a damn for the body; 'e's all for the spiritooal nater, like old Meditations there. Now *Wishnyou Lucksmi* an' that lot is the Preservers. They eats an' drinks 'earty, like me. So it stands to reason, sir, don't it? that 'e's a *Shiver*, and I'm a *Wishnyou Lucksmi*.' He stood up under pretence of giving a wipe round a valve with the oily rag he held, and looked out to the horizon where the sun was setting, like a huge red signal right on the narrowing line. 'So,' he went on after a pause, 'that's why I wouldn't 'ave 'arm come to old Meditations. 'E's a *Shiver*, I'm a *Wishnyou Lucksmi*. That's what *I* am.'

His meaning was quite clear, and I am not ashamed to say that it touched me.

'Look here,' I said, 'take care you don't run over that old chap some day when you are drunk, that's all.'

He bent over another valve, burnishing it. 'I hope to God I don't,' he said in a low voice. 'That'd about finish me altogether, I expect.'

We returned the next morning before daybreak; but I went on the engine, being determined to see how that bronze image looked on the permanent way when you were steaming up to it.

'You ketch sight of 'im clear this side,' said Craddock, 'a good two mile or more; ef you had a telescope ten for that matter. It ain't so easy t'other side with the sun a-shining bang inter the eyes. And there ain't no big wave as a signal over there. But Lordy! there ain't no fear of my missin' old Meditations.'

Certainly, none that morning. He showed clear, first against the rosy flush of dawn, afterwards like a dark stain on the red ribbon.

'I'll run up close to him to-day, sir,' said Craddock, 'so as you shall see wot 'e's made of.'

The whistle rang shrill over the desert of sand, which lay empty of all save that streak of red with the dark stain upon it; but the stain never moved, never stirred, though the snorting demon from the west came racing up to it full speed.

'Have a care, man! Have a care!' I shouted; but my words were almost lost in the jar of the brake put on to the utmost. Even then I could only crane round the cab with my eyes fixed on that bronze image straight ahead of us. Could we stop in time—would it move? Yes! no! yes! Slower and slower—how many turns of the fly-wheel to so many yards?—I felt as if I were working the sum frantically in my head, when, with a little backward shiver, the great circle of steel stopped dead, and Craddock's voice came in cheerful triumph—

'There! didn't I tell you, sir? Ain't 'e stiddy? Ain't 'e a-subdooin' of mortality beautiful?' The next instant he was out, and as he stooped to his task he flung me back a look.

'Now, sonny, you'll 'ave to move. You're in the way—the permanent way, my dear.'

That was the last I saw of him for some time, for I fell sick and went home. When I returned to work I found, much to my surprise, that Craddock was in the same appointment; in fact, he had been promoted to drive the solitary passenger train which now ran daily across the desert. He had not been on the spree once, I was told; indeed, the R.E., who was of the Methodist division of that gallant regiment, took great pride in a reformation which, he informed me, was largely due to his religious teaching combined with Departmental Discipline.

'And how is Meditations?' I asked, when the great rough hand had shaken mine vehemently.

Craddock's face seemed to me to grow redder than ever. ''E's very well, sir, thanking you kindly. There's a native driver on the Goods now. 'E's a *Shiver-Martha Davy* lot, so I pays 'im five rupee a month to nip out sharp with the stoker an' shovel 'is old saint to one side. I'm gettin' good pay now, you know, sir.'

I told him there was no reason to apologise for the fact, and that I hoped it might long continue; whereat he gave a sheepish kind of laugh, and said he hoped so too.

Christmas came and went uneventfully without an outbreak, and I could not refrain from congratulating Craddock on one temptation safely over.

He smiled broadly.

'Lor' bless you, sir,' he said, 'you didn't never think, did you, that Nathaniel James Craddock, which his name was given to 'im in Holy Baptism, I do assure you, was going to knuckle down that way to old *Hommipuddenhome*? 'Twouldn't be fair on Christmas noways, sir, and though I don't set the store 'e does on 'is spiritooal nater, I was born and bred in a Christyan country, I do assure you.'

I congratulated him warmly on his sentiments, and hoped again that they would last; to which he replied as before that he hoped so too.

And then *Holi* time came round, and, as luck would have it, the place was full of riff-raff low whites going on to look for work in a further section. I had to drive through the bazaar on my way to the railway station, and it beat anything I had ever seen in various vice. East and West were outbidding each other in iniquity, and to make matters worse, an electrical dust-storm was blowing hard. You never saw such a scene; it was pandemonium, background and all. I thought I caught a glimpse of a corn-coloured beard and a pair of blue eyes in a wooden balcony among tinkling *sútáras* and jasmin chaplets, but I wasn't sure. However, as I was stepping into the inspection carriage, which, as usual, was the last in the train, I saw Craddock crossing the platform to his engine. His white coat was all splashed with the red dye they had been throwing at each other, *Holi* fashion, in the bazaar; his walk, to my eyes, had a lilt in it, and finally, the neck of a black bottle showed from one pocket.

Obedient to one of those sudden impulses which come, Heaven knows why, I took my foot off the step and followed him to the engine.

'Comin' aboard, sir,' he said quite collectedly. 'You'd be better be'ind to-night, for it's blowin' grit fit to make me a walkin' sandpaper inside and out.' And before

I could stop him the black bottle was at his mouth. This decided me. Perhaps my face showed my thoughts, for as I climbed into the cab he gave an uneasy laugh. 'Don't be afraid, sir: it's black as pitch, but I knows where old Meditations comes by instinck, I do assure you. One hour an' seventeen minutes from the distance signal with pressure as it oughter be. Hillo! there's the whistle and the baboo a-waving. Off we goes!'

As we flashed past a red light I looked at my watch.

'Don't you be afraid, sir,' he said, again looking at his. 'It's ten to ten now, and in one hour an' seventeen minutes on goes the brake. That's the ticket for *Shivers* and *Martha Davy*; though I *am* a *Wishnyou Lucksmi*.' He paused a moment, and as he stood put his hand on a stanchion to steady himself.

'Very much of a *Wishnyou Lucksmi*,' he went on with a shake of the head. 'I've 'ad a drop too much, and I know it; but it ain't fair on a fellar like me, 'aving so many names to them, when they 're all the same—a eatin' an' drinkin' lot like me. There's Christen[8]—you'd 'ave thought he'd 'ave been a decent chap by 'is name, but 'e went on orful with them *Gopis*—that's Hindu for milkmaids, sir. And Harry[9]—well, he wasn't no better than some other Harrys I've heard on.— And Canyer,[10] I expect he could just about. To say nothin' of *Gopi-naughty*;[11] and naughty he were, as no doubt you've heard tell, sir. There's too many on them for a pore fellar who don't set store by 'is spiritooal nater; especially when they mixes themselves up with *Angcore*[12] whisky, an' ginger ale.'

His blue eyes had a far-away look in them, and his words were fast losing independence, but I understood what he meant perfectly. In that brief glimpse of the big bazaar I had seen the rows of Western bottles standing cheek by jowl with the bowls of *dolee* dye, the sour curds and sweetmeats of *Holi*-tide.

'You had better sit down, Craddock,' I said severely, for I saw that the fresh air was having its usual effect. 'Perhaps if you sleep a bit you'll be more fit for work. I'll look out and wake you when you're wanted.'

He gave a silly laugh, let go the stanchion, and drew out his watch.

'Don't you be afraid, sir! One hour and seventeen minutes from the distance signal. I'll keep 'im out o' 'arm's way, an' willing, to the end of the chapter.'

He gave a lurch forward to the seat, stumbled, and the watch dropped from his hand. For a moment I thought he might go overboard, and I clutched at him frantically; but with another lurch and an indistinct admonition to me not to be afraid, he sank into the corner of the bench and was asleep in a second. Then I stooped to pick up the watch, and, rather to my surprise, found it uninjured and still going.

Craddock's words, 'ten minutes to ten,' recurred to me. Then it would be twenty-seven minutes past eleven before he was wanted. I sat down to wait, bidding the native stoker keep up the fire as usual. The wind was simply shrieking round us, and the sand drifted thick on Craddock's still, upturned face. More than once I wiped it off, feeling he might suffocate. It was the noisiest, and at the same time the most silent journey I ever undertook. Pandemonium, with seventy times seven of its devils let loose outside the cab; inside Craddock asleep, or dead—he might have been the latter from his stillness. It became oppressive after a time, as I remembered that other still figure, miles down the track, which was so strangely bound to this one beside me. The minutes seemed hours, and I felt a distinct relief when the watch, which I had held in my hand most of the time, told me it was seventeen minutes past eleven. Only ten minutes before the brake should be put on; and Craddock would require all that time to get his senses about him.

I might as well have tried to awaken a corpse, and it was three minutes to the twenty-seven when I gave up the idea as hopeless. Not that it mattered, since I could drive an engine as well as he; still the sense of responsibility weighed heavily upon me. My hand on the brake valve trembled visibly as I stood watching the minute-hand of the watch. Thirty seconds before the time I put the brake on hard, determining to be on the safe side. And then when I had taken this precaution a perfectly unreasoning anxiety seized on me. I stepped on to the footboard and craned forward into the darkness which, even without the wind and the driving dust, was blinding. The lights in front shot slantways, showing an angle of red ballast, barred by gleaming steel; beyond that a formless void of sand. But the centre of the permanent way, where that figure would be sitting, was dark as death itself. What a fool I was, when the great circle of the fly-wheel was slackening, slackening, every second! And yet the fear grew lest I should have been too late, lest I should have made some mistake. To appease my own folly I drew out my watch in confirmation of the time. Great God! a difference of two minutes!—two whole minutes!—yet the watches had been the same at the distance signal?—the fall, of course! the fall!!

I seemed unable to do anything but watch that slackening wheel, even though I became conscious of a hand on my shoulder, of some one standing beside me on the footboard. No! not standing, swaying, lurching——

'Don't!' I cried. 'Don't! it's madness!' But that some one was out in the darkness. Then I saw a big white figure dash across the angle of light with outspread arms.

'Now then, sonny! yo're in the way—the permanent way.'

.   .   .   .

The inspector paused, and I seemed to come back to the sliding whir of the trolly wheels. In the distance a semaphore was dropping its red arm, and a pointsman, like a speck on the ribbon, was at work shunting us into a siding.

'Well?' I asked.

'There isn't anything more. When a whole train goes over two men who are locked in each other's arms it is hard—hard to tell—well, which is *Shivers Martha Davy*, and which is *Wishnyou Lucksmi*. It was right out in the desert in the hot weather, no parsons or people to object; so I buried them there in the permanent way.'

'And those are tombstones, I suppose?'

He laughed. 'No; altars. The native *employés* put them up to their saint. The oval black upright stone is Shiva, the Destroyer's *lingam*; those splashes are blood. The flat one, decorated with flowers, is the *salagrama*,[13] sacred to Vishnu the Preserver. You see nobody really knew whether old Meditations was a *Saiva* or a *Vaishnava*; so I suggested this arrangement as the men were making a sectarian quarrel out of the question.' He paused again and added—

'You see it does for both of them.'

The jar of the points prevented me from replying.

Notes

1 Marjoram.
2 Tent-pitchers—men employed in measuring land.
3 *Om mi pudmi houm.* The Buddhist invocation.
4 *Shiva.*
5 *Mata devi.*
6 *Vishnu Lukshmi.*
7 *Holi,* the Indian Saturnalia.
8 *Kristna.*
9 *Hari.*
10 *Kaniya.*
11 *Gopi-nath.* These are all names of Vishnu in his various Avatars.
12 *Encore.*
13 A fossil ammonite.

Part 3

KIPLING'S RAILWAY KINGDOM

18

RUDYARD KIPLING, 'AN ESCAPE NORTHWARDS', IN *OUT OF INDIA: THINGS I SAW AND FAILED TO SEE IN CERTAIN DAYS AND NIGHTS AT JEYPORE AND ELSEWHERE* (NEW YORK: G. W. DILLINGHAM, 1895), PP. 116–119

The Englishman came to Jodhpur at mid-day, in a hot, fierce sunshine that struck back from the sands and the ledges of red-rock, as though it were May instead of December. The line scorned such a thing as a regular ordained terminus. The single track gradually melted away into the sands. Close to the station was a grim stone dak-bungalow, and in the verandah stood a brisk, bag-and-flask-begirdled individual, cracking his joints with excess of irritation. He was also snorting like an impatient horse.

Nota Bene.—When one is on the road it is above all things necessary to "pass the time o' day" to fellow-wanderers. Failure to comply with this law implies that the offender is "too good for his company;" and this, on the road, is the unpardonable sin. The Englishman "passed the time o' day" in due and ample form. "Ha! Ha!" said the gentleman with the bag. "Isn't this a sweet place? There ain't no ticca-gharries, and there ain't nothing to eat, if you haven't brought your vittles, an' they charge you three-eight for a bottle of whiskey. An' Encore at that! Oh! it's a sweet place." Here he skipped about the verandah and puffed. Then turning upon the Englishman, he said fiercely: "What have you come here for?" Now this was rude, because the ordinary form of salutation on the road is usually: "And what are you for?" meaning "what house do you represent?" The Englishman answered dolefully that he was travelling for pleasure, which simple explanation offended the little man with the courier-bag. He snapped his joints more excruciatingly than ever: "For pleasure! My God! For pleasure! Come here an' wait five weeks for your money, an' mark what I'm tellin' you now, you don't get it then! But per'aps your ideas of pleasure is different from most people's. For pleasure! Yah!" He skipped across the sands towards the station, for he was going back with the down train, and vanished in a whirlwind of luggage and the fluttering of female-skirts: in Jodhpur women are baggage-coolies. A level, drawling voice spoke from an inner room: " 'E's a bit upset. That's what 'e is! I remember when I was at Gwor-lior"—the rest of the story was lost, and the Englishman set to work to discover the nakedness of the dak-bungalow. For reasons which do not concern the public, it is made as bitterly uncomfortable as possible. The food is infamous, and the charges seem to be willfully pitched about eighty per cent. above the tariff, so that some portion of the bill, at least, may be paid without bloodshed, or the unseemly defilement of walls with the contents of drinking-glasses. This is shortsighted policy, and it would, perhaps, be better to lower the prices and hide the tariff, and put a guard about the house to prevent jackal-molested donkeys from stampeding into the verandahs. But these be details. Jodhpur dak-bungalow is a merry, merry place, and any writer in search of new ground to locate a madly improbable story in, could not do better than study it diligently. In front lies sand, riddled with innu-merable ant-holes, and, beyond the sand, the red sandstone wall of the city, and the Mahomedan burying-ground that fringes it. Fragments of sandstone set on end mark the resting places of the faithful, who are of no great account here. Above everything, a mark for miles around, towers the dun-red pile of the Fort which is also a Palace. This is set upon sandstone rock whose sharper features have been worn smooth by the wash of the windblown sand. It is as monstrous as anything in Dore's illustrations of the *Contes Drolatiques* and, wherever it wanders, the eye comes back at last to its fantastic bulk. There is no greenery on the rock, nothing but fierce sunlight or black shadow. A line of red hills forms the background of the city, and this is as bare as the picked bones of camels that lie bleaching on the sand below.

Wherever the eye falls, it sees a camel or a string of camels—lean, racer-built *sowarri* camels, or heavy, black, shag-haired trading ships bent on their way to the Railway Station. Through the night the air is alive with the bubbling and howl-ing of the brutes, who assuredly must suffer from nightmare. In the morning the chorus round the station is deafening. A camel has as wide a range of speech as an elephant. The Englishman found a little one, crooning happily to itself, all alone on the sands. Its nose-string was smashed. Hence its joy. But a big man left the station and beat it on the neck with a seven-foot stick, and it rose up and sobbed.

Knowing what these camels meant, but trusting nevertheless that the road would not be *very* bad, the Englishman went into the city, left a well-kunkered road, turned through a sand-worn, red sandstone gate, and sank ankle-deep in fine reddish white sand. This was the main thoroughfare of the city. Two tame lynxes shared it with a donkey; and the rest of the population seemed to have gone to bed. In the hot weather, between ten in the morning and four in the afternoon all Jodhpur stays at home for fear of death by sun-stroke, and it is possible that the habit extends far into what is officially called the "cold weather;" or, perhaps, being brought up among sands, men do not care to tramp them for pleasure. The city internally is a walled and secret place; each courtyard being hidden from view by a red sandstone wall except in a few streets where the shops are poor and mean.

In an old house now used for the storing of tents, Akbar's mother lay two months, before the "Guardian of Mankind" was born, drawing breath for her flight to Umarkot across the desert. Seeing this place, the Englishman thought of many things not worth the putting down on paper, and went on till the sand grew deeper and deeper, and a great camel, heavily laden with stone, came round a corner and nearly stepped on him. As the evening drew on, the city woke up, and the goats and the camels and the kine came in by hundreds, and men said that wild pig, which are strictly preserved by the Princes for their own sport, were in the habit of wandering about the roads. Now if they do this in the capital, what damage must they not do to the crops in the district?

19

RUDYARD KIPLING, 'NAMGAY DOOLA', FROM *MINE OWN PEOPLE*, IN *WORKS*, 15 VOLS. (NEW YORK: LOVELL, N.D.), I, PP. 31–37

ONCE upon a time there was a king who lived on the road to Thibet, very many miles in the Himalaya Mountains. His kingdom was 11,000 feet above the sea, and exactly four miles square, but most of the miles stood on end, owing to the nature of the country. His revenues were rather less than £400 yearly, and they were expended on the maintenance of one elephant and a standing army of five men. He was tributary to the Indian government, who allowed him certain sums for keeping a section of the Himalaya-Thibet road in repair. He further increased his revenues by selling timber to the railway companies, for he would cut the great deodar trees in his own forest and they fell thundering into the Sutlej River and were swept down to the Plains, 300 miles away, and became railway ties. Now and again this king, whose name does not matter, would mount a ring-streaked horse and ride scores of miles to Simlatown to confer with the lieutenant-governor on matters of state, or assure the viceroy that his sword was at the service of the queen-empress. Then the viceroy would cause a ruffle of drums to be sounded and the ring-streaked horse and the cavalry of the state—two men in tatters—and the herald who bore the Silver Stick before the king would trot back to their own place, which was between the tail of a heaven-climbing glacier and a dark birch forest.

Now, from such a king, always remembering that he possessed one veritable elephant and could count his descent for 1,200 years, I expected, when it was my fate to wander through his dominions, no more than mere license to live.

The night had closed in rain, and rolling clouds blotted out the lights of the villages in the valley. Forty miles away, untouched by cloud or storm, the white shoulder of Dongo Pa—the Mountain of the Council of the Gods—upheld the evening star. The monkeys sung sorrowfully to each other as they hunted for dry roots in the fern-draped trees, and the last puff of the day-wind brought from the unseen villages the scent of damp wood smoke, hot cakes, dripping undergrowth, and rotting pine-cones. That smell is the true smell of the Himalayas, and if it once gets into the blood of a man he will, at the last, forgetting everything else, return to the Hills to die. The clouds closed and the smell went away, and there remained nothing in all the world except chilling white mists and the boom of the Sutlej River.

A fat-tailed sheep, who did not want to die, bleated lamentably at my tent-door. He was scuffling with the prime minister and the director-general of public education, and he was a royal gift to me and my camp servants. I expressed my thanks suitably and inquired if I might have audience of the king. The prime minister readjusted his turban—it had fallen off in the struggle—and assured me that the king would be very pleased to see me. Therefore I dispatched two bottles as a foretaste, and when the sheep had entered upon another incarnation, climbed up to the king's palace through the wet. He had sent his army to escort me, but it stayed to talk with my cook. Soldiers are very much alike all the world over.

The palace was a four-roomed, whitewashed mud-and-timber house, the finest in all the Hills for a day's journey. The king was dressed in a purple velvet jacket, white muslin trousers, and a saffron-yellow turban of price. He gave me audience in a little carpeted room opening off the palace court-yard, which was occupied by the elephant of state. The great beast was sheeted and anchored from trunk to tail, and the curve of his back stood out against the sky line.

The prime minister and the director-general of public instruction were present to introduce me; but all the court had been dismissed lest the two bottles aforesaid should corrupt their morals. The king cast a wreath of heavy, scented flowers round my neck as I bowed, and inquired how my honored presence had the felicity to be. I said that through seeing his auspicious countenance the mists of the night had turned into sunshine, and that by reason of his beneficent sheep his good deeds would be remembered by the gods. He said that since I had set my magnificent foot in his kingdom the crops would probably yield seventy per cent. more than the average. I said that the fame of the king had reached to the four corners of the earth, and that the nations gnashed their teeth when they heard daily of the glory of his realm and the wisdom of his moon-like prime minister and lotus-eyed director-general of public education.

Then we sat down on clean white cushions, and I was at the king's right hand. Three minutes later he was telling me that the condition of the maize crop was something disgraceful, and that the railway companies would not pay him enough for his timber. The talk shifted to and fro with the bottles. We discussed very many quaint things, and the king became confidential on the subject of government generally. Most of all he dwelt on the shortcomings of one of his subjects, who, from what I could gather, had been paralyzing the executive.

"In the old days," said the king, "I could have ordered the elephant yonder to trample him to death. Now I must e'en send him seventy miles across the hills to be tried, and his keep for that time would be upon the state. And the elephant eats everything."

"What be the man's crimes, Rajah Sahib?" said I.

"Firstly, he is an 'outlander,' and no man of mine own people. Secondly, since of my favor I gave him land upon his coming, he refuses to pay revenue. Am I not the lord of the earth, above and below—entitled by right and custom to one-eighth of the crop? Yet this devil, establishing himself, refuses to pay a single tax . . . and he brings a poisonous spawn of babies."

"Cast him into jail," I said.

"Sahib," the king answered, shifting a little on the cushions, "once and only once in these forty years sickness came upon me so that I was not able to go abroad. In that hour I made a vow to my God that I would never again cut man or woman from the light of the sun and the air of God, for I perceived the nature of the punishment. How can I break my vow? Were it only the lopping off of a hand or a foot, I should not delay. But even that is impossible now that the English have rule. One or another of my people"—he looked obliquely at the director-general of public education—"would at once write a letter to the viceroy, and perhaps I should be deprived of that ruffle of drums."

He unscrewed the mouthpiece of his silver water-pipe, fitted a plain amber one, and passed the pipe to me. "Not content with refusing revenue," he continued, "this outlander refuses also to beegar" (this is the corvee or forced labor on the roads), "and stirs my people up to the like treason. Yet he is, if so he wills, an expert log-snatcher. There is none better or bolder among my people to clear a block of the river when the logs stick fast."

"But he worships strange gods," said the prime minister, deferentially.

"For that I have no concern," said the king, who was as tolerant as Akbar in matters of belief. "To each man his own god, and the fire or Mother Earth for us all at the last. It is the rebellion that offends me."

"The king has an army," I suggested. "Has not the king burned the man's house, and left him naked to the night dews?"

"Nay. A hut is a hut, and it holds the life of a man. But once I sent my army against him when his excuses became wearisome. Of their heads he brake three across the top with a stick. The other two men ran away. Also the guns would not shoot."

I had seen the equipment of the infantry. One-third of it was an old muzzle-loading fowling-piece with ragged rust holes where the nipples should have been; one-third a wire-bound matchlock with a worm-eaten stock, and one-third a four-bore flint duck gun, without a flint.

"But it is to be remembered," said the king, reaching out for the bottle, "that he is a very expert log-snatcher and a man of a merry face. What shall I do to him, sahib?"

This was interesting. The timid hill-folk would as soon have refused taxes to their king as offerings to their gods. The rebel must be a man of character.

"If it be the king's permission," I said, "I will not strike my tents till the third day, and I will see this man. The mercy of the king is godlike, and rebellion is like unto the sin of witchcraft. Moreover, both the bottles, and another, be empty."

20

RUDYARD KIPLING, 'THE MAN WHO WOULD BE KING', IN *WORKS*, 15 VOLS. (NEW YORK: LOVELL, 1899), V, PP. 92–99

"Brother to a Prince and fellow to a beggar if he be found worthy."

THE Law, as quoted, lays down a fair conduct of life, and one not easy to follow. I have been fellow to a beggar again and again under circumstances which prevented either of us finding out whether the other was worthy. I have still to be brother to a Prince, though I once came near to kinship with what might have been a veritable King and was promised the reversion of a Kingdom—army, law-courts, revenue and policy all complete. But, to-day, I greatly fear that my King is dead, and if I want a crown I must go and hunt it for myself.

The beginning of everything was in a railway train upon the road to Mhow from Ajmir. There had been a Deficit in the Budget, which necessitated traveling, not Second-class, which is only half as dear as First-class, but by Intermediate, which is very awful indeed. There are no cushions in the Intermediate-class, and the population are either Intermediate, which is Eurasian, or native, which for a long night journey is nasty, or Loafer, which is amusing though intoxicated. Intermediates do not patronize refreshment-rooms. They carry their food in bundles and pots, and buy sweets from the native sweetmeat-sellers, and drink the roadside water. That is why in the hot weather Intermediates are taken out of the carriages dead, and in all weathers are most properly looked down upon.

My particular Intermediate happened to be empty till I reached Nasirabad, when a huge gentleman in shirt-sleeves entered and following the custom of Intermediates, passed the time of day. He was a wanderer and a vagabond like myself, but with an educated taste for whisky. He told tales of things he had seen and done, of out-of-the-way corners of the Empire into which he had penetrated, and of adventures in which he risked his life for a few days' food. "If India was filled with men like you and me, not knowing more than the crows where they'd get their next day's rations, it isn't seventy millions of revenue the land would be paying—it's seven hundred millions," said he; and as I looked at his mouth and chin I was disposed to agree with him. We talked politics—the politics of Loaferdom that sees things from the underside where the lath and plaster is not smoothed off—and we talked postal arrangements because my friend wanted to send a telegram back from the next station to Ajmir, which is the turning-off place from the Bombay to the Mhow line as you travel westward. My friend had no money beyond eight annas which he wanted for dinner, and I had no money at all, owing to the hitch in the Budget before mentioned. Further, I was going into a wilderness where, though I should resume touch with the Treasury, there were no telegraph offices. I was, therefore, unable to help him in any way.

"We might threaten a Station-master, and make him send a wire on tick," said my friend, "but that'd mean inquiries for you and for me, and I've got my hands full these days. Did you say you are traveling back along this line within any days?"

"Within ten," I said.

"Can't you make it eight?" said he. "Mine is rather urgent business."

"I can send your telegram within ten days if that will serve you," I said.

"I couldn't trust the wire to fetch him now I think of it. It's this way. He leaves Delhi on the 23d for Bombay. That means he'll be running through Ajmir about the night of the 23d."

"But I'm going into the Indian Desert," I explained.

"Well *and* good," said he. "You'll be changing at Marwar Junction to get into Jodhpore territory—you must do that and he'll be coming through Marwar junction in the early morning of the 24th by the Bombay Mail. Can you be at Marwar Junction on that time? 'Twon't be inconveniencing you because I know that there's precious few pickings to be got out of these Central India States—even though you pretend to be correspondent of the *Backwoodsman*."

"Have you ever tried that trick?" I asked.

"Again and again, but the Residents find you out, and then you get escorted to the Border before you've time to get your knife into them. But about my friend here. I *must* give him a word o' mouth to tell him what's come to me or else he won't know where to go. I would take it more than kind of you if you was to come out of Central India in time to catch him at Marwar Junction, and say to him:— 'He has gone South for the week.' He'll know what that means. He's a big man with a red beard, and a great swell he is. You'll find him sleeping like a gentleman with all his luggage round him in a Second-class compartment. But don't you be afraid. Slip down the window, and say:—'He has gone South for the week,' and he'll tumble. It's only cutting your time of stay in those parts by two days. I ask you as a stranger—going to the West," he said with emphasis.

"Where have *you* come from?" said I.

"From the East," said he, "and I am hoping that you will give him the message on the Square—for the sake of my Mother as well as your own."

Englishmen are not usually softened by appeals to the memory of their mothers, but for certain reasons, which will be fully apparent, I saw fit to agree.

"It's more than a little matter," said he, "and that's why I ask you to do it—and now I know that I can depend on you doing it. A Second-class carriage at Marwar Junction, and a red-haired man asleep in it. You'll be sure to remember. I get out at the next station, and I must hold on there till he comes or sends me what I want."

"I'll give the message if I catch him," I said, "and for the sake of your Mother as well as mine I'll give you a word of advice. Don't try to run the Central India States just now as the correspondent of the *Backwoodsman*. There's a real one knocking about here, and it might lead to trouble."

"Thank you," said he simply, "and when will the swine be gone? I can't starve because he's ruining my work. I wanted to get hold of the Degumber Rajah down here about his father's widow, and give him a jump."

"What did he do to his father's widow, then?"

"Filled her up with red pepper and slippered her to death as she hung from a beam. I found that out myself and I'm the only man that would dare going into the State to get hush-money for it. They'll try to poison me, same as they did in Chortumna when I went on the loot there. But you'll give the man at Marwar Junction my message?"

He got out at a little roadside station, and I reflected. I had heard, more than once, of men personating correspondents of newspapers and bleeding small Native States with threats of exposure, but I had never met any of the caste before. They lead a hard life, and generally die with great suddenness. The Native States have a wholesome horror of English newspapers, which may throw light on their peculiar methods of government, and do their best to choke correspondents with champagne, or drive them out of their mind with four-in-hand barouches. They do not understand that nobody cares a straw for the internal administration of Native States so long as oppression and crime are kept within decent limits, and the ruler is not drugged, drunk, or diseased from one end of the year to the other. Native States were created by Providence in order to supply picturesque scenery, tigers, and tall-writing. They are the dark places of the earth, full of unimaginable cruelty, touching the Railway and the Telegraph on one side, and, on the other, the days of Harun-al-Raschid. When I left the train I did business with divers Kings, and in eight days passed through many changes of life. Sometimes I wore dress-clothes and consorted with Princes and Politicals, drinking from crystal and eating from silver. Sometimes I lay out upon the ground and devoured what I could get, from a plate made of a flapjack, and drank the running water, and slept under the same rug as my servant. It was all in the day's work.

Then I headed for the Great Indian Desert upon the proper date, as I had prom-ised, and the night Mail set me down at Marwar Junction, where a funny little, happy-go-lucky, native-managed railway runs to Jodhpore. The Bombay Mail from Delhi makes a short halt at Marwar. She arrived as I got in, and I had just time to hurry to her platform and go down the carriages. There was only one Second-class on the train. I slipped the window and looked down upon a flaming red beard, half covered by a railway rug. That was my man, fast asleep, and I dug him gently in the ribs. He woke with a grunt and I saw his face in the light of the lamps. It was a great and shining face.

"Tickets again?" said he.

"No," said I. "I am to tell you that he is gone South for the week. He is gone South for the week!"

The train had begun to move out. The red man rubbed his eyes. "He has gone South for the week," he repeated. "Now that's just like his impidence. Did he say that I was to give you anything?—'Cause I won't."

"He didn't," I said and dropped away, and watched the red lights die out in the dark. It was horribly cold because the wind was blowing off the sands. I climbed into my own train—not an Intermediate Carriage this time—and went to sleep.

If the man with the beard had given me a rupee I should have kept it as a memento of a rather curious affair. But the consciousness of having done my duty was my only reward.

Later on I reflected that two gentlemen like my friends could not do any good if they foregathered and personated correspondents of newspapers, and might, if they "stuck up" one of the little rat-trap states of Central India or Southern Rajputana, get themselves into serious difficulties. I therefore took some trouble to describe them as accurately as I could remember to people who would be interested in deporting them: and succeeded, so I was later informed, in having them headed back from the Degumber borders.

21

RUDYARD KIPLING, 'LETTERS OF MARQUE', IN *WORKS*, 15 VOLS. (NEW YORK: LOVELL, 1899), XII, PP. 5–9

I

EXCEPT for those who, under compulsion of a sick certificate, are flying Bombaywards, it is good for every man to see some little of the great Indian Empire and the strange folk who move about it. It is good to escape for a time from the House of Rimmon—be it office or cutchery—and to go abroad under no more exacting master than personal inclination, and with no more definite plan of travel than has the horse, escaped from pasture, free upon the countryside. The first result of such freedom is extreme bewilderment, and the second reduces the freed to a state of mind which, for his sins, must be the normal portion of the Globe-trotter—the man who "does" kingdoms in days and writes books upon them in weeks. And this desperate facility is not as strange as it seems. By the time that an Englishman has come by sea and rail *via* America, Japan, Singapur, and Ceylon, to India, he can—these eyes have seen him do so—master in five minutes the intricacies of the *Indian Bradshaw*, and tell an old resident exactly how and where the trains run. Can we wonder that the intoxication of success in hasty assimilation should make him overbold, and that he should try to grasp—but a full account of the insolent Globe-trotter must be reserved. He is worthy of a book. Given absolute freedom for a month, the mind, as I have said, fails to take in the situation and, after much debate, contents itself with following in old and well-beaten ways—paths that we in India have no time to tread, but must leave to the country cousin who wears his *pagri* tail-fashion down his back, and says "cabman" to the driver of the *ticca-ghari.*

Now, Jeypore from the Anglo-Indian point of view is a station on the Rajputana-Malwa line, on the way to Bombay, where half an hour is allowed for dinner, and where there ought to be more protection from the sun than at present exists. Some few, more learned than the rest, know that garnets come from Jeypore, and here the limits of our wisdom are set. We do not, to quote the Calcutta shopkeeper, come out "for the good of our 'ealth," and what touring we accomplish is for the most part off the line of rail.

For these reasons, and because he wished to study our winter birds of passage, one of the few thousand Englishmen in India on a date and in a place which have no concern with the story, sacrificed all his self-respect and became—at enormous personal inconvenience—a Globe-trotter going to Jeypore, and leaving behind him for a little while all that old and well-known life in which Commissioners and Deputy Commissioners, Governors and Lieutenant-Governors, Aides-de-camp, Colonels and their wives, Majors, Captains, and Subalterns after their kind move and rule and govern and squabble and fight and sell each other's horses and tell wicked stories of their neighbors. But before he had fully settled into his part or accustomed himself to saying, "Please take out this luggage," to the coolies at the stations, he saw from the train the Taj wrapped in the mists of the morning.

There is a story of a Frenchman who feared not God, nor regarded man, sailing to Egypt for the express purpose of scoffing at the Pyramids and—though this is hard to believe—at the great Napoleon who had warred under their shadow. It is on record that that blasphemous Gaul came to the Great Pyramid and wept through mingled reverence and contrition; for he sprang from an emotional race. To understand his feelings it is necessary to have read a great deal too much about the Taj, its design and proportions, to have seen execrable pictures of it at the Simla Fine Arts Exhibition, to have had its praises sung by superior and traveled friends till the brain loathed the repetition of the word, and then, sulky with want of sleep, heavy-eyed, unwashed, and chilled, to come upon it suddenly. Under these circumstances everything, you will concede, is in favor of a cold, critical, and not too impartial verdict. As the Englishman leaned out of the carriage he saw first an opal-tinted cloud on the horizon, and, later, certain towers. The mists lay on the ground, so that the splendor seemed to be floating free of the earth; and the mists rose in the background, so that at no time could everything be seen clearly. Then as the train sped forward, and the mists shifted, and the sun shone upon the mists, the Taj took a hundred new shapes, each perfect and each beyond description. It was the Ivory Gate through which all good dreams come; it was the realization of the gleaming halls of dawn that Tennyson sings of; it was veritably the "aspiration fixed," the "sign made stone," of a lesser poet; and over and above concrete comparisons, it seemed the embodiment of all things pure, all things holy, and all things unhappy. That was the mystery of the building. It may be that the mists wrought the witchery, and that the Taj seen in the dry sunlight is only, as guide-books say, a noble structure. The Englishman could not tell, and has made a vow that he will never go nearer the spot, for fear of breaking the charm of the unearthly pavilions.

It may be, too, that each must view the Taj for himself with his own eyes, working out his own interpretation of the sight. It is certain that no man can in cold blood and colder ink set down his impressions if he has been in the least moved.

To the one who watched and wondered that November morning the thing seemed full of sorrow—the sorrow of the man who built it for the woman he loved, and the sorrow of the workmen who died in the building—used up like cattle. And in the face of this sorrow the Taj flushed in the sunlight and was beautiful, after the beauty of a woman who has done no wrong.

Here the train ran in under the walls of Agra Fort, and another train—of thought incoherent as that written above—came to an end. Let those who scoff at overmuch enthusiasm look at the Taj and thenceforward be dumb. It is well on the threshold of a journey to be taught reverence and awe.

But there is no reverence in the Globe-trotter: he is brazen. A Young Man from Manchester was traveling to Bombay in order—how the words hurt!—to be home by Christmas. He had come through America, New Zealand, and Australia, and finding that he had ten days to spare at Bombay, conceived the modest idea of "doing India." "I don't say that I've done it all; but you may say that I've seen a good deal." Then he explained that he had been "much pleased" at Agra, "much pleased" at Delhi, and, last profanation, "very much pleased" at the Taj. Indeed, he seemed to be going through life just then "much pleased" at everything.

22

RUDYARD KIPLING, 'AMONG THE RAILWAY FOLK', IN *WORKS*, 15 VOLS. (NEW YORK: LOVELL, 1899), VII, PP. 65–93

A railway settlement

JAMALPUR is the headquarters of the East India Railway. This in itself is not a startling statement. The wonder begins with the exploration of Jamalpur, which is a station entirely made by, and devoted to, the use of those untiring servants of the public, the railway folk. They have towns of their own at Toondla and Assensole; a sun-dried sanitarium at Bandikui; and Howrah, Ajmir, Allahabad, Lahore, and Pindi know their colonies. But Jamalpur is unadulteratedly "Railway," and he who has nothing to do with the E. I. Railway in some shape or another feels a stranger and an interloper. Running always east and southerly, the train carries him from the torments of the northwest into the wet, woolly warmth of Bengal, where may be found the hothouse heat that has ruined the temper of the good people of Calcutta. The land is fat and greasy with good living, and the wealth of the bodies of innumerable dead things; and here—just above Mokameh—may be seen fields stretching, without stick, stone, or bush to break the view, from the railway line to the horizon.

Up-country innocents must look at the map to learn that Jamalpur is near the top left-hand corner of the big loop that the E. I. R. throws out round Bhagalpur and part of the Bara-Banki districts. Northward of Jamalpur, as near as may be, lies the Ganges and Tirhoot, and eastward an offshoot of the volcanic Rajmehal range blocks the view.

A station which has neither Judge, Commissioner, Deputy, or 'Stunt, which is devoid of law courts, *ticcagharies*, District Superintendents of Police, and many other evidences of an over-cultured civilization, is a curiosity. "We administer ourselves," says Jamalpur, proudly, "or we did—till we had local self-government in—and now the racket-marker administers us." This is a solemn fact. The station, which had its beginnings thirty odd years ago, used, till comparatively recent times, to control its own roads, sewage, conservancy, and the like. But, with the introduction of local self-government, it was ordained that the "inestimable boon"

160

should be extended to a place made by, and maintained for, Europeans, and a brand-new municipality was created and nominated according to the many rules of the game. In the skirmish that ensued, the Club racket-marker fought his way to the front, secured a place on a board largely composed of Babus, and since that day Jamalpur's views on government have not been fit for publication. To understand the magnitude of the insult, one must study the city—for station, in the strict sense of the word, it is not. Crotons, palms, mangoes, *mellingtonias*, teak, and bamboos adorn it, and the *poinsettia* and *bougainvillea*, the railway creeper and the *bignonia venusta*, make it gay with many colors. It is laid out with military precision to each house its just share of garden, its red brick path, its growth of trees, and its neat little wicket gate. Its general aspect, in spite of the Dutch formality, is that of an English village, such a thing as enterprising stage-managers put on the theaters at home. The hills have thrown a protecting arm round nearly three sides of it, and on the fourth it is bounded by what are locally known as the "sheds"; in other words, the station, offices, and workshops of the company. The E. I. R. only exists for outsiders. Its servants speak of it reverently, angrily, despitefully or enthusiastically as "The Company"; and they never omit the big, big C. Men must have treated the Honorable the East India Company in something the same fashion ages ago. "The Company" in Jamalpur is Lord Dufferin, all the members of Council, the Body-Guard, Sir Frederick Roberts, Mr. Westland, whose name is at the bottom of the currency notes, the Oriental Life Assurance Company, and the Bengal Government all rolled into one. At first, when a stranger enters this life, he is inclined to scoff and ask, in his ignorance, "*What* is this Company that you talk so much about?" Later on, he ceases to scoff; for the Company is a "big" thing—almost big enough to satisfy an American.

Ere beginning to describe its doings, let it be written and repeated several times hereafter, that the E. I. R. passenger carriages, and especially the second class, are just now horrid—being filthy and unwashen, dirty to look at, and dirty to live in. Having cast this small stone, we will examine Jamalpur. When it was laid out, in or before the Mutiny year, its designers allowed room for growth, and made the houses of one general design—some of brick, some of stone, some three, four, and six roomed, some single men's barracks and some two-storied—all for the use of the employés. King's Road, Prince's Road, Queen's Road, and Victoria Road—Jamalpur is loyal—cut the breadth of the station; and Albert Road, Church Street, and Steam Road the length of it. Neither on these roads or on any of the cool-shaded smaller ones is anything unclean or unsightly to be found. There is a dreary village in the neighborhood which is said to make the most of any cholera that may be going, but Jamalpur itself is specklessly and spotlessly neat. From St. Mary's Church to the railway station, and from the buildings where they print daily about half a lakh of tickets, to the ringing, roaring, rattling workshops, everything has the air of having been cleaned up at ten that very morning and put under a glass case. There is a holy calm about the roads—totally unlike anything in an English manufacturing town. Wheeled conveyances are few, because every man's bungalow is close to his work, and when the day has begun and the offices of the "Loco." and "Traffic" have soaked up their thousands of natives and hundreds of Europeans, you shall pass under the dappled shadows of the trees, hearing nothing louder than the croon of some bearer playing with a child in the veranda or the faint tinkle of a piano. This is pleasant, and produces an impression of Watteau-like refinement tempered with Arcadian simplicity. The dry, anguished howl of the "buzzer," the big steam whistle, breaks the hush, and all Jamalpur is alive with the tramping of tiffin-seeking feet. The Company gives one hour for meals between eleven and twelve. On the stroke of noon there is another rush back to the works or the offices, and Jamalpur sleeps through the afternoon till four or half-past, and then rouses for tennis at the institute.

In the hot weather it splashes in the swimming bath, or reads, for it has a library of several thousand books. One of the most flourishing lodges in the Bengal Juris- diction—"St. George in the East"—lives at Jamalpur, and meets twice a month. Its members point out with justifiable pride that all the fittings were made by their own hands; and the lodge in its accouterments and the energy of the craftsmen can compare with any in India. But the institute is the central gathering place, and its half-dozen tennis-courts and neatly-laid-out grounds seem to be always full. Here, if a stranger could judge, the greater part of the flirtation of Jamalpur is carried out, and here the dashing apprentice—the apprentices are the liveli- est of all—learns that there are problems harder than any he studies at the night school, and that the heart of a maiden is more inscrutable than the mechanism of a locomotive. On Tuesdays and Fridays, the volunteers parade. A and B Compa- nies, 150 strong in all, of the E. I. R. Volunteers, are stationed here with the band. Their uniform, gray with red facings, is not lovely, but they know how to shoot and drill. They have to. The "Company" makes it a condition of service that a man must be a volunteer; and volunteer in something more than name he must be, or some one will ask the reason why. Seeing that there are no regulars between Howrah and Dinapore, the "Company" does well in exacting this toll. Some of the old soldiers are wearied of drill, some of the youngsters don't like it, but—the way they entrain and detrain is worth seeing. They are as mobile a corps as can be desired, and perhaps ten or twelve years hence the Government may possibly be led to take a real interest in them and spend a few thousand rupees in providing them with real soldiers' kits—not uniform and rifle merely. Their ranks include all sorts and conditions of men—heads of the "Loco." and "Traffic," the "Com- pany" is no respecter of rank—clerks in the "audit," boys from mercantile firms at home, fighting with the intricacies of time, fare, and freight tables; guards who have grown gray in the service of the Company; mail and passenger drivers with nerves of cast-iron, who can shoot through a long afternoon without losing temper or flurrying; light-blue East Indians; Tyne-side men, slow of speech and uncom- monly strong in the arm; lathy apprentices who have not yet "filled out"; fitters, turners, foremen, full assistant, and sub-assistant station-masters, and a host of others. In the hands of the younger men the regulation Martini-Henri naturally goes off the line occasionally on hunting expeditions.

There is a twelve-hundred yards' range running down one side of the station, and the condition of the grass by the firing butts tells its own tale. Scattered in the ranks of the volunteers are a fair number of old soldiers, for the Company has a weakness for recruiting from the Army for its guards who may, in time, become station-masters. A good man from the Army, with his papers all correct and certificates from his commanding officer, can, after depositing twenty pounds to pay his home passage, in the event of his services being dispensed with, enter the Company's service on something less than one hundred rupees a month and rise in time to four hundred as a station-master. A railway bungalow—and they are as substantially built as the engines—will cost him more than one-ninth of the pay of his grade, and the Provident Fund provides for his latter end.

Think for a moment of the number of men that a line running from Howrah to Delhi must use, and you will realize what an enormous amount of patronage the Company holds in its hands. Naturally a father who has worked for the line expects the line to do something for the son; and the line is not backward in meeting his wishes where possible. The sons of old servants may be taken on at fifteen years of age, or thereabouts, as apprentices in the "shops," receiving twenty rupees in the first and fifty in the last year of their indentures. Then they come on the books as full "men" on perhaps Rs. 65 a month, and the road is open to them in many ways. They may become foremen of departments on Rs. 500 a month, or drivers earning with overtime Rs. 370; or if they have been brought into the audit or the traffic, they may control innummerable Babus and draw several hundreds of rupees monthly; or, at eighteen or nineteen, they may be ticket-collectors, working up to the grade of guard, etc. Every rank of the huge, human hive has a desire to see its sons placed properly, and the native workmen, about three thousand, in the locomotive department only, are, said one man, "making a family affair of it altogether. You see all those men turning brass and looking after the machinery? They've all got relatives, and a lot of 'em own land out Monghyr-way close to us. They bring on their sons as soon as they are old enough to do anything, and the Company rather encourages it. You see the father is in a way responsible for his son, and he'll teach him all he knows, and in that way the Company has a hold on them all. You've no notion how sharp a native is when he's working on his own hook. All the district round here, right up to Monghyr, is more or less dependent on the railway."

The Babus in the traffic department, in the stores, issue department, in all the departments where men sit through the long, long Indian day among ledgers, and check and pencil and deal in figures and items and rupees, may be counted by hundreds. Imagine the struggle among them to locate their sons in comfortable cane-bottomed chairs, in front of a big pewter inkstand and stacks of paper! The Babus make beautiful accountants, and if we could only see it, a merciful Providence has made the Babu for figures and detail. Without him, the dividends of any company would be eaten up by the expenses of English or city-bred clerks. The Babu is a great man, and, to respect him, you must see five score or so of him in a room a hundred yards long, bending over ledgers, ledgers, and yet more ledgers—silent as the Sphinx and busy as a bee. He is the lubricant of the great machinery of the Company whose ways and works cannot be dealt with in a single scrawl.

The shops

THE railway folk, like the army and civilian castes, have their own language and life, which an outsider cannot hope to understand. For instance, when Jamalpur refers to itself as being "on the long siding," a lengthy explanation is necessary before the visitor grasps the fact that the whole of the two hundred and thirty odd miles of the loop from Luckeeserai to Kanu-Junction *via* Bhagalpur is thus contemptuously treated. Jamalpur insists that it is out of the world, and makes this an excuse for being proud of itself and all its institutions. But in one thing it is badly, disgracefully provided. At a moderate estimate there must be about two hundred Europeans with their families in this place. They can, and do, get their small supplies from Calcutta, but they are dependent on the tender mercies of the bazaar for their meat, which seems to be hawked from door to door. There is a Raja who owns or has an interest in the land on which the station stands, and he is averse to cow-killing. For these reasons, Jamalpur is not too well supplied with good meat, and what it wants is a decent meat-market with cleanly controlled slaughtering arrangements. The "Company," who gives grants to the schools and builds the institutes and throws the shadow of its protection all over the place, might help this scheme forward.

The heart of Jamalpur is the "shops," and here a visitor will see more things in an hour than he can understand in a year. Steam Street very appropriately leads to the forty or fifty acres that the "shops" cover, and to the busy silence of the loco. superintendent's office, where a man must put down his name and his business on a slip of paper before he can penetrate into the Temple of Vulcan. About three thousand five hundred men are in the "shops," and, ten minutes after the day's work has begun, the assistant superintendent knows exactly how many are "in." The heads of departments—silent, heavy-handed men, captains of five hundred or more—have their names fairly printed on a board which is exactly like a pool-marker. They "star a life" when they come in, and their few names alone represent salaries to the extent of six thousand a month. They are men worth hearing deferentially. They hail from Manchester and the Clyde, and the great iron-works of the North: pleasant as cold water in a thirsty land is it to hear again the full Northumbrian burr or the long-drawn Yorkshire "aye." Under their great gravity of demeanor—a man who is in charge of a few lakhs' worth of plant cannot afford to be riotously mirthful—lurks melody and humor. They can sing like north-countrymen, and in their hours of ease go back to the speech of the iron countries they have left behind, when "Ab o' th' yate" and all "Ben Briarly's" shrewd wit shakes the warm air of Bengal with deep-chested laughter. Hear "Ruglan' Toon," with a chorus as true as the fall of trip-hammers, and fancy that you are back again in the smoky, rattling, ringing North!

But this is the "unofficial" side. Go forward through the gates under the mango trees, and set foot at once in sheds which have as little to do with mangoes as a locomotive with Lakshmi. "The "buzzer" howls, for it is nearly tiffin time. There is a rush from every quarter of the shops, a cloud of flying natives, and a procession of more sedately pacing Englishmen, and in three short minutes you are left absolutely alone among arrested wheels and belts, pulleys, cranks, and cranes—in a silence only broken by the soft sigh of a far-away steam-valve or the cooing of pigeons. You are, by favor freely granted, at liberty to wander anywhere you please through the deserted works. Walk into a huge, brick-built, tin-roofed stable, capable of holding twenty-four locomotives under treatment, and see what must be done to the Iron Horse once in every three years if he is to do his work well. On reflection, Iron Horse is wrong. An engine is a she—as distinctly feminine as a ship or a mine. Here stands the *Echo*, her wheels off, resting on blocks, her underside machinery taken out, and her side scrawled with mysterious hieroglyphics in chalk. An enormous green-painted iron harness-rack bears her piston and eccentric rods, and a neatly painted board shows that such and such Englishmen are the fitter, assistant, and apprentice engaged in editing that *Echo*. An engine seen from the platform and an engine viewed from underneath are two very different things. The one is as unimpressive as a cart; the other as imposing as a man-of-war in the yard.

In this manner is an engine treated for navicular, laminitis, back-sinew, or whatever it is that engines most suffer from. No. 607, we will say, goes wrong at Dinapore, Assensole, Buxar, or wherever it may be, after three years' work. The place she came from is stencilled on the boiler, and the foreman examines her. Then he fills in a hospital sheet, which bears one hundred and eighty printed heads under which an engine can come into the shops. No. 607 needs repair in only one hundred and eighteen particulars, ranging from mud-hole-flanges and blower-cocks to lead-plugs, and platform brackets which have shaken loose. This certificate the foreman signs, and it is framed near the engine for the benefit of the three Europeans and the eight or nine natives who have to mend No. 607. To the ignorant the superhuman wisdom of the examiner seems only equalled by the audacity of the two men and the boy who are to undertake what is frivolously called the "job". No. 607, is in a sorely mangled condition, but 403 is much worse. She is reduced to a shell—is a very elle-woman of an engine, bearing only her funnel, the iron frame and the saddle that supports the boiler.

Four-and-twenty engines in every stage of decomposition stand in one huge shop. A traveling crane runs overhead, and the men have hauled up one end of a bright vermilion loco. The effect is the silence of a scornful stare—just such a look as a colonel's portly wife gives through her *pince-nez* at the audacious subaltern. Engines are the "livest" things that man ever made. They glare through their spectacle-plates, they tilt their noses contemptuously, and when their insides are gone they adorn themselves with red lead, and leer like decayed beauties: and in the Jamalpur works there is no escape from them. The shops can hold fifty without pressure, and on occasion as many again. Everywhere there are engines, and everywhere brass domes lie about on the ground like huge helmets in a pantomine. The silence is the weirdest touch of all. Some sprightly soul—an apprentice be sure—has daubed in red lead on the end of an iron-tool-box a caricature of some friend who is evidently a riveter. The picture has all the interest of an Egyptian cartouche, for it shows that men have been here, and that the engines do not have it all their own way.

And so, out in the open, away from the three great sheds, between and under more engines, till we strike a wilderness of lines all converging to one turn-table. Here be elephant-stalls ranged round a half-circle, and in each stall stands one engine, and each engine stares at the turn-table. A stolid and disconcerting company is this ring-of-eyes monsters; 324, 432, and 8 are shining like toys. They are ready for their turn of duty, and are as spruce as hansoms Lacquered chocolate, picked out with black, red, and white, is their dress, and delicate lemon graces the ceiling of the cabs. The driver should be a gentleman in evening dress with white kid gloves, and there should be gold-headed champagne bottles in the spick and span tenders. Huckleberry Finn says of a timber raft, "It amounted to something being captain of that raft." Thrice enviable is the man who, drawing Rs. 120 a month, is allowed to make Rs. 150 overtime out of locus. Nos. 324, 422, or 8. Fifty yards beyond this gorgeous trinity are ten to twelve engines who have but in to Jamalpur to bait. They are alive, their fires are lighted, and they are swearing and purring and growling one at another as they stand alone. Here is evidently one of the newest type—No. 25, a giant who has just brought the mail in and waits to be cleaned up preparatory to going out afresh.

The tiffin hour has ended. The buzzer blows, and with a roar, a rattle, and a clang the shops take up their toil. The hubbub that followed on the prince's kiss to the sleeping beauty was not so loud or sudden. Experience, with a foot-rule in his pocket, authority in his port, and a merry twinkle in his eye, comes up and catches Ignorance walking gingerly round No. 25. "That's one of the best we have," says Experience, "a four-wheeled coupled bogie they call her. She's by Dobbs. She's done her hundred and fifty miles to-day; and she'll run in to Rampore Haut this afternoon; then she'll rest a day and be cleaned up. Roughly, she does her three hundred miles in the four-and-twenty hours. She's a beauty. She's out from home, but we can build our own engines—all except the wheels. We're building ten locos, now, and we've got a dozen boilers ready if you care to look at them. How long does a loco. last? That's just as may be. She will do as much as her driver lets her. Some men play the mischief with a loco. and some handle 'em properly. Our drivers prefer Hawthorne's old four-wheeled coupled engines because they give the least bother. There is one in that shed, and its a good 'un to travel. But eighty thousand miles generally sees the gloss off an engine, and she goes into the shops to be overhauled and refitted and replaned, and a lot of things that you wouldn't understand if I told you about them. No. 1, the first loco. on the line, is running still, but very little of the original engine must be left by this time. That one there, came out in the Mutiny year. She's by Slaughter and Grunning, and she's built for speed in front of a light load. French-looking sort of thing, isn't she? That's because her cylinders are on a tilt. We used her for the mail once, but the mail has grown heavier, and heavier, and now we use six-wheeled coupled eighteen-inch, inside cylinder, 45-ton locos. to shift thousand-ton trains. *No!* All locos. aren't alike. It isn't merely pulling a lever. The Company likes its drivers to know their locos., and a man will keep his Hawthorne for two or three years. The more mileage he gets out of her before she has to be overhauled the better man he is. It pays to let a man have his fancy engine. A man must take an interest in his loco., and that means she must belong to him. Some locos. won't do anything, even if you coax aud humor them. I don't think there are any unlucky ones now, but some years ago No. 31 wasn't popular. The drivers went sick or took leave when they were told off for her. She killed her driver on the Jubbulpore line, she left the rails at Kajra, she did something or other at Rampur Haut, and Lord knows what she didn't do or try to do in other places! All the drivers fought shy of her, and in the end she disappeared. They said she was condemned, but I shouldn't wonder if the Company changed her number quietly, and changed the luck at the same time. You see, the Government Inspector comes and looks at our stock now and again, and when an engine's condemned he puts his dhobimark on her, and she's broken up. Well, No. 31 was condemned, but there was a whisper that they only shifted her number, and ran her out again. When the drivers didn't know, there were no accidents. I don't think we've got an unlucky one running now. Some are different from others, but there are no man-eaters. Yes, a driver of the mail *is* somebody. He can make Rs. 370 a month if he's a covenanted man. We get a lot of our drivers in the country, and we don't import from England as much as we did. 'Stands to reason that, now there's more competition both among lines and in the labor market, the Company can't afford to be as generous as it used to be. It doesn't cheat a man though. It's this way with the drivers. A native driver gets about Rs. 20 a month, and in his way he's supposed to be good enough for branch work and shunting and such. Well, an English driver'll get from Rs. 80 to Rs. 220, and overtime. The English driver knows what the native gets, and in time they tell the driver that the native'll improve. The driver has that to think of. You see? That's competition!

Experience returns to the engine-sheds, now full of clamor, and enlarges on the beauties of sick locomotives. The fitters and the assistants and the apprentices are hammering and punching and gauging, and otherwise technically disporting themselves round their enormous patients, and their language, as caught in snatches, is beautifully unintelligible.

But one flying sentence goes straight to the heart. It is the cry of Humanity over the task of Life, done into unrefined English. An apprentice, grimed to his eyebrows, his cloth cap well on the back of his curly head and his hands deep in his pockets, is sitting on the edge of a tool-box ruefully regarding the very much disorganized engine whose slave is he. A handsome boy, this apprentice, and well made. He whistles softly between his teeth, and his brow puckers.

Then he addresses the engine, half in expostulation and half in despair, "Oh, you condemned old female dog!" He puts the sentence more crisply—much more crisply—and Ignorance chuckles sympathetically.

Ignorance also is puzzled over these engines.

Vulcan's forge

IN the wilderness of the railway shops—and machinery that planes and shaves, and bevels and stamps, and punches and hoists and nips—the first idea that occurs to an outsider, when he has seen the men who people the place, is that it must be the birthplace of inventions—a pasture-ground of fat patents. If a writing-man, who plays with shadows and dresses dolls that others may laugh at their antics, draws help and comfort and new methods of working old ideas from the stored shelves of a library, how, in the name of Commonsense, his god, can a doing-man, whose mind is set upon things that snatch a few moments from flying Time or put power into weak hands, refrain from going forward and adding new inventions to the hundreds among which he daily moves?

Appealed to on this subject, Experience, who had served the E. I. R. loyally for many years, held his peace. "We don't go in much for patents; but," he added, with a praiseworthy attempt to turn the conversation, "we can build you any mortal thing you like. We've got the *Bradford Leslie* steamer for the Sahib-gunge ferry. Come and see the brass-work for her bows. It's in the casting-shed."

It would have been cruel to have pressed Experience further, and Ignorance, to fore-date matters a little, went about to discover why experience shied off this question, and why the men of Jamalpur had not each and all invented and patented something. He won his information in the end, but did not come from Jamalpur. *That* must be clearly understood. It was found anywhere you please between Howrah and Hoti Mardan; and here it is that all the world may admire a prudent and far-sighted Board of Directors. Once upon a time, as every one in the profession knows, two men invented the D. and O. sleeper—cast iron of five pieces, very serviceable. The men were in the Company's employ, and their masters said: "Your brains are ours. Hand us over those sleepers." Being of pay and position, D. and O. made some sort of resistance and got a royalty or a bonus. At any rate, the Company had to pay for its sleepers. But thereafter, and the condition exists to this day, they caused it to be written in each servant's covenant, that if by chance he invented aught, his invention was to belong to the Company. Providence has mercifully arranged that no man or syndicate of men can buy the "holy spirit of man" outright without suffering in some way or another just as much as the purchase. America fully, and Germany in part, recognizes this law. The E. I. Railway's breach of it is thoroughly English. They say, or it is said of them that they say, "We are afraid of our men, who belong to us, wasting their time on trying to invent."

Is it wholly impossible, then, for men of mechanical experience and large sympathies to check the mere patent-hunter and bring forward the man with an idea? Is there no supervision in the "shops," or have the men who play tennis and billiards at the institute not a minute which they can rightly call their very own? Would it ruin the richest Company in India to lend their model-shop and their lathes to half a dozen, or, for the matter of that, half a hundred, abortive experiments? A Massachusetts organ factory, a Racine buggy shop, an Oregon lumber-yard, would laugh at the notion. An American toy-maker might swindle an employé after the invention, but he would in his own interests help the man to "see what comes of the thing." Surely a wealthy, a powerful and, as all Jamulpur bears witness, a considerate Company might cut that clause out of the covenant and await the issue. There would be quite enough jealousy between man and man, grade and grade, to keep down all but the keenest souls; and, with due respect to the steam-hammer and the rolling-mill, we have not yet made machinery perfect. The "shops" are not likely to spawn unmanageable Stephensons or grasping Brunels; but in the minor turns of mechanical thought that find concrete expressions in links, axle-boxes, joint packings, valves, and spring-stirrups something might—something would—be done were the practical prohibition removed. Will a North country-man give you anything but warm hospitality for nothing? Or if you claim from him overtime service as a right, will he work zealously? "Onything but t' brass," is his motto, and his ideas are his "brass."

Gentlemen in authority, if this should meet your august eyes, spare it a minute's thought, and, clearing away the floridity, get to the heart of the mistake and see if it cannot be rationally put right. Above all, remember that Jamulpur supplied no information. It was as mute as an oyster. There is no one within your jurisdiction to—ahem—— "drop upon."

Let us, after this excursion into the offices, return to the shops and only ask Experience such questions as he can without disloyalty answer.

"We used once," says he, leading to the foundry, "to sell our old rails and import new ones. Even when we used 'em for roof beams and so on, we had more than we knew what to do with. Now we have got rolling-mills, and we use the rails to make tie-bars for the D. and O. sleepers and all sorts of things. We turn out five hundred D. and O. sleepers a day. Altogether, we use about seventy-five tons of our own iron a month here. Iron in Calcutta costs about five-eight a hundred-weight; our costs between three four and three-eight, and on that item alone we save three thousand a month. Don't ask me how many miles of rails we own. There are fifteen hundred miles of line, and you can make your own calculation. All those things like babies' graves, down in that shed, are the moulds for the D. and O. sleepers. We test them by dropping three hundred weight and three hundred quarters of iron on top of them from a height of seven feet, or eleven sometimes. They don't often smash. We have a notion here that our iron is as good as the Home stuff."

A sleek, white, and brindled pariah thrusts himself into the conversation. His house appears to be on the warm ashes of the bolt-maker. This is a horrible machine, which chews red-hot iron bars and spits them out perfect bolts. Its manners are disgusting, and it gobbles over its food.

"Hi, Jack!" says Experience, stroking the interloper, "you've been trying to break your leg again. That's the dog of the works. At least he makes believe that the works belong to him. He'll follow any one of us about the shops as far as the gate, but never a step further. You can see he's in first-class condition. The boys give him his ticket, and, one of these days, he'll try to get on to the Company's books as a regular worker. He's too clever to live." Jack heads the procession as far as the walls of the rolling-shed and then returns to his machinery room. He waddles with fatness and despises strangers.

"How would you like to be hot-potted there?" says Experience, who has read and who is enthusiastic over *She*, as he points to the great furnaces whence the slag is being dragged out by hooks. "Here is the old material going into the furnace in that big iron bucket. Look at the scraps of iron. There's an old D. and O. sleeper, there's a lot of clips from a cylinder, there's a lot of snipped-up rails, there's a driving-wheel block, there's an old hook, and a sprinkling of boiler-plates and rivets."

The bucket is tipped into the furnace with a thunderous roar and the slag below pours forth more quickly. "An engine," says Experience, reflectively, "can run over herself so to say. After she's broken up she is made into sleepers for the line. You'll see how she's broken up later." A few paces further on, semi-nude demons are capering over strips of glowing hot iron which are put into a mill as rails and emerge as thin, shapely tie-bars. The natives wear rough sandals and some pretense of aprons, but the greater part of them is "all face." "As I said before," says Experience, "a native's cuteness when he's working on ticket is something startling. Beyond occasionally hanging on to a red-hot bar too long and so letting their pincers be drawn through the mills, these men take precious good care not to go wrong. Our machinery is fenced and guard-railed as much as possible, and these men don't get caught up by the belting. In the first place, they're careful— the father warns the son and so on—and in the second, there's nothing about 'em for the belting to catch on unless the man shoves his hand in. Oh, a native's no fool! He knows that it doesn't do to be foolish when he's dealing with a crane or a driving-wheel. You're looking at all those chopped rails? We make our iron as they blend baccy. We mix up all sorts to get the required quality. Those rails have just been chopped by this tobacco-cutter thing." Experience bends down and sets a vicious-looking, parrot-headed beam to work. There is a quiver—a snap—and a dull smash and a heavy rail is nipped in two like a stick of barley-sugar.

Elsewhere, a bull-nosed hydraulic cutter is rail-cutting as if it enjoyed the fun. In another shed stand the steam-hammers; the unemployed ones murmuring and muttering to themselves, as is the uncanny custom of all steam-souled machinery. Experience, with his hand on a long lever, makes one of the monsters perform; and though Ignorance knows that a man designed and men do continually build steam-hammers, the effect is as though Experience were maddening a chained beast. The massive block slides down the guides, only to pause hungrily an inch above the anvil, or restlessly throb through a foot and a half of space, each motion being controlled by an almost imperceptible handling of the levers. "When these things are newly overhauled, you can regulate your blows to within an eighth of an inch," says Experience. "We had a foreman here once who could work 'em beautifully. He had the touch. One day a visitor, no end of a swell in a tall, white hat, came round the works, and our foreman borrowed the hat and brought the hammer down just enough to press the nap and no more. 'How wonderful!' said the visitor, putting his hand carelessly upon this lever rod here." Experience suits the action to the word and the hammer thunders on the anvil. "Well, you can guess for yourself. Next minute there wasn't enough left of that tall, white hat to make a postage-stamp of. Steam-hammers aren't things to play with. Now we'll go over to the stores . . . "

Whatever apparent disorder there might have been in the works, the store department is as clean as a new pin, and stupefying in its naval order. Copper plates, bar, angle, and rod iron, duplicate cranks and slide bars, the piston rods of the *Bradford Leslie* steamer, engine grease, files, and hammer-heads—every conceivable article, from leather laces of beltings to head-lamps, necessary for the due and proper working of a long line, is stocked, stacked, piled, and put away in appropriate compartments. In the midst of it all, neck deep in ledgers and indent forms, stands the many-handed Babu, the steam of the engine whose power extends from Howrah to Ghaziabad.

The Company does everything, and knows everything. The gallant apprentice may be a wild youth with an earnest desire to go occasionally "upon the bend." But three times a week, between 7 and 8 P.M., he must attend the night-school and sit at the feet of M. Bonnaud, who teaches him mechanics and statics so thoroughly that even the awful Government Inspector is pleased. And when there is no night-school the Company will by no means wash its hands of its men out of working-hours. No man can be violently restrained from going to the bad if he insists upon it, but in the service of the Company a man has every warning; his escapades are known, and a judiciously arranged transfer sometimes keeps a good fellow clear of the down-grade. No one can flatter himself that in the multitude he is overlooked, or believe that between 4 P.M. and 9 A.M. he is at liberty to misdemean himself. Sooner or later, but generally sooner, his goings-on are known, and he is reminded that "Britons never shall be slaves"—to things that destroy good work as well as souls. Maybe the Company acts only in its own interest, but the result is good.

Best and prettiest of the many good and pretty things in Jamalpur is the institute of a Saturday when the Volunteer Band is playing and the tennis courts are full and the babydom of Jamalpur—fat, sturdy children—frolic round the bandstand. The people dance—but big as the institute is, it is getting too small for their dances—they act, they play billiards, they study their newspapers, they play cards and everything else, and they flirt in a sumptuous building, and in the hot weather the gallant apprentice ducks his friend in the big swimming-bath. Decidedly the railway folk make their lives pleasant.

Let us go down southward to the big Giridih collieries and see the coal that feeds the furnace that smelts the iron that makes the sleeper that bears the loco. that pulls the carriage that holds the freight that comes from the country that is made richer by the Great Company Badahur, the East Indian Railway.

Part 4

ANGLO-INDIAN JUNCTIONS

NONLINEAR FUNCTIONS

23

RABINDRANATH TAGORE,
'A JOURNEY WITH MY FATHER',
IN *MY REMINISCENCES*
(LONDON: MACMILLAN, 1917),
PP. 77–81, 86–87

My shaven head after the sacred thread ceremony caused me one great anxiety. However partial Eurasian lads may be to things appertaining to the Cow, their reverence for the Brahmin is notoriously lacking. So that, apart from other missiles, our shaven heads were sure to be pelted with jeers. While I was worrying over this possibility I was one day summoned upstairs to my father. How would I like to go with him to the Himalayas, I was asked. Away from the Bengal Academy and off to the Himalayas! Would I like it? Oh, that I could have rent the skies with a shout, that might have given some idea of the How!

On the day of our leaving home my father, as was his habit, assembled the whole family in the prayer hall for divine service. After I had taken the dust off the feet of my elders I got into the carriage with my father. This was the first time in my life that I had a full suit of clothes made for me. My father himself had selected the pattern and colour. A gold-embroidered velvet cap completed my costume. This I carried in my hand, being assailed with misgivings as to its effect in juxtaposition to my hairless head. As I got into the carriage my father insisted on my wearing it, so I had to put it on. Every time he looked another way I took it off. Every time I caught his eye it had to resume its proper place.

My father was very particular in all his arrangements and orderings. He disliked leaving things vague or undetermined, and never allowed slovenliness or makeshifts. He had a well-defined code to regulate his relations with others and theirs with him. In this he was different from the generality of his countrymen. With the rest of us a little carelessness this way or that did not signify; so in our dealings with him we had to be anxiously careful. It was not so much the little less or more that he objected to, as the failure to be up to the standard.

My father had also a way of picturing to himself every detail of what he wanted done. On the occasion of any ceremonial gathering, at which he could not be present, he would think out and assign the place for each thing, the duty for each member of the family, the seat for each guest; nothing would escape him. After it was all over he would ask each one for a separate account and thus gain a complete impression of the whole for himself. So, while I was with him on his travels, though nothing would induce him to put obstacles in the way of my amusing myself as I pleased, he left no loophole in the strict rules of conduct which he prescribed for me in other respects.

Our first halt was to be for a few days at Bolpur. Satya had been there a short time before with his parents. No self-respecting nineteenth-century infant would have credited the account of his travels which he gave us on his return. But we were different, and had had no opportunity of learning to determine the line between the possible and the impossible. Our Mahabharata and Ramayana gave us no clue to it. Nor had we then any children's illustrated books to guide us in the way a child should go. All the hard-and-fast laws which govern the world we learnt by knocking up against them.

Satya had told us that, unless one was very very expert, getting into a railway carriage was a terribly dangerous affair—the least slip, and it was all up. Then, again, a fellow had to hold on to his seat with all his might, otherwise the jolt at starting was so tremendous there was no telling where one would get thrown off to. So when we got to the railway station I was all a-quiver. So easily did we get into our compartment, however, that I felt sure the worst was yet to come. And when, at length, we made an absurdly smooth start, without any semblance of adventure, I felt woefully disappointed.

The train sped on; the broad fields with their blue-green border trees, and the villages nestling in their shade flew past in a stream of pictures which melted away like a flood of mirages. It was evening when we reached Bolpur. As I got into the palanquin I closed my eyes. I wanted to preserve the whole of the wonderful vision to be unfolded before my waking eyes in the morning light. The freshness of the experience would be spoilt, I feared, by incomplete glimpses caught in the vagueness of the dusk.

When I woke at dawn my heart was thrilling tremulously as I stepped outside. My predecessor had told me that Bolpur had one feature which was to be found nowhere else in the world. This was the path leading from the main buildings to the servants' quarters, which, though not covered over in any way, did not allow a ray of the sun or a drop of rain to touch anybody passing along it. I started to hunt for this wonderful path, but the reader will perhaps not wonder at my failure to find it to this day.

Town bred as I was, I had never seen a rice-field, and I had a charming portrait of the cowherd boy, of whom we had read, pictured on the canvas of my imagination. I had heard from Satya that the Bolpur house was surrounded by fields of ripening rice, and that playing in these with cowherd boys was an everyday affair, of which the plucking, cooking and eating of the rice was the crowning feature. I eagerly looked about me. But where, oh where was the rice-field on all that barren heath? Cowherd boys there might have been somewhere about, yet how to distinguish them from any other boys, that was the question!

By this time I was rid of my blue manuscript book and had got hold of a bound volume of one of Letts's Diaries. I now saw to it that my poetising should not lack any of the dignity of outward circumstance. It was not only a case of writing poems, but of holding myself forth as a poet before my own imagination. So when I wrote poetry at Bolpur I loved to do it sprawling under a young cocoa-nut palm. This seemed to me the true poetic way. Resting thus on the hard unturfed gravel in the burning heat of the day, I composed a martial ballad on the "Defeat of King Prithwi." In spite of the superabundance of its martial spirit, it could not escape an early death. That bound volume of Letts's Diary has now followed the way of its elder sister, the blue manuscript book, leaving no address behind.

We left Bolpur, and making short halts on the way at Sahebganj, Dinapore, Allahabad and Cawnpore we stopped at last at Amritsar.

An incident on the way remains engraved on my memory. The train had stopped at some big station. The ticket examiner came and punched our tickets. He looked at me curiously as if he had some doubt which he did not care to express. He went off and came back with a companion. Both of them fidgeted about for a time near the door of our compartment and then again retired. At last came the station-master himself. He looked at my half-ticket and then asked:

"Is not the boy over twelve?"

"No," said my father.

I was then only eleven, but looked older than my age.

"You must pay the full fare for him," said the station-master.

My father's eyes flashed as, without a word, he took out a currency note from his box and handed it to the station-master. When they brought my father his change he flung it disdainfully back at them, while the station-master stood abashed at this exposure of the meanness of his implied doubt.

The golden temple of Amritsar comes back to me like a dream. Many a morning have I accompanied my father to this *Gurudarbar* of the Sikhs in the middle of the lake. There the sacred chanting resounds continually. My father, seated amidst the throng of worshippers, would sometimes add his voice to the hymn of praise, and finding a stranger joining in their devotions they would wax enthusiastically cordial.

24

FANNY BULLOCK WORKMAN AND WILLIAM HUNTER WORKMAN, *THROUGH TOWN AND JUNGLE: FOURTEEN THOUSAND MILES A-WHEEL AMONG THE TEMPLES AND PEOPLE OF THE INDIAN PLAIN* (LONDON: T. F. UNWIN, 1904), PP. 6, 48, 63–64, 66, 102, 204–207, 226

One of the most important conditions of a cycle journey in India and one of the most difficult to arrange for is a suitable lodging-place at night. Before the existence of railways this question was easier to solve than at present, for then, when the only means of communication was by stages on the highways, these were provided at intervals of ten to twenty miles with dak bungalows, where travellers could put up with a fair degree of comfort.

On the building of the railways travel was diverted from the highways, and many of the bungalows being no longer needed were discontinued. Others still in use have been permitted to get out of repair, their furniture has become worn and broken, the china deficient, and the khansamahs who look after them decrepit, so that stopping in them is not what it was in the palmy staging days.

For this reason it is not convenient to leave the railway lines for long, and some highways, which, were they provided with bungalows, would furnish the shortest and best route, have to be avoided and others of inferior construction followed. In many of the large towns and smaller cities the dak bungalows are still a live institution being well appointed and well kept. In these the traveller is more comfortable than in the ordinary Indian hotel.

We had a list of Indian dak bungalows, which was published with one of the railway guides, but it was incomplete and also misleading, in that it indicated bungalows at some places where none existed. It had been compiled years before, and had never been corrected. The question as to where the next night's lodging would be found was ever a burning one, and all too often we could get no information on this point at the place where we were putting up. Hence, unless there was some large town which we were fairly sure of reaching at night, we found it advisable to avoid cross-country roads and keep as near the railways as possible, for, at the worst, shelter could be obtained in the waiting-room of some country station, where we could and did on several occasions sit the night out on uncomfortable straight-backed chairs. This method of repose did not serve to relieve fatigue any too well after a hard day's ride nor to fortify us for the next day's equally severe exertion.

Combined with lodging was the question of food. Wherever a bungalow with a khansamah or a large railway station with a buffet was found, there was no trouble as to food.

There is one peculiarity common to Indians of every race, religion, condition, and class—except perhaps the highest, which is too well-bred to show it—viz., curiosity. Without any apparent motive they put a string of questions nearly always the same to us on all occasions, the answers to which could not possibly be of any importance to them. These were, "Where do you come from? When did you leave there? What service do you belong to? What is your business here? How long do you stop? Where are you going?" In some cases, not satisfied with these, they asked us if we were bicycle agents. They could not understand otherwise, why we should take the trouble to travel on cycles.

These questions were answered as prudence dictated. After some experience we found it convenient to cut off too much impertinence by looking wise and mysteriously hinting we were on secret service making an examination of the district, which usually had the effect of putting an end to further questioning. But, as in Spain, where the customs have many points of resemblance to those of the East, we could not get the people to do much for us, till their curiosity had been satisfied.

At Jalarpet Junction there was no bungalow, so we were obliged to pass the night in the waiting-room at the railway station, which was comfortable as such places go. At the larger railway stations the men's and women's waiting-rooms are provided with two or three cane couches each, and a dressing-room containing a washstand, pitcher, hand-basin, commode, and sometimes an iron bath-tub. If one is so fortunate as to be the sole occupant of the room, one can pass a fairly comfortable night; but usually one's rest is disturbed by the snores of other occupants, the screeching of locomotive whistles, the rumble of trains, the harsh and discordant shouting of natives on the platform, and the incoming of passengers. On several occasions parties of natives invaded the waiting-room and camped on the floor, making so much noise that sleep was impossible.

The waiting-rooms of the small stations possess only a table, straight-backed chairs, and wooden settees, and in these comfort is out of the question. One learns to doze on the wooden settees and even sitting upright on the chairs, but refreshing sleep cannot be obtained.

THE road to Mysore passes over the undulating plateau to Neddivattam near its northern edge. When we travelled over it the rounded hills were covered with dry grass, which in the fine lighting assumed a rich brown colour and a silky lustre, in strong contrast to which were the sholas with their clinging forests of fresh vivid green and red, out of which jutted great masses of white and coloured rhododendrons, the whole forming one of the pictures so delightful to the eye in India, where at the same moment winter, spring, and summer, seem to join hands.

As we wheeled down the Gudalore ghat, a wilder country than that on the Mettupalaiyam side unfolded itself to view. Several thousand feet below in the foreground lay the foot-hills of Mysore clothed with dense jungle, beyond which the pomegranate-toned plains vibrated under the brilliant sky, a unique vista even in this land of varied jungle scenery.

After reaching the foot-hills the road for the next twenty-six miles ran up and down, and finally ascended over a pass. It was not a metalled road, and it was in a most disgusting condition, being badly cut up by heavy carts and covered with dust to a depth of three to four inches. In many places it was impossible to ride over it. It ran through heavy jungle, which lay cool and green on either side, but it itself had no trees of any kind to temper the vertical rays of the midday sun, under which we toiled through the thick dust.

The jungle of this region conforms to one's preconceived ideas of tropical jungle derived from tales of the East, of areas covered with rank vegetation, where vast masses of bamboo form an impenetrable barrier; where giant trees rise thick, smothered with snaky creepers, which hang in interlacing festoons from their lofty tops; where here and there openings occur through which the sunlight falls aslant prostrate decaying trunks, and tall grass borders a pool of sluggish water, into which a moss-covered bough falls with a splash, that makes one shiver even at a temperature of 85°; where the air is heavy and silent, the breeze never blows, and the birds never sing, a fitting place for the lairs of fierce wild beasts; where, with nerves ajar, one is ever expecting that something uncanny may happen to break the spell cast upon the jungle world.

About two o'clock p.m. at a cross road by a stream, where there was a serai patronised by natives, we found our bearer with the luggage. He had been despatched the morning before from Ootacamund with a bullock cart by a shorter route with orders to meet us at Gundlupet at ten o'clock a.m. on this day. Here he was some four hours behind time and still fifteen miles from Gundlupet.

The cart with the luggage was standing under a tree, the bullocks were grazing near by, and the bearer and driver were enjoying a siesta in the shade in the most nonchalant manner. We speedily interrupted their repose, and demanded an explanation of the failure to be at the appointed rendezvous, which it was easily in their power to reach. The bearer, with rolling eyes and excited manner, said they had met three wild elephants on the road a short distance ahead, on account of which they feared to venture further. We ordered them to yoke the bullocks at once and follow us, as we proposed to go on, elephants or no elephants. There are plenty of wild elephants in the region, but we had our own opinions as to the truth of the bearer's statement.

Our bearer was a Madrasi, who came with us from Ceylon. He rejoiced in the name of Jacob, by which it will be understood, that he was nominally a Christian, and had been under the influence of the missionaries. We engaged him, before we had heard of the general opinion regarding Christian Indians. He was by no means a fool. He could read, write, and speak, English as well as Tamil, and usually appeared well.

He had not been long in our employ, when we noticed certain things about him that seemed somewhat out of the ordinary course. He was not always on hand when wanted, and he was very unfortunate. On the afternoon when we visited the Great Temple at Madura, he accompanied us so handsomely dressed in a clean white ruffled tunic, purple turban, and scarlet kummer-band, that we felt rather proud to have such a trim-looking servant with us. After we had finished with the gopura, we told him he could have the remainder of the afternoon to himself, but must be on hand to serve us at dinner.

Dinner-time came but no bearer. Two hours more passed and he did not appear. About ten o'clock in the evening he came in looking rather wild but with his clothing intact. As a reason for his failure to return sooner he said, that, after our departure, the temple parasites, who had been so importunate with us, had set upon him in a body, and during his struggles to free himself had robbed him of ten rupees.

Two weeks later at Mahabalipur he came to us and said, his shirt, which he had left hanging on the bungalow wall, had been relieved of three ruby studs. A few days after this at Madras, some hours after receiving his box delivered by the railway agent with ours, he brought it to us, and showed us that the lock had been forced, and said that two shirts, a pair of gold sleeve buttons, and some money, had been stolen from it. An appeal to the railway agent resulted in a denial that the box had suffered while in his charge. At Ootacamund he suddenly became lame, and could not do his work, and now an apparition of wild elephants prevented him from carrying out his orders.

We reached Tiptur, a town on the railway, on the afternoon of the fourth day after leaving Mysore. Our bearer had been ordered to go to that place, which was only a day's ride by rail from Mysore, and await us at the bungalow. On our arrival at the bungalow the khansamah said he had seen nothing of the bearer or our luggage. We were in consternation at this information, for we needed the services of the bearer and still more our luggage after four days of hard riding in the heat and dust. We did not know what to do, but as something must be done, we decided to do the first thing that suggested itself, viz. to make inquiries at the railway station.

On going to the station we found our luggage piled up in a corner in the rear and the bearer lying beside it in a most bedraggled condition helplessly intoxicated. When aroused he looked at us with the dazed expression we had previously noted, and could give no coherent account of where he had been during the three preceding days.

Here we had at last the solution of the problem of his many misfortunes and his sins of omission. He was possessed of the devil of intemperance too strongly to warrant any hope of its being cast out. It was evident he would no longer suit our purpose, which required that a servant should at least be able to exercise such faculties as he might possess. Accordingly, thankful that the matter was no worse, we paid him his wages on the spot and gave him a return ticket to Colombo. Thus ended our first lesson with a Christian servant.

Over the greater part of the state of Mysore and to the north over the districts of Anantipur, Kurnool, Bellary, and well into Hyderabad, the rolling surface of the country is dotted with bare granite hills much broken and covered with great rounded boulders, many of which are balanced one upon another.

The people here were the darkest in colour of any we saw in India, and were as black as any African could possibly be, but they did not have the coarse features and woolly hair of the negro.

AFTER a long summer in Kashmir and amongst the mountains of Ladakh, Nubra, and Suru, and a short time amongst those of Sikkim, the beginning of November found us at Darjeeling preparing to initiate our second winter of Indian travel by a pioneer run to Calcutta, a journey which no one had as yet attempted on the cycle.

Two roads were indicated on the maps but neither was fully carried out, and information as to which was the better route or whether either was practicable could not be obtained at Darjeeling. The Himalayan Railway had so completely superseded the former means of communication by coach, that neither magistrates nor P.W.D. officials nor those of the railway could tell where the carriage roads ran or in what condition they were in.

One railway official, ignoring the question about the turnpike, of which he knew nothing, apparently in good faith—though loyalty to the interests of the railway corporation might be suspected of fathering his remarks—suggested the danger of encountering tigers and wild elephants in the Terai at the base of the hills. He regaled us with stories of the first-named animals lying about near the railway line sunning themselves in the early morning and "never opening their eyes, when the train went whizzing by," and of attacks on the train by the latter, which rendered its retreat up the line prudent. If these savage animals made so little account of so formidable an object as a railway train, what could two unarmed cyclists expect?

In spite of the fact that we had travelled extensively on our cycles in many lands, including several thousand miles in India, and might be expected to understand the matter of equipment, when our purpose became known to our acquaintance in Darjeeling, advice of all kinds was poured in upon us without regard to its applicability to our case.

Ladies in particular advised the carrying of wadded quilts, although we were descending into tropical heat, and at the same time suggested the indispensability of sun umbrellas in addition to our topis, as the heat of the sun in the plains would be especially dangerous after a sojourn in the hills. Also dark glasses could not be neglected.

As a prophylactic against the malaria which infests the Terai large doses of quinine were strongly urged, and for other emergencies oil of eucalyptus, and mustard, and chlorodyne. Had we acted on this and other well-meant advice and tried to take with us half of the articles recommended, our cycles might have broken down under their loads, and certainly we should not have had strength to propel them.

Our intended journey would occupy eight days, and at least six nights would have to be spent in villages with primitive accommodations away from the railway, so that we could not have the assistance of our servant and baggage. The accessories needful for this time filled all satchels to overflowing, and made formidable parcels for the handlebars. One of these parcels was surmounted by the light tin tea-kettle, always a useful and at times an indispensable article.

On a brilliant morning we wheeled away from the famous hill station attended by an escort of half-clothed screaming Bhutian children. At Ghoom the highest point on the road above Darjeeling began the grand downward run of 7,000 feet, thirty-eight miles in length, to the hazy plains of Bengal. The road, which crosses the railway several hundred times, zigzags down the long arête on which the village of Kurseon stands. The gradient is easy, but on this occasion we found the descent fatiguing on account of the condition of the road, which had been cut up at nearly every crossing by the narrow wheels of heavily laden carts, thus necessitating great care in riding.

The descent of this arête recalled in certain ways our cycling days among the arêtes of the Grande Kabylie in front of the Djurjura range in Algeria, with the difference that there the Lalla Khredeja formed the chief motif de paysage and here the more imposing Kanchenjanga.

On reaching Kurseon the cord holding the kettle, which from its airy platform had furnished a "danse Macabre"-like obligato all the way from Darjeeling, slipped, and the kettle rattled off over the railway ties and deposited itself in front of the up-coming mail train. A native dexterously rescued it from its perilous position, and it was restored to its place on the top of the pyramid crowning the handlebar.

Following and crossing the snaky curves of the Himalayan Railway, as it circles around from spur to spur, the road plunges downward, now over hillocks of glistening tea plant, again through deepening jungle dark with tropical trees and trailing creepers, or blazing with brilliant bushes touched here and there by the noonday sunshine struggling through the tangled foliage above. And just here in the thick of the jungle was the place for the tiger to lie dozing, but none appeared, nor were any wild elephants encountered on the watch to dispute our passage. Not even the shrill wail of the jackal was heard, only the loud continuous chirp of the cicadas combined with the weary puff of the up-coming goods train reminded us we had left the snows for the tropical plains of the Terai.

We put up at the Siliguri bungalow at the foot of the hills. The following day's run of sixty miles to Kissenganj in the heat and dust over the lumpy remains of the post road caused us to be vividly conscious of the fact, that the bracing mountain atmosphere had been exchanged for the steamy lifeless air of the plains. The stuffiness of the lower world, so noticeable when leaving the mountains of Europe in September, is still more marked in the plains of Bengal in November. In cycling out of Kashmir in October or November the case is quite different, for scarcely a more agreeable climate can be found than that of the Punjab at this season with its bright days and cool mornings and evenings.

From Kissenganj to Purneah, forty-two miles, the road improved somewhat. Twenty miles from the former shortly before Dingra Ghat a large river was crossed in the police boat. Some miles south of Purneah the post road brings up at Caragola, from which at that time no means of crossing the Ganges existed, so we took a train at Purneah for Sahibganj Ghat, where a steamer connecting with the train takes passengers some miles down the river to Sahibganj on the south bank.

The Gangetic plain at this point is a sandy desert scored by changes in the river bed, and the maintenance of even fair roads is out of the question. We therefore had to take another train to Bhagalpur some hours to the west, whence a good road runs south through the flourishing towns of Suri and Dhumka for a hundred and seventy-five miles to Scynthia, where train must again be taken for Burdwan fifty-three miles away on the Grand Trunk Road.

Whatever it may have been in the beginning the worship of Jagannath has now become a business, which furnishes employment to thousands of attendants. Where a hundred thousand pilgrims are at times assembled in a single day, many priests are required to officiate, many attendants to direct the movements of the multitude, many cooks to prepare their food, and many temple girls to dance at the ceremonies.

In addition to those employed in and around the temple, it is said, that agents are sent to all parts of India to induce pious Hindus to make the pilgrimage to Jagannath. These inform themselves carefully as to the pecuniary circumstances of their intended victims, and approach only those who are wealthy or well-to-do. The information gathered and the names of those who agree to go are forwarded to the temple priests, who thus know what demands they can make on the purses of the devotees when they arrive. The pilgrimage is made on foot except in case of the highest class. Before the days of railways it often involved a march of two thousand miles or more and may now one of several hundred, but the sacrifice of time, effort, and money, is considered none too great for the end in view, the sight of the god, which cleanseth from all sin.[1]

The temple reached, it is a question of rupees whether the pilgrim beholds Jagannath from near or from far, or indeed at all. Even to the faithful the only open sesame is money. He is told, the nearer the view of the god the greater the efficacy of a pilgrimage. His privileges are regulated by the amount of means known to be at his disposal. But to obtain only an ordinary view he must pay a round sum. If he has not the amount demanded with him in money, he is required to sign a bond for it binding on himself and his descendants, which is collected to the last anna. Many a Hindu family is impoverished for several generations by the drain thus created by the religious fervour of an ancestor.

The most authentic information as to the temple and present ceremonies is contained in the account of Mitra, who being himself a Hindu was accorded opportunities for inspection and study enjoyed by no other writer.

Note

1 The opening of the Orissan Railway has changed all this. The vast majority of pilgrims of every class now go to Puri by rail. At the festival seasons the crowd is so great that the railway is taxed to its utmost capacity. A railway official stated that more than 300,000 rupees had been taken at Puri for tickets in a single day.

25

WALTER DEL MAR, *THE ROMANTIC EAST: BURMA, ASSAM, & KASHMIR* (LONDON: A. AND C. BLACK, 1906), PP. 106–110

Assam

THE most prominent buildings in Chittagong are the offices of the Assam-Bengal Railway, on the top of one hill; and, on the top of another, the post-office, circuit-court, and dak bungalow, all under one roof. Chittagong presents no special feature of interest; but it is the headquarters of the race of lying, quarrelsome, Moslem boatmen and longshoremen employed in the Bay of Bengal, along its coasts, and up the rivers emptying into it, as the Lascars are similarly employed in the Arabian Sea. There are no European books on sale in Chittagong, nor any newspapers; and it appears that the ticket-seller at the railway station does not even read his company's time-tables, as he said he had never heard of, or sold a ticket to, Kamarbandha Ali, a station 460 miles from Chittagong up the main line.

The Assam-Bengal railway is a metre-gauge line open from Chittagong to Tinsukia in the Brahmaputra valley, a distance of 574 miles, with branches aggregating about 165 miles in length. In addition to the very exceptional damage, amounting to over £90,000, it received in the earthquake of June 12, 1897, when over 1500 people were killed in Assam, the railway is subject to annual damage during the rains in the difficult hill section, and elsewhere on the line. For it must be remembered that one place in the Khasi Hills north-west of the railway holds the world's record for rainfall, and after the rains trains are liable to interruptions, even if the line is not in places entirely carried away, and constant labour is required to keep the line in working condition.

The closest connection we could make involved a wait of eight hours at Laksam Junction, so we took the train down to Chandpur on the east bank of the Meghna, one of the great rivers formed by the junction of the Ganges and the Brahmaputra. There we waited for the Calcutta mail, which comes down by steamer from Goalundo, and had our dinner in the restaurant-car on the way back to Laksam. During the night we skirted the western and northern borders of Hill Tippera, and the next day was spent in traversing the hill section between Badarpur, the junction for the Silchar branch, and Lumding, the junction for Gauhati. After crossing the Surma river the line goes up the Jatinga river valley amid hills to Damchara. The section between this station and Lumding was open for traffic on the 1st of December 1903. The railway first follows the right bank of the Jatinga, which runs between heavily-wooded hills, and the scenery begins to be very pretty.

All along the railway are posts showing the miles and quarter-miles from Chittagong, and the tunnels are also numbered; No. 2 being at the 272nd mile-post, and No. 3 goes through a landslip. Farther on, near another landslip, was the wreck of a recently derailed train. There was a hot controversy as to the cause of the accident, some ascribing it to excessive speed, others to faults in the permanent way. However that may be, the railway cuttings are certainly too steep, and work is going on all along this section reducing their pitch. The natives work with a sort of hoe called a khodali, and are usually armed with a big knife similar to the Burmese dha, which they call a dao. The valley broadens between the 278th post and Harangajao, which is between the 282nd and 283rd post, where the rail level is 489 feet above the sea.

There is plenty of big game to be found in Assam, including rhinoceros, elephant, leopards, the wild buffalo, and tigers. Shortly before we came through, a man had been found dead on the railway, mauled by a tiger, and we saw at Harangajao the body of a leopard which was killed on the line only a few hours before we arrived there. At this station two engines are attached to the train, one in front and one in back, and the real ascent begins. The gradient most of the way is 1 in 37, and there is a succession of tunnels and viaducts up to the summit, which is in tunnel No. 15, just before Jatinga station in the Cachar hills (294th mile), where the rail level is 1855 feet above the sea. The hills are less thickly wooded on the other side of the watershed, but there is more timber after Mahur. There are other streams to cross and further tunnels until, after threading No. 32, the line runs through a level jungle of bamboos and pampas-grass to Langting (343 miles). Three miles farther on there is a grave covered with a white marble cross by the side of the line.

After Lumding, where we changed into the dining-car, the railway goes across country to Dhansiri station, and then down the Dhansiri valley. After Manipur Road, from where there is a cart-road to Manipur going south-west to Kohima and then south, the railway runs in the Sibsagar district with the Naga hills lying to the east. It was about three o'clock in the morning when we pulled up at Kamarbandha Ali station, where we found kind friends whose tea-gardens are in this district.

26

ROBERT MAITLAND BRERETON, *REMINISCENCES OF AN OLD ENGLISH CIVIL ENGINEER, 1858–1908* (PORTLAND, ORE.: IRWIN-HODSON, 1908), PP. 11–16

During 1866–7 the line was completed to Bhosawell, near the Taptee river, and the point of junction of the Nagpore branch with the main line to Calcutta. The catastrophe attending the failure of the viaducts and bridges on No. 12 contract at this period caused the board to send out their consulting engineer in 1867 to make a thorough examination of the masonry construction of the entire system. After his careful examination he prepared a schedule of all works requiring reconstruction. This was called a "reconstruction schedule." A specified fund, called "The Casualty Fund," was provided from periodical contributions from revenue to meet the cost of reconstruction. Very serious delay in the completion of the through line from Bombay to Calcutta was the outcome of the contract system, which then received its death-blow.

The contractor-firms of the main line from Bhosawell to Jubbulpore and of the Nagpore branch threw up their contracts. The board in London, with the approval of the government, decided to appoint two chief engineers for the entire system. I was appointed chief engineer of the North-Eastern, or Calcutta and Nagpore, division, and Mr. Henry LeMesurier chief engineer of the South-Eastern, or Madras, division. He had been one of the resident engineers on the East Indian Railway. Mr. Walter Knox was appointed the company's agent in Bombay. He remained with us only sixteen months, and was succeeded by Mr. LeMesurier, who also retained the chief engineership of the South-Eastern division.

I entered on this appointment in July, 1868, and undertook to carry out for the company the unfinished construction to completion of my division, with the aid of my carefully selected staff of old G. I. P. brother officers. I completed the junction with the East Indian line at Jubbulpore on March 8, 1870, a period of nineteen months. This was fully eighteen months sooner than the board, the agent, the consulting engineer, or the government railway engineers considered possible when I started in. I was considered rash by many when, in the spring of

1869, I reported to the board that "all the mass of work in hand will be success-fully completed in May, 1870," and for giving Lord Mayo, the Viceroy, the same assurance. How was it done in that short period? The answer is: In the first place, I was most fortunate in having at my back and call a splendid staff of every grade, whose heart was in their work; who possessed a thoroughly practical knowledge of construction in every branch and skill and perseverance in overcoming every kind of obstacle and difficulty; who believed in me and trusted me to the core. In the second place, I adopted the American system in railway construction; that is, I had temporary rail-tracks constructed across the rivers and nullahs to enable us to get the bridge work and permanent way materials hauled ahead during the dry season of the year, as during the rainy season the roads through the black soil of the Nerbudda valley were impassable for about four months, and all this heavy material from England had to come from Bombay. We hustled Mr. Warden Mor-rice, the excellent storekeeper in Bombay, almost out of his wits to supply our requirements; also Mr. Henry Conder, the able and active general traffic manager, who was everlastingly being coaxed into lending extra aid in the rapid forward-ing of our freight. I owed much of my success to his cordial co-operation during the whole of that strenuous period. This period—now that I look back upon it—formed the most strenuous one of my entire professional life. It was a hustle and a bustle through the hottest and the wettest portions of the year. In 1869 a violent outbreak of cholera swept through the Nerbudda valley, followed by a terrible famine. Thousands of our native workmen fled from the works. Hundreds died from cholera and famine in these districts. Cholera gave me a taste of its grip, but my soul fought for its body and won. My staff was greatly discouraged by this condition of affairs. Fate seemed determined to balk our best efforts, but *nil desperandum* was the voice we listened to, and *Opitulante Deo* (God helping), my old family motto, was my trust. During this period neither my staff nor I had any let-up from our strenuous efforts, except during the Christmas week of 1869, when I had the pleasure of entertaining them and their wives and other friends from Nagpore, Khandeish, Nassick, Poona and Bombay, at Bhosawell. Then and there we enjoyed an all-round good time with cricket, music and dancing. Some of my staff and I were lovers of "shikar," but during this time the tigers, pan-thers, bears, wild boar, sambhar, chetal, antelope, bustard, florikin and quail in the jungles and plains, along the line through Asseerghur, the Nerbudda valley and Berar, were left undisturbed by us. The third attribute to my success was in my being always enabled to get on well with all classes of the natives. I was but a poor Hindoostanee and Mahratta linguist. I knew just enough of the language to make myself understood and to guess at what they were talking about. I had small knowledge of simple medicinal and surgical appliances, which also helped them to like me.

They all seemed to like and respect me during my sojournings amongst them in the Admednuggur, Khandeish, Berar, Nagpore, Asseergur, Nerbudda valley and Deccan districts. Sir Salar Jung bears testimony to this mutual good will in his long letter to me of December 24, 1866, a copy of which will be found in the appendices. My love for shikar and animals and birds of all kinds kept me on good terms with the Bheels—after they had quieted down—and the jungle folks in Berar, Nagpore, Asseergur and Deccan (Hyderabad) districts. Salar Jung lent me two of his elephants for a time, which enabled me to bag a few tigers.

At last, on the seventh of March, 1870, two months sooner than I had promised the company in the spring of 1869, the through and unbroken line between Bombay and Calcutta was ready for the Viceroy and the Duke of Edinburgh to open to the public on the morrow. On Monday, March eighth, we got the two trains from Bombay, containing the Viceroy and the Governor of Bombay—Sir Fitzgerald Seymour—and their staff, and another special containing Sir Salar Jung and other guests, through to Jubbulpore at 7:30 P. M. The Duke of Edinburgh, who came from Calcutta by the East Indian line, had arrived at 4 P. M. Then and there the Viceroy—Lord Mayo—with the silver-plated hammer provided for the occasion, struck the silver key that connected the G. I. P. rail with the E. I. rail. H. R. H. the Duke of Edinburgh gave it an extra royal tap; thus was our achievement perfected. That eighth of March day was an awfully anxious and fatiguing one for me and the staff. Our worthy locomotive superintendent—C. W. Hawkins—in his zealous pride for the appearance of his department, had put his newest and gorgeous locomotives to haul the Viceroy's train into Jubbulpore. The engine machinery being new, worked, Oh! so stiffly, and the boilers were "priming" all the way from Hurda to Jubbulpore, so that it took twelve hours to run the distance of 128 miles, which could have been covered in six hours if older rolling stock had been used.

Among our guests on this opening ceremony were H. E. the Commander-in-Chief, Sir William Mansfield; The Resident at Hyderabad, Mr. Charles Saunders (whose father and family I knew well when I was a young engineer on the Great Western Railway, of which he was for many years the secretary); Sir Alfred Spencer; Mr. John Morris, Chief Commissioner of the Central Provinces; H. H. the Maharajah Holkar; H. H. the Maharajah of Kewal; H. H. the Maharajah of Punnah; the Rajah of Negode; the Rajah of Myhere, and Sir Salar Jung, the Nizam's great minister, who had left Hyderabad for the first time in his life, to attend this opening and the durbah which followed. A part of what the Viceroy and Governor-General spoke on this occasion I have given in the appendices. For the further entertainment of the Duke of Edinburgh a "drive" of a great stretch of tiger and deer-haunted jungle was organized by Mr. Malcolm Low, assistant commissioner, and other officials. In this it was said over two thousand natives were employed to form a line of beaters. On the day after this I took H. R. H. to open the Towa River viaduct; this he named "The Alfred" viaduct. After that he went to Bombay.

A month later I had to seek a rest for mind and body, and obtained two months' leave of absence from the agent. Lord Mayo had invited me to Simla, as he wanted to consult me concerning future extensions of the railway system in India being carried out by the government of India. This matter he had referred to in his speech at Jubbulpore. The success attending this rapid completion of the line by the company's engineering staff astonished the supreme and local governments, and greatly gratified the traveling and commercial public. It had served to open the eyes of all India to what could be done by English civil engineers, free from red-tapism and backed by intelligent and liberal-minded authorities at home and in India. At Simla I met many old friends, and made many new ones. In July, 1870, there occurred a great public sensation caused by the catastrophe at Allahabad through the fall of new barrack buildings, and also by the failure of others at Jubbulpore. The Governor-General wished me to serve with Colonel Anderson, R. E., on a committee to investigate and report on these buildings, and telegraphed to Bombay to obtain the agent's consent to my doing so; this was granted.

After I had completed this work for the government of India, I returned to Bombay, in August, 1870. I had not received a word of recognition or thanks for my services from the board or from the consulting engineer in London since the completion of the line. The only person at home who had been connected with the board that I knew well was Mr. Hugh Childers, M. P.; he had been chairman. I had written him a full description of the opening. His reply I have given in the appendices. I found on arriving in Bombay that Mr. LeMesurier, the agent, had received instructions from the board to terminate my services with the company. He never told me or wrote me about this, and I have never seen or heard the managing director's directions in this matter.

What he did do was to get Colonel Trevor, R. E., the secretary to the Government Railway Department, to inform me. Of course I felt it keenly, though the warm farewell I received from the staff gave balm to the wound. On my return to London in October, I saw the managing director at the office, but I never saw the members of the board, and was never asked to attend it.

The managing director said he regretted that my services had been terminated, and asked me if I would be willing to return to India as chief engineer of the entire line, with Mr. LeMesurier as agent. Of course I declined this proposition, as my place had already been filled by a worthy member of the old staff, and Mr. LeMesurier and I could never have worked together harmoniously. He had been neither generous nor helpful to me during the last year of my hard efforts. The managing director informed me that the board had not liked my going to Simla to recruit, and that it did not like the Governor-General's remarks, made at the opening dinner, regarding the future policy of the government of India concerning further railway construction in India. No pecuniary reward for my services, outside of the salary due, was offered me. I was received with comparative coolness by the consulting engineer and by the then government director of the Indian Railway Companies.

The Duke of Argyll—then Secretary of State for India—received me very kindly. Lord Mayo had written in my favor to him. He presented me at the levee held in March, 1871, and entered my name on the list for future consideration for the C. S. I. honor. Sir William Baker, to whom Sir Henry Durand had written about me, also showed me much kindness, and Lord Lawrence, ex-Viceroy and ex-Governor-General, did the same; also Sir Cecil Beadon and several others prominent in Indian affairs. The fact was, I had antagonized the contractor element in London by showing what the company's engineering staff could do without the contract-system. Furthermore, I had annoyed the consulting engineer by having rejected a lot of wood-sleepers ("ties" these are termed in America), which had been sent to India. These were not up to the dimensions of the specification; the wood was of inferior quality, and the creosoting was insufficiently done. The government engineers had seen these sleepers and had supported me in my action. My greatest satisfaction arose from the undeniable fact that the achievement of success was solely due to the efforts of the oldest members of the company's engineering staff, who began their services under those able chief engineers, Mr. James J. Berkley and Mr. Robert W. Graham. Thus ended my fourteen years of professional services in India. I had, on the whole, enjoyed a happy and most interesting life there.

27

C. O. BURGE, *THE ADVENTURES OF A CIVIL ENGINEER: FIFTY YEARS ON FIVE CONTINENTS* (LONDON: ALSTON RIVERS, 1909), PP. 73–74, 98–101

A CURIOUS circumstance in connection with my Indian appointment may be mentioned to show how an apparently trivial detail may often lead to a considerable result. There were some four or five other appointments made at the same time by the Madras Railway Co., who were to be my employers, and calling at their London office, I asked by what mail steamer I was expected to start. The reply was that either the next one or the one after would do; so, not having any special reason for delay, I secured the only berth vacant in the first steamer, the other engineers following in the next ship a fortnight or a month later. On reaching Madras, and stating and verifying my previous experience, I was at once appointed to the entire charge of the only railway construction division then vacant, the filling of which was a matter of urgency. The rest, most of them just as experienced and well qualified as I, but arriving later on the scene, became only assistants to others of my position, and in consequence they were left years behind me in subsequent promotion, owing not so much to absence of qualifications as to want of opportunities of showing them.

A much later instance of apparent chance leading to important results occurs to me, that of a friend whom I shall call Professor Proteid. He had some success at home in the particular science which he cultivated, but his health requiring a more genial climate, he emigrated, hoping to turn his knowledge to account in one of the southern colonies. He went out in a sailing ship, and as the vessel was entering the port of destination, a man on board the steam-tug which came alongside, preparatory to towing the ship up the harbour, was reading the local paper. Proteid having been months at sea, and anxious to know what was going on in the world, asked the man to lend him the paper, which was handed up.

After reading the news, his eyes lighted on an advertisement from one of the Colonial Government Offices, asking for applications for an important appointment in the very department of science in which he was specially proficient. But the moment after which no application would be received was within an hour of the time when he saw the advertisement, and the ship was still some distance from the quay, while he did not know how far the office might be from the landing-place. Proteid scribbled an application, collecting his credentials, and almost counted the slow throbs of the little steamer as she struggled on with the huge ship behind her up to the wharf, where with needless care, as he thought, the latter was gradually warped alongside. He had only ten minutes left. Jumping ashore, he hailed a cab and reached the office, panting upstairs and handing in his application to the Secretary within a few seconds of the time named. On the latter asking Proteid how long he had been in the colony, the reply, much to his astonishment, was, "About ten minutes."

The great characteristic of railway construction work in India is the enormous rivers which have to be crossed, these being often twice or thrice the width of the Thames at London, but, unlike that waterway, having an almost dry bed at certain seasons for several months together. At other times of the year they often carry torrents of water which would sweep away everything but the very strongest structures in bridge piers. In order to economise carriage of steel and other material for the great bridges which are thus required, their construction is usually delayed till the line is practically completed up to the site, when the rails are continued across the dry bed of the river, so that the material carried by trains may be delivered for the bridge and the works beyond. So long are these dry periods, that not infrequently the railway is even opened for public traffic with the trains running through the river beds pending the completion of the larger bridges.

It is perhaps unnecessary to say that natives, including women, do all the construction work of the Indian railways. I had nearly as many women as men at shifting earthwork, the men digging it out and the women carrying it in baskets on their heads to where it was required. Native artisans are also skilful, the carpenters having an advantage over Europeans in using three limbs in their work. Being exceedingly lithe and supple, the carpenter seizes the wood on the bench with one uplifted foot, which is as grasping as a Jew money-lender, having his two hands free for the plane or chisel.

On account of the cheapness of labour all sorts of makeshift contrivances are used instead of mechanical power, as we know it. Man's and bullocks' work do everything in conjunction with the inevitable bamboo. India is unthinkable without bullocks and bamboos. A special instance of this is the raising of water from wells and from bridge foundations by the bullock *mot*. A great bag of hides lifts the water by means of a rope carried over a pulley to a pair of bullocks, who work down a steep inclined plane, thus utilizing their weight as well as their power. Another means of doing the same work by men's weight only is the *picotta*. This is formed by a tall bamboo fixed upright, to which are slung by ropes two or three cross bamboos bound tightly together. The attachment is in the middle of the cross-piece, which is thus free to swing vertically like a see-saw. From one end hangs a bucket dipping into the well, while an agile native, steadying himself by a light handrail attached to the cross-bar, works the latter alternately up and down by running along the bar, thus lifting the full bucket, which is emptied by another coolie into the channel, and dropping it down again by running back along the bar in the reverse direction.

The first appearance of the locomotive in the jungle is like that of the foul fiend himself to the unsophisticated native. The engine appears long before the opening of the railway, it being used by the construction engineer as soon as the rails are laid, so as to draw wagons carrying various materials for the works, and also frequently ballast. Hence, as "bandy" is the generic name for any vehicle in Southern India, the terrible machine soon acquired its name of "Ballaster-Bandy," which stuck to it for all time, even when used in the regular traffic after the line was opened. I well remember, on one occasion, a great crowd of villagers assembling at the rail end awaiting the first arrival of the expected monster, concerning which village rumour had been busy. It moved up quietly enough and stopped, upon which the natives, who are as curious as cows, thronged round it and almost under its wheels.

Here was the driver's opportunity; so he suddenly let off steam in all directions. The phenomenon, so familiar to us, of the white and loud hissing steam, was absolutely new to the unsuspecting coolies, who were scattered like a bursting rocket.

When railways were first introduced into India, the English contractors thought that English navvies were essential to their construction, and they were accordingly imported, but it was soon found that the climate was unsuitable for European manual work, and though the native could not rival the white man in the amount of work done, his wages were small enough to overbalance this, and so white labour ceased. The English railway navvy of the mid-Victorian period belongs to an extinct species. He was very different from the labourer of the present day, when railway construction has practically ceased at home, and machinery has so largely supplanted manual effort. He had the thews and sinews of a prize-fighter, and an enormous capacity for work, and, unfortunately, at times for drink. I suppose it was the latter propensity which led to an order by the Madras Government censuring some of the navvies for seizing and carrying off some native policemen, whose sense of duty led them to interfere in a drunken row. It was only a few years before my time, and it was said that each navvy took two constables, one under each arm, and chucked them outside the railway fences.

Owing to a scarcity of local labour at one time, some Afghans, Pathans, and Kandaharis were sent to me from the North—fine fellows, with almost Italian complexions, and good workers, but very quarrelsome, being always armed with dangerous-looking knives. Their features, or sometimes the absence of them, showed that they usually settled their differences by private enterprise without troubling Government legal machinery. Apart from these little scrimmages among themselves, with which it was wise policy not to interfere, I found them easy to manage, as indeed I have found in dealing since with semi-civilized races in various other parts of the world, when rigid justice is dealt out to them.

195

28

FRANK A. SWETTENHAM, *THE REAL MALAY: PEN PICTURES*, SECOND ED. (LONDON: JOHN LANE, 1907), PP. 37–42

In the Malay sketches contained in this and a previous volume, I have endeavoured to portray, as exactly as I could, the Malay as he is in his own country, against his own most picturesque and fascinating background. I will not here make further reference to him, beyond saying, broadly, that he deeply resented our first coming, and has lived to change his mind. His conversion has been slow, as might be expected with one so constituted and with such traditions, but still it is so genuine that he will candidly confess both the original feeling and the present recantation. The position he occupies in the body politic is that of the heir to the inheritance. The land is Malaya, and he is the Malay. Let the infidel Chinese and the evil-smelling Hindu from Southern India toil, but of their work let some share of profit come to him. They are strangers and unbelievers; and while he is quite willing to tolerate them, and to be amused, rather than angered, by their strange forms of idolatry, their vulgar speech in harsh tongues, and their repulsive customs, he thinks it only fitting that they should contribute to his comfort and be ready to answer to his behests. The Malay hates labour, and contributes very little to the revenues in the way of taxation. He cultivates his rice-fields, when he is made to do so by stern necessity, or the bidding of his headmen, and he is a skilful fisherman, because that is in the nature of sport. He plays at trade sometimes, but almost invariably fails to make a living out of it; because, having once invested his capital in a stock, he spends all the money he receives for sales, and then finds he has no means to continue his business. And yet, he is a delightful companion, a polite and often an interesting acquaintance, and an enemy who is not to be despised. He has aspirations. He loves power and place, and his soul hankers after titles of honour. In all these desires his women-folk are keenly interested. They apply the spur, and will readily consent to become the man's mouthpiece, when they think the good things of this world can be got by judicious flattery or tearful pleading.

The Chinese have, under direction, made the Protected States what they are. They are the bees who suck the honey from every profitable undertaking.

A thorough experience of Malays will not qualify an official to deal with Chinese—a separate education is necessary for that, but it is a lesson more easy to learn. It is almost hopeless to expect to make friends with a Chinaman, and it is, for a Government officer, an object that is not very desirable to attain. The Chinese, at least that class of them met with in Malaya, do not understand being treated as equals; they only realise two positions—the giving and the receiving of orders; they are the easiest people to govern in the East for a man of determination, but they must know their master, as he must know them. The Chinese admire and respect determination of character in their rulers, and hold that it is a characteristic as necessary as the sense of justice. The man who possesses the judicial mind, but is too weak to enforce his own judgment, will never be successful in dealing with Chinese.

Until Governor Sir Cecil Smith exorcised the secret society demon, the Chinese made the Straits Settlements the happy hunting-ground of all those societies forbidden in their own country. But in the Malay States it was different. From the very first these guilds, these centres of crime and oppression, with powers of combination for revolt against every form of government, were absolutely forbidden, and in Perak it was for many years a capital offence to belong to any such organisation. Under present conditions the Chinese are the bone and sinew of the Malay States. They are the labourers, the miners, the principal shopkeepers, the contractors, the capitalists, the holders of the revenue farms, the contributors of almost the whole of the revenue; we cannot do without them.

The Hindu, the Tamil, the native of Southern India, is, by comparison, a poor thing; oily in body, cringing in demeanour, and maddening in speech. But for all that he is very useful, whether as a labourer on a plantation, a cattle keeper and cart driver, a washerman, or a barber. The Malay States would be glad to get more of these people; and they have this advantage over the Chinese, that while the Indian women and children emigrate with the men of the family, the Chinese do not. Out of a population of, say, 200,000 Chinese, there are only 3000 women.

The stewardship of British officers in the Malay States has lasted for twenty-five years, and it may be interesting to enumerate some of the visible results of their "advice," which is now, with greater candour, admitted to be control.

One hundred and seventy-five miles of railway have been built and equipped with rolling-stock, out of current revenues; and extensions, aggregating much the same mileage, are, as already stated, now under construction, and should be completed in 1902. This seems a small achievement, dawdling and slow beyond belief; but neither the city of London nor the War Office has taken any interest worth speaking of in the Malay Peninsula, and, so far, there has been a total absence of that rivalry with foreign powers which seems to add a special value to some remote countries, without any very evident attractions of their own. Therefore the Malay States have had to rely upon their own resources, and, first, to provide funds to meet the ordinary expenses of government, after satisfying the reasonable demands of a number of native chiefs; secondly, to construct roads, public buildings, and other necessary works; and, lastly, to find a surplus from the annual revenues with which to build railways. It is only now that a comparatively insignificant sum has been borrowed to push on the railways a trifle more rapidly than would otherwise have been possible. More than half the cost of the present extensions must be supplied from general revenues. More than 2000 miles of excellent roads and 1000 miles of telegraphs have been made and paid for out of revenue. Five important schemes of waterworks have been completed, and much has been done for irrigation, on which it is intended to spend about $700,000 in one district. Lighthouses have been erected, wharves provided, prisons, hospitals, schools, barracks, and handsome public offices constructed. A trigonometrical survey of the Western States is being pushed on, public gardens have been laid out, and museums instituted. A good deal has been spent on experimental agriculture, and the States are alive to the immense importance of encouraging all forms of permanent and profitable cultivation.

Some figures will best illustrate the rapid advancement and present importance of the States. The first year of which it is possible to give any statistics is 1875, and on the opposite page is the record of revenue, at intervals of five years, down to 1895, with the actual returns for 1898.

The combined revenues of the four States amounted, last year, to over $9,000,000, and for the present year they will exceed $11,000,000, which means that, in the time British Residents have controlled the finances of the Protected States, they have succeeded in increasing the revenues over twenty-fold, and Ceylon is now the only English Crown colony which can show higher figures.

29

MALCOLM WATSON, *THE PREVENTION OF MALARIA IN THE FEDERATED MALAY STATES*, PREFACE BY RONALD ROSS (LIVERPOOL: LIVERPOOL SCHOOL OF TROPICAL MEDICINE, 1911), PP. 111, 121, 134

Apart from the evidence of the children, the history of the making of the railway which runs over the Pass, records severe malaria, especially at Ayer Kuning and Bukit Gantang, where large cuttings and a tunnel had been made. While the Malays native to Bukit Gantang who had acquired immunity in their childhood could live in the valley, the non-immune Tamils on the railway construction suffered severely. We often see Javanese who generally have acquired immunity in their childhood, living in places which Tamils have had to abandon.

I may here remark that the spleen rates of Malay children in their Kampongs is not comparable with that of Tamil immigrants on an estate, since among the latter the non-immune new arrivals of all ages up to ten form a larger proportion of the total population than do the new-born of the Malays. While a number of the Malays in the higher ages will already have acquired immunity and lost the enlargement of the spleen, the Tamils at all ages will still be suffering from the disease.

Places newly populated by an immigrant coolie population showing a spleen rate of 100 may really differ considerably in the amount of malaria present.

Anophelines of Bukit Gantang Valley. During the four days (16 to 19 November, 1909) 26 adult Anophelines were taken in the houses of the 'islands,' or as the places are locally known as Kampong Paya and Bendang Siam. They were the following:—

M. rossii	10
M. albirostris	6
M. sinensis ... ...⎱	9
M. barbirostris ... ⎰	
Myzorhyncus umbrosus x.	1
	26

I am unable to give any evidence as to the termination of the experiment. The manager states that as long as the coolies were there they did not suffer from malaria, but that on account of their terror it was impossible to keep them there long. He strongly suspected they left the lines at night and went to other unprotected lines. He also informed me that the coolies said the lines were very close, and that they would often lie outside in a blanket at night. The lines had a wooden ceiling, and as they also were more enclosed than other lines are, it is probable they were close.

I had, unfortunately, to leave this experiment, and therefore am unable to draw any conclusions. Doubtless the F.M.S. Government will take an early opportunity of testing the value of mosquito-proof lines on the railway extensions now being carried out towards the Siam States, where malaria will be as serious an obstacle as it has been in the previous railway and other public works.

In view of the knowledge we now possess of the method of ridding estates of malaria, the question of the practicability of mosquito-proof coolie lines is of less concern to the estates than it was, when it appeared that years might elapse before an estate could be made healthy.

XIV.—Conclusions from Malayan observations. The conclusions I would draw from these observations are:—

(1) That both flat and hill land in Malaya before opening are very malarious, and blackwater fever has been found on both.

(2) That hundreds of square miles of the flat land of Malaya have been freed from malaria by simply draining and felling the jungle.

(3) That the cost of these rural anti-malaria measures in Malaya (where labour is dear) is about £3 sterling an acre, being two pounds to drain and one pound to fell the heavy virgin jungle. This expenditure at the same time is the first step in agriculture, and the land has then acquired a considerably increased value.

(4) That this freedom from malaria coincides with the disappearance of an Anopheline which breeds in undrained jungle, and does not breed in open earth drains when kept clear of weeds and flowing.

(5) That certain hilly land intersected by ravines, although opened and drained, is as malarious as when first opened.

Variation of death-rate with spleen-rate

The issue of the Indian Immigration Report for 1909 enables me to produce the chart showing the variation of the death-rates of 1909 with the spleen-rates of 1909, and for the purpose of comparison I have also included in the chart the death-rate of 1908, and what I imagine would be the curve of the death-rates were quinine not given systematically on any of the estates. The exact spleen-rates of the groups have been used in this chart instead of the middle values.

The death-rate uninfluenced by quinine

(a) Public works.—Those who have seen the terrible death-rate on public works in the Federated Malay States, such as the Ampang and Ulu Gombak Water Works of Kwala Lumpor, the Ayer Kunning Water Works of Klang, the Changkat Jong Water Works of Teluk Anson, the Ayer Kunning railway tunnel near Taiping, will readily believe, I think, that a death-rate of 300 per 1,000 is no exaggeration. As Daniel says: 'Under such circumstances in Malaya, malaria is as severe and prevalent as in bad parts of Africa.'

Part 5

COLONIAL RAILWAYS
Third-class passengers, famine, and
the drain

JOHN L. STODDARD, *LECTURES*, TEN VOLS. (BOSTON: BALCH, 1899), IV, INDIA, PP. 23–24

A wail from India's coral strand

I'm weary of the loin-cloth,
   And tired of naked skins;
I'm sick of filthy, knavish priests
   Who trade in human sins:
These millions of the great unwashed
   Offend both eye and nose;
I long for legs in pantaloons
   And feet concealed in hose.

A wail of human misery
   Is ringing in my ears;
The sight of utter wretchedness
   Has filled my eyes with tears;
The myriad huts of mud and straw
   Where millions toil and die
Are blots upon this fertile land
   Beneath an Orient sky.

I'm weary of the nasal rings
   And juice-discolored lips;
I cannot bear these brown-skinned brats
   Astride their mothers' hips;
I loathe the spindling Hindu shanks
   With dirt encrusted hard;
I'm nauseated by the hair
   That reeks of rancid lard.

I'll ride no more in little cabs
   That serve as railroad-cars,
Each barely twenty feet in length
   And swayed by countless jars;

My bones are racked by traveling
  In India's jerky way:
Far better weeks in Pullman cars
  Than one night in Cathay!

I'm sick at heart (and stomach too)
  Of India's vile hotels,
Whose rooms are drearier and less clean
  Than many prison cells;
Where servants swarm like cockroaches
  Yet nothing can be had,
And where your private "boy" alone
  Prevents your going mad.

I'm weary of the sun-hats too
  Like toad-stools made of pith;
I'm sick of Buddha's "sacred tooth"
  And every other myth.
Good-bye to whining mendicants
  Who show their loathsome sores!—
I'm glad to take the steamer now,
  And sail for other shores.

31

MAHATMA GANDHI, *THIRD-CLASS IN INDIAN RAILWAYS* (LAHORE: GANDHI PUBLICATIONS LEAGUE, 1917), PP. 3–7

I have now been in India for over two years and a half after my return from South Africa. Over one quarter of that time I have passed on the Indian trains travelling third class by choice. I have travelled up north as far as Lahore, down south up to Tranquebar, and from Karachi to Calcutta. Having resorted to third class travelling, among other reasons, for the purpose of studying the conditions under which this class of passengers travel, I have naturally made as critical observations as I could. I have fairly covered the majority of railway systems during this period. Now and then I have entered into correspondence with the management of the different railways about the defects that have come under my notice. But I think that the time has come when I should invite the press and the public to join in a crusade against a grievance which has too long remained unredressed, though much of it is capable of redress without great difficulty.

On the 12th instant I booked at Bombay for Madras by the mail train and paid Rs. 13–9. It was labelled to carry 22 passengers. These could only have seating accommodation. There were no bunks in this carriage whereon passengers could lie with any degree of safety or comfort. There were two nights to be passed in this train before reaching Madras. If not more than 22 passengers found their way into my carriage before we reached Poona, it was because the bolder ones kept the others at bay. With the exception of two or three insistent passengers, all had to find their sleep being seated all the time. After reaching Raichur the pressure became unbearable. The rush of passengers could not be stayed. The fighters among us found the task almost beyond them. The guards or other railway servants came in only to push in more passengers.

A defiant Memon merchant protested against this packing of passengers like sardines. In vain did he say that this was his fifth night on the train. The guard insulted him and referred him to the management at the terminus. There were during this night as many as 35 passengers in the carriage during the greater part of it. Some lay on the floor in the midst of dirt and some had to keep standing.

A free fight was, at one time, avoided only by the intervention of some of the older passengers who did not want to add to the discomfort by an exhibition of temper.

On the way passengers got for tea tannin water with filthy sugar and a whitish looking liquid miscalled milk which gave this water a muddy appearance. I can vouch for the appearance, but I cite the testimony of the passengers as to the taste.

Not during the whole of the journey was the compartment once swept or cleaned. The result was that every time you walked on the floor or rather cut your way through the passengers seated on the floor, you waded through dirt.

The closet was also not cleaned during the journey and there was no water in the water tank.

Refreshments sold to the passengers were dirty-looking, handed by dirtier hands, coming out of filthy receptacles and weighed in equally unattractive scales. These were previously sampled by millions of flies. I asked some of the passengers who went in for these dainties to give their opinion. Many of them used choice expressions as to the quality but were satisfied to state that they were helpless in the matter; they had to take things as they came.

On reaching the station I found that the ghariwala would not take me unless I paid the fare he wanted. I mildly protested and told him I would pay him the authorised fare. I had to turn passive resister before I could be taken. I simply told him he would have to pull me out of the ghari or call the policeman.

The return journey was performed in no better manner. The carriage was packed already and but for a friend's intervention I could not have been able to secure even a seat. My admission was certainly beyond the authorised number. This compartment was constructed to carry 9 passengers but it had constantly 12 in it. At one place an important railway servant swore at a protestant, threatened to strike him and locked the door over the passengers whom he had with difficulty squeezed in. To this compartment there was a closet falsely so called. It was designed as a European closet but could hardly be used as such. There was a pipe in it but no water, and I say without fear of challenge that it was pestilentially dirty.

The compartment itself was evil looking. Dirt was lying thick upon the wood work and I do not know that it had ever seen soap or water.

The compartment had an exceptional assortment of passengers. There were three stalwart Punjabi Mahomedans, two refined Tamilians and two Mahomedan merchants who joined us later. The merchants related the bribes they had to give to procure comfort. One of the Punjabis had already travelled three nights and was weary and fatigued. But he could not stretch himself. He said he had sat the whole day at the Central Station watching passengers giving bribe to procure their tickets. Another said he had himself to pay Rs. 5 before he could get his ticket and his seat. These three men were bound for Ludhiana and had still more nights of travel in store for them.

What I have described is not exceptional but normal. I have got down at Raichur, Dhond, Sonepur, Chakradharpur, Purulia, Asansol and other junction stations and been at the 'Mosafirkhanas' attached to these stations. They are discreditable-looking places where there is no order, no cleanliness but utter confusion and horrible din and noise. Passengers have no benches or not enough to sit on. They squat on dirty floors and eat dirty food. They are permitted to throw the leavings of their food and spit where they like, sit how they like and smoke everywhere. The closets attached to these places defy description. I have not the power adequately to describe them without committing a breach of the laws of decent speech. Disinfecting powder, ashes, or disinfecting fluids are unknown. The army of flies buzzing about them warns you against their use. But a third-class traveller is dumb and helpless. He does not want to complain even though to go to these places may be to court death. I know passengers who fast while they are travelling just in order to lessen the misery of their life in the trains. At Sonepur flies having failed, wasps have come forth to warn the public and the authorities, but yet to no purpose. At the Imperial Capital a certain third class booking-office is a Black-Hole fit only to be destroyed.

Is it any wonder that plague has become endemic in India? Any other result is impossible where passengers always leave some dirt where they go and take more on leaving.

On Indian trains alone passengers smoke with impunity in all carriages irrespective of the presence of the fair sex and irrespective of the protest of non-smokers. And this, notwithstanding a bye-law which prevents a passenger from smoking without the permission of his fellows in the compartment which is not allotted to smokers.

The existence of the awful war cannot be allowed to stand in the way of the removal of this gigantic evil. War can be no warrant for tolerating dirt and overcrowding. One could understand an entire stoppage of passenger traffic in a crisis like this, but never a continuation or accentuation of insanitation and conditions that must undermine health and morality.

Compare the lot of the first class passengers with that of the third class. In the Madras case the first class fare is over five times as much as the third class fare. Does the third class passenger get one-fifth, even one-tenth, of the comforts of his first class fellow? It is but simple justice to claim that some relative proportion be observed between the cost and comfort.

It is a known fact that the third class traffic pays for the ever-increasing luxuries of first and second class travelling. Surely a third class passenger is entitled at least to the bare necessities of life.

In neglecting the third class passengers, opportunity of giving a splendid education to millions in orderliness, sanitation, decent composite life and cultivation of simple and clean tastes is being lost. Instead of receiving an object lesson in these matters third class passengers have their sense of decency and cleanliness blunted during their travelling experience.

Among the many suggestions that can be made for dealing with the evil here described, I would respectfully include this: let the people in high places, the Viceroy, the Commander-in-Chief, the Rajas, Maharajas, the Imperial Councillors and others, who generally travel in superior classes, without previous warning, go through the experiences now and then of third class travelling. We would then soon see a remarkable change in the conditions of third class travelling and the uncomplaining millions will get some return for the fares they pay under the expectation of being carried from place to place with ordinary creature comforts.

32

'THIRD-CLASS PASSENGER
COMPLAINTS AND INDIAN
PILGRIMS', FROM EAST INDIA
RAILWAY COMMITTEE, 1920–21.
*REPORT OF THE COMMITTEE
APPOINTED BY THE SECRETARY
OF STATE FOR INDIA TO ENQUIRE
INTO THE ADMINISTRATION AND
WORKING OF INDIAN RAILWAYS.*
VOL. I. (LONDON: HIS MAJESTY'S
STATIONARY OFFICE FOR THE
INDIA OFFICE, N. D.), PP. 54–55

167. We received many complaints regarding the treatment of third class passengers. The third class passenger, his grievances are of long standing and have often been recognised. Stress was laid upon them by Sir Thomas Robertson in his report of 1903, and—more especially with regard to mela traffic—by the Pilgrim Committees of a few years ago, whose reports showed plainly that even with the insufficient means of transport available more might easily be done for the passengers' comfort; it might, for instance, be necessary in exceptional circumstances for passengers to travel in trucks, but the trucks could at least be cleaned beforehand. We may quote the following sentence from the letter dated 27th September 1916, from the Sanitary Commissioner to the Government of India, submitting the reports of the Pilgrim Committees:—

> "The Government of India can hardly be aware of the amount of ill-feeling and ill-will towards themselves that these two conditions (viz. (1), overcrowding of ordinary trains and pilgrim specials, and (2) the use of goods wagons to carry pilgrims) engender."

168. As voiced before us, the complaints of third class passengers still continue under the following heads:—

(*a*) Overcrowding, to the extent at times of double or even more than double the approved carrying capacity.
(*b*) Inaccessibility and insanitary condition of w.c.'s in third class carriages for long distance journeys.
(*c*) Dirty condition of third class carriages.
(*d*) Inadequate water supply on station platforms.
(*e*) Inadequate food supply arrangements.
(*f*) Inadequate waiting sheds or waiting rooms.
(*g*) Insufficient booking office facilities.
(*h*) Uncivil treatment by railway staff.

169. In India, with its vast population, normally sedentary, but at intervals—sometimes of months, sometimes of a year, sometimes of several years—flocking in enormous numbers to melas (fairs or fêtes) or on pilgrimages to holy places, occasional overcrowding is inevitable. To construct and equip the railways so that on rare occasions they should be able to accommodate without inconvenience traffic out of all proportion to the normal is evidently impossible. And so long as the present shortage of funds persists serious hardship is unavoidable. But when it comes to overcrowding as a constant everyday affair, carried to the length that Members of the Committee have seen with their own eyes—passengers by regular trains perched in the luggage racks and in suburban services hanging on outside or squatting on the steps of the coaches, it is another matter. Serious measures must be taken to deal with it. It cannot be done away with till funds are provided on a scale sufficient to allow of railways being brought up all round to a much higher standard of efficiency. But even with restricted facilities something more might be done by measures such as borrowing stock to the utmost possible extent from other lines to meet exceptional local pressure, and by strict supervision of matters such as enforcing cleanliness and the provision of drinking water. We consider that in such ways as these the utmost efforts should be made to minimise the inconveniences to which the lower class passengers are subjected.

170. We were told by the Agent of the East Indian Railway that the Railway Board had recently disallowed any capital expenditure, even to provide such things as installation of additional water supplies or erection of waiting sheds, as they did not directly improve the movement of traffic. Whatever the shortage of funds, we cannot think that if an order so sweeping as this was given it was in the general interest.

171. The view has been urged upon us that the third class passengers suffer relatively more than other users of the railways from the lack of adequate facilities, and that, though they contribute by far the greater part of the coaching earnings and nearly one-third of the entire railway revenue, their requirements have

received less attention than those of the organised traders and more vocal classes of passengers. There is a strong feeling on the part of the Indian public that the improvement of the conditions under which the mass of the passengers travel has a priority claim.

172. In this connection we may refer to the existence on a few lines of a special class of official, known as Passenger Superintendents, who are engaged at some of the principal stations in looking after the comfort and convenience of the lower class passengers. These officials are usually retired Indian Army officers, who give much assistance to travellers. The evidence given to us shows that their services are appreciated, where they exist, and we recommend an extension of the employment of such officials.

33

M. GANDHI, 'THE QUESTION OF REAL CONVENIENCE', *YOUNG INDIA* 2, 8, FEBRUARY 25, 1920, PP. 1–2

Not long ago the appellate bench of the Allahabad High Court gave its decision in a case in which an Indian had been convicted under section 109 of the Railway Act for having willfully entered a third class compartment reserved for Europeans and Anglo-Indians and refusing to leave it when asked to do so. The defence of the appellant was that he was within his rights to enter the compartment as the Railway Act did not empower the authorities to reserve a compartment for a particular class of passengers. Their Lordships however upheld the conviction maintaining that it was merely a case of providing for the general convenience of the travelling public and that such a reservation was therefore legitimate and did not involve racial preference. They however observed that if any citizen of the country found anything objectionable in the rule, his remedy lay through the authority of the Governor-General-in-Council and he had certainly not been left to work out the remedy himself by a deliberate breach of the rule.

    •   •   •   •   •   •   •   •

Now with regard to the first observation of their Lordships, while we do not dispute their ruling so far the particular Act is concerned, we do dispute the plea advanced by their Lordships that it is merely a case of providing for the general convenience of the travelling public wherein no racial preference or oppression is involved. Apparently their Lordships seem to be totally unacquainted with the condition of the 3rd class Indian passenger who like his brother European or Anglo-Indian 3rd class passenger pays the same fare and is therefore privileged to enjoy the same right, comfort and convenience as the latter, but who as a rule is crammed up and packed like sardines and not surely human beings, on almost every railway. Where then is the ground for belief that the Railway Companie by providing this special reservation for one class of passengers have at heart and are at all anxious to provide for 'the accommodation and convenience of their passengers *generally*?' Even if this phrase 'providing for the general convenience of the travelling public' were interpreted the other way as it was done in a case of similar nature in the Bombay High Court viz., that the mass of 3rd class travelling public, the orthodox Hindu, does not like certain habits of the European and the Anglo-Indian such as eating beef or mutton, it cannot be a sufficient excuse for and does not justify this exclusive reservation. For when an Indian knowingly and of his sweet will comes and occupies the compartment-provided there is accomodation—it follows that he has no such scruples and objections against the European's habits etc. An instance of this nature can be cited of the Kathi-awar Railway where compartments are reserved for untouchables, but if any other member of the travelling public desires to share the accommodation, he can do so, provided the number does not exceed the prescribed limit.

We do not however grudge our European or Anglo-Indian brother the neces-sary comfort and convenience he, as a human being, is entitled to. But as it is, the accommodation provided by reservation for the Europeans and Anglo-Indians is much out of proportion both as to their number and necessary convenience. This does not mean that because we are herded up like cattle and thrown in a hell we want them also to share our fate. But what we want is that regard should be paid and provision be made, at least for some meagre convenience of the Indian pas-senger as well. Otherwise the feeling of racial preference and oppression crops up howsoever much one may like to disregard it.

Then as regards their Lordships' second observation on the right of an indi-vidual to seek remedy in a breach of a rule, our views are already wel-known. A deliberate breach of a rule which is believed to have no legal, much less a moral sanction is not an offence. Of course we always say that this is a remedy to be applied when it is absolutely necessary to get a wrong righted and when all other methods of lesser efficacy such as petitioning and appealing have failed. In this particular instance, however, we are of opinion that instead of going to the Governor-General to get this particular rule of reserving compartments for Europeans and Anglo-Indians rescinded, it would be far more valuable, and to our mind effective, if we directed our united energies in getting the root cause of such complaints permanently removed by pressing on the Railway companies the need of providing greater accommodation and convenience for the large mass of 3rd class passengers, than exists at present.

34

'TREATMENT OF INDIANS ABROAD', *YOUNG INDIA* 2, 44, NOVEMBER 3, 1920, 7

Pariahs within the empire

Let me take you in thought to British East Africa, where I have lived day by day with Indians in Indian homes. On every side out there the Indian is marked by the badge of inferiority, although he was the pioneer settler in the country. Things have come to such a pass that contact with Indians is regarded by many English men and women as contaminating. The Indian is not allowed to sit in a public rickshaw in which a European has sat. The Indian is not allowed to travel in a railway carriage in which a European may travel. The Indian is kept out of railway station refreshment rooms as far as possible, where any Europeans may be taking their meals. The Indian is discriminated against in the railway station bungalows and not allowed to occupy rooms in which Europeans may wish to sleep. The Indian is now at last by law, and statute, and ordinance, to be segregated strictly in every part of his residential life, so that even if he possesses property in certain European quarters, he will not be allowed to live there. Such a policy of the Ghetto is to be strictly carried out, not merely by the order of the ruling White Race in East Africa, but by the direct order and pronouncement of the Colonial Secretary of State in London, at the Colonial Office, Whitehall, Lord Milner. For Lord Milner himself has just formulated his ultimate decision, that strict segregation must be carried out, not only in residential quarters in East Africa but as far as possible in commercial quarters also. Remember, please remember, that this decision will not remain an East African decision only. It will be taken up in every British Colony which has not practised segregation already. It will be a precedent for every Colonial Governor. It will affect Uganda as much as East Africa. It will pass on to the Tanganyika territory and to Nyasaland and to Zambesi, reaching even to Rhodesia, where, on the whole, up to the present Indians are comparatively well treated. The popular cry of the White Race will be raised, racial hatred will be fanned into a flame, and no Governor in Africa will be strong enough to resist the claim, that will now be made by settlers, who will say, quite truly, that Lord Milner himself has given his ultimate decision from the very centre of the British Empire at Whitehall *that Indians must be segregated.*

Segregation means degradation

I wish to tell you emphatically, for a fact, that *segregation* means *degradation*. I have lived in such segregated areas called Indian locations, and I have seen face to face the degradation and the humiliation and the injustice of it all. My heart has burnt with shame and indignation that my own people, my own English people should treat another race like that.

Mahatma Gandhi has written quite plainly that Indians under such condition are 'Pariahs within the Empire.' That phrase is quite literally and exactly true. They are 'untouchables' That is their exact position. Let me give you some incidents, which will show you the truth of that statement. I was in Johannesbrug station, waiting for the mail train which was to take me to Durban. When it came in, somewhat late, Ramdas, the son of Mahatma Gandhi, went into the compartment with my writing case in order to reserve my seat for the night journey. A young English lad (who was on his way back to school after the holidays) seized hold of Mahatma Gandhi's son and would have struck him a blow if I had not prevented it. A few moments later, the conductor, who was an Englishman, was about to do the same. He shouted out to Ramdas: 'Get out you—,' using an unmentionable word. This all happened within thirty seconds; and Ramdas would have been brutally assaulted twice, if I had not been behind him to prevent it. Mahatma Gandhi's son was a 'pariah', an 'untouchable', who contaminated by his very presence that European compartment.

The Law of Karma

An Indian gentleman, in that very city of Johannesburg in Africa, said to me one day: "Mr. Andrews, now what is it to be an 'untouchable'? We have been treating millions of our fellow-countrymen as 'untouchables' in India itself, and now we have been made to feel what it is to be untouchables ourselves. The Law of Karma is working itself out." It appeared to me that the logic here again was irresistible. The Law of Karma, as he truly said, was working itself out. The golden rule of conduct, which I have already stated, must be applied here just as impartially as I have tried to apply it before to my own countrymen: "Whatsoever ye would that men should do unto you, even so do unto them." If we do not like to be troated as 'pariahs' and 'untouchables' ourselves, we must not treat others as 'pariahs' and 'untouchables.' If we would wish Englishmen to respect us and give us independence, we must respect our own brothers in India and give them independence. We must not keep them any longer in a servile condition, if we wish ourselves to be free.

I will tell you another incident. I was in the railway station at Nairobi, in East Africa, and a group of Indian gentlemen were standing with me, who were man of wealth, property, and higher education. An African porter came by and intentionally and insultingly pushed one of these Indian gentlemen, with a neer on his countenance, which showed that he had done it on purpose. An Englishman, who was near by, laughed at it, and the African porter was pleased to receive the Englishman's approbation. This action made me blaze with fury and indignation, because I knew how Africans had then been prompted to insult Indians in this manner, simply in order to wound Indians' feelings and make them feel their utter humiliation. My friend was at some distance from me when it all happened. He then came quickly across to me and said: Mr. Andrews, did you see that? This is what we have to suffer. We are insulted like that every day of our lives in some way or another. If I were not obliged to make money for my family, I would leave East Africa to-morrow. To live in this country is to sink lower and lower in self-respect. I told him that he should either stay in the country to help his fellow-countrymen out of all this terrible bondage, or else he should leave it. I said that I could not believe *any* compensation in the way of money making could make up for this loss of self-respect.

35

M. GANDHI, 'CARPING CRITICISM', *YOUNG INDIA* 3, 19, MAY 11, 1921, 146

Carping criticism—Often do young men criticise the conduct of leaders without just cause. The latest instance that has come to my notice is rather striking. A special train was arranged for a visit to Mirpur Khas from Hyderabad during my recent visit to Sindh. This was too much for a correspondent. He thought that the leaders had indulged in a waste of national funds. I had not stopped to inquire the reason why the special was arranged. He advised me to cancel the special and give a day more to Sindh and save the money. If he had inquired into the matter, the friend would have discovered that without the special it was impossible to take me to Mirpur Khas, that I could not have given a day more to Sindh without disturbing the rest of the programme, that it was necessary for me to go to Mirpur Khas and that the expense was comparatively small. Criticism of public men is a welcome sign of public awakening. It keeps workers on the alert. Those who pay have a right to ensure economy. There is undoubtedly an extravagance often noticed about popular demonstrations, much money is spent in tinsel splendour. The expense is often thoughtless. And we are likely to gain by fearless criticism of public expenditure or general conduct of public men. But all such criticism must be well informed and thoughtful. All carping criticism must be avoided.

Whilst on the question of railway travelling, I must remark that there is still noticeable a desire to avoid 3rd class travelling. I am sorry to say that, being no longer physically able to travel 3rd class, I am deprived of the inestimable experiences of third class railway travelling. It affords an opportunity of contact with the national mind which nothing else does. It enables one to render service which cannot be otherwise rendered. I would therefore urge all workers to avoid 2nd class travelling save in rare cases. No one perhaps knows better than I do the discomfort of 3rd class railway travelling. I put it down partly to callous railway management and partly to bad national habits that ignore the convenience of the neighbours. Observant workers travelling 3rd class would efficiently deal with the disregard both of the management and the passengers. There is no doubt that 2nd class travelling is not within the reach of the masses. And national servants may claim to privileges not enjoyed by the latter.

M. K. G.

36

SIR RICHARD TEMPLE, 'THE BENGAL FAMINE (1874)', IN *THE STORY OF MY LIFE*, 2 VOLS. (LONDON: CASSELL, 1896), I, PP. 229–248

HAVING started by railway from Serampore near Calcutta late in the evening, with my Staff, Mr. Buckland and Mr. Hart, I reached Patna, the capital of Behar, the next morning. This was in January 1874; and I could not help looking back on my arrival there as a neophyte in the Service in 1848, twenty-six years previously. The sentiments which I had felt at Lahore, at Nagpore, at Hyderabad, now came back to me. Though I had recently given six of the best years of my life to council in the cabinet, yet I knew that my real *métier* was rather in the field where I was now to be severely exercised.

The situation, which had developed itself and had to be encountered by Lord Northbrook's Government, was in this wise. The population whose crops had been injured or destroyed by drought and who were threatened more or less with famine, dwelt between the left or north bank of the Ganges and the Himalayas. They numbered about twenty millions of souls, though the danger to some of them was in a greater to others in a lesser degree. There was no surplus rice in India to supply their need. That had to be brought by sea from Burmah to Calcutta, by the British India Steam Navigation Company, then under the able chairmanship of Sir William Mackinnon. From Calcutta it was conveyed by the East India Railway Company to the right or south bank of the Ganges. It was thus collected chiefly at or near Patna, partly also at various stations lower down the river. So far we had the help of two great European companies with the best mechanical appliances. But then came the rub, the tug of contest for me. The base of my operations was a mighty river, now low indeed, but soon to rise and widen daily with the melting of the Himalayan snows. These vast quantities of grain were to be carried down the steep river-bank and laden on flotillas of boats, to be towed across by tug-steamers to the opposite bank, and thence to be hauled up to the dépôts. From the dépôts they were to be taken away by bullock-carts to the famine-stricken villages, distant from twenty-five to fifty miles. This transport must be on a gigantic scale, and under the command of one chief transport officer. For this command I obtained the able services of Colonel (afterwards Sir Charles) Macgregor. I spoke to the Commander-in-Chief, Lord Napier of Magdâla, regarding further assistance, and he said that the Army was for the service of the country. I thus had the assistance of many excellent military officers, Europeans, and of many of the smartest among the Native officers. I also had the zealous help in the field of my old secretary, Colonel Harry Rivett-Carnac, now Aide-de-Camp to the Queen.

Crossing the Ganges, I and my Staff made a rapid tour through the threatened districts. The soil was fertile but depended entirely on rainfall for its productiveness. The country was one of the most densely peopled regions in the world. The further we advanced from the river and the nearer towards the mountains, the sharper became the indications of the coming famine. I perceived that the worst parts would be those lying between the town of Darbhunga and the British frontier adjoining Nepaul. From the dépôts at Darbhunga, supplies would presently have to be drawn for vast multitudes of persons who would otherwise perish. At that place the transport resources, for succour to the suffering villages, would have to be gathered. But it was forty miles distant from the nearest point on the Ganges. We could, indeed, land the stores at that point; but to drag them thence for this distance was a formidable, though not an impossible, task. So I proposed that a light railway should be made from that point to Darbhunga at the rate of a mile a day. Lord Northbrook approved, and the work was entrusted to Captain Stanton of the Royal Engineers. Then all the Civil officers in these districts helped to collect carts and bullocks in tens of thousands. Requisitions were made on every village, and readily complied with by the cart-owners who were thankful for the employment. Thus the whole strength of the Government and of the people was thrown into the operation. I caused the earliest supplies to be collected in the tracts where the famine was expected to appear first. In this work I was constantly associated with two young Civil servants whom I shall never forget—Mr. Magrath since deceased, and Mr. (now Sir Charles) Macdonnell at present the Lieutenant-Governor of the North-Western Provinces.

I then found one peculiar precaution to be indispensable, namely a house-to-house visitation in every village to discover whether hapless persons were pining at home, in hunger but without complaint. According to my information there were such persons to be found in most places. But if we were to wait till they asked for relief, we should find them past remedy. From my knowledge of the Native character, I was not surprised at this peculiar phase of it. So I caused the visitation to be made effectual for its benevolent purpose.

Having taken every precaution that could be thought of for Behar, I left the work in the hands of Mr. (afterwards Sir Steuart) Bayley and under him, in the charge of Mr. Metcalfe. I then recrossed the Ganges, my object being to visit the region lying at the base of the Eastern Himalayas. My way thither was by that very Rajmehal where, as a young man, twenty-six years before, I had a horrid journey. On the opposite side of the Ganges I halted at the ruins of Gour, which were most imposing though they afforded little more than traces of their pristine grandeur. Close to them I had a great dépôt and transport station. In my tent I could hear the creaking and rolling of the cart-wheels in the nocturnal hours right under the walls of the ruined mosque. I perceived that the distress in these districts would be more widely spread, but less intense than in Behar. Having made the necessary arrangements there, I hastened back to Behar having received reports indicating that near Darbhunga the famine might be on us sooner than we had expected. Having further strengthened my line of defence in that quarter, I returned to Calcutta, to report everything to Sir George Campbell before his departure.

I had always been on the friendliest terms with him, and I, with my wife, stayed with him during these days at Belvedere, the Government House of Bengal, near Calcutta. I well remember our sitting together at afternoon tea for the last time. Presently the sound of martial music and the tramp of horse were heard, as the guard of honour from the Governor-General came to escort Sir George to the railway station on his departure for England, viâ Bombay. That evening my wife and I went out to dinner. Coming home afterwards to Belvedere, we could scarcely believe that the house was our own for awhile. The next day the same sounds were heard, and Colonel Earle (afterwards the well-known General), the Military Secretary, came to accompany me, as I was to pay my State visit to the Governor-General on assuming the Government of Bengal. Naturally, the greetings between me and Lord Northbrook were cordial. I had not exchanged such greetings since the days when I used to meet Sir John Lawrence. At that moment, uppermost in the minds of us both, was the famine crisis. He inquired anxiously, and I replied that every precaution had been taken throughout the vast field of operations. I said, moreover, that a detailed estimate of the cost, both gross and net, after allowing for recoveries, was nearly ready, and would be submitted to him within the shortest possible time. I would then, while still at the capital, ask for the sanction of the Government of India to this estimate, before returning to the field. Accordingly, I obtained the approval of the Government of India to the estimate, which covered the months up to the middle of the following autumn. I wished for this formal sanction, knowing that public opinion, with generous impetuosity, will often urge commanders and administrators to transcendent efforts, overlooking the expense at the moment—and will afterwards be offended when, on the successful completion of the work, the cost comes to be defrayed. I meant to make it clear that the instructions from supreme authority to me, to undertake operations of unprecedented magnitude, were given with a full knowledge of what the cost would be. Fortunately, at the end of it all, I was able to report that we had worked within this estimate.

I held a hastily arranged reception for the Native nobles and gentry of Calcutta, and explained to them that there would be more leisure thereafter for these courtesies, if my efforts to save the lives of their countrymen should be blessed with success. I presided at one meeting of the Legislative Council of Bengal. There was a Municipal Bill, in which my friend Mr. (afterwards Sir Stuart) Hogg was officially concerned. He had asked me to secure its second reading before my departure, and I made a speech to the Council which helped in securing that result. I then said a few respectful and complimentary words to the Council, and begged them to excuse my absence for a while from their deliberations, owing to the exigencies of the time. I gave some verbal and confidential instructions to the Chief Secretary to the Government of Bengal, Mr. (afterwards Sir Rivers) Thompson, which enabled him to despatch a mass of current business. That same evening, towards the end of April, I set out by night train for Behar, leaving my wife at Belvedere.

The principal officer with me in the field was my Famine Secretary, Mr. (now Sir Charles) Bernard, who was my old friend of the Central Provinces, and who had been for some time holding high office under Sir George Campbell. I had also Mr. Charles Buckland as my Private Secretary, and Captain Spence as my Aide-de-Camp. As we alighted from the train on the Ganges bank, I greeted Colonel Macgregor at his post in the centre of the relief operations. The scene had changed for the worse since I was there in January. The sun was hot, the air dusty, the river broader and browner. The convoys, the flotillas of boats, the tug-steamers, together made a combination of bustling activity. Crossing the river at a point lower down, I found the light railway to Darbhunga nearly finished.

At Darbhunga I was glad to meet Mr. Metcalfe, Mr. Macdonnell, Mr. Magrath, and to settle with them the final measures for fighting the famine which was now face to face with us. We regarded this famine as an enemy that would attack us along a line extending over hundreds of miles. On the point opposite Darbhunga his onslaught would be the earliest and the fiercest. At that point, then, I would be present, and see that when he came on he should be repelled in the proper way. Accordingly, he did come just about the time we expected, and his attack was all the more critical because certain mistakes had been made by some local authorities, which I had to rectify by my own action. At the first blush I thought that, after all my care, some lives would be lost, and the effect of that, at the outset of our campaign, would have been bad. For several days I had to gallop about with Magrath, and especially with Macdonnell, in the dust and glare under a burning sun. Thus everything was put right; food-grain was brought in the nick of time to the mouths of the imperilled people, and so the enemy was beaten off in the old way. I had now found the way for coping with the famine in its hardest form, by experiments carried out successfully under my own eye.

What had succeeded here would *a fortiori* succeed more easily all along our line. I was therefore able to issue further and immediate instructions throughout the whole area of relief operations, whereby the famine, now imminent, would be met as fast as it appeared from point to point, day after day. I had established telegraphic communication with most points of danger, and thus I was assured that we had the advantage of an auspicious beginning, that, contrary to the misgivings and vaticinations in many quarters, no lives were being lost, and that not even the humblest and the poorest had succumbed.

Then, too, were apparent the results of the house-to-house visitation, village by village, which I had instituted during my first visit to Behar in January. Multitudes of famishing people, too proud, or too apathetic, to apply for relief, had been searched out and taken away from the homes where they had laid themselves down to die. These had been collected in troops at various centres where they could be properly fed. I used to have these emaciated creatures marshalled in a sitting posture, in order to assure myself that their condition was being improved. The melancholy of these parades was relieved by the certainty that, once discovered, the sufferers would be rescued from starvation. Those who were affected by disease—and smallpox was then appearing in many places—were collected in field hospitals under medical care.

I now saw that the light railway from the Ganges bank to Darbhunga the centre of distress, the bullock-cart transport, the relief operations generally, were in working order, and that the people were safe from famine in this the worst part of Behar for some weeks to come. But this was only a part of the distressed area; other operations equally large were going on in several other quarters; and my care was demanded for all alike. I therefore sought a spot which should be just behind the centre of the whole work, and that place without doubt was Monghyr. So I took a house there, perched on a high cliff. The railway to Calcutta ran between the base of this cliff and the right bank of the Ganges. From my perch I could descry with a telescope my several bases of operations, facing northwards. On my extreme left were the transport-flotillas of Behar plying from morn to eve. On my extreme right, in the Rajmehal direction, were the barges unloading the food-grain destined for Northern Bengal. Despite the intense heat, every hour had to be utilised in order that the last ton of grain might be in its place by the middle of June, after which date the rains might stop all transit work.

From this vantage point at Monghyr, I used to appear quickly by rail, by boat, or on horseback, at any point where affairs might not be going on quite rightly. I also held what we called Relief Councils, at which my principal officers were present comparing notes. But for a few days fortune was very unkind to me personally. Whether from exposure to inclemency of climate, or from breathing field-hospital air, or from whatever cause, horrid boils broke out on my limbs; these not only spoilt my riding but even prevented any locomotion. I concealed my pains as long as I could, fearing lest public anxiety should arise if it were to be whispered that anything was the matter with me. At length I was confined to the house for a brief while. Just at that moment my wife came up from Calcutta, to wish me good-bye before starting for England. When she had to leave, it was grievous for me to be unable to descend the long flight of steps from my home to the railway station to see her off. But from my balcony I listened to the train as it passed along the base of the cliff and whisked her away. I was, however, very soon out again, and took care to telegraph to the Governor-General from the field, in terms which showed that I must be on horseback, in order to counteract any rumours that might have arisen regarding my indisposition. It was clear, however, that there ought to be a highly qualified medical man in charge of me personally during these emergencies. I accordingly obtained the valuable services of Surgeon-Major (now General) Staples, who remained with me continuously and assiduously for many months.

So the mill of famine relief went grinding along for many weeks, with dreary yet resistless force. For millions and millions of people sustenance must be provided.

For those who were able-bodied some sort of employment was to be found. To those who produced money wherewith to purchase, food grain had to be sold. Empty grain-markets, where buyers could congregate, were replenished. Those who could not work, and were penniless, had to be fed gratuitously. Thus vast quantities of grain were dispensed, partly in return for labour, partly on account of cash received, and partly in charity. By the 1st of May complete discipline had been established not only among all the relief and transit establishments including some hundreds of thousands of men, but also among the people concerned, numbering many millions. During the month of May it operated noiselessly but effectually; and the guerdon of success remained with us, for there was no loss of life.

The situation of Monghyr suited my purpose so remarkably well, that it attracted the notice of Mr. Archibald Forbes, the talented correspondent of the London "Daily News," who had been residing in Behar all this time, and had rendered national service by accurate and impartial observations, which had often corrected misapprehension in the public mind. He visited me at my perch there, and said that the place was quite a strategic position from which the famine, like an armed enemy, could be combated. I took him for a breezy gallop to the Moslem shrine in the neighbourhood, and told him how, twenty-six years before, I made my first sketch there.

But from the middle of June, affairs entered upon a new phase. The transit work was over; and supplies of food grain for several months were in the right places for all the people dependent upon us. Meanwhile at dawn of each day as I woke in my elevated verandah in the perch at Monghyr, I looked towards the eastern horizon for rain-clouds. Very early one morning I beheld that horizon dark with masses of vapour rolling up. So the rains set in, and immediately hundreds of thousands left our relief works to go and till their fields. But soon the rains ceased for a while, and we feared that what had happened in several historic famines would happen to us now, namely that the failure of the rains in one year would be followed by a similar disaster in the next. We were indeed quite prepared for this dread contingency, and had the reserve stocks in the dépôts to carry us over the autumn, up to the time when transport operations could, if necessary, be resumed. Still the effect on the public mind of this cessation, or suspension, of the rains became marked at once. The borders of the distressed areas enlarged themselves day by day. In districts, not reckoned as distressed, the grain dealers, expecting further scarcity, shut up their granaries or raised their prices, and grain riots began to appear in North-Eastern, even in Eastern, Bengal.

Meanwhile the rivers had risen so far as to afford me the means of rapid communication by water. My vessel the "Rhotas" had been ordered up from Calcutta, and was moored near the base of my cliff at Monghyr. She was a State barge, called a "flat" in the Indian Marine, and was attached to a powerful river steamer, the "Sir William Peel." On board of her I and my Staff were conveyed at railway speed down the Ganges in flood to Eastern Bengal. Thence she took us easily and swiftly, backwards and forwards to many parts of the general relief area. In the dry season the Ganges had been a cruel impediment to me, but now the river was of the utmost convenience as affording me rapid transit. I remained on board this vessel till the end of the famine relief.

I thus reached Dacca the capital of this river-kingdom, and there met Lord Northbrook who had come from Calcutta in his State barge. We cordially exchanged felicitations on the providential deliverance of our people from famine. On that occasion some honours were being publicly bestowed on Nawab Abdul Ghani, the foremost man in the large Moslem population of Eastern Bengal. In his speech Lord Northbrook, addressing the people under my charge, commended to them in the kindest terms my conduct during the famine relief operations. Such an utterance, coming from him, strengthened my influence.

Early in July the rains began again, this time descending with a regularity and copiousness that dispelled anxiety. Week by week people went off our hands in vast numbers, and our expenses were proportionably reduced. We could, however, by no means break up our organisation or relax our precautions, because the August rains might fail. It was the failure of these very rains in the previous year that had caused the present famine. Thus though the body of our system became attenuated, the framework, the backbone and skeleton, so to speak, of our organisation was kept up, ready for any crisis that might still supervene. In August, however, the latter rains came in such a providential manner that, humanly speaking, the coming harvest was secure. Still many relief operations would be necessary until the new crops should begin to come in. So the great organisation, though shrunken in proportions, was in its vitality preserved till nearly the end of September. About that time I assembled the last of my Relief Councils at Monghyr, and with their advice decided to break up the organisation. Some critics remarked humorously that I had dismissed the famine with costs! I was then thankful to report to the Governor-General that the famine relief operations were over, that there had been no decrease of the population from hunger, and not more than the normal rate of disease, that all establishments were being reduced, and all expenses ceasing, that the only remnant would be the stock of reserve grain, prepared for an emergency from which we had been mercifully spared.

It was now lawful for me, after all I had borne and suffered during nine weary months, with unabating strain, to seek some comparative repose in my beloved Himalayas. At dawn one morning as I left my pretty cabin in the "Rhotas" where much successful business had been done, I felt a wrench and a regret. But in a few moments I was rolling along in a one-horse van, with my face set towards the mountains of Darjeeling. The next day I was at the Lieutenant-Governor's house there, called "The Shrubbery," with my faithful companions, Bernard, Buckland, Staples and Spence. After the relaxing atmosphere of my river-kingdom in Bengal, I drank in the Alpine air. I saw for the first time the rising sun cast his beams on the snow-masses of Kinchinjunga, and seem to set the mighty summits on fire. But the tension on my mind had been so severe for a long time that I could not bend my thoughts, scarcely even turn my eyes, to the picturesque. I found myself riding amidst matchless scenery, and yet making no sketches. The house had not been recently inhabited by my immediate predecessors, and had become damp from disuse. However we improvised fires, and then I buckled myself to prepare a final Report on the late famine. The station as a health-resort was out of season and almost deserted, so I was quite free from distraction. With the skilled and valued help of Mr. Bernard, my Report was ready by the end of October, and was then transmitted to the Governor-General.

Before returning to Calcutta I made a rapid journey through Orissa to see the system of canals for irrigation recently completed in that Province. I there saw the notorious car of Jaganath which was no longer permitted to crush its victims, and had long been out of use for any save ceremonial purposes. I chanced to witness at one of the temples a strange scene of excitable fanaticism. Some foreign strangers by mistake tried to enter forbidden precincts. The raving fury, and mad passion of the priests and attendants would have provoked bloodshed, had not the arm of secular authority been stretched forth to keep the peace. I visited the Hindu remains called by sailors the Black Pagoda, because being on the shore it serves as a landmark at sea. I rode along the wide sands, the desolate strand almost underneath the sculptured ruins of the wondrous structure. From seawards the heavy surf fell with a melancholy resonance on the shore, as if chaunting the dirge of departed grandeur. I fancied that Dickens would have liked to hear this when he was expressing the thought of what the wild waves were saying.

In November I proceeded to Belvedere to meet my wife who was returning from England. After that, the crowning scene occurred in the history of the Bengal famine, so far as I was concerned. The leading Natives of Bengal and Behar, as representing the entire community, wished to render public thanks to me for my conduct during the famine. The Bengal men declared that they would express their sentiments in English. The Behar men said that they would prefer to thank me in their own language, Hindustani, which I perfectly understood. I had fixed a day for receiving them all at Belvedere, when the sad news was received from England by telegraph of my father's death after a short illness. The leading newspaper of the Natives in Calcutta said that the Lieutenant-Governor, having succoured others, was now himself in grief. After a delay of a few days, the two important deputations from Bengal and Behar were ceremoniously received by me in the State apartments at Belvedere. Certainly it was to me the most memorable reception that I ever held. The spokesman for the Bengalis, in English, was Raja Degumber Mitter a thoroughly representative man. The two addresses, the one in English, the other in Hindustani, were much to the same effect. They summarised comprehensively the dimensions of the calamity which had been impending, and the various measures by which it had been averted. They thanked me, personally, in the most hearty and explicit manner for my efforts on behalf of their imperilled countrymen. They claimed for these efforts the most complete success. Then they went on to thank in similar terms the Government of India, whose lieutenant I was, and especially the Governor-General who had conceived the plan of relief and had placed me in power to execute it. They adverted to the British public opinion at home which had supported us throughout. In reply I claimed their gratitude for the Governor-General and the Government of India. I acknowledged the good conduct of their countrymen at large throughout the crisis, the munificence of all the Natives in the vast area of distress who could afford to give—the self-reliance of the poor who, instead of being pauperised by relief, relinquished the bounty of the State the moment that prosperity returned—the universal charity in all the villages, which both before and after the famine obviated the necessity of a poor-law—the fortitude with which all classes of both sexes had faced the common danger—and I called them to join me in thanking Providence for having mercifully preserved us.

37

VAUGHAN NASH, *THE GREAT FAMINE AND ITS CAUSES* (LONDON: LONGMANS, GREEN, 1900), PP. 12–13, 102–104, 110–114, 144–152, 163–165, 175–182, 229

Town and cantonment are getting their water by bullock transport. Even the engines on the line, like the cattle, are reduced to picking up water where they can. We were stopped yesterday for supplies at a nullah near Visapur, which the railway people have been tapping. The farmers in the villages are doing their best to drive wells down to the water, and Government has been lavish in making advances to help them, but the successive droughts seem to have left the earth bone dry to a depth never known before, and little comes of the ryots' efforts. The central horror of this famine lies in the fact that the misery and torment of a water famine have to be endured together with a famine of food for people and fodder for beasts.

In ordinary famines, or even in normal times when the work on his farm grows slack, the ryot will leave his home and go off to Bombay in search of work, or he will take to bullock-driving, or try to pick up a labourer's job on the irrigated lands in the north. But this year plague and famine have shut the door in his face, and no work is to be had. The Mahratta ryot is a hardy fellow; but what can he do when the cattle have gone to the butcher, when the last grains of the famine crop have been eaten, when the money-lender will not lend another pie, and the bucket comes empty up the well? In the first place, he will send his wife and children to the relief works, and try if he can struggle on alone; and probably after a time he will give that up as a hopeless job and go to join his family at the famine camp. This, I am told, is the first famine that has found the farmers in any numbers on the relief works. At some of the camps in the Poona district there are 40 per cent. of Mahrattas, most of them farmers or members of farmers' families, working and sleeping in the same camp with beggars and with mahars, who sweep the villages and eat the flesh of famine-stricken bullocks. A fair test this of the extremity of the cultivator.

As to relief measures, two points are pretty clear, and they apply to Rajputana generally. Without the railways, large districts must have been isolated from all possible food supplies, and unless the famine relief had been organised on a generous and effective scale the railways would have been useless, except for carrying away the train-loads of hides and bones. As it is, they have been bringing grain into the country from the North and Northwest, and the unfinished railway which is to connect Karachi and Calcutta has been giving a large amount of employment for famine labour. Of course there are plenty of districts far away from the rails, but they are not beyond the reach of camel and railway service combined.

The task of concerting relief measures has been an anxious one for all concerned. The Government of India is not only the governor of British provinces, but the protector of the people in the Native States, and it was bound to see that precautions were taken against the evil day. What was the policy of the native princes going to be? Some of them had no money in the treasury, others were known or suspected to be indifferent as to what became of their subjects, and not a Rajah had before been called upon to steer his ship through a tempest that threatened annihilation. The Viceroy, at any rate, lost no time in declaring his policy, and he decided early in the day to give the native rulers a strong lead. He offered loans on easy terms to the States that wanted money; he sent to Rajputana, as Famine Commissioner, Major Dunlop-Smith, who won his spurs in Hissar at the last famine in the Punjaub, and he offered the services of Staff Corps men, engineers, and doctors. Nobody could have given more practical or strenuous encouragement to the chiefs, and Lord Curzon may to-day fairly congratulate himself on the way in which his challenge was accepted. With a few exceptions, the princes both in Rajputana and other districts have set manfully to the task of saving life, and so far as I can judge, the famine organisation in Rajputana has been as successful as could be expected. There have been several cases in which the native princes have shown a signal public spirit and capacity for effective leadership. The young Maharajah of Bikanir took his place at the head of the famine organisation from the start. He set works going in the desert, organised a system of grain supply, and turned over to the famine service the camel corps of the Imperial service which Lord Dufferin invited the Native States to organise. Again, the Maharajah of Marwar, the young nephew of Sir Pertab Singh, found himself with a dry treasury in the autumn, and no prospect of revenue; for in these States "no crop no revenue" is still the rule. He borrowed three million rupees from the Government of India, and, with the help of his own Ministers and a little knot of Englishmen who for the last six months have been toiling like galley slaves, a relief organisation has been built up which would do no discredit to a British district. I have seen something, and heard more, of the good work that is being done in Marwar; and coming as I did from British territory, expecting to find confusion and inadequacy in the organisation, the results have astonished me.

I mentioned in my last letter that cholera was raging in Jodhpur, and I have since heard that outbreaks have occurred in most of the famine camps. At Pali town—a place which gave its native name to the plague—there is a serious epidemic, but happily no fresh cases have appeared in the camp or poorhouse for some time back. At a tank work fifteen miles to the east, where nearly 30,000 wanderers had been collected, things have not gone so well, as a panic set in, and more than half the people scattered themselves over the desert, carrying the pestilence with them. The same thing on a smaller scale has happened at other camps, and it is easy to understand why the towns and villages, not in Marwar alone, but in other Rajputana States, are being desolated by the scourge. Cholera, indeed, is in the air. I travelled from Jodhpur with one of the engineers of the railway. A telegram was put into his hand saying that a man with cholera had been taken out of the train that followed ours, and a few stations farther on another telegram was handed to him announcing the man's death. My fellow-passenger to Jaipur was a doctor knocked up by overwork, who had been fighting the cholera in the northern districts. An English officer on famine service in the deserts since November came in on his camel to Pali fit for nothing but a rest at home. I open the newspaper, and find that cholera has broken out at Godhra, and that a hundred bodies are lying unburied at the camp that I visited a fortnight ago. Brahma Nund, famine officer to the Marwar Durbar, who came with me in the train from Pali to Marwar junction, was visiting a camp a short time back when he saw a man fall. Then another fell, and another. Next day a hundred and ninety people were down with the cholera, most of the officials had fled, the camp was in panic, and the sweepers would not touch the bodies. Brahma Nund collected fresh workers around him, told the people that it was a holy service, and no defilement to see to the sick and bury the dead, and in due time fairly beat the cholera out of the camp. A line from the book of Ramayan, he told me, was running in his head during the struggle; he wrote it for me in my notebook, and here it is—"Disadvantage, advantage, life, death, fame and infamy rest in the hands of God."

I am afraid there can no longer be any doubt that a calamity of the most appalling kind is beginning to break over India, and that hundreds of thousands of poor wretches who have been reduced by want and by the hardships and unnatural conditions of life in the famine camps will go down before the blast. The odds are too great against the handful of Englishmen who are fighting on the other side. Here in Rajputana there are twenty Staff Corps men and a few engineers and doctors, and besides them must be reckoned the Residents, the story of whose efforts to save the people would make a chapter in English history worth the reading, if it could only be written. Look at the map, and consider what chance this little band of Englishmen, backed by an occasional Brahma Nund, can have against the pestilence. Nor is the rest of India so vastly better off in point of establishment. A thousand, or even five hundred, British officers, commissioned and non-commissioned, and another five hundred doctors might turn the scale. The existing service is not strong enough to grapple with famine, let alone cholera.

I must go back now for a moment to describe another part of the Marwar machinery of relief—I mean the collecting depôt. One of the difficulties the State has had to face is the recall of the multitude of Marwaris who have strayed into other districts. Many have come back by road, but immense numbers have been fetched by train, and Marwar Junction, where a collecting camp is established, is one of the principal depôts for the reception of these wanderers, who are fed up for a few days and then passed on to one of the famine camps. The camp proper has had to be dismantled because of the cholera, and I found four parties, each about a thousand strong and arranged in huge circles on an open stretch of sandy ground, their fires beginning to blaze in preparation for the evening meal. Here were all sorts and conditions of men—potters, oil extractors, camel breeders, beggars, thieves, drummers, cultivators. Most of those I talked to were wanderers who had returned from Central India, leaving their cattle dead behind them, and often enough some member of the family as well. A woman who sat with her boy had left her husband and a girl of twelve at Indore, and two of her children had died since their return to their own land. There have been many deaths at the collecting house. The doctors tell me that the condition in which thousands of wanderers have come back is such as to make their final recovery impossible. They may do their work at the famine tanks and eat their rations like the rest, but their bodies cannot be properly nourished, and if they get back finally to their own villages it will only be to die.

Here in Jaipur State the famine is less severe than it is in Marwar, and in many districts there has been a fair supply of fodder. Moreover, there are appreciable stretches of country where irrigation works have enabled the people to hold out longer than they would otherwise have done.

In the Central Provinces

It is a far cry from Simla to the Central Provinces, whether you look at the thermometer or the distance to be travelled. For most of the way the railway skirts the western famine frontier. First there is a long stretch of Punjaub to be traversed, then you find yourself in the North-west Provinces, which have escaped the famine owing to a sufficient rainfall, touching at cities with Mutiny names, and passing close to the borders of Rajputana. And finally you cut across the barrier of the Central India States, in all of which the famine is more or less severe, and come out upon the region that has been described as the boss of the Indian shield, and which, topography apart, is the very equator for heat. When I left the train at Jubbulpur and stepped out into what ought to have been the cool of the evening, I had skirted the greater part of the famine region, but the breadth of the Central Provinces still lay to the south, and beyond that again the enormous tract of Hyderabad and Berar.

The Central Provinces were constituted in 1861 by the union of the outlying dependency of the North-west Provinces (the Saugor-Nerbudda territories) with the estreated dominions of the Rajah of Nagpur. "These tracts," so a Government report informs you, "include the mass of jungle-covered hills which have given asylum to the aboriginal tribes in their retreat before the advancing tide of Hindoo immigration." Twenty-one thousand square miles are under the Forest Department, and in 1891 there were 18,000 square miles of large zamindari (landlord) estates, said to be in great part waste, and another 20,000 square miles lying uncultivated in private hands, most of it hilly and rocky ground, which the authorities say it would not pay to cultivate. Roughly, then, the Central Provinces include some of the richest land in India, with tracts of virgin soil that have only been opened up within the last thirty years—and also some of the poorest. It is emphatically a half-developed territory, and for mixture of tribes I suppose it cannot be surpassed. The land system is described as forming the connecting link between the proprietary communities of the North-west Provinces and the landlord settlement of Bengal. The revenue settlement is not made with each individual cultivator as in Bombay and Madras, nor with entire village communities, as in the North-west and, nominally, in the Punjaub, but with landlords who were drawn from the class of revenue farmers, and in a moment—as it seems to some—of aberration forcibly endowed by the Government with the lands of the State. For the rest the tenants have quite recently been safeguarded in respect to their occupancy rights by a most stringent law. Their rents are fixed by the Government when the periodical revenue settlement is made with the landlords, concerning which, however, and the effect of the system of land assessment on the condition of the people, I must postpone comment till I have had time for pushing my inquiries further. As to the extent and acuteness of the famine, it may be gauged by the fact that out of a population of ten and three-quarter millions in the districts affected, close upon a million and three-quarters are on Government relief, and it is expected that the number will be increased to two millions before the monsoon bursts. In Raipur, the great rice-growing district, 600,000, or 40 per cent. of the people, are on relief, and in Bilaspur, the neighbouring division, which I hope to visit, a quarter of a million. Happily the people have been spared a fodder famine, and there is food and to spare for all the beasts in the Government forests; but the rains were wholly insufficient to grow rice, and in the grain-growing districts the autumn and spring crops were very small. The scarcity of water is growing acute, and wells, tanks, and streams are drying up on every hand; but in the eastern district, from which I write, the land looks far less baked than in the rest of the famine districts, and I believe that the authorities hope for a sufficient supply for drinking purposes throughout the provinces.

It is impossible to speak too highly in praise of the relief work which has been carried on ever since the autumn. In the famine of 1897 the Government was too late in the field, and a heavy toll was paid before measures of relief could be organised; but the lesson has been well learned, and directly the failure of the autumn crops declared itself, a systematic campaign was organised by the Chief Commissioner, and pushed forward twenty-four hours ahead of every movement of the enemy. The campaign has no doubt been costly, and it has absorbed an army of organisers, but on the other hand it has kept the people from starvation, and when the monsoon bursts the two millions of agriculturists will be in good heart and trim for getting their farms in hand again. Till a week or so back, when the cholera drew ahead, the death-rate for the Central Provinces was normal, and if that is not a test of triumphant organisation, I do not know what is. The Government has opened village relief works and kitchens at the people's own doors; it has gone to the Gonds and Bhils, and other aboriginal tribes, and offered them work at grass-cutting and road-making in the forests, and wherever there was a sign of genuine distress, relief works on a larger scale have been opened. Not a district has been neglected, and out of all the scores of thousands who have come in across the borders, not a starving wanderer from the Native States has been sent empty away. And with all this the rate of wages has been sufficient to keep the people in good condition; fining below the minimum is rare, and the penal minimum is, so far as I can gather, unknown. What has been the moral effect of this policy? Have the people flocked from their villages at the invitation of the Sirkar when they might have stayed at home? Are they skulking at their ease on the works, where the Government is feeding them? These are the questions which I have been putting to officials of all grades in the service, and seeking to answer for myself in the villages as well as on the works. I cannot pretend to give a conclusive reply, but I think that I can shed a little light on some very vexed questions which these recurrent famines are raising to a point of Imperial importance.

First as to the labour problem. The policy of the famine authorities has been to exact a fair task from the people, and to do this it was necessary to have competent supervision, and enough of it, to see that the camps were not so large as to endanger discipline, and to hit upon a means of payment that would give the people a clear idea of the relation between work and wages. They began by paying their works superintendents double the salary paid in the last famine, and enough officers, engineers, and non-commissioned officers were imported to keep watch and ward over the whole gigantic system of relief that had of necessity to be built up on a basis of native officialdom. This, as I have said, was costly in the first instance, but then the famine in these parts has emphatically not been run on the cheap. Further, it was decided that not more than five thousand, or at the outside six thousand, people were to be employed at once on any one work—a provision that has kept the famine camps from degenerating into mobs. And, finally, the payment of wages was to be made daily, and the daily task so marked out as to be comprehensible to a child. A system of moderate fining was introduced for cases of contumacy, but it was provided that no one should be fined twice in the same week until the attention of a superior officer had been called to the matter, so that inquiry should be made as to whether the fault lay with the workers, the supervision, or the material. The result of all this patient and laborious contriving is that the great majority of the people are earning the maximum wages, and are in good heart and good condition, and that a vast addition in the shape of tanks, roads, and railway work has been made to the wealth of the provinces. So much for the work. That the policy will prove itself really costly in the long run I venture to doubt. Whether the relief has sapped the people's independence is a more difficult question to bring to the test. The view of those who are entitled to speak with the highest authority is that of two evils it was better that a certain number should be admitted to the works who were not absolutely destitute than that any risks should be run of reducing the really needy to a state of starvation by barbed-wire deterrents. They frankly admit that a certain percentage of people who might have eked out a living in their villages have come upon relief; but in regard to this class it is pointed out that when the famine is over their savings will be available for making a fresh start, and to this extent the drain on Government and charitable aid will be reduced. No one can blind himself to the dangers that lurk in the erection of a system of out-relief on this colossal scale, but I cannot say that the officials are despondent as to the results, whilst the chief desire of the people themselves, who are employed at a distance from their homes, is to get back again as soon as may be. That is so, at any rate, in the case of the farmers. Till there is grain to feed them, it would be foolish to expect the labourers to be in any hurry to return. At the best of times their existence is a hard and precarious one.

In company with a member of the Civil Service I have been visiting some of the villages in the Hoshangabad division, and the evidence I have gathered, coupled with the testimony of the officers in charge of village districts, goes to show that the bulk of the people have elected to make a brave fight against the famine, surrendering only when there is no choice left to them. Riding out through the fields, you are struck at once by the amount of work that is going on in the way of ploughing, harrowing, and weeding.

Down here in the Central Provinces the relief has been organised with such grasp and thoroughness and the whole famine service is drilled to such a point of efficiency, that the prospect may be faced with something like composure. In the Raipur district matters are worse, the cholera having declared itself in forty-five camps; but the numbers attacked are only a tithe of those in the Bombay Presidency, and as the people have confidence in the officials, and all the camps are of manageable dimensions, there is no panic.

There is a serious flaw in the general famine organisation on which I must say a word before closing this letter. Here in the Central Provinces, any quantity of Government fodder, cut and uncut, is going begging, whilst away in the Punjaub and Rajputana and Gujerat, the last of the beasts are dying of hunger. The fact is that there is no fodder famine if you take India as a whole, any more than there is a grain famine. But whereas the Government is paying the people to get rice from Bengal and Burmah and grain from the North-west Provinces and the Punjaub, and the grain dealers and the railways are finding it worth their while to bring the food to the place where it is wanted, no such organisation, with the exception of a handful of cattle camps, exists for keeping the cattle alive. The fault lies partly with the Government, who began by demanding an absurdly high price for the fodder, partly with the railway companies, which either will not, or cannot, supply the rolling stock, and in any case find the transport of grain more profitable than that of pressed fodder. Between the two the mischief has been done. A spurt has lately been given to the Bombay demand by a big reduction of price, but the railway companies refuse to provide anything like enough trucks; and I suppose that is why the Lieutenant Governor of the Punjaub has given up all hope of bringing fodder into his province as a bad job. And yet the Forest Officer at Hoshangabad tells me that he is advertising his fodder in seven newspapers, and that the slackness of demand is such that the grass-cutting operations, carried on by famine labour, are being stopped. The Forest Department has a pretty long queue of sins waiting at its door for the day of reckoning, and so have the Indian railway companies, and the two of them may now apportion the responsibility as best they may for the catastrophe which has robbed India of her cattle. So far as the Government of India and the provincial governments are concerned, their position is one of confessed helplessness. Surely it would have been better to spend a little money and energy in saving the cattle, even at the risk of annoying the railway companies, than to fall back on loans for buying fresh cattle, if indeed they are anywhere to be got.

It is, perhaps, a question whether the most generous treatment permitted by the famine code would have kept the Gujeratis in anything approaching to fair condition. Here, in Broach, where for some weeks the harshest treatment that I have seen in India was meted out, the state of the people beggars description. The "deterrent" element, on which the Bombay Government lay such stress, has had full play with a vengeance, but when the history of the famine comes to be summed up, I doubt if the result will be paraded as a success. The net effect of it on the works has been semi-starvation, sickness, and an appalling death-rate, and in the villages, starvation on a wholesale scale amongst the people who were "deterred," by the harshness of the tests, from going upon the works. There is a point at which relief becomes a greater evil than misery and privation, and to the mind of the Gujerati this point was reached when the wages on the works were cut down to the skeleton standard. It is too late to repair the damage, now that the test has shown the people to be really and truly famine-stricken, and the buried hoards of grain and ornaments to be figments of the Secretariat's imagination. The rules have, indeed, been relaxed, but the people have lost confidence, and multitudes have been reduced to that awful state in which the body wastes and shrivels, no matter how much food is put into the stomach. The finest wheat and the best champagne would be useless now. And on top of all this a raging visitation of cholera is sweeping the country. Of this final catastrophe I can do no more than give you a colourless sketch. The kites and jackals are gorging themselves, and the air is thick with the stench of the dead, who are dying faster than they can be burned or buried. Every one of the works in the districts of Ahmedabad, Broach, Kaira, and Panch Mahals has been attacked. In Kathiawar it has been almost as bad. The cholera is of the most virulent kind, and the first instinct of the people has been to fly from the camps, in the hope of reaching their homes alive. It has been a race between cholera and starvation, a grand hunt of death with scores of thousands of the refugees at the famine camps for quarry. The panic is estimated to have driven about half the people from the works in the Ahmedabad district, and I suppose that something like a hundred thousand souls have joined in the flight in Gujerat alone. The number of the dead is unknown, but it must be reckoned by scores of thousands. In some instances the native officials ran off when the cholera came, leaving the sick to die without medicine or help. At Godhra a handful of Englishmen, including the collector and the medical officer, had to collect and burn nearly a thousand bodies with their own hands. Dr. Klopsch, of the *American Christian Herald*, who is over here distributing the fund which his readers have contributed, was at Dohad, forty miles further west, just after the breaking up of the works, and he tells me that he could not free himself from the stench of the dead for a couple of days. He was in Russia during the recent famine, and, in his opinion, the stress of suffering in Gujerat, leaving the cholera out of account, is worse than anything he saw there.

Gujerat in May

WHEN I was here a few weeks ago things seemed to be about as bad as bad could be; but all that was hideous and heartrending in the condition of the people has been intensified in the weeks that have passed. Cholera has come, the last of the few remaining cattle are dying, and under this burning sky, which shows no signs of the expected rains, the hearts of the people are failing them for fear. They have fought against death a long and unavailing fight, enduring sufferings that no Western race could bear; now they sit with bowed heads awaiting death. They have no hope to buoy them up, poor wretches. The skies are as brass; but supposing the rains were to fall to-morrow, how are the fields to be ploughed and sown without bullocks or seed, and where is the food to come from to keep life in cultivator and labourer, and how are the children to live when the strength of the mothers is spent and the cow that used to give the "baba" milk is dead?

An impression seems to exist at home that directly the monsoon breaks a transformation scene is to take place, Government and philanthropy between them supplying all that is wanted to set the life of the fields in motion once more. I wish I could see any traces of such a thing here. In Broach—the richest and most heavily assessed district in Bombay Presidency—there is no evidence whatever of the approach of this happy change, and two incidents that have come under my notice point quite the other way. A practical effort was lately made by the Commissioner to keep the remnant of the plough cattle from death. A large grant was secured from the Famine Fund for supplying fodder at a low price—two rupees per 1000 lbs.—and arrangements were made for bringing up quantities from the Central Provinces, where, as I wrote last week, tens of thousands of tons are waiting for customers. Here was good tidings. The people came to the town in crowds when the first consignment arrived, and their gratitude for this Heavensent respite for their dying beasts was touching to see. "Tell the Englishmen," said a ryot, "that all our cattle would have died if it hadn't been for them." But, alas, for the sequel! The railway companies, after the first few hundred tons were carried, turned their attention elsewhere. Remonstrances, petitions were in vain. The Government of India were appealed to, but they declared that they could do nothing. The railway remained deaf and obdurate. And so it has come about that the last hope of saving the beasts has had to be abandoned. "Give us fodder, give us fodder," was the burden of the despairing chorus that I heard in the villages yesterday. "We can manage for ourselves. We live on half our usual food, and it is poor, coarse stuff—rice from Burmah and jowar, instead of cadgeree and ghi; but help us to keep our cattle alive. We work where we can find work, and we are hungry. But if our cattle have no food, what use are our carts, and how shall we plough our fields?" It seemed cold comfort to tell these men that England will help—for what good will the help be later on when the beasts are all dead?—but it was the best that I could offer them.

The second incident is of the same order, but this time it is the Government grant for buying cattle that has missed fire. A large order—large in actual numbers, but small in relation to the need—was given for bullocks to the cattle owners in Bhopal State, where cattle happened to be plentiful. The cattle were to be delivered at thirty rupees a head, and the authorities waited anxiously for their arrival. They are still waiting, and if in the course of weeks the cattle should arrive they will probably be too late. In any case, if there is no fodder in Broach they may just as well stay in Bhopal. I asked an Englishman, who has had business relations with Gujerat for nearly forty years, whether this deadlock was, in his opinion, avoidable. His verdict is that with energy and organisation the pressure could be overcome. But these are qualities that appear to be lacking in Indian railway management.

The physical condition of the people is steadily deteriorating, and the death-rate has gone up again in the past month.

But the flight has been general enough to scatter the cholera broadcast through towns and villages, and to throw the relief machinery out of gear. Baroda has fared better, but in Rajputana the havoc has been something frightful, the recorded deaths from cholera amounting in places to nearly 5 per cent. of the population, and 10 per cent. in some of the Bhil districts. The works in Tonk, Udaipur, Sirohi, Marwar, and Ajmere were nearly dislocated, Udaipur faring worst. Colonel Adams, Administrative Medical Officer in Rajputana, is amongst the victims.

Now that the deluge has come the Government is taking measures. Additional officers, recruited from all parts of India, are being poured into Gujerat, and the Commissioner, Mr. Lely, who is looked up to by the people as their father and protector, has been granted something like a free hand. The new policy is to start works close to the villages, so that the refugees on their arrival shall find help within reach, and every nerve is being strained to get the organisation set on foot while there is a chance of saving life.

The cultivator of Bombay and the Punjaub who has come under the money-lender's thumb is denied this protection. He has no security and no rights.

To say that the tendencies I have been describing must in the nature of things make for famine, is perhaps to labour the obvious. They make for famine at every step in the road from independence to serfdom. We are muzzling the mouth of the ox which treads out the corn. The ryot's produce is the money-lender's, and he can no longer put by for famine if he would, nor can he be expected to work with the will and energy of a free man. The fat years are for the bunya, the lean kine for the ryot. Even the unencumbered cultivator no longer stores his grain now that the railway is ready to whisk it off.

But is the money-lender, after all, the man of destiny, who as capitalist and organiser may yet direct the energies of the ryot to a higher plane, and, after the friction of the transition is over, open a new chapter of prosperity? Judged by present facts, the answer is no, and yet again no.

38

ROMESH CHUNDER DUTT, *OPEN LETTERS TO LORD CURZON ON FAMINE AND LAND ASSESSMENTS IN INDIA* (LONDON: K. PAUL, TRENCH, TRÜBNER, 1900), PP. 124–125, 305, 314–315

Another point which is connected with famine and which famine brings into dis-agreeable prominence is that something must be radically wrong when the failure of rain means failure of irrigation even in extensive tracts set down as tank-fed, tracts which are therefore not solely dependent—*mana-vari* as we call them in our Presidency—on the fall of rain. Now that it is declared in the budget that the programme of purely protective railway works has been practically exhausted, one big drain on the famine grant may be said to be at an end and the prospects of irrigation may be taken vastly to brighten; for there has all along been a contrast, as it was bound to be, between the way the claims of the railway and the claims of irrigation were respectively met. I say "as it was bound to be," because the cause of railway is virtually the cause of enterprise, of commerce of manufacture, of railway rolling stock and of ambitious engineering; and the representatives of each and all of these necessarily unite their lusty voices and focus their cultured and energetic intelligence on it—a species of advantage which the unlettered and inert peasantry can never hope to command.

The cause of the raiyat population must, of course, be the cause of the whole staff of Executive Government, embracing all grades from the topmost to the lowest round in the ladder; and it augurs well for that population that, even in this year of sore and straitened circumstances, no less than a crore of rupees is granted for their special benefit, although large slices of it are ear-marked for specific irrigation works and although only a small fraction is available this year for the creation, extension and the repairs of the vast number of tanks and reser-voirs, which play no insignificant part in aggravating or diminishing the ill-con-sequences of absent rains. Let me take my own Presidency for an example. There a large part, if not the major part, is dependent on tanks, reservoirs and similar contrivances to catch and collect water: and yet it is a mere toss-up whether they should be empty and bring on famine for want of rains, as in the year before last, or whether they are filled, partially at least, as this year, and render scarcity scarce. Such instances cannot but prove that something more than the excavation of canals on a grand scale remains to be done and redone continuously and at frequent cost.

Permit me to point out that I have not in this or in any other letter made any statement which I am not prepared to prove. "Mr Dutt," your correspondent writes, "lays special stress on the fact of so much money going out of India in the shape of interest, loans, &c. Just so. But he does not say how much capital was spent on those undertakings." The Blue-book on Indian railways can surely supply this information to your correspondent. I produced that Blue-book before the Currency Committee in November 1898, when I was examined as a witness, and showed that the railway system has caused a net loss of over fifty millions to the Indian revenue—*i.e.*, to the Indian people; that it was still causing us an annual loss of about two millions; and that this loss was greatly owing, not to the construction of the main lines needed for famine protection purposes, but to local lines constructed for special interests, and often under pressure from capitalists in this country. It is this practice which I protest against. No sane man objects to paying interest on capital spent; but every reasonable man objects to adding to India's indebtedness by the construction of fresh lines under guarantee of profits from the Indian revenues when the people of India do not ask for those fresh lines, do not want them, and cannot afford to have them. An endeavour should be made in times of peace to reduce India's public debt, and thus to reduce the money which goes out of India as interest.

The general opinion among the people of India is that, now that the great military lines have been constructed, now that the lines really required for famine protection have been laid down, the Government should not directly or indirectly make the people's money responsible for further lines. The impression is that India is not rich enough to construct those new lines which are being multiplied from year to year; that it is an unsound, hurtful, and disastrous policy to continuously add to the national debt of India in order to construct these new lines which the people do not want, and which the country's finances do not justify. The impression is that pressure is brought to bear upon the Government by influential classes of capitalists and manufacturers for opening such new lines for serving special interests, and that the Government, with every desire to be honest and impartial, sacrifices the interests of the people, because the people are not constitutionally allowed to express and enforce their views as against the views of the influential classes. The impression is (to use the words of the late Sir George Campbell, sometime Lieutenant-Governor of Bengal) that when British capitalists have put their money in losing concerns in India, people in London bully and abuse the Government of India to get the concerns taken over, and eventually they are successful. There may or may not be some truth in these impressions; but the demand that the Indian people's money should not be invested on new lines of railway in India, or on the road from Burma to China, without consulting the people's wishes, is just and reasonable. To borrow money in England to an unlimited extent to further extend the railway system in India or outside India proper, is for the Indian Government a policy of extravagance and of injustice to the people.

It is necessary to further elucidate our remarks by a reference to the history of the Import Duties of India? It will be in the recollection of most Indian officials that the Government of India and Government at home have repeatedly made "graceful concessions," and have sacrificed Indian revenues, because the people of India have no constitutional power to back their Government and to resist unjust demands. But the end is not yet. On the 9th of this month (August 1898), the Secretary of State for India was asked in the House of Commons to admit British manufacture in India at a further reduction of one-fourth the duty on foreign goods, after the example of Canada. Lord George Hamilton declined to do so, but the assailants have only to persist to carry their point. Neither Conservatives nor Liberals are strong enough to resist for any length of years such demands backed by twenty or thirty or forty solid votes in the House. And unless the people of India are allowed the constitutional right to stand by their Government, and to defend their national revenues and their national interests, the humiliating sight will be witnessed again and again of the British Government in India knowingly and openly sacrificing the interests of the people of India under the mandate of British voters at home.

39

DADABHAI NAOROJI, *POVERTY AND UN-BRITISH RULE IN INDIA* (LONDON: S. SONNENSCHEIN & CO., 1901), PP. 193–196, 227–229

Railways

I may take railways to represent public works. The benefits generally derived from railways are these: they distribute the produce of the country from parts where it is produced, or is in abundance, to the parts where it is wanted, so that no part of the produce is wasted, which otherwise would be the case if no facility of communication existed. In thus utilising the whole produce of the country, the railway becomes directly a saving agent, and indirectly thereby helps in increasing the production of the country.

It brings the produce to the ports at the least possible cost for exportation and commercial competition for foreign trade, and thus indirectly helps in obtaining the profits of foreign trade, which are an increase to the annual income of a country.

Every country in building railways, even by borrowed capital, derives the benefit of a large portion of such borrowed capital, as the capital of the country, which indirectly helps in increasing the production of the country. Excepting interest paid for such borrowed capital to the foreign lending country, the rest of the whole income remains *in the country*.

But the result of *all* the above benefits from railways is ultimately realised and comprised in the actual annual income of the country.

The misfortune of India is that she does not derive the above benefits, as every other country does.

You build a railway in England, and, say, its gross income is a million. All the employés, from the chairman down to the common labourer, *are Englishmen*. Every farthing that is spent from the gross income is so much returned to Englishmen, as direct maintenance to so many people *of England*, and to England at large, as a part of its general wealth. Whether the shareholders get their 5 per cent., or 10 per cent., or 1 per cent., or 0 per cent., or even lose, it matters not at all to the whole country. Every farthing of the income of the million is fully and solely enjoyed by *the people of the country*, excepting only (if you borrowed a portion of the capital from foreign parts) the interest you may pay for such loan. But such interest forms a small portion of the whole income, and every country with good railways can very well afford to pay. All the benefits of railways are thus obtained and enjoyed by *the people of the country*.

Take the case of the United States. India and the States are both borrowers for their railways (the latter only partially), and they both pay interest to the lending countries. They both buy, say, their rails, machinery, etc., from England, the States buying only a portion. So far, they are under somewhat similar circumstances; but here the parallel ends. In the United States every cent. of the income of the railway (excepting the interest on the foreign loan) is the income of *the people of the country*—is a direct maintenance for the people employed on it, and an indirect property of the whole country, and remaining *in* it.

In India the case is quite different. First, for the directors, home establishments, Government superintendence, and what not, in England, a portion of the income must go from India; then a large European staff of employés (excepting only for inferior and lowest places or work left for Natives) must eat up and take away another large portion of the income; and to the rest the people of the country are welcome, with the result that, out of their production which they give to the railways, only a *portion* returns to them, and *not the whole*, as in all other countries (except interest on foreign loan), and the diminution lessens, so far, the capacity of production every year. Such expenditure, both in England and India, is so much direct deprivation of the natural maintenance of as many people of India of similar classes, and a loss to the general wealth and means of the people at large. Thus the whole burden of the debt is placed on the shoulders of the people of India, while the benefit is largely enjoyed and carried away by the people of England; and yet Englishmen raise up their hands in wonder why India should not be happy, pleased, and thankful! Some years ago I asked Mr. J. Danvers to make a return, in his annual Railway Report, of the salaries and every other kind of disbursement on Europeans, both in England and India. If I remember rightly (I cannot just now lay my hands on the correspondence), he was kind enough to promise he would try. But I do not know that this information has been given. Let us have this information, and we shall then know why India does *not* derive the usual benefits from railways; how many Europeans displace as many Natives of the same class, and deprive them of their natural means of subsistence (some 3,600 in India, and all those in England), and what portion of the income the people of India do not see or enjoy a pie of.

Instead, therefore, of there being any "railway wealth" to be added to the annual production or income of India, it will be seen that there is much to be deducted therefrom to ascertain what *really* remains for the use of its own people; for the income of railways is simply a portion or share of the production of the country, and what is eaten up and taken away by Europeans is so much taken away from the means of the people.

It is no wonder at all that the United States have their 70,000 or more miles of railways, when India, under the *British Government*, with all its wonderful resources, with all that good government can do, and the whole British wealth to back, has hardly one-tenth of the length, and that even with no benefit to the people of the country. In short, the fact of the matter is that, as India is treated at present, all the new departments, opened in the name of civilisation, advancement, progress, and what not, simply resolve themselves into so much new provision for so many more Europeans, and so much new burden on exhausting India. We do pray to our British rulers, let us have railways and all other kinds of beneficial public works by all means, but let *us* have their natural benefits, or talk not to a starving man of the pleasures of a fine dinner. We should be happy to, and thankfully, pay for such European supervision and guidance as may be absolutely necessary for successful work; but do not in Heaven's and Honesty's names, talk to us of benefits which *we do not* receive, but have, on the contrary, to pay for from our own. If *we* are allowed to derive the usual benefits of railways and other public works, under such government as the British—of law, order, and justice—we would not only borrow £200,000,000, but £2,000,000,000, and pay the interest with as many thanks, with benefit both to ourselves and to England, as India would then be her best and largest commercial customer.

The real important question, therefore, in relation to public works is, not how to stop them, but how to let *the people of the country* have their full benefits. One of the most important parts of England's great work in India is to develop these public works, but to the *people's* benefit, and not to their detriment—*not that they should slave, and others eat.*

The Commission suggests the institution of an Agricultural Department, and a very important suggestion it is. But they soon forget that it is *for India* this is required, that it is at India's expense it has to be done, that it is from India's wretched income that this expenditure has to be provided, and that India cannot afford to have more blood sucked out of her for more Europeans, while depriving so much her own children; in short, that Native agency, under a good English head or two, would be the most natural and proper agency for the purpose. No; prostrate as India is and for which very reason the Commission was appointed to suggest a remedy, they can only say, "More Europeans," as if no such thing as a people existed in India.

Were any Englishman to make such a proposal for England, that French or German youths be instructed at England's expense, and that such youths make up the different public departments, he would be at once scouted and laughed at. And yet these Commissioners thoughtlessly and seriously suggest and recommend to aggravate the very evil for which they were expected to suggest a remedy.

I appeal most earnestly to his Lordship the Secretary of State for India, that, though the department suggested by the Commissioners is very important, his Lordship will not adopt the mode which the Commissioners have suggested with good intentions, but with thoughtlessness about the rights and needs of India; that, with the exception of some thoroughly qualified necessary Europeans at the head, the whole agency ought to be Native, on the lines described by the Commissioners. There can be no lack of Natives of the kind required, or it would be a very poor compliment indeed to the educational exertions of the English rulers during the past half-century.

A new danger is now threatening India. Hitherto India's wealth *above* the surface of the land has been draining away to England; now the wealth *under* the surface of the land will also be taken away, and India lies prostrate and unable to help herself. England has taken away her capital. That same capital will be brought to take away all such mineral wealth of the country as requires the application of large capital and expensive machinery. With the exception of the employment of the lower class of bodily and mental labourers, the larger portion of the produce will, in several shapes, be eaten up and carried away by the Europeans, first as servants, and next in profits and dividends; and poor India will have to thank her stars that she will get some crumbs in the lower employments of her children. And great will be the sounding of trumpets of the wealth found in India, and the blessings conferred on India, just as we have sickeningly dinned into our ears, day after day, about railways, foreign trade, etc.

Now, this may sound very strange, that, knowing full well the benefits of foreign capital to any country, I should complain of its going to India. There is, under present circumstances, one great difference in the modes in which English capital goes to every other country and India. To every other country English capitalists *lend*, and there is an end of their connexion with the matter. The *people* of the country use and enjoy the benefit of the capital in every way, and pay to the capitalists their interest or dividend, and, as some capitalists know to their cost, not even that. But with India the case is quite different. English capitalists do not merely lend, but with their capital they themselves invade the country. The produce of the capital is mostly eaten up by their own countrymen, and, after that, they carry away the rest in the shape of profits and dividends. The people themselves of the country *do not* derive the same benefit which is derived by every other country from English capital. The guaranteed railways not only ate up everything in this manner, but compelled India to make up the guaranteed interest also from her produce. The remedy then was adopted of making State railways. Now, under the peculiar circumstances of India's present prostration, State works, would be, no doubt, the best means of securing to India the benefits of English capital. But the misfortune is that the same canker eats into the State works also— the same eating up of the substance by European employés. The plan by which India can be really benefitted would be that all kinds of public works or mines, or all works that require capital, be undertaken by the State, with English capital and *Native* agency, with so many thoroughly competent Europeans at the head as may be absolutely necessary.

Supposing that there was even extravagance or loss, Government making up any deficiency in the interest of the loans from general revenue, will not matter much, though there is no reason why, with proper care, a Native agency cannot be formed good enough for efficient and economic working. Anyhow, in such a case the people of India will then really derive the benefit of English capital, as every other country does, with the certainty of English capitalists getting their interest from the Government, who have complete control over the revenues of India, and can, without fail, provide for the interest.

For some time, therefore, and till India, by a change in the present destructive policy of heavy European agency, has revived, and is able to help herself in a free field, it is necessary that all great undertakings which India herself is unable to carry out, for developing the resources of the country, should be undertaken by the State, but carried out chiefly by Native agency, and by preparing Natives for the purpose. Then will India recover her blood from every direction. India sorely needs the aid of English capital; but it is English *capital* that she needs, and not the English invasion to come also and eat up both capital and produce.

As things are taking their course at present with regard to the gold mines, should they prove successful great will be the trumpeting of India's increased wealth; whilst, in reality, it will all be carried away by England.

In the United States the people of the country enjoy all the benefits of their mines and public works with English capital, and pay to England her fair interest; and in cases of failure of the schemes, while the people have enjoyed the benefit of the capital, sometimes both capital and interest are gone. The schemes fail, and the lenders of capital may lament, but the people have enjoyed the capital and the produce as far as they went.

I have no doubt that, in laying my views plainly before the Secretary of State, my motives or sentiments towards the British rule will not be misunderstood. I believe that the result of the British rule *can be* a blessing to India and a glory to England—a result worthy of the foremost and most humane nation on the face of the earth. I desire that this should take place, and I therefore lay my humble views before our rulers without shrinking.

Part 6

RAILWAYS AND THE SPREAD
OF EPIDEMIC DISEASE

40

R. SENIOR WHITE, 'STUDIES IN MALARIA AS IT AFFECTS RAILWAYS', RAILWAY BOARD TECHNICAL PAPER 258 (PART I), (REPRINT), *INDIAN MEDICAL GAZETTE*, LXII (CALCUTTA: GOVERNMENT OF INDIA, 1928), 55–59

Malaria Research Officer, Indian Research Fund Association, Formerly Malariologist, Bengal-Nagpur Railway

FROM the point of view of the Malariologist a railway is a Euclidean straight line. It might therefore be thought that any attempt to control malaria along its route would be foredoomed to futility, unless powers of entry and work on surrounding property were granted. For this reason very little has in the past been attempted towards the control of malaria on railways. The railhead port of Talaimanaar on the Ceylon Government Railway was reported on by James (1912), but no anti-mosquito measures other than screening seem to have been undertaken. The Khulna branch of the Eastern Bengal Railway was the scene of a quinine campaign (Eastern Bengal Railway press, 1925), which, as might have been expected, proved futile, though some valuable statistics and experience were gained from it. Though the St. Louis South-Western Rail Road in the United States of America have conducted anti-malaria operations at a cost of $800, (Rs. 2,400, approx.), per mile of track with excellent results, it was not until the writer was appointed Malariologist to the Bengal-Nagpur Railway that any Indian railway made any serious attempt to deal with the malaria affecting it. It is hoped that the account of various anti-malaria operations given in the present paper will convince the administrations of the various railways of India that the control of malaria as it affects their operations is not only practicable, but economic.

I.—Malaria during railway construction

Whilst it is a commonplace of the text-books that railway construction in the tropics, with its 'aggregation of labour,' is nearly always associated with fulminant epidemics of the disease, yet in the past little has been done to obviate such happenings. Medical aid to the victims has usually been liberally forthcoming, but this is of small comfort to the engineer whose work has been brought to a standstill. "A death a sleeper" is a vivid generalization on the happenings on, for instance, the building of the ghat section of the Great Indian Peninsula Railway, the Beira Railway in East Africa, the Indo-Ceylon connection of the Ceylon Government Railway, though it is doubtful if even approximate figures exist to prove or disprove such assertions.

The Amda-Jamda' branch of the Bengal-Nagpur Railway, built through the hills of the Singhbhum district of Chota Nagpur in 1923–24, proved yet again what is the price of opening up communications in hyper-endemic country without the help of the expert. In the worst length the Engineer staff were doubled, in the hope that one officer out of each pair would be in a state to do duty; labour died, or bolted, in such numbers that work was finally undertaken by a Pioneer Regiment from the Frontier. In the circumstances it is hardly to be wondered at that the cost of the branch line considerably exceeded the estimate.

It was shortly after this unfortunate experience that the same Railway had to undertake another construction in notoriously malarious country, namely the Raipur-Vizianagram Railway, which is being built to serve the new Imperial port of Vizagapatam. Of the 309 miles separating the two towns 261 have to be constructed on one sanction.

The malaria map of India, (Christophers, 1926), leaves a large patch on the route of this railway blank, 'Probably hyper-endemic hill areas.' As will be shown at the end of this section, investigations by the writer have partly filled this gap in our ignorance, but meantime it suffices to be said that between seventy and eighty miles of the route lie within 'The Agency,' as described by the inhabitants of the Northern Circars, or in 'Madras,' as used by the people of the Orissa Feudatory States.

There are malarious tracts of general evil reputation in many parts of India. The Terai of the Eastern Himalayas, the Northern slopes of the Khasia Hills behind Gauhati, Lahore Cantonments (Mian Mir), most of Chota Nagpur in Bihar and Orissa, the foot of the Nilgiris, (where, incidentally, the station staff of Kallar leave for healthier quarters by the last train of the day and are brought back by the first train in the morning), to name but a few, are all notorious for their 'feverishness,' but it is probable that no locality in the whole Indian Empire has such a dreadful reputation as 'The Agency.' "Completed Agency Service" is an asterisked qualification in the Madras medical cadre list! The planter goes to the Duars expecting malaria, the Forest Officer of Singhbhum faces it with some equanimity, but 'going to the Agency' in Northern districts of Madras is a matter for bated breath! Though it may be legitimately argued that 'wind-up' to this extent has a psychological effect in inducing any attack to assume an ultra-serious nature, there is still no doubt that this is the largest hyper-endemic tract in the Empire. How serious conditions really are is set forth in cold statistics in the report of Perry (1915).

The experience of the surveys for the Raipur-Vizianagram Railway was fully confirmative of the deservedness of the evil reputation of this district. (*a*) The whole route was surveyed by officers of the now defunct East Coast Railway in 1883–86. Two years were spent on reconnaissance before a route was found across the Eastern Ghats practicable for a railway, two years more in actual survey. The records of this party are apparently lost, and what casualties they suffered is not known, but the writer stumbled on the grave of one of the engineers of the party, twenty miles south of the Madras frontier, in December 1926, being the next occasion since 1886 when the whole route was traversed by railway officers. (*b*) In 1897 a further survey was started from the southern end also by the East Coast Railway. This party broke down from malaria 99 miles from Vizianagram, or after traversing barely forty miles of the hyper-endemic zone. (*c*) In 1907 yet another party essayed a re-survey, but likewise broke down after achieving only two miles more than their predecessors of ten years previous. (*d*) Lastly, in 1923, the twenty-four miles across the summit of the range were again re-surveyed. By this time the railway from Vizianagram to Parvatipuram (48 miles), was opened, and motor transport was available to a certain extent. Three months only, January to March, were spent in the field, and the Engineer in charge of the party left railhead with all his staff duplicated. On completion, only 25 per cent. were effective.

Meanwhile, another survey across Jeypore State to the west of the line under consideration had cost the lives of two officers of the party.

Such was the record when actual construction was sanctioned in 1925. Work was started from both ends, but the Northern end, from Raipur, (District IV), being in healthy country for the first thirty miles, need not be considered at present.

The District Engineer for the Southern end, (District I), took up his station in May 1925. In consultation with the Assistant Surgeon in charge of his medical arrangements he pitched a large base camp four miles north of Parvatipuram between a hill foot and a tank. All went well. The rains arrived, streams rushed down from the hills above, and nothing happened. Early in September of that year the writer was appointed, and proceeded to Parvatipuram. He had been assured in Calcutta that the unhealthy country did not begin for at least ten miles north of this base camp. The rains were practically over and the whole area at the hill foot was a mass of seepage, which with the cessation of actual precipitation was starting breeding. The grass of the camp was squashy under foot, and footprints filled up with water, which swarmed with larvæ, mostly *A. culicifacies*. Within a quarter of a mile of the camp was a village, spleen rate 25 per cent. It was obvious that, with the approaching hatching out of the first generation, an outbreak was impending. Accordingly, before any further work could be undertaken, this ill-placed base camp, which with its stores was too large to move, had to be protected. The plan for this, as typical of the protection scheme subsequently evolved for actual construction operations, is given in Chart II.

Even before drains could be cut promiscuous oiling of the principal areas was undertaken, the drains being cut subsequently to concentrate the seepage water and to dry out the intervening land. It will be noticed that hill foot contour drains were not used. They would have been far better, and far less expensive in upkeep than the herring-bone system put in, but speed was in this case the essence of the contract. Labour, at that time, was scarce and poor, as no actual importations had yet been made and the local labourer is disinclined for hard work of any kind, whilst contour drains would have involved difficulties with the stony hill foot soil. As it was, fresh seepages were always breaking out between drains, involving the putting in of additional ones, as is seen by those marked 'A' on the plan. However, the crude scheme worked, and an outbreak in the camp was averted, although the nearby village unprotected on three sides, suffered its usual autumn outbreak. This was not only valuable as a demonstration to the engineers of what would have otherwise happened to the camp, but served as a very convenient source of blood films, as free medicines were offered in return for blood at the laboratory and medical tents.

Having secured a protected base, the next point, which, of course, had the Malariologist been appointed sufficiently early, should have been the initial undertaking, was an examination of malarial incidence along the route. As at that period opening of construction was only authorized for the first thirty-eight miles from railhead, detailed survey was only carried out so far, conditions beyond not being examined at that time.

The information thus elicited was fully confirmatory of the appearance and reputation of the district, though disturbing to the engineers, who imagined that in working up to mile 86 they were running through fairly healthy country, halting at the edge of the real danger zone. A five mile length was discovered (mile 62 to 67), where the spleen rates are as high as they are likely to be anywhere in the world.

Armed with this information the Acting Chief Medical Officer and the writer in conference with the heads of the Engineering Department and the District Engineer, proposed that when actual work was started the contractors should not be allowed to string out their labour all along their lengths, as is apparently the invariable custom in railway construction, but should be forced to concentrate them in camps, at the rate of two camps per three mile length, on sites capable of anti-mosquito protection, to be selected by the Malariologist, in consultation with the District Engineer in respect of convenience for work, where practicable. This method of working was novel to the contractors, who are usually men from Kutch, of no particular education, and accustomed to use up their coolies as they do their tools, with no concern about their health until this reaches a point when it affects them financially, for which reason a certain amount of opposition was incurred, and for a considerable time unauthorized camps kept springing up, which had to be dealt with.

It was manifestly impossible to carry out a detailed mosquito survey of the whole thirty-eight miles prior to choosing sites, and such had to be selected 'by eye' in the first instance. Detailed surveys of selected sites were then undertaken as fast as possible, and protection plans for each drawn out and formulated. Owing to the necessity of providing each of a dozen contractors with at least one camp from which he could commence operations and locate his coolies, who were commencing to arrive, much dodging up and down the route was necessary. This, in a country with unbridged roads in so vile a state of disrepair as North Madras was very wasteful of precious time. In spite of a repair shop at base camp, cars were continually going out of action through the appalling tracks over which they were run, whilst late rains often brought down floods which rendered all or any of the unbridged rivers impassable for a day or more. Had more than thirty-eight miles been commenced at one time it would have been impossible to keep pace with demands for camps and simultaneously oversee actual drainage and oiling operations, indicating that in future, camps should be sited and protection therefor organized well ahead of actual importations of labour. As it was, contractors located in some comparatively healthy lengths had to be left without protection for some weeks, with more or less ill effects. It must, however, be remembered that all this organization work was a new thing, without any precedent save Panama, and there was no financial liberty on the scale of the great American undertaking.

Immediately following survey and drainage operations it was necessary to organize oiling. This was done with crude oil, applied to running water by swabs previously soaked in it staked in the channel or by spraying machines of the 'Four Oaks' pattern. Much of the country was very rough, and the coolie needed a free hand for movement. The type with the self-contained pump with which pressure is raised prior to being carried was therefore preferable to the type in which one hand pumps whilst the other directs the spray. The 3-gallon capacity machine, charged, was also found rather too heavy for use in rough country, and the 2½-gallon machine was preferred. Its smaller capacity, however, involves greater waste of time whilst further supplies are brought from the sub-depôt established at each camp. Machines constantly needed minor repairs, and the staff was placed under an ex-sergeant of Royal Engineers as chief inspector, which class of man alone seems to have sufficient organizing capacity and initiative to carry out the details of a rather complex organization.

As soon as possible returns were started to keep check on the results of the work. These were never completely satisfactory, and, in the writer's opinion, never could be so without undue expenditure. The medical staff of a construction consists of an Assistant Surgeon with each District Engineer, and one Sub-Assistant Surgeon per twenty mile length, and it is manifestly impossible that each man should visit each of a dozen camps daily and make out a sick return, in addition to running an out-patient dispensary at his headquarters. All that could be arranged for was that each contractor should submit a daily return of the approximate number of coolies in each camp and the number of cases of fever occurring during the day. *Bokhar* is an elastic term covering many other diseases than malaria. Again, great difficulty was experienced in getting the contractor to record only fresh cases each day, and in several cases deliberate falsification was proved, in the hope of getting enhanced rates of work such as are sometimes paid in ultra-feverish country. Finally, reliance in any form on the contractors had to be abandoned, and resort had to be made to the Sub-Assistant Surgeons obtaining 'figures' once each week by enquiry from the coolies themselves. In any case, one thing is certain that the statistics do not err on the side of under-statement!

Even against this handicap, the results amply justified the measures taken. For ten months for which records had been obtained up to the time of the writer's departure for other work, the daily incidence of malaria never reached 2 per cent. of the total strength, a figure which the engineers considered negligible. It may be claimed, in fact, that construction through this hyper-endemic tract has proceeded with a lower morbidity from malaria than any large engineering work hitherto undertaken in India. The mortality from the disease has been *nil*.

These results, moreover, were not obtained at any inordinate cost. Once the organization was got into working order, which took between three and four months, the upkeep charges, which consisted of the salaries of the inspector and his assistant, the drain maintenance and oiling coolies' pay, oil, and the running of a vanette car for travelling, together with a proportion of the cost of the malariologist and his establishment at headquarters, only amounted to Rs. 18 per mile of construction per month, a negligible amount in the vast sums involved in railway construction.

Several instances occurred indicating what would have happened had the ordinary construction methods been followed in such country, and, I think, proving the financial justification for anti-malaria measures on work of this nature. (*i*) Camp Rambudrapurain at mile 60 had to be located too near the village of that name, with a spleen rate of 60 per cent. There was a particularly contumarious contractor on this length who during an interrogaum flatly refused to carry out the orders of the malaria section. The Assistant Engineer acting in charge of the District engaged him in a correspondence instead of taking instant measures. A fortnight was wasted by all concerned except the mosquitoes! An outbreak occurred and about forty coolies bolted. (*ii*) A camp, (not shown on the map), was put up at mile 61½, mainly to house coolies engaged in transport of stores across the Solawa nullah nearby whilst it was impassable for lorries during the monsoon. Owing to a misunderstanding it was not protected immediately. The fever rate was 12 per cent. On starting protection it fell in two months to 3 per cent.

Railway construction has the further disadvantage from the malariologist's point of view that conditions are never static. The camps were surveyed and protected on the original lie of the country. In few did conditions as shown on the plans endure for long. Streams were diverted for engineering purposes, embankments caused pools behind them, seepages were exposed by borrow pits. Fresh breeding places were thus created almost in a night, and once the writer had ceased to reside in and devote his whole time in the district, the sanitary inspector had to meet every emergency as it arose, without waiting for the next visit of the malariologist.

Only a man of exceptional initiative and experience can successfully fill such a post of Sanitary inspector, and though, on subsequent inspection, the writer at times found that water which could only have produced harmless species like *vagus* was being treated, it was extremely rarely that he found a dangerous breeding place overlooked. Such never failed to declare its presence by a rise in the fever rate of the camp affected within a fortnight. A small outbreak at camp mile 591 was traced to some seepage on a hillside in dense bush that had been overlooked in the original survey. It was then just dry, but spraying all the huts after temporary evacuation was necessary to deal with the infected anophelines which they harboured.

It must be also remembered that the majority of the coolies engaged for construction work are infected prior to arrival, and [Illegible Text] numerous gametocyte carriers among them. Many camps showed one or two days enhanced malaria incidence following rain or cold snaps. In every case absolutely no breeding could be found around them, nor anophelines in the huts. They could only have been in the nature of general relapses. How little the *kutcha* huts used by coolies on constructions afford protection from wet or cold and how suitable they are, with their leafplait walls, for barbouring anophelines, Fig. 2 shows.

A failure may be as in tructive as a success, and the following is an account of one such. Thirty miles north of Parvatipuram lies Ravaguda, one of the two small towns of the Vizagapatani Agency Tracts. The spleen rate of the town is in the neighbourhood of 40 per cent., which is low compared with many of the surrounding villages. The Government dak bungalow is nearly a mile away from the town, and has a most evil reputation amongst touring officers of Government. An Assistant Engineer with staff took up his quarters in and around it at the start of construction, and suffered no ill effects during the monsoon. It was not until early in December that this place could be attended to. The bungalow is situated on a cape of high land, with the gorge of the Rayaguda river, on one side and a deep ravine with nearly vertical cliffs on the other.

The river gorge breeds a certain amount of *A. culicifacies* in backwaters with *Spirogyra* after the rains subside, but the ravine is much the more dangerous, being full of setpage sprangs at the foot of the cliffs, which collect into a small stream with a *Ranunculus*-like plant interwaven with *Spirogyra* growing thickly on its edges. An irrigation channel, grass edged, takes off and follows the stream, and some of the rice fields near the mouth of the ravine are perennially wet through seepage. The whole area swarmed with *A. funesing*. The measures taken consisted of clearing off all the marginal vegetation of the stream, (this had to be reported almost weekly), and rough weeding the seepage area, so that the oil had a chance of reaching the larva, but the rice field, with unreaped stubble over mud so soft and deep as to render it largely impassable, defied protection by oiling. That a certain amount of improvement was affected is shown by the fact that the engineer and his staff escaped serious malaria, but the health of the former gradually went downhill, and he lead to be invalided. To test the efficacy of the control the writer slept without a not for one night only in the middle of the monsoon in the dâk bungalow, and contracted benign [Illegible Text] malaria, but the oiling was two days overdue owing to flooded rivers rendering earlier arrival impossible, and as the oil was being washed away almost as soon as applied at that time of year, it is possible that more [Illegible Text] than usual were managing to breed up. The place can only be deals with efficiently by considerable engineering works involving either transforming the ravine into a lake by a series of dams to bury the seepage, or the lowering of the entire ravine level to dry out the margins of the stream and get the seepage into the main channel, (Fig. 4). As the whole bottom is sand, this latter would need never ending upkeep. In addition the rice land containing seepage would have to be [Illegible Text] and effectively under-drained. Here we have an instance where temporary methods of control fail.

The assistant engineer stationed at this place was moved, when failure was proved, to a healthy and protectable site north of the town.

41

J. A. SINTON, 'THE EFFECTS OF MALARIA ON RAILWAYS', *RECORDS OF THE MALARIA SURVEY OF INDIA* 5, 4 (DECEMBER 1935), 471–476

In those countries where malaria prevails, the tax which this disease levies upon railway systems in all stages of their activities has been noted by many observers. Malaria may not only delay for many years the initiation of great schemes of transport, with associated development of natural resources, but may also have a very marked effect in hindering the construction of railways and in increasing the cost of such work. Even after they have been constructed, malaria may add largely to their operation costs, from its effects in reducing the number and the quality of the available labour force. The latter may also require a higher wage and greater privileges on account of its exposure to sickness. This leads to an increase in transport charges, and so an inhibition of the proper development of the natural resources of the area served by the railroad. These factors give rise to a vicious cycle whereby not only is the interest obtained from the capital outlay small, or negligible, but also the high transport charges lead to a diminished traffic, which has little encouragement to increase and so to swell the profits of the line.

The malarious nature of a district may prevent the development of railway facilities in a locality for many years. This may be due not only to the difficulties encountered in surveying the route for such lines, to a realisation of the enormous difficulties which the disease would place in the way of obtaining and retaining an adequate labour force for the construction, and to the great expense which this would entail, but also to the difficulties which the disease would place in the way of the commercial development of the area served and upon which factor the profits of the railway would depend.

Senior-White and Newman (1932) state that 'during the survey of the line at Laing-Biang (Indo-China) in 1900, there was in the eight months a mortality of 77 per cent in the Europeans and 80 per cent in the natives'. The former author (Senior-White, 1928) has described the difficulties and disasters that malaria caused to the parties which attempted to survey the course of a railway line through the very malarious hill tracts of the Madras Presidency from Vizianagram to Raipur in 1883, 1897 and 1907. These parties were unable to complete the survey because of the ravages of malaria. The successful party in 1923 spent only 3 months in the field (January to March) and 'the engineer in charge of the party left railhead with all his staff duplicated. On completion, only 25 per cent were effective'. 'Meanwhile, another survey across Jeypore State to the west of the line under consideration had cost the lives of two officers of the party'. The difficulties encountered in the early surveys helped to hold back the construction of this line for 40 years.

While malaria may place great obstacles in the path of survey parties, these difficulties only afford some indication of the obstruction which this disease may cause to the construction gangs. The financial loss at the former stage is infinitesimal as compared with that in the latter.

'It will probably be admitted by all in a position to judge that there is nothing so expensive as ill health among the labour forces on the construction of a line, it is impossible to estimate the financial loss to Government of say two or three good construction engineers being invalided home on account of a preventable disease. In how many instances are estimates exceeded and difficulties multiplied tenfold due to sickness amongst the labour? Therefore, from a business point of view, everything should be done to maintain the whole of the employés, from the Chief Engineer down to the lowest paid coolie in a good and efficient state of health' (Clemesha, 1917).

'Whilst it is a commonplace of the textbooks that railway construction in the tropics, with its "aggregation of labour", is nearly always associated with fulminant epidemics of the disease (malaria), yet in the past little has been done to obviate such happenings' . . . . ' "A death a sleeper" is a vivid generalisation on the happenings' (Senior-White, 1928). As instances of such events in other countries, Senior-White (1928)[1] quotes the construction of the Beira Railway in East Africa, and the Indo-Ceylon connection of the Ceylon Government Railway Bostock (1911) notes that the heavy death rate during the building of the Pretoria-Delagoa Bay line forced malaria upon public notice. Thomas (1911) draws attention to difficulties which malaria placed in the way of the building of a line along the Madeira River, to connect Bolivia and Brazil—'Several attempts have been made to build this line, and each time malaria has raged among the workers. A most virulent form of fever occurs, which has at times incapacitated 50 per cent to 80 per cent of the total working force'. Senior-White and Newman (1932)[*] also cite the instances of the Congo and the Indo-China Railways:—

'In Yunnan, in 1905, in the region of the Lower Namti, in 5,000 coolies from Tien-Tsin who were working on the first 15½ miles, there were about 3,000 casualties, almost all due to malaria. Many died on the spot and gangs abandoned the place, dying along the road while they attempted to flee from this murderous locality. In 1907, in a gang of 170 which had arrived a month and a half earlier, there were 18 dead, 60 ill and 40 bolted. In another gang of 150, 35 were gravely ill, 50 were hardly in a state to stand up and 51 had run away'.

James (1920) reports that, in railway work at a port in Ceylon, the area acquired an evil reputation because of malaria. From the statistics available, it would appear that an ordinary unskilled labourer only put in about 18 working days in the month, and the death rate among the labour force was 46 per mille of the average daily strength.

India has not been without her tragedies and difficulties during railway construction in the past. McCombie Young (1911) remarks upon the very high mortality among the coolies employed in building a branch of the Eastern Bengal State Railway through the Malda district of Bengal in 1903–1907.[2] Clemesha (1917), in speaking of the construction of the line between Kishangunj and Siliguri in Bengal, states that 'the amount of sickness and desertion on the part of the coolie labour was very high indeed, and the Railway Board are probably better acquainted than I am with the large cost of the work due to delays and enhanced rates to contractors caused by the lack of proper medical arrangements'. Denham (1925) reports a high incidence of malaria during the construction of the Pyinmana-Taungdwingyi Railway in Burma. In one section the number of new cases of this disease in relation to the amount of labour employed was 2·4 per cent in May, but rose to 54·7 per cent in December.

Suhrawardy (1928) points out the necessity for 'reducing the incidence of the disease and the inefficiency caused by it at construction centres', while Senior-White (1928) speaks of the trouble experienced from malaria during the construction of the Ghat section of the Great Indian Peninsula Railway.

The Malaria Commission of the League of Nations (1930) mention 'the Ambda-Jambda line in Singhbhum (Orissa), notorious for the enormous toll of sick and dead from malaria during its construction'.

Senior-White (1928) gives further particulars of this line and says 'the Ambda-Jambda branch of the Bengal-Nagpur Railway, built through the hills of the Singhbhum district of Chota Nagpur in 1923–24, proved yet again what is the price of opening up communications in hyperendemic country without the help of an expert. In the worst length the engineer staff were doubled, in the hope that one officer out of each pair would be in a state to do duty; labour died, or bolted, in such numbers that work was finally undertaken by a Pioneer Regiment from the Frontier. In the circumstances it is hardly to be wondered at that the cost of the branch line considerably exceeded the estimate'. Wats (1924) also gives some details of this outbreak—'from the commencement of the work, the engineer in charge informed me, malaria was rife amongst them (the temporary military labour force) reducing their capacity to 50 per cent and at the end of the work each man had to be given 3 months' leave to recuperate his health'.

Senior-White (1928) reports upon the difficulties which malarial sickness caused in the construction of the Saranda Tunnel, also situated in the hyperendemic Singhbhum area of Orissa. This tunnel was first made in the eighties of last century. No precise information is available as to the malaria rate at that time, but from deduction this must have been very high. 'It is said that mortality and bolting among the labour so disorganised the accounts that the gangs were paid, shift by shift, as they emerged from the workings. Several of the Cornish miners who formed the subordinate tunnelling staff died of malaria, or more probably of blackwater, for which the district is notorious'. As this line serves the iron ore mines of Orissa, it was later found necessary to double the track through the tunnel. Work was started in August 1925, and in this month malaria was responsible for an incapacitation rate of 21 per cent, which rose to 34 per cent in November, when the Assistant Surgeon died of blackwater fever and the office staff was so disorganised that no further records are available until the end of the epidemic in March 1926. By this time all the non-immune labour had practically disappeared, and had been replaced by local aborigines.

These quotations give some indication of the trouble and loss which malaria may cause during the construction of railway lines in areas where malaria prevails. Even when the construction has been completed, the financial and labour difficulties of the company are not finished, for this disease may exact a heavy toll upon the health and efficiency of the staff.

The epidemic of malaria in the Punjab in 1908 was first brought prominently to public notice by the sudden disorganisation of the train service, due to fever among the employees of the large railway centre, Lahore. At Bombay, 'the guards, porters and sweepers belonging to the G. I. P. Railway were attacked, and so many of the former were prostrated that at one time during the height of the epidemic (1908) as many as ten of the local trains had to be cancelled' (Bentley, 1911b).

Apart from such exceptional conditions, malaria causes a serious obstruction to the efficient and economical working of railway systems in many parts of India. The Lumding Railway Junction in the forest area of Assam was at one time so malarious that its abandonment was seriously considered.

A special investigation of malarial conditions in the railway colony at Myitnge in Burma was undertaken by Williams (1919) on account of the wide prevalence of the disease affecting especially the labour in the railway workshops. Denham (1925) reports that, on one section of the line in Burma, the percentage of railway employees attending hospital monthly for malaria varied from 3 in February to 19·2 in July.

Several medical officers of the Eastern Bengal Railway have drawn attention to the losses which malaria causes to the workers and the administration of this line which serves a very malarious tract of country. Suhrawardy (1928) points out the danger that malaria may break out in a serious form at important and large stations, and 'cause inefficiency amongst important classes of our running and operating staff'. Bishop (1926) studied the effects of malaria upon the staff of the Khulna branch of the same line from September 1924 to March 1925. He reports that, out of a staff of 861 individuals and 1,027 dependents, about 27·3 per cent suffered from primary attacks of the disease, and 11·0 per cent with recurrent attacks. In 18 stations with a staff less than 15 persons each, 50 per cent of this population suffered from malaria during the period under review. In 6 stations with a staff of 15 to 30 persons, the percentage was 40; in 3 stations with a staff of 30 to 100, it was 23 per cent, and in 2 with a staff over 100 it was 16 per cent.[3] Sladen (1927) records that, at Ishurdi station during the month of September 1925, there were 3,207 days of certified sickness from all causes among a staff of 617 individuals, and, of these lost days, 2,565, or more than 4 per person, were due to malarial sickness. One year later, after anti-malarial measures had been in operation, the total loss was only 696 days during the same month, of which 53 were due to malaria. Sladen estimates that the cost of a man being off-duty from sickness is Re. 1 per diem (this he thinks an underestimate). Taking this figure it means that the Eastern Bengal Railway lost, at Ishurdi alone, Rs. 2,565 during the one month of September 1925. This officer also points out the loss to the railway of sick leave to its staff—'These long absences from duty were and still are a heavy cost to the Administration'.

The subject of the losses due to malaria was also investigated by Rao (1928) in the Lalmanirhat district of the same railway. He estimates that the loss was Rs. 27,367 in this one district during 1924, from days lost due to malarial sickness among the staff, in 1925 it was Rs. 35,957, and in 1926 it was Rs. 24,248, allowing the financial loss to be Re. 1 per diem. The Agent of this line states that, during 1923, out of 48,000 employees, the number of sick treated as outpatients by the railway medical staff was 89,904, of which about one-third were due to malaria (Sladen, 1927). During 1925 there were more than 120,000 cases of sickness amongst the staff and their dependents. 'The railway lost the service of each member of the staff for one week, or, in the aggregate, nine hundred work years, as a consequence'.

Senior-White (1928) gives details of the difficulties which malaria caused at Dangaoposi station on the Bengal-Nagpur Railway—'Things began to go wrong in August, when the line had been open five months, with the onset of the monsoon. Within a few weeks conditions had become so bad that the station was almost at a standstill' . . . . 'At the end of October there was hardly a single member of the staff who had escaped malaria, which was still raging with almost undiminished intensity. Relief men were doing most of the work and going down themselves'. He gives figures showing the days lost, the percentage of the staff attacked, etc., which 'indicate how complete was the disorganisation owing to absences'. He points out that such outbreaks are characterised by an inordinate delay in getting the traffic moving again when they affect important centres. He also records that 'within the last three years at least three of the largest railways in this country have experienced similar outbreaks, all of them on a large scale, affecting more important division points than the one here described'.

Notes

1 These authors have described in some detail the relationship of malaria to many phases of railway activity.

2 McCombie Young (1911) attributes the epidemic conditions, which appeared among the local population of the Malda district at this time, to the 'tropical aggregation of labour' on the railway works. Clemesha (1917) quotes other instances where railway construction works have been responsible for a heavy malarial incidence in their neighbourhood.

3 The cost of anti-malarial operations *per capita* of the population is greater at small than at large stations. As pointed out by Senior-White (1928), in such small stations the absence of a man for duty is more felt, and occasions greater disorganisation—maybe in main line train-working—than at larger stations, whilst relief is less easily obtainable.

42

R. NATHAN, *THE PLAGUE IN INDIA, 1896, 1897,* 4 VOLS. (SIMLA: GOVERNMENT CENTRAL PRINTING OFFICE, 1898), I, PP. 291–297

Measures to prevent the spread of infection by land

Discussion of principles—land quarantine and the stoppage of railway traffic

The early efforts made to prevent the spread of plague infection by persons travelling by land are described in succeeding sections of this chapter. The whole subject of the principles governing these efforts came under careful discussion in February and March 1897, in connection with proposals to impose quarantine against the Bombay Presidency or to prohibit third class railway traffic from stations within the Presidency.

On the 13th February the special Calcutta Medical Board urged that all persons leaving Bombay, Karachi or other infected places should be detained for ten days under observation. The Government of Bombay then suggested the expediency of imposing quarantine against the Bombay Presidency, posts being established on the border at suitable places, generally a long distance on the Bombay side of the frontier. It was also suggested by the Government of Bombay that third class railway passenger traffic might be temporarily suspended along certain sections of the line of communication. On the 4th March the Lieutenant-Governor of the Punjab proposed that, plague having broken out in Sukkur, an endeavour should be made to check the advance of the disease into the Punjab by the imposition of ten days' quarantine at some place within the southern portion of the province, cordons being thrown out at right angles to the railway and river extending some distance west into the Dehra Ghazi Khan district and east into the Bahawalpur State. On the 16th March the Agent to the Governor General in Rajputana telegraphed a proposal that, plague having become endemic in the native state of Palanpur near the Rajputana border, people from Palanpur should be prevented from travelling northwards by rail.

The Government of India having carefully considered these proposals, and having taken the opinion of their sanitary adviser, decided that there were insuperable objections both to the imposition of land quarantine and to the prohibition of third class railway traffic from infected districts. In arriving at these conclusions, the Governor General in Council was mainly influenced by the following considerations.

All experience in India, including that of an attempt that had recently been made by the Commissioner in Sind to impose quarantine at Sukkur, showed that the imposition of absolute land quarantine was ineffectual. In a previous chapter the failure to protect the Ahmedabad district by quarantine during the 1812 to 1821 epidemic has been noticed, and also Dr. Ranken's condemnation against the strict land quarantine imposed during the Pali outbreak of 1836 and the failure of that quarantine to protect the route through Merwara. In 1876 a committee was appointed in the Punjab to consider the question of land quarantine against cholera, and reported that strict land quarantine was impossible in India.

The Government of India were convinced that an endeavour to quarantine the Bombay Presidency, a large portion of which was infected when the discussion took place, would be no more efficacious than previous efforts of a like nature. No extensive cordon in India can be expected to be proof against attempts to evade it, and an endeavour to establish a cordon along the great length of the Bombay frontier could not possibly succeed. Besides being ineffectual the attempt would be likely to lead to mischievous results. In the first place, it would distract attention from the important measures of observation and sanitary improvement. In the second place, it would occasion an unjustifiable amount of hardship and suffering, and it would give opportunities for oppression and extortion. In the third place the aggregation of large bodies of people on the borders of the infected area under circumstances rendering proper sanitary administration very difficult or even impossible presents conditions very favourable to the spread of disease and may occasion serious epidemic outbreaks. The imposition of land quarantine is also contrary to the accepted principles for the treatment of epidemic disease. The Dresden Sanitary Conference of 1893 was opposed to land quarantine; and declared (Chapter V, Annexure I) that only persons suffering from cholera or presenting cholera-like symptoms should be detained. That conference was composed of the delegates of a number of European states possessing national frontiers, customs lines, and national and trade interests, all tending to facilitate quarantine regulations, and it declared against land quarantine under circumstances far more favourable to its adoption than those which exist in India. The delegates of Her Majesty's Government at the Sanitary Conference held at Venice in February and March 1897 to devise measures to prevent the spread of plague were instructed to urge the acceptance of the principles of the Dresden Convention, and in the convention framed by that conference those principles were re-affirmed. In chapter I, section III of the regulations prescribed by the Venice Convention, it is stated that modern methods of disinfection should be substituted for land quarantine; and in chapter II, section V, the rule is laid down that land quarantine should no longer be enforced, and that only persons presenting symptoms of plague should be detained. After prescribing these principles the conference made the concession, in order to cover the difficulties which were likely to be experienced by certain

Governments in preventing the importation of plague into their countries by land routes, that during the prevalence of plague every country had the right to close its land frontiers either in part or in whole against all traffic.

The Government of India also considered that the suggestion to stop third class railway traffic from infected districts could not be adopted. The precaution could be evaded by breaking the railway by a road journey across the frontier. It would make invidious distinctions between classes and would cause great inconvenience and hardship. It would also be ineffective, inasmuch as it would offer no check to the spread of the disease otherwise than by railway, and would not prevent the chance of infection being carried by persons choosing to take first or second class tickets. It would also greatly increase the chance of infection being carried by other means than the railway. Prevented from travelling by rail the inhabitants would scatter over the country-side, and find an egress by ways which would render inspection and control difficult or impossible. The stoppage of third class railway traffic is, equally with the imposition of absolute land quarantine, opposed to the principles of the Dresden Convention of 1893 and the Venice Convention of 1897.

Guided by these considerations, the Government of India negatived the proposals for the imposition of land quarantine and the partial stoppage of railway traffic, and in the place of these measures prescribed the precautions detailed in the succeeding portions of this chapter. They stated that all travellers from infected districts should be inspected by a medical officer, and that any persons deemed likely to carry infection should be detained under observation in suitable segregation shelter and under proper sanitary supervision until the danger of their spreading infection was past. In determining whether travellers should be detained or not, inspecting officers were directed to exercise the widest discretion, and they were instructed that any person who was at all suspicious either by reason of his appearance, symptoms or the dirty condition of his clothes or effects should not be permitted to proceed without being placed under observation. It was also prescribed that the class of persons, who when they enter a town can neither be traced nor depended on to give information of plague, should be treated as suspicious. Similar instructions were given with regard to persons, such as labourers and emigrants, who travel in bodies. With these precautions were combined measures for the disinfection of the personal effects of travellers likely to carry infection, for the supervision at their destination of travellers from infected districts, and generally for the detection of plague cases on their occurring in any town or village in the threatened provinces. The Government of India hoped that these measures would protect the rest of India against the Bombay Presidency with the least possible amount of interference with intercourse and without avoidable hardship. The established fact that isolated cases of plague are not difficult to stamp out if they are at once detected and due precautions taken, lent additional force to this expectation, which was on the whole justified by the result.

In a telegram, dated the 17th March, the Government of Bombay, whilst accepting the decision of the Government of India against the proposal to impose general quarantine against the Bombay Presidency, urged that land quarantine should be permitted at selected places within the Presidency. They gave the following reasons.

In accordance with the custom of the country in dealing with cholera, the inhabitants of healthy villages in the Thana and Surat districts had already imposed quarantine against villages infected with plague. In some towns and villages specially liable to infection limited quarantine had been imposed with good results by District Magistrates and Political Agents. Quarantine even if not thoroughly effective checks large movements of people, and persons flying from an area, where active remedial and disinfecting operations are anticipated, avoid going to a town where quarantine has been imposed. Quarantine need not be absolute, but it is specially important to apply it to the class of people, who when they enter a town can neither be traced nor depended on to give information of plague among them. Medical inspection, though valuable, does not detect cases that are only incubating, and the experience of the city of Bombay had shown that cleansing operations cannot check plague, unless accompanied by measures for the detection of all new cases—a procedure requiring a larger staff than can be supplied in most country towns. With regard to the stoppage of third class railway traffic, the Government of Bombay stated that it would not be carried out except in particular cases and for most cogent reasons. The Government of India recognised that the villagers in threatened districts might and should be allowed to protect themselves by voluntary action, and that it was desirable to treat as suspicious persons who on entering a town can neither be traced nor depended upon to give information of plague among them. They were, however, entirely averse from the imposition of compulsory quarantine between different local areas. They accordingly replied in a letter, dated the 29th March, that the general objections against land quarantine, which they considered to be overwhelming, hold good in the case of the imposition of quarantine by one local area against another local area. Such quarantine, it was remarked, besides being opposed to the principles which have been repeatedly affirmed by those who have most studied the subject, is sure to be ineffectual and to give rise to hardship and oppression, and may very possibly foster outbreaks of the disease. The only circumstances under which strict compulsory quarantine is possible and likely to be effectual is when the outbreak occurs in a small place, the inhabitants of which can be easily and securely isolated away from the area of infection, and then the isolation must be most carefully regulated and controlled and proper sanitary precautions must be taken. The operations at Khandraoni in the Gwalior State, described in Chapter IX, were instanced as an example of the successful imposition of strict segregation on a small scale. Here the circumstances were exceptionally favourable, inasmuch as the village is small, it was found easy to isolate the inhabitants outside the area of infection, and a commissioned medical officer of experience was deputed to the spot, and the adoption of all possible sanitary precautions and the prevention of oppression and extortion thus secured. The larger the place and the less complete its isolation, the greater become the difficulties, and the point is very soon reached when they are insurmountable.

The revised general rules for the control of remedial and preventive measures in the Bombay Presidency, issued by the Government of Bombay on the 29th March, contained the following two rules authorising the imposition of local land quarantine:—

"*Rule 26.*—District Magistrates are empowered, when they consider it necessary, to impose quarantine at any place or places against any other place or places."

"*Rule 29.*—A District Magistrate, with the sanction of the Commissioner, is empowered to prohibit inter-communication between any place and any other places."

At the request of the Government of India the Government of Bombay cancelled these rules and substituted the following rule in accordance with the prescribed principles:—

"*Rule 29.*—Plague authorities specially appointed by a Commissioner for this purpose are authorised to prevent the passage of suspicious persons from any town, village or local area, or into any town, village or local area to which this rule may be applied by the Commissioner, unless such persons have been detained in a place of observation for a period prescribed by the Commissioner: and unless, if arrangements for disinfection of their clothing, baggage, etc., have been made under the Commissioner's orders, such disinfection has been effected. Such plague authorities shall have the widest discretionary power, subject to the general or special orders of the Commissioner, to decide what person shall be considered 'suspicious' for the purposes of this rule. So long as he remains in a place of observation under this rule, no person shall be allowed to communicate, except with the permission of the plague authority, with persons outside the limits of the place. He shall obey such orders as may be issued by the plague authority for the cleanliness or protection from infection of the persons, property or quarters of the persons detained."

At the time of the recrudescence the Government of Bombay appointed a committee of experienced officers to devise, if possible, further means of preventing people from leaving infected localities and entering other places until suitable precautions have been taken with respect to them. The outcome was the issue by the Government of Bombay, on the 5th October 1897, of a set of rules to control the egress of persons from infected localities. A copy of these regulations is given in Appendix VIII. Broadly, the rules are intended to prohibit persons from travelling from infected localities to other places without a pass granted by the plague authority appointed for the purpose, and they provide that if it is considered necessary, the pass shall not be granted until the person has been disinfected and detained under observation in an observation camp. The rules further explain generally the circumstances under which passes may be granted without previous detention, and permit certain classes of persons to travel without passes. With regard to the particular case of railway traffic the rules prohibit booking within fifteen (increased by a later notification to twenty) miles of the infected locality in the case of persons who have not (*a*) a pass, if they come from the infected locality, or (*b*) a certificate from the village officer that they have been residing in the village and have just left it, if they come from a locality outside the infected area.

After a careful consideration of these rules, the Government of India were constrained to point out that their general tenor was such as to give an indirect encouragement to land quarantine, and that the plague authorities charged with working them might easily, unless their action were carefully supervised, utilise them for the imposition of such quarantine. Allusion was again made to the grave objections which had from the outset been taken to the imposition of land quarantine, and it was observed that this view had been endorsed by the recent Sanitary Conference at Venice, and must be strictly followed by the authorities in India.

The form of the rules was also considered open to objection inasmuch as it exempts from their operation certain classes of persons such, for instance, as Europeans and Government and railway servants, and, with the sanction of the District Magistrate, their families and attendants. The Government of India stated that they were totally opposed to any interference with the ordinary avocations of persons who are not sick or suspicious, but in their opinion it is wrong to exempt special classes of persons from the operation of the rules. The principle which should govern the rules is that they should apply to all classes, but that detention should be enforced only in the case of such persons as are, in the exercise of the wide discretion which should be entrusted to the responsible officer, considered suspicious.

In addition to the above criticisms the Government of India stated their conviction that these elaborate rules for the control of the movement of people from infected localities would be powerless to check the spread of the disease unless they were accompanied by stringent measures to suppress the malady within the infected areas. In the absence of such measures the compulsory detention of the inmates in infected localities tends to foster the growth of the epidemic, and to establish plague foci whence the disease may not improbably spread with even greater virulence than if no measures had been devised to prevent the egress of the inhabitants. They, therefore, impressed upon the Government of Bombay that the most important object to aim at is, not the control of the movement of the people, but the adoption of such well-devised and stringent measures as will prevent the occurrence of plague cases from engendering fresh dangerous plague centres, whence the infection will certainly spread in spite of all efforts to confine it.

43

JAMES KNIGHTON CONDON, 'RAILWAY INSPECTION', *THE BOMBAY PLAGUE, BEING A HISTORY OF THE PROGRESS OF PLAGUE IN THE BOMBAY PRESIDENCY FROM SEPTEMBER 1896 TO JUNE 1899* (BOMBAY: EDUCATION SOCIETY, 1900), PP. 141–146

The adoption of measures for the prevention of the conveyance of plague infection by Railway passengers engaged the attention of Government as early as October 1896, as soon as it was found that plague had become established, and was spreading in the Town and Island of Bombay. The authorities of the G. I. P. and B. B. & C. I. Railways were consulted as to the best method of securing adequate inspection arrangements, and before plans were developed, a telegram was received from the Government of India on the 12th October 1896, urging the adoption of a systematic examination of Railway passengers. Measures were soon organized for the systematic and careful examination of all passengers leaving Bombay by through trains at Grant Road on the B. B. & C. I. Railway line, and at Victoria Terminus on the G. I. P. Railway line, under Section 47 (*d*), 71 and 117 of the Railway Act (No. IX of 1890). Meanwhile active steps had been taken by local bodies in most of the important places in the Presidency for their own protection, and by the 22nd of October 1896 it was decided to make arrangements for the medical examination of arrivals at those places where it did not already exist. At about the same time Government were informed that the Southern Mahratta Railway Company had of their own accord instituted arrangements for the inspection of passengers travelling on their line at Poona, Miraj, Belgaum, Londa, Hubli, Gadag, and Hotgi.

Soon after (about the middle of December) the large exodus from Bombay made it impossible for the then existing staff in Bombay to cope with the work. A better and more comprehensive system, to be worked by an adequate staff, was therefore introduced; and from the 4th of February 1897 Government decided to stop the inspection of through passengers in Bombay, and, instead, to provide for the examination of all passengers in down through trains at Kalyan and Palghar Stations on the G. I. P. and B. B. & C. I. Railway lines respectively, and to employ at each of these stations a large staff of Inspecting Medical officers under Commissioned Medical officers. Observation Camps and Plague Hospitals were rapidly erected at those places, and rules giving the powers for all necessary procedure were published on the 10th February 1897, under the Epidemic Diseases Act (Act III of 1897). These rules were shortly after applied also to Bhusawal (for the protection of the Central Provinces, Bengal and Calcutta), to Ahmedabad (for the protection of Káthiáwár and Rájputána), to Hotgi (for the protection of the Southern Maratha Country, Hyderabad and Madras), and to Londa (for the protection of Goa, Mysore and Madras).

Inspection posts under these rules were subsequently established at various places in the Presidency, e. g., Poona, Rajevadi, Dhond and Manmad, and the system of barrier inspections already in force for the inspection of arrivals at important places was improved and extended.

Under Government Resolutions No. 522–88-P., dated the 1st February 1897, and 1072–542-P., dated the 27th February 1897, Surgeon-Major (now Lieut.-Colonel) A. F. W. Street, D.S.O., I.M.S., Deputy Sanitary Commissioner, who had been placed on special duty in connection with the plague in January 1897, was appointed to control and supervise all measures for the Medical Inspection of passengers by railway, in and near Bombay, and at Dhond and Manmár and other stations in the Presidency. This control he exercised until the end of April 1897, when, in consequence of an accident, he was compelled to proceed to Europe on privilege leave. The control of the Mofussil inspections then passed into the hands of District Officers, while that of those in and near Bombay were made over by Government Resolution No. 2914–2994-P., dated the 27th May 1897, to Surgeon-Captain W. E. Jennings, who supervised and controlled the measures in Bombay, until he was appointed in May 1898 to act as Health Officer of that Port.

In the Thana District, at the beginning of 1898, when medical inspection arrangements there gave way to the detention camp system, camps were opened at Bandra and Kalyan. These camps were placed in Surgeon-Major Street's charge from the 1st of February 1898 until the 6th April 1898, when they passed to the control of the Collector of Thana.

On the 23rd of February 1897, a list of infected areas was published and arrivals from such areas were compelled to furnish their names, addresses, business, &c., to the local authorities, who were thus able to maintain an efficient watch over them.

In April 1897 disinfection of the baggage of Railway passengers was instituted at Hotgi and Bhusawal. Later on, when plague had spread to several towns in the mofussil, and continued to spread, and it was found inexpedient to arrange for a wide-spread medical inspection so thorough as to influence its course materially, a number of Observation Camps were established in selected parts of the

Presidency for the purpose of disinfecting and detaining for observation all third class passengers from infected areas.

In the meanwhile, Bombay became practically free, and, to prevent its re-infection, all passengers coming into Bombay City, whether by sea or rail or road, were examined, and such as came from infected areas and were likely to carry infection, including third class passengers by rail, were detained for observation in Camps. This arrangement lasted until the recrudescence of plague in December 1897.

Local, through, barrier, frontier and mofussil inspections with disinfection Observation Camps, and other regulations to prevent infected or probably infected people from travelling, remained in force till after the middle of the year 1898, modified by local indications from time to time; as, however, there seemed little prospect of a speedy termination of the epidemic, and as it was considered that many of the regulations in force, such as detention and others, which practically close the channels of daily business, etc., were inexpedient as permanent features of plague administration, a modified system, known as the Surveillance System, was introduced in October 1898, which is laid down and described in Government Resolution No. 5772–5864-P. of 17th October 1898. The chief features of this new system were—

(a) systematic and careful medical examination of each traveller;
(b) careful disinfection of suspicious articles;
(c) correct ascertainment and record of the location of travellers after they have been permitted to enter a town;
(d) special regulations for travellers who could not be depended upon to give a trustworthy account of their residence and movements, or were suspicious, whether by reason of their appearance or symptoms, or the dirty condition of their clothes or effects.

On the 4th November 1898, Captain W. E. Jennings, I. M. S., was appointed Supervising Medical Officer, Railway Medical Inspection, to susperintend the working of the new system in the Presidency proper. His duties, detailed at length in Government Resolution No. 6130–6228-P., dated the 8th November 1898, were briefly as follows, viz.:—

(i) To report from time to time at what places medical examination should, in his opinion, be conducted and at what places discontinued;
(ii) to be responsible for the efficiency of the examination at each place, for the arrangements for the comfort of the public, and generally for carrying out the provisions of Government Resolution No. 5772–5864-P., dated the 17th October 1898;
(iii) to keep a list of infected stations for the purpose of special plague-marking of railway tickets; and
(iv) to inspect Surveillance Registers at Railway stations.

During the month of January 1899, barrier inspection of all departures from Broach Station was instituted on the B. B. & C. I. line, and in March 1899 an inspection and disinfection post was instituted at Dohad on the Godhra-Rutlám line for the protection of Rájputána and Central India, and also a barrier inspection of all arrivals at Wathar on the Southern Maratha line for the protection of Wai, Panchgani and Máhábleshwar.

Though railway inspections have been in force for more than two years, yet the plague has spread. But, the area and duration of its prevalence considered, its dissemination has been very gradual: and there can be little doubt that it has been largely checked by this measure. The following causes have combined to discount its utility:—

(*a*) The impossibility, when the measures would have been most useful, of obtaining sufficient staff on account of the large demand made on the Medical Department for Plague, Famine, Cholera, and Frontier Campaigns, all at the same time, and the consequent delegation of inspection work to temporary medical subordinates; who, though doubtless equally zealous, were yet less qualified.

(*b*) Evasion by travellers, *i.e.*, alighting before arrival at, and walking past inspection-station; booking to intermediate non-infected stations, &c.

(*c*) The conveyance of infection by road.

(*d*) The impossibility of detecting cases in the incubation stage.

On the other hand there is much to demonstrate the value of the system as a preventive measure. Statistics go to illustrate that it is a powerful deterrent against those travelling, who are actually suffering from plague, and also against those travelling, who are probably infected: for out of many hundreds of thousands of passengers examined, only an infinitesimal number were found to be actually suffering from plague, and, out of many thousands detained for observation, a comparatively small number developed plague. It is almost certain that all actual plague cases, and all those who have commenced to sicken for plague, are detected, and only those incubating for plague escape.

The inspection establishments were made up of officers of the following classes, *viz.*, Commissioned Medical Officers, English Doctors and Lady Nurses, Government Assistant Surgeons and Hospital Assistants, Indian Medical graduates and native practitioners, medical students, Indian trained nurses and female inspectors specially instructed to assist in inspection work, and clerical, police and menial staff.

The following statement gives in a tabular form the period during which the Revised Regulations were in force, the number of passengers detained, the number of plague cases detected (and of deaths among them), the numbers of those disinfected and subjected to the clinical thermometer test, and the total expenditure at each station up to the week ending 2nd June 1899. It also contrasts in a general way the comparative efficiency of the Revised Regulations and the Detention Camp system (which was in force during the epidemic of 1897–98).

A comparison of the tables brings out the fact that under the Detention Camp system at 12 stations during an average period of 5·4 months each, out of 131,074, people detained (for ten days), 201 cases of plague were detected, and the total cost was over Rs. 1,85,000. Under the Revised Regulations at 14 stations during an average period of 5·7 months each, out of 19,302 people detained (for observation only), 413 cases of plague were detected, and the total cost was under Rs. 1,03,030, including cost of monsoon shelters for 1899.

Part 7

RAILWAYS AND CRIME

44

L. F. MORSHEAD, *REPORT ON THE POLICE ADMINISTRATION IN THE BENGAL PRESIDENCY* (CALCUTTA: BENGAL SECRETARIAT BOOK DEPOT, 1907), PP. 36–38

Railway police

79. The total number of cases, both cognizable and non-cognizable, reported to the Railway Police during the year was 10,348 against 8,658 in 1906.

The increase is almost entirely in cognizable crime, which rose by 1,609 cases. Except on the Eastern Bengal State Railway, where a rise of 300 cases under class VI is attributed to the increased activity of the Agents of the Society for the Prevention of Cruelty to Animals, the increase is almost entirely under class V (Minor offences against property), which includes missing goods cases.

All the four Railway systems contribute, in proportion, fairly evenly to the general increase, a fact which indicates that one reason for the rise is the recent division of the Railways into smaller charges, resulting in the maintenance of closer supervision and less concealment of petty crime.

Other reasons for the increase are—

(1) Increase in the volume of traffic.
(2) Extensions of jurisdiction, viz., the grand chord and the Ondal-Sainthia chord on the East Indian Railway, and the Bhujodih-Gomoh, the Purulia-Ranchi and the Jharsuguda-Sambalpur extensions on the Bengal-Nagpur Railway.
(3) The scarcity prevailing throughout the year.
(4) On the East Indian Railway, the activity of three gangs of Railway thieves at Auta, near Lakhesarai, at Jhajha and at Ondal respectively. Repressive measures against these have been taken.

Out of 6,681 true cognizable cases which occurred, convictions were obtained in 1,887 cases, 2,106 persons being convicted out of 2,576 tried. The percentage of convictions to cases decided was 89·5 against 88·9 in 1906 and that of persons convicted to persons tried 81·7 against 80·3.

Strikes.—During the year a serious strike occurred amongst the European and Eurasian drivers and guards on the East Indian Railway. The strike commenced at Assansole on the 18th November 1907 and spread rapidly all over the line. At Assansole, where the strikers took possession of the engine sheds and practically held up all traffic, it was found necessary to requsition the services of a company of European troops from Calcutta to maintain order, whilst detachments from the Military and Armed Police companies were stationed at Howrah and other places to prevent intimidation and violence. Except for one or two isolated cases of assault it is satisfactory to note that nothing serious occurred, and after some days, during which traffic on the line was practically paralysed, an amicable settlement of their differences was arrived at between the Company and their servants.

On the 24th of November, out of sympathy with the strikers on the East Indian Railway, a number of the guards on the Bengal-Nagpur Railway also went out on strike, but were speedily induced by the Railway authorities to resume work.

The pointsmen at Chakradharpur also struck work, but the firmness displayed by the authorities and the dismissal of the ringleaders brought this strike also to a speedy termination.

On the Bengal and North-Western Railway a strike occurred in the Railway workshops at Samastipur. It subsided, however, within a week.

On the Eastern Bengal State Railway a strike occurred on the 7th December amongst the shunters, native drivers and firemen at Sealdah and Chitpur. The Manager by employing European soldier drivers in their places succeeded in keeping the majority of the trains running, seeing which, the strikers expressed their willingness to return to work. The majority were allowed to do so, but the ringleaders were dismissed.

Rioting.—A case occurred at Goalundo in which the Assistant Station Master was assaulted when travelling by trolley at night. Suspicion falling on some police with whom he had a misunderstanding, a Constable, Dafadar and a Chaukidar were put on their trial, but were acquitted by the trying Magistrate, who held the evidence of identification to be unsatisfactory.

At Dinajpur a serious case occurred in which two Europeans of the name of Lazarus were attacked and beaten on the platform by some students. Fifteen persons were sent up for trial; of whom 9 were discharged and 6 convicted under section 147, Indian Penal Code.

Some of the more important Railway cases are briefly reported below:—

Thefts.—An old offender abstracted Rs. 1,000 in Currency Notes and Rs. 100 in cash from the person of a passenger. He was convicted and sentenced to 7 years' rigorous imprisonment.

One Gopi Sahu, a running train thief, was caught between Bhadrak and Balasore while in the act of stealing a box belonging to a European passenger containing £150. He was convicted and sentenced to 2 years' rigorous imprisonment.

A passenger's box containing gold ornaments and clothing to the value of over Rs. 5,000 was stolen from a train by an up-countryman. The accused was arrested in Calcutta while attempting to dispose of a lump of gold, and placed on his trial, but was finally discharged for want of evidence.

A parcel containing specie booked from Bhita to Howrah by a passenger train was stolen from the guard's brakevan. Two railway servants were put on their trial, but were acquitted.

A bag belonging to one Mr. Condon containing valuables and cash valued at Rs. 2,000 was stolen from a second class compartment. A Muhammadan named Noor Muhammad was arrested with the property by a constable at Barauni station. He was convicted and sentenced to rigorous imprisonment for one year.

A bale of silk was stolen from the platform of the Howrah station during the absence of the chaukidar on duty. One Debi Kalwar, a notorious receiver of stolen property, was subsequently arrested in possession of the silk and sent up with four others for trial. All were convicted and sentenced to terms of imprisonment ranging from five to seven years.

82. *Robbery.*—On the Eastern Bengal State Railway ornaments to the value of Rs. 40 were snatched from the person of a native lady travelling between Goalundo and Panchuria. No clue was obtained in this case.

83. *Drugging.*—While travelling from Bolpore to Azimganj, a passenger was drugged and robbed of Rs. 2,540. No trace of the poisoners could be discovered.

On the Bengal Nagpur Railway a passenger was accosted by a woman who decoyed, drugged and finally robbed him of Rs. 3,000 in notes at Purulia. This case was investigated by the Criminal Investigation Department and ended in the arrest of the culprit at Jubbulpore. This case has already been noticed in the report on the Criminal Investigation Department.

84. *Dacoity.*—In two cases men escorting money from the Railway stations on the Eastern Bengal State Railway were attacked by dacoits. One case remained undetected and the other ended in discharge for want of sufficient evidence.

In another case two men were sent up for trial on a charge of having looted Rs. 600 from the booking office at Chingripota Railway station. The Magistrate discharged the accused as he did not believe the Station Master's identification, and thought his conduct after the occurrence suspicious. The Magistrate seems to have taken a correct view of the case which was of a decidedly suspicious nature.

85. *Railway accidents.*—There were 1,120 deaths from accidents against 1,053 in 1906. Of these 66 were found to be cases of suicide.

86. *Obstructions.*—There were 48 true cases of obstruction against 63 in 1905. The decrease is satisfactory. The Police sent up 9 cases for trial. Of these 2 cases

with 4 persons ended in conviction and 7 cases with 7 persons ended in acquittal. The most serious of these occurrences was that which occurred on the Bengal Nagpur Railway on the 5th December, an attempt being made to wreck the special train conveying His Honour the Lieutenant-Governor, about 12 miles south of Kharagpur.

45

S. T. HOLLINS, *THE CRIMINAL TRIBES OF THE UNITED PROVINCES* (ALLAHABAD: GOVERNMENT PRESS, 1914), PP. 2–5, 90–94, 109–110, 115–117

Occupation.—The Aherias have found that there is little to be made by hunting in the highly cultivated canal-irrigated Doab. Most members of the tribe lead honest lives as cultivators, and others maintain themselves by making baskets, collecting honey, gums, &c., which they sell in the towns and villages. Some Aherias however, are vagrants, and as thieves, burglars, and robbers they are amongst the most active and determined criminals in the provinces. Children learn to steal at an early age, and by the time they are 15 or 16, they are expert enough to join expeditions. Gangs of from ten to twenty men leave their homes periodically and go on lengthy expeditions to distant parts of the country. They are absent for several months and when they return home, they generally have sufficient plunder with them to maintain themselves and their families in leisured ease for the rest of the year. Before a gang sets out, arrangements are made that a local Bania should keep the women and children supplied with food during the absence of the men. In some instances however, those of the community who have become tenants or landowners, agree to look after the women and children till the men return. The gang then sets out in small parties of two or three in order to avoid observation, and they generally represent themselves as pilgrims on their way to one of the Hindu holy places. They wander through villages in small parties and ask for alms, but they are ever on the lookout for an opportunity to pilfer and steal. They lift things from passing carts, and they visit pilgrim camps and steal articles of jewellery from women while they are asleep. When committing more serious crime, a large number of them assemble at an appointed place. A leader is chosen and they all obey his orders implicitly. They take up their position on a piece of rising ground near a main road and watch the carts and travellers that pass by. They then select a likely looking cart, and open their attack with a shower of kankar. This generally puts the cart, men to flight, and they then loot the cart at their leisure. They conceal their plunder in an old well or in the jungle and then disperse. Some days later they recover the stolen property and dispose of it through middle-men. If a member of the gang is captured, the leader remains behind and spares no expense to secure his release. They are also skilful burglars, and generally mark down a house some days before they actually break into it. Such houses are always on the outskirts of a village where they can be successfully raided before an alarm can be raised. During recent years, Aherias have acquired some reputation as railway thieves. They snatch parcels through the windows of passenger trains and climb on to goods trains by night and open wagons and throw some of the contents out on the line. They mark the place where they throw bundles out of wagons by counting the number of telegraph poles to the next station. When the train slows down, they alight, and then go back along the line to pick up their plunder. When out on an expedition, the members of a gang associate with each other as little as possible, and notify their whereabouts to each other by means of jackal cries. When they return to their homes, the proceeds of the expedition are divided up amongst the tribe.

Criminal history.—The records of the F. P. B., Allahabad, show over 1,600 convictions against members of the tribe in the United Provinces. When arrested Aherias represent themselves as Ahirs, Bahelias, Banjaras, Dhakpachas, Gadarias, Jogis, Karwals, Khatiks, Lodhs, Malis, and Pasis.

Badhaks

Origin.—The Badhaks are a vagrant criminal tribe and claim that they are of Rajput descent. They are closely allied to the Baurias and Bahelias, and their ancestors are said to have been a mixed community of both Musalman and Hindu outcastes. There is little doubt that they are of mixed origin and are on the same level as Kanjars, Sansias, and other similar vagrants. They admit vagrants and bad characters of all descriptions to their tribe.

Customs, &c.—Their ceremonies are of the usual low caste type, and their special deity is KALI to whom they offer goats. They eat game and vermin such as foxes, jackals, and lizards, and they believe that jackal's meat fortifies them against the inclemencies of winter.

Occupation.—As a class Badhaks have no regular occupation, though some of them are cultivators on a small scale whilst others cut grass, and collect jungle-produce. They are of a vagrant disposition, and can with difficulty endure the tedium of a regular life, and gangs of men leave their homes at various periods and wander about the country in the garb of Faquirs. They pose as religious mendicants, but are ever on the lookout for an opportunity to enrich themselves by crime. They are not as skilful criminals as some of the other gipsy tribes in the provinces, but they are always ready to pilfer and steal, to break into houses and lift cattle, and even to commit highway robberies, when they can do so without incurring undue risk. One of their favourite methods of committing crime is to attach themselves to a party of pilgrims by representing themselves as devout men, and then stealing all their property when a suitable opportunity occurs. In former days they were suspected of being poisoners, and it is on record that they frequently drugged people and decamped with their property. In the vicinity of their homes they only commit petty thefts, such as stealing the clothes of men working in the fields, cutting standing crops, &c., but when they go off on distant expeditions, they go in for the more serious forms of crime mentioned above. The women of the tribe are also addicted to petty thefts, and the children are taught to pilfer and steal from their earliest days.

Efforts to reform the tribe have been made at various times, but they have never been successful, as the Badhak has an utter contempt for honest employment and the greatest repugnance to a regular life.

Criminal history.—The records of the F. P. B., Allahabad, show close upon 100 convictions against the present members of the tribe in these provinces.

Pasis

Origin.—The Pasis are a Dravidian tribe found chiefly in the eastern districts of the Province of Agra and in most of the districts of Oudh. The term is apparently derived from the Sanskrit word *Pashika*, "one who uses a noose." The original occupation of the Pasis appears to have been the tapping of various kinds of date trees for sap which they fermented into liquor. There are various traditions as to the origin of the tribe. One is to the effect that once upon a time when a man was killing cows in the jungle, Parasu Ram who happened to be at hand let drops of his sweat fall on the grass and so raised five men to life to put a stop to the slaughter of these sacred animals. Hence arose the name Pasi from the Hindi word *Pasina* "sweat." When these five men had rescued the cows they demanded wives from Parasu Ram. At that moment a Kayasth girl happened to be passing, and Parasu Ram made her over to these five Pasis. She thus became the mother of the Kaithwas, a subcaste of the tribe. Another legend tells how a devotee called Kuphal was offered a boon by Brahma and he asked that he might be perfected in the art of thieving, a request that was granted him. One of his descendents named Karan had two wives, one a Kshatrin and another an Ahiran. From the former sprang the Raj Pasis and the Bhils and from the latter the Khatiks. Some of the Raj Pasis maintain that they are descended from the Bai Rajput hero Tilok Chand, who, they say, was a Bhar king. They therefore claim that they are akin to the Bhars. The folklore of Partabgarh shows that Pasis, Arakhs, Khatiks, and Pachars all belong to the same tribe. One legend sets forth that the original Pasis had a great fight with the Raja of Newa. Some of them were cowards and hid themselves behind a *khat* (bed), hence they were called Khatiks. Others hid themselves behind *arka* plants and were thus named Arakhs. All through Oudh the Pasis have traditions that their ancestors were once lords of the country and that Pasi kings reigned at Sandila, Dhaurahra, Mitauli, and Ramkot.

From the different traditions it can safely be surmised that there is a close affinity between the Pasis, Arakhs, Motis and Khatiks, and the general appearance and customs of the members of these communities indicate that they are closely allied. The Pasi tribe has over three hundred sub-sections, and from the names applied to these various sections, it is obvious that the term Pasi is a purely occupational one, and includes a number of distinct tribes whose only connection is their common occupation of extracting juice from the date palm.

Amongst the most important sub-sections of the tribe are:—

The Ahirs, Aherias, Arakhs, Bahelias, Bhils, Baurias, Bachas, Bairasis, Chaurasis, Chunaralis, Dhanaks, Gujars, Gwalas, Khatiks, Kaithwas, Mangtas, Pachars, Pasmangtas, Parasramis, Raj Pasis, Rewas and Tarmalis.

Customs, &c.—All questions relating to marriage and caste are decided by the tribal council. Most of the subcastes are endogamous, some of them however intermarry. Divorce is allowed, but divorced women and widows are permitted to marry again. Concubinage as a rule is not tolerated. If a woman is detected in an intrigue, the relations on both sides have to give a tribal feast, and then the offenders are admitted to caste. If the woman's paramour is an outsider, she is permanently expelled from the tribe. There is no fixed price for a bride, but a girl's parents are expected to give something to the relations of the bridegroom. Women of other castes are not introduced into the tribe, but if a woman becomes pregnant by a stranger and the child is born in her husband's or her father's house, it is recognised as a Pasi of pure blood. Marriage ceremonies are of the usual low caste type. The dead are cremated, but those who die of a disease are usually buried. Adoption is permitted and adopted sons are admitted to full rights of succession. There are various tribal deities in different localities. Thus, some sub-sections of the tribe worship BANDI MAI, a form of DEBI, whilst others worship the PANCHON PIR and RAM THAKUR. When small-pox breaks out, SITLA MAI is worshipped by the women. Spirits are believed to occupy old trees, and a pig is offered to them on certain occasions. Pasis eat everything except the flesh of the cow, buffalo, alligator, monkey, horse, jackal, and lizard. The women take their food after the men have finished eating. As a class, Pasis are addicted to tobacco and liquor. The women usually wear bracelets, necklaces, nose-rings, ear-ornaments, and heavy pewter anklets, whilst the men affect ear-ornaments and hang gold coins round their necks.

Occupation.—A few are landholders, but most of them are labourers, collectors of palm juice, and makers of grind stones. On the whole, however, they bear an indifferent reputation, and as early as 1849, they were well known as thieves, robbers, thags and professional poisoners. Up to a few years ago, large bodies of them were retained by the wealthy landowners and petty chiefs of Oudh as body guards and mercenaries. They were expert archers and rendered invaluable assistance in the various quarrels in which the different chiefs were constantly engaged, they enforced the prompt payment of rents, and they cost their employers little, as they lived on the country-side. They have now ceased to be retained to any large extent, by men of position, and the majority of them have settled down to a regular life. They all have the predatory spirit, however, and numbers of them lead a roving life of crime, and their wanderings extend from Dehra Dun to Mandalay. Writing of them in 1904, Mr. Bramley says of them in his report on Inter-Provincial crime. "The Pasis of Oudh are hereditary robbers and thieves, as also are those in the Gopiganj and Bhadoi Parganas of the Mirzapur District who were renowned in former times for their daring dakait raids into Rewah and Central India . . . . The tribe is therefore one with distinctly criminal tendencies, which even in these days . . . . when not held in proper control, are apt to develop to an alarming extent, and in certain districts, such as Allahabad, Partabgarh, Rae Bareli, North Mirzapur and west Jaunpur, the Pasis are a perfect pest to their law-abiding neighbours and are still employed in gangs by refractory landowners for purposes of crime. There is also ample evidence indicating, that like other predatory tribes, they have taken full advantage of the facilities afforded by our improved Railway system for making long raids into Bengal and other Provinces for the sole purpose of committing crime. Moreover, the descendants of the old Mirzapuri Pasi dakaits, now finding that Rewa and Central India no longer furnish the same attractions as of yore, have taken to boats and combined with the Mallahs, and have for years past travelled down the great deserted water-ways of Bengal unobserved, and have regularly looted the riverain Districts in Eastern Bengal and Assam . . . Like the Bhars and others, they have been attracted by certain industries in Bengal, and thus large numbers migrate annually to Calcutta, Burdwan, Rangpur, Pabna, Dacca, and Mymensingh, in all of which districts, Pasis have been convicted of offences varying from dakaitis to petty thefts. They do not appear to be settling down in Eastern Bengal and Assam to the same extent as the Bhars and Dusadhs, but being criminals of a pronounced type, they are a far more dangerous lot than either of the others, and do not hesitate to resort to violence when necessary . . . There is a mass of evidence on record to show that they invariably work with the zamindars, and even the police, of their home districts at their backs, and thus instead of settling down in Eastern Bengal, the criminal Pasis mostly all return every year to their homes laden with booty, from which the local magnates are paid appropriate *nazarana*." Numerous gang cases in the United Provinces and in Bengal during recent years show that the Pasis frequently join with other castes and tribes for the purpose of committing organised crime. When committing thefts, a number of men and women of the gang will form a long line, one behind the other, in a crowd. The first man on the line will steal something and pass it along the line down to the last man who will promptly go off with it to some appointed place. The women do not generally take part in dakaitis, but the men show great daring in holding up carts and passengers. Sticks and stones form their usual weapons, but they sometimes carry fire-arms. Both the men and the women of the tribe are experts at administering poison. They get into conversation with a party of travellers and then travel in company with them. When a suitable opportunity presents itself, they poison or drug the whole party and then decamp with all they can lay hands on. They are thus a dangerous body of criminals, and require constant police surveillance. A feature of their organization is the place of eminence the women attain in the tribe, and many of the most dangerous Pasi gangs of the present day, are under the leadership of women.

Criminal history.—It is impossible to give an accurate account of the criminal history of the tribe, as Pasis invariably give wrong names and addresses when arrested. Some idea of their depraved instincts can, however, be gathered from the fact that the files in the Criminal Investigation department office show 474 convictions against the members of the tribe in these Provinces.

Occupation.—Most of the sub-castes of the tribe, such as the Dhobis, Lodhas, Nais, Kurmis, Sunars, Telis, &c., have regular trades, as their names imply, and may therefore be dismissed without further reference. The genuine Sanauria however is a born thief and vagrant and has a supreme contempt for a regular life and settled employment.

They first came to notice in 1851 when they were reported from Gwalior as adept *uthaigiras*. The term *uthaigir* aptly describes their criminal methods, which have remained substantially the same for generations. The advent of railways has merely facilitated and not altered their *modus operandi*. They are not a wandering tribe, but have fixed residences where the women and children remain while the men and boys go off on thieving expeditions. It is a rule of the tribe that a theft may not be committed within 100 miles of their home, and it is another rule that theft must not be committed with violence, or after dark, or by the light of the moon. On this account they are also known as Chandravehdis. Gangs of 50 or 60, known as *Nals*, leave their homes under *mukhias* or *naldars* after the Dasehra and remain absent for periods which may extend up to two or three years. On arriving at their hunting ground, which is generally a place over one hundred miles from their homes, these gangs select their beats, and separate, after arranging a place where they all are to reassemble some months later. When they meet again, they divide up their spoils, and if each man's share comes to Rs. 40, they return to their homes and devote themselves to sowing the *kharif* crop. Otherwise they part again and exploit the country, till they acquire sufficient property to bring each man's share up to the standard minimum. Formerly all these gangs were accompanied by a number of camels and ponies to carry their plunder, but now these methods of transport have been largely supplanted by the railway. A gang on arriving at some fixed destination breaks up into parties of four or five adults known as *upardars* and each party is accompanied by one or two boys of ten or twelve years of age known as *chhawas* or *chhappas*. The *upardars* get into conversation with a likely looking person and engage his attention whilst the *chhawa* watches his opportunity and runs off with all his property. They are skilful railway thieves and are to be found travelling on all the railways of Central India. Two or three of them get into a carriage together and one of them picks up a bundle belonging to one of the passengers. This is passed from one to another, and is finally thrown out of the window near a station, the exact place being marked by the number of telegraph posts to the next station. They all alight at the station, and then go back along the line and pick up their booty. They also mix with passengers at a railway station, and when a man is taking his ticket, a *chhawa* decamps with his property, whilst the others jostle him by pretending to shoulder their way to the ticket office. Similarly, they get into conversation with shopkeepers and keep them occupied whilst confederates steal all that they can lay their hands on in the shop. Such articles are passed on from one man to another and are generally concealed outside the town before the shopkeeper can disengage himself from his entertaining customers.

In 1874 the Sanaurias of Lalitpur were proclaimed under the Criminal Tribes Act, but this measure was attended with little success. The Act could only be applied to the members of the tribe who were settled in the locality, and could not be put into effect against the vagrant members of the tribe who took care to remain far beyond its sphere of influence.

The Sanauria of the present day therefore remains a light fingered soldier of fortune, and is never happier than when he is engaged in pilfering and thieving.

Bhamptas

Origin.—The Bhamptas are believed to have originally come from Southern India and they are now chiefly found in the Bombay Presidency and in the adjoining Native States. They are recognised by the Sanaurias of Lalitpur as a branch of their tribe, and their manners and customs and methods of committing crime indicate that they are closely allied to the Sanauria community. They have settled down in several districts in the Bombay Presidency, but Bhamptas are to be found wandering all over Northern India. In Bombay they are known as Ghantichors (bundle thieves), Khisa-katru (pocket-cutters) Kalwadru, Kamatis, Oochlis, Pathruts, Takáris, Tudug Wadri and Vadáris. They admit Muhammadans and Hindus of all respectable castes to their tribe, and are always ready to adopt outcaste children.

Customs, &c.—Bhamptas are a very mixed tribe and conform to no particular type. They are below the average height, and some are fair, whilst others are very dark. All are wiry and active rather than powerful and robust. The women are comely, but have a low standard of morality. The men dress well and live in a superior style, but do not go in for unnecessary display. The women dress like Marathas or Brahman women, and usually wear nose-rings. They tattoo their hands and faces, the left hand being more profusely tattooed than the right. Every Bhampta community has a headman who presides at all caste meetings, and is universally respected. The customs and ceremonies of the tribe are of the usual type, but it is said that a girl is never given in marriage till her suitor has proved himself a dexterous thief. They have an ordeal by which a suspected person has to plunge his hand into a pot of boiling oil to establish his innocence. If his hand is not blistered, he is adjudged innocent of the charge brought against him.

Occupation.—Bhamptas follow the ordinary rustic callings, and occasionally the more wealthy trade in a small way as merchants. Some have acquired a good deal of land in the villages in which they have settled, others are small tenants, whilst the poorer classes work in the fields as labourers. But settled occupation does not appeal to them as a class, for they are all born thieves and pilferers. From their childhood they are taught to steal, and they are freely chastised by their parents if they show any inaptitude for their hereditary calling. They first steal toys from other children, and in order to do so, they entice their playmates to secluded spots by offering them sweetmeats. Thus they gradually become proficient, and eventually they are fully qualified to take part in the expeditions of the grown up members of the tribe. Gangs of 8 or 10 leave their homes periodically disguised as well-to-do Marathas. They visit a big town or place of pilgrimage and hire a house and represent themselves as traders or sight-seers. Their air of respectability places them beyond suspicion, and while one or two of them remain in the house to keep up appearances, the others visit the bazaars or bathing ghats and pick pockets wholesale. Some of them get into conversation with shopkeepers or pilgrims, and keep them occupied whilst their confederates steal their property. Occasionally they start a row in a bazar and during the confusion that ensues, they appropriate property of all kinds and pass it on from one to another till it ultimately reaches a confederate on the outskirts of the crowd, and he at once goes off with it to the house that they have rented. When they have thoroughly exploited one town, they move off to another and continue their operations till it is time to move on again. Sometimes they lay themselves out to study the history of a village, and then they visit that village and represent themselves as learned men who can reveal the past and foretell the future. They substantiate their words by referring to some event that has taken place in the village, and it then generally happens that one of the villagers invites them to stay with him. When they get a suitable opportunity they invariably decamp with most of his possessions. But it is as railway thieves that the Bhamptas are best known in Northern India and in thieving in passenger halls, goodsheds, and running trains they are second to none. Some of them jostle a traveller in the passenger hall whilst a confederate steals his property, and others offer to buy tickets for passengers and decamp with the money entrusted to them, whilst their companions cover their retreat. In trains they throw bundles out of the window of a carriage and mark the place by the number of telegraph poles to the next station. They then alight and go back along the line and pick up the property they have secured. Occasionally two of them will get into a crowded carriage at night and one of them will pretend to go to sleep on the floor, politely intimating that it will be more comfortable for the others if he does so. He then proceeds to open or cut into the bundles placed under the seat, whilst his confederate covers his movements by casually letting his blanket fall over his head and shoulders. Gangs travelling about the country have a common rendezvous and generally keep in touch with one another. When leaving an encampment they leave marks on the ground or arrange their cooking stones in a certain way to indicate to others of the gang who may be following them the direction they have taken. Stolen property is generally buried as soon as acquired, and it is then got rid of as soon as the hue and cry has subsided. It is disposed of through goldsmiths, liquor vendors and such people and the proceeds are remitted by the Bhamptas to their homes by money order. Property stolen in one Province, however, is often openly sold in another, and it frequently happens that bundles of stolen property are sent to their homes by touring gangs.

46

M. PAUPARAO NAIDU, *THE HISTORY OF RAILWAY THIEVES WITH ILLUSTRATIONS & HINTS ON DETECTION*, FOURTH ED. (MADRAS: HIGGINBOTHAMS, 1915), PP. 4–19

Bhamptas

Regarding the Bhamptas, it must be observed that the best description of them has already been given by Colonel Portman, and it would be almost vain to attempt to better it except, perhaps, in a few minor details. The Bhamptas are a class of people who reside in the Deccan, chiefly in the Poona, Satara, Nasik and Ahmadnagar Districts of the Bombay Presidency, and who earn their livelihood as professional thieves and pick-pockets.

> "And live they must, and live they will
> "On cursed mammon gotten ill."

They are known also by special names in other places, viz. "Takari" in Nasik, "Uchlya" in Satara, "Gantichor" and "Vadari" in Ahmadnagar, and "Senoria" in some other districts of the Bombay Presidency. They are known as Bhamptas all over India. They exist in every province in India under different names, and travel over all the Railway lines. Their criminal propensities have acquired such a notoriety that in Northern India the word Bhampta has become a bye-word for a thief, no matter to which class of thieves the particular individual belonged. Even so, the word Chain in Bengal or Kepmari in Madras signifies a thief of no class in particular.

2. As these Bhamptas talk broken Telugu, Colonel Portman thinks that they must have come originally from the Nizam's territories, or from some Telugu country; and this view is correct inasmuch as the house or family names of these men comprise of words of Telugu origin, such for instance as Bhuminore (agriculturists), Guvvanore (bird catchers), Munigalore (followers of Munisvara), Kaliputtinore (descendants of Kali), Pappanore (dealers in dhal), Panthipattinore (pig

288

rearers), Yeddumoralore (merchants who carry their goods on bullocks), God-dalore (workers with axe), which are all derived from the Telugu words *Bhumi, Guvva, Munisvara, Kali, Pappu, Panthi, Yeddu* and *Goddali*. They also talk Hindustani. They talk and dress usually like the Mahrattas of the Poona and Satara districts. They have certain words and phrases which are known only to themselves. When engaged in the Telugu districts, they talk Mahratti and Canarese; and when in Mahratti and Canarese countries, they talk Telugu. Their domestic language is Telugu and their women talk Telugu more freely, though in a rather corrupt form than other languages. They tell me that they once belonged to the clan of "Poosala Dasaries" who still sell beads in the Telugu country. They make certain signs with their eye-lids and fingers which are totally unintelligible to others.

3. They are Hindus, and they worship the goddess "Kali," whose principal temple to which they resort, is in the village of Konali in the Akalkote State, under the Political Agent of Sholapur; and there they frequently assemble in gangs, before and after their raids, to worship the goddess for luck to attend them, or for the success they have achieved.

4. It is impossible to classify them under any particular caste or creed as excepting the low caste Malas or Chumbars, Madigas or Dheds, Ramosi and Mangs, they admit all castes of men from Brahmins to Boyas. Recruits thus enlisted, after being duly initiated into the mysteries of thieving, become Bhamptas, and intermarry with the members of the community.

5. The Bhamptas are sub-divided into two groups, *viz.*, "Jadaw" and "Gaekwad." These divisions are exogamous, that is, "Jadaws" do not marry with "Jadaws," or "Gaekwads" with "Gaekwads"; but the members of the two divisions intermarry one with another. During their wanderings, they occasionally come in contact with women of bad character, whom they take as concubines and eventually treat as wives. They even kidnap young boys of all castes, whom they adopt and bring up to their profession. It is said that Chinya, a Bhampta Naik, adopted as his sons, (1) Metya of the Wani or oil-monger class from Guzerat, (2) Munya of the Marwadi class, (3) Mahadya of the Sutar or blacksmith class, and several other boys.

6. A Police Sub-Inspector of Satara Taluq, who had the help of some Bhampta informants in an important recent case, says that some 12 families originally entered the Bombay Presidency about a hundred years ago from Telingana and divided into three batches of four each, one settling in Poona district; the second in Kholapur and Sangli States; and the third in Satara district in the village of Limb in Satara Taluq. There still exists at this Limb village the tomb of "Chinnappa", one of their prominent leaders. Till recently, Bhamptas before starting on an excursion, used to visit this tomb and worship there, so that luck may attend them. After some successful efforts at house-breakings and thefts and the accumulation of some wealth, this Limb batch shifted to the village of Rui in Koregaon Taluq which is more convenient for their "business" owing to jungles and hills being close by wherein they may conceal themselves for days obtaining food and other supplies from their wives and other relations. At Rui, they constructed

strong permanent houses with elevated places, in those of the leaders, whence old women and boys always keep a watch for any Government officers, particularly Police, who may visit the village. These houses have doorways communicating with the houses of other ryots so that they may escape through them when their houses are surrounded. Similarly the other two batches that settled in Kholapur and Sangli States and Poona districts prospered in their thieving excursions and scattered also into Ahmednagar, Nasik and Sholapur districts. Thus these settlements in their flourishing condition became very prolific and their number may be roughly calculated at some thousands at present. They have kept up their matrimonial connection where they happen to be and have thus formed a distinct community, as no honest outsider would condescend to join them.

7. An old man aged about 80 years called Malhari Kandu still lives in the village of Rui in Koregaon Taluq in Satara district. He is the richest man in the village with property worth about 50,000 rupees and has four sons, *viz.*, Esu, Bapu, Thukaram and Sakharam. These latter organise gangs of Bhamptas from various places advancing loans to them for the maintenance of their families during their absence.

8. The next man in importance in Rui village is Chendria alias Rama Chandar. This man with about half a dozen convictions to his credit, has risen in importance by hoarding up the sale proceeds of his booty to the extent of over 10,000 rupees. He is the son of Chinya referred to in para. 5 who was brother of Malhari Kandu. This Chandria was till 1911 also organizing gangs by advancing loans and sending them out to commit crime, but he took care not to go with them having had unfortunate experiences in several places. He has since been arrested in the Poona gang case and convicted.

9. There is another important man named Parasu Dowlu, aged 70, living at Moregaon in Bhimtadi Taluq of Poona district. He has four sons Gulba, Thukaram, Mari and Visvanath, all in very good circumstances. They also organise gangs and travel on various Railway lines. Almost all the Bhamptas of Poona and Satara districts depend upon these three families for loans or help in times of need. Parasu Dowlu and his son Gulba have since been arrested in the Poona gang case.

10. Before the introduction of railways, these people, like the Bauris and other leading criminal tribes, confined themselves to wandering about the country in gangs, visiting all large towns and villages, especially those where fairs were being held or any festivals celebrated, for the purpose of thieving and picking pockets. They had one remarkable peculiarity; their trade was carried on only by day, never after dark. With the opening of railways, however, having soon found out that thefts could easily be committed in trains, they quickly took to this new way of enriching themselves, and gave up their old custom of thieving only between sunrise and sunset, because they discovered that darkness favoured their designs on the persons or property of travellers; and it may be said that all successful thefts in trains are committed by them only during the night. As the different lines of railways are extending, they are also increasing in number every day, and spreading in all parts of India, committing their depredations.

11. In August 1884, Lieutenant-Colonel Brown, the Acting Superintendent of Police on the G. I. P. Railway, obtained from Government, on his own recommendation, a conditional pardon for two Bhamptas, named Methya Chinya and Ranya Satwa, who made a clean breast of their profession from *alpha* to *omega*. It was only through the information obtained from these two men that his successor Colonel Portman, referred to in the introduction, was able to seize cartloads of stolen property consisting of various jewels, cloths, vessels, etc., of different places, from the houses of Bhamptas in the villages of Baburdi and Moragaon in the Soopha Taluq, Poona District. It was through these very men that Colonel Portman was able to collect their history.

12. Their mode of committing crime is for about ten Bhamptas with one or two women to start from home and split into two or three batches, after arranging to meet again on a certain day in a fixed place. On a newly opened railway, they engage a house in some large town of importance, calling themselves railway contractors, and travel by turns during the nights, always taking care that the house is never vacant. Each batch of men go to a station dressed in some sort of disguise or in good ordinary clothes, taking a canvas or carpet bag, or at least a bundle with them, and purchase tickets for some place far or near. In their bag or bundle they invariably have one or two coloured turbans, two or three coats, a knife, a pair of scissors, a mirror, a chisel about six inches long and half an inch broad, a long tin-case of chunam, "Vibhuthi," "Namam" and "Sreechurnam," to put different marks on their foreheads, a string of beads and a few old cloths. They also carry trinkets such as rings, bangles, buttons, nose rings, etc., of very trifling value, which their females expose for sale on road-sides to show ostensibly to the public that it is their means of livelihood. They make the other passengers understand that they are on a pilgrimage to Ramesvaram, Tirupati, Hampi, Jagannadh, Kasi, Haridwar, or any other religious place on the railway line in which they fix their game. They look out for passengers also having bags which seem likely to contain anything valuable, and they follow such persons into the same carriage, and, sitting near, endeavour to enter into conversation, and ask them where they are going and at what station they intend alighting. After a time, when it begins to get dark, or, if it is already dark, the other passengers begin to drop off to sleep. Then one of the Bhamptas, on the pretext of making them more comfortable, lies down on the floor, and covers himself with a large cloth under the pretence of going to sleep, while his confederrate, stretching his legs on to the opposite seat, spreads out his cloth, thus more or less screening the man lying beneath. This latter, when all appears quiet, begins manipulating the bag he has spotted under the seat, to feel with his hands if anything valuable is there, and if he cannot succeed in getting his hand into the bag, he takes from his mouth a small curved knife, which all Bhamptas carry concealed between their gum and upper lip, and with that he rips the seams of the bag and takes out what he finds. If the curved knife is not sharp enough to cut the canvas, he uses the other knife he has with him, and if the article spotted be a tin or wooden box, he makes use of the chisel in forcing it open, generally at the lock, and transfers the contents to his bag or bundle, or passes

up what he had stolen to his confederate, and, at the next station, the two get out of the carriage, and either leave the train altogether, or get into another carriage. Should there be any complaint of loss, they throw the things out of the window.

13. If the passenger discovers the loss while they are still in the same compartment, suspects them and complains to the Police Constable at a Railway station, the latter searches their bags or bundles, finds no stolen property to be sure, and lets them off. Then they go back along the line and recover the property. Or, instead of cutting open the bag, they quickly, when the owner is asleep, exchange bags and sneak away at the first opportunity, and the unfortunate victim discovers what has happened only a little too late, perhaps on arriving at his destination, when of course he reports the loss to the Police, who naturally find great difficulty in tracing up the thief. If the passenger keeps his bag below his head, and is wary enough not to give them any scope in the train, they will also get down at the station with him, and as generally this passenger lies down in the station or choultry near it till morning, these Bhamptas go with him to the same spot, and misrepresenting to him that they are merchants from some place far or near, manage to sleep near him. During their conversation they will inspire him with such confidence that he, taking them for honest travellers, relaxes his vigilance over his bag in proportion, nay more, feels positively happy in their company. They will then take the first opportunity to walk away with his bag in the dark, and will be several miles off before he goes and complains to the Police. Most of these budmashes have a notoriety for clearing at a stretch astoundingly long distances. These men will, as a rule, steal anything, however small in value, and it is needless to say that sometimes they make heavy hauls, much to the detriment of railway passengers. They also contrive to remove stealthily articles from the pockets of travellers purchasing tickets at the booking offices, as in the crowd the passengers do not notice what is going on, much less perceive who the thief is.

Mr. Kennedy, Inspector-General of Police, Bombay, in his book on the criminal classes of the Bombay Presidency, gives the following account of the signs used by Bhamptas when they wish to warn one another:—

"One Bhampta warns another by first coughing and then clearing the throat; this is done quietly if police are about or noisily if the person to be warned is at a distance and the coast is clear. He never points with the hand or finger, does not look in the direction from which danger is expected, but points with the elbow while scratching his head, working his elbow backwards. If a Bhampta is awaiting the arrival of a train in which he expects friends and notices the police are watching him, he will twist one end of his shoulder cloth (*uparni*) round one arm to indicate that he is tied up; and if he intends his friends not to alight, he will scratch his head and work his elbow in the direction the train is moving. This means 'I am watched, continue your journey.' There is no slang for 'come here,' the elbow movement does instead of a word."

14. Bhamptas do not confine their operations merely to the railway which passes through their district. They also proceed in gangs on the Madras and Southern Mahratta Railway, and South Indian Railways, the Great Indian Peninsular

Railway, the Mysore and the Nizam's State Railways, the Bombay-Baroda and Central Indian Railways, the Rajputana Railway, the Bengal-Nagpur Railway, the East Indian Railway, the Oudh and Rohilkund Railway and others. They generally choose one line and start in a gang of about ten or twelve men with one or two women for some place on that line, and, fixing a central place as a rendezvous, proceed by twos and threes to prey upon the public, returning to their homes either after they succeed, or if they are afraid they are suspected, or when they are released from jail. When returning with the booty, the stolen jewels are secured round the waist of a woman, who will travel in a carriage reserved for females. The stolen cloths will be concealed in bedding, which is generally carried by the men; but usually they send the women in advance with all the valuables. When there is no female, the chief man will carry the jewels in his waist, under the disguise of a respectable contractor or a merchant.

15. It may be interesting to the readers to know an instance of their doings on the Bezwada-Madras line traced by me in January 1900. A party of nineteen men and three women, belonging to the gangs of Rui, Karati, Poojeechivadi, Hale, Wadagaon and Konali, started towards Bezwada. The party split up into two gangs of eleven each. On their way they had good hauls, and Maniram and Byri with the two women named Manku and Ranu, returned to their places from Hyderabad with a large quantity of the property stolen. Of the remaining eighteen Bhamptas, eight men confined their operations to the Bezwada-Madras line and made Nellore their headquarters, while the remaining nine men and the woman Sunderabai chose the Nizam's Guaranteed State Railway as their field of operations, and made a good haul before they were all arrested by the Secunderabad Railway Police.

16. The eight persons encamped at Nellore, hired a decent house belonging to one Inala Appayya Chetty at Santhapet, close to the Pennar river, on the 11th December 1899, and called themselves railway contractors. From that day till the end of the month they kept travelling up and down, and ascertained for themselves at which of the railway stations there were no Constables, and which of the stations were considered to be important. Every night four of them went out, while the other four remained at home. On the 30th December they stole the tin-box of the Nazir of Amalapuram Court, Godavari District, which contained 28 rupees worth of property. On the 2nd January 1900, some jewels were stolen from a passenger's bundle, but no complaint was lodged about the loss at the time. On the 5th January, a big theft involving a thousand rupees' worth of jewels, belonging to the wife of the Superintendent of Sangam Anicut, was committed between Nellore and Bezwada, and the complaint was made to me in person by the lady with sobs and cries. The wooden box from which the jewels had been removed was examined by me, and from the marks of a chisel or nail left on the lid at the lock, I was convinced that it must have been the work either of a Bhampta or of a Kepmari. I took immediate steps to detect the case by tracing out this professional thief, and deputed Constables to the different stations to watch all the passengers closely, as this culprit must take train somewhere to reach his place of abode. One

Bhampta, named Nathu, was caught at Sulurpet with stolen property as he was alighting from the train, the complainant who missed his property having been sharp enough to discover the loss and to complain at once. While he was being searched by the Nellore Station-house Officer, his three associates, who held tickets from different places, bolted from the platform in the dark, but were eventually arrested in the village of Tada. Their names are Gangaram, Nama and Maru. No stolen property was found upon them.

17. Before the 20th January 1900, no less than ten thefts were committed by them. On the morning of the 21st, two more Bhamptas, Rama and Bapu, with over 500 rupees' worth of property in their possession, were arrested by a beat Constable while they were dragging themselves along the road under the influence of liquor. The same evening another Bhampta, named Pakira *alias* Balaram, was arrested at Nayudupeta railway station by a Railway Police Constable. I presume that this man had evidently concealed all the property he had in his possession, and arrived at that station to go to Nellore to inform his other associates of the arrest of their comrades.

18. On the 25th January, when the train was about to start, the eighth man, Chendria *alias* Rama Chandar, got into the train at Nellore at 1 A.M., when a Platform Constable, suspecting him to be a Bhampta, and having no time to search his bundles, pointed him out to the two Constables of the travelling section in the train. These Constables, in their turn, conveyed the suspicion to the Station-house Officer of Bapatla, who was also in the same train, and he searched him at Bitragunta and found over a thousand rupees' worth of jewels and cloths with him. This man was perhaps leaving Nellore finally, as the place was getting too hot for the gang after so many arrests in quick succession.

19. As every one of them was going out of Nellore, and the thefts were being committed on both sides of Nellore, I was convinced that these Bhamptas fixed Nellore as their headquarters. On making a searching enquiry I learnt that the house of Appayya Chetti, referred to above, had been engaged by them, and as it was found locked, I broke the lock open in the presence of some witnesses, and found in the house a portion of the stolen property connected with four of the cases mentioned above.

20. In four cases the boxes were broken open with chisels. In two cases the boxes were carried bodily away. In two cases the railway bags were cut open, and in the remaining two the property was removed from bundles. Property connected with eight cases was traced to them, and the Head Assistant Magistrate of Gudur sentenced them all to imprisonment varying from one to four years.

21. In the year 1901 just about its close, the people of Rajahmundry were startled by a series of thefts committed both in the Bazaar street and on the bank of the Godavari, the cases numbering over half a dozen in the space of about a fortnight.

Closely on the heels of these, came a clever pick-pocketing of about Rs. 10 committed on the station platform in broad daylight. Immediately after the complaint of this last case was received by me in my capacity of Railway Police Inspector, I went to work, and, suspecting that there was a professional gang located somewhere in the town or in its neighbourhood, I held a thorough scrutiny, and with the help of the local officers, traced out a gang of nine Bhamptas and their women and children in three of the huts in the washerman quarters of Innespet about a mile and a half from the Railway station.

The three huts were immediately searched, when, besides a medley of trifling trinkets of all sorts, were found a few postal letters from their homes in Ahmednagar taluq received by them at Dharwar, Dond Junction, Allahabad, Calcutta and Khurda. These letters disclosed that they sent home several money orders and parcels including two watches, and that they were then on a tour through India starting in February 1901 from Dharwar where one of them had a conviction for theft. They then travelled through the Bombay Presidency to Dond Junction whence they sent some money orders. Then they had been to Allahabad wherefrom they sent two watches and some money. In June the gang reached Howrah, where a few of its members seem to have been bound over for good behaviour by a Calcutta Magistrate. In August the whole gang squatted at a hamlet close to the Railway Station of Khurda Road under the patronage of the village *Saraparakar*, who, falling in love with a young widow of theirs, connived at the questionable life of the gang, who committing a few thefts near Midnapur and Puri, some of the members were caught and convicted. The Police too got scent finally of their unwelcome presence at Khurda Road.

Finding the place thus becoming too hot for them, they came down to Rajahmundry, leaving the young widow to the Saraparakar's amours probably with the object of keeping up his connection with the gang.

The finger prints taken and sent to the different bureaux elicited the above convictions in Dharwar and Calcutta that year.

Six of the men arrested at Rajahmundry were bound over for good behaviour by the Joint Magistrate of Godavari.

22. A gang of twenty-four men started about January 1909 for Calcutta and engaged three small houses there between the two Post offices of New Bara Bazaar and Hithabadi near Harrison Road. They split into several parties and made temporary encampments in Goalando and Damukdia in Eastern Bengal, on the Railway lines of which they had arranged to work. Between January 1909 and September 1910, they had such heavy hauls on different Railways, that they successfully sent about 180 money orders to the value of eight thousand rupees from the above two Post offices of Bara Bazaar and Hithabadi, but only six of the gang were traced and convicted for thefts and four more bound over for good behaviour. About twenty-five of these money orders were received by Chendria of Rui and the rest to the other leaders and their families in different places.

47

REPORT OF THE RAILWAY POLICE COMMITTEE, *1921* (SIMLA: GOVERNMENT MONOTYPE PRESS, 1921), PP. 2–5

The grievances of the public in regard to the protection of goods

8. It is the public who suffer most from theft on the railway, and it was a complaint from the Upper India Chamber of Commerce that ultimately led to the appointment of the Committee. It seems appropriate therefore that the grievances of the public and of the commercial community in particular should be given first place in a discussion of the arrangements made for the protection of goods on the railways.

9. The case as represented to us is that theft and pilferage from goods in transit are on the increase; that they have attained a magnitude which reflects serious discredit on the police and railway administrations; that in regard to a large portion of the goods traffic the railways are so completely protected under the different forms of risk-note that they are careless of the interests of the public, and that conditions exist and are allowed to continue which make theft and pilferage both easy and safe. As to the nature of these conditions, we mention briefly those in regard to which we have heard complaints in practically every part of India.

Much of the thieving, it is alleged, is done by the railway staff. There is no effective supervision, and the misdeeds of those below are winked at by those who are supposed to control them.

Purely mechanical methods of protection, again, are ignored. A loaded wagon is secured by a piece of string. Goods yards are generally thoroughfares. They are for the most part badly lighted and imperfectly protected by fencing. The shed accommodation is as a rule inadequate, and the consignments lie about at the mercy of the evil-disposed. It almost seems as though the convenience of the thief was consulted in the construction of the wagons. Projections and attachments enable him to board them in motion. In some of the older wagons, manholes help him to gain access to the contents. The flap door when closed admits of the insertion of a knife by means of which bags are slit, and the same method of extraction is used through the crevices of wooden floors, while the contents of open wagons are an easy prey.

Delays in transit, too, are now general. Each day that the goods are allowed to lie booked or unbooked in the yard before despatch, each day that they are detained at transhipment stations, each halt by the roadside and each shunt into a siding means so much more exposure to depredation.

And in face of all this, it is claimed that the railways and the police do nothing. Dishonesty on the part of railway subordinates is said to be encouraged by superficial enquiries and inadequate punishments: they are allowed to protect and screen themselves by insisting unreasonably on risk-notes and clear receipts, and to burke complaints by a refusal of open delivery where theft is suspected. As for the police, their work is marred by a desire to shirk responsibility, difficult investigations are not pressed home, and culprits are rarely brought to book.

10. Some of the witnesses we have heard have given us rough estimates of the extent of their losses. The representative of the Tata Iron and Steel Company said that of the consignments of fruit, fish and vegetables to the industrial colony at Jamshedpur, scarcely one per cent reached their destination intact. The Mysore Chamber of Commerce stated that one-half of every consignment of coal was pilfered by women who carry their spoil away openly in baskets. A firm of provision merchants in Bombay estimated that 10 per cent of their consignments suffered. At Chittagong a professor who is interested in a co-operative society informed us that if they could get their consignments through without loss, it would mean a saving to their members of 25 per cent. The representative of the Indian Tea Association, the members of which import large quantities of rice for the use of the garden coolies, stated that until recently 20 per cent of their consignments had been pilfered. In the United Provinces thefts of fruit were so notorious that the local Government itself moved in the matter, and in the instructions which were issued by the Oudh and Rohilkhand Railway, in their weekly gazette of June 27th 1919, it was admitted that apparently "not a single parcel of fresh fruits can reach its destination without suffering from the attacks of thieves."

The evidence of official figures in regard to losses

11. Some of the charges set forth in the last chapter it is unnecessary for us to discuss. The delays in transit are due to shortage of rolling stock, and the defects in wagons largely to the difficulty of replacing or improving old stock owing to the war. But it cannot be denied that several of the counts in the indictment are true. In this chapter, we shall show how far the official figures for claims, losses and crime support the general allegations as to the extent and growth of the evil. In the two following chapters we shall deal with the more specific charges against the railways with regard to—

(*i*) inefficiency and dishonesty on the part of subordinates and lack of supervision,

(*ii*) neglect of mechanical means of protection, and

(*iii*) indirect encouragement of theft by the risk-note system, etc.

After discussing the case against the railways we shall proceed to consider the criticisms made against the police.

12. There can be no question that losses by theft and pilferage have increased. So far as the increase is due to causes other than those into which it is our duty to enquire, it is generally attributed to the rise in the cost of living. No statistics are available to show the full extent of the evil, but in ten years the amount paid in compensation by seven of the principal railways has risen from 11·95 lakhs to 70·27 lakhs. In the same period the goods earnings on these railways rose from 25·37 crores to 38·44 crores. In other words an increase of 52 per cent in the goods earnings was accompanied by a rise of 488 per cent in compensation and the percentage of the goods earnings paid in compensation rose from ·47 to 1·83. The bulk of the increase has occurred since 1917.

In six years, the number of reports has risen 64 per cent on the Bombay, Baroda and Central India Railway, 125 per cent on the East Indian and no less than 244 per cent on the Great Indian Peninsula. On the North-Western and the Bengal-Nagpur lines, the number has more than trebled in ten years.

14. These statistics, however, require some explanation. They include a number of claims and reports which have nothing to do with theft or pilferage. The amount paid in compensation covers damage to goods by fire, water and accident, and loss by misdespatch and misdelivery. From 15 to 20 per cent should probably be allowed on this account. Then again owing to the rise in prices, the 488 per cent increase in compensation means a much smaller increase in the quantity of goods lost, and there is evidence to show that claims have received an artificial stimulus from the growth of claims agencies. Similarly, in a large proportion of cases in which goods are reported lost, they are found on enquiry merely to have been left behind or misdirected or carried beyond their destination.

On the other hand, much is lost for which compensation is never claimed. The goods may have been sent at owner's risk, or a clear receipt may have been given before the loss was discovered or the owner may not think it worth while to make a claim. It is impossible to estimate the amount of the losses for which no claim is made, but the total must be very large indeed.

15. The Police figures of reported crime show that thefts from running goods trains increased from 6,898 in 1915 to 11,227 in 1919, and thefts from goods sheds and transhipment stations from 4,479 in 1915 to 7,476 in 1919. Convictions in the former were 336 in 1915 and 598 in 1919, and in the latter 989 and 1,778, respectively. The odds therefore taking India as a whole, are nearly twenty to one in favour of the man who robs a running train, and it is not surprising that the occupation is growing in popularity.

The railways themselves suffer as much as the public. Six hundred maunds of coal are said to be stolen every day at Asansol at the present time, and last year on the East Indian Railway alone thefts of mineral oil belonging to the Company amounted to nearly a quarter of a million gallons.

298

We think the evidence justifies the conclusion that the total value of the property stolen on railways in India does not fall short of a crore of rupees per annum. The number of offences, if all the petty pilferages are included, must run into millions. Of these, in 1919, only 33,555 were reported to the police and of the reported cases less than 16 per cent resulted in conviction.

16. The figures are startling. Fortunately, the remedies, we believe, are simple. We accept the principle first laid down in 1882 and ever since adhered to, that the railways must be held responsible for the safe custody of property entrusted to them, and in our view the present situation has arisen because the obligations which flow from that principle have not been sufficiently regarded. The problem is in the main one of prevention, and as such falls primarily within the province of the railways.

The guarding and handling of goods

(i)   Watch and ward

17. We shall consider first of all the watch and ward staff, its recruitment, personnel, strength and organization. Each department has its own watchmen, but it is those employed by the Traffic Department for the protection of stations, goods-yards and goods-sheds with whom this Committee is mainly concerned.

18. *Recruitment.*—Traffic watchmen are appointed by the District Traffic Superintendent, or by station masters and traffic inspectors subject to his confirmation. The character of the men is supposed to be verified by enquiry from the police after appointment and before confirmation. Other precautions are sometimes taken. At Howrah, the candidate has to produce a surety. On the South Indian Railway he has to get a recommendation from some official or private person of known respectability. It is not found possible to maintain lists of candidates as the men who apply cannot usually wait for employment. They are recruited from practically all castes, though sweepers, chamars and members of criminal tribes are generally excluded. Most of the railway officers who have given evidence express a preference for pensioners or at any rate for men who have served in the army or the police, and on several railways special rates of pay have been sanctioned for men of this class.

19. *Personnel*—On almost every line, the officials complain of the quality of the men employed. Pensioners are difficult to obtain and when obtained are often past work. The other watchmen too are frequently old and decrepit, and unequal to personal conflict with able-bodied thieves. They are usually recruited in the neighbourhood and from the same class as the menials. They have friends among the local bad characters, and not infrequently combine with their old associates and the less upright of the station staff in theft and pilferage.

This is the picture as drawn by railway officials themselves. In Bombay and Madras we were told by police officers of cases in which ex-convicts and men who had been dismissed from the railway and the police were employed as watchmen. In the United Provinces, an experienced superintendent said they were mostly criminals. An inspector on the Bengal and North-Western Railway says, "It is an open secret that no chaukidar pays for his food but helps himself". Another inspector classes them with the menials whom he regards as responsible for all the pilferage that goes on.

48

ABSTRACT OF EVIDENCE RECORDED BY THE RAILWAY POLICE COMMITTEE, 1921 (CALCUTTA: SUPERINTENDENT GOVERNMENT PRINTING, 1921), PP. I–IV, 1–8

Questions to be answered by railway police officers

1 Do you consider that the system of having the Watch and Ward establishment under the Traffic Department works satisfactorily? If not, what are the defects and what remedies would you suggest? Do you consider any improvement in the class of men enlisted desirable? (Page 1.)

2 What is the system—

   (*a*) of checking goods at time of loading, unloading and transhipment;
   (*b*) of supervising the staff employed in handling goods;
   (*c*) of fastening and sealing wagons;
   (*d*) of seal checking, and;
   (*e*) of guarding loaded wagons in yards and on running trains.

   Do you consider the systems in force satisfactory? (Page 9.)

3 Are the lighting and fencing-in of goods sheds and transhipment sheds satisfactory? (Page 17.)

4 Are pilferage or thefts from:—

   (*a*) goods sheds of goods booked or unbooked;
   (*b*) transhipment yards;
   (*c*) goods trains; and
   (*d*) passenger trains (luggage booked or unbooked) frequent on the length of railway in your charge and do the railway police take any cognizance of such cases, or measures to prevent such losses? If not, do you consider that they should do so? (Page 20.)

5 Are pilferages from consignments of particular classes of goods:—(*a*) arms and ammunition, (*b*) fresh fruit, (*c*) liquor, (*d*) fish—numerous on the length of railway in your charge?

What special arrangements are made for the protection of such consignments? (Page 24.)

6 Are reports of shortages or missing goods from seal-intact wagons made to the railway police for enquiry?
What is the system in force with regard to the registration and investigation of such cases? (Page 28.)

7 How far is such pilferage, as takes place, due to the act or connivance of the railway staff? (Page 34.)

8 Are cases of shortages from wagons with broken seals registered and investigated as thefts immediately on report being made? (Page 36.)

9 What are the arrangements in force regarding seal checking? What is the strength of the special force (if any) told off for this duty, and is it carried out at all stations and out posts where there are railway police or only at the boundaries of jurisdictions? (Page 38.)

10 Are railway police sent out at night with goods trains for the purpose of Watch and Ward? If so, please furnish brief particulars of the arrangements so made. If not, what measures are taken to prevent thefts from goods trains? (Page 41.)

11 Are head constables and constables deputed as train guards with all night trains for the protection of passengers and their property? If so, what is the system in force? How many men are employed and for how many hours are they so employed? Is the system effective? (Page 44.)

12 Are such guards deputed with day trains? (Page 48.)

13 Are cases of forged currency notes received at stations or in cash offices, registered by the railway police? If not, how are such cases dealt with? (Page 49.)

14 Is there much unreported loss or crime? If so, why are reports not made? (Page 50.)

15 Is railway crime mostly the work of local thieves? Where do most offences occur as regards (a) passengers and their luggage, (b) goods (e.g., in stations, at goods sheds, etc.)? (Page 54.)

16 Is there any want of co-operation between the railway and the district police in British India or in Native States? (Page 57.)

17 Can you instance any cases of malpractices on the part of railway and police subordinates which have come under your own immediate observations, and can you suggest an measures for checking such malpractices? (Page 64.)

18 Under what rules and by whose orders are members of the Railway Police Force at present recruited, transferred, promoted, etc., and do you consider that the system requires alteration? Is the quality of the officers and men satisfactory? (Page 67.)

19 Is service in the railway police popular? Is the *personnel* interchangeable with that of the district police? (Page 72.)

20 Are there complaints of too frequent transfers of gazetted officers? (Page 77.)

21 Have you a system of fixed travelling allowance? If not, are you in favour of such a system for officers and men? (Page 78.)

22 Are quarters provided for officers and men? (Page 80.)

23 Is life in the railway police service regarded as unhealthy? (Page 82.)

24 Are punishments or rewards more frequent than in the district police? (Page 84.)

25 Are you of opinion that the present allocation, strength and working of the police are satisfactory? In what particulars, if any, are alterations required? (Page 85.)

26 What railway police reserve is there, and have you any proposals to make regarding the sufficiency or allocation of the police reserves on the railway or railways with which you are connected? (Page 90.)

27 Is there any want of co-operation between the members of the railway staff and the railway police, and are you aware of any ill-feeling between the subordinates of the two departments? (Page 93.)

28 Is any more effective system of *liaison* possible, *e.g.*, by deputing railway officers to the railway police and police officers to the railway temporarily or by employing police officers permanently in the claims branch? (Page 99.)

29 What are the principal difficulties encountered in railway police investigations? What have you to suggest for their removal? In particular have you reason to complain of (1) delay in reporting, (2) difficulties due to reference to other jurisdictions, (*e.g.*, district police or railway police of another division or province) or to railway authorities? (Page 102.)

30 What are the rules regarding the investigation of cases occurring within railway limits and providing for the co-operation of the district police in the investigation of such cases? Are these rules satisfactory? (Page 110.)

31 What is the present rule defining the limits of railway police jurisdiction and do you consider it satisfactory? (Page 113.)

32 Have you any system for the special training of railway police officers and men? Do you think such a system is likely to give useful results? (Page 117.)

33 Have you a special detective staff? If so, describe its organisation? Do you consider this system likely to improve detection? (Page 119.)

34 What are the arrangements in force for the prosecution of railway cases? Are they satisfactory? (Page 124.)

35 The railway police are at present organised on a provincial basis. Would any other system of organisation in your opinion be an improvement on this, *e.g.*, (*a*) imperialisation, (*b*) an organization which would take the railway system as the unit and make the Superintendent of Police for most purposes the Head of a Railway Department, (*c*) a system under which the railway police were amalgamated with the district police. (Page 127.)

36 Are the railway police liable to be called on to provide special guards in times of unrest, strikes, etc.? If so, can such arrangements be made without interfering prejudicially with the general work of the railway police? (Page 138.)

37 How are the Superintendents' charges distributed in your province? (Page 140.)

38 Have you any further suggestions to make on matters germane to the present enquiry? (Page 141.)

Questions for railway officers

1 How are the members of the Watch and Ward establishment appointed and supervised? (Page 147.)
2 From what castes are the men drawn, and is any enquiry as to character made before appointment? (Page 150.)
3 Is an improvement in the class of men enlisted desirable? (Page 153.)
4 Do you consider that the system of having the Watch and Ward establishment under the Traffic Department works satisfactorily? If not, what are the defects and what remedies would you suggest? (Page 156.)
5 What is the system:

(a) of checking goods at time of loading, unloading and transhipment;
(b) of supervising the staff employed in handling goods;
(c) of fastening and sealing wagons;
(d) of seal checking, and
(e) of guarding loaded wagons in yards and on running trains,

Do you consider the systems in force satisfactor? (Page 164.)
6 Are the lighting and fencing-in of goods sheds and transhipment sheds satisfactory? (Page 175.)
7 Are pilferages or thefts from:

(a) goods sheds of goods booked or unbooked;
(b) transhipment yards;
(c) goods trains, and
(d) passenger trains (luggage booked or unbooked) frequent on your railway, and do the Railway Police take any cognizance of such cases, or measures to prevent such losses? If not, do you consider that they should do so? (Page 179.)

8 Are pilferages from consignments of particular classes of goods: (a) arms and ammunition, (b) fresh fruit, (c) liquor, (d) fish, numerous on your railway? What if any special arrangements are made for the protection of such consignments? (Page 189.)
9 Are reports of shortages or missing goods from seal-intact wagons made to the railway police for enquiry? If not, how are such cases dealt with, and what is the system of investigation in cases investigated by the railway authorities? What are the main difficulties encountered? (Page 195.)
10 What is the difference between the arrangements made for the safety of:—

(a) goods at owner's risk, and
(b) goods carried at railway risk? (Page 202.)

11 How far is such pilferage as takes place due to the act or connivance of the railway staff? (Page 204.)

12 Is there any want of co-operation between different departments of the same railway or between different railways in regard to claims? (Page 208.)

13 Are you of opinion that the present allocation, strength and working of the police on your railway are satisfactory? In what particulars, if any, are alterations required, in your opinion? (Page 212.)

14 Is there any want of co-operation between the members of the railway staff and the railway police, and are you aware of any ill-feeling between the subordinates of the two departments? (Page 221.)

15 Is any more effective system of *liaison* possible, *e.g.*, by deputing railway officers to the railway police and police officers to the railway temporarily or by the employment of police officers in the claims branch of the Traffic Department? Page 226.)

16 Is any system of rewards in force in the Claims Department, *e. g.*, are rewards given for recovery of goods:—

    (*a*) in proportion to the value of goods recovered;
    (*b*) out of the sums set apart by the railway administration to cover claims,
    (*c*) out of fines? (Page 230.)

17 Are fines imposed as punishments by the railway authorities in cases where negligence or connivance in regard to losses is proved or suspected? (Page 231.)

18 Is there much unreported loss or crime? If so, why are reports not made? (Page 233.)

19 The Railway Police are at present organised on a provincial basis. Would any other system of organization, in your opinion be an improvement on this, *e.g.*, (*a*) imperialisation, (*b*) an organization which would take the railway system as the unit and make the Superintendent of Police for most purposes the Head of a Railway Department; (*c*) a system under which the Railway Police would be amalgamated with the District Police. (Page 236.)

20 Can you give any instances of malpractices on the part of railway or police subordinates which have come under your own immediate observation? and can you suggest any measures for checking such malpractices? (Page 245.)

21 Have you any suggestions to make on any other points germane to the enquiry? (Page 248.)

Questions to be answered by trades associations, members of the public, etc.

1 What is the number of members of your Association? (Page 253.)

2 Are the members firms or individual members of firm? (Page 253.)

3 In what classes of consignments are the members mainly interested? (Page 253.)

4   In what classes of consignments are complaints of pilferage, theft or shortage most common? and on what Railway? (Page 256.)

5   Are these consignments mainly sent (1) by passenger train or goods train, (2) at Railway risk or owner's risk? (Page 259.)

6   Are complaints increasing in number? If so, can any explanation be given? (Page 263.)

7   If complaints are common, have you any suggestions as to the measures which should be adopted to give greater security? (Page 268.)

8   Do you consider that goods stations are adequately lighted and fenced? (Page 475.)

9   At what stage do you suspect that pilferages, etc., are generally made? (Page 277.)

10   Do you send your own men to book the consignments, see them into the wagon, and take delivery? (Page 282.)

11   Have you any complaints about specific malpractices, *e. g.*, pressure brought to give clear receipt without examination of goods, etc.? (Page 285.)

12   Have you any suggestions to make about the arrangements for the safety of passengers? (Page 289.)

13   Do you consider that the treatment and investigation of claims is satisfactory? Is there any special complaint as to particular classes of claims? Are claims promptly dealt with? (Page 292.)

14   Have you any suggestions to make for the improvement of the methods of dealing with claims? (Page 299.)

15   Have you any other suggestions to make germane to the inquiry? (Page 302.)

ABSTRACT OF EVIDENCE

RECORDED BY THE

RAILWAY POLICE COMMITTEE

QUESTIONS TO BE ANSWERED BY RAILWAY POLICE OFFICERS.

Question No. 1.—Do you consider that the system of having the Watch and Ward establishment under the Traffic Department works satisfactorily? If not, what are the defects and what remedies would you suggest? Do you consider any improvement in the class of men enlisted desirable.

United provinces

Mr. Kaye, Inspector-General of Police, was of opinion that there should be a separate Railway Department for Watch and Ward under a superior officer, with travelling Inspectors and Jemadars. Appointments, punishment and general control should be in his hands. The existing arrangement on most railways was very unsatisfactory. There were many complaints that members of the Watch and Ward were commonly utilised for other duties. As far as possible, military pensioners should be employed. Improvement was chiefly a question of expense.

Mr. Begbie, Deputy Inspector-General, considered that the Watch and Ward staff was undermanned and inadequately paid with the result that a great deal of pilferage was done by the staff. The lighting arrangements were inadequate even at stations like Moghal Serai, Allahabad, Cawnpore and Tundla, so that even with a larger staff, the protection of wagons could not be satisfactory. What was required was a strong staff, a better-paid staff and, if possible, a responsible official at their head. The department ought to be under some responsible officer of the railway who should welcome suggestions from the head of the railway police.

Mr. Acock, Superintendent of Police, considered that in big yards the Watch and Ward should be under the railway. Pensioned sepoys were a satisfactory class but the majority of indigenous coolies were criminals. A special officer not below the rank of Assistant Traffic Superintendent should be solely in charge. It was impossible for station masters in large yards like those at Lucknow, Saharanpur, Moradabad and Moghal Serai to exercise any efficient supervision. It was difficult for the present low class chowkidar to make out his case against other members of the yard staff who were also subordinates of the station master. The station master was a transportation officer in the main and would not willingly entertain charges of theft against his staff. The watch and ward staff urgently needed an officer to fight their battles for them.

Mr. Bell, Superintendent, Railway Police, stated that the present staff was inefficient. Railway chowkidars were underpaid and were on duty for too many hours at night. *Ex*-Jemadars and *ex*-Army sepoys should be employed and should be under the supervision of a European Sergeant at large stations. The whole force should be under a gazetted officer belonging to the railway or railway police, preferably the latter.

Mr. Fitzpatrick, Deputy Superintendent of Police, considered that there should be a separate department of the railway under the District Traffic Superintendent with separate Inspectors to supervise the Watch and Ward. He recommended the employment of Army pensioners.

Inspector Macleod suggested a separate department under the railway.

Inspector Murphy suggested that there should be a separate supervising staff controlled by the District Traffic Superintendent personally, or by one of his Assistants. The staff should have nothing to do with station masters. If the Watch and Ward establishment were transferred to the railway police, matters would not improve.

Mr. Sharpe, Superintendent, Railway Police, was of opinion that the system was very unsatisfactory. No reliable supervision or control was exercised over the staff. Chowkidars turned up late for duty and absented themselves with impunity. The distribution of duties was left to the station master's clerk, but an examination for instance at Moghul Serai would show that he merely maintained a list of chowkidars and did not arrange the duties at all. The Jemadar of the chowkidars did not distribute his force to the best possible account. Instead of 10 men in the yard only 2 would be found. The others would be in the station master's office, the parcels office and the luggage office. Thefts occurred frequently during the duty of particular chowkidars without their being taken to task. The Traffic Department which controlled the chowkidars had little knowledge of the numerous thefts reported and less interest in the matter, regarding it solely as an evil with which the Government Railway Police should deal. The efficiency of the latter was usually judged by their failure to deal successfully with yard thefts, but they had no control over the staff. The obvious remedy was to make over the Watch and Ward system *en bloc* to the Railway Police. Additional police should be appointed for the purpose. Failing this, a better class of chowkidars, *ex*-military men, should be appointed with better pay and prospects. Adequate lighting and fencing-in of yards was also an urgent necessity.

Inspector Farrant was of opinion that an inferior class of men was employed and that supervision was practically non-existent. He suggested that the Watch and Ward should be placed under the control of the Railway Police provided that the Railway Authorities made better fencing and lighting arrangements and that the pay of the staff was considerably increased. A superior class of man should be enlisted such as military or police pensioners.

Prosecuting Inspector Khairat Nabi stated that the strength was insufficient and the class of men unsuitable. Gurkhas and retired sepoys or other Government servants of the same status should be appointed with better pay and prospects. Transfers should be made after every 12 months. The appointment of local men should be avoided. There should be a jemadar or daffadar over every 12 chowkidars and 1 Watch and Ward Inspector over the whole force. The Inspector's duty would be to maintain a register of attendance and to detail the duties of jemadars and the men under him and to see that they were carried out. Every big station should have 1 Inspector and small stations should be grouped under such an official. The duties of chowkidars and jemadars should not be more than 6 hours at a time. Railway Police Constables should not be entrusted with Watch and Ward duties. There was the danger of cases failing in court in the absence of witnesses independent of the Police. Courts placed more reliance on other witnesses than on the Police. The Police could make surprise visits when necessary, but the responsibility of watching the goods should remain with the Railway Department.

Sub-Inspector Abdul Aziz considered that *ex*-Army sepoys or a good class of men of any community would be more reliable and useful than the present staff; but such men should not be kept at any station for more than a year.

Sub-Inspector Pearey Shankar complained of lack of supervision over the Watch and Ward staff and stated that the arrangement of duties was invariably left in the hands of station masters' clerks who had no experience or aptitude for such work. The Watch and Ward establishment should either be placed under the Police or under a Non-Commissioned Army officer. The class of men recruited was also very inferior. Men who had served the best part of their lives elsewhere were enlisted. They were generally unreliable, and with the inadequate pay they received and the great amount of temptation that presented itself before them while doing their duty and their physical incapacity to defy thieves, they easily fell in with the local bad characters. To ensure good work it was necessary—(1) that they should be given a living wage, (2) that they should be enlisted from men of high caste and proper enquiry should be made regarding their character; and (3) a standard of height and chest measurement and medical examination should be insisted upon.

Bombay

Mr. Robertson, Inspector-General of Police, thought that at the basis of the matter was the responsibility of the Railway Companies for the safety of the goods in their charge. The existing division of responsibilities between the Police and the Railway Companies represented by the classification "Crime and Order" and "Watch and Ward" was sound in principle and should be maintained. The duties included in these terms were set out in detail in paragraph 48 of the Report of the Railway Police Committee, 1907. It was not necessary to revise the definitions except in the case of guarding running goods trains. He suggested that the staff should be properly organised and a system of progressive pay instituted. A lower supervisory staff of Havildars and Jemadars and a higher supervisory staff of Inspectors should be appointed. Control should be removed from station masters and handed over entirely to the District Traffic Superintendent who would work through his staff of Inspectors. It should be a Railway service and the Police should have no control. Seal checking should be one of the duties of the reformed Watch and Ward staff. He thought that the guarding of goods while in motion was as much the duty of the Watch and Ward as was the guarding of them while lying in goods sheds.

Mr. Holman, Deputy Inspector-General, was of opinion that the Watch and Ward staff should be made independent of other departments and placed under a Superintendent attached to the Claims Department. The Watch and Ward staff would not be satisfactory until they were adequately paid, organised and supervised.

Mr. O'Brien, Superintendent of Police, Bombay, Baroda and Central India Railway, said that it was unsatisfactory to have one agency to prevent and another to detect. There was no proper supervision of the Watch and Ward and he would unify control of Watch and Ward and Police. Station masters had too much to do to spare time for supervision.

Mr. Austin, Deputy Superintendent of Police, Great Indian Peninsula and Madras and Southern Mahratta Railways, stated that the system of having the Watch and Ward establishment under the Traffic Department did not work satisfactorily. Men past work were enlisted, and no enquiry was made as to their antecedents with the result that in some cases *ex*-convicts were entertained. The Watch and Ward should be placed under Police supervision and better pay should be given. At present under the Traffic Department no notice was taken of Police reports. A reformed Watch and Ward might enquire into missing goods cases and report to the Superintendent of Police. An experienced Traffic Officer might be appointed Superintendent of the Watch and Ward.

Sub-Inspector Rage agreed with Mr. Austin's remarks.

Mr. Guider, formerly Deputy Inspector-General of Police, Bombay Presidency and now Watch and Ward Superintendent, Bombay, Baroda and Central India Railway, stated that he did not think that the system was satisfactory. The principal defects were (1) the haphazard method of appointing watchmen without regard to their caste, age, physical or mental condition or character, (2) the entire absence of any efficient supervision over their work. The supervision exercised by the Traffic staff was practically *nil* due chiefly to the inability of the staff to spare time, besides attending to their other and more important duties. The Watch and Ward should be made a separate department of the Railway under a responsible head with assistants to supervise the work. A better class of men, preferably *ex*-military men, should be employed on a better wage and the staff should be provided with quarters and uniform. The hours of duty which at present were 12 at a stretch should be reduced. He had been appointed temporarily as Superintendent of the Watch and Ward on the Bombay, Baroda and Central India Railway, and was at present collecting material to submit proposals for its organization and working. A small beginning had been made by employing an Inspector and several Head Watchmen and Watchmen at Baroda marshalling yard with jurisdiction as far as Ahmedabad in the north and Bombay in the south. The results for the brief period that the system had been working had been encouraging, the number of thefts from wagons, chiefly in Baroda marshalling yard, having diminished. His idea was that there should be a sufficient number of watchmen at each station effectively to guard all the goods sheds, yards, platforms and wherever shunting and other handling of goods took place. He saw no objection to chaukidars of all departments being organized into one force for each railway. The class of men now obtained was not satisfactory. When there was a vacancy some one said that the applicant was his brother and he was appointed at once. No enquiry was made about his character. A sufficiently large number of *ex*-military men was now available. They had been accustomed to discipline and had more sense of responsibility than the ordinary chaukidar. At the same time he would not exclude local men altogether, because they were very useful, having a knowledge of the people and of the surrounding country. It was essential that the staff should be provided with quarters, otherwise there was sure to be discontent. At some stations where watchmen were included in the menial staff they were provided with quarters but a large number of them were not so provided and did not even live at the station where they were employed. The men would be liable to transfer. The lowest unit would vary according to the size of the yard and the location of the station and would depend on the length and number of stations intervening. A duffadar or havildar might be appointed to look after 10 or 15 stations or if they were unimportant, the number might be increased. There were chaukidars at most stations on the Bombay, Baroda and Central India Railway, but at many there were only one or two men. It would be necessary under the new scheme to arrange for the supervision of these men by travelling inspectors and duffadars. One feature of the new scheme had been to remove the control of the Watch and Ward from the hands of the station staff. The reasons that led to this change were that the station staff never paid any attention to the Watch and Ward nor were they able to do so. Station Masters' time was taken up in attending to business in the station and on the platform. They had not the time to go to the yard to see whether the watchmen were on the alert or whether they were present or not. Choukidars were supposed to be on duty in the goods sheds and yards, but actually they went to a corner and went to sleep. The hours of duty were too long to expect any reasonable man to keep himself awake being from 6 o'clock in the evening to 6 o'clock in the morning. One man had to look after half a mile of yard where hundreds of wagons were being shunted up and down. It stood to reason that he could not effectively supervise all that was taking place during the shunting operations. Another reason for the change was the feeling that men would be better wachmen if removed from the control of the station staff, because the Indian Station Master utilized them on duty for which they were never intended, for instance, as house orderlies. One man was found serving as a *paniwala*. He had not heard any reason given that there would be less risk of their colluding with the station staff in regard to thefts and pilferages if removed from their control, but from his own personal experience he believed that there was a great deal of collusion between the station staff and chaukidars in regard to the proceeds of thefts. Station Masters got supplies of things they generally used and when the choukidars supplied them they enjoyed a certain amount of immunity from discipline. They looked after their own interests as well. With regard to the suggestion that if a well disciplined force were instituted it might be possible to cut down the staff, he thought that later some attempt might be made in that direction when things had improved, but he did not think that it would be possible in the beginning. On the contrary, it would be necessary to increase the staff. It would be necessary to put the men into uniform and to arm them with a weapon, say the *dharia* used in Gujerat which had a sort of bill book at the end of a long stick. It was a very formidable weapon. The men must have something with which to defend themselves in the case of attack by armed men. In reply to a question whether it was proposed to enlist the men under any Act, he stated that there was no enactment under which the men could be enlisted but he though it very desirable that there should be some sort of authority or power to arrest, and for superior officers, to make searches. The men of course had certain powers of arrest under the Railway Act, like any other Railway servant, but as regards the question of arresting men outside the jurisdiction of the Railway, they ought to be vested with some legal authority and made additional policemen under the Police Act. There was such a provision in the local Police Act. They should be given jurisdiction in the adjoining areas as it might be necessary to follow up cases and make inquiries and even make searches. They ought to have power to search without waiting for the local police. The headman of the village was very often the receiver of stolen property purloined from the railway. He was averse from rendering any assistance and would put all sorts of difficulties in the way of the railway investigating staff. Promptness was everything in an inquiry and these men should have the power of arrest and making searches. With regard to the suggestion that the provision in the Bombay City Police Act under which the Police were entitled to arrest a man who was in possession of property under suspicious circumstances (the onus of proving that he was innocent being on the man who was arrested) should be applied to the Railways he thought that the idea was excellent. It was intended that he should look after the whole of the Bombay, Baroda and Central India line, both metre gauge as well as broad gauge. The charge would be unwieldy for one man to supervise effectively and he thought that an assistant would be necessary. In the first instance he would ask for a Policeman because he was more accustomed to exercise supervision over disciplined men, but when the force was placed on a permanent footing he did not think that it should necessarily be officered by Policemen.

Ahmedabad

Mr. Fitzpatrick, now Catering Superintendent, Bombay, Baroda and Central India Railway but formerly an Inspector in the Railway Police, was of opinion that the Watch and Ward should be done by the Police because under the present system those responsible for Watch and Ward lacked (i) the power to summon, (ii) the power to search. Detection was absolutely eliminated in these circumstances. He thought that appointments in the Watch and Ward should either be made pensionable or that the advantages of the Provident Fund should be extended to them so that some hold could be secured over the members. If the Watch and Ward were properly run the Railways could prevent crime but they would never be able to detect it. Every Traffic Inspector should be a police officer and he should have the power to search and to summon. He should work under the Superintendent of Police who would be entirely responsible for the Watch and Ward.

Mr. Lallubhai Hargovindas, Public Prosecutor, Godhra (Panch Mahals), mentioned that during 1920 he had been employed to prosecute many railway theft cases in the Panch Mahals, the value of property stolen totalling about 7 lacs, chiefly from consignments from the Egerton and Dhariwal Mills to Dohad and Jekot. They were all goods train thefts while the train was in motion. He was of opinion that in many of these cases the watchmen were concerned as they were in touch with the thieves in the surrounding villages. He did not agree that the increase in thefts was solely due to the rise in prices. He ascribed the increase a great deal to the notion held by the Police that their responsibility had ceased after the system of watch and ward by the Railway was instituted in 1911. The main thing was supervision and that they did not get now-a-days. Station Masters sat in their bungalows and never gave an eye to the watchmen.

Inspector Garside on special duty with the Bombay, Baroda and Central India Railway as Watch and Ward Inspector, stated that the Watch and Ward should be organised as a separate department under a railway officer. A European with Police experience should control the members of the Watch and Ward. His duty as Watch and Ward Inspector was to keep the whole Watch and Ward staff awake, which was most essential because most of the thieving that was going on was being done by railway servants in the larger yards and this had been going on simply because nobody had been keeping the Watch and Ward awake. The number of the Watch and Ward was insufficient at large stations. He had not arrived at any conclusion as to the criterion which should be adopted for fixing the strength of the Watch and Ward, which depended very largely on circumstances. One man was sufficient if alert, to guard both sides of wagons. The quality of the Watch and Ward was fairly satisfactory. He was enlisting *ex*-soldiers who had been demobilised, but not pensioners, as the latter were too old as a rule.

Madras

None of the witnesses considered the system satisfactory. The main defects mentioned were:—(1) the right type of man was not appointed, (2) the supervision was inadequate.

Mr. Thomas, the Inpector-General, said that the head watchman was not a person of sufficient authority and, to have the station master as the executive head, was the worst possible arrangement. The station master did nothing whatever to stop pilferage. He had known a station master object to a suggestion from a policeman that he should do something to stop it. The general pay in Madras was Rs. 15 which was quite insufficient. An improvement in the class of men was necessary, the type of men employed in the Police being satisfactory. Greater scrutiny regarding their antecedents was also necessary. The hours of work should be greatly curtailed. At present the average watchman worked from dusk till dawn. He thought that it would be advisable to place the watch and ward under Police control, something on the line of the arrangements existing in the Kolar Goldfields. There ought to be one European supervising officer.

Mr. Hannyngton, Deputy Inspector-General, Criminal Investigation Department, said that more responsibility for crime should be put on the Watch and Ward. The Police did not supervise them officially, but in practice they did when thefts were bad.

Mr. Windle, Superintendent, Railway Police, Trichinopoly, suggested that if it were not possible to put the Police in control the Watch and War I should be encouraged to have a greater sense of responsibility by granting them gratuities and extending to them the advantages of the General Provident Fund. The railways would probably raise objections as these suggestions if adopted would mean a great increase in expenditure. A third possibility would be to get a business man to take over the whole thing on contract. Enquiries into autecedents should be made through the Railway Police. He had known of cases in which the South Indian Railway had employed dismissed policemen as watchmen.

Inspector Doraisamy suggested that the Watch and Ward should be made to deposit a certain sum in advance. This system had been tried with success in the Madras and Southern Mahratta Railway. Men of better physique and better sense and younger men were required. At present ordinary street coolies who were past work were recruited.

Inspector Krishnayya suggested shorter hours.

Bengal

Mr. Bradley, Superintendent, Railway Police, Howrah, stated that the system, as at present worked was far from satisfactory. Till quite recently the men were miserably paid. Their pay was increased lately but an incremental system should be introduced. The staff was undermanned, overworked and ill-organised. In Asansole and Bandel 25 and 33 per cent. of the men were convicted in specific cases of theft during 1920. He had to employ detectives and extra men for patrols before he could get things right at Asansole but had got good information by paying for it. At Asansole the yard was surrounded by a criminal population. A separate Watch and Ward Department should be created with an officer at its head immediately subordinate to the General Traffic Manager, with assistants at selected places on the line. The force should be organised on military or police lines with proper hours for duty and rest. There should be a reserve under a subordinate officer for duty at places where outbreaks of thefts occurred. The alternative was to place the duty of the Watch and Ward in the hands of the Police but he was not in favour of this idea.

Mr. Ezechiel, Superintendent, Railway Police, Sealdah, mentioned that the Watch and Ward jemadars who were *ex*-sepoys were too old. As the watchmen were drawn from the same class as the menials they were afraid to report them. There should be more *ex*-soldiers.

Inspector D. N. Mukherjee stated that a committee was appointed some time ago to enquire into the Watch and Ward system at Howrah. The members were all experienced subordinate officers of the railway and they were unanimous in condemning the organisation. In his opinion the best arrangement would be for the Police to take over the Watch and Ward duty and to do away with the present system. At present the Police were responsible for the detection of crime but the prevention was entrusted to a different organisation. From the Police point of view this arrangement was faulty. The Police did the Watch and Ward on the jetties of the Port Trust and thefts were less common there.

Inspector S. C. Banerjee said that the hours were too long and there should be an efficient supervising staff.

Assam

The Assam Government was of opinion that the Watch and Ward should remain under the Railway Authorities.

Mr. Giles, Superintendent, Railway Police, stated that the question of Watch and Ward was considered by the Railway and Police authorities with special reference to Chittagong jetties between the years 1910 and 1912 when the Railway was altogether opposed to Police control except under conditions which would have nullified the advantages from the point of view of the Police Department. As regards the general question of Watch and Ward the Railway would oppose any suggestion to replace their men by the Police under purely Police control. It would lead to difficulties, and perpetual quarrelling if the Watch and Ward at railway stations were done by Railway chowkidars under Police supervision. Special training of constables would also be necessary before it could be done with good results. It would then lead to the detection of malpractices on the part of railway subordinates as well as on the part of police themselves.

Inspector Syed Hashmatullah did not consider the system satisfactory. The number of the Watch and Ward should be increased and there should be an independent supervising officer. They should be enlisted from a better class of men and no miscellaneous duty such as fetching water, making purchases in the bazar, etc., should be imposed upon them.

Inspector Upendra Chandra Deb was of the same opinion.

Bihar and Orissa

Mr. Ezechiel, Superintendent, Railway Police, Patna, stated that the system of having the Watch and Ward under the Traffic Department was satisfactory but the following defects existed:—(*a*) The number of chowkidars was too small to be of any practical use. (*b*) The chowkidars were poorly paid and were not given the benefits of the Provident Fund. (*c*) They were enlisted without any enquiry being made as to their character and past history, (*d*) There was no supervision. There should be a dafadar over every group of 10 chowkidars. Chowkidars should be eligible for promotion to the post of dafadar and men doing the work of dafadars should be given better posts in the Traffic Department. Better working would probably be obtained if the Watch and Ward were placed under the Police.

Mr. Cook, Superintendent, Railway Police, Kharagpur, did not consider that the system was satisfactory. The men employed were of low class and were ill-paid and had no training. They personally committed thefts of foodstuffs. Pensioned sepoys would probably be the best men to employ.

Babu P. D. Misra, Deputy Superintendent of Police, considered the system satisfactory except for supervision. He suggested the appointment of a special staff for the purpose. Supervision and checks by station masters and goods clerks were nominal. Gurkhas and retired military men had proved a failure as chowkidars. He quoted his experience at Asansol where after a short time they became receivers. The present class was suitable if paid sufficiently and properly supervised. They should not be allowed to remain at one station for any length of time and should be severely punished for negligence and handsomely rewarded for good work.

Inspector Indar Sen Sachar did not consider that the present system was satisfactory for the following reasons:—(*a*) An unsatisfactory class of men was recruited. (*b*) Want of discipline and indefinite nature of duties. (*c*) Unlimited terms for which a chowkidar was posted at different stations. Transfers of chowkidars depended entirely on their ability to keep the establishment clerks in the office of the District Traffic Superintendent in a good humour. Owing to their position under the Station Master if the latter happened to be slack or dishonest, which was the rule rather than the exception he had to connive at what the chowkidars did to supplement their small pay. "It is an open secret that no chowkidar pays for hi food but helps himself from the stock of booked and unbooked consignments in the goods shed which are in his charge." The Railway Police should not undertake the Watch and Ward of railway property as that system had been condemned, but each Railway District should have a Watch and Ward Department and chowkidars should be recruited in consultation with the Superintendent of Railway Police. A mixed class of men should be recruited, preferably *ex*-soldiers and Gurkhas. Chowkidars should not remain at stations for longer than a year. For every ten stations there should be a dafadar whose duty should be the supervision of the work of chowkidars. Above him there would be a Sergeant under orders of the District Traffic Superintendent, who would be responsible for the supervision of the Watch and Ward staff in his jurisdiction and would be constantly on tour. The railway authorities should either take the loan of an officer of the rank of Sub-Inspector of Police from the Police Department or at least appoint men of that status and qualification in the post. The Watch and Ward staff should not be under station masters. The number of chowkidars to be employed at a particular station should be fixed in consultation with the Superintendent of Police, and when traffic conditions demanded the District Traffic Superintendent should augment this number from a small reserve. The practice of station masters employing temporary local men in vacancies and reporting the matter to the District Traffic Superintendent for approval should be abolished.

Inspector Fouzdar Narain Kuar was not in favour of the present system, the defects being:—(1) Insufficient staff. (2) Nature of supervision. (3) Underhand practices. (4) Poor pay. (5) No verification of character. The force should be under the control of the Police for the sake of better discipline. Chowkidars should have a chance of rising to the post of dafadar, constable and even head-constable in the case of good work. If possible, *ex*-Army men should be recruited. At present there was no control over the working of chowkidars. If they went to sleep in the yard when supposed to be on duty there was nobody to take them to task. They imagined that their duty was simply to report to the station master on duty when they found any seal broken in the yard.

Central Provinces

Mr. Deighton, Inspector-General of Police, did not consider that the system worked satisfactorily. The remedy was to enforce responsibility on the Traffic Department. Four-fifths of the crime reported arose from defective supervision. The pay of the upper subordinates of the Traffic Department was insufficient to keep them from temptation. Railway Companies paid enormous sums annually in compensation for goods lost or stolen and if a really substantial salary was given it would result in a corresponding decrease in compensatory expenditure, enormous saving of time and work and loss to merchants.

(*1*) *Messrs. Hurst,* (*2*) *Mayberry,* (*3*) *Glackan,* (*4*) *Sharif Muhammad Khan,* (*5*) *Mazhar Naqi, and* (*6*) *Baij Nath Kaula,* all thought that the present system was unsatisfactory.

Defects specified were:—

(*a*) Inadequate control (1), (3) and (4).

(*b*) Lack of supervision (1), (4) and (5).

(*c*) Poor quality—

    (i) Old and feeble (4), (5).

    (ii) Bad characters (4), (5).

    (iii) Poor class (2), (3).

(*d*) Men were local men and were kept too long in one place (5).

(*e*) Hours were too long (5).

Suggestions mentioned were:—

(*a*) Employ pensioners (3).

(*b*) Put Watch and Ward under Police permanently (5) or temporariily (4).

(*c*) Transfers of railway menials to be reported to Police (4).

Hyderabad (Deccan)

Mr. Crawford, Deputy Inspector-General, Railway Police, thought that the system was not satisfactory because the persons often responsible for pilfering were either the immediate superiors or colleagues of the watchmen who were not sufficiently supervised. Their hours were too long; they were on duty for 12 hours at a stretch, *i.e.,* from 7 A.M. to 7 P.M. and from 7 P.M. to 7 A.M. No care was taken to see that the men on duty from 7 P.M. to 7 A.M. did not work on their own during the day and come to work in the evening to lie down and sleep. The strength of the Watch and Ward was not insufficient. It was the supervision that was bad. Watchmen should be placed under a gazetted officer of the Railway who should enlist and control them. This officer should be known as Superintendent of Watchmen and his head-quarters should be at the head-quarters of the Railway Police Superintendent so that they might confer and work together to prevent crime. He could have some men under him to inspect the watchmen. They could also enquire into cases of theft and shortage and help the railway considerably. Men of any class made watchmen but pensioned sepoys and policemen who had been subjected to discipline and sentry duty were preferable. Their hours should be from 12 noon to 12 midnight and 12 midnight to 12 noon. It was not the proper duty of the Police to do Watch and Ward work. (Mr. Crawford added that in Hyderabad the Watch and Ward duties were performed by the Railway Police.)

317

Rajputana

Mr. Ashdown, Inspector-General, Railway Police, considered that the Watch ard Ward establishment should be under the control of the Police. At present the actual supervision was most defective as the Traffic Department could not devote any time to it except at the cost of neglecting their proper duties. If the Watch and Ward were placed under the control of the Police they would be better supervised. The Police would also be in possession of the antecedents of the men and would maintain a permanent record regarding them. If the Traffic Department were unwilling to relinquish all control over the establishment, it should be possible to allow it to continue to enlist the men (the present class was satisfactory provided the Police had some power of *veto* in the case of men of bad character), to leave all supervision to the Police and to grant both departments joint powers of dismissal. If supervision was made over to the Police, it would be necessary to increase the strength of Head Constables and Sub-Inspectors. It would, however, be possible for the Railway Companies to organise their Watch and Ward as a regular service. The Bombay, Boroda and Central India Railway had taken steps to do so. There would be no objection to the Watch and Ward being organised as separate branch of the Traffic Department with a gazetted officer at its head. Powers of supervision should be given to the Police together with authority to exclude men of bad character or to dismiss them with the concurrence of the Railway officer in charge of the department. This arrangement would not lead to friction but he would prefer that the Watch and Ward should be under the control of the Police. In the case of the District Police the chowkidari establishment was under the District Superintendent of Police although it was controlled by the District Magistrate. People who had to watch and take care of property should be more or less under the control of the Police if they were to be expected to minimise losses or to prevent crimes.

Sind

Mr. Barker, Superintendent, Railway Police, Karachi, was of opinion that the system was not satisfactory. The present arrangement for Watch and Ward which was done by chowkidars enlisted in a haphazard manner by the Traffic Department and practically uncontrolled was a very weak spot in the prevention of crime. A better method would be the employment of men under Section 22B of the District Police Act, IV of 1890, which would ensure the enlistment of a suitable type of men, a lequate control over them and prospects of promotion. The Railway would pay for the force but would have no voice in its control in the same way as private persons and firms, such as Ralli Brothers, obtained additional police which were controlled by the Police Department while the firms paid for services rendered. The present chowkidars were at the beck and call of station masters and others and did very little Watch and Ward. The chowkidars placed on guard over consiguments were often so ignorant and in many cases so old that when questioned they could not give the number of packages placed under their charge. It would be possible to surmount the present difficulties by having a regularly organised Watch and Ward service on each railway if the chowkidar was not at the beck and call of station masters and others.

Khan Saheb Mubarak Ali Hyder Ail, Inspector of Police, was of opinion that the system of having the Watch and Ward under the Traffic Department was not satisfactory. Chowkidars were employed on low pay, while their enlistment, discharge and dismissal were made on the recommendations and at the discretion of station masters, therefore they had to work in consultation with them. The men employed were useless. This work ought to be entrusted to the Police and men should be specially selected for the purpose. They should be made to understand that they would be rewarded by promotion for good work and that they would be held responsible for proper watch and ward.

Punjab

Mr. Farquhar, Inspector-General of Police, stated that the existing force of chowkidars at large centres should be replaced by regular police because the members of the latter force could be transferred from one duty to another and in that way could be prevented from forming cliques and gangs which could not be ensured with chowkidars who were residents of the locality. Where there was a police station with an Inspector and perhaps a Deputy Superintendent, control and supervision could be easily exercised over the Watch and Ward. He did not advocate such an arrangement in small places because the Watch and Ward would be thoroughly slack and there would be no discipline. Moreover thefts at small stations were comparatively easy to locate, at any rate, much easier than in big yards like Lahore, Delhi and Rawalpindi. Replacing the chowkidari staff at large stations by Railway Police would not transgress the principle that the railway were responsible for the safe custody of goods in their charge. The men would be additional police and would be paid for by the railway. That arrangement would be better than the system of having a regular Watch and Ward service in the Railway with gazetted officers at the head, because even under such an arrangement the chowkidars could not be transferred whereas there were police buildings at every large station. The North-Western Railway did not provide quarters for their chowkidars.

Mr. Stead, Assistant Inspector-General, did not consider that the system was satisfactory, the chief defects being:—(*a*) Want of supervision, and (*b*) Poor quality of the staff. He would replace the Watch and Ward chowkidars by additional police under the Railway Police at large centres maintaining the present arrangement of chowkidars under the Traffic Department at minor stations only. Such an arrangement would entail extra expenditure for the Railway because the Police received pensions and were clothed and housed. They were also better paid than the chowkidars and they got leave. He had discussed the suggestion with the Agent and other Railway officials and he did not think that they were hostile to the proposal.

Khan Bahadur Abdul Hakim, Deputy Superintendent of Police, did not consider the system satisfactory, the chief defects being (*a*) employment of incompetent hands, (*b*) want of supervision. He was of opinion that the Watch and Ward should be under the supervision of station house officers or that they should be replaced by additional police. His experience went to show that the goods clerks were hand in glove with the chowkidars and were implicated in pilferages. Another argument against the system was that the chowkidars did the work of private servants for the clerical staff. Furthermore, it was a common complaint in his jurisdiction that the Railway could not obtain sufficient chowkidars: for instance, 40 chowkidars were sanctioned for Rawalpindi but there were actually only 9 chowkidars on the roll. The Railway paid their Chowkidars Rs. 17 per mensem whereas the Police started on Rs. 17–8 and rose to Rs. 20. They also received extra Re. 1, as an allowance and had many chances of promotion to the post of Head-Constable and Sub-Inspector. Sub-Inspectors generally rose from constables.

Part 8

THE RAILWAY AS OASIS
Egypt, the Near East, and the Middle East

49

ISABELLA F. ROMER, *A PILGRIMAGE TO THE TEMPLES AND TOMBS OF EGYPT, NUBIA, AND PALESTINE IN 1845–6*, 2 VOLS. (LONDON: R. BENTLEY, 1846), PP. 98–100

Since I have been here I have had an opportunity of hearing the great question of a railroad across the Desert to Suez much discussed. It would be presumptuous in me to venture an opinion of my own as to its *practicability*, but I can bear full testimony to its being a most *desirable* object, not only as regards the commercial interests of England, but in facilitating the progress of the overland travellers to and from India, and converting that which is now the most fatiguing part of the journey into the easiest and most agreeable. It generally happens that the two mails meet here, the steamer belonging to the Transit Company at Alexandria bringing the Indian passengers who have landed there from Southampton, and depositing them at Cairo, where they are allowed a very short time to enjoy themselves, after having been stowed away in the Nile Steamer for thirty-six hours closer than the inmates of a slave-ship. They are then packed into vans provided by the Transit Company, in which they are jumbled across the Desert, and generally reach Suez in the space of twenty-four hours or so, their baggage, provisions, &c. being sent upon camels and asses. At Suez they are at once embarked in the Red Sea steamer, *et vogue la galère!* The passengers coming from India exactly reverse this line of march, but they are exposed to greater suffering and inconvenience; for, after a long sea-voyage, with its concomitant miseries, they are hurried across the Desert without delay, and such among them as are in too invalid a state to be able to support the rough vans, are put into a sort of sedan chair, which is suspended between two donkeys, and thus they are trotted across the dreary waste.

Now, could the great desideratum of a rail-road across the Desert be accomplished, all this suffering would be obviated, for *in less than three hours* the Indian passengers would be transported, baggage and all, from Cairo to Suez, and *vice versâ*. In short, the terminus would be established at Boulac, the port of Cairo; and the rail-road would thus run without interruption from the Red Sea to the Nile, and would enable travellers to go *overland* from London to Calcutta, *viâ*

Marseilles, without ever having recourse to post-horses, except for a few stages between Paris and Chalons-sur-Saone!

As in all places local politics take precedence of general ones, I have heard the *pour et contre* of the railway question much canvassed since I have been in Cairo; and it has been my good fortune to form the acquaintance of one who has the power of explaining the advantages accruing from such an undertaking better than any one else could possibly do, as by him and by his late brother, Galloway Bey, the original idea was conceived of thus as it were diminishing the distance between the Red Sea and the Nile, and squeezing the weary passage of the Desert into an agreeable three hours' morning drive. These gentlemen submitted their great plan to Mohammed Ali, who possesses both genius to appreciate and energy to execute such a conception, were he left to his own unbiassed judgment; and so much did he *then* approve of it that he empowered Messrs. Galloway to send for machinery and rails to England in order to commence operations.

50

JAMES HINGSTON, *THE AUSTRALIAN ABROAD ON BRANCHES FROM THE MAIN ROUTES ROUND THE WORLD* (MELBOURNE: W. INGLIS, 1885), P. 348

Our train has a breakdown that occasions two hours' detention near to a native village, which, with my new acquaintance, I go to visit. It is the most wretched of sights. A collection of low-built huts—mere pigsties of places, and wholly unfit for human habitation. They appear in the distance, huddled together, like so many mud-made beehives. A space of about two feet separates each of them, which is all of street that there is to these mud-mound villages. To enter one of these horrible collections of dwellings is a sore trial to the eyes and nose, as also to the sympathies of the sentimental. Every hand, down to that of the infant in arms, is held out for begging, and one cannot fail to give where there is such crushing evidence of need. There is not a vestige of furniture in these hovels. The aborigines of Australia are, all things considered, better off. In the lowest depths there is said to be yet a deeper, and so with this poor land-labourer. He is liable, I am told, any day to be driven away to a distance to work, as a slave, on public works at the slave's pay of a daily handful of grain and the lash. Mehemet Ali in 1820–1 had a canal—the Mahmoodieh canal, which runs for a distance of seventy miles from Cairo to Alexandria—dug by an average hundred and fifty thousand of these poor oppressed wretches, daily employed for nearly two years. They died in hundreds at the work, the total loss of life on the undertaking being thirty-eight thousand. No tools were provided for them. The women laboured equally with the men, and were forced to scoop the earth out with their hands, and carry it away in the miserable rag of an apron that is their chief covering. Taxes are collected at any time that money is wanted. The collection is organised by officials called in gradation Finance Minister, Mudir, Mamour, Sheik Elbeled, Sarraf, and another official who carries the stick that, applied to the soles of the feet, compels payment, if torture can do so.

To the honour of the English be it said that in the public works for which British contracts were taken, which were of course paid for by British-borrowed money, the contractors refused slave labour, and paid honestly for the work done. Such was done also in the construction of the Suez Canal. It is impossible to imagine how astonished the Egyptians must have been at such fair treatment. England must get and keep Egypt some day, if only to pay herself back something of her loans, and to protect her dearly-bought interest in the canal. There can be no one in Egypt who has to work and pay taxes but must say the sooner the better. "It is a consummation devoutly to be wished" by all who have the interest of humanity—to say nothing of Egypt—at heart.

Cairo is reached at last. Its minarets glittering in the setting sun's rays are vis-ible long before it is reached. It is impossible to keep one's seat and one's head inside the carriage, though my French friend tells me that I shall see quite enough of it from the easier point of view to be got from a donkey's back. The station is a large one, and so is the mob of people about it—quite preparing one for the big city beyond, which surprises one by its size, as also by its busy and bustling look. All nationalities seem mixed up in it, and the endless donkeys and their drivers help to mix them up still more. The streets get more thickly crowded as we prog-ress, and the noise of the donkey-drivers is a distinct characteristic at once percep-tible, and is also the shout of those "avant-couriers" who run in front of most of the vehicles to help clear the way. The importance of the coming vehicle is seen in the number of these forerunners. One thinks of the honours paid of old in giving to some one "a carriage and horses and fifty men to run before him."

51

C. F. GORDON CUMMING, *VIA CORNWALL TO EGYPT* (LONDON: CHATTO & WINDUS, 1885), PP. 102–104

Those yellow slippers, too, are worthy of notice. The orthodox bright yellow dye with which the leather is stained is obtained from the rinds of pomegranates. Every blue-robed woman whom you meet probably carries on her head a great flat basket of fruits and vegetables, her little marketing for the day; or else on her shoulder sits a quaint Eastern baby, and a group of bigger children clustered round her—little creatures whose large, calm eyes would be so beautiful were it not for flies and filth; but, alas! as some one suggested, "What is beauty without soap?" (and, indeed, soap seems a thing unknown in Egypt, or at least wonderfully precious, judging from the prices charged for washing!) As to these poor dark-eyed little ones, their mothers keep them filthy on purpose, lest any one passing should admire them, and so excite the envy of evil spirits.

Moreover, they believe it strengthens the sight to paint the eyelids of even the youngest baby with khol, a mixture of soot and antimony, which is carefully applied with a silver bodkin. This certainly makes the eye look immensely large, but painfully unnatural. Then, the amount of ophthalmia is something frightful. It is due chiefly to the intense dryness of the atmosphere and the subtle, impalpable dust which for ever floats in the air above the crowded city. Exceeding dirt also does its part; while the swarm of flies which cluster on the sores, and there revel undisturbed, are a sight to fill you with disgust. Of course they carry infection to the next eye on which they settle, and so the loathsome disease spreads, and that with such frightful rapidity that sometimes the whole eye is reduced to a mere opaque pulp within twenty-four hours, even when the sufferer is otherwise in perfect health. The consequent amount of blindness is startling; and I believe the computation is that one man in six has lost the sight of either one or both eyes.

Even where actual blindness does not exist, the powers of vision are singularly defective, and when it became necessary for the railway, in selecting its servants, to test their sight, it was found that a very small minority of the candidates could distinguish a red signal from a green one at a distance of a hundred yards. I believe this is partly the reason that so large a proportion of the company's servants are Europeans.

It is said that in the time of Mahomet Ali many children were artificially made blind of one eye to exempt them from the conscription; indeed, grown-up men voluntarily blinded themselves to avoid the hated service, forgetting that the wilful destruction of one eye might always involve the loss of both. A gentleman who was travelling in Egypt, not very long after that time, told me that of his eight boatmen two had lost one eye, a third was nearly blind of both, four had purposely knocked out three upper teeth on the right side, to avoid biting cartridges, while the eighth had chopped off the trigger finger from the right hand. He adds, that in a whole day he had failed to notice one peasant working in the fields who was what he termed a sound man, that is, one who had not subjected himself to some such voluntary mutilation to escape conscription. Mahomet Ali, however, hit on the expedient of raising a one-eyed regiment, so as to utilize as many as possible of these refractory subjects.

The ravages of ophthalmia tell cruelly on the beauty of the Egyptian women. Too often the dark blue veil, which just reveals one dreamy brown eye, conceals a hideous chasm in the place where its fellow should be.

How little Moore can have suspected so prosaic a cause when he describes

> "The mask that shades
> The features of young Arab maids,
> A mask that leaves but one eye free
> To do its best in witchery."

The said mask, or rather veil, is the inevitable yashmak—a mantle veiling the whole head and figure, and fastened across the nose by a brass ornament, so as just to leave an opening for the eyes (or eye, as the case may be). With the poor, this veil is invariably of a deep blue, dyed with indigo; but richer folk wear black silk, and their attendants white linen, and when the wind blows back this covering it reveals indoor raiment of vivid colours, beautifully embroidered.

52

HADJI KHAN (GAZANFAR ALI), ARMIN VAMBERRY AND WILFRID SPARROY, *WITH THE PILGRIMS TO MECCA* (LONDON: J. LANE, 1905), PP. 83–84, 87

Two trains start from Port Said to Suez every day, one in the forenoon and one in the evening. The line as far as Ismailia is a narrow tramway having a gauge of 2ft. 8in.; the cars are consequently both narrow and uncomfortable, and take about three hours to do the journey. On my bidding good-bye to the dragoman I had engaged, he assured me that he was far too devout a Muslim to fleece so pious a pilgrim as myself, and he would not accept a centime more than five francs for the boat, the carriage, and his special services. It was from him that I first heard of the outbreak of cholera in Arabia—a report that was unfortunately confirmed at Suez, whither I journeyed in the discomfort of a dust-storm and a hot easterly wind. We arrived at Ismailia at one o'clock, or thereabouts, having left Port Said at a quarter to ten o'clock. This place, when the canal was being cut, was the headquarters of the workmen; but now it has sunk in importance, many of the buildings having actually fallen in ruins. Some of the managers of the company, however, are still living there, and the best houses in the town are at their disposal. Employment is provided on the canal for some hundred and twenty pilots, most of whom are Greeks and Frenchmen, though a few Englishmen have been recently added to the staff. The railway from Cairo to Suez, which belongs to the Egyptian Government, passes through Ismailia and picks up the passengers for Suez who have travelled so far by the Canal Company's toy line. Henceforward the journey was made in comfort, for the line, though a single one, is a standard British gauge and the train provided with an excellent waggon-restaurant. Nearly all the passengers on board were Arabs and low-class Europeans in the third-class compartments. We stopped at three stations on the way, and every time it happened we were greeted by a weird chorus of Arab song, of which the burden was the "Wondrous names of God and the virtues of His Prophet." I was somewhat amused to hear the words, "Not I, by God!" in reply to my inquiry as to whether or not a certain Arab would be good enough to fetch a bottle of soda water for me. For I, being unused to the climate, had suffered tortures from thirst in the scorching heat and driving dust-clouds, the intervals between the stages being extremely long and tedious—in fact, it took the train seven hours and a quarter to cover the hundred miles that separate Port Said from Suez. Nor was the prospect of a sort to slake the thirst of the weary pilgrim. All along the line hugs the right bank of the canal, and nothing is to be seen except the soft white sand of the glowing desert, unless it be an occasional patch of green grass or a cluster of date trees, irrigated by the fresh-water canal newly cut in order to conduct the much-needed water from a spot near Cairo to Port Said and Suez, the latter a place which stands in sore want of the cleansing and refreshing element.

On my arrival at the station a dragoman, one of the plagues of Egypt, joined himself to my suite, informing me with glib mendacity that he carried both Arabia and the Land of the Pyramids in his pocket, whereas, as a matter of fact, he had not once left his native town. However, as I could not shake the fellow off, I made the best of a bad bargain by taking him out shopping with me. First, I bought a deep crimson fez with a long black silk tassel and a straw lining. Though it looked both cool and fanciful, and was therefore pleasing to my Oriental eye, I am not certain that a turban would not have been more in keeping with the complete Arab suit which I subsequently purchased. This consisted of a thin linen shirt, a pair of trousers, and two long and graceful robes. The shirt was worn as long as a night-shirt, it had no collar, and the roomy sleeves were left open at the wrists. The trousers were more interesting, and of a curious shape and an odd material, being made of thin white calico, and so cut that whereas an elephant's thigh could scarcely fill the ample width of the uppermost part, one had the greatest difficulty in slipping the feet through the lower ends which clung tightly round the ankles. As for the two robes, which were long enough to cover the nether garments, the inner one was made of the finest silk, striped in successive colours of red, yellow, and green, and was left entirely open in front, but the left breast overlapped the right, to which it was buttoned from the armpits downwards. The outer habit of a blueish colour served as a cloak to the inner one, was made of the same material, and cut in precisely the same way. No socks were worn, and the shoes were not unlike ordinary slippers, with this exception, that they were turned up at the toes.

53

NORMA LORIMER, *BY THE WATERS OF EGYPT* (LONDON: METHUEN, 1909), PP. 1–3, 425–427

Journeying to Cairo

CAIRO, *Nov.* 1907

I AM in Egypt—I have seen the desert, I have felt the sunshine, I have bowed my head before the Sphinx. Dear friend, it is all fermenting inside my benumbed brain, none of it will come to my pen—I must write just now of lighter things, of things which in the aggregate make up Egypt, but which are not Egypt, as the desert is Egypt, as the sunshine is Egypt, as the Sphinx is Egypt. Time and custom will, I suppose, allow me to talk and write glibly about these paramount things in this overwhelming land of the Pharaohs; at present you of all people will understand how impossible it is.

Landing in Alexandria is even more alarming for a *dame seule* than landing in Syracuse, and I have often told you what that means!

After what I have seen of Mohammedan life in Tunis and Turkey, I am prepared to love Mohammedan Egypt as I love Catholic Italy.

In the busy station, which was in the wildest confusion, congested by a ship-load of passengers of all nationalities embarking themselves on one small train for Cairo, I saw a stately Arab spread out his prayer-mat close to the wall of the stationmaster's office, the one spot free from luggage, and commence his evening prayer. As though alone in the desert or before the sacred *mihrab* of a mosque, he stood for some moments at the end of his mat with folded hands and closed eyes. He seemed to be listening to some voice speaking to his ears alone, then suddenly he dropped to his knees and touched the mat three times with his forehead. For at least ten minutes he prayed, now in perfect silence, now in chanting monotones, with that peculiar intonation which is as intimately connected with the Koran as a curate's voice is associated with the litany. The engines shrieked, the European passengers lost their manners and their seats in their noisy nervousness about their luggage, but that unmindful Moslem prayed on. At the very last moment, when the guard, and the engine-driver, and the stationmaster, and I think the stoker and the porters, had all agreed with each other by mystical signs and glances that the train might make a start, he picked up his mat, put on his shoes and shouldered his *goullah* of unbaked clay. On his back was a sweeping bundle of green sugar-cane, a brown-and-white striped bag full of only an Eastern could have told what, and a meek black kid, which with Christian resignation allowed its legs to be tied together round his neck. With that scorn of hurry which gives the Arab his "Christ-like" dignity, he walked across the platform and stepped majestically into the slowly moving train.

I was lost in admiration.

The way he had timed that prayer was perfect. That he had not skipped or slurred a single passage, you may be sure. The way I had been deceived into thinking, in that medley of verbacious Italians, yelling Orientals, and shrieking engines, that he was alone with his God, was also perfect.

Little did I dream that these mystic eyes which seemed to be thinking of what they did not see, had kept a sharp look-out on the occult passes of the moving spirits of the train!

But such is the East; nothing that matters is ever divulged. An Arab will talk his head off about all that does *not* matter, and keep as perfect silence as any living thing could about all that you wish to know.

My first impressions of the East are already a little dimmed, yet not a week has passed since I landed. The mud villages which I saw for the first time on my journey from Alexandria to Cairo, and which gave me such keen pleasure, I now take for granted; you will say no wonder, for they all look the same, just as though they had grown up out of the sand they stand in. The houses are always mud-brown, without one touch of colour or bit of stone masonry to break their outline; they are very low and very dirty, yet to me the picture they create is quite beautiful.

The great oasis of the Libyan desert

CAIRO, *May 5th*, 1907

About our journey to the great oasis

WHAT actually fired us into going to the oasis was the fact that before the Oasis Company laid their railway line across the desert, and that was only six months ago, it used to take, by the shortest route, sixty hours on camel, that was from Gorgah a distance of one hundred and twenty miles.

The route from Esneh is one hundred and thirty-eight miles; and the route from Assiout, which is part of the road by which slaves were formerly brought into Egypt from Darfûr and Kordofân, is one hundred and twenty-six miles from the Nile.

Dr. Budge in his guide-book says the journey generally takes from five to six days by camel. Now we left Cairo at 6.30 p.m., had a most comfortable bed and dinner on board the train, and arrived at the Western Oasis at about sundown next evening. It seemed almost incredible that we could have done that same six days' journey by camel in that short space of time by train, and have done it too as easily and comfortably as though we had been travelling from Paris to Nice. The *wagon lits* in Egypt are very cool and comfortable, for they are built of wicker-work, and everything about them is extremely modern and well planned to alleviate the trials of a dusty journey. Our friend at court, the manager of the Oasis Railway, had told some one at the Oasis settlement to have the rest-house for travellers ready for our arrival; and he had got food sufficient for three days waiting for us at the base, which our faithful Mohammed Ali took up with us. He was for these three days our cook, maid, house-parlour maid, and dragoman all in one.

On our return journey to Cairo the up express, the famous *train-de-luxe* of Egypt, stopped for us at the base, which, let me mention, is the junction where we left the Egyptian State railway for the new desert railway belonging to the Oasis Company. Stopping at the base was an act of courtesy on the company's part, who are always most anxious to do what they can to make tourists' journeys by rail enjoyable. Certainly their express well deserves its name, for it is extremely luxurious.

I thought it was charming of our friend, the manager of the Oasis line, and of his friends who lived with him at the base, to pretend so splendidly that they were glad to see us, for we got off the train at a horribly early hour—it was just dawn—and landed ourselves on their hospitality for some hours. I must say that the sight of Lorna may have made the pretence a little easier, for, no matter what sort of a night she has passed, she always makes her appearance as fresh and smiling as though the world had been created on purpose for her enjoyment each new day.

Our breakfast in the grey dawn carried my thoughts back to my journey across Canada, in the early days of the Canadian Pacific Railway. The wooden house close to the line, the total absence of any other habitations, the happy open-air life led by the little colony of Englishmen, whose daily lives were entirely connected with the line, in one way or another; it all spoke to me of the days when I used to visit the young engineers, whose houses were dumped down like Bedouin tents along the track of the great Canadian Pacific Railway. The one great difference was, that life in Egypt is built on more luxurious lines, for the native has a genius for cooking and doing domestic work; whereas in Canada, unless you are far enough west to come in touch with the Chinese immigrant, you very often have, or had in those days, to do your own cooking as well as your own washing. At the base there was no want of comforts, or even luxuries. As we ate the beautiful dinner our friends gave us on our return journey, I could not help thinking how very well men can get along without women when they have native servants to do every conceivable thing for them, and when they can order the latest records for the pianola and gramophone to make their long evening hours amusing.

We ate our lobster cutlets to the accompaniment of Arab songs, and sipped our liqueurs and black coffee in rocking chairs on the wide verandah, under the opulence of a desert moon and the splendour of a night-blue sky ablaze with stars,—southern stars that radiated like little suns,—while Madame Melba sang her famous song in *La Bohème* in the very best gramophone style.

It was really beautiful, for the instrument was far enough away for us to lose the hissing sound, and Madame Melba's voice in the clear air was as perfect as in the opera-house at Covent Garden. Squatting on the desert sand in front of us were little groups of listening natives; with the moonlight pouring down upon their dark clear-cut faces and slender limbs, they made a striking contrast to our party.

Indeed, the scene was full of picturesque contrasts—contrasts between things ancient and modern, Oriental and European: the white *jebbas* of the natives, their carefully turbaned heads, the tweed suits of the Englishmen, their pink sun-burnt faces; the vast stretch of desert sand, the limitless starry sky; and, most incongruous of all, the railway train and the gramophone.

On our journey onwards from the base to the Oasis we sat in the engineers' car, which had windows all round it, so that we saw as much of the scenery as though we had been travelling on camels in the old way; and this again reminded me of my long journeys in the "observation cars" of Canada.

54

E. L. BUTCHER, *EGYPT AS WE KNOW IT* (LONDON: MILLS & BONN, 1911), PP. 6–16, 22–23, 153–155

To be an Englishman at the head of a Government department in those days, was to occupy a position something like that of a great English lord of the manor in medieval times. Our power over the natives stopped short of life and death. We could put people into prison, keep them there for years, or take them out again, at our will and pleasure, without inquiry or formality of any kind. When I first went to the Pyramids, with but one companion, I found two sheep being roasted whole over a fire in the desert to furnish our luncheon. When we travelled it was in a special train, and, according to our rank, provision for so many "wives" must be made to accompany us. My brother, I found, was entitled to eight "harem" on his train, all of whom I represented in my own person. Once when we woke up in the morning at a desert station we found *four* specials waiting for our orders. It happened in this wise.

We started on a journey of inspection at six o'clock one morning, and drove to Boulak da Krur. For at that time Boulak da Krur was the nearest station where you could touch the line to Assiout—it went no farther south—or in the other direction to Tel el-Baroud, where it joined the main line to Alexandria. It was to Tel el-Baroud that we were bound, and our journey was for the most part through desert, but you could generally see the distant fringe of green which marked the course of the Nile. The fresh water canal, by the side of which the line passes for a considerable distance, did not at that time produce even the thinnest line of vegetable life along the water's edge. Now, thanks to my brother, the line runs through miles of plantations, producing telegraph poles and a particularly valuable fibre. Then, owing to the loose and crumbling sand, it needed to be constantly cleaned out; and some way from Cairo we passed a band of several thousand fellahs engaged in that work. It was curious to see them swarming like ants in the distance, for they spread thickly over a mile or two of the way. They were a wild-looking and open-mouthed multitude, in rags more or less picturesque, as they paused in their slow going to and fro with baskets of sand to watch us go by. They had no tools, only these baskets, which they filled down by the water's edge and carried up to empty on the top of the bank. A dreary dawdling kind of work it seemed, much as if they had tried to ladle out the water with tea-spoons. They were presided over by patriarchal-looking old men with long flowing robes, white turbans, and thick sticks. This was the "corvée," a system which we have long since abolished. At one station we all got out and strolled round in the sunshine to inspect the one tree in the place, by an old water-wheel still in use, though a steam pump had been provided close by and apparently never worked. Here the land was no longer desert, but stretched away on either hand in a flat, green plain, covered with heavy crops of beans, wheat, and barley. The native villages were not half so unpicturesque as I imagined they would be. It is true they are merely built of dried mud with flat roofs; but they have a way of piling the houses one above another on the rising ground, so that the straight lines and small round pigeon-towers are decidedly effective when relieved by a background of blue sky, and surmounted by the straight stems and feathery crowns of the palms.

By and by we reached Baroud, the limit of our day's inspection. I sat in the station and took a sketch of what could be seen through the arches while E. was busy, and then we went out and wandered about the country. As soon as we could, we started on our return journey. E. wanted to get back in time for a Board Meeting the same afternoon, so we went along rather fast, though when we got into the desert again a strong wind was blowing the sand across the line and piling it up in great drifts against the few obstacles it encountered.

It was the sand which drove us off the line. We had been shaking badly for some time, it was very hot, and we were all silent and sleepy when the shaking increased violently, there was a plunge forward, a crash, and E., Mohammed, Ghulamshah and I found ourselves all mixed up in a heap. We were all extracted from the carriage, but I soon came back again to sit inside it, though at a curious angle, as nothing could be done but send off messengers to the nearest station—seven miles—to telegraph and wait for help. After sketching I tried to write a letter, and when driven by wind and sand and noise to desist, I solaced myself by reading Latimer's *Sermon of the Ploughers*, and studying the features of the scene.

It was two o'clock when we broke down, and we waited till it grew dark without any change in the position of affairs. It grew also very cold, and as I had expected to be home in the heat of the day, I had nothing except a thin cloak to put over my muslin dress, and had to take one of E.'s rugs. It was impossible to keep the wind out of the carriage, as the jar had shaken the windows, so that they did not fit properly. We had candles fortunately, and outside the Arabs lighted a fire on the sand and cowered round it.

No one came, and we began to think we were abandoned in the desert for good, but we afterwards heard that they had been busy enough about us at both ends of the line. On hearing the news by telegram, two specials were dispatched, one after another, from Alexandria; while at Boulak, when they at length heard of our accident, one of the clerks got an engine and started off to our rescue. But as we had effectually blocked the desert line he had to go up the main line to Baroud and come down again. Meanwhile we poor creatures were roused into life about half-past eight by the welcome sound of a train whistle, and beheld the lights of the first Alexandrian engine, which had taken all this time to get down to us. It had only a second-class carriage attached of an antediluvian character—much worse than an English third, and with no glass in any of the windows. Altogether, as we could not get home without going up to Baroud and down the main line, which would have taken us half the night, E. decided that we had better pass the night at the station next on the way to Tel el-Baroud. So we stopped there and got out in a scene of wild confusion. Every one stood round with lanterns and all vociferated together in Arabic. E. explained to me that they wanted me to go into the station-master's harem instead of passing the night in the waiting-room. I agreed, glad of the new experience, for this was a little out-of-the-way desert station without even a village near it.

The stationmaster, a fussy little man with a shawl tied round his neck, immediately led me up a rough stone staircase and battered furiously at a wooden door, shouting something in Arabic. A woman opened the door with many exclamations, and we came into what I suppose was a kind of hall, as it was destitute of all furniture. The harem consisted of four rooms all opening into one another. In the second there was a broad divan running half round the room and a bedstead. Almost the only other thing in the room was a brazier full of charcoal, which stood on the floor in one corner. By the side of the bed a little carpet was spread out, and upon it a woman was saying her prayers in Oriental fashion. She did not look round or appear in any way conscious of the entrance of an English stranger, though I suppose such an event could never have happened before in her life. I waited till her prayers were finished, when she came forward and greeted me. We could not of course speak to each other, as neither she nor any of the rest could speak any European language, and I knew exactly five words of Arabic, none of which suited the present emergency. By and by the stationmaster came back again and took me into room No. 3, where I was again seated on a divan, and through the open door of No. 4 could see another woman bustling about with bedclothes, and evidently preparing her own bed for me. Meanwhile the stationmaster was bundling up and down stairs with quilts, etc., for E.'s comfort. I observed that he never came into the inner rooms without leaving his shoes on the threshold of No. 3.

After a little time they had completed all possible preparations in my honour, and the master, nerving himself for a final effort, came up to me, scrabbled at his own mouth with his hand and ejaculated the beautiful French sentence, "Mungey? Mungey?" I politely declined and spoke to him in French, but it was a failure. Evidently he had exhausted all the resources of his learning in that direction, so he only led me to the door of No. 4, and signed to me to enter.

This room was smaller, and contained two beds, one had been made up on the floor and the other spread with a clean quilt for me. Both had mosquito curtains of native muslin. Under the bed I perceived the family store of bread piled upon the floor; there were also some boxes in one corner filled with wearing apparel, and a lamp in the window-sill. Here I found a very pretty little woman very anxious to be friendly and talkative; but neither of us managed to make out much of what the other wished to say. As soon as the women disappeared, I seized the opportunity to get out of the bed into which they had insisted on my climbing just as I was, and took off my boots and out-of-door things. At this juncture they both reappeared, and seeing my stockinged feet upon the carpet the little woman immediately dived down to the bottom of one of her boxes, and produced a pair of new slippers carefully packed in paper, which she gave me to put on. Then they led me to the toilette table in the next room and pointed out to me with great pride a veritable watchpocket nailed upon the wall. As, however, I happened to have left my watch at home, I could not gratify them by making use of it, and soon retreated to my bed again. In a few minutes I found them on their knees again outside my curtains, through which they poked up to me tiny cups of a liquid which I think was meant for tea, made in a coffee-pot. After this they retired, but I heard them chattering and laughing together in the outer room for a long time before my pretty friend came in and got into the other bed. I pretended then to be asleep—not that I did sleep much that night

When it grew light I began to wonder what was the next step. I had no means of communicating with E., and he had not told me any probable time for starting. Every one else was snoring peacefully, and I did not like to disturb them, so I lay still. Suddenly, however, I heard the stationmaster in the outer room shouting to me, "Locomotive! Coming!" two words of English with which he must have carefully primed himself for the occasion. I jumped out of bed and made a hasty toilet. Downstairs I found E., looking rather exhausted after his night on the divan of an Egyptian railway station room, several natives, and Mr. A., who by working all night had managed to get our own special train up, and ready for use. That was how four specials came to be waiting for us at once in the days of Ismail Pasha.

I took for granted at the time that I had been in the private house of a Mohammedan, but I know now that nothing could have been more unlikely. In those days it was impossible to find a sufficient number of educated Mohammedans for such positions; even now, after a generation of education and with every desire on the part of English officials to favour Mohammedans, it is not common to find a Moslem stationmaster. The despised Christian Egyptians of the old race are still appointed, though grudgingly, to posts where both intelligence and trustworthiness are required.

The songs of the people are generally found to reflect popular feeling better than any other form of expression, and Egypt is no exception to the rule, though perhaps the monotonous recitative of the labourers at work should rather be called a chant than a song. Here are three specimens from different periods. The first is a translation made by one who listened to the chant of the labourers at work on the Suez railway when it was first built. In the time of Ismail it is perhaps unnecessary to remind my readers that the labour was both forced and unpaid.

Chant of the men

Strophe:—We are all in rags, we are all in rags,
Antistrophe:—That the shiekh may be dressed in cloth.

Chant of the children

Boys:—They starve us, they starve us;
Girls:—They beat us, they beat us;
Boys:—But there's some one above,
         There's some one above,
Girls:—Who will punish them well,
         Who will punish them well.

Years pass, Ismail is gone, forced labour is not altogether abolished, but the labourers are properly treated and paid. Here is the chant of the men at work on a Government undertaking under an English official.

Strophe:—The Pasha has a thick stick.
Antistrophe:—But his pockets are full of gold.

Years pass again, and an Englishman pauses to listen to the chant of the labourers at work on the building of Lord Cromer's house. It is very short and simple:

Strophe:—The howaga is good;
Antistrophe:—The howaga is good.

The "howaga" is now a title given to any European foreigner. It originally signified, I believe, a merchant.

One day Mohammed came in to say that there was a native servant outside who wanted to know where he should find his master. I, not unnaturally, asked who his master was, and was gravely informed that he had forgotten his master's name, but had come to us because he was an Englishman. I went out to the front gate to investigate. There was an old native, with a *carro* (native cart) quite full of obviously English luggage, and leading a dog by a string. On being questioned, he said that his master was an Englishman stationed in one of the provincial towns— I have forgotten which—that yesterday this Englishman had received a telegram, and had at once risen and gone to Cairo by train. Then he, the servant, had received a telegram bidding him pack up everything and bring it to Cairo. So he had collected his master's effects and come to Cairo, but the people at the railway station (implied contempt for their intelligence) could not tell him where his master was, and had told him to go and ask the Priest of the English. And would my excellency be good enough to tell him.

I again asked his master's name and was told that he could not remember it. I asked if he knew the department to which he belonged. Yes (promptly), it was the Irrigation. I went in and got the directory, from which I slowly read to the man all the names of Englishmen in the Irrigation. He shook his head sadly, he could not recognise one. That did not surprise me, for nicknames are as common in Egypt now as they were a thousand years ago, and very few Englishmen are known to the natives by their proper names. I then went and examined the solid leather portmanteaux. Not a label of any kind, not even an initial. A bright idea struck me, and I called the dog to examine his collar, but that too was blank. But I had some reason to suppose that some of the Irrigation officers would be meeting at a certain house in Cairo that afternoon, so finally I sent a man to guide the old native to that house, and told him to sit upon the doorstep till his master appeared. He went off obediently, and I suppose my conjecture was right, for he did not return, nor did I ever discover who his master was.

E. L. BUTCHER, *THINGS SEEN IN EGYPT* (LONDON: SEELEY, SERVICE AND CO., 1914), PP. 177–178

After the Mahmal itself follows a larger or smaller procession, according to whether it is the first or second progress of the carpet. On the first occasion it is not packed up in the howdah, but displayed on wooden frames, which are carried by relays of natives. There will often be one or two of the beautiful old litters in which great Moslem ladies used to go on pilgrimage with a suitable retinue. These are slung between two camels, gaily caparisoned in scarlet cloth, like all the rest who take part in the procession. The camels are one behind, the other before the litter, and the ladies, though secluded themselves, have a good view of everything that goes on.

The pilgrims go by train to Suez, and then take steamer to Jeddah. It was a sad blow to the old conservatism of Islam when the holy carpet and the holy people were thrust into railway carriages. Sinister rumour says that a telegraph-wire injured the pyramid-shaped top of the Mahmal, which was a bad omen; but, fortunately, nothing came of it. As it is, even in these days of comparative luxury, the pilgrims brave many hardships. They suffer from fatigue and heat and close-packing, and the fevers generated by these conditions; but those who do get back are happy men, and troops of friends will hail their returning feet.

When the chief dangers of the long journey are over, and the pilgrims are well on their homeward way, they will write letters to their fathers and brothers and all their home-keeping kinsfolk, pouring forth gratitude to God, who, by the mouth of His servant Abraham, enjoined men to make a pilgrimage to the house of their God.

Then those friends who have stayed behind paint on the whitewashed walls of the houses pictures of locomotive engines, and ships, and palm-trees, and raging lions, to show how the occupant has travelled by land and sea, and has braved dangers from wild beasts, but is now returned safe and sound; and when he is nigh to the city they bring him on his way with torches and music, so that the coming back, as well as the going forth, of the Mahmal is a time of festivity and joy.

FRANCIS E. CLARK AND HARRIET E. CLARK, *OUR JOURNEY AROUND THE WORLD* (HARTFORD, CONN.: A. D. WORTHINGTON, 1896), PP. 377–380, 383–389

There is almost nothing to see in Ismalia except the donkeys and the donkey boys. The latter are ubiquitous and most persistent. They meet you at the landing; they thrust their donkey in your face and eyes as soon as you step ashore. They plant him before you, broadside on, to bar your further progress, unless you mount and ride. They sound his praises in every note of the gamut. After all other recommendations fail, they plead with you to take him because of his "lovely black eyes." One boy even recommended his donkey to us as a "riglar masher." If they suspect you of being an American, they will cry out, "Take my donkey, Master," "My donkey is Yankee Doodle," "My donkey's name is Washington," while one boy gravely assured us, thinking that he surely would secure our patronage thereby, that his animal rejoiced in the name of "Washy-Washington."

We tarry in Ismalia no longer than is absolutely necessary, for stranger sights lure us on to the City of the Califs.

Taking the railway at Ismalia, a journey of a few hours brings us to the ancient city of Cairo. The first part of the way lies through the desert, and a most uncompromising and undeniable desert it is. The yellow sand hems in the narrow railway track on every side, and there is scarcely a green thing far or near to refresh the eyes. Still, barren as is the country, its people are of never-failing interest. Every railway station is bright with the colors of the curious costumes of men and women. Here is an orange seller, for instance, with her face entirely covered by a hideous black veil, with only a slit large enough for two piercing black eyes to shine through. Over her nose is a curious brass contrivance like a great supplementary nose, which seems to attach the veil to the upper part of the headdress. Here is another woman with a heavy water jar on her head, which she carries, standing proudly erect, in a way that shows that she has been used to such burdens from her earliest girlhood. At another station we see a whole family of Arabs squatting upon the platform, the women veiled as those we have already described, though the little girls are allowed to go with uncovered faces. For the most part, they are a stupid, degraded lot of human beings, with nothing of aspiration in their eyes, and no desire to be anything but the hewers of wood and the drawers of water which they and their ancestors have been for so many centuries.

After a few miles of this desert journey, we grow rather listless and indifferent to that which may be seen outside the car window, but suddenly we are aroused from our indifference by an entrancing sight of green fields and fertile gardens and waving palm trees. It is as though we had come into a fairy land, out of a very prosaic workaday world. And indeed we have entered fairy land, and the magician that works the wonder is none other than old Father Nile. He sends out his life-giving waters, and whatever he touches springs into new life and blossoms like the rose. The line of demarcation between the desert and the well-favored lands of the Nile is clear and distinct; one moment the train is in the arid purgatory of the desert, the next it is in the smiling paradise of the oasis.

And this first fertile tract to which we have come is none other than the Goshen of the Bible. No wonder that the aged Jacob rejoiced when his long pilgrimage was over and he entered into this fair land. We can understand better than ever before the great power that Joseph must have enjoyed to be able to secure this goodly land for his father and his unbrotherly brothers.

Off in the distance, but a little way from the railway track, are the fields where the Israelites made bricks without straw, and perhaps our eye rests upon the very place where Moses, rendered indignant beyond the power of control at the cruelties which were heaped upon his suffering fellow countrymen, slew the Egyptian, and became an exile from the court where he might have reigned as a prince, "choosing rather to suffer affliction with the people of God than to enjoy the pleasures of sin for a season." Our hearts throb within us as we look out on these historic sights, and realize that these were the same sandy plains, the same green fields, watered then as now, "with the tears of the Nile," while the same cloudless Egyptian sky bent over them as over us. Out here rode in majestic state the famous Prime Minister of the Pharaohs, the young man who, by his own virtue and force of character, raised himself from the position of a captive peasant to a prince of the realm. These roads, too, were trodden by the feet of Aaron, the High Priest, by Miriam, the tuneful singer; and along these same highways rumbled the chariot wheels of the great Pharaohs, who, as world-conquering rulers, have never been equaled by Greek or Roman, Turk or Briton.

We see very little, however, to remind us of the magnificence of the Pharaohs, or of the state in which Joseph traveled in those early days. Most of the villages which we pass are mean collections of wretched mud houses. Their four walls rise scarcely higher than the head of a man, and except for an occasional mosque, with its slender minaret, there is no attempt at architectural beauty or embellishment of any kind. Most of the lower classes who swarm at the railway stations, and whom we see from the car windows, wear around their necks charms, written on paper, and sewn up in leather. They are ignorant and superstitious to the last degree, and not only protect themselves, but their cattle in the same way. Every man, as he passes a saint's tomb, it is said, mumbles a prayer without stopping, and, saints' tombs being very numerous, a mumbled prayer is always on his lips. Some of the great saints are appealed to on every possible occasion. If a man sneezes, or is afflicted with the hiccoughs, or turns his ankle in the streets, he adjures his favorite saint. Even if his legs are stiff as he rises from his seat, he exclaims, "O Virgin Mary!" Their ignorance is beyond all comprehension, the education even of the upper classes being confined to the narrow limits of the Koran. Not one of them can be convinced that the earth is not flat, while they agree thoroughly with Parson Jasper in his dictum that "the sun do move."

An Egyptian school is a curiosity. The pupils sit on the floor, study their lessons aloud, rocking back and forth, and they make the schoolroom about as noisy as a ward political meeting. I generally knew where a schoolroom was at least half a minute before I reached its doors. The master squats on the floor, or stands among his pupils, who are seated in rows or promiscuously scattered through the apartment. Their lessons are given to them upon slates or large cards, and they sit rocking back and forth and studying aloud.

A learned priest, which means a man learned in the mysteries of the Koran, indignantly walked out of an examination hall in Cairo recently, when told that the scholars were there taught that the earth was round. No such heresy would he allow to have place even for a moment in his theology. Every other man is to a Mohammedan an infidel; and not only an infidel, but a miserable and despicable infidel, at that, who deserves stoning and torture and death, though the laws unjustly interfere in his behalf. Even the children will greet the Europeans on the street with the exclamation: "Ya Nusrani!" (O Nazarene). The donkey boy calls out to his ass, as he prods him with a sharp stick: "Go along, you son of a pig, get on, you son of a Nazarene!"

It is said by those who have lived long in Egypt, that the centuries of oppression under hard task masters, and the subserviency to a false and degrading religion, have not only dulled the moral and intellectual faculties of the Egyptians, but have deadened even their physical senses as well. A traveler and resident for ten years in Egypt says that the sense of pain is very small among the lower classes, that their olfactory nerves are also extremely dull, that they cannot distinguish one person from another by his footsteps, and not easily by his voice, and that they never hear a slight or distant sound, or notice a whisper.

In the interior of the poor houses, whose outer walls we see from the train, is no furniture worthy of the name. A few mats, a sheepskin, a basket or two, kettles for heating water, and a small array of wooden dishes, is all that we find within the hut, and this hut is shared by the hens and the ducks, the goats, and the sheep of the establishment, as well as by the human inhabitants, while the cows and buffaloes would have no hesitation in pushing their way within the doors, were they wide enough to receive them.

Almost the only food of the laboring classes is a kind of bread made of sorghum flour or of Indian corn, wheaten bread being eaten only by the wealthy classes. For supper, however, we are told, even the poorest cause a hot repast to be prepared. This usually consists of a highly salted sauce made of onions and butter, or, in the poorer houses, of butter and linseed oil.

Around the low table the various members of the family sit, while each member dips his piece of bread, held in his fingers, into this common family sauce. In addition to this, buffaloes' and goats' milk, and in the summer, cucumbers and pumpkins are the only addition. Of course, this meagre bill of fare and this wretched manner of life applies to the lower classes only. There is an aristocracy in Egypt, as there is everywhere else, that clothes itself in purple and fine linen and lives upon the fat of the land. But the poverty of the masses is almost beyond description.

Poor as it is, the common people of Egypt were probably never so well off as they are to-day. From the time of the Israelites they have lived the lives of serfs. Oppressed by the original Pharaohs, doubly oppressed by each succeeding dynasty, their lives held cheaper than the very dirt of the street, hundreds of thousands of them sacrificed in the digging of every great canal and the building of every gigantic pyramid; it is only within the memory of the present generation that attention has been called to the wretched condition of the Fellahin, and that anything has been done for their relief. Since the English have acquired a dominating control in Egypt, their beneficent rule has been felt as in other Eastern lands. Order has come out of chaos, justice has succeeded to tyranny, and theoretically, at least, the tiller of the soil can assert his rights as well as the proudest descendant of the Pharaohs. As a matter of fact, there is doubtless still very much of oppression and iniquitous taxation, for the work of centuries cannot be undone in a moment, or the rights of a people secured by a single decree. However, Egypt is on the high road to recovery. Every succeeding year sees a better state of affairs in the land of the Nile, and the common people, at least, should devoutly give thanks for the interference of John Bull and his redcoats.

But among our fellow-passengers are many others besides the Fellahin of the Nile. There are grave Mohammedan dignitaries. Some of these Moslems wear green turbans, showing that they are descendants of the great prophet himself, for no others are allowed to wear this color. The scholars wear a broad, evenly-folded turban of a light color, and it is said that the orthodox length of a believer's turban is seven times that of his head, being equivalent to the whole length of his body, in order that the turban may afterwards be used as the wearer's winding-sheet, and that this thought may familiarize him with the prospect of death.

The Copts, some of whom we also see among our fellow-passengers, or among the loungers at the railway station, wear a dark blue turban, and the Jews a turban of yellow, since these were the colors decreed in the fourteenth century.

One of the most characteristic things of any country is the way in which the children are carried. As may well be believed, such luxuries as baby carriages are unknown in the East. In China and Japan the babies are strapped upon the backs of their mothers; in India they are carried upon their thighs; while in Egypt they are perched upon their mother's shoulders, the little legs hanging down before and behind, while they lean over on their mother's head, and frequently go to sleep in this seemingly uncomfortable position.

Of course beggars are very common. You cannot step off the railway trains, or into the mosques, or turn the corner of the streets, without being besieged by some new claimant for charity. Thin, scrawny, diseased hands are thrust into your face at every turn, and your loathing repugnance is more often excited than pity, by the horrible specimens of humanity that dog every footstep. Men with noses and chins eaten away by cancer, with eyes sealed and corroded by countless sores, with finger joints twisted and gnarled by rheumatism, or with handless stumps gradually being eaten away by leprosy, confront us at every turn until one has to harden himself against these sights, or else flee incontinently within doors, and lock himself away from all his fellow-men.

Instead of politely saying good morning to the passing stranger, the beggar cries out to every European, "Backsheesh, backsheesh!" (A gift, a gift.) The wise traveler responds to all such salutations, "Ma fish, ma fish!" (I have nothing for you). Or, if he wishes to vary the formula, he will say, "Allah yatik" (May God give thee). This often answers in place of backsheesh, and the beggar will go away quite as contented as if he had received what he asked for.

A very common sight in the great cities, as well as in the smaller towns, is the water carrier with his goat-skin of water, which looks like the great bloated carcass of an animal carried on his back. He still plies his trade in the city of Cairo, although the city is well supplied with water from the new water-works. Still, he passes along the street, with his heavy goat-skin on his shoulders, crying out at the top of his lungs, "Ya auwad Allah!" (May God recompense me). Nevertheless, notwithstanding his pious cry, he will be very much disappointed if any one took a draft from his goat-skin and left all the recompense to Allah.

On feast days, especially the birthdays of the saints, pious Moslems, desirous of securing an easy entrance into paradise, frequently hire one of these water carriers to supply all comers with water gratuitously. Then the water carrier shouts in a loud tone, "Sebil Allah ya' atshan ya moyeh!" In this way he invites all to drink freely, but he is very careful to turn to his employer, who usually stands near him with a good deal of ostentation, saying, "God forgive thy sins, oh dispenser of the drink offering, God have mercy on thy parents!" To which they who are partaking of the water reply, "Amen. God have mercy on them and on us." After numerous blessings of a similar kind have been interchanged, the sakka hands the last cup of water to his employer with the words: "The remainder for the liberal men, and paradise for the confessor of the unity. God bless thee, thou dispenser of the drink offering."

Many of the other cries that one hears in the street or in the railway station are equally curious. The cry of the orange merchant and the itinerant fish peddler at home are quite unintelligible, though spoken in one's own language, and it can easily be imagined that the street cries of Egypt are quite beyond the comprehension of the passing tourist. So, without shame, we must confess that we have consulted our guide book at this point for the interpretation of these cries.

There is a man with a thin jelly made of starch and sugar. He is crying out, "O sugar for a nail, O confection!" which unintelligible cry indicates that he is willing to barter his jelly for a nail or piece of old iron.

There is a vender of lemons, who calls out to us as we pass by, "God will make them light, O lemons!" We turn to Baedeker to find that he means to say, in his highly figurative and poetic language, that God will help him to sell his lemons, and thus make his baskets light.

Another long cry of twenty syllables rings out on the air, which, being interpreted, reads as follows: "Help, O help, the lupins of Embabeh are better than almonds! O how sweet is the little son of the river!" This cry, too, must be interpreted, when we find that it means that the peas which this vender has to sell require to be soaked in river water some time before they are boiled. On this account they are called "Sons of the river," and their praises are thus sung by this poetical child of the desert.

By these various sights and sounds and cries of street vender and beggar, we are welcomed to Cairo, the magic city of the Orient, and find ourselves in the country of the Arabian nights, the capital city of the Cailifs.

57

LOUISA JEBB WILKINS, *BY DESERT WAYS TO BAGHDAD* (LONDON: T. NELSON & SONS, [1912]), PP. 55–87

The dawn of the Baghdad Railway

THERE is something very weird and uncanny in the terminus of a railway in the middle of a wild and desolate country such as this. The Monster runs his iron fangs into the heart of its desolation and shoots you into it like a ball out of a cannon's mouth. Roaring and hissing and sending out jets of flame, he comes racing through the darkness to a certain definite spot; here he discharges you in the blackness of night and subsides. Next morning when you awake he is gone, and you are left to shift for yourself as best you can. But there is a certain human friendliness about this Monster while you are travelling with him. He seems to draw all the signs of life out of an apparently dead country and collect them at the stations for you to see. Great warehouses filled with sacks of corn testify to the productiveness of a country which, judging it from the train window after harvest time, one would dismiss as mere barren soil; an occasional MacCormick's "Daisy" reaper awaiting delivery on a side platform, native carts hanging about, and truck-loads of empty sacks tell the same tale. Groups of peasants, idly gossiping, gathered together by the whistle which heralds the Monster's approach, belie the impression of an uninhabited land; for Turkish villages are carefully designed so as not to attract attention. When one's eye gets more familiar with the seemingly uniform colour of the landscape, varied only by light and shade, one becomes aware of the low, flat-topped, mud-brick houses, which, even at close quarters, often seem but part of the natural rock.

Even the unchanging East is powerless once the Monster's fangs have taken hold; he alone of all influences comes to stay and leave his mark.

Slowly, perhaps, but very surely, he undermines with irresistible persistence the customs and habits which from time immemorial have held their own against the religious, educational, or military forces of stronger nations.

This particular spot has long been the battlefield of the East and the West; now one, now the other, has had temporary ascendance; in the long run the East has always conquered.

But already we can see what a power the East has to reckon with in the railway. For one thing it attacks the Eastern in one of his vital points—his conception of

Time. Time waited for him when he had but camels to load; but the railway will not wait for him; the Monster screeches and is off. Sunrise or two hours after sunrise is not one and the same thing to him. Relentless as day and night he comes and goes, and there is no cheating him as the Eastern cheats Time.

But the railway is cheating the East out of its time-worn customs and ideas, and there is a certain sadness in the evidences of transition. All down the line picturesque native costumes are being replaced by ugly European clothes. The men wear terrible fancy trouserings from Manchester; the women spend more money on dress—and unfortunately it is European dress—and less on the old-fashioned wedding feasts. The turnover of the shops in the larger towns has increased fourfold in the last ten years. The bazaars are now a medley of stalls exhibiting native manufactures side by side with cheap trinkets from England and loud flannelettes from Italy. The price of wheat has doubled; and with that of wheat the prices of other exports have also risen. Opium, wool, mohair, hides, and salt are amongst the products of these great plains.

Two short days' ride from Nicæa had brought us to Mekidje, a station on the Anatolian Railway half-way between Haida Pasha and Eskishehr. The single line went as far as Konia, and one train ran each way every day. It stopped for the night at Eskishehr, continuing the journey next morning.

We arrived at the station some hours before the train was due, and sat in the stationmaster's strip of garden, for there did not seem anything else to do. We said good-bye to the Zaptiehs and to the muleteers who were returning to Brusa, and watched them slowly disappear down the road we had come. Then we heard the low, familiar tinkle of camel bells and a score or more of laden animals paced slowly into the open ground round the station. They have a more discreet and tuneful way of announcing their arrival than the Monster, and when they appear on the scene they do so in a more dignified, calmer manner. Having arrived also, they do not look as if they were off again the next minute; they look as if they had come to stay for ever, and they give you time to think. One by one, in answer to a word of command, they knelt down in the dust, and the great baskets holding the goods were unfastened and rolled about on the ground. Their owners seemed too slack to do any more. They let them lie there while they looked at the sun. The Monster is slowly replacing these carriers of the East; but their day is not yet done by a long way, for they must feed him from the interior. His life is still dependent on the life of those he is working to destroy.

At last we heard his distant shriek. Down upon us he came, dashing up all in a minute, in such a splutter and such a hurry, waking us all up. Officials rushed up and down the platform, and swore at the natives who were loading our baggage. Everybody talked at once to everybody else, and the Monster hissed impatiently, noisy even when he was standing still.

There were not many passengers; in a first-class carriage a Pasha travelled in solitary state; all his harem were delegated to a second-class carriage, where the blinds were pulled down. In the third-class were a few natives, who leaned out of the windows and gossiped with the camel owners, idle witnesses of the busy scene.

But the Monster is getting impatient; he hisses furiously and finally gives a warning shriek. Then off he goes, and we take a last look at the kneeling camels, munching away as unconcernedly as if their destroyer had never invaded their peaceful country.

Mekidje is practically at sea-level; Eskishehr is a tableland two thousand feet high; we had therefore a steady rise on the whole journey up the valley formed by the Kara Su, a river which has its source in the neighbourhood of Eskishehr. On each side rounded hills shut out the horizon, save where here and there a tributary valley would reveal, through steep-sided gorges, a distant view of purple ridges with snow-clad tops.

It was night when we arrived at Eskishehr, and we groped our way to the Grand Hôtel d'Anatolie, kept by Greeks. It was at this hotel that we first met Hassan, who was destined to play such a large part in our future travels. He was an Albanian Turk, and had been introduced to us by our friends in Constantinople, whom he accompanied on their shooting expeditions in this district. They had written to ask him to look after us during our brief stay at Eskishehr.

Ibrahim brought him into our room, and there he stood silently, after salaaming us in the usual way.

Ibrahim was a tall man, but Hassan towered above him. He wore a huge sheepskin coat, which added to his massive, impressive look.

X looked up words in her Turkish book.

"They told us you would look after us here?" she said.

"As my eyes," he answered very quietly and simply. And thus began one of those friendships on which neither time nor distance can leave its mark.

Two days later X asked him whether he would accompany us on the next stage of our journey, across the Anatolian Plateau and the Taurus Mountains to Mersina.

"Will you come with us and guard us well?" she said. He dropped on one knee and kissed her hand.

"On my head be it," he said.

Eskishehr, before the days of the railway, was a purely Turkish town; it displayed the usual chaos of mud-brick and wooden houses, with their lower windows carefully latticed over for the concealment of the women; of narrow, winding bazaars, here a display of brightly coloured clothes and rugs, there a noisy street of smithies and carpenters' shops; and rising above it all the minarets of half a dozen mosques.

But the railway's mark is on it to-day. The population has been increased by some five thousand Tartars and Armenians, whose houses, planted together near the line, have a neat, modern, shoddy look, contrasting with the picturesque squalor of the ancient Turkish town.

The railway is slowly attacking the stronghold of the Turkish peasant, extending his operations on the wasted stretches of cultivable land, and slowly opening out dim vistas of prosperity athwart his present apathy. In the same way the railway is slowly affecting the town merchant. But one shudders here at the effect of prosperity unaccompanied by civilising influences. For in the rich merchant of the town you have the Turk at his worst. The simple, hospitable Turkish peasant is made of good stuff; the Turkish soldier of rank and file, if his fanatical tendencies are not encouraged, is equally good; the official Turk is corrupt, but only because the particular method of administering his country's laws obliges him to be so; the educated Turk of Constantinople is rapidly becoming a civilised being. But the rich middle-class Turk of towns has nothing to be said for him. The Christians have taught him to drink, and he is rich enough to keep a large harem. We had an introduction to one such person in Eskishehr. The polished Turkish phraseology of welcome could not conceal the coarseness and vulgarity of his mind, and we were glad to escape to the sacred inner chambers, where a very young and pretty woman sat in lonely state, the latest addition to his harem. There she sat, draped in the softest silks of gorgeous colourings, surrounded with all the evidences of luxury and comfort, as sulky as a little bear.

We were accompanied by a Greek lady, who talked French and Turkish and acted as our interpreter; but never a smile or more than a word could be drawn out of the cross little thing. She simply stared in front of her with an expression of acute boredom in her beautiful eyes. A good-natured, elderly serving-woman, who stood at the door, explained matters. She had been very much pampered at home, and she had had a good time; she saw all her young friends at the baths, the social resort for Turkish ladies. The rich merchant had been considered a great *parti;* but already she had had enough of it. She never went out except for an occasional drive in a closed carriage. She was tired of embroidery work, she was tired of eating sweets, she was tired of smoking, she was tired of her fine dresses. *Aman*, but it would come all right—and the serving-woman winked and nodded, and stroked her mistress's listless hand.

"Is it always like this?" we asked the Greek lady.

"Ah, mon Dieu! not at all! This man is very jealous, and she may not see her friends. He heaps on her what money can buy and thinks that is enough. But with the poor it is different. You will see. There is a wedding to-day in a poor family. I will arrange for you to go. Mon Dieu! no, it is not always thus. La pauvre petite."

The room in which we sat was draped in the usual Turkish manner with magnificent curtains in rich Eastern colourings. Round three walls ran low divans covered in the same way. There was not such a room in Eskishehr we were told. Had the decorations stopped there, and we had been able to forget the unfortunate prisoner, the general effect would have been decidedly pleasing. But as we sat there our eyes were kept glued, by some horrible attraction, on the glitter of a cheap gilt frame of the gaudiest description, containing a crude coloured print of the German Emperor; below this stood a gimcracky little table covered with a cheap tinselled cloth, on which was placed a glass and silver cake-basket in the vilest of European taste. It hit one terribly in the eye. It was a jarring note in the Monster's work.

We took leave of the sulky little lady, and left her once more to her sweets and her embroideries in the long, weary hours of lonely splendour.

We had only seen the second act of this bit of Turkish drama; when the curtain went down for us we had had enough of it.

But we were about to see Act I. in different surroundings. The Greek lady kept her word, and in due course we found ourselves ushered into the house of the bridegroom. The preliminary ceremonies had already begun—in fact they had been going on all day. There sat the bride at the end of a room which had been cleared of everything except the low stool which she occupied alone. She was a lumpy looking girl of seventeen or so, and sat there motionless with downcast eyes. On the floor sat dozens of women, packed as tight as the room could hold. The bride might neither look up nor speak, which seemed hard, for every woman in the room was both looking at her and speaking about her; the hubbub was terrible.

She rose as we entered and kissed our hands; this much is apparently allowed on the arrival of strangers. The Greek lady explained that she was obliged to stand until we asked her to sit down again, and that she might not look at us. This was a good deal to ask on such an occasion; European ladies are not, as a rule, guests at the wedding of the Turkish poor, and we caught one or two surreptitious peeps from under her long eyelashes. We joined the throng on the floor and continued to gaze at her as every one else did. Marriage customs in general, and her own affairs in particular, were discussed for our benefit, the Greek lady interpreting in torrents of voluble French.

"She may not speak to her husband for forty-eight hours. When he comes in he will lift the veil and see his bride for the first time. Then he puts a girdle round her waist and it is finished. His mother chose her for him. If he does not like her, no matter, he can choose another, for he is getting good wages, and can afford to keep two."

By and by a large tray was brought in, piled up with rounds of native bread and plates of chicken. It was placed on a low stool in the centre of us all, and, following everybody's example, we grabbed alternate bits of chicken and bread. Then followed hunches of cake made of nuts and honey.

We were still eating when we heard a noise of singing and musical instruments outside; it became louder and louder, and finally stopped by the house.

"They are singing 'Behold the bridegroom cometh,' " said the Greek lady; "the man is being brought in a procession of all his friends"

The food was hastily removed, and all the guests were marshalled into an adjoining room, which already seemed as full as it could hold of babies and children and old hags, who presumably had been left to look after the younger ones. We were allowed to remain while the finishing touches were put on the bride. Her face was first plastered all over with little ornaments cut out of silver paper and stuck on with white of egg; then she was covered over entirely with a large violet veil. And so we left her sitting there, sheepish and placid in the extreme, in strange contrast to the voluble Greek lady and the excited friends. We met the bridegroom in the passage. He kissed his father, and stood first on one foot and then on the other. His mother took him by the shoulders, opened the door of the room we had just left, and shoved him in. Let us hope that the silver ornaments did their work and made his bride pleasing in his sight when he lifted the violet veil. What she thought of him need not concern us any more than it did her or her friends, for such thoughts may not enter the minds of Turkish brides.

The show was over. The curtain of the first act had gone down for us. It gave promise of a more successful drama than the one we had previously witnessed.

It is 267 miles or thereabouts from Eskishehr to Konia. It took us a good fifteen hours by rail. We were now on the summit of the tableland; the bounded river valley gradually gave way to long stretches where signs of cultivation were more apparent. We were getting into the great wheat-growing district, which the railway is causing to extend year by year. At Karahissar, a town of 33,000 inhabitants, a gigantic rock with straight sides and castellated top rises abruptly out of the plain, and from here another corn-growing valley merges into the great plain stretching away to the north. Mount Olympus, whose base we had skirted on leaving Brusa, could be very dimly discerned on the sky-line.

Then darkness set in, and the Monster ran steadily on with us into the unknown. Towards eight o'clock there was a sudden stop; it had come to the end of its tether.

We had left Calphopolos and Ibrahim at Eskishehr, and now only Constantin remained as a link with civilisation. Hassan had appeared at the station at Eskishehr, prepared to accompany us round the world if need be. He wore a brown suit of Turkish trousers and zouave under his sheepskin cloak. His pockets bulged rather, so did the wide leather belt which he used as a pocket, otherwise his worldly goods were contained tied up in a white pocket-handkerchief.

And so we arrived at Konia. Behind us was the railway, leading back to the things we knew, to the things we should hope to see again; before us was the plain, leading us to strange new things, things we should, perhaps, just see once and leave behind for ever.

The iron Monster had dumped us down and was no further concerned with us; if we would go further it must be by taking thought for ourselves.

There were horses and arabas to hire, there were provisions to lay in, there was the escort of Zaptiehs to be procured and the goodwill of the authorities to be obtained. We had letters of introduction to Ferid Pasha, then Vali of the Konia vilayet and since Grand Vizier of Constantinople. He was not as other Valis; he was called the great and the good, and had established law and order in his province. There need be no fear of brigandage while we were within the boundaries of his jurisdiction.

The Government building, the Konak, occupied one side of the square in which stood our hotel, and we sent Hassan across to pay our respects. But Ferid Pasha was away, which caused us great disappointment; we could only see his Vekil, the acting Governor.

Taking Hassan and Constantin with us, we went up the long flight of steps and down a corridor leading to the Vali's room. Peasants and ragged soldiers hung about the passage, and black-coated Jewish-looking men hurried in and out. A soldier showed us the way, holding back the curtains which concealed the entrance to various rooms, and from behind which the mysterious looking Jews were continually creeping.

The Vekil sat at a table covered over with official documents; a divan, higher and harder than those we had seen in private houses, ran round two walls, on which squatted several secretaries, holding the paper on which they wrote on the palms of their left hands. Beside the Vekil sat an old Dervish priest, and next him the Muavin, the Christian official appointed after the massacres to inform Valis of the wishes of Christians, and better known amongst those who know him as "Evet Effendi" (Yes, Effendi).

X was getting fluent in matters of Turkish greeting; she now reeled off a suitable string in reply to theirs. Hassan stood beside us, grave and dignified, and we noticed that all the men greeted him very courteously. X then endeavoured to explain our desire to travel to Mersina and requested the services of a suitable escort. Owing to limitations in her knowledge of the Turkish vocabulary, the nearest she could get to it was that the Consul at Mersina loved us dearly and wished us to come to him. Matters were getting to a deadlock; the officials appeared to be asking us what was the object of our journey, and we could only insist on the intense love of our English Consul.

Suddenly another visitor was ushered in, and for the first time since leaving Nicæa the strange sound of the English tongue fell upon our ears. The newcomer was Dr. Nakashian, an Armenian doctor living in Konia.

He at once acted as interpreter. Officialdom for once put no obstacles in the way, and an escort was promised us for the journey. The Vekil inquired whether we should like to see the sights of Konia; and on our replying in the affirmative, he arranged that we should be taken round that afternoon; Dr. Nakashian also promised to accompany us.

Accordingly we sallied out later on horseback with Hassan. Dr. Nakashian was mounted on a splendid Arab mare. The Government Protection, in the shape of two Zaptiehs and a captain, followed in a close carriage. We started off very decorously, but the Arab mare became excited and plunged and galloped down the street; our horses caught the infection, and we followed hard; the Government Protection put its head out of each window and shouted; the driver lashed his jaded horse, and the rickety carriage lurched after us in a cloud of dust. The natives lining the streets shouted encouragingly; finally we landed at the Dervish mosque. Dervishes are strong in Konia. Their founder is buried here, and his tomb is an object of pilgrimage. The chief feature of the mosque is its wonderful polished floor, where the dancing ceremonies take place.

At Konia, perhaps more than at Eskishehr, one is struck with the railway's influence in the passing order of things. There are many fine buildings in the last stages of decay in this ancient city of the Seljuk Turks; the palace, with its one remaining tower, the fragments of the old Seljuk walls found here and there in the middle of the modern town, the mosques lined with faïence, beautiful even in its fragments. Contrast with this the squalor and the dirt of the present Turkish streets, the earth and wood houses, enclosed in walls of earth, the apathetic natives, and the general feeling of stagnation and decay.

Then, outside the town, the railway appears; modern European houses spring up round it—offices for the Company and an hotel. A whiff of stir and bustle brought in along with the iron fangs of the Monster brings a sense of fresh life to these people, whose existence seemed one long decay of better things, like that of the ruins amongst which they spend their days.

And everywhere there was a whisper of yet closer touch with civilisation. The Anatolian Railway stops at Konia, but its continuation under the name of the Baghdad Railway was everywhere in the air. No one spoke openly about it; its coming seemed enveloped in such a shroud of mystery that one felt there was a sort of halo around its birth. At first one mentioned it baldly by name; and at once the official would put on his most discreet and impressive manner and refer to the will of Allah; the merchant would nod mysteriously and then wink with evident satisfaction. "It comes! oh yes, it comes! but it is better not to talk of it yet." And the Zaptieh would sigh heavily, thinking of his unpaid wages, and say, "Please God, it comes," and then look hastily round to see who had overheard him.

And so at last we also learnt to speak of the Coming of the Monster with bated breath and lowered tones, and were duly infected with the impressiveness of his arrival—the arrival of the Being whose touch was to bring new life into this dead land.

It was on the morning of the third day after our arrival at Konia that we made the plunge into the great plain from the spot where the Monster had left us. We collected in the square in front of the Konak. There were two covered arabas to convey the baggage, and in one of these Constantin and Hassan also rode; X and I rode horses, and had saddle-bags slung under our saddles. Our escort consisted of three Zaptiehs, a Lieutenant, Rejeb, and an ancient Sergeant, Mustapha.

The head of the police accompanied us a few miles out of the town.

Slowly, riding at a foot's pace, we left it all behind, the squalid streets, the modern houses, the scraggy little trees; the lumpy road became a deeply rutted track bordering stubble fields; lumbering carts passed us, squeaking terribly as the wheels lurched out of the ruts to make way for us. The track became an ill-defined path, along which heavily laden pack-animals slowly toiled, raising clouds of dust. Turning in our saddles, all we could see of Konia was the minarets of its mosques standing above a confused blur on the horizon line.

There is a strange fascination in watching the slow disappearance of any object on the horizon, when that horizon is visible at every point round you. The exact moment never comes when you can state the actual disappearance of the object. You think it is still there, and then you slowly realise that it is not. And when you have realised this, you turn round again in the saddle once for all, and set your face steadily towards the horizon in front of you, which for so many hours on end has nothing to show and nothing to tell you, and yet whose very emptiness is so full of secret possibilities and hidden wonder.

We had got beyond the point where one met others on the road; we had now become our own world, a self-contained planet travelling with the sun through space. When he disappeared over the horizon line we pitched our camp and waited for his reappearance on the opposite side. At the first glimmer announcing his arrival the tents were hauled down, the arabas loaded up, and by the time his face peeped over the line we were in our saddles, ready once more to follow him to his journey's end.

It is a great half-desert plain, this part of Anatolia; desert only where it is water-less, and very fertile where irrigation is possible. In places it seemed to form one huge grazing ground; now it would be herds of black cattle munching its coarse, dried-up herbage; now flocks of mohair goats, now sheep, herded by boys in white sheepskin coats, tended by yellow dogs. Then we knew that a village would be somewhere about, although we did not always see it; for here too the villages are the colour of the surrounding country and perhaps only visible in very clear sunlight.

Or it might be that we would ride slowly through a cluster of mud huts, and the yellow dogs would rush out and bark furiously at us, while the men and children stared silently, too listless even to wonder. At times we would stop in a village for our midday meal, sitting in the shade of its yellow mud walls. The Zaptiehs would stand round us and keep off the dogs until some of the village men would appear and call them away with a half-scared look—for the Zaptieh is the tax-collector, and they suffer from extortion at his hands.

We visited the women in their houses, and found them always interested and friendly. Turkish was becoming more intelligible to us, and the conversation usually took the same form:—

"Who is your father?"
"He is a Pasha in a far country."
"Where are your husbands?"
"We have no husbands."
"How is that?"
"In our country the women are better than the men, and the men are afraid of us."

Then our clothes are fingered all over and the cost of everything on us is asked. We rise to go, and they hang on to us and implore us to come again. But the sun has already begun to dip on his downward course, and we must hurry after him.

Then would follow hours when no attempt at cultivation, or sign of herds and flocks, would be visible, and the desert country was only relieved by wonderful effects of mirage, in which we would chase elusive pictures of mountains and lakes and streams.

One had time to take it all in: the wonderful exhilarating air, the silent stretches, the long, monotonous days of the shepherd boys, marked only by the gathering in of their flocks at night.

How will it be when the Monster comes, roaring and snorting through these silent plains, polluting this clear air with his dust and smoke? At first these haughty, resentful shepherds will stand aloof from the invasion, the yellow dogs will bark in vain at the intrusion. Then slowly its daily appearance will come to them as the sun comes in the morning and the stars at night. Unconsciously it also will become a part of the routine of their lives. They will not cease to look at it with wonder, for they have never wondered. They will accept it, as they accept everything else. But use it? That is a different tale. It will be a long fight; but the Monster has always conquered in the end.

On the third day we rode into Karaman. A medieval castle crowns the town, and is visible at some little distance across the plain.

The old sergeant, Mustapha, startled us by suddenly greeting it from afar:—

"Ah, Karaman, you beautiful Karaman, city of peace and plenty. Ah, Karaman, beloved Karaman!"

And the Zaptiehs, taking up the refrain, made the silent plains ring with "Karaman! beautiful Karaman!"

We pitched our tents on a grass plot in the centre of the town. Constantin began preparing the evening meal, and the natives hung round in groups staring at us, or bringing in supplies of fuel and milk and eggs. A seedy-looking European pushed his way up to our tent and began storming at us in French.

"But it is impossible for you to camp here—it is not allowable; you must come at once to my house. There is nothing to say."

X and I tried to rouse our bewildered minds out of the Eastern sense of repose into which they had sunk through all these days. We concluded that Karaman must possess an urban district council, and that we were breaking some law of the town.

We pressed for further enlightenment.

"But do you not see all these people looking at you? It is not for you to camp here. My house is ready for you. There are good beds and it is dry, but this . . . " and he waved his hand at our preparations. "It is not possible; there is nothing to say."

By this time Hassan and Rejeb, into whose hands we had been entrusted for protection, came up and stood over us, looking threateningly at our gesticulating, excited friend.

"I do not understand," I said. "Who says that we may not camp here?"

"But it is I that say it; it is not possible. My house is ready; there is nothing to say."

"Who are you?" I said.

"I am an Austrian," he answered. Then he lowered his voice, in that mysterious manner which we associated with the coming of the Monster. "I am here," he said, in an undertone, "as agent commercial du chemin de fer Ottoman."

"Very good," I answered; "and now tell us why we cannot camp here."

"But it is damp," he said; "look at the mud."

"Oh, is that all?" I said. "We are much obliged to you for the offer of your house, but we always sleep out."

"But I have good beds," he said, "and a dry room at your service. There is nothing to say."

At this point Rejeb could contain himself no longer. He spoke sternly to the Austrian in Turkish.

"What do you want?" he said. "These ladies are under my protection. What are you saying to them?"

The man poured out volumes of Turkish; Rejeb and he had a violent altercation, which seemed to be ending in blows.

"Come, come," I said to the man, "enough of this. We are much obliged to you for your offer of hospitality, but we prefer to remain outside."

He seemed totally unable to understand that this could be the case. "If it is myself you do not care about," he said, in a crestfallen manner, "I can easily move from the house. The beds are clean and they are dry."

We finally consented to spend the evening at his house, and accompanied him through the streets, Rejeb and Hassan following closely on our heels. He showed us into a stuffy little sitting-room. Every corner was crammed with gimcracks; the whole place reeked of musty wool chairbacks.

Then we followed him upstairs; we must at any rate "look at the beds"—he evidently thought the sight of them would prove irresistible.

On calmer reflection the beds were, doubtless, no worse than the ordinary type to be found in commercial country inns; but to us, coming out of the sweet and wholesome atmosphere of the yet untainted plain, they seemed to be the very embodiment of stuffiness and discomfort. The windows, which had evidently not been opened for some time, were heavily draped, so as to effectually exclude all light and air even when open.

"There, now do you see? It is clean, it is dry. There is nothing humid here; but out there it is exposed, it is damp, it is not allowable."

We waived the question for the moment, reserving our forces for a later attack, and returned to the sitting-room, where a native woman was preparing the evening meal. We questioned our host on the arrival of the railway. He admitted being there to tout for trade *in case* it came; but who could tell, in a country like this, what would happen? Mon Dieu! it was a God-forsaken country, and all the inhabitants were canaille; there was no one he could associate with. He counted the days till his return. "When would that be?" "Ah," then he became mysterious once more and looked round at the door and window: "Ah, God knows; might it come soon!"

The serving-woman appeared and said that our men wished to see us; they had been sitting on the doorstep ever since we entered the house and refused to go away. The Austrian went out to them; high words ensued, and we looked through the door. The Austrian, crimson with rage, was gesticulating violently and pouring out torrents of unintelligible Turkish. Rejeb stood in front of him, hitting his long riding-boot with his whip and answering with some heat. Above him towered Hassan, very calm and very quiet, slowly rolling up a cigarette and now and then putting in a single word in support of Rejeb.

The Austrian turned to us. "Can you not send these men away, ladies? It is an impertinence. They refuse to leave you here unless they themselves sleep in the house. They say they have orders never to leave you, but surely they can see what I am!"

We calmed him down as best we could, and insisted on our intention of returning to our tents. He could not understand it, and I should think never will. But we got away, Rejeb and Hassan one on each side of us. When we were out on the road in cover of darkness both men burst into loud roars of laughter.

"Have we not done well, Effendi?" they said. "We have rescued you from the mad little man. The great doctor in London, has he not said, 'You shall sleep in the tent every night'?"

And, gathering round our camp-fire in the damp and the mud, we rejoiced with Hassan and Rejeb over their gallant assault and our fortunate escape.

Two days' further ride brought us to Eregli. We approached it in the dusk, riding during the last hour through what appeared to be low copse wood. The place seemed low and damp; we rode past the door of the khan, and the men besought us to go there instead of camping outside. Constantin said he was ill, the arabajis said their horses would be ill. But Rejeb and Hassan took our side and we had the tents pitched on a spot which seemed dry in the darkness. Next morning we awoke to find ourselves encircled by a loop of the river and in a dense white mist. It was so cold that the milk froze as we poured it into the tea. We ate our breakfast with our gloves on, walking up and down to keep warm.

Constantin said that he was still ill; the arabajis said their horses were now ill; but that was because the khan was comfortable. We decided, however, to give them a day's respite and ride out ourselves to Ivriz in search of the Hittite inscription at that place.

An hour's ride took us clear of the mists, and the sun came out hot and strong. Our road lay up a gorgeous richly wooded river valley. For the first time on our journey we realised what the absence of water and trees had meant. Our horses' feet crackled over brown and red autumn leaves; autumn smells, crisp and fresh, filled the air; brown trout darted from under dark rocks in the stream. Away through gaps in the low encircling hills we got sudden visions of two gigantic white-topped mountain peaks, the first suggestion of our approach to the Taurus barrier.

Ivriz is a good three hours' ride from Eregli, and lies high on one of the lower hills. We left our horses in the village and climbed on foot to the spot where the river, rushing suddenly out of the bowels of the earth, has formed a cave in the limestone cliff. Below this the stream had cut its way through the rock, leaving steep sides of bare stone which tell a tale of untold geological age. At one point the ground shelved out on a level with the bed of the stream, and the waters here swept round a corner, so that the face of the rock overlooking them was almost hidden from any one on the same shore.

It is on this face that the Hittite inscription is carved. A god, with a stalk of corn and a bunch of grapes in his hands, stands over a man who is in an attitude of adoration before him.

There it stands, hidden from the casual observer, visited by no one but the native who comes to cure his sickness in the sacred waters of the cave above.

Away in the desolate hills, off the track of man, the god has looked down on the waters of the river through all those æons since the days of the Hittites, which count as nothing in the time which it took this same river to carve its bed out of the eternal hills. How much longer will its solitude be left unviolated? The "agent commercial du chemin de fer Ottoman" is established at Eregli as elsewhere. When the iron Monster comes bellowing into Eregli his shriek will be heard in these silent hills, and following in his footsteps countless hordes of tourists will invade this sacred spot.

With something akin to a feeling of shame I turned my Kodak on him; and a sorrowful thought of the many who would be following my example in the years to come shot across my mind.

It was the sixth day after leaving Konia, and we were in full view of the Taurus Mountains. We were crossing the same stretch of barren plain, with its occasional patches of cultivation, its hidden villages with the flocks and herds trooping in at sundown. But the bounded horizon changed our conception of it; it was no longer a limitless plain. The nearer ranges stood out in dark purples and blues; behind and above towered the snow-clad heights which, looking down on to the Mediterranean shores, knew of the life and bustle of its sea-girt towns.

We had come out on the other side of the unknown plain and the aspect of things was changed. What drew us on now was not the mystery of unexplored space, but the feeling that here was a great barrier to cross. We were about to share with these heights the knowledge of what lay on the other side. But there was more than this—we were about to do what the Monster might possibly fail to do. As we drew near the barrier, the mysterious allusions to his approach all took the form of pointing at this barrier. "So far and no further he may come," they seemed to say.

As I rode with Mustapha up a long, winding pass on the outskirts of the range he pointed at the valley below us. "The Turkish Railway," he said solemnly.

A long line of laden camels wound slowly up the opposite side; for a full quarter of a mile they covered in single file the road winding up out of the valley. I pulled my horse up, and Mustapha stopped his alongside of mine. We both bent our heads forward and listened. The sound of their tinkling bells came faintly across the valley to us; the low, musical tones, the quiet, measured movement, all was in keeping with the towering mountains and the still, clear air. Hassan rode up with the other men and joined us. He put his hands up to his mouth and gave a shrill, prolonged whistle in exact imitation of the engine we had left at Konia. The men looked at one another and laughed. Then they shrugged their shoulders and pushed on up the path.

Part 9

RAILWAYS AND THE
RE-PARTITIONING OF
BRITISH AFRICA

58

THOMAS JOSEPH WILLANS, *THE ABYSSINIAN RAILWAY* (LONDON: 1870), PP. 163–176

When the Advance Brigade of the expedition arrived in Annesley Bay, in the latter part of October, 1867, they brought with them enough rails and sleepers to lay a mile of tramway, and a dozen light trucks to work it. It was originally intended to place the grand depôts some distance inland, and it was considered that a light line between them and the piers would be necessary. Rails were at once laid from about 100 yards above high water mark down the shelving sandy beach, as far as it was practicable to continue the line. A great saving in labour was made by landing stores at all stages of the tide direct from the Arab boats into the waggons, which were run out into the water alongside the former. Small branch lines at other points were constructed for conveying sand to raise a portion of the fore-shore. Rails were laid upon the stone pier as it progressed, which were of utility for landing purposes, and assisted greatly in its construction.

In the middle of November, as soon as it was known that the Sooroo Pass would be the main route to the Abyssinian Highlands, Lieutenant Colonel Wilkins (the Commanding Royal Engineer) directed that a survey for a light railway should be made from the landing place to Koomayleh at the entrance to the pass. The orders regarding the line were to save cuttings and embankments as much as possible, and, to effect this, to diminish the radii of the curves and increase the gradients. Although the distance between Zoulla and Koomayleh by road was only 12¾ miles, twenty miles of rails and sleepers were sent for, as it was considered prac-ticable—and if the expedition had been prolonged it would have been advanta-geous—to have continued the railway for the first six miles up the Sooroo Pass. A small fitting shop was also indented for and all the requisites and rolling stock for repairing and working the line when completed. In making the survey it was found very difficult to determine the proper waterway required for the numerous water-courses, then dry, which would have to be crossed. For the first two miles the country bore evidence of being at times flooded, and it was decided not to raise an embankment, but merely to give sufficient waterway for the ordinary channels, and to allow the whole line to be nundated in the time of an unusual flood. It would have been imprudent not to have provided some outlets, as there was no certainty that the line would not be required during the rainy season. An alluvial plain extended from the coast to the foot of a low ridge of extinct volca-noes, about six miles inland. Over this portion, part of which was covered with low thorny jungle, little more was necessary than levelling the inequalities of the ground to make it ready for the sleepers. After the sixth mile a broken country was reached, and the line entered a large stony ravine, through which it wound for the next mile and-a-half, by a succession of sharp curves and steep gradients, the object being to save any heavy work which, at this portion of the railway, would have been doubly difficult from the necessity of providing the working parties with water from a distance of four miles, for the latter was not procurable at a nearer point until the end of February, and then only in a limited quantity.

From this low ridge, a short descending gradient brought the railway on to the Koomayleh plain. Hence the natural inclination of the country towards the Sooroo Pass was about 1 in 40, so, although pretty uniform in slope, it was necessary to have recourse to curves and a winding tortuous line to obtain the necessary limiting gradient of 1 in 60. This entailed crossing the natural drain-age of the country, and consequently the construction of many small culverts and bridges. Fortunately, rock was not met with on any portion of the railway, although for the last few miles the ground was very stony, and strewn with large boulders, evidently washed down from the hills. The total length of the line between the landing place and Koomayleh was a little over eleven miles and a quarter, or about a mile and a quarter less than the road made by the Quartermas-ter General's Department.

The survey having been completed in the middle of December, the laying of the line was at once commenced. A company of native sappers worked for a short time in levelling the ground and forming the approaches to the Hadas bridge. The gangs of plate-layers not having yet arrived from Bombay, intelligent Chi-nese carpenters were employed to spike down and fish-plate the rails; and a small party of Shohoes, under a native non-commissioned officer, brought up rails and sleepers.

At the commencement of the expedition the reconnoitring party brought with them from Aden a number of 25-ft. and 12-ft. iron girders for barrack floors, in the anticipation that they would prove useful. On the railway, four bridges, containing a total of six spans of 25 feet, and several small 12-ft. culverts were made of them, as the girders intended for the purpose did not arrive until the end of January. The safe load on each pair of girders being only 9 cwt. per lineal foot, they had to be supported in the centre by two uprights resting on a horizontal sill.

The Hadas bridge (see Pl. I) was made in this manner, the girders resting on trestles buried 5 feet below the bed of the river. In the middle of June I examined it carefully, after this temporary structure had stood, for 5½ months, the continual passage of trains over it. There had been no settlement nor displacement, although the river had risen to within 10 inches of the bottom line of the girders; nor were the uprights, supporting the latter, worn or frayed by the hammering of the engine and waggons.

The sketches of this and bridge No. 7 (Plate II), are not intended to serve as models, but merely as examples of constructions which answered, without failure, the purpose for which they were intended. As no timber was sent especially for the railway, it was impossible to secure the sizes and quantities required for the bridges. We were compelled to use wood of the dimensions which could be be spared to us by other departments.

The railway cannot be said to have been properly commenced until the middle of January, when gangs of plate-layers and coolies, plant and stores, arrived from Bombay. The Hadas bridge and branch line being completed, the work was pushed on in the direction of Koomayleh, but the progress was very slow, on account of the want of spikes for fastening down the rails, and the limited supply of material which could daily be landed at the over-crowded pier.

Throughout the expedition, but more particularly during the first three months from its commencement, it was very difficult to find out what stores a ship was loaded with when she arrived in Annesley Bay. The Commissariat Department had the charge of shipping everything; and often a portion of a ship's cargo had to be changed, at the last moment, in Bombay, for something more emergently required in Abyssinia. The railway seemed more than usually unlucky, for rails were sent without spikes, rendering them useless; when the latter were procured, it was found that the augers (for boring holes in the sleepers) had been left behind to come in another ship. I may mention that the laying of the line was greatly expedited by the artizans of the Punjaub Pioneer Regiment (23rd), who made excellent augers, and repaired those daily broken on the works. Their workshop was on the ground in the burning sun, and a few simple tools, carried on a mule, were all they required to turn out augers better adapted for boring the hard wood of the sleepers, than those of English make.

Two engines and a sufficient number of trucks to form two trains were landed in the middle of January, and immediately the resources of the railway were taxed to the utmost in bringing up the commissariat and military stores from the piers to the store sheds. So great indeed were the demands on the two piers during the first three months of the year, that it was with the greatest difficulty the railway plant and stores were landed. So many trains were in requisition for other purposes, that it was almost impossible to keep the plate-laying parties at the end of the line supplied with material. In January, gangs of the Army Works Corps, an organised body of coolies, commenced to arrive from Bombay. Owing, however, to the great demand for labour there, and the objection that the natives of India have to cross the sea, the men composing it were physically much below the ordinary standard of native labourers, and the artizans, as a rule, were very indifferent workmen. They were especially intended for the railway, and were supposed to be about 1,200 strong; but I do not believe there were ever more than half this number employed upon it. Some gangs, composed of Chinese, picked up in Bombay, worked exceedingly well, gave no trouble, and were very useful in carrying heavy weights. Under the efficient direction of officers detailed for the purpose, the Army Works Corps did a great deal of valuable work, and were used for many duties which could not have been performed by Sepoys.

The head-quarter wing of the 23rd Punjaub Pioneer Regiment (about 400 strong), under Major (now Lieutenant-colonel), Chamberlain was detached for work on the railway in the middle of January. They continued about 2 months employed on its construction and proved most useful, working with great alacrity under the most trying circumstances. These men, admirably organised, equipped, and clothed, and accustomed to make hill roads in India during peace time, were especially adapted for this work. Captain (now Major) Darrah, R.E., was in charge of the railway during the whole time of its construction. He had as assistants two engineer subalterns (Lieutenant Pennefather, late Madras, and Lieutenant Willans), and Lieutenant Graham, 108th Regiment; Lieutenant Phillpotts, R.N., was also attached to the railway for the purpose of landing plant and material, and making the necessary arrangements for discharging the vessels in the harbour, containing railway stores. Lieutenant Baird, R.E., arrived in the end of February, and took over at once the onerous duties of traffic-manager. Lieutenant Pennefather, R.E., had charge of the account department; for the large staff of civilians, for working the line, entailed a series of complicated accounts, the responsibility of which rested with Captain Darrah. The commissariat arrangements and tenting devolved upon Lieutenant Graham. The special duties which were allotted to each officer, did not prevent his being employed with the working parties, when he had available leisure, but the principal portion of the outdoor work, and the construction of the line with its bridges, was done by Captain Darrah, assisted up to the middle of March by Lieutenant Willans. There was a great want of non-commissioned officers, especially those having a knowledge of Hindoostanee; indeed, only one Sergeant of the Royal Engineers (Madras Sappers and Miners) was available as an overseer on the railway works. Some men of the 4th (King's Own) Regiment were employed as platelayers, carpenters, and clerks, and afterwards some of the 45th Regiment as carpenters and blacksmiths. A few of them remained on the work until the end of the expedition, although as a rule they joined their regiment when they marched from Zoulla.

During the month of January, about four miles of railway over the sandy plain, and three sidings at Zoulla, were made. The latter, though taking but few men to construct, gave a great deal of trouble, owing to the want of skilled labour necessary to lay them properly, and the interruption to the traffic they caused, when the line was broken up to insert them. From the first day that a locomotive got up steam, the additional difficulty of supplying it with water was imposed upon us.

The tank engines, with moderate work, consumed about 1,000 gallons a-day; and at the first the experiment was tried of mixing a small amount of salt water with the condensed, to economize, as far as possible, the latter. It was found, however, not to answer, for although some locomotives are constructed to use salt water, the priming, in one case, was so great with water in the slightest degree brackish, as to render the engine almost useless, and to cause a much larger quantity of condensed water being required than when it was solely fed from the latter source. A small condenser on the pier was given up exclusively for railway purposes. It did not yield, however, enough water, and the deficiency had to be supplied by the slow and laborious process of pumping from water-boats brought alongside the pier. Engines when detained on the line had often to leave their trains and run down to the pier to take in water, and in some cases even to draw their fires, not having enough water to bring them down there, causing very great delay, inconvenience, and loss.

The discovery of water at points along the line was almost, if not actually, essential to the success of the railway. Major Chamberlain recognizing the great necessity for obtaining it, detached several parties of skilled well-sinkers from the 23rd Punjaub Pioneers to dig wells in likely places in the alluvial soil. After several trials, a hot spring was met with 55 feet below the surface of the ground, and about 3½ miles from Zoulla. The temperature of the water when raised was 120 deg. F., but by exposing it in open barrels for a day it became as cool as the water from the shipping. Although it contained a considerable amount of saline matter, it was not undrinkable, and worked moderately well for the engines. Soon two other wells were sunk, and the yield, amounting to about 12,000 gallons per diem, enabled us to establish tanks there for watering the engines, and to give up entirely the troublesome and precarious supply at the pier. It also allowed us to move out working parties ahead of the plate-layers, which had before been almost impracticable, as water had to be brought by railway from Zoulla for their use, and the Engineer officers were supposed to make arrangements for doing so. I can hardly overstate the previous delays and difficulties we encountered owing to the uncertainty and shortness of the water supply. One and a half gallons per diem were supposed to be allotted to each man, not an over abundant supply where work was carried on all day under a burning sun and often through parching dust storms. But until we got our own wells there was no certainty whether the apportioned amount would be given or not at the watering places. Often after working from daylight until noon, the natives could not cook their food, owing to the water-ration not having been served out, and the afternoon's work had to be postponed until a small supply was obtained. That it was unavoidable, no one can doubt, and my only reason for stating it is to give some idea of the difficulties, other than engineering, in our way.

In the commencement of February, the railway had nearly reached to the foot of the low hills, about six miles from the coast. Captain Darrah therefore applied for the military working parties to be increased, in order that the plate-laying might not be delayed by the earthwork. A well was also commenced at the site of the railway bridge in the stony ravine, in hopes that water might be obtained, and the camps moved on there, for marching the men nearly three miles from their present camp to their work, entailed great loss of time. As the responsibility of providing water for the working parties devolved upon Captain Darrah, it would have been very hazardous and imprudent, with the experience gained by our previous difficulties at Zoulla, to have sent a large number of men to a place where there was no water, and where it would have had to be brought upon mules from a long distance, to supply them.

About the middle of February, a wing of the 2nd Grenadier Regiment (Bombay Native Infantry) was despatched for work on the railway. The plate-laying, however, advanced slowly, for the rails had nearly all to be straightened, and many of them to be cut, being very much worn, crooked, and of odd lengths. When the government of Bombay determined that the railway plant, stores, and rolling stock should be sent entirely from India, it was found that light rails of the same pattern were not obtainable for the number of miles required. The railways at Madras, Kurrachee, and Bombay, were indented upon, and the result was that we were supplied with rails of no less than five different patterns.

For the first two miles a single flanged fish-plated rail, weighing about 45lbs. a yard was used, which answered very satisfactorily, made an easy road, and was everything that was required. Then for the next four miles we were compelled to lay down those sent from Kurrachee, single-flanged rails, weighing about 50 lbs. to the yard, and having joint-chairs instead of fish-plates. They had been in use for many years on the harbour works at Kurrachee; taken up and laid down several times; bent to fit sharp curves, and cut to suit the original line; so that when they arrived in Zoulla, a great portion of them were useless. So bad were they, that if the expedition had lasted another year, we should have been compelled to substitute other rails for them, and on more than one occasion the engine has gone off the line, owing to a rail having broken between two sleepers. The use of joint-chairs instead of fish-plates, the former being of wrought iron and very bad, made a very rough line, and the want of proper ballast rendered it worse. A small quantity of single-flanged rails, weighing 40 lbs. to the yard, were sent from Bombay, and had been fitted there in the government workshops with fish-plates and bolts. Unfortunately, the holes in the plates and rails were not at uniform distances apart, and the bolts fitted the holes so tightly as to allow of no play. This rendered the straightening and adjustment of the line almost impossible, and although they were well suited for the work, we were obliged to reject them.

A double-headed fish-plated rail, with chairs, weighing 65 lbs. a yard, was purposely left until the heavy gradients and sharp curves were reached. A rail with chairs takes considerably more time to lay than a single-flanged one with spikes; it is not, therefore, so well adapted for rapid work as the more temporary rail. Its weight was also against its use, as with chairs it cannot have weighed less than 95 lbs. a yard; but there was no comparison between the finished lines of the two descriptions. The smooth travelling on the part of the railway laid with the double-headed rail, and the ease with which it was kept in repair, almost repaid for the increased trouble and delay in laying it. A quantity of 30 lbs. and 35 lbs. rails were also sent with cast-iron joint chairs, but they were too light to lay on the main line, and were used only on sidings; they here showed how badly they were adapted for fast traffic, by bending between the sleepers.

The rolling stock was, however, a much greater source of trouble than the rails.

Six locomotives were shipped from Bombay, but owing to the great difficulty in landing them, and the time and skilled labour required to put them together, only four were used on the railway.

No. 1. A tank engine, although just turned out of the railway workshops at Bombay, after running for a fortnight, had to be supplied with new driving wheels. It had six wheels, two pairs of which were coupled, and with great difficulty ran round the curves, owing to there being no play in the axle boxes.

No. 2. Another small tank engine (6 wheeled) was very well adapted for the line, although old. The boiler tubes were worn out, and had to be replaced in Abyssinia.

Nos. 3 and 4 were also tank engines with only 4 wheels each; this gives great facility for running round curves, although dangerous for fast traffic. These loco-motives were of a cheap description and old, having been in use for many years at Kurrachee. The working parts of the machinery were outside the wheels, an arrangement very badly suited for a sandy plain where dust storms were of con-stant occurrence, as the sand penetrated into the exposed parts, and soon wore away the bearings. All these engines were very light, weighing with coal and water from 16 to 20 tons each; none of them were powerful, and the best one could only draw 15 small loaded trucks up an incline of 1 in 60.

Sixty waggons were sent for working the line. They were the ordinary trol-lies, without springs. They had originally belonged to a reclamation company in Bombay, and having been used for running only two or three miles at a time along a railway, were not furnished with grease boxes, and were not adapted for a longer journey. The axle bearings being of cast-iron, and open to the driving sand, were soon worn through; indeed, I have known a truck thus incapacitated by a fortnight's running on the line. Gun metal bearings were sent for to Bombay and arrived in May, but few trucks were fitted with them. The want of springs and spring buffers were great causes of wear and tear to the rolling stock. The line being rough, and every truck being loaded to its utmost capacity, the jarring and oscillation increased the traction, more especially where there was no give or take from the springs, and everything was dead weight on the engine. Coupling chains were broken and coupling bars pulled out from the waggons at starting. The boxes containing the spare coupling chains had been left behind at Bombay, or were beneath several hundred tons of railway iron on board ship. From all these causes combined we were always very short of trucks, and at least 40 per cent., were continually under repair, or condemned as unfit for further service. In May, some open waggons with springs and spring buffers were sent from Bombay; their axles were too far apart to run easily round the curves, but several were altered and fit-ted with covers and seats to form passenger carriages.

On the 19th February, about half the line being completed, and a siding made at the Quartermaster General's road, this portion of the line was opened for traffic. From this date almost all the commissariat stores were brought up by rail from Zoulla, the baggage animals removed to Koomayleh, and the enormous expense of providing them with condensed water at the former place, greatly reduced in consequence. The railway was now taxed to its utmost to bring up these supplies, four to seven trains being required daily for the purpose, and at the same time to keep the plate-laying parties in material.

Two small iron girder bridges were built close to the Quartermaster General's road, No. 5 of two spans of 20 feet, and No. 6 one span of 25 feet. The trestles for both were prepared in Zoulla, and when brought to the site, it took three days to complete the bridges. The earthwork of the railway commenced here, for hitherto it had been only levelling the ground, and forming approaches to the bridges; but as the working parties were strong, there was no unnecessary delay to the plate-laying, on account of its being unfinished. Fortunately the Punjaub Pioneers again found water at the site of bridge No. 7, 70 feet below the bed of the dry water course, and sunk a well there, which was a model of neat and good work. The camps were moved close to this spot, but the supply of water was not enough for everyone, and 1,200 gallons a day had to be brought up by railway from the Pioneer well.

Commencing at bridge No. 7, the line wound through the ravine with an ascending gradient of 1 in 91 and with numerous curves up to the heaviest cutting and sharpest curve on the line which was about 3,500 feet from the bridge. The depth of the former was about 9 ft., and the radius of the latter 870 ft. To meet the increased labour so urgently required at this time, the other wing of the 2nd Grenadier Regiment Bombay Native Infantry, was sent to join the railway camp; but at the very end of February the Punjaub Pioneers were ordered to the front and their place supplied by a weak wing of the 45th Regiment. To say that we were great losers by the exchange, is no slur on the latter regiment, for they were numerically about one-third less than the Pioneers, had had no previous training in using the pick and shovel, and were incapable of the severe work in the burning sun, which came almost naturally to the Indian troops. The Grenadier Native Infantry Regiment, stimulated by the unusual sight to them of European soldiers being called upon to furnish working parties, increased their exertions, and until the close of the expedition, in the most intense heat, laboured with such alacrity as to call for special commendation in the report of the Commanding Royal Engineer.

The Skew Bridge (No. 7), see Pl. II, was commenced in the first week in March, and finished in ten days. At the same time four small 12-feet girder culverts were constructed, and on the 15th of March the rails had been laid up to the Koomayleh plain. In the latter part of January, Lieut. (now Captain) Merewether, R.E., was directed by the Commanding Royal Engineer to commence the earthwork of the line from Koomayleh. At first there was some difficulty in obtaining working parties, but having a company of the Madras Sappers at his disposal, being furnished with some military labour, and neither the cuttings nor the embankments being heavy on this portion of the line, the work was reported completed up to the end of the Koomayleh plain, in the middle of March. Very unfortunately, however, owing to Captain Merewether having been on the sick list, and unable to superintend the work in person, it was found that the line had not been accurately enough marked out, that on the curves the radii were not the same at different points on the same curve, and consequently a large portion of the line had to be rejected. The company of Madras Sappers and Miners excavated a well on the Koomayleh plain, where water was obtained 90 feet below the surface, in sufficient quantity to supply the railway. The camp was therefore moved and pitched close to this well. The wing of the 45th Regiment left for the front about the 28th March, and consequently the whole work devolved upon the 2nd Grenadiers and the Army Works Corps. Shortly afterwards the head-quarters wing of the Grenadiers was withdrawn, and replaced by a wing of the 18th Bombay Native Infantry.

In the latter part of March, a new siding was finished about 3 miles from Koomayleh, and 9 from Zoulla, and the new portion of the line reported to the Commanding Royal Engineer, as ready to be opened for traffic. The 50 lbs. single flanged rails (Kurrachee) were, however, so very bad, that he thought it advisable to substitute for them the new fish-plated rail (65 lbs.) with chairs. Fortunately almost all the extension consisted of the latter rail, and although there was some delay in replacing the former, where it had been laid, this extra portion was open to traffic on the 28th March. The heat had now become so intense that it was impossible to get the same amount of physical labour from the workpeople as heretofore. The railway progressed slowly, the energies of the officers being directed to the working of the line, as well as to its construction. The watering, coaling, shunting, and repairing abstracted men who otherwise would have been pushing on the construction. In the end of April, the fall of Magdala being known, the Commanding Royal Engineer thought it advisable to terminate the line when it had reached about one mile from Koomayleh, and to prepare for the great traffic which it would have to bear on the return of the troops. A loop-line and station sheds were accordingly made at the terminus.

The total quantity of line laid was 12 miles 106 yards, although the length of the main line was under 11 miles, the difference being made up by sidings and a branch line to one of the piers. From the middle of May to the close of the expedition in the middle of June, the railway was taxed to its utmost working capabilities in conveying troops, baggage, and stores. The arrangements for working the line had been much improved. Telegraph stations were placed at Zoulla, Pioneer wells, and the Koomayleh terminus. Watering tanks were erected at the Pioneer wells, which was the main watering place on the line; a stand pipe and tank were fixed at the siding in Koomayleh plain; and a fire engine stationed at the bridge in Stony Ravine, to supply the engines with water. At the Pioneer wells sheds had been built for repairing engines and waggons; sidings, for the rolling stock to remain in at night, constructed; and all the civilian employés camped there close to their work.

A commodious station was made at Zoulla, which proved very convenient, although most of the trains ran direct down to the piers. The working hours on the railway commenced daily at 4.30 a.m., and often were not over till past ten in the evening. Three trains only could be made up, as many of the waggons were hors-de-combat, and it was only by the most strenuous exertions that the locomotives could be kept in working order. The nights were devoted to their repair, but they got worse and worse daily. At the end it was found that two of them were not worth the labour and expense of re-embarkation, and they were accordingly abandoned.

As regards the question whether this railway might not have been better and more quickly made by a civil contractor than by officers of the corps with military and organized labour, I think the evidence is in favour of the latter. An English firm could not have employed European navvies in the burning sun on the shores of the Red Sea, and the labour must have been brought from either Egypt or India. It would have taken more time for a contractor to have organized and despatched gangs of Egyptians to Zoulla than for the Bombay government to have sent the necessary labour from India; for it should be remembered that it was not determined by the government of Bombay to have a railway until the end of November, 1867.

When the guarantee of the state, and the promise of high pay, failed to bring a good class of Coolie from India, a contractor would have had little prospect of securing any but the most indifferent hands, as labour was in great demand for the other departments of the expedition. All the officers on the railway were accustomed to employ natives on the public works in India, were acquainted with their language, and understood their management, qualifications which can be rarely met with out of the government service, and which can scarcely be over-rated. Where neither food nor water was to be purchased, where no local labour was obtainable, where even shelter for workmen had to be imported, and where all the stores had to be landed at an overcrowded pier, it is hardly probable that a contractor could have made his own arrangements for everything, without the help of the military departments. It required all the influence of the Royal Engineer officers to procure such necessary assistance as barges for landing plant and stores, accommodation at the pier for discharging them, trains to bring up the material to the plate-laying parties, besides rationing the men, and providing them with water. The above can surely be done at the place of debarkation of an army better by officers than civilians.

We did not complain of the want of skilled labour on the Abyssinian railway, we could have pushed on much faster if the plate-laying parties had been supplied with a sufficient amount of good material, for the latter had to be largely rejected on account of its inferiority. Plate-laying is easily learned, and men accustomed to work together will soon understand the orders of a foreman. No great speed is required on a military railway, and, consequently, the line may be laid much more roughly than on an ordinary line, where it is requisite to run quick trains.

I venture to add the following remarks suggested by our experience in Abyssinia. A narrow gauge line is most preferable for a military railway, as the waggons are lighter, run round the sharp curves with greater facility, and when they run off the line are more easily got back again, than those made for a broad guage. In construction, a short heavy gradient on a straight line, is preferable to a sharp curve as an alternative. Trains can rush at the former and overcome the resistance (which only acts one way) by their momentum. On a curve there is the liability of running off the line, and the resistance, which is very considerable on a rough one, acts both ways. Our sharpest curve on the Abyssinian railway had a radius of 870 feet, and was on an incline of 1 in 91. With a narrower gauge than the Indian

(5 feet 6 inches) we might have adopted even a smaller radius. The heaviest gradient was 1 in 60, often combined with sharp curves.

A single flanged rail weighing about 40 lbs. per yard is most suitable for a military railway. It should be fish-plated, and in lengths of 24 feet. If wooden sleepers are used, the rail is most quickly fastened to them for a temporary line by 4 inch spikes nailed into the sleepers, which are first bored with an auger. Considerable trouble is found, however, when this method is adopted, in keeping the line in gauge round sharp curves, and also at points. Chairs decidedly should be used for the latter if possible. Where there are only light tank engines, 9 sleepers to each rail will suffice, those at each side of the fish-plates, centrically, 2 feet apart, and the remainder about 2 feet 9 inches. It will be found convenient, and plate-layers say it makes a much easier line, to have the fish-plates on each line of rail exactly opposite each other. This necessitates cutting a rail on long curves, where the inner line is shorter than the outer one.

Iron pot-sleepers would be well adapted for a military railway. The Commanding Royal Engineer in Abyssinia sent to Bombay for them, but they could not be obtained for a light rail. Iron pot-sleepers would be easily carried and loaded on railway trucks (the wooden ones were continually dropping off the waggons). The tie rod connecting the former could, without difficulty, be fixed in its place by an ordinary soldier or Sepoy, and the line can never be out of gauge when once laid. The pot-sleeper, being in two parts, is carried with much greater ease than the unwieldy wooden one, which is very awkward for men unaccustomed to lift heavy weights.

The small wrought-iron girders made up in Bombay for Abyssinia, were well adapted for bridges. They were in two lengths, 14 and 22 feet, answering for spans of 12 and 20 feet. They were calculated for a working load of 1 ton per running foot, rather in excess of our requirements. The weight of the larger one was about a ton, and it was conveyed and put up without difficulty. Girders of 30 cwt. would not be inconveniently large, if it were desirable to increase the spans of the bridges. Wooden trestles make good temporary piers, and 3-in. sheet piling, driven by heavy mallets, retains small embankments well at the abutments. The bridges on the Abyssinian railway were not good examples of construction, as there was no timber sent especially for them; this should not be neglected in future, and it was with great difficulty that wood of any description was obtained.

It is impossible to give a correct estimate of the number of men required to carry rails and sleepers to keep the above parties supplied with material, as the lengths of the leads varied very much. On an average, where the ballast trains came up to the end of the line, as it was laid, about 120 men (natives) were employed in carrying rails and sleepers, and in unloading trains.

The rate of progress in Abyssinia with the single flanged rail, without chairs, where there was no delay on account of the want of rails, &c., was nearly 400 yards a-day (10 working hours); when the double flanged rail with chairs was used it was much less, being about 250 yards.

Tank engines are no doubt the best adapted for a temporary line; they are more powerful for their weight, and, consequently, can be made lighter than those with tenders, and require no turn-tables, as they run either end foremost with equal facility. They are, however, very destructive to the line for their weight, and require trouble and experience in working them.

The trucks should have their axles as close almost as the wheels on each side will permit, and should be small and light. Those we used weighed about two tons, but they required more power to drag than those properly made with springs, and three tons in weight.

All waggons should have springs, and also spring buffers. Economy alone can preclude these being furnished; the rougher the line, the more needful and advantageous are waggons of this description.

Sides to waggons are useful, but the catches for letting one side down should not be liable to be jerked up by the motion of the train. I have seen several waggons thrown off the line by their contents falling on the rails, owing to defective catches which became loosened.

Covered waggons would be convenient for some purposes, but would not answer for trusses of forage, &c., and in a hot climate could not be used for troops, unless constructed with several large doors. We found in Abyssinia that the ordinary small waggons were not suited for carrying rails, the length of the latter (24 feet) obliging them to be placed on two waggons, and often causing one of the trucks to run off the line at the first curve. Waggons should be made on purpose for rails and sleepers, especially where there are no appliances for loading high trucks. The platform should not be higher than 4 feet, so that the rails and sleepers can be easily lifted on to them. For a line with sharp curves, it would be advantageous to use bogies.

We may conclude that we had to execute in our workshops the maximum amount of repairs, in proportion to the traffic and length of the line, that can well be incurred on any railway.

A very complete fitting shop was sent from Bombay, including steam lathes, stationary engines, quarters for mechanics, &c. It was never put up, and proved more in the way than otherwise; for any careful packing arrangements made in Bombay were altogether neutralized by the vessel which brought them going ashore in the Red Sea, and by her cargo being transferred to another ship. We were, therefore, often obliged to land heavy machinery to procure useful stores, buried beneath it in the hold of the vessel.

The civil establishment, picked up in Bombay at a short notice, and without increased rate of pay being offered to them, could scarcely be expected to give satisfaction, although in some instances we met with valuable services. Some of the employés were dismissed, and their places supplied by promoting those who seemed deserving men. We lost through casualties and dismissal about 25 per cent. of the European civilians, and they were always a source of trouble and anxiety to us, and I think it would be advisable to substitute for them, as far as possible, men from the ranks.

Intelligent non-commissioned officers would make good station masters, as their most important duty is to obey orders. Guards could be furnished in the same manner. Pointsmen and signalmen could easily, if required, be supplied from the ranks. Engine drivers and foremen plate-layers are about the only men whose places could not be filled from the army or navy. Firemen and fitters can be supplied from the latter; and for some time on the Abyssinian railway, the duties of locomotive foreman were efficiently performed by one of the engineer officers kindly lent for the purpose from H.M.S. "Octavia."

The Abyssinian railway was a great success, if we may gauge it by the amount of assistance it gave to the expedition, by the saving in money it effected by allowing the baggage animals, at an early date, to be taken away from Zoulla (where they were drinking condensed water at an enormous cost), and by the help it gave to the Land Transport Corps, in enabling them to send these animals to the front; by the celerity and dispatch with which by its aid stores were landed and brought up to the store sheds; and by the rapidity and ease with which the troops and their baggage were brought back and re-embarked at once.

It cannot be taken as an example of the time in which a military railway ought to be constructed, if there were no impediments in its way. From this point of view it was often judged by civilians as a failure; but as an auxiliary to the expedition, and as an additional means of transport, no one, who had anything to do in connection with it, can have doubted its extreme utility.

Constructed under the most unfavourable circumstances, in extreme heat, which sometimes reached 180° F. in the sun, with indifferent materials and bad rolling stock, it nevertheless proves how necessary in future it will be to provide all our military expeditions with a light railway at their points of debarkation.

59

RUDYARD KIPLING, *THE LIGHT THAT FAILED*, IN *WORKS*, 15 VOLS. (NEW YORK: LOVELL, 1899), III, PP. 296–303

"I am very content." He stroked the creaseless spirals of his leggings. "Now let us go and see the captain and George and the lighthouse boat. Be quick, Madame."

"But thou canst not be seen by the harbor walking with me in the daylight. Figure to yourself if some English ladies——"

"There are no English ladies; and if there are, I have forgotten them. Take me there."

In spite of his burning impatience it was nearly evening ere the lighthouse boat began to move. Madame had said a great deal both to George and the captain touching the arrangements that were to be made for Dick's benefit. Very few men who had the honor of her acquaintance cared to disregard Madame's advice. That sort of contempt might end in being knifed by a stranger in a gambling hell upon surprisingly short provocation.

For six days—two of them were wasted in the crowded Canal—the little steamer worked her way to Suakin, where she was to pick up the superintendent of lighthouses; and Dick made it his business to propitiate George, who was distracted with fears for the safety of his light-of-love and half inclined to make Dick repsonsible for his own discomfort. When they arrived George took him under his wing, and together they entered the red-hot seaport, encumbered with the material and wastage of the Suakin-Berber line, from locomotives in disconsolate fragments to mounds of chairs and pot-sleepers.

"If you keep with me," said George, "nobody will ask for passport or what you do. They are all very busy."

"Yes; but I should like to hear some of the Englishmen talk. They might remember me. I was known here a long time ago—when I was some one indeed."

"A long time ago is a very long time ago here. The graveyards are full. Now listen. This new railway runs out so far as Tanai-el-Hassan—that is seven miles. Then there is a camp. They say that beyond Tanai-el Hassan the English troops go forward, and everything that they require will be brought to them by this line."

"Ah! Base camp. I see. That's a better business than fighting Fuzzies in the open."

"For this reason even the mules go up in the iron-train."

"Iron what?"

"It is all covered with iron, because it is still being shot at."

"An armored train. Better and better! Go on, faithful George."

"And I go up with my mules to-night. Only those who particularly require to go to the camp go out with the train. They begin to shoot not far from the city."

"The dears—they always used to!" Dick snuffed the smell of parched dust, heated iron, and flaking paint with delight. Certainly the old life was welcoming him back most generously.

"When I have got my mules together I go up to-night, but you must first send a telegram to Port Said, declaring that I have done you no harm."

"Madame has you well in hand. Would you stick a knife into me if you had the chance?"

"I have no chance," said the Greek. "*She* is there with that woman."

"I see. It's a bad thing to be divided between love of woman and the chance of loot. I sympathize with you, George."

They went to the telegraph-office unquestioned, for all the world was desperately busy and had scarcely time to turn its head, and Suakin was the last place under sky that would be chosen for holiday-ground. On their return the voice of an English subaltern asked Dick what he was doing. The blue goggles were over his eyes and he walked with his hand on George's elbow as he replied—

"Egyptian Government—mules. My orders are to give them over to the A. C. G. at Tanai-el-Hassan. 'Any occasion to show my papers?"

"Oh, certainly not. I beg your pardon. I'd no right to ask, but not seeing your face before I——"

"I go out in the train to-night, I suppose," said Dick, boldly. "There will be no difficulty in loading up the mules, will there?"

"You can see the horse-platforms from here. You must have them loaded up early."

The young man went away wondering what sort of broken down waif this might be who talked like a gentleman and consorted with Greek muleteers. Dick felt unhappy. To outface an English officer is no small thing, but the bluff loses relish when one plays it from the utter dark, and stumbles up and down rough ways, thinking and eternally thinking of what might have been if things had fallen out otherwise, and all had been as it was not.

George shared his meal with Dick and went off to the mule-lines. His charge sat alone in a shed with his face in his hands. Before his tight-shut eyes danced the face of Maisie, laughing, with parted lips. There was a great bustle and clamor about him. He grew afraid and almost called for George.

"I say, have you got your mules ready?" It was the voice of the subaltern over his shoulder.

"My man's looking after them. The—the fact is I've a touch of ophthalmia and I can't see very well."

"By Jove! that's bad. You ought to lie up in hospital for a while. I've had a turn of it myself. It's as bad as being blind."

"So I find it. When does this armored train go?"

"At six o'clock. It takes an hour to cover the seven miles."

"Are the Fuzzies on the rampage—eh?"

"About three nights a week. 'Fact is I'm in acting command of the night-train. It generally runs back empty to Tanai for the night."

"Big camp at Tanai, I suppose?"

"Pretty big. It has to feed our desert-column somehow."

"Is that far off?"

"Between thirty and forty miles—in an infernal thirsty country."

"Is the country quiet between Tanai and our men?"

"More or less. I shouldn't care to cross it alone, or with a subaltern's command for the matter of that, but the scouts get through in some extraordinary fashion."

"They always did."

"Have you been here before, then?"

"I was through most of the trouble when it first broke out."

"In the service and cashiered," was the subaltern's first thought, so he refrained from putting any questions.

"There's your man coming up with the mules. It seems rather queer——"

"That I should be mule-leading?" said Dick.

"I didn't mean to say so, but it is. Forgive me—it's beastly impertinence I know, but you speak like a man who has been at a public school. There's no mistaking the tone."

"I am a public school man."

"I thought so. I say, I don't want to hurt your feelings, but you're a little down on your luck, aren't you? I saw you sitting with your head in your hands, and that's why I spoke."

"Thanks. I am about as thoroughly and completely broke as a man need be."

"Suppose—I mean I'm a public school man myself. Couldn't I perhaps—take it as a loan y' know and——"

"You're much too good, but on my honor I've as much money as I want . . . . I tell you what you could do for me, though, and put me under an everlasting obligation. Let me come into the bogie truck of the train. There is a foretruck, isn't there?"

"Yes. How d'you know?"

"I've been in an armored train before. Only let me see—hear some of the fun I mean, and I'll be grateful. I go at my own risk as a non-combatant."

The young man thought for a minute. "All right," he said. "We're supposed to be an empty train, and there's no one to blow me up at the other end."

George and a horde of yelling amateur assistants had loaded up the mules, and the narrow-gauge armored train, plated with three-eighths inch boiler-plate till it looked like one long coffin, stood ready to start.

Two bogie trucks running before the locomotive were completely covered in with plating, except that the leading one was pierced in front for the nozzle of a machine-gun, and the second at either side for lateral fire. The trucks together made one long iron-vaulted chamber in which a score of artillerymen were rioting.

"Whitechapel—last train! Ah, I see yer kissin' in the first class there!" somebody shouted, just as Dick was clambering into the forward truck.

"Lordy! 'Ere's a real live passenger for the Kew, Tanai, Acton, and Ealin' train. *Echo*, sir. Speshul edition! *Star*, sir."—"Shall I get you a foot-warmer?" said another.

"Thanks. I'll pay my footing," said Dick, and relations of the most amicable were established ere silence came with the arrival of the subaltern, and the train jolted out over the rough track.

"This is an immense improvement on shooting the unimpressionable Fuzzy in the open," said Dick, from his place in the corner.

"Oh, but he's still unimpressed. There he goes!" said the subaltern, as a bullet struck the ouside of the truck. "We always have at least one demonstration against the night-train. Generally they attack the rear-truck where my junior commands. He gets all the fun of the fair."

"Not to-night though! Listen!" said Dick. A flight of heavy-handed bullets was succeeded by yelling and shouts. The children of the desert valued their nightly amusement, and the train was an excellent mark.

"Is it worth while giving them half a hopper full?" the subaltern asked of the engine which was driven by a Lieutenant of Sappers.

"I should just think so! This is my section of the line. They'll be playing old Harry with my permanent way if we don't stop 'em."

"Right O!"

"*Hrrmph!*" said the machine gun through all its five noses as the subaltern drew the lever home. The empty cartridges clashed on the floor and the smoke blew back through the truck. There was indiscriminate firing at the rear of the train, a return fire from the darkness without and unlimited howling. Dick stretched himself on the floor, wild with delight at the sounds and the smells.

"God is very good—I never thought I'd hear this again. Give 'em hell, men. Oh, give 'em hell!" he cried.

The train stopped for some obstruction on the line ahead and a party went out to reconnoiter, but came back cursing, for spades. The children of the desert had piled sand and gravel on the rails, and twenty minutes were lost in clearing it away. Then the slow progress recommenced, to be varied with more shots, more shoutings, the steady clack and kick of the machine guns, and a final difficulty with a half-lifted rail ere the train came under the protection of the roaring camp at Tanai-el-Hassan.

"Now, you see why it takes an hour and a half to fetch her through," said the subaltern, unshipping the cartridge-hopper above his pet gun.

60

ANNIE BRASSEY, *THE LAST VOYAGE:* *1887* (LONDON: LONGMANS, GREEN, 1889), PP. 435–437

The visit of President Kruger, of the Transvaal, to President Brand, of the Free State, was a prominent topic at the time of our visit. It had led to the delivery of a speech by Mr. Kruger, in which he had declared the determination of the Boers to preserve their complete independence. In the Cape Colony people are more interested in the establishment of railway communication with the new gold-fields within the borders of the Transvaal than in the question of political union. As yet a certain reluctance is manifested by the Boers to establish railway communication with the Cape. An English company has made a railway from Delagoa Bay to the Transvaal frontier, and the line will shortly be extended to Pretoria. In the mean-while the people of the Cape Colony are desirous of extending their system of railways, already 1,483 miles in length, into the interior. Considerable discoveries of gold have recently been made within the limits of the Transvaal, but close to the border, and all the workers at the mines are Englishmen from the Cape Colony. There is no reason to doubt that permission to establish railway communication with this newly discovered goldmining district will be ultimately granted.

Among the Boers of the Transvaal a large number are friendly to the English. Once connected with the Cape by railway, and by a Customs union, which has been much under discussion, the Cape Colony and the Transvaal will be for all practical purposes of trade united. A divided administration of government in a country of such wide extent is an unmixed advantage.

It was particularly gratifying to hear from Mr. Hofmeyr, the head of the Dutch party in the Cape Parliament, and a most able representative of the Colony in the late Colonial Conference, how entirely satisfied his people are to live under British rule as now conducted. The Dutch colonists at the Cape have no personal relations with Holland. They look back upon their former connection as an inter-esting historical association; but the protection which England affords against the occupation of the Cape by some other foreign power is a practical boon, and one greatly valued. There is a party at the Cape which regards with disfavour the dependence of the present Premier, Sir Gordon Sprigg, on the Dutch vote, or, as it is called, the Africander Bond. From another point of view we may hail with satisfaction the success which an Englishman has achieved in winning the con-fidence of the Dutch. While conducting the government to their satisfaction, he is thoroughly loyal to his own nationality. Baron Hübner speaks in discouraging tones of our position at the Cape. A much more cheerful impression was conveyed by the present able Governor, Sir Hercules Robinson, and by other eminent men whom I had an opportunity of consulting.

Judging from such indications as came under our personal notice, the native races, so far from being a source of weakness, are a great strength to the colony. The Indians in North America, the Maoris in New Zealand, the aborigines of Australia, have disappeared or dwindled away before the white man. The Zulus and Kaffirs have proved themselves capable of adopting and promoting civilisation. They show in numerous instances a high appreciation of the blessings of education. They are ready to labour on the farms, on the railways, and in the mines. They are content to live under the rule of a superior race.

61

FRANK VINCENT, *ACTUAL AFRICA; OR, THE COMING CONTINENT* (NEW YORK: D. APPLETON & CO., 1895), PP. 208–210, 295–296, 298–306, 312–314, 376–379, 414–415, 419–428

I remarked one day on which there was a difference of 45° between 6 A. M. and 4 P. M.——45° to 90°. At about eleven o'clock we reached Wadi Halfa, 802 miles from Cairo. The houses of the town are scattered along the eastern bank for several miles, and are mostly single-story mud huts; a few of them are of two stories, and have whitened walls. Groves of palms line this bank, but the opposite is all desert. Wadi Halfa is so called from the halfa (called alfa throughout Barbary) or coarse grass which springs up everywhere outside the irrigated portions of land. The town is about in latitude 21° 50′ north and longitude 31° 20′ east. It contains 4,000 Egyptian troops, officered by Englishmen. A permanent garrison has been stationed here since the war in the Soudan. There are many negro soldiers, and these are said to be quite as brave as the Egyptians, and much truer. There are several mud forts, mounting small repeating guns, and outlying citadels for pickets in every direction on the summit of the ridges and knolls and even upon the opposite bank of the river. The town itself contains nothing of any special interest, but there is a narrow-gauge railway running from here around the cataract, which it is worth employing for a trip as far south as possible.

The second cataract begins a few miles south of Wadi Halfa and extends about seven miles. The railway was laid down by the English a number of years ago to transport troops and stores above the cataract. It at first ran a distance of eighty-six miles to Ferket, but fifty miles of it were afterwards destroyed by the Mahdists, who threw the rails into the river and used the sleepers to boil their kettles and cook their food. The telegraph wire they twisted together to form their spurs. Thirty-six miles of this road have been put in order by the Egyptian army, and trains are now run regularly on Mondays and Thursdays at 8 A. M., returning at 4 P. M. The line extends to a place called Sarras, where is a large fort and camp, the outpost of the Egyptian army, all beyond this being since 1885 in the hands of the Mahdists. Thursday was the day on which we had arrived, and the train having gone out regularly in the morning, it was necessary for us to engage a special train, which we did at the rate of about $2.50 each for the excursion. There were some twenty of us, and so the railway people received $50.00. We had first to get permission of the military authorities, and then a guard of twelve soldiers, armed with Martini-Henry rifles, being deputed to accompany us, we left at 2 P. M. The carriages were of miniature pattern, the third-class passengers having to stand in open vans. The rolling-stock was of English manufacture. Our small but powerful locomotive was curiously enough called the "Gorgon." No train, even of goods, is allowed to run without an escort of soldiers. The little road in leaving Wadi Halfa passes the large walled enclosure of the garrison and the level space used as a parade, drill ground and shooting range, and then heads across the desert until it reaches the banks of the Nile, which it follows to Sarras. We crossed a number of Arab cemeteries, the graves being placed close together, and only marked by low head and foot stones and covered with white pebbles. We soon entered the region of the cataracts—rapids and rocks similar to those in the first cataract. Along the banks were hills composed wholly of smoothly-rounded rocks, in the river were thousands of rocky and sandy islets, about which the muddy Nile roared and ran— some of these islets only large stones, others great heaps of them, others rocks with banks of sand, and still others large islands, cultivated and tree-or shrub-covered, and inhabited. The river was hereabouts several miles in width, and the black polished rocks and swirling water made a very extraordinary picture. The first cataract cuts through granite, but the second through ferreous sandstone boulders, which are stained and coated with Nile mud as those at Assouan-Philæ. At Sarras, the present terminus of the line, we found an Egyptian garrison in camp, and upon a neighboring isolated rock a strong fortress. The troops consisted of a battalion of infantry, a company of cavalry and a small camel-corps. The camels especially attracted our attention and admiration, being all of them white and fine animals. We found three English officers in charge of the outpost. The river continues southwards, between high banks, of about the same width, but is said to be scarcely navigable for a long distance. Sarras is the farthest point to which travellers are now permitted to go—it is in about latitude 21° north, or a thousand miles from the Mediterranean. We arrived back at Wadi Halfa at 7 P. M.

A few of us rose early the next day and made an excursion to the famous rock of Aboosir, which is about the centre of the cataract region, upon the west bank, the object being to get the view from thence of the cataract. We crossed diagonally to the opposite shore, a distance of about three miles, where we found donkeys to take us over the desert to our destination. I had so small a donkey that I actually feared he might trip over my feet. A very strong breeze from the northwest was blowing, and we were able to stem the strong current in about an hour. The donkeys carried us for a short distance along the river bank and then took a direct line across the desert to the great rock. The undulating surface was covered with fine deep sand. All about us were curious low, weather-worn outcroppings of rock. In an hour and a quarter we had made the distance of six miles. The rock rises solitarily about fifty feet above a huge cliff facing the river and three hundred feet above it. It not only affords a capital prospect of the second cataract, but of the country in every direction. In the south the long range of blue mountains is that of Dongola, 150 miles distant. The third cataract is near them. The view over the Nile is one of grandeur but of savage desolation. The polished black rocks look like heaps of coal or carbon crystals as they sparkle in the sunlight. The rapids on the western side of the river are much larger than those upon the eastern, and one sees better here the myriads of small islands which dot and break up the Nile into so many swirling streams. The roar of these rapids is plainly heard, but is not so prodigious as some travellers and geographers have maintained. The desert side of the rock of Aboosir is carved with thousands of names of visitors. Among them I noticed several of famous explorers and Egyptologists—those of Belzoni, Champollion, Warburton and Lord Lindsay. We returned to Wadi Halfa at noon, and our steamer almost immediately thereafter started upon the return voyage to Philæ. The strong head wind did not neutralise the power of the strong current, and we proceeded down stream at nearly double our upward rate. We arrived at Aboo Simbel at 5 P. M., and spent two hours in studying the splendid old temple, both exterior and interior.

In the morning we found lying near us a little Egyptian gun-boat, which came in late the previous night. It was a "sternwheeler" of much the same model as our own boat. It mounted a small Hotchkiss gun in an iron turret forward, and two Nordenfeldt guns on a little deck above. The steamer was plated with bullet-proof sheets of iron.

As my steamer was to remain in port for a day or two, I availed myself of the opportunity to make an excursion by rail to the Portuguese frontier and the town of Komati Poort, some sixty-three miles distant. The daily train started at 7 A. M., and I could spend about three hours at Komati Poort and return to Lorenzo Marquez by 6.30 P. M. The railway is of narrow gauge. The locomotives have been built in England and the cars and vans either in Holland or Germany, that is to say, their parts have been made there, and brought out and put together here. A Dutch company has the contract for continuing and completing the road to Pretoria. Komati Poort is really a few miles beyond the Portuguese frontier, in the Transvaal. I was therefore only able to buy a "round" ticket to Ressano Garcia, the actual frontier station, and then to purchase another there to Komati Poort. The cars were diminutive little affairs, built partly on the English and partly on the American plan. You could pass from end to end of the train. The cars were of four classes, those of the first having comfortable leather-covered seats. The fourth were simply open freight cars, in which the natives stand or lie like animals. There were however but few passengers. The blacks proved interesting. They belonged mostly to the Amatonga and Swazi tribes. The men were of good size and muscular; the women were fat and sleek. All were very dark, with short woolly hair, in which one or two feathers were generally stuck, not, as one would think, for ornament, but to use in scratching the head. These gave a funny look indeed to the faces beneath them. The natives were always chatting, laughing and skylarking. The dress of the women was simply two pieces of gay-colored calico or cotton, the one worn as a chemise, the other as a gown. They wore much jewelry: silver finger rings and buttons in their ears, bangles around their wrists, and rings of copper around their ankles. The men were clothed only in loin cloths, over which were suspended two pieces of an animal's skin, a flap before, another behind. They had sometimes many yards of copper or brass wire coiled about their ankles, sometimes several strings of coins or shells, or both. They often wore charms of bone or shell about their necks. Occasionally you might see one who had eked out his scanty costume with a European-made vest or hat, or a military coat. One fellow strutted up and down the platform of one of the stations with a pair of antelope horns fastened to his neck and standing out from his head in a very diverting fashion. These natives are either employed upon the railway or the plantations of foreigners. Many of them live in hamlets along the line, where the women till the fields and the men and boys bring food—chickens, eggs, fruit and bottles of milk—to the stations to sell to passing travellers. We followed the banks of the English river for a short distance, and then turned away and pursued a northwest course to our destination. The country throughout was of the same general character, low and level, and covered with grass and scrubby trees. You especially remarked the juxtaposition of vegetation belonging to widely separated zones. There were many species of palms and cacti, and a great number of calabash trees. At the stations were little else than the necessary railway buildings, and no towns appeared between them. The scattered houses of the natives were made of grass in beehive form, with an entrance not two feet in height. I saw many half-naked women at work in the fields, using great clumsy hoes, and often smoking pipes. Sometimes they had a child strapped to their backs. Much maize and wheat seemed to be grown, but the greater part of the country was simply covered with coarse grass and with a squat sort of tree with gnarled branches. I noticed very few cattle, and these were not of good appearance. The scenery was altogether tame until the end of the journey was approached. Here we followed the banks of the Incomati river for a considerable way and then saw a distant chain of mountains to the left. These trend north and south, and are called the Lombobo Range. They serve as a division between the possessions of Portugal and the Transvaal. The southern frontier of the former is only seventy miles south of Delagoa Bay. Komati Poort consists of about a score of European houses, and a small settlement of blacks lying on the gentle slope of a wide valley. It boasts a hotel, many drinking saloons, and a few shops of provisions and miscellaneous manufactured goods. I was attracted to one of the latter by the great quantity of horns of animals peculiar to South Africa lining the verandah. I found Koodoo horns selling for 15 shillings a pair, Buffalo £2, Hartbeest 5 shillings, Sable Antelope £2, and the skull of a Hippopotamus for £4.

Natal

AT five o'clock we crossed the bar, and passing the long break-waters, slowly entered the port of Durban and drew up at the wharf, making fast in line with a dozen or more vessels of medium tonnage. On shore were various shipping offices and a large brick hotel. Cars were standing on several tracks of railway. Tugs were busy hauling lighters. A 'bus stood near by, and a uniformed customs official was at the gangway. I realized that I had reached a thoroughgoing British Colony. Making a simple "declaration" regarding my baggage, it and myself were soon bundled into a carriage, and all started for the town, two miles distant. A tramway connects the port and a suburb, called Addington, with Durban, but it was not running at the early hour of our arrival. We drove rapidly along a broad, clean, macadamised avenue, lined with small single-story cottages surrounded by beautiful trees and flowers, and turning into one of the three principal parallel streets of the city, passed a small but neat hotel, some Law Courts, and then the handsome Town Hall, appearing beyond and above a fine park, furnished with the conventional bandstand. Opposite this park was the hotel to which I had been recommended. And a more extraordinary structure I have never beheld in any part of the world. Apparently the citizens of Durban and visitors from this section of Africa dislike to mount staircases, for this hotel is but a single story in height, and is therefore spread over several acres. The front gardens were ablaze with lovely flowers which exhaled the richest perfumes. Entering I found halls like lanes running in every direction and most of them lined with pots of flowers and plants, and hung with heads and horns of South African game. Passing through a number of offices, reception-rooms and corridors, I came out into a large paved courtyard full of flowers and vines, and furnished with a fountain. Here were placed rows of great reclining-chairs, and on every side were rooms for guests. I wandered about, discovering one by one all the apartments necessary for the equipment of a first-class hotel, but this I did at great risk of getting lost. Flitting about in every direction with bare feet were Hindoo (Madrassee) servants, neatly and cleanly clad in white tunic and trousers, and wearing graceful white turbans. I afterwards found the hotel to be as well arranged and comfortable as it was novel and curious. Durban has a population of 30,000, of which number about one-half are English, one-quarter negroes, and one-quarter natives of India.

In the afternoon I took a long drive through the city and out into the country to the top and along the crest of the Berea. Here there is a small hotel which commands, on the one side, a splendid view over the town, the port and the ocean, and upon the other, of the beautiful green hills and valleys of the interior. The view in this direction reminded me of many parts of England, with its general style of park-land, groves of trees and open country. There were cultivated here also much sugar-cane, tea, coffee, and tropical fruits and vegetables. Right at one side of the very English-looking hotel and surrounding gardens, stood a mango tree and a huge roffia palm. The principal roads are broad and macadamised. A tramway line runs nearly the whole length of the Berea. The open cars are drawn by three horses harnessed abreast. The country houses are of pleasing architecture, and some of them of brick and two stories in height, of Queen Anne style, surrounded by extensive grounds laid out in lawns, flower-gardens and paths, would be no discredit to a watering place like Long Branch. There is a very good Botanical

Garden on the Berea, to which the public are admitted free. A small greenhouse contains a capital collection of orchids.

I reached the Umgeni river on the north and returned by the great plain upon which lies Durban, and which would contain a city three times the size. In the evening we had very heavy rain, which as the rainy season is coming on, will occur frequently now, and to which is due the deep rich green of the verdure all about the city and extending along the coast of the colony for a distance of about thirty miles inland. This has caused Natal to be called the "Garden of South Africa." Here tropical agriculture generally prevails. To this region succeeds one where English styles of farming are carried on, and wheat, oats, barley and Indian corn are grown. Next comes the veldt or grazing country, where sheep-farming and the breeding of horses and cattle are the chief pursuits of the inhabitants.

The streets of Durban always afford interesting sights and scenes. As with the commingling of the vegetal products of two zones in this semi-tropical colony, so with the varied and picturesque blending of things English and things African, of life and customs at home and of those adopted abroad. In the first place Durban is a very pretty and lively town. It is laid out at right angles, with very wide macadamised streets and flagged sidewalks. The majority of the buildings are but a single-story in height, and are made of brick and plaster with iron roofs, although plain brick and even stone are rapidly coming into use. There are many fine and useful public buildings. The Town Hall, near the centre of Durban, would be an ornament to any city. It occupies an entire square and is built of a gray sandstone, with a lofty tower in which a clock strikes the hours, halves and quarters, together with additional chimes. In the centre of the building is a large hall, with gallery and stage suitable for political meetings, concerts and balls. Other parts are occupied by the Post Office, the Museum, and the various municipal offices. The Museum, which is free to the public, is small but interesting, being devoted almost exclusively to collections from Natal and South Africa generally. There are minerals, shells, coins, animals, plants, and the dress and weapons of native tribes. All are well arranged and carefully labelled. Near the Town Hall is a public swimming bath, admission to which is little more than nominal. The swimming tank is ninety feet long, thirty broad, three feet deep at one end and eight at the other. Durban boasts of a pretty little theatre, which has two galleries and eight stage-boxes. It is used at present only by travelling companies. There are also a free public library and reading-room. In short, most of the institutions thought necessary at home are here represented, and it is with difficulty one comes to believe one's self actually in "savage" Africa. There are but few cabs in Durban, but there is the tramway, with its one-and also two-deck cars, and there are regular stands of single and double 'ricshaws, a sort of baby-carriage, like those in use in Japan, where the idea originated, pulled by a native at a fast trot and costing a sixpence by the course. These vehicles are used also in Ceylon, and might with advantage be introduced elsewhere. Very odd it is to see occasionally in the streets—amid smart English drags, and dog-carts with tandem teams, and young men astride bicycles—huge four-wheeled wagons holding four tons and drawn by nine yoke of sturdy oxen. Curious also are the native policemen with their helmets and uniforms like those of the London police, but with knee-breeches only, their chocolate-colored calves being quite bare. They are picked men, however, and of fine physique. The streets are diversified and enlivened also by the features and costumes of the different neighboring tribes, of Zulus, Swazis, Amatongas, Basutos, and Pongos, to all of whom the general name of Kaffir seems to be indiscriminately applied. Then there are, moreover, Banians, Chinese, Madrassees, Boers and various European nationalities. The principal exports of Port Natal are wool, sheep-and ox-skins, and sugar.

Having seen everything of interest in Durban, I left for the gold-fields and diamond-mines of the interior. My objective for the former was the city of Johannesburg, in the centre of the diggings, which is in a general northwesterly direction from Durban and is reached by 304 miles of railway to the borders of the Transvaal Republic, and then 135 miles by coach—the total distance by this route being therefore 439 miles from the coast. It is traversed in forty-eight hours, including brief stoppages for food and sleep. The railway is eventually to be extended from the frontier of Natal across the Transvaal to Johannesburg. There are several lines of railway running from different parts of South Africa towards Johannesburg, but only one—that from Cape Town—as yet reaches it; by the others the latter part of the journey has always to be made by coach. As the tariff is very high, and the coaches used in the interior cannot carry much baggage, I sent nearly all of mine by sea to Cape Town, there to await my arrival. An express train leaves Durban daily at 6 P. M. for Charlestown, the present terminus, arriving at 11.30 A. M. the following day. The coach is advertised to leave half an hour later. The railway is a narrow-gauge single-track, the road-bed is "metalled," the bridges are of cut stone, and the signals embody the latest improvements. At the station I found a short train of small carriages arranged in three classes, with a baggage van and powerful locomotive. Owing to the hilly character of the country and its rapid rise from the sea the line is very tortuous. There were not many passengers of the first and second class, but two carriages were crowded with Kaffirs. For a long distance from Durban the country was covered with the suburban residences of her citizens, and with fruit and vegetable gardens. The broken character of the surface, and the intense green of the glossy verdure had a very pleasing appearance. In two hours' time we had ascended 2,500 feet and reached another climate. Much tea and many bananas were grown hereabouts. We saw several huts of the Zulus and numbers of these nearly wholly nude people. In two hours more we had reached Maritzburg, the capital, a pretty town about half the size of Durban. Here I purchased for five shillings a "sleeping-ticket," which entitled me to have brought into my compartment a heavy blanket, a sheet and two pillows, this being the nearest approach to a sleeping-car yet known upon this road. In the fine, large, brick station in which we halted were trucks bearing great piles of this bedding, which natives wheeled opposite each compartment and gave to those willing to pay the extra price. It was removed early in the morning at another station. We stopped several times for refreshments, there being a choice offered of sitting at a table for a regular meal, or getting a lunch at a bar. The bars were always large and profusely supplied with "wet goods." The English governor of Natal resides at Maritzburg. Ladysmith, a little village of iron-roofed houses, which we reached at half-past five the following morning, is 3,300 feet above the sea. As we went on I saw that we had attained an entirely new style of country—undulating plains, for the most part treeless, and with a range of mountains, the Drakensburg, to the westward. One part of this range, nearly due west of Ladysmith, is 10,000 feet high. The Drakensburg forms the dividing line between Natal and the Orange Free State. We passed many Kaffir kraals or villages, with their circular enclosures for cattle, around which were placed their beehive-shaped grass and reed huts. On the grassy plains were occasionally to be seen small herds of cattle or flocks of sheep. English or Boer farms were few and far between. At Newcastle, a small town 268 miles from Durban, and nearly 4,000 feet above it, we halted for breakfast. From here on, the engineering of the road was quite remarkable. It was full of loops, horseshoe curves, sometimes almost complete circles, steep grades, and in one place several tangents, the locomotive pulling first at one end of the train and then at the other. Coal of seemingly good quality was being mined at several points upon the railway between Newcastle and Charlestown. Four or five miles from the latter we passed through a rough ridge in a long tunnel. Charlestown I found to be a small village of two or three long, wide streets, with houses of hasty and flimsy construction, and everything betraying a temporary town, for when the railway is continued it will relapse into merely a station. Charlestown is 5,400 feet above the sea-level.

At the side of the depot stood our coach, which I was surprised to find was of the "Concord" pattern, from New Hampshire, U. S. A. It was a huge structure, swung upon great leather straps, and carried twelve passengers inside and six outside. It was drawn by a team of eight mules and two horses, the latter leading. We employed mules over the rougher parts of the road, but elsewhere the teams consisted entirely of horses. All these animals were in fine condition, fat, strong and willing. Forty pounds only of baggage was allowed free to each passenger, all above that having to be paid for at a dear rate. The baggage having been weighed and our tickets shown, we took our seats, the coach being about half full. I therefore was able to obtain an outside seat, while reserving that in the inside which I had engaged for shelter in case of rain. There mounted before me two Boers, the one the driver, the other the conductor, a man whose duty it was to tend the break and castigate the team. I was surprised to find the driver employed but two pairs of reins, one being for the wheelers and the other for the leaders, though the latter passed through rings in the headstalls of all the others, with an outside rein attached to each animal. This arrangement was as admirable as simple, for the team was at all times under complete control. The driver was moreover exceedingly expert, but no less so was the conductor, who was armed with a whip of which the bamboo stock was about twelve feet in length, with a leather lash of at least twenty feet. With a team of horses this was not much used, but with one of mules it was in almost constant application. The wielding of it is an art which

I never tired of watching. The Boers will hit any part of any animal of the team that they wish, easily reaching the leaders and slashing them right and left with lightning rapidity, accompanied with snaps of the lash like the report of a pistol. They also have many peculiar cries for instructing or encouraging their animals. The team draws by a long chain attached to the pole of the coach. The stages varied from an hour to an hour and a half in length, and we alternated a trotting with a galloping pace. Our speed would vary from eight to ten miles an hour. At some of the stations there would be a store and hotel, and perhaps three or four other houses, at others only the stable of galvanised iron sheets. The stores contained a very miscellaneous collection of the necessities of life and travel in the interior of South Africa. As we drew up the fresh teams would always be standing in line, ready to be "put to" by their native hostlers in five or ten minutes' time.

Leaving Charlestown and entering the Transvaal, we found ourselves in that vast prairie of smoothly undulating land called the veldt. Not a tree or bush was in sight, nothing but smooth pasture. The road is merely a track across this vast sea of grass. It is like the steppes of Central Asia. There are some distant low hills to be seen, but owing to the wavy character of the surface, extensive views are not often possible. We would pass many miles of country without seeing a single house or meeting a person. The Boer homesteads are neat little structures, always surrounded by such trees as can be made to grow. We would occasionally meet their owners driving in a sort of two-wheeled gig, covered with a canvas hood, and drawn by a pair of horses or maybe a four-in-hand team. Occasionally we would pass natives walking to Johannesburg and carrying upon their backs all their worldly goods, consisting of a pair of shoes, a blanket and a pail or kettle of food. These people work in the mines for a few months, and then return home to spend what they have earned, or it may be to live in luxury for several years. We passed many of the great wagons going in either direction, loaded with wool and hides, or with all sorts of merchandise and provisions. The rear part of many of the wagons was covered with a canvas hood and here the transport men sleep and keep their cooking utensils and personal effects. Each wagon has a huge break attached to the rear-wheels and worked with a screw from behind. The oxen are driven by a man on foot with a long whip like that already described, though a native boy, called a forelouper, generally leads the first yoke by a leather strap attached to their horns. The oxen are fastened to the wagons by long chains or wire cables, and they pull with light and comfortable yokes. These animals were all large and sleek, though I was told that in the dry season they become very lean and ill-favored. Frequently by the side of the road you will see several of these teams "outspanned," unharnessed or unhitched, as we should say, for rest and feeding. At frequent distances along the road stones are set up informing the transport men that teams may feed thereabouts, or in other words these are public outspanning places. The land belongs to Boer farmers, but they have such enormous farms that they permit this use of their pasture at stated spots. I found the track for the most part very good, being as smooth and hard as the floor of a house, though on the latter part of the journey, owing to recent rains and a rougher surface, we were a good deal shaken and jostled. During the afternoon we stopped at a wretched little inn for dinner. This meal consisted only of chicken, rice and potatoes with tea and coffee, all bad, and the chicken sufficiently hard and tough to macadamise a road. We reached the town of Standerton about seven in the evening, first crossing the Vaal river—the principal branch of the great Orange river—upon a fine iron bridge resting on stone pillars. The stream was at that time not more than a hundred feet in width, but its banks plainly showed that before the end of the rainy season it became many times that width, with a swift current that would ill brook obstacles. Standerton is a straggling sort of village of small single-story houses, with a great shed of a hotel and a pretty stone church. It has, like all South African towns, enormously wide streets, and some attempts have been made at introducing the blue gum or eucalyptus trees of Australia. In the gardens of several of the houses you see peach and other fruit trees, though all seem to thrive with difficulty. In the hotel was a large billiard-table, and a bar which was constantly crammed with Boer citizens. We had a passable dinner, slept two in each room, about ten feet square, and were called at half-past four in the morning to dress, drink a cup of coffee, and re-enter the coach.

The stars were shining brightly, and we found our overcoats none too heavy in the fresh light air. At eight we halted fifteen minutes to partake of a bad Boer breakfast and then went on to Heidelburg, which we reached at half-past one. This town, lying on the slope of a smooth range of hills, is larger and more important than Standerton, though like the latter its only fine building is its church. After an unsatisfactory dinner at the hotel, we started on for Johannesburg. I speak so much of our meals because this being one of the shortest and most travelled routes to the gold-fields, one expects and is entitled to far better accommodation. The road became wet and heavy but we kept steadily on, passing herds of splendid cattle and large flocks of sheep and goats. We crossed the track of the new railway running between Johannesburg and Pretoria, which was completed a few months later. And about here we obtained our first view of a suburb of Johannesburg. The last stage was a short one of but six miles, and soon after entering upon it, we crossed a ridge from whose summit we had a good general view of the range of hills called the Witwatersrand, or simply Rand, for brevity, in which lies the reef now being worked for gold. This reef extends in a general east and west direction for some forty or fifty miles, and all around the horizon we saw the wooden towers containing the hauling-gear of the shafts, and the smoke-pipes and buildings of the batteries or stamping mills.

The railway does not go directly there by the shortest route, but one has to pass through the Orange Free State from north to south, and having entered Cape Colony, to cross westwardly to a railroad which extends from Cape Town to Vryburg in British Bechuanaland and passes Kimberley *en route*. You reach this line at De Aar Junction, almost at a point equidistant from Johannesburg and Cape Town. The time consumed on the journey of 1,013 miles between these two latter points is fifty-six hours, and the first-class fare, exclusive of meals and "tips," is £11. 12s. Every Monday a "saloon sleeping and dining train," consisting of first-class carriages only, leaves Johannesburg by this route, and every day of the week there is an ordinary train of three classes, which completes the distance in about five hours' more time. The line had only been opened directly through to Cape Town about two months before my visit to the Transvaal. When extended to Pretoria it will cover a total distance of 1,050 miles. There was talk also of the Western System, or Kimberley route, being continued to Johannesburg, a distance of 250 miles. All these railroads are of a three-and-one-half foot gauge, are of single-track, and belong to the Cape Colony Government, with the exception of the roads in the Transvaal, which are being built for that government by the "Netherlands Company of South Africa." My train started at the rather uncomfortable hour of 5.15 A. M. There were about a dozen carriages, drawn by a very powerful locomotive with six small driving-wheels. Some of the carriages were labelled as passing through direct to Port Elizabeth or East London, ports on the southeast coast, or to Cape Town or to Kimberley. Then there were a number of dilapidated old freight-cars which had been cheaply fitted for excursions. These were at that time running to the local and foreign exhibition being held at Kimberley, to which cheap return rates were being offered by all the railroads. I found the Orange Free State Railway to be well made, with a stone-ballasted track, substantial stone and iron bridges, and frequently pretty and commodious little station-houses, built of a hard cut stone. All along the road were wretched huts of Kaffirs, who had been employed in building it, or were now engaged in keeping it in order. Some of the huts were made of pieces of sheet iron, others of iron sleepers, others of old rugs. The country through which we passed all day was simply the veldt, a great tree-less rolling prairie, with but very few farmhouses, and still fewer villages. The stations ordinarily contained only the buildings appropriate to the railway service, and a miserable little store, hotel and bar. Our speed was slow and we made long stops at seemingly unimportant places. Meals of not very good quality, and with little or no attendance, were served at the uniform rate of two-and-sixpence per head. Occasionally you might see several ox-wagons with their great teams "trek-king," or travelling, away across the plains. On leaving Johannesburg we passed for a long distance through a mining region. There were plenty of shafts and mills, and great heaps of "tailings." These were gold diggings, but upon reaching the frontier of the Orange Free State I noticed many coal mines. About three o'clock the next morning we passed through Bloemfontein, the capital of the Orange Free State, a small town of low houses, though of a picturesque appearance, in strong contrast to the surrounding prairie. The government of this State is carried on through legislative powers vested in an assembly called the Volksraad, as in the Transvaal. There are fifty-eight members, who are elected by their constituents for the term of four years. The Executive power rests in the President, who is elected by suffrage of burghers throughout the State.

Going on from Bloemfontein, the character of the country changed somewhat, being much more rough and hilly. This kind of surface is here styled the Karroo, and it is mostly covered with a low scrub called Karroo bush. In this part of the State I saw many great flocks of sheep and goats, and a few of ostriches. The latter sitting close together, with their long necks craning directly upwards, made an odd sight. The railway is not yet fenced, and the engineer had frequently to blow his whistle to scare away animals, and sometimes we had to come to a "dead-stop," since the railway company are obliged to pay for any destruction of life. The line will eventually be fenced, as are the Natal railways. The southern border of the State is the Orange river, which we crossed upon a fine iron-girder and stone-pier bridge, about 1,200 feet long and fifty or sixty feet above the water. The river is crooked, very muddy, and not very deep, but subject to floods in the rainy season that greatly increase its depth and velocity. We were now in Cape Colony proper and still in the Karroo, great undulating plains from which spring here and there curious peaked or table-topped hills with almost precipitous flanks. Not a tree, other than such as have been planted, appears. In the valley of the Orange river and other smaller streams which we crossed there was a little verdure, consisting of dwarf trees and bush. At the De Aar Junction we found a train that had just arrived from Kimberley, and was going on to Cape Town, after attaching several carriages of our train destined for the same point. From De Aar to Kimberley the distance is 147 miles. Late in the evening we crossed the Orange river again, and by a bridge similar to that just mentioned. To sum up, the greater part of the country through which we passed from Johannesburg to De Aar and to Kimberley was simply a vast, wind-swept, treeless, grass-or bush-covered upland steppe. We reached Kimberley at half-past two the following morning, and I was driven at once to a comfortable little three-story brick hotel, situated near Market Square.

On our return we arrived at Benguela early in the morning, and in the afternoon I made an excursion to Catumbella, with which it is connected by a narrow-gauge railway fifteen miles in length. There is one train each way every day. The cars are miniature. Those for the first-class had transverse seats, covered with cushions, and were open on every side, with canvas curtains to ward off the fierce sun; the second-class passengers had to content themselves with benches, and the third to squat upon the floor, or stand. There were, besides, several platform cars for freight. The little railway has been built some ten years, and is owned by a Portuguese Company. The speed attained is about ten miles an hour, though occasional stops have to be made to keep up a sufficient head of steam. We had quite a full train. The road runs all the way across level sandy plains, which are covered with a coarse scrub of thorns and bushes, with a few baobabs. On one side was the sea, on the other a low range of barren mountains. Nearing Catumbella, however, the scene changed. Much vegetation and many villages appeared. There were great groves of the palm-oil trees and, by the ocean, of cocoanut-palms. The native huts were of wattle and mud sides and grass-thatches, surrounded by thick fences of coarse grass.

We reached Catumbella in one hour and a half, there being no stations on the road. Just above the point at which the journey terminated were two knolls, upon one of which was a fort and upon the other the residence of the mayor of the town. I walked to a Dutch trading-house for whose manager, Mr. Kamerman, I bore a letter of introduction. I crossed on the way the Catumbella river—a swift, shallow, muddy stream, here perhaps three hundred feet wide—upon a neat iron bridge. The town lies on level ground, bounded on every side, except that towards the sea, by a circle of steep bare hills and by its side winds the river, its banks bordered by beautiful tropical trees. Further up country this river contains both crocodiles and hippopotami. A road leads from the town to the sea, some four or five miles distant, where are several factories engaged in the salt trade. Catumbella consists of two or three long straggling macadamised streets. It is a town of single-story houses, and contains a population of about one hundred whites—Portuguese and Dutch—and some two thousand natives. It is a great trading centre. A trade route from the distant interior terminates here, or rather it actually terminates at Benguela, to which the railway has been built for its accommodation. A carriage road, which runs much of the way alongside the railway, is also used by the Europeans for carts, mules and hammocks, while the natives pass on foot. Behind the town you see the trails of the carriers passing over the steep hills. They enter the interior by the valley of the river, which affords an easier route than is available to the eastward of Benguela. Caravans of natives are coming and going throughout the year. All day long you see them toiling over the hill, each bearing upon the head or shoulder a bundle of India-rubber, hides or gum copal, or a bag of wax or orchilla, or a small tusk or tooth of ivory. Physically these carriers are generally very ugly, being thin and misshapen, and many being afflicted with loathsome diseases. Both men and women are nearly naked and children wholly so. The few rags which they wear are filthy, but no more so than their bodies. Yet many of them, especially the children, have bright, intelligent faces. The women wear brass and iron wire bangles and anklets, necklaces of beads, and all, both men and women, attach fetish charms in small boxes or cylinders about their necks. Some of these caravans number two hundred people, and come from several hundred miles in the interior, being months upon their journey. Those living nearer make perhaps two visits a year. At the busiest season there are sometimes as many as ten thousand carriers temporarily staying in the town. The products and goods are brought chiefly by the natives of Bailundo, Bihé, Caconda and Ganguellas. For what they bring they are paid in barter by the many Portuguese traders, whose shops are filled with cheap cotton cloths, beads, wire, head-kerchiefs and clothing, gin and aguardiente, ordinary cheap guns, powder and last, but not least, old silk tall hats. A native of any means and pretensions to gentility is never happy until he has bought a high silk hat, with which, and wearing probably nothing else than a dirty loin cloth, with a pipe in his mouth, and being more or less under the influence of liquor, he struts about town, a very ridiculous show to a foreigner, but an object of admiration and envy to all his compatriots. These natives generally remain in Catumbella only so long as their credit is good, when they walk in easy stages back to their distant villages. They carry only an earthenware pot for cooking their manioc, a gourd for water, a stick to assist their climbing in difficult places, and perhaps a rusty old flint-lock musket, which has been tightly bound with strips of hide from end to end with the idea or hope that this will prevent its explosion.

I remained over night in Catumbella and took the morning train back to Benguela. We carried with us some thirty or forty laborers who were going to Prince's and St. Thomas' islands under contract to work for five years in the coffee and cacao plantations. Each wore around the neck a tin badge inscribed with his or her number, the name of the plantation, and the locality. These people had been neatly fitted out with gay-colored cotton suits and fancy caps, of all which finery they seemed exceedingly proud. I breakfasted with the governor, Senhor Francisco de Paula Cid, Junior, and received from him a fine collection of photographs, and much interesting information concerning Benguela. This gentleman was formerly a captain in the navy. The provincial and district governors, who have great power, are by tradition naval officers, while the chiefs of the counties into which the districts are divided, are, as a rule, officers of the army. The counties are again divided into townships, which are presided over by resident traders or, often, educated natives. I also received a number of similar courtesies from the governor at Loanda, but why should I specialise?—one is always sure of favor and hospitality from a Portuguese official. Governor Paula Cid told me that in the year 1887 the exports of Benguela took a sudden jump upwards, owing to the appearance in the markets of a new kind of India-rubber, which is extracted from the roots of a small shrub that grows spontaneously on the banks of certain rivers in the interior. This rubber is not so good as the Brazilian, but is found in greater quantity and is more readily extracted. The value of the exports in 1892 was 1,466 contos of reis (or about $1,650,000) and of this total, rubber amounted to 1,207 contos, wax coming next with 188, and ivory next with but 34 contos. In the same year the district of Benguela produced 3,000,000 litres of aguardiente, most of which was sent to London and St. Thomas. The value of the importation in 1892 was 900 contos. The port of Benguela is annually visited by an average of 100 vessels, of which number 70 are steamers and the remainder ships. The two principal rivers of the district are the Kunene and the Kubango which flow from the north to the south and west, and whose banks, some four or five thousand feet above the sea-level, are very fertile. Between these two rivers are found several sorts of iron, and in great quantities. Some mines of copper and sulphur, and some small traces of gold are met with upon the high plateau. The climate here is excellent, and well-suited to Europeans. There is in Benguela a branch of the *Banco Nacional Ultramarino*, the business of which in 1892 amounted to over $3,000,000. We received on board a large shipment of India-rubber, wax and orchilla, and left for Novo Redondo, where we received more cargo, and then went on to Loanda, arriving at noon on the following day.

Before leaving Loanda I witnessed "Carnival" as celebrated by the natives and Portuguese. It lasted three days, during which time the blacks did not work, but kept on a perpetual spree, consuming great quantities of aguardiente. There were processions in *bal-masqué* costume by day and night, and fireworks also at all times. The order of the processions was something like this: there was a march, then a halt and dance, a grand "walk-round" to the music of tom-toms, mandolins and tambourines, the whole accompanied with much singing and chanting. The

395

dances were quite barbaric, and the din of the native music was terrific. The other people would crowd around at these halts and clap their hands and laugh like the children they are. Very many of the maskers copied the uniforms of generals, with cocked-hats, much gold-lace and decorations. There were, besides, many ridiculous caricatures. These simple people save their wages and prepare for these carnivals for weeks beforehand. Flags were displayed all over the city, which was thoroughly *en fête*. On the last afternoon there was a procession of the Portuguese in gayly-decked carriages, and a great pelting of bonbons and flowers quite in the style of the *bataille des fleurs* at Nice. Many were in fancy-dress. At night a military band discoursed very agreeable music in the little park upon the hill near the governor's palace.

Stanley said years ago that the vast resources and capabilities of the Congo basin would be practically useless, and it would be impossible to introduce men, material and commerce to develop the country until a railway should be built around the cataracts. All goods and luggage have to be transported on the head and shoulders of lazy, irresponsible natives. And besides, it is often difficult to get enough men, although in the past four years as many as 50,000 carriers have been employed in the transport service. A ton of goods is conveyed from London to the Lower Congo for £2, but costs £50 for carriage from Matadi to Stanley Pool. A railway is, however, at last in process of construction around this chief physical obstacle to the admission of commerce and civilisation. The route was surveyed in 1888, and the work was undertaken in January, 1890, by a Belgian company, whose government liberally subscribed to the capital and gave them also valuable concessions. It is calculated that 25,000,000 francs will cover all cost of construction and rolling-stock, and pay interest on the capital during the estimated seven years of its construction. When this road is completed inner Africa will be within a few weeks of the capitals of Europe. The length of the line, which is to be run from thirty to fifty miles distant from the left bank of the river—south of the usual caravan route—will be 268 miles. Only the first twenty-five or thirty miles of this present any serious engineering difficulties. The gradients are comparatively easy and sharp curves will only be required in the first section. But three rivers of any size will need to be bridged—the M'poso, the Kivilu, and the Inkissi. The longest of the bridges will only be 300 feet. At all places where large torrents occur steel aqueducts are building that will carry the floods down the hills and under the railway track. The line starts at Matadi and terminates near the station of Kinchassa, on Stanley Pool, where the trucks of goods can be unloaded directly into the river steamers. The railway is now completed but thirty miles. Matadi has been a base of supplies for railroad and steamship operations for several years past. Very many employes of the railroad are quartered here. Five years ago there were only two buildings and ten Europeans here, but to-day the town contains 300 Europeans—besides the railway employes, officials of the State, traders and missionaries—fifty more than Stanley left behind him in the entire Congo region, when he returned to Europe after founding his stations. The white population includes Belgians, French, English, Germans, Dutch, Italians,

Swedes, Americans and Greeks. Fully one-third of the entire railway work has centered in the thirty miles recently completed, for this has been built under very adverse circumstances, much of it having been blasted out of solid and very tough quartzite rock, and the rest being in an exceedingly hilly region. Within ten miles from Matadi the road mounts, 1500 feet. This, however, is the worst part of the line, and progress is now expected to be rapid. There are about 200 whites and 2,000 natives engaged in building the road, of whom nearly half came from various points on the Guinea coast. At present seven locomotives and thirty cars are on the tracks, and have been kept busy carrying railway material and provisions as the road advanced.

There are some half dozen iron buildings of the factory at Matadi—warehouses, a general dining-saloon, dormitories, offices, etc.—all of which are raised upon brick pillars some ten feet or so above the ground. The chief products in which the company deals are ivory and rubber, the first being the chief item. The tusks are of all sizes from one foot to eight in length. The rubber comes to market in little lumps the size of small oranges, half a dozen of which are strung together, and a porter's load of them is then sewed up in a long narrow sack. Several of the great iron warehouses are filled with miscellaneous merchandise to barter for the ivory and rubber, for no money is yet used in central Congo. Powder and wire at present represent gold, and beads, silver. Besides these are great quantities of crockery, huge boxes of knives, and large bales of Manchester cottons, secondhand European hats and clothes, earthenware statuettes and ornaments, coarse American smoking tobacco, and flint-lock muskets worth about $1.50 each.

On March 28th, everything being in readiness, we began our journey. We took with us a total of seventy porters, including those for the tents, the hammocks and the provisions. My tent was one of the English make of Edgington, a wall-tent about eight feet square, with an exterior "fly" or roof above, which serves as a capital break for very hot sun or very heavy rain. My camp bed was of canvas, with leather-covered cushions for mattress, and a very necessary mosquito-netting. My hammock was of canvas, with an awning of the same material, like that previously used in Angola. I had six bearers for it. The two iron trunks contained all needful clothes. The porters were all Congo boys or men, rather slight and undersized black people, wearing only a loin cloth and some ornaments, such as a bead necklace, a brass bangle around the ankle, or an iron bracelet. All were more or less tattooed, or, rather, marked by gashes, upon the chest, back and shoulders. It was, however, in the dressing and arrangement of the hair that their supreme ingenuity seemed to be employed. A few wore it in its natural short woolly state. Some twisted it into little strings two or three inches long and matted together with palm oil, their heads thus resembling our window-mops. A few had their hair trained and gummed together on the crown, like a woman's chignon with us. Nearly all had their front teeth filed to points, a few only had the upper ones notched, which always gave them a disagreeable expression when opening the mouth. All these people were exceedingly dirty and odoriferous. For the caravan journey they are paid in goods of an equivalent value of forty francs, and they must find their own food. This latter does not incommode them, for it consists generally of manioc, bananas and palm-oil kernels. They do not require any food or drink when starting in the morning on a day's march, but eat whenever a halt is made, and always have a big feed at night. They are quite like children, and their wants are almost nothing. Each one, as I have said, carries a load of about sixty pounds. They are marshalled and kept in order by a head-man, who is styled the captain.

As the new railway virtually follows the caravan road for a short distance, we determined to take advantage of this, and had chartered a train to carry us to the terminus, about fourteen miles from Matadi, and then we were to walk some three miles further and camp. We crowded all our men, with their loads, into two open cars, and started from the factory about eight o'clock in the morning. The road is a very narrow-gauge and the rails are fastened in "chairs" directly to the iron sleepers, without the use of any spikes. There are many steep grades and many short curves. At first you follow the bank of the Congo to the entrance of the M'poso river, and then turn directly south up the valley of this brawling stream. As soon as we leave Matadi I notice some small rapids extending nearly across the Congo. The banks on each side are high and steep. Vivi, with its single house, is nearly opposite the mouth of the M'poso. The falls of Yellala are four or five miles above. After running some distance along the banks of the M'poso, whose yellow flood rushes swiftly over a rocky bed far below us, we cross the river upon the single span of an iron girder bridge. Then we turn more to the east and wind through an exceedingly hilly country, rising rapidly until we reach the height of 1,500 feet. Then we gradually descend until the terminus is reached. The road so far runs through a hilly, grass-covered and treeless region, excepting only in the narrow valleys of some of the streams, where you see a few oil palms, baobabs, cotton-woods, and other less well-known trees. The rolling-stock of the line is all of Belgian manufacture. The engineers are white men, and their assistants natives of the Guinea coast, who are quite clever at their work. We pitched our tents near the temporary house of the chief of this section of the railway, and took breakfast with him in his cool and comfortable grass thatched and walled *salle-à-manger*. The general direction of the caravan road to Stanley Pool is northeast. The first half of the way it runs at some distance from the river, but the second half is nearer and follows almost its exact course.

Early the next morning we started on our route and followed the graded embankment of the railway to its end, where some of the officials hospitably invited us to rest and take lunch with them. The country had been very hillocky, and covered with grass and scrubby trees. It was not cultivated, nor settled. The few habitations we saw were those of the men at work upon the railway. After lunch we continued on through much swampy ground, and grass ten or twelve feet in height, which so filled the path that we had a hard struggle to get through it. In some of the wettest places I had to quit the hammock and take to the back of the strongest of my men. We had some difficulty in finding the caravan road after leaving the line of the railway, but succeeded at last, and arrived at the State station of Congo da Lemba early in the evening. This station has been made upon the level summit of a long ridge. There were half a dozen houses, grass topped and sided, and some large gardens of peas, maize, bananas and ground-nuts. Round about were several monster baobabs. We camped, and started on at six in the morning, the road being a mere trail winding up and down very steep hills. In the valleys were dense forests and brooks and rivers. We forded one of the latter called the Bembizi, and, about noon, crossed the Lufou on a chain suspension bridge a hundred feet long, and halted at a State station of a few huts, one of which was for the use of white travellers, while an open shed was for the carriers. An Egyptian was in command here. The bridge had been made by the State. A narrow place being chosen, the chains had been secured to huge baobabs on each bank. It was then about twenty-five feet above the water, but weeds attached to the guy ropes spoke plainly of a rise of the river of many feet, during the wet season. This river has a swift current, and empties into the Congo. From the tops of some of the ridges we had very extensive views of the surrounding country—hilly, grass-covered and for the most part treeless save in the valleys and depressions. The sun was terrific, and the bits of forest through which we passed were like Turkish baths to us. The great heat and malarious air, and the rough steep roads together make a journey of five hours and fifteen miles a good average day's work. In fact, this is the customary length here, the afternoon being employed in looking after the carriers and their loads, bathing, changing clothes, reading, writing, sleeping, preparing for dinner, etc. The houses of the State, which may be used by white travellers, are simple grass and reed made structures, with a verandah all around, and generally two rooms, without furniture other than, possibly, a rude couch made of split bamboo.

We took to the road at 6.30 A. M., and kept steadily on until we reached another State station, nicely situated on a high plateau, and surrounded by gardens of man-ioc, sweet potatoes, beans, tomatoes, maize, bananas, pimentoes, pineapples and ground-nuts. At each of these stations there is always a sign-board giving in hours the distance to the next in each direction. After breakfast we went on an hour further to Banza Manteka, where, upon the levelled top of a ridge, about 1,300 feet above sea-level, is one of the American missionary stations, with church, school-house, etc. There is a small native village in the immediate neighborhood. From here there are very extensive and beautiful views of the hilly region, whose rich green color proves most attractive.

Soon after arrival a perfect tornado of wind and rain broke over us. We were making our journey, unfortunately, in the middle of the rainy season, or, rather, of that styled the "long rains," for there are two of these seasons in the Congo State, and so every afternoon or night we might expect rain. We were hospitably entertained at the mission and, much refreshed, went on early in the morning. The country became more open and there were great plains covered with grass. We halted at one station to rest, and to allow the men an opportunity to buy food from half a dozen native women, who had come from some neighboring villages with manioc, maize, bananas and palm-kernels. They bore their produce in large and well-made funnel-shaped baskets. Our men bought this food with gay-colored handkerchiefs and coarse, blue glass-beads. We then went on for a couple of hours more, the sun beating upon us with tremendous force, and halting near another station, made camp on the bank of a small and swift stream, running northwesterly into the Congo. A chain was stretched here across the river between two trees, and a large canoe attached to this served as a primitive but serviceable ferry. Our porters are quite a study, and afford me much amusement. In the morning as soon as they prepare their loads they start off, without partaking of any food, straggling along the track for a mile or so, only anxious to get to the previously-understood halting-place as soon as possible. Sometimes, when tired, they rest by the roadside, and if they happen to have any food, eat it, often making little fires to boil their manioc or roast their maize. If we ourselves halt anywhere they occupy this time in taking a regular breakfast. As soon as we get to our camping-place they all throw down their loads and squat beside them, very close together, watching everything that we do. If there is shade they utilise it, but if not, sit quite contented in the blazing sun. When they are quite rested they begin their cooking and gabbling, both of which continue until they go to sleep, about nine in the evening. In sleeping they lie down upon the ground without pillow, mat, or covering, ordinarily, though sometimes they have a piece of cotton cloth over them. As for us, we have breakfast or luncheon soon after arriving in camp, placing our table under a tree, or in one of the tents. If we are near one of the many small rivers, we always indulge in a bath before dinner. This meal is served late in the evening, and, after a brief chat and smoke, we go early to bed to get fortified for the morrow's march. We live well, for, besides all our tinned provisions, we have with us two milch goats, a crate of live fowls, and several demijohns of Portuguese wine, and cases of claret and hock. Fresh eggs and fruit are often to be bought from the natives who visit the stations. The country to-day was uncultivated and uninhabited, at least to any extent near our route. Though we have our hammocks we walk a good deal, in order to vary our travel. We met many caravans of fifty and even a hundred men, carrying ivory and rubber down to Matadi. A large tusk was a load for one man, and was carried upon the head, resting upon a small cushion and being supported by one or both hands. The rubber was enclosed in long and narrow baskets of palm-leaf, carried upon either the head or shoulders.

On the caravan road

WE broke camp at our usual early hour, and our porters forded the river, which came a little above their waists. The country through which we then passed was hilly but smoother than heretofore. We halted for breakfast at one of the State buildings, a rather good quality of house, with grass-roof and reed-mat sides. On a rough pole outside floated the flag of the Congo State. The custodian—a black man—lived in a hut at one side. There was also, near at hand, a large open shed for the use of the porters. After our meal we went on for three hours more over a good, clayey track, and through many bosky glens. Several small streams were crossed upon bridges made of trunks of small trees plastered with clay. At every muddy pool our men drank enormously of water which no white man could have touched with impunity. The heat was very great, and our clothes were as wet with perspiration as if they had been thrown in a river. Late in the afternoon we reached the Kuilu, a deep and swiftly flowing river, about two hundred feet wide. It is said to abound with crocodiles, though we did not happen to see any. We were ferried over this stream in an enormous canoe made from a single tree trunk, and found one of the stations on the opposite bank. These State stations, I may explain, occur regularly upon the caravan road, at distances of about four hours' march—distances in the Congo, as in Madagascar, being estimated by hours, not miles—all the way from Matadi to Leopoldville. We camped in a shady grove of palm and other trees. The chief of the station treated us to fresh palm wine, which had a flavor closely approaching that of the milk of a cocoanut which has become slightly fermented. During the two following days we marched through much grass twenty feet high, which formed a cover over the path where the heat was stifling. We had distant views of a fine range of mountains in the northeast. There were terrific tornadoes at night. On the third day we reached the pretty valley, the town, and the river of Lukungu. It was a large open valley, with a few trees. At one side were a number of iron-roofed buildings belonging to the missionaries, and upon a knoll in the centre was the station, while in several directions stood little native villages. We rested a short time, and then pushed on, crossing the Lukungu upon a suspension bridge made of wire cables, with a roadway of small tree trunks. We then had some deep swamps to wade and some steep hills to climb. We stopped for breakfast on one of the latter, and greatly enjoyed the wide and fair prospect. At night, not finding a suitable camping place near water, we hired a hut—a building made of reeds, with a cylindrical roof. This is the usual native house hereabouts. They are about eight feet wide, the same high, and twelve long. It rained very heavily all the night.

We made an early start, and after an hour got glimpses of the Congo, lined by low hills. From here we gradually descended to the bank of the river and to the town of Manyanga, having first to cross by canoe a small stream that here enters the Congo. Manyanga consists of the houses of the chief of the station, those of the Belgian Commercial Company, and a small native settlement. Just beyond, some swirling rapids, that would be quite impassable for a steamer, fill the entire Congo. But from here large whale-boats descend the river as far as Isanghila. Formerly the Zanzibaris operated these boats, and were accustomed to sing while at their work. No Zanzibaris are now on the river, but their wild songs remain, having been learned by the Congo natives—an utter novelty for them. On the opposite side of the river upon the top of the high bank is the French station of Manyanga North and a Dutch factory, which are in the territory called French Congo. The river is crossed in huge canoes, formed of single tree trunks, or in one of the large iron whaleboats, and, though the current is strong and eddies abound, quick and safe ferriage is made. The river is about a mile wide here, and contains many small, and a few very large, fish. All kinds are esteemed by the natives and some are relished by Europeans. Huge crocodiles also abound.

We were forced to remain two weeks at Manyanga awaiting porters, ours only having been engaged as far as this. The special cause of delay in our case was that, it being the height of the rainy season, a less number of natives than usual were upon the road on account of their dislike to ford deep rivers, to wade through swamps, and to forego dry places in which to camp. There is also at this time of year less likelihood of there being a variety and quantity of food in the markets, which are held for their use at varying intervals along the caravan route. They are thus apt to become sick, and, unless absolutely necessary, the most of them prefer to work only during the dry season—from May to November—when it is always easy to get as many porters as one wants. When the railway is completed, however, this whole cumbersome system will be done away with, for the caravan-road will then be deserted by Europeans, and used only by those of the natives whose villages are in its immediate vicinity. Several times a number of carriers came in to Manyanga, but not enough for our wants, and we could not detain them till others came. While awaiting these people we paid a visit across the river to the French post of Manyanga North, to the neighboring Dutch factory, and to a factory of the Belgian Commercial Company situated an hour's walk from the river. We crossed in one of the large iron whaleboats, first rowing up the river along the shore for a considerable distance, and then heading almost directly across. The current was very swift, but with our men vigorously rowing, and the assistance of a small three-cornered sail, we were able to get over in an hour. Upon arriving we had a stiff climb to the top of the hills, where are the factory and the post. These consisted of half a dozen houses each. From them we had a most splendid view up and down the river, over the surrounding country, and the great rapids almost at our feet. After a walk to the Belgian factory—a few dwellings and warehouses—also situated on the top of a smoothed hill—we returned and breakfasted with the chief of the French post, M. Croz, and in the late afternoon recrossed the river to our temporary home.

At last we obtained the requisite number of porters, and started for Leopoldville. On leaving Manyanga the road at once mounts the hills which border the river, and so continues on, with extensive views of the country in every direction. It was still the same character of surface, grass-land scantily covered with scrubby trees and bushes. Many great land-slides and deep gullies appeared, the different colors of the soil showing very brilliantly. The villages were mostly at a distance from the caravan route. The road had in many places been cleared of vegetation to a width of some ten or twelve feet; it was hard and dry. The streams were greatly swollen, and one of them we had to swim. It was not broad but deep, and had a very swift current. There had once been a bridge over it, but this had been swept away by some flood. A strong liana was stretched across, and to this the porters clung with one hand while supporting their burdens upon the head with the other. In crossing two of the men lost their footing and dropped their loads into the water, which unfortunately were trunks containing our clothes, all of which, of course, were completely soaked, and some of our books and maps were quite ruined. It was an accident that frequently happens during the rainy season. We also traversed several rapid streams either on narrow wooden bridges, erected by the State, or sitting upon the shoulders and clinging to the heads of our men. We heard the songs of many birds, and saw a few crows and ducks, and a few small snakes. Many carriers passed us, the most of them bearing tusks of ivory.

The highest point on the road from Matadi to Leopoldville is 1,650 feet above the sea, and about here we enjoyed a very fine and extensive survey of the Congo, bounded by ranges of steep hills, down which coursed several streams, with large cataracts plainly visible. The scenery was really interesting, a thing not always to be said of the Congo region. Near one station a market was being held on the top of a round hill. The people, who had come from all the neighboring region, were arranged in a large circle of three or four ranks, squatting upon the ground. The sellers were nearly all women. There was a good variety of local produce, but no manufactures. Perhaps four hundred people were present—half of whom were dealers—and their chaffering produced a perfect Babel. These markets are held regularly twice a week. They are generally only for food. You see manioc in several styles, cooked and uncooked and ground into flour, palm oil and kernels, beans, maize, salad, fowls, eggs, plantains, sweet potatoes, mushrooms, peanuts, peppers, tobacco, large fish from the Congo, several kinds of fruit, etc. These things will be bartered for cheap blue cotton cloth, colored handkerchiefs, and bits of coarse brass wire, shaped like staples. These last pass for change, and are generally carried in large bunches. They serve also for bracelets and anklets, when their ends are fastened together, and for many useful, as well as these ornamental, purposes. The asking and taking price are widely divergent. With us the people demanded such exorbitant sums that it required much patience to make any purchases at all. They seemed quite indifferent about the disposal of their wares, that were placed before them in covered baskets to prevent thieving, which greatly prevails. We, however, were repaid by observing the market. The venders, as I have said, were mostly females, and many of them had their babes slung upon their backs. The unmarried girls were nude to the waist, the married women covering their breasts only by small—too small—square pieces of cloth attached by strings around the shoulders. Otherwise they were more scantily dressed than even the men. They wore huge brass rings upon their ankles, two and three together, and so heavy were these that pieces of cloth had to be fastened under them to save the skin. Necklaces and circlets of beads about the head were also worn. The men, besides, wore necklaces and bracelets, and nearly always a bone or tooth or piece of wood, as a fetish. Many of the women had their hair dyed red, and several of the men had their faces painted in bright colors, generally, however, there were only three or four short lines extending outwards from the corners of their eyes. They looked for all the world like the home-made demons of our pantomimes. But as usual it was in the arrangement of the hair that the greatest attempts at fashion were displayed. Though they had but little, they tortured that little into a dozen different patterns, giving it a variety of partings, longitudinal, circular and vertical, twisting it into a mop of little curls, turning it into a miniature coil at the back of the head, cutting all but a long strip from the centre of the forehead to the nape of the neck, which at a distance had the effect of a Roman helmet, while still others had all the head shaved. Very few of the men had any beard, and this was always thin and scanty. Both men and women are accustomed to smoke pipes, made of hard wood, in which they burn tobacco that is mild enough, but hardly what we should call of good flavor. The men are exceedingly fond of the fresh palm wine, which they call malafou, and which, taken in large quantities, proves very intoxicating. Both sexes are of small stature, and most of the men are meagre, but some have fine development of chest and shoulders. The poverty of their diet, or at least the general absence of meat, and the privations and hardships of their existence would account for their physical condition, and explain their short lives, for rarely do you see old, gray-haired or wrinkled people. They seem, however, to have great endurance, if not very great strength. But all—men, women and children—were exceedingly dirty and strong-smelling. They were a laughing, good-natured set, always ready for a joke, though their chief pleasure in life seemed to be a big feed.

62

HENRY M. STANLEY, *THROUGH SOUTH AFRICA* (LONDON: SAMPSON LOW, MARSTON, 1898), PP. 4–19, 22–23, 76–79

The new railway

Considering that we have come all the way from London, 7300 miles away, to celebrate the arrival of the locomotive at Bulawayo, such questions may sound ungrateful, and considering that last night at the banquet every speaker had something favourable to say of the Bechuanaland Railway and its builders, such questions may be supposed to indicate disagreement with the general opinion. There is really no necessity to suppose anything of the kind. Both the builders and the railway deserve praise. The fact that some eight trains have already arrived at Bulawayo, and that every passenger expresses himself warmly as to the condition of the line, and the pleasure derived from the journey, ought to satisfy everyone that the railway is ready for traffic, and will serve for many years, I hope, to connect Bulawayo with Cape Town.

But I want my readers to thoroughly understand what has been done, without prejudice to Bulawayo, the railway, or its builders. I am not so surprised at the railway, as at the length of time people in South Africa were content to be without it. The whole country seems to have been created for railway making. It offers as few difficulties as the London Embankment. Hyde Park is extremely uneven as compared with it. For nearly a thousand miles the railway sleepers have been laid at intervals of thirty inches on the natural face of the land; the rails have been laid across these, and connected together; the native navvies have scraped a little soil together, sufficient to cover the steel sleepers; and the iron road was thus ready for traffic. In March, 1896, the railway was but a few miles beyond Mafeking—say, about 880 miles from Cape Town—on November 4, 1897, it is 1360 miles in length from Cape Town, showing a construction of 480 miles in 19 months. There is nothing remarkable in this. The Union Pacific Railway between Omaha and Denver progressed at three, four, even five miles a day, over a much more irregular surface; but then, of course, the navvies were Irishmen, who handled the shovel like experts, and the rails with the precision and skill of master workmen. Natives could not be expected to attain the proficiency and organisation of the American Celts.

Our special train left Cape Town on Sunday at 4 P.M. A corridor train of six coaches, marked Bulawayo, at an ordinary provincial-looking station, seemed somewhat strange. Had it been marked Ujiji, or Yambuya, it could not have been more so. Three of us were put in a compartment for four. The fourth berth was available for hand luggage. Soon after starting we were served with tea and biscuits, and were it not for the flat wilderness scenery we might have imagined ourselves in an International sleeping car. Time tables were also furnished us, from which we learned that we were due at Kimberley, 647 miles, at 10.15 P.M. on the next day, November 1; at Mafeking, 870 miles, at 3.12 P.M. on November 2; Palachwe, in Khama's country, 1132 miles, at 12.47 P.M., November 3; and at Bulawayo, 1360 miles, at 9.30 A.M. on November 4, which would be ninety hours at fifteen miles per hour.

It took us an hour to cross the Lowry Strait, which at no very distant period must have been covered by sea and separated the Cape Peninsula from the Continent.

At 5.30 we arrived at the Paarl, 35 miles, a beautiful place suggestive of Italy with its vineyards, gardens and shrubbery, and lovingly enfolded by the Drakenstein Range. With its groves of fir and eucalyptus, bright sunshine, and pleasant-faced people, with picturesque mountains round about, it seemed a most desirable place.

The Paarl Station and others we passed bear witness to the excellence of Cape railway administration. The names of the stations were boldly printed on japanned iron plates, and though the passage of so many trains crowded with distinguished strangers had drawn large assemblages of the Colonists, male and female, whites, mulattoes, and negroes, the cleanliness and orderliness that prevailed were very conspicuous.

At 6 P.M. we had passed Wellington, 45 miles, which went to prove the rate of travel. This town also drew from us admiring expressions for its picturesque situation in one of the folds of the Drakenstein, for the early summer green of its groves, vineyards, and fields, and its pretty white houses. I thought, as I marked the charming town and its church spires, and the sweet groves around, what a contrast it was to the time when the Hottentot reared his cattle in the valley, and the predatory bushman infested the neighbourhood, and preyed on ground game and goats.

On the platform, among those who welcomed our coming, were a dozen Radical shoemakers lately arrived from Leicester. They charged Colonel Saunderson, M.P., my fellow traveller, with an expressive message to Mr. Labouchere. It is too forcible and inelegant for print, but it admirably illustrates the rapidity with which Radicals become perverted by travel.

Darkness found the train labouring through the mountainous defile of the Hex River. We could see but a loom of the rugged heights on either side, but from all accounts this part of the line is one of the show places which strangers are asked to note.

At daylight we were well on the Karroo, which at first sight was all but a desert. However, we were not long on it before we all took to it kindly. The air was strangely appetising, and we could not help regarding it with benevolence. The engineers who designed the line must have been skilful men, and by the track, as the train curves in and out of narrowing valleys and broadening plains, we are led to suppose that the Continent slopes gently from the interior down to Table Bay. The railway is a surface line, without a single tunnel or any serious cutting. The gradients in some places are stiff, but a single engine finds no difficulty in surmounting them.

At 4 P.M. of November 1 we reached the 458th mile from Cape Town, so that our rate of travel had been nineteen miles the hour. On tolerably level parts our speed, as timed by watch, was thirty miles; stoppages and steep gradients reduce this to nineteen miles.

We were fast asleep by the time we reached Kimberley. Night, and the short pause we made, prevented any correct impressions of the chief city of the Diamond Fields. At half-past six of November 2 we woke up at Taungs, 731 miles. The small stream over which we entered the late Crown Colony of Bechuanaland serves as a frontier line between it and Griqualand.

The first view of the country reminded me of East Central Africa, and I looked keenly at it to gauge its capabilities. To a new-comer it would not seem so full of promise as it was to me. It would appear as a waterless region, and too dry for a man accustomed to green fields and flowing rivers, but I have seen nothing between the immediate neighbourhood of the Missouri River and the Rocky Mountains to surpass it, and each mile we travelled in Bechuanaland confirmed that impression. Every few miles we crossed dry watercourses; but, though there was no water in sight, it does not derogate from its value as farm land. The plateau of Persia is a naked desert compared to it, and yet Persia possesses eight millions of people, and at one time contained double that number. The prairies of Nebraska, of Colorado, and Kansas are inferior in appearance, and I have seen them in their uninhabited state, but to-day they are remarkable for the growth of their many cities and their magnificent farming estates. All that is wanted to render Bechuanaland a desirable colony is water, so that every farm might draw irrigating supplies from reservoirs along these numerous watercourses. For Nature has so disposed the land that anyone with observant eyes may see with what little trouble water could be converted into rich green pastures and fields bearing weighty grain crops. The track of the railway runs over broad, almost level, valleys, hemmed in by masses of elevated land which have been broken up by ages of torrential rains, and whose soil has been swept by the floods over the valleys, naturally leaving the bases of the mountains higher than the central depression. If a Persian colonist came here he would say: "How admirable for my purpose! I shall begin my draining ditches or *canauts* from the bases of those hills and train them down towards the lower parts of these valleys, by which time I shall have as many constant and regular running streams as I have ditches, and my flocks and herds and fields shall have abundance of the necessary element." A thousand of such Persians would create thus a central stream with the surplus water flowing along the valley, and its borders would become one continuous grove. As the

Persians would do, the English colonists whose luck it may be to come to this land may also do, and enrich themselves faster than by labouring at gold mining.

These dry river-beds, now filled with sand, need only to have stone dams built across, every few hundred yards, to provide any number of reservoirs. They have been formed by rushing torrents which have furrowed the lowlands down to the bed rock, and the depth and breadth of the river courses show us what mighty supplies of water are wasted every year. As the torrents slackened their flow, they deposited their sediment, and finally filtered through underneath until no water was visible, but by digging down about two feet, it is found in liberal quantities, cool and sweet.

Even the improvident black has discovered what the greenness of the grass shows, that, though water is not visible, it is not far off. At one station the guards told me that they could find plenty of water by an hour's digging, which was a marvel to many of our party. I was told in Khama's territory that Khama, the chief, owned eight hundred thousand head of cattle before the rinderpest made its appearance and reduced his stock by half. If true, and there is no reason to doubt it, it shows what Bechuanaland might become with trifling improvements.

Before we came to Vryburg, the continuous valley had broadened out into a prairie, with not a hill in sight. The face of the land was as bare as though ploughed. By 4 P.M. we had come to the 850th mile, showing that the rate during the last twenty-four hours had been sixteen and a third miles an hour. Since Taungs, 731 miles, we had been closely skirting the Transvaal frontier, while to the west of the line lay what was once the mission-field of Livingstone and Moffatt. An hour later we arrived at Mafeking, on the Moloppo River, a tributary of the Orange River. Mafeking will always be celebrated in the future as the place whence Jameson started on his desperate incursion into the Dutch Republic. The Moloppo River contains lengthy pools of water along its deepened course, but the inhabitants of Mafeking are supplied by copious springs from Montsioa's old farm. The town lies on the north, or right bank, and is 870 miles from Cape Town. It is 4194 ft. above the sea. Already it has been laid out in broad streets which are planted with trees, and as these are flourishing they promise to furnish grateful shade in a few years. Outside of the town there is not a tree in sight, scarcely a shrub, and consequently it is more purely a prairie town than any other. Due east of it lies Pretoria, the Boer capital, about 180 miles distant, and it may be when the Boers take broader views of their duty to South Africa at large, and their own interests, that they will permit a railway to be constructed to connect the two towns, in which case the people of Mafeking cannot fail to profit by having exits at Delagoa Bay, Durban, and Cape Town. It will be passing strange also if the neighbourhood of Mafeking will not be found to contain some of the minerals for which the Transvaal is famous. The Malmani Gold Field is about 50 miles off, and the Zeerust Lead and Quicksilver Mine but a trifle further. For the growing of cereals it ought also to be as distinguished as the neighbouring state, for the soil is of the right colour.

On leaving Mafeking we were in the Bechuanaland Protectorate, a country of even greater promise than the Crown Colony. The next morning (November 3) we were well into Khama's country, 1071 miles from Cape Town. A thin forest of acacia trees, about 20 ft. in height, covered the face of the land. The soil was richly ochreous in colour. The grass was young and of a tender green, and the air cool and refreshing. The railway constructors must have rejoiced on finding so little labour required to perform their contract in this section. By skilfully chosen curves they were enabled to easily surmount any unevenness on the surface, and nothing more was required than to lay the steel sleepers on the ground, cross them with the rails, and add a few spadefuls of earth to complete the railway. The train runs wonderfully smooth and steady, and we experienced less discomfort than on some English trains I know. This is naturally due in a great measure to the slower and safer rate of speed we travel, and the newness of the rolling stock. During the whole day we were not once reminded by any jolt, jar, or swaying, of any imperfections, and our nights were undisturbed by loose play of rails or jumping.

At Three Sisters, 388 miles from Cape Town, we were at the highest altitude of the line, being 4518 ft. above the sea. Thence to Bulawayo, a thousand miles, the greatest variation in altitude is 1500 ft.; but were it not for the Railway Guide we should never have supposed that the variation was over 100 ft., so imperceptible are the ascents and descents of the line.

Magalapye Station (1088 miles) consisted of a third-class carriage and a goods van laid on three lengths of rail. We were halted nearly an hour near the Magalapye River, and learned that we were sixty miles inside of Khama's country. Improvements are proceeding to make the line more secure during the torrential season. At present it descends into the bed of the broad stream of sand, and here, if anywhere, a smart rainfall would destroy the line. Consequently, a high embankment has been made, stone piers have been built, and an iron bridge will span the river at a sufficient height. Here we heard also that one of the special trains ahead of us had suffered an accident from the explosion of an oil engine, which generated the electric light, resulting in the burning of two men, one of them badly.

The Magalapye River is one of those sandy watercourses so common in South Africa. To provide water for the station a broad ditch was cut across the sandy course, which was soon filled with clear and excellent water—enough, in fact, to supply a small township. It is to be hoped that all the guests noted this and carried away with them the object lesson.

The sight of this suggested to me that there was an opportunity for a genius like Rhodes to do more for South Africa than can be done by the discovery and exploitation of gold fields. A company called the United South African Waterworks might buy land along the principal watercourses, build a series of stone dams across them, clean out the sand between them, and so obtain hundreds of reservoirs for the townships that would certainly be established in their neighbourhood.

Beyond Palachwe (1132 miles) the thorn trees begin to disappear, and leafier woods, which resemble dwarf oak, take their place, though there are few trees higher than twenty feet. The soil is good, however, despite the fact that each dry season the fires destroy the grasses and the loams which are necessary for their nourishment. Most of the stations in this part are mere corrugated iron cottages, or railway carriages, temporarily lent for the housing of the guards.

At each halting place since arriving in Bechuanaland, we have been made aware how quickly the Englishman's generous disposition serves to teach natives to become beggars. Italy, Switzerland, Egypt, have thus suffered great harm. From Taungs to Palachwe, crowds of stalwart and able-bodied natives of both sexes have flocked around the kitchen-car to beg for bread, meat, and kitchen refuse. It is a novel and amusing sight at present, but in the course of time I fancy this practice of patronising beggars will make a callous and offensive breed that will not easily be put off with words.

At Shashi River, 5 P.M., the three special trains lay close together, because of the difficult gradient leading out of the bed of the river. While the engines assisted the trains up the steep, I came across an impromptu presentation of an address by the Mayor of Cape Town to Mr. Logan, the caterer of the excursion parties. According to what was said, we were all made to believe that we could not have been better served had the first European caterer undertaken the provisioning, to which no one could make objection, and a duly signed testimonial to that effect was presented to that gentleman. The scene, however, seemed odd at unknown Shashi, and strongly illustrated a racial characteristic for speechmaking and presentation of testimonials.

On the morning of November 4 we saw as we looked out of the carriage that the country was a continuation of that of the previous day. It was still as level, apparently, as a billiard table. We were drawing near to Bulawayo—were, in fact, due there about 9 A.M. We had been led to expect a more tropical vegetation, but as yet, though we were only sixty miles off, we saw no signs of it, but rather a return to the thorn bush of the Karroo and Southern Bechuanaland. One variation we noted, the rocky kopje is more frequent. These curious hill-heaps of rock are remnants of the primeval table-land that rose above the present face of the country from 100 to 300 feet. The sight of these curious kopjes deepened the idea that the seat of the "Killer," Lo Bengula, would be found on a high eminence, protected by a cluster of these kopjes, but we looked long in vain for such a cluster of hills. Even the sight of a lordly tree would be welcomed, for the tame landscape was growing monotonous. The absence of scenery incidents did not diminish our friendly sympathies towards Rhodesia, and we made the most of what was actually visible, the blue sky, the dwarf trees, the low green herbage which dotted the ground in the midst of wide expanses of tawdiness, the burnt grass tussocks, which we knew would in a few days be covered as with a carpet of green. We see the land just before the season changes, and signs of vivifying spring approaching are abundant. A few days ago the first rains set in. The last two nights have witnessed a wonderful exhibition of electric display in the heavens, and severe thunderstorms have followed. In another fortnight it is said the plains will have become like a vast garden.

At thirty-five miles from Bulawayo we came to the Matoppo Siding. The engineers stopped for breakfast at a restaurant and boarding house! which was a grass hut 20 feet long. Near by a diminutive zinc hut was called "General Store." Several tarpaulins sheltered various heaps of miscellanea. There a Matabele servant of a fur trader informed us that Lo Bengula was still alive, near the Zambesi, happy with abundance of mealies and cattle, and that any white man approaching his hiding-place would be surely killed, but that if any large number of white men went near him, he would again fly.

At the 1335th mile from Cape Town an accident to the special train ahead of us retarded us four hours. The engine, tender, water tank, and bogie car ran off the track. No one was hurt, fortunately, and by 1 P.M. we were all under way again, though the first lunch we were to have eaten together at Bulawayo was necessarily changed to the first dinner.

At 2.30 we were on the alert to catch a first view of Bulawayo, and at 2.55 P.M. a few stray gleams of white, seen through the thorn bush, were pointed out to us as the capital of Matabeleland. We had passed the famous Matoppo Hills to the right of us, but, excepting for their connection with the late war, there was nothing interesting in them. They consist of a series of these rocky kopjes of no great height, lying close together, mere wrecks of the crest of a great land wave, terrible enough when behind each rocky boulder and crevice a rifleman lies hidden, but peaceful now that the war is over, and the white man has made himself an irremovable home in the land.

As was said, we entered Bulawayo a few minutes later, and saw the crude beginnings of a city that must, if all goes well, grow to a great distinction. As a new-comer with but an hour or two's experience of it, I dare not venture upon saying anything more. We heard that the Governor, Sir A. Milner, had already officiated at the ceremony of opening the line, that his speech was not remarkable for any memorable words, that he had given the Victoria Cross to some trooper for gallant conduct in the field. I heard that Sir Alfred had also read a despatch from Mr. Chamberlain, which was to the effect that at the opening of the railway to Bulawayo he was anxious to send a message to the settlers assembled to celebrate the event. He sympathised with their troubles, but he was gratified to think that there was a happier future in store for them. The railway would be a stimulus to every form of enterprise, and would effectually bind the north and south together.

There was a little speech delivered by Commandant Van Rensburg on Monday night, which, perhaps, will be thought by London editors of no importance, but it was most gratifying to me, inasmuch as I had become possessed with the same ideas. He said that it was generally supposed that without gold Rhodesia could not exist, but he differed from that view, as, he was certain in his own mind, it would remain an important country because of its many agricultural products, its native wood, coal, cement, etc., etc. He had come to the conclusion that Rhodesia was as fit for agriculture as any part of South Africa, though he had been rather doubtful of it before he had seen the land with his own eyes. That is precisely my view. It is natural that the large majority of visitors who have come here to satisfy themselves about the existence of gold in Rhodesia should pay but little attention to what may be seen on the surface; but those who have done so now know that Rhodesia has a great agricultural future before it.

Several hundreds of men, eminent in divers professions, have come from England, America, the Cape, Orange Free State, Natal, Basuto and Zulu Lands, the Transvaal, Bechuanaland, and Northern Rhodesia, to celebrate the railway achievement by which this young Colony has become connected with the oldest Colony in South Africa. In any other continent the opening of five hundred miles of new railway would be fittingly celebrated by the usual banquet and the after-dinner felicitations of those directly concerned with it; but in this instance there are six members of the Imperial Parliament, the High Commissioner of the Cape, the Governor of Natal, scores of members of the Colonial Legislatures, and scores of notabilities, leaders of thought and action, bankers, merchants, and clergy from every colony and state in the southern part of this continent. They all felt it to be a great event. Few events of the century surpass it in interest and importance. It marks the conclusion of an audacious enterprise, which less than ten years ago would have been deemed impossible, and only two years ago as most unlikely. It furnishes a lesson to all colonising nations. It teaches methods of operation never practised before. It suggests large and grand possibilities, completely reforms and alters our judgment with regard to Africa, effaces difficulties that impeded right views, and infuses a belief that, once the political and capitalist public realises what the occasion really signifies, this railway is but the precursor of many more in this continent.

This was my first day's introduction to the moral condition of Johannesburg. But to begin at the beginning. On arriving at midnight at the frontier of the Transvaal, near the Vaal River, the train was stopped in the open veld until daylight, for Boer officials require daylight to make their conscientious examination of passengers and their luggage. Half-an-hour after dawn the train moved over the Vaal Bridge, and we were soon within the grip of the Boer Custom House. I was told later that the officials were insolent; but I saw nothing uncommon, except a methodical procedure such as might belong to a people resolved to make a more than usually thorough search. The officials came in at the rear end of the carriage, locked the door behind them, and informed us we were to go out before them. The male passengers were ushered into one corrugated-iron house, the females with their respective searchers behind them into another. One burly passenger had diamonds concealed on his person, but his clothes were only slightly felt. A small pale clergyman just behind him, however, received marked attention, and was obliged to take off his boots, and every article of his baggage was minutely scrutinised. Probably some of the women searchers performed their duties just as thoroughly. My servant was asked to pay duty on some of my shirts, but he refused to pay anything, on the ground that the shirts had been repeatedly worn and washed.

The distance to Johannesburg from the frontier was but an hour and a half of ordinary running, but from the time we neared the Vaal River it occupied us eleven hours. A reporter from the *Star* had come aboard at the frontier station, and from him we learned a few facts regarding Johannesburg, such as that the uitlander miners intended to starve the burghers out by closing the mines, that the Australians were leaving in crowds, and though there were three Presidential candidates in the field, Kruger was sure to be returned for a fourth term, as General Joubert was known to be weak, and Schalk Burger almost unknown.

The Transvaal veld was much greener, and more rolling, than that of the Orange Free State. Johannesburg came into view about 9 A.M.; but instead of making direct for it, the train sheered off and came to a halt at Elandsfontein, six miles east. It was then we first obtained an intelligent comprehension of the term "Main Reef," to whose production of gold the existence of Johannesburg is due. Its total length, I am told, is 38·5 miles, to be accurate, and along this a chain of mines, well equipped and developed, exists, out of which, however, only ten miles of the reef can be profitably worked under the present economic circumstances. The working of the remaining twenty-eight miles depends mainly upon the removal of the burdens, upon low wages, abundant labour, cheap transport, etc. The richer and dividend-paying section of the Reef contains such mines as the Langlaagte, Paarl Central, Crown Reef, Pioneer, Bonanza, Robinson, Worcester, Ferreira, Wemmer, Jubilee, City and Suburban, Meyer and Charlton, Wolhuter, George Goch, Henry Nourse, New Heriot, Jumpers, Geldenhuis, Stanhope, and Simmer and Jack. To either side of Elandsfontein runs a lengthy line of chimney stacks, engine houses, tall wooden frames, supporting the headgear, stamp mills, with clusters of sheds, huts and offices, hills of white tailings, and ore. To the westward these become more numerous, and as the train moved from Elandsfontein towards Johannesburg, it clung to the side of a commanding ridge by which we obtained a panoramic view of mine after mine, each surrounded by its reservoirs, hills of tailings, lofty stores of ore, iron sheds, mills, offices, and headgear structures, until finally they occupied an entire valley. Presently, while we still clung to the ridge, we saw that the scattered cottages, with their respective groves, were becoming more massed, and looking ahead of them we saw the city of Johannesburg, filling the breadth of a valley, girdled by a thin line of tall smoke stacks, and dominated by two parallel lines of hills, the crests of which rose perhaps 300 ft. or so above the city. The scent of eucalyptus groves filled the air, for now the ridge on our right was given up to cottages, villas, mansions, each separated by firs, eucalyptus, flower gardens, and varied shrubberies, the whole making a charming sight, and a worthy approach to the capital of the mining industry.

63

JOSEPH CONRAD, 'HEART OF DARKNESS', IN *YOUTH, AND TWO OTHER STORIES* (NEW YORK: MCCLURE, PHILLIPS & CO., 1903), PP. 71–80. ORIGINALLY PUBLISHED IN *BLACKWOODS MAGAZINE* 165, 1,000–1,002 (FEBRUARY, MARCH, AND APRIL 1899), 193–220, 479–502, 634–657

Nowhere did we stop long enough to get a particularized impression, but the general sense of vague and oppressive wonder grew upon me. It was like a weary pilgrimage amongst hints for nightmares.

"It was upward of thirty days before I saw the mouth of the big river. We anchored off the seat of the government. But my work would not begin till some two hundred miles farther on. So as soon as I could I made a start for a place thirty miles higher up.

"I had my passage on a little sea-going steamer. Her captain was a Swede, and knowing me for a seaman, invited me on the bridge. He was a young man, lean, fair, and morose, with lanky hair and a shuffling gait. As we left the miserable little wharf, he tossed his head contemptuously at the shore. 'Been living there?' he asked. I said, 'Yes.' 'Fine lot these government chaps—are they not?' he went on, speaking English with great precision and considerable bitterness. 'It is funny what some people will do for a few francs a month. I wonder what becomes of that kind when it goes up country?' I said to him I expected to see that soon. 'So-o-o!' he exclaimed. He shuffled athwart, keeping one eye ahead vigilantly. 'Don't be too sure,' he continued. 'The other day I took up a man who hanged himself on the road. He was a Swede, too.' 'Hanged himself! Why, in God's name?' I cried. He kept on looking out watchfully. 'Who knows? The sun too much for him, or the country perhaps.'

At last we opened a reach. A rocky cliff appeared, mounds of turned-up earth by the shore, houses on a hill, others, with iron roofs, amongst a waste of excavations, or hanging to the declivity. A continuous noise of the rapids above hovered over this scene of inhabited devastation. A lot of people, mostly black and naked, moved about like ants. A jetty projected into the river. A blinding sunlight drowned all this at times in a sudden recrudescence of glare. 'There's your Company's station,' said the Swede, pointing to three wooden barrack-like structures on the rocky slope. 'I will send your things up. Four boxes did you say? So. Farewell.'

"I came upon a boiler wallowing in the grass, then found a path leading up the hill. It turned aside for the bowlders, and also for an undersized railway-truck lying there on its back with its wheels in the air. One was off. The thing looked as dead as the carcass of some animal. I came upon more pieces of decaying machinery, a stack of rusty rails. To the left a clump of trees made a shady spot, where dark things seemed to stir feebly. I blinked, the path was steep. A horn tooted to the right, and I saw the black people run. A heavy and dull detonation shook the ground, a puff of smoke came out of the cliff, and that was all. No change appeared on the face of the rock. They were building a railway. The cliff was not in the way or anything; but this objectless blasting was all the work going on.

"A slight clinking behind me made me turn my head. Six black men advanced in a file, toiling up the path. They walked erect and slow, balancing small baskets full of earth on their heads, and the clink kept time with their footsteps. Black rags were wound round their loins, and the short ends behind waggled to and fro like tails. I could see every rib, the joints of their limbs were like knots in a rope; each had an iron collar on his neck, and all were connected together with a chain whose bights swung between them, rhythmically clinking. Another report from the cliff made me think suddenly of that ship of war I had seen firing into a continent. It was the same kind of ominous voice; but these men could by no stretch of imagination be called enemies. They were called criminals, and the outraged law, like the bursting shells, had come to them, an insoluble mystery from the sea. All their meager breasts panted together, the violently dilated nostrils quivered, the eyes stared stonily uphill. They passed me within six inches, without a glance, with that complete, deathlike indifference of unhappy savages. Behind this raw matter one of the reclaimed, the product of the new forces at work, strolled despondently, carrying a rifle by its middle. He had a uniform jacket with one button off, and seeing a white man on the path, hoisted his weapon to his shoulder with alacrity. This was simple prudence, white men being so much alike at a distance that he could not tell who I might be. He was speedily reassured, and with a large, white, rascally grin, and a glance at his charge, seemed to take me into partnership in his exalted trust. After all, I also was a part of the great cause of these high and just proceedings.

"Instead of going up, I turned and descended to the left. My idea was to let that chain-gang get out of sight before I climbed the hill. You know I am not particularly tender; I've had to strike and to fend off. I've had to resist and to attack sometimes—that's only one way of resisting—without counting the exact cost, according to the demands of such sort of life as I had blundered into. I've seen the devil of violence, and the devil of greed, and the devil of hot desire; but, by all the stars! these were strong, lusty, red-eyed devils, that swayed and drove men—men, I tell you. But as I stood on this hillside, I foresaw that in the blinding sunshine of that land I would become acquainted with a flabby, pretending, weak-eyed devil of a rapacious and pitiless folly. How insidious he could be, too, I was only to find out several months later and a thousand miles farther. For a moment I stood appalled, as though by a warning. Finally I descended the hill, obliquely, towards the trees I had seen.

"I avoided a vast artificial hole somebody had been digging on the slope, the purpose of which I found it impossible to divine. It wasn't a quarry or a sandpit, anyhow. It was just a hole. It might have been connected with the philanthropic desire of giving the criminals something to do. I don't know. Then I nearly fell into a very narrow ravine, almost no more than a scar in the hillside. I discovered that a lot of imported drainage-pipes for the settlement had been tumbled in there. There wasn't one that was not broken. It was a wanton smash-up. At last I got under the trees. My purpose was to stroll into the shade for a moment; but no sooner within than it seemed to me I had stepped into a gloomy circle of some Inferno. The rapids were near, and an uninterrupted, uniform, headlong, rushing noise filled the mournful stillness of the grove, where not a breath stirred, not a leaf moved, with a mysterious sound—as though the tearing pace of the launched earth had suddenly become audible.

"Black shapes crouched, lay, sat between the trees, leaning against the trunks, clinging to the earth, half coming out, half effaced within the dim light, in all the attitudes of pain, abandonment, and despair. Another mine on the cliff went off, followed by a slight shudder of the soil under my feet. The work was going on. The work! And this was the place where some of the helpers had withdrawn to die.

"They were dying slowly—it was very clear. They were not enemies, they were not criminals, they were nothing earthly now,—nothing but black shadows of disease and starvation, lying confusedly in the greenish gloom. Brought from all the recesses of the coast in all the legality of time contracts, lost in uncongenial surroundings, fed on unfamiliar food, they sickened, became inefficient, and were then allowed to crawl away and rest. These moribund shapes were free as air— and nearly as thin. I began to distinguish the gleam of the eyes under the trees. Then, glancing down, I saw a face near my hand. The black bones reclined at full length with one shoulder against the tree, and slowly the eyelids rose and the sunken eyes looked up at me, enormous and vacant, a kind of blind, white flicker in the depths of the orbs, which died out slowly. The man seemed young—almost a boy—but you know with them it's hard to tell. I found nothing else to do but to offer him one of my good Swede's ship's biscuits I had in my pocket. The fingers closed slowly on it and held—there was no other movement and no other glance. He had tied a bit of white worsted round his neck—Why? Where did he get it? Was it a badge—an ornament—a charm—a propitiatory act? Was there any idea at all connected with it? It looked startling round his black neck, this bit of white thread from beyond the seas.

"Near the same tree two more bundles of acute angles sat with their legs drawn up. One, with his chin propped on his knees, stared at nothing, in an intolerable and appalling manner: his brother phantom rested its forehead, as if overcome with a great weariness; and all about others were scattered in every pose of contorted collapse, as in some picture of a massacre or a pestilence. While I stood horror-struck, one of these creatures rose to his hands and knees, and went off on all-fours towards the river to drink. He lapped out of his hand, then sat up in the sunlight, crossing his shins in front of him, and after a time let his woolly head fall on his breastbone.

"I didn't want any more loitering in the shade, and I made haste towards the station. When near the buildings I met a white man, in such an unexpected elegance of get-up that in the first moment I took him for a sort of vision. I saw a high starched collar, white cuffs, a light alpaca jacket, snowy trousers, a clean necktie, and varnished boots. No hat. Hair parted, brushed, oiled, under a green-lined parasol held in a big white hand. He was amazing, and had a penholder behind his ear.

"I shook hands with this miracle, and I learned he was the Company's chief accountant, and that all the bookkeeping was done at this station. He had come out for a moment, he said, 'to get a breath of fresh air.' The expression sounded wonderfully odd, with its suggestion of sedentary desk-life. I wouldn't have mentioned the fellow to you at all, only it was from his lips that I first heard the name of the man who is so indissolubly connected with the memories of that time. Moreover, I respected the fellow. Yes; I respected his collars, his vast cuffs, his brushed hair. His appearance was certainly that of a hairdresser's dummy; but in the great demoralization of the land he kept up his appearance. That's backbone. His starched collars and got-up shirt-fronts were achievements of character. He had been out nearly three years; and, later on, I could not help asking him how he managed to sport such linen. He had just the faintest blush, and said modestly, 'I've been teaching one of the native women about the station. It was difficult. She had a distaste for the work.' Thus this man had verily accomplished something. And he was devoted to his books, which were in apple-pie order.

"Everything else in the station was in a muddle,—heads, things, buildings. Strings of dusty niggers with splay feet arrived and departed; a stream of manufactured goods, rubbishy cottons, beads, and brass-wire set into the depths of darkness, and in return came a precious trickle of ivory.

"I had to wait in the station for ten days—an eternity. I lived in a hut in the yard, but to be out of the chaos I would sometimes get into the accountant's office. It was built of horizontal planks, and so badly put together that, as he bent over his high desk, he was barred from neck to heels with narrow strips of sunlight. There was no need to open the big shutter to see. It was hot there too; big flies buzzed fiendishly, and did not sting, but stabbed. I sat generally on the floor, while, of faultless appearance (and even slightly scented), perching on a high stool, he wrote, he wrote. Sometimes he stood up for exercise. When a truckle-bed with a sick man (some invalided agent from up-country) was put in there, he exhibited a gentle annoyance. 'The groans of this sick person,' he said, 'distract my attention. And without that it is extremely difficult to guard against clerical errors in this climate.'

"One day he remarked, without lifting his head, 'In the interior you will no doubt meet Mr. Kurtz.' On my asking who Mr. Kurtz was, he said he was a first-class agent; and seeing my disappointment at this information, he added slowly, laying down his pen, 'He is a very remarkable person.' Further questions elicited from him that Mr. Kurtz was at present in charge of a trading post, a very important one, in the true ivory-country, at 'the very bottom of there. Sends in as much ivory as all the others put together . . . . ' He began to write again. The sick man was too ill to groan. The flies buzzed in a great peace.

"Suddenly there was a growing murmur of voices and a great tramping of feet. A caravan had come in. A violent babble of uncouth sounds burst out on the other side of the planks. All the carriers were speaking together, and in the midst of the uproar the lamentable voice of the chief agent was heard 'giving it up' tearfully for the twentieth time that day . . . . He rose slowly. 'What a frightful row,' he said. He crossed the room gently to look at the sick man, and returning, said to me, 'He does not hear.' 'What! Dead?' I asked, startled. 'No, not yet,' he answered, with great composure. Then, alluding with a toss of the head to the tumult in the station-yard, 'When one has got to make correct entries, one comes to hate those savages—hate them to the death.' He remained thoughtful for a moment. 'When you see Mr. Kurtz,' he went on, 'tell him from me that everything here'—he glanced at the desk—'is very satisfactory. I don't like to write to him—with those messengers of ours you never know who may get hold of your letter—at that Central Station.' He stared at me for a moment with his mild, bulging eyes. 'Oh, he will go far, very far,' he began again. 'He will be a somebody in the Administration before long. They, above—the Council in Europe, you know—mean him to be.'

"He turned to his work. The noise outside had ceased, and presently in going out I stopped at the door. In the steady buzz of flies the homeward-bound agent was lying flushed and insensible; the other, bent over his books, was making correct entries of perfectly correct transactions; and fifty feet below the doorstep I could see the still tree-tops of the grove of death.

"Next day I left that station at last, with a caravan of sixty men, for a two-hundred-mile tramp.

"No use telling you much about that. Paths, paths, everywhere; a stamped-in network of paths spreading over the empty land, through long grass, through burnt grass, through thickets, down and up chilly ravines, up and down stony hills ablaze with heat; and a solitude, a solitude, nobody, not a hut. The population had cleared out a long time ago. Well, if a lot of mysterious niggers armed with all kinds of fearful weapons suddenly took to traveling on the road between Deal and Gravesend, catching the yokels right and left to carry heavy loads for them, I fancy every farm and cottage thereabouts would get empty very soon. Only here the dwellings were gone too. Still I passed through several abandoned villages. There's something pathetically childish in the ruins of grass walls. Day after day, with the stamp and shuffle of sixty pair of bare feet behind me, each pair under a 60-lb. load. Camp, cook, sleep, strike camp, march. Now and then a carrier dead in harness, at rest in the long grass near the path, with an empty water-gourd and his long staff lying by his side. A great silence around and above.

64

'LIONS', *THE SPECTATOR*, MARCH 3, 1900, PP. 307–308

The lions that stopped the railway

SPEAKING in the House of Lords of the progress of the Uganda Railway, Lord Salisbury mentioned that among the unexpected difficulties encountered were a pair of man-eating lions, which stopped the works for three weeks, before they were shot. As some five thousand men were at work on the line, their intimidation by two lions seems almost incredible. Yet it is a fact that so dreadful was the pressure exercised by the constant attacks of this pair of man-destroying wild beasts, and so cumulative the fear caused among the Indian labourers by the sight and sound of their comrades being dragged off and devoured, that hundreds of these industrious workmen, trained on similar duties under the service of the Government of India, abandoned their employment and pay, and crying out that they agreed to work for wages, not to be food for lions or devils, rushed to the line as the trains for the coast were approaching, and flinging themselves across the metals, gave the engine-drivers the choice, either of passing over their bodies, or of stopping to take them up and carry them back to Mombasa. Many of these men were not timid Hindoos, but sturdy Sikhs. Yet the circumstances were so unique, and the scenes witnessed from week to week so bloody and appalling, that their panic and desperation are no matter for surprise. Lord Salisbury understated the facts. Though the *works* were stopped for three weeks, the lions' campaign lasted, with intervals of quiet when one or other had been wounded, from March till the end of December. In this time they killed and ate twenty-eight Indians, and it is believed at least twice this number of natives, Swahilis and the like; besides wounding and attacking others. They attacked white engineers, doctors, soldiers, and military officers, armed Abyssinian askaris, sepoys, bunniahs, coolies, and porters. Some they clawed, some they devoured, some they carried off and left sticking in thorn fences, because they could not drag them through. At first they were contented to take one man between them. Before the end of their career they would take a man apiece on the same night, sometimes from the same hut or camp-fire. The plain, unvarnished tale of this "prehistoric revival" of the position originally held by man in the struggle for existence against ravenous beasts is set out at considerable length and detail in the *Field* of February 17th and February

420

24th by Mr. J. H. Patterson, one of the engineers of the line, who, after months of effort and personal risk, succeeded in breaking the spell, and killing both the lions, which the natives had come to regard as "devils," that is, as equivalent to were-wolves, and guided by the local demons.

The parallel to the story of the lions which stopped the rebuilding of Samaria must occur to every one, and if the Samaritans had quarter as good cause for their fears as had the railway coolies, their wish to propitiate the local deities is easily understood. If the whole body of lion anec dote, from the days of the Assyrian Kings till the last year of the nineteenth century, were collated and brought together, it would not equal in tragedy or atrocity, in savageness or in sheer insolent contempt for man, armed or unarmed, white or black, the story of these two beasts. The scene of their exploits was only one hundred and thirty miles from the coast, in the valley of a cool and swift stream, the Tsavos River. Filled by the melting of the snows on Kilimanjaro, bordered with palms and ferns, and at a further distance by a dense and impassable jungle of thorns, its banks became suddenly the camping ground of thousands of hardworking Indian railwaymen, who slept in camps scattered up and down the line for some eight miles. Into these camps the lions came, thrusting their gigantic heads under the flaps of the tents, or walking in at the doors of the huts. Their first victim was a Sikh jemadar, taken from a tent shared by a dozen other workmen, the next a coolie. Then they raided the camps regularly until the local length of rail was finished, and the bulk of the men moved up country out of the lions' beat. But some hundreds were left behind, to build bridges and do permanent work. It was then that the lions' reign of terror began, which ended in the complete stoppage of an Imperial enterprise supplied with every mechanism and appliance of civilisation, from traction engines to armed troops.

Perhaps the strongest evidence of the pressure to which these beasts subjected the dominant biped man is that they forced him to become arboreal. If the setting of blood and bones were not so ghastly, the scene would provoke a smile. After hundreds had fled some three hundred still remained, for whom the engineer, worn out by want of sleep himself, and by constant tracking of the lions by day and sitting up by moonlight, endeavoured to find safe quarters by night, when they might be seen "perched on the top of water-tanks, roofs, and bridge-girders. Every good-sized tree in camp had as many beds lashed to it as its branches would bear. So many men got up a tree once when a camp was attacked that it came down, the men falling close to the lions. Strange to say, they did not heed them, but then they were busy devouring a man they had just seized."

The fearful shrieks of the victims rang in their ears night after night, till no one knew whose turn would come next. Sound men lay and listened to the cracking of bones and the tearing of limbs within fifty yards of the place where they were, and sick men in hospital expired from sheer terror as they listened to the monsters quarrelling over their feast. Twenty shots were fired in the dark at the sound of the lions eating a man, and they finished him to the last bone. They would spring over the highest thorn "boma," pick up a man and trot round with him looking for the best way out, as a cat carries a rat. Every one will ask, why were these men not armed? The answer is that the ordinary coolie does not know the use of arms, but that, even when the lions were fired at, unless actually hit, they cared nothing. Unlike nearly all wild beasts, they feared neither fire, nor firearms, nor lamps, nor white men. One sprang on an officer's back, tore off his knapsack, and then carried off and ate a soldier who was following him. They prowled round and round white men in *machans* (sheltered by the dark), trying to stalk them. One was caught in an ingenious trap, made of two cages of steel rails, in one of which were three sepoys armed with Martinis. The lions had become so used to walking into huts that the trap itself was an extra inducement to be bold, and they looked on the sepoys as bait. The sepoys lost their heads as the lion bounced about, and blazed off in every direction but the right one, though they could have touched the imprisoned beast with their rifles. At last one bullet hit the catch of the door and released the lion. Another was shot in the back with slugs. A week later it tried to stalk Mr. Patterson, who was sitting in a tree, and after stalking him like a Boer sharpshooter from bush to bush till within twenty yards, was wounded, and next day was killed. The other had been shot by Mr. Patterson shortly before, after the pair had marched round and round him for two hours as he sat up over a kill they had made. It was a huge maneless lion 9 ft. 8 in. long and 3 ft. 9 in. high. Its last meal had been an African native. The other was 9 ft. 6 in. long, and 3 ft. 11 in. high. Both beasts killed men solely for food, though the country round swarmed with every description of game dear to lions. Only when the men had run away, or taken to trees, of slept in iron huts, did they kill goats or donkeys. They ate every portion of the men's bodies except the top of the skull and sometimes the hands. It is said that in the island of Singapore tigers have actually assembled and multiplied in order to eat the Chinese coolies now employed on the plantations. But the records of the East do not supply an instance in which six thousand men and a Government organisation were baffled and defied by two man-eaters.

To what a distance the whole story carries us back, and how impossible it becomes to account for the survival of primitive man against this kind of foe! For fire—which has hitherto been regarded as his main safeguard against the carnivora—these cared nothing. It is curious that the Tsavos lions were not killed by poison, for strychnine is easily used and with effect. Poison may have been used early in the history of man, for its powers are employed with strange skill by the men in the tropical forest, both in America and West Central Africa. But there is no evidence that the old inhabitants of Europe, or of Assyria, or Asia Minor ever killed lions or wolves by this means. They looked to the King or chief, or some champion, to kill these monsters for them. It was not the sport but the duty of Kings, and was in itself a title to be a ruler of men. Theseus, who cleared the roads of beasts and robbers; Hercules, the lion-killer; St. George, the dragon-slayer, and all the rest of their class owed to this their everlasting fame. From the story of the Tsavos River we can appreciate their services to man even at this distance of time. When the jungle twinkled with hundreds of lamps, as the shout went on from camp to camp that the first lion was dead, as the hurrying crowds fell prostrate in the midnight forest, laying their heads on his feet, and the Africans danced savage and ceremonial dances of thanksgiving, Mr. Patterson must have realised in no common way what it was to have been a hero and deliverer in the days when man was not yet undisputed lord of the creation, and might pass at any moment under the savage dominion of the beasts.

65

J. H. PATTERSON, *THE MAN-EATERS OF TSAVO AND OTHER EAST AFRICAN ADVENTURES* (LONDON: MACMILLAN AND CO., 1910), PP. 61–74

Chapter VI

The reign of terror

THE lions seemed to have got a bad fright the night Brock and I sat up in wait for them in the goods-wagon, for they kept away from Tsavo and did not molest us in any way for some considerable time—not, in fact, until long after Brock had left me and gone on *safari* (a caravan journey) to Uganda. In this breathing space which they vouchsafed us, it occurred to me that should they renew their attacks, a trap would perhaps offer the best chance of getting at them, and that if I could construct one in which a couple of coolies might be used as bait without being subjected to any danger, the lions would be quite daring enough to enter it in search of them and thus be caught. I accordingly set to work at once, and in a short time managed to make a sufficiently strong trap out of wooden sleepers, tram-rails, pieces of telegraph wire, and a length of heavy chain. It was divided into two compartments—one for the men and one for the lion. A sliding door at one end admitted the former, and once inside this compartment they were perfectly safe, as between them and the lion, if he entered the other, ran a cross wall of iron rails only three inches apart, and embedded both top and bottom in heavy wooden sleepers. The door which was to admit the lion was, of course, at the opposite end of the structure, but otherwise the whole thing was very much on the principle of the ordinary rat-trap, except that it was not necessary for the lion to seize the bait in order to send the door clattering down. This part of the contrivance was arranged in the following manner. A heavy chain was secured along the top part of the lion's doorway, the ends hanging down to the ground on either side of the opening; and to these were fastened, strongly secured by stout wire, short lengths of rails placed about six inches apart. This made a sort of flexible door which could be packed into a small space when not in use, and which abutted against the top of the doorway when lifted up. The door was held in this position by a lever

424

made of a piece of rail, which in turn was kept in its place by a wire fastened to one end and passing down to a spring concealed in the ground inside the cage. As soon as the lion entered sufficiently far into the trap, he would be bound to tread on the spring; his weight on this would release the wire, and in an instant down would come the door behind him; and he could not push it out in any way, as it fell into a groove between two rails firmly embedded in the ground.

In making this trap, which cost us a lot of work, we were rather at a loss for want of tools to bore holes in the rails for the doorway, so as to enable them to be fastened by the wire to the chain. It occurred to me, however, that a hard-nosed bullet from my ·303 would penetrate the iron, and on making the experiment I was glad to find that a hole was made as cleanly as if it had been punched out.

When the trap was ready I pitched a tent over it in order further to deceive the lions, and built an exceedingly strong *boma* round it. One small entrance was made at the back of the enclosure for the men, which they were to close on going in by pulling a bush after them; and another entrance just in front of the door of the cage was left open for the lions. The wiseacres to whom I showed my invention were generally of the opinion that the man-eaters would be too cunning to walk into my parlour; but, as will be seen later, their predictions proved false. For the first few nights I baited the trap myself, but nothing happened except that I had a very sleepless and uncomfortable time, and was badly bitten by mosquitoes.

As a matter of fact, it was some months before the lions attacked us again, though from time to time we heard of their depredations in other quarters. Not long after our night in the goods-wagon, two men were carried off from rail-head, while another was taken from a place called Engomani, about ten miles away. Within a very short time, this latter place was again visited by the brutes, two more men being seized, one of whom was killed and eaten, and the other so badly mauled that he died within a few days. As I have said, however, we at Tsavo enjoyed complete immunity from attack, and the coolies, believing that their dreaded foes had permanently deserted the district, resumed all their usual habits and occupations, and life in the camps returned to its normal routine.

At last we were suddenly startled out of this feeling of security. One dark night the familiar terror-sticken cries and screams awoke the camps, and we knew that the "demons" had returned and had commenced a new list of victims. On this occasion a number of men had been sleeping outside their tents for the sake of coolness, thinking, of course, that the lions had gone for good, when suddenly in the middle of the night one of the brutes was discovered forcing its way through the *boma*. The alarm was at once given, and sticks, stones and firebrands were hurled in the direction of the intruder. All was of no avail, however, for the lion burst into the midst of the terrified group, seized an unfortunate wretch amid the cries and shrieks of his companions, and dragged him off through the thick thorn fence. He was joined outside by the second lion, and so daring had the two brutes become that they did not trouble to carry their victim any further away, but devoured him within thirty yards of the tent where he had been seized. Although several shots were fired in their direction by the *jemadar* of the gang to which the coolie belonged, they took no notice of these and did not attempt to move until their horrible meal was finished. The few scattered fragments that remained of the body I would not allow to be buried at once, hoping that the lions would return to the spot the following night; and on the chance of this I took up my station at nightfall in a convenient tree. Nothing occurred to break the monotony of my watch, however, except that I had a visit from a hyæna, and the next morning I learned that the lions had attacked another camp about two miles from Tsavo—for by this time the camps were again scattered, as I had works in progress all up and down the line. There the man-eaters had been successful in obtaining a victim, whom, as in the previous instance, they devoured quite close to the camp. How they forced their way through the *bomas* without making a noise was, and still is, a mystery to me; I should have thought that it was next to impossible for an animal to get through at all. Yet they continually did so, and without a sound being heard.

After this occurrence, I sat up every night for over a week near likely camps, but all in vain. Either the lions saw me and then went elsewhere, or else I was unlucky, for they took man after man from different places without ever once giving me a chance of a shot at them. This constant night watching was most dreary and fatiguing work, but I felt that it was a duty that had to be undertaken, as the men naturally looked to me for protection. In the whole of my life I have never experienced anything more nerve-shaking than to hear the deep roars of these dreadful monsters growing gradually nearer and nearer, and to know that some one or other of us was doomed to be their victim before morning dawned. Once they reached the vicinity of the camps, the roars completely ceased, and we knew that they were stalking for their prey. Shouts would then pass from camp to camp, "*Khabar dar, bhaieon, shaitan ata*" ("Beware, brothers, the devil is coming"), but the warning cries would prove of no avail, and sooner or later agonising shrieks would break the silence and another man would be missing from roll-call next morning.

I was naturally very disheartened at being foiled in this way night after night, and was soon at my wits' end to know what to do; it seemed as if the lions were really "devils" after all and bore a charmed life. As I have said before, tracking them through the jungle was a hopeless task; but as something had to be done to keep up the men's spirits, I spent many a weary day crawling on my hands and knees through the dense undergrowth of the exasperating wilderness around us. As a matter of fact, if I had come up with the lions on any of these expeditions, it was much more likely that they would have added me to their list of victims than that I should have succeeded in killing either of them, as everything would have been in their favour. About this time, too, I had many helpers, and several officers—civil, naval and military—came to Tsavo from the coast and sat up night after night in order to get a shot at our daring foes. All of us, however, met with the same lack of success, and the lions always seemed capable of avoiding the watchers, while succeeding at the same time in obtaining a victim.

I have a very vivid recollection of one particular night when the brutes seized a man from the railway station and brought him close to my camp to devour.

I could plainly hear them crunching the bones, and the sound of their dreadful purring filled the air and rang in my ears for days afterwards. The terrible thing was to feel so helpless; it was useless to attempt to go out, as of course the poor fellow was dead, and in addition it was so pitch dark as to make it impossible to see anything. Some half a dozen workmen, who lived in a small enclosure close to mine, became so terrified on hearing the lions at their meal that they shouted and implored me to allow them to come inside my *boma*. This I willingly did, but soon afterwards I remembered that one man had been lying ill in their camp, and on making enquiry I found that they had callously left him behind alone. I immediately took some men with me to bring him to my *boma*, but on entering his tent I saw by the light of the lantern that the poor fellow was beyond need of safety. He had died of shock at being deserted by his companions.

From this time matters gradually became worse and worse. Hitherto, as a rule, only one of the man-eaters had made the attack and had done the foraging, while the other waited outside in the bush; but now they began to change their tactics, entering the *bomas* together and each seizing a victim. In this way two Swahili porters were killed during the last week of November, one being immediately carried off and devoured. The other was heard moaning for a long time, and when his terrified companions at last summoned up sufficient courage to go to his assistance, they found him stuck fast in the bushes of the *boma*, through which for once the lion had apparently been unable to drag him. He was still alive when I saw him next morning, but so terribly mauled that he died before he could be got to the hospital.

Within a few days of this the two brutes made a most ferocious attack on the largest camp in the section, which for safety's sake was situated within a stone's throw of Tsavo Station and close to a Permanent Way Inspector's iron hut. Suddenly in the dead of night the two man-eaters burst in among the terrified workmen, and even from my *boma*, some distance away, I could plainly hear the panic-stricken shrieking of the coolies. Then followed cries of "They've taken him; they've taken him," as the brutes carried off their unfortunate victim and began their horrible feast close beside the camp. The Inspector, Mr. Dalgairns, fired over fifty shots in the direction in which he heard the lions, but they were not to be frightened and calmly lay there until their meal was finished. After examining the spot in the morning, we at once set out to follow the brutes, Mr. Dalgairns feeling confident that he had wounded one of them, as there was a trail on the sand like that of the toes of a broken limb. After some careful stalking, we suddenly found ourselves in the vicinity of the lions, and were greeted with ominous growlings. Cautiously advancing and pushing the bushes aside, we saw in the gloom what we at first took to be a lion cub; closer inspection, however, showed it to be the remains of the unfortunate coolie, which the man-eaters had evidently abandoned at our approach. The legs, one arm and half the body had been eaten, and it was the stiff fingers of the other arm trailing along the sand which had left the marks we had taken to be the trail of a wounded lion. By this time the beasts had retired far into the thick jungle where it was impossible to follow them, so we had the remains of the coolie buried and once more returned home disappointed.

Now the bravest men in the world, much less the ordinary Indian coolie, will not stand constant terrors of this sort indefinitely. The whole district was by this time thoroughly panic-stricken, and I was not at all surprised, therefore, to find on my return to camp that same afternoon (December 1) that the men had all struck work and were waiting to speak to me. When I sent for them, they flocked to my *boma* in a body and stated that they would not remain at Tsavo any longer for anything or anybody; they had come from India on an agreement to work for the Government, not to supply food for either lions or "devils." No sooner had they delivered this ultimatum than a regular stampede took place. Some hundreds of them stopped the first passing train by throwing themselves on the rails in front of the engine, and then, swarming on to the trucks and throwing in their possessions anyhow, they fled from the accursed spot.

After this the railway works were completely stopped; and for the next three weeks practically nothing was done but build "lion-proof" huts for those work-men who had had sufficient courage to remain. It was a strange and amusing sight to see these shelters perched on the top of water-tanks, roofs and girders—anywhere for safety—while some even went so far as to dig pits inside their tents, into which they descended at night, covering the top over with heavy logs of wood. Every good-sized tree in the camp had as many beds lashed on to it as its branches would bear—and sometimes more. I remember that one night when the camp was attacked, so many men swarmed on to one particular tree that down it came with a crash, hurling its terror-stricken load of shrieking coolies close to the very lions they were trying to avoid. Fortunately for them, a victim had already been secured, and the brutes were too busy devouring him to pay attention to anything else.

66

C. O. BURGE, *THE ADVENTURES OF A CIVIL ENGINEER: FIFTY YEARS ON FIVE CONTINENTS* (LONDON: ALSTON RIVERS, 1909), PP. 154–155

But the worst wild beasts with which I had to deal were human. In order to induce labourers to come into such a district, wages at high rates were offered, and even then the white men were, to a large extent, the most cut-throat-looking rascals that I ever had to deal with—ship deserters and others of all nations, Greeks, Italians, French, and English. Besides these, were imported Zulus, Kaffirs, Basutos, who were specially sent with their headmen from the eastern provinces and Zululand. Some of these had come across country under the leadership of a Captain R—, a rollicking Irishman who had gained their confidence, and spoke some of their languages fluently. He trusted them so much that he was unarmed on his long journey, only carrying a shillelagh or knobkerry, as it is locally named.

On arrival of his party at the town where the Karoo districts began they were met by the Minister for Native Affairs. He made them all sit round in a circle under a spreading tree, and made a speech to them in their native language, they every now and then giving grunts of satisfaction as he assured them of the fatherly care which they would receive. I shall not easily forget the scene, the two or three white men, and, squatting round, the hundreds of lightly-clothed savages eagerly listening and, through their chiefs, occasionally putting in a question. Camped on the works, the chiefs or headmen did nothing, but were necessary for keeping order among the tribes for which each was responsible, foremen having to be separately employed to direct the work. The Zulus were splendid men physically, and worked well. At each throw of the shovel they shouted in concert, "Cetewayo!" with a long stress on the penultimate syllable. He was then their king with whom we afterwards contended in the Zulu war.

67

CHARLOTTE MANSFIELD, *VIA RHODESIA: A JOURNEY THROUGH SOUTHERN AFRICA* (LONDON: S. PAUL, 1911), PP. 161–168

With a feeling of deep gratitude to H.H. the Administrator and Mrs. Wallace for their great kindness and hospitality, I left Livingstone and boarded the train bound for Kafue. Although the ham had disappeared in so cruel a manner, yet I went forth armed with a tea-basket filled with plenty of food for the journey. On the train was a Native Commissioner, whom I had previously met, and we decided to join food forces and picnic together; he had fish and I had fowl, and so the journey was enlivened with a veritable feast.

At Kalomo Station I saw a herd of tame elands standing with some cattle close to the railway; they looked quite happy, and were as tame as the cows. Kalomo was at one time the seat of the Administration for N.W. Rhodesia, but the site proved so unhealthy that the officials were transferred to Livingstone. The advocacy of Kalomo as a health resort is said to have been the only mistake ever made by the great explorer Livingstone. It proved to be quite the reverse, and it was at considerable cost that the change of the seat of the Administration was made.

The Native Commissioner who travelled by the same train was accompanied by a bitch and litter of pups, and when we arrived at his destination, I said I should quite miss the wee beauties, and he replied:

"If I thought you wouldn't throw him away, I would give you one."

"But I should love one," I cried, as the train was moving, and the result was that a little black pup was thrust back hurriedly through the carriage window. After that the little mongrel was my constant companion. I named him "Ugly."

Rarely have I seen a more beautiful sight than the floods around Kafue. The river had overflowed its banks to such an extent, that for considerably over a mile the land had become transformed into a beautiful lake, a huge surface of water covered with water-lilies. These flowers, of exceptionally large growth, were of the most delicate shades of pale mauve and white; their long stems, like tubes of india-rubber, could be seen deep down in the clear water.

Kafue Station was quite unapproachable. The stationmaster, armed with the mail bag, bravely set forth on a raft to deposit the letters on the coach, which, meanwhile, had been detached from the engine. I stood on the front platform, and was keenly interested in watching the arrangements for dragging the coach through the water to the bridge, on which another engine was waiting.

A very stout rope was fastened to the coach, and a hundred natives, like athletes in a tug-of-war, seized the rope, and with much shouting pulled with all their might. The funniest sight was the head-boy cracking a long whip and beating, not the boys but the water, as with wild gesticulations he urged them on. It took over an hour to drag the coach through the mile and a quarter of water-lilies.

In front of us the bridge, a structure of thirteen spans, and each span a hundred feet, but around on either side water glistening in the glory of the African sun, above the blue of the sky, a canopy of azure edged with flametinged clouds, away in the far distance green trees and verdant land, and, flying across the space between a radiant heaven and a beautiful earth, large birds with white and grey plumage—it was a sight to dwell for ever in one's memory.

On the bridge the waiting engine was attached, and also the white coach of the doctor, who twice a week journeyed down from Broken Hill. I was kindly invited by the doctor to join him and another man for dinner, and later, in dense darkness, we arrived at Broken Hill.

That night I made my first acquaintance with a hut, for a very comfortable one was given to me to sleep in. This hut, I learn, is hereafter to be called Mansfield Lodge in honour of my visit.

I remained three days in Broken Hill, and during that time received much consideration from all the officials. And what a jolly party they were! I used to take my meals at their united mess, and one day they proclaimed a half-day's holiday so that I might tell all their fortunes. What a picture they made, seated round the table, so eagerly watching the cards!

The tall, handsome sergeant was called Maude because his name was Allen, and another man was called Lottie, his surname being Collins; in fact, all had nicknames, but unfortunately I have forgotten them. One man played the piano quite well and sang many songs. The Magistrate was the best banjo player I have heard off the professional platform, and the cheery Government Agent, well, he is universally known as a man who is only unhappy when he is not helping someone. He even tried to find me some reliable doves! but it was not to be.

Doves seem to be the musical sparrows of Africa. How plentiful they are, how tame, but yet how elusive if one is on shooting bent! The cooing of the doves is a sound as much associated with Africa as the humming of the veld beetle, the singing of the crickets, and the croaking of the frogs.

Wherever there are trees, there are doves, graceful birds of soft, pale grey plumage; their voices are sweet and low yet very distinct as they coo to each other at sundown, that sweet, brief period between flaming day and starlit night. When out in the wilds one wishes to find water; the doves will lead you there, for thither they fly every evening. There are doves everywhere, near the towns, in the gardens, and again hundreds of miles away from the railway—truly the doves are one's most constant companions, and yet how wild they are!

Armed with a gun, and dreaming of a possible pie, you follow the cooing of a dove. Now it is on the right, you are quite certain, and turn in that direction; then, as though playing a game of touch-about, "coo coo" sounds far away on your left; then you fancy, in fact you are sure, that you see two fly to a tree in front of you, you throw up a stick to dislodge them, for it isn't good sport to shoot a bird on a bough; "coo coo" sound the gentle mocking voices behind you, and you decide that shooting doves may be good exercise for your legs, but you need not overburden yourself with cartridges!

Quite a number of people, I find, are under the erroneous impression that the recently opened railway into Congo territory, of which Broken Hill is the terminus, is another link in the original route of Rhodes's scheme of a Cape to Cairo railway, and that the Tanganyika Concessions Mines are situated near Lake Tanganyika; they are even further distant than is the Victoria Falls Power Company in Johannesburg from the Victoria Falls—with which it has no connection whatsoever save that it has usurped the name.

The rails, when they leave Broken Hill, branch off to the north-west instead of to the north-east, and lead no nearer Cairo from the Rhodesia end than before. This new railway is certainly of benefit to Rhodesia, because it brings more traffic through, but what would really put N.W. and N.E. Rhodesia on the same commercial footing with Southern Rhodesia would be a railway from Broken Hill to Tanganyika, or as near the lake as sleeping-sickness regulations permit, taking the route past Serenje, Mpika, Kasama, and Abercorn. The last-named place must not be confounded with the Abercorn in the Salisbury district of Southern Rhodesia, which has recently acquired notoriety on account of newly discovered gold finds. Abercorn, in N.E. Rhodesia, is within a few miles and within sight of Lake Tanganyika.

Doubtless one day the railway will embrace these 540 miles, and then, indeed, will the country prove a rich harvesting ground for farmers; the land is so cheap now that it should prove a good investment for those who can afford to wait.

At Broken Hill there is a very interesting bone cave, discovered only within the last two years; it contains remains of animals which are supposed to have existed before the Stone Age.

Excavations are being made, and developments are watched with interest, by Dr. McKnight, who is very enthusiastic about the subject and quite an authority on the relics, a number of which he has examined. So far no human remains have been discovered, but many bones of animals now extinct have been unearthed. The cave probably became at some time hermetically sealed, and the teeth and bones have been preserved by the proximity of zinc, this same zinc which is the despair of the shareholders of the Broken Hill lead mine, for so far it has been impossible to separate the two minerals, and the lead is therefore impure and cannot be smelted. Experiments are still being made, and hopes are entertained that a successful process may yet be discovered. A fortune awaits the man who finds it, because at present these mines are worthless.

68

JOHN R. RAPHAEL, *THROUGH UNKNOWN NIGERIA* (LONDON: T. W. LAURIE, 1914), PP. 43–53, 130–138

Zungeru to Kano

"THE line is the thing," to modify Hamlet's phrase. To get the track into working order at the earliest possible day, that is the object of all concerned in the construction of a railway, once it has been started. You must have rails laid, locomotives, carriages. All subsidiary matters can be improvised provisionally. It is not necessary to wait until "the last button on the soldiers' leggings" has been fixed. Thus, on the section from Zungeru to Kano a number of things remain to be done before there is the completeness which is seen south of the Niger.

To anybody with whom time is a consideration, a railway, instead of the old method along the cart-road of 282 miles to Kano, is an unspeakable boon.

Some novel travelling features appear on Zungeru Station. There has not been sufficient time to enrol a full staff and therefore one must make one's own arrangements for getting heavy packages into or from the train. First-class passengers can enjoy the unusual experience of obtaining from the Stationmaster partly printed labels, writing on them the destination, then hunting for a glue-pot and themselves affixing the labels. It is a case of every man his own porter. We are not at a fashionable resort, and all who have to do the job undertake it in a laughing spirit.

Directly the train moves off you realise you are on your own resources. Private, or even official, hospitality cannot extend to a train where everybody is expected to look after himself in all things for nearly half a week. A 50-foot coach is partitioned into four divisions, all quite bare. In a division—you may be fortunate in having two—you must rig up your little home: a sitting and dining-room by day; a sleeping apartment at night. Each end of the coach has a stove, where the cooks can prepare meals.

Minna—38 miles—is reached in two hours, and here the night is spent. In the hot weather passengers put their camp-beds on the open platform, arranging them under the projecting roof if rain threatens.

Arrival of the train at Minna marks a busy time, for the line upwards from Baro joining, passengers who have come by the river route are waiting to continue the journey northwards, or others may have come down from that direction.

Amidst all the bustle of people coming and going, of the excitement of sorting baggage for carriers, of piles of bales and boxes being moved, of loud whistling of locomotives and of shunting engines, I saw a white-robed figure go on his knees, turn his face to the east and bend his head in devotion. It was a Mohamedan silently offering up evening prayer. Religious duty was louder to him than the babel resounding around. He was not ashamed to speak with his Maker in sight of the multitude.

Yet there are worthy folks at home who seek to send missionaries to these people to teach them to worship the same God but in a different way. Why is the money and the energy expended on such missions—which are practically hopeless in Mohamedan countries like this—not deflected to the better purpose of mitigating the vice, the crime and the preventible poverty in the great cities of the United Kingdom, where the triple evils stalk abroad in the daylight, unabashed, unashamed.

At Minna Station one must see Mr A. Newport, the stalwart traffic inspector. I say one "must," because the first time travelling over the line there are enquiries which have to be satisfied. For instance, change of train is made for the journey continued early next morning. Further, it may not have occurred to a traveller, even thinking out all requirements to the most minute detail, that wood for a fire on the train to cook food would be necessary. Finally, one's filter may not be within easy access and condensed water be needed for preparing the evening meal.

In all these, and perhaps other instances, Mr Newport is of incalculable aid and value. Whatever the multitude of matters pressing upon him for immediate attention, he always seems willing to accept one more without impatience or irritation. But if everybody going through Minna leaves all these things to be supplied by Mr Newport, it is likely that he will not have a sufficiency of them to satisfy everybody's expectations. Maxim and moral: When travelling in Nigeria never depend on supplying from another's provisions that which you have wilfully neglected to provide for yourself.

At Minna Station one may also meet Mr E. H. Biffen, Traffic Superintendent of the Baro-Kano Railway, uniformly genial and courteous, and ever ready to do all in his power to help a traveller; and on the platform there will probably be Mr J. Oldfield, Traffic Assistant, who seconds the manner of his chief.

On waking up at Minna Station one realises more fully than on the previous afternoon what it is to be on one's own resources for bodily needs. Sufficient condensed water had been economised for breakfast, but, in a tropical country above all, some kind of wash, at least once a day is almost as necessary for comfort as food, and for preference the operation is performed on getting out of bed.

Just at 6 o'clock, as I was wondering, after an hour's cogitation, what was to be done in a distinctly uncomfortable predicament, mental relief came. Looking out of the window I saw my native servant—for the time being maid-of-all work, cook, steward, and general factotum—Oje, trudging along towards the stationary train with a pail on his head, and by the manner of balancing the utensil it was clear that it contained water. Without being told, Oje had set out and discovered water.

How did he come to divine its presence in a place where he had not previously been and of which he had never heard? I asked him. He said he saw a footpath from the railway and sagely concluded it must lead somewhere. That somewhere, he deduced, was likely to be a native village. A village was sure to be near a stream or other water. He would go and investigate.

I do not mean that Oje argued all these points in their logical sequence, after the manner of a Sherlock Holmes; instinct told him at once.

The water had come from a shallow, stagnant, well-nigh dried-up water course. It looked yellow, and on being shaken took the consistency of thick soup. Still, it was water, and for that relief much thanks.

Oje—poor, friendless Oje, hundreds of miles from home and parents—had more prescience than his master—employer is a word I would sooner use—more prescience than any white man on the train. A chapter could easily be written of Oje. He deserves it, is worthy of it. He is always helpful, frequently a pleasant companion to speak with, and occasionally a comfort to talk to in the silent evenings when flying insects make writing impossible, in spite of his limited vocabulary of even pidgeon English. His devotion is staunch and unmistakable. I shall remember Oje with many kindly sentiments when thousands of miles of sea and land separate us, and when, perhaps, I am tramping through the lands of another continent.

The prospect of an unwashed state happily past, as the train spins along one can heartily enjoy the free-and-easy existence, as one sits on a camp chair and, facing the open door of the "saloon," tries to catch the breeze stimulated by the running train. It seems more enjoyable than the luxury of the boat express. Your pail containing water may leak; no matter, you *must* effect a repair on the spot, and that is done by drawing a rag into the hole. You discover that you have no bread for breakfast and that none was to be bought at Minna Station; no matter, a tin of biscuits from your food boxes will serve instead. You find out that the firm who made up the food boxes have omitted the sugar; no matter, some other passenger will help you out. Whatever your petty troubles, they are lost sight of in the feeling that you are in your own little compartment, within its walls living in your own way, distant from the stilted and artificial manners which clog life at home.

The celerity with which the Baro-Kano Railway was constructed—its junction with the Lagos Railway is at Minna—and the instant and remarkable success it has proved have caused an "overrunning of the constable" in the provision of rolling stock. You may notice that the first-class coaches are patched up in parts. As a matter of fact, I believe that a number were to have been broken up, having been discarded by home lines, but the call for accommodation was so pressing that as many as could be made serviceable were again put on the rails. So you see the result of two or three worn-out carriages being made into a single sound one; sides and floor, with some doors from other carriages screwed on to form a complete article.

The demand on the part of third-class passengers—of course, all natives—was much greater. It was not merely a case of the construction of the finished track outstripping the supply of carriages; the number of passengers carried had exceeded the utmost expectations. It was estimated that the total receipts for the last financial year, 1911–12, April to March, would amount to £10,000, but they totalled £46,000. It is clear that on this line, as in the case of most in the United Kingdom, the third-class passenger is to be the stand-by of income for human freight. Apart from the fact that there are few Europeans in the country—I should say less than 700 to a native population of 10,000,000—averaging the 255 miles between Minna and Kano, the respective proportions are: first-class, seven Europeans; second-class, two or three Europeans; third class, 150 natives.

The supply of ordinary third-class coaches was utterly insufficient. Every type of truck has had to be used in addition, or the passengers left. All canvas sheetings obtainable for roof coverings did not suffice, and as native travellers clamoured to be carried in any way so long as only they were carried, low side trucks were put on, and then high ones, containing coalite and other goods in transit on which the passengers wished to sit.

It should be borne in mind that these people have always been in the habit of moving from one place to another—these Hausa traders—and they quickly grasped the advantage and the comfort of riding in trains at a low charge instead of tramping along bush paths or caravan roads. By means of using the railway they could do as much business in one day, with less marching, as they formerly did in a month.

And how these people enjoy the train ride! No party of school-children on their one-day-a-year excursion more so. See them crowded as the proverbial sardines, laughing, joking, happy, with legs dangling over the sides of the goods trucks. When Lugard projected, Girouard put in hand, and Eaglesome carried out the railway from Baro to Kano they builded better than they knew.

The track between Zungeru to Minna takes a gentle rise; the latter is 500 feet higher than the former. The country traversed is wooded and fertile, but depopulated, the effect of the cruel slave-raiding descents from the north, which devastated districts, leaving, as evidence of the visitation, burnt-down villages, the inhabitants all either dragged off to slavery or put to the sword on the spot. The land sunk into disuse and desolation.

British power has stopped it for ever, at least, as long as British power is supreme. But decades must pass before tillers are again on the soil. When they are the wide acres of Northern Nigeria will give agricultural produce on a scale that will bring great prosperity to the Protectorate and render it of value to territories beyond its borders, exporting perhaps foodstuffs, and certainly those essential oils for which manufacturers in Europe are searching the tropics.

Immediately after leaving Minna, in the first six miles the rise is 300 feet. The track then becomes fairly level, frequently crossing tributaries of the Kaduna River, the largest of which is the Kogin Serekin Pawa. From this the line follows the valley of the Kugo River, climbing 30 miles to the Zaria Plateau, which is

436

touched at Bakin Kasua, 70 miles south of Zaria City and 19 before reaching the Kaduna. Then a drop of approximately 400 feet to Kaduna Station.

Over certain parts of the track, where temporary work has quite recently been superseded by that of a lasting character which has not yet hardened and settled, the train proceeds very gingerly, for it is heavily laden and must needs be hauled with caution and knowledge.

Most of the stations consist of a bank of gravel, levelled as a platform would be, with a 10 feet by 12 feet corrugated iron box, which holds telegraph instruments—the eyes and ears for safe conduct of the line—and is also the Stationmaster's office. Two or three huts near by are the domiciles of the staff, comprising a telegraphist, a pointsman, and a labourer, all natives. A pointsman is necessary, as, although the line is a single track, every station has a loop for trains passing each other. At stations of a very minor type the Stationmaster is also telegraphist.

At intervals the engine halts for sustenance. A tank is set up, sometimes quite in bush country but always near streams which are never completely dried up, and water forced into the tank by a hand-pump worked by "boys," who live in huts near by. The railway engineers have made small dams across the streams as safeguards for supply.

Every three or four miles are gangs of eight to ten "boys," who live in a small settlement of their own, and, under a headman, pay attention to the track, supervised by a European platelayer, who has charge of 25 to 30 miles of line.

There is unmistakable evidence of approaching Kaduna. The line broadens out to four tracks and there are other adjuncts of a locomotive depôt. Kaduna has also the importance of being the headquarters of the Director of Railways. In the absence on vacation of Mr Eaglesome, I spent the evening—the train stays overnight—with the Deputy Director, youthful Mr E. M. Bland, referred to in the Zungeru chapter.

Among the entertainments in the way of sightseeing and instruction which he gave me was a walk across the adjacent Kaduna River railway bridge. I was lured on unsuspectingly and, I am sure, innocently on the part of Mr Bland. He never guessed—nor will he know until he sees these lines in print—of the ordeal it was to the visitor. The Kaduna Bridge is 660 feet long. The rails are fixed to sleepers the spaces between which are open to the river below.

In the middle of the track is a narrow sheeting of iron and along this Blondin-like tight-rope strode the Deputy Director, I tremulously following. Had I half an idea that he intended going beyond the first few inches I would either have invented some excuse for turning back or have boldly asked to be excused on the score of a sudden headache or something of the kind. I certainly expected every minute that this exasperatingly cruel guide would stop. When we reached midway across I wondered why on earth he was continuing the walk. Only that I did not trust myself to turn round on the narrow pathway I would have returned forthwith.

Mr Bland never ceased to speak of points of interest left and right, throwing a directing finger first in one direction and then in another, I more or less mechanically answering in monosyllables, the slippery, heavy nails in my boots striking the narrow metal pathway ominously, and, scarcely lifting my eyes from it all the time, I thought of people I knew in England, conjuring up what they would say to my having come to my end by falling through into the waters beneath Kaduna Bridge, instead of going under by the more heroic malarial fever.

Once Mr Bland, indicating a notable landmark, turned round to make the matter clearer, and on my quickly replying with a "Yes," as though I saw and understood everything—earnestly praying he would get over the bridge at the earliest possible moment—he remarked that I was looking the wrong way and that the object to which he referred was half-a-mile off the opposite side of the bridge.

At last we were across, and I glanced around to discover a boat by which we could row or paddle back. Before I could gain breath to utter a word out spake Mr Bland. He said how sorry he was that he could not indulge in canoeing, as he did at home—he is a Canadian—as there was no craft of any kind for miles.

Then we must go back over that few-inches-wide iron path! Why were engineers so madly stupid as to place such an ordeal under the uncertain feet of an enquiring journalist? However, there was no alternative. A repeated 660 feet of mental tribulation and we were safe on the other bank.

Immediately I developed a wonderful power of conversation and comment on all the Deputy Director had told me during those horrible perambulations from bank to bank. In my exuberance of spirits I felt I wanted to slap him on the back. Oh, yes, I now saw quite distinctly and with eagerness the concrete piers on which the temporary bridge was laid for construction purposes, and a little higher up the river I recognised, visually, the ford used in the old days of the caravan road from the north.

The Bauchi Light Railway

GOING down the railway from Kano the traveller opens his eyes widely at Zaria Station. At Kano there is no platform and no station. Time had not been sufficient to build either. Passengers climb into the train from the rails. For 90 miles southwards—to Zaria—the same conditions exist, with this difference, that there are not so many people to see the engine and carriages and their human freight as at the terminus. At Kano a small corrugated iron shed for the telegraph instruments, a mud house for the office, and a board indicating the place are all that mark the spot. You thoroughly realise you are in a country only recently opened.

But, arriving at Zaria, instead of a single track there are seven wide gauge—3 feet 6 inches—four narrow gauge—2 feet 6 inches—tracks and commodious engine sheds, a large building being put up to warehouse the increasing quantities of tin which the Government expects from the tin fields.

White railway officials hurry hither and thither with an air of bustle, hustle and business, and, most striking of all at first sight, a station with an upper story for the administration staff. As you look nearer you notice that the roof is merely of iron and that the ornamented woodwork appears somewhat crude in its first coating of green paint. But, coming from where there are none of these adjuncts, the general appearance of Zaria Station is imposing, and, although tiny by comparison, the thought occurs of Euston, Paddington or Waterloo. Men coming upwards from the Coast may not be impressed by these things, for they have recently been where larger dimensions rule.

Bound for Bauchi, at Zaria Station the traveller takes the first turning to the right, literally so, as he walks from one side to the other of the island platform for the continuation of his journey. But the continued progress is not quite so promptly accomplished as may be imagined from this description.

The boat train from Lagos, which should leave on the previous Friday evening, is due at Zaria 11 a.m. on Tuesdays. The traveller must wait till next morning, as it is not possible to transfer luggage, etc., from the boat train to the one going to the foot of the Bauchi Plateau in time to reach that destination the same day, and, as the Bauchi line is fresh and unballasted, the service cannot safely be carried on during darkness. The night is therefore spent in a rest-house, for which a charge of 2s. is made. Next morning at 7 a.m., the train starts from Zaria Station for Rahama, turning eastwards and forming an angle to the main line.

I will not work myself into a state of uncontrollable excitement and frenzy over the Bauchi Light Railway having been laid down a narrower gauge than the line of which it is a branch, nor will I belch forth fire and fury, in the shape of epithets of stupidity and ignorance, against whoever decided on the gauge. I will content myself with saying that it would have been better to have had the uniform gauge and thus avoid the delay and expense of breaking bulk on transfer. The line was laid down at a time of emergency and was largely an experiment, for then the exact direction of the main tin deposits had not been determined. The prime object was to have rail transport for the tin as quickly as possible and for as long a distance as the £200,000 given by the Home Government would cover.

There is no need to weep and wail and tear one's hair about the thing, for it is merely temporary. Embankment and bridges have been built to take the wider gauge and the rolling stock is easily convertible to use on that measurement.

You in England, as many do here, may laugh at this little line, which needs a day to traverse 88¼ miles, sometimes not doing it in that period. You may call it ironically, as people do here, the Bauchi Express or the Bauchi Flyer, but I must admit I was never so thrilled at any mechanical means of traction, never so impressed by any trial trip of a gigantic ocean liner, never so moved by participating in the initial run of a train at home embodying some new feature intended to make the public admire, I was never so thrilled by any one of such many departures in which I have taken part as I was when the train started round the iron curve from Zaria for Rahama.

One must indeed possess a dulled imagination not to have one's feelings stirred by contemplation of this line running through quite new country where it seems but yesterday a white man had scarcely trod. Who can go over this line and omit to think of John Eaglesome and his staff for having given them in the course of a few months means of transportation on a course where everybody is feverishly eager to get to his destination at the earliest possible moment, for nowhere more than in mineral prospecting is time, every minute of it, money.

You may rate me too ecstatic. But trek 90 miles along unmade paths in the extreme hot season or in the excessively wet season. Then say what you would give for a railway lift from starting-point to finish.

The first 14½ miles of rails are second-hand. They are taken from the old tram-way which ran from Barijuko, on the Kaduna River, to Zungeru previous to the advent of the Lagos Railway. The remaining 5½ miles of rails of the tramway are being used for the trollies which take the refuse from Zungeru every morning. The old tramway station is re-erected as the central market shed in Zungeru native village. That is the way they administer in Northern Nigeria. Nothing is wasted. Lugard had left when that was done, but his spirit and methods remained. Complaints are heard in England of extravagance and wastefulness by public departments. I wonder whether the appointment of Sir Frederick Lugard to control the spending departments in London would effect a remedy.

Passengers on the Bauchi Light Railway have a plain van with a sliding door the height of the coach. A van serves for two men, who must bring chairs and, in case of the train being detained overnight en route, beds, and also make their own arrangements for cooking. The demand for accommodation frequently exceeds the supply; and that men be not delayed, the traffic staff provides a similar van but one usually used for goods. Such a van will not have the cooling, protecting matchboard under the iron roof, and persons using a van of that kind should therefore remember that a helmet, or at least some headcovering, is a wise provision against sun troubles.

Vans have a small compartment at each end for native servants, but there are no stoves. Should, however, there be a delay during the journey, passengers' cooks get out and kindle a fire on or near the track. That is the chance for a hot meal. There are seven stations: Awai, Soba, Duchi-n-Wai (for the Berrida and neighbouring tin mines), Karre, Kudara (for the Wassaku Concessions), Worroko and Rahama.

The first 10 miles passed are open, flat country, having slight bush, with sections here and there under cultivation for guinea corn. Near Awai, 17 miles from Zaria, can be seen the remains of a walled town. The wall, now quite thin, has been worn away by the weather to a few feet in height, broken and irregular at top, and within it thick trees of many years' growth and wild grass demonstrate that where thousands of souls lived and where their children might be dwelling today has been destroyed utterly, the dead fruit of fierce tribal warfare. A few straw, circular huts belong to recent comers who are tilling bits of the desolate city.

At 10 o'clock, whilst at Soba Station, word came that the heavy rain of the night had caused a washout of the line some miles ahead. Questions were asked whether we should have to tramp the remaining distance to Rahama. "Oh, no; it would only mean a stay of about four hours."

Now, you folks at home, delayed at a tiny village station would probably exhaust the interest of the place in a few minutes and relieve the tedium of waiting by gloomy maledictions or settle down to fitful and impatient reading. Not so out here. We are all philosophers at such trifles. We know that a day's set programme may at any moment be completely upset by the elements. One of the passengers, Mr D. Bannerman, of the Northern Nigeria (Bauchi) Tin Mines, complacently unlocked his gun case, shouldered a rifle and, accompanied by a little party, sallied forth in the bush to look for sport and perchance bring something fresh back for the dinner pot, arranging with the engine-driver that a long loud whistle should notify that telegraphic word had come that that washout was near being remedied. Mr Bannerman was back well before a start was made, at 2.45.

Thiry-five miles from Zaria the Duchi-n-Wai hills loom in front, only the tips of them, above the dark green of trees, now much closer, which on both sides have closed in the view to a mile or so. They soon give way left and right to fields less freely timbered, with an occasional acre bearing guinea corn.

It had been clear when we left Soba that the journey could not be completed that day, so on reaching Duchi-n-Wai, at 4.15, a stop was made for the night. Cooks cut wood for fires from trees near and commenced preparations for dinner.

With two camp-beds up and mosquito curtains there is not much room for other furniture in a van. Folding chairs and tables are therefore brought and put on the rails, and along the side of the train they are ranged, each with its hurricane lamp amidst plates and dishes.

The native servants make their fires the other side of the train, sit round them and join together in song, sleeping on the ground, in the open, which they prefer to inside the carriages.

Six o'clock next morning another start was made. At Bibin, between the 60 and 61 miles' boards, high, rocky hills are within a few hundred yards of the line. As the engine stops for water and you glance backwards, it looks as though the train had entered a very narrow opening. In front is a similar view. Going out of this gorge there is again grassy plains studded with trees.

We had left Kudara Station, 66 miles from Zaria, and were thinking of an easy, plain spin for the rest of the journey, when occurred a sudden severe jolting, the more pronounced as the sleepers are of metal and not covered by gravel: we were derailed. There was just a semblance of panic among some of the passengers and one rather excitedly jumped from the train. We had been going round a curve and doing it slowly, at 6 miles an hour, so there was not much danger of being upset. The train was quickly stopped. The driver gave the double whistle which is a distress signal and tells all who know railway language that there is a mishap.

It happened that near by was the hut of Mr Robert Brown, Bridging Foreman, who had gone in to read a letter from his wife, in England, which the train had dropped a few minutes earlier. Running out and seeing what had occurred he had a trolly put on the line and sent word to the temporary workshed at Kudara Station for hydraulic jacks and other implements. The double whistle had also brought hurrying to the spot Richard Brown, driver of a ballast train a quarter-of-a-mile away. Never have I seen men work with more energy than these two and the driver of the train, J. Swainson, did on that tropically hot morning. Swainson had ordinary jacks on the engine, and a start was made with them. Of the seven coaches, three had been derailed, each 26 feet long and weighing about 8 tons.

Everyone who has duties keeping him in this country speaks some Hausa. It is especially necessary for persons who are in constant direction of natives. A large gang at work on construction—for the line is not nearly finished, and is only open unofficially for the convenience and assistance of transport to and from the tin fields—had been summoned and Robert Brown disclosed his linguistic acquirement as his men ran to and fro at his orders.

But there are some words for which the Hausa tongue has no equivalent, and these words have become incorporated in their pristine freshness into local vocabularies. Thus, it sounded amusing to hear, "Kow jack; Muzza muzza." ("Bring the jack, quickly, quickly.") Sharply also were called the orders to "Kow crowbar," "Kow slewing bar" and "Kow" half-a-dozen other things given their English names.

By the exertions of the two Browns and Swainson (who had all along been obliging in every way he could to the passengers) the three derailed coaches were lifted back on the rails, and in an hour-and-a-half from the time of the accident the train was again running. As it moved off we gave a hearty cheer for the Browns and for Swainson.

No further incidents marked the trip.

Part 10

AUSTRALIANA AND ABORIGINES

Possession and dispossession

69

SAMUEL CALVERT, ENGRAVING, 'SKIPTON JACKY JACKY AND HIS TRIBE AT THE OPENING OF THE BEAUFORT RAILWAY', SEPTEMBER 7, 1874

Figure 69.1 Samuel Calvert, Engraving

EASTERN EXCURSIONISTS. THE EARLY MORNING TRAIN AT SPENCER STREET STATION (MELBOURNE, VICTORIA), MAY 4, 1881

Figure 70.1 Eastern Excursionists

JAMES HINGSTON, *THE AUSTRALIAN ABROAD ON BRANCHES FROM THE MAIN ROUTES ROUND THE WORLD* (MELBOURNE: W. INGLIS, 1885), PP. VIII–IX, 151–153

"J. H." on "travel

[Argus, 10th February, 1885.]

AT the MAYOR'S LUNCHEON to MR. J. A. FROUDE, the historian, and to LORD ELPHIN-STONE, at the TOWN HALL, MELBOURNE, on 9th February, MR. HINGSTON being called upon to reply (with LORD ELPHINSTONE) to the Toast of "TRAVEL," spoke as follows:—

"Travellers in times past have had a very bad character. (Laughter.) They have, unhappily, been stigmatised as the tellers of lies—'travellers' tales,' as they are called in proverbial language. (Laughter.) It originates, I believe, from the book of Job, which is generally believed to be the oldest book in the world. Therein we have prominent mention of one who has been misconceived as the prototype of all travellers. When asked on his appearance among a number of good men what he had been doing, Satan answered, 'Going to and fro upon the earth, and walking up and down therein.' (Laughter.) This plain, straightforward reply contains the condensed essence of all that has been said by all travellers up to the present time. (Hear, hear.) For that reason the world has mixed up all travellers with this first one. (Laughter.) Most of those who migrated to Australia were satisfied they had had enough of travel in coming hither. (Laughter.) Four months of a sea voyage is a very satisfactory time of it. Those who have experienced it understand to the full the 'sea sorrow' mentioned by Shakspeare in 'The Tempest.' (Laughter.) They have mostly only two desires towards the end of the voyage—the first is to get ashore and stay there—(laughter)—and the second is to punch the head of the man who wrote the joyful song of 'A Life on the Ocean Wave.' (Laughter.) The author of 'Home, Sweet Home,' is known never to have had a home—(laughter)—and it is my belief that the writer of 'A Life on the Ocean Wave' was never at sea at all. (Laughter.) Australians have really nothing whatever to travel for. (Hear, hear.) They can, in their mind's eye, see all the world in the accounts of it supplied to them through the press by those who follow the footsteps of Job's traveller in going about the earth, for, it is to be hoped, better reasons. They have no need to travel for change of climate—the climate changes often enough here. (Laughter.) Of scenery Australasia supplies every sort, and all of the finest samples. (Hear, hear.) In the mountaineering way there is enough for the Alpine Club on the snow-covered peaks between Beechworth and Gipps Land, and anything further wanted in that line is to be found in Mount Cook and the vast glaciers of New Zealand—that grand land for the picturesque. (Applause.) For coast scenery there is no equal in the world to that of the West Coast Sounds, and for lakes it will be hard indeed if the grand ones of New Zealand do not satisfy. (Hear, hear.) For strange people there is no need to seek out of Australia. Its population comprises varieties of the human race from all parts, and good samples, too—the pick of the world's basket. (Laughter.) For fortune there is no occasion for the Australian to go further afield. If he can do anything he can do it to best purpose in Australasia, and if he can do nothing he is as well or better off here than anywhere. (Laughter.) Any man can make his fortune in Australia by the simple method of minding his own business. (Laughter.) The Australian not satisfied with the land he has settled in, would likely not be satisfied in any of Mahomet's seven heavens. He would be always wanting to explore the other six. (Laughter.) It is of Australia and such dissatisfied ones of its people that Monckton Milnes, the poet, had in mind when writing—

> 'A man's best things are nearest him—
>   Lie close about his feet;
>   But 'tis the distant and the dim
>   He ever strives to greet.'

(Hear, hear.) Such people are as inquiring in their way as Mrs. Hemans' famous child in its anxiety as to the whereabouts of the 'Better Land.' (Laughter.) Having no faith that they have already found it, they go hence, on some vamped-up excuse or other, really seeking if there be any better place than Australia. That they all come back here is answer enough to all such inquiries. (Hear, hear.) If these Australians go abroad by the Overland Route, they see, in Ceylon and India, Crown colonies which teach them the value of the free colonies of Australia. (Hear, hear.) They see their less fortunate kinsmen toiling and perspiring under a tropical sun for fortune, while those in Australia can make here both fortune and fame. In Ceylon and India there are no parliamentary honours to be got—no £300 a year to begin with, with £1500 a year to follow when a fellow gets into the Ministry. (Laughter.) Neither in those colonies, nor in all America, are any titles to be got, such as we get here when we attain to the Chief Secretaryship, and to the Chairmanship of either House of Parliament. All the titles to be got in America are insignificant beside knighthood. Who cares to be called, as almost everybody is in the States, general, colonel, or 'old hoss?' (Laughter.) The returned traveller from Australia comes back to it a wiser and a gladder man. (Hear, hear.) He sees how imperfect his education has been, how little he knows, and how much he has to unlearn of the nonsense stuffed into him in early days. (Laughter.) He has seen that his beliefs, prejudices, and prepossessions have been all matters of education, and that had he been left a baby in India he might have been brought up as a good Thug, or if left on the Cannibal Islands have done as cannibals do. (Laughter.) He has had the self-conceit knocked out of him, and has gained, instead, that self-respect, which teaches him to respect others and those distinctions of character which he had before thought to be but heresies, faults, and failings. (Hear, hear.) He has been a rolling stone in his travels, and finds that it is not moss but polish that gives a stone any value. (Hear, hear.) He has had his sharp corners rubbed off, and is himself rubbed up and brightened mentally and intellectually. (Hear, hear.) I have said that there is work in Australia for everybody who can do anything, but I do not wish to falsely raise the hopes of our distinguished visitor and guest. (Laughter.) Australia is the happy place, and Australians the happy people that, alike, have no history. ('Hear, hear,' and applause.) Although there is no work here for the historian, there is plenty for one who can write 'Short essays upon great subjects.' ('Hear, hear,' and laughter.) Australia is a great subject, and the shortest thing to be said about it is that those who come to it know well indeed the advantages of such travelling as they have already done, if they never travel further." (Laughter and applause.)

"Oh, yes; look at Bradshaw—there is one in the office, I daresay.

And to Bradshaw we referred, and that was confirmatory of our idea, which was that we could start from Sydney at nine in the morning, get to Bowenfells, and see the wounderful descending terraces of zigzags there; get something to eat there, and drink toasts in honour of Christmas Day and all friends far away, and then return at night by the train—set down in Bradshaw as starting at twelve— and sleep all the way back to Sydney. The excursion was desirable on several grounds. The Zigzag Railway, beginning its ascent of the Blue Mountains at Lapstone Hill, was an engineering wonder. Nothing can be shown to equal it in Europe, nor on the huge railway across the American continent, though two ranges of mountains have to be passed in its course. That was one reason; another was, that the air of the Blue Mountains was a good change from that of Sydney, and the scenery, the finest that the eye could delight in; and, further still, there was the greater reason of the journey affording something to do on a day when it is most miserable to be shut up in a city where one knew nobody, and to think that every one was enjoying the Christmas festival of friendship save and except one's own isolated self.

Fine and fair broke the morning, and punctually we all met at the railway-station. To save any after remorse, extra care was taken by us to enquire as to the return train from Bowenfells at twelve that night. Bradshaw might be wrong. He had not erred, we were told, and no further care remained. A very pleasant feeling that!

The carriages were large and the seats broad, well adapted for sleeping, we said, on our night journey back. The windows, too, were of the right height and size for our having a long look around at all which was to come in our way. It came very soon, too, for we were quickly whisked up to the foot of the ascent, and our train began to go up stairs. We will pause for a moment—though our train did not—just to breathe. The Blue Mountains of New South Wales stretch away from within a short distance of Sydney to the neighbourhood of Bathurst, a good day's journey right through. The trouble to reach the far-away summit, up the steep side, is only the beginning of trouble. When the top of one mountain is gained, the tops of all the others have to be crossed; for it is a huge jumble of mountains that has to be traversed, with dark wooded and rocky valleys every-where between and around. Through the whole long length of that line there is scarcely a straight hundred yards of road. It is zigzag up the side, zigzag on the top, and zigzag to the bottom, when the ride is over. When it is over, it is not a ride that will be forgotton.

We remember ascending a staircase in a square tower in a Belgian town, up which we went some twenty-five steps forward to a landing, and then faced about to go twenty-five more steps to another landing, and then right about again, and so on to the top. That is the way that the Zigzag is ascended on Lapstone Hill, with this little difference, that in ascending the tower staircase, we faced about at each turn, which the train does not. The engine pulls up for half a mile or so, and then pushes for another half mile, and then another pull, and a repeated push, and so lugged and pushed, the level earth is left quickly far away beneath us. All heads are out of the windows now, looking over at the staircase-like road down away below us, and up which we were dragging a few minutes past. The feeling is decidedly new and sensational. The landscape, too, lights up, as it were, differently as each further ascent is made, and larger views around obtained. The head gets giddy at some stages of the journey, where but a little projection of earth or stone seems to be between the roadside and all that lies so very far away down there. We think that if our iron horse were but to bolt, or to become restive and upset the coach, how little talk about it we should be likely to have after the accident. It is seen, however, that the engine is of the strongest and largest the gauge of the line of the broadest, and, though but a single line of rails, we see plainly that the traffic on this wonderful line is not such as to lead to any fear of other trains running into us before or behind. The idea that there is but one train a day—and that probably the same engine takes it back again—allays all nervousness on that score. The Blue Mountains line was not constructed, we believe, with any idea of its being a paying concern. The country it "opens up" must be a long way ahead, for the mountain tops we have now reached, and the dark valleys all around us can be only dwelling-places for opossums, wild cats, and eagle-hawks, now and for ever. The tops of the mountains afford payment in scenery for all the trouble in getting thither. Our train now and henceforward takes to a serpentine movement, and that unceas-ingly. On looking out of the window—and all heads are outside—we see either the engine or the last carriage of the train about broadside on to us, always one or the other. In and out, and winding about everywhere, did the makers of this difficult road go to find their way. How they ever found it and made any road whatever is all the astonishment. Cuttings through here and there in short tunnels—cuttings down on this side and on that, and now and again on both sides—filling up of great gaps, and making winding viaducts over others—was of the work to be done everywhere. We never tire of looking out of the windows. The trouble is that we cannot look out on both sides at once.

The scenery varies at every turn, and the turn is every minute, and the views are of the finest on both sides—wild ravines of torn and upheaved rock, with no speck of vegetation or trace of life of any kind—darkly-wooded valleys of all depths and variety of characteristics, on which the sun and the driving fleecy clouds make picturesque effects of light and shade—are to be seen from one side or another in endless profusion. Little stations are reached every now and then and stopped at, apparently for form's sake. The idea of taking up passengers from the population hereabouts never enters the mind. We have got beyond passengers and taxes. A man might dwell here and never get into the census. In times gone by a monastery would have been perched upon one of the lonely peaks, or on the side of one of these inaccesible valleys, after some holy hermit had chosen such place for his peculiar life, and got sainted for so doing. It may happen so yet, for that which has been will be. An oasis comes at last, when One Tree Hill, or Mount Victoria, is reached. A most delightful spot is this, as it naturally would be, considering all the difficulty in getting to it. From here the Weatherboard Falls can be seen, which Von Guerard has so well painted. Here, also, is a huge valley, which has been bridged with evidently great labour and expense. On the one side of this bridge the view is into the wildest of rocky and craggy depths, and on the other into a long, cultivated valley of green fields and farms. It is as if this bridge parted the goats and their rocky residence upon the left hand from the sheep and their green pastures upon the right. There are two good hotels at One Tree, and a road that leads on to Hartley, distant some few miles, and connected with kerosene-produce, and coal. A week could be very well spent about here by those wishing for that time's breath of mountain air.

We got on by the rail after this towards Bowenfells, through similar scenery of mount and valley to that which we had seen all the morning. Towards three o'clock we came to the descending zigzag—the downstairs-going business—and to our journey's end. This descending zigzag far exceeds, in every novelty, the ascending one. It is a stupendously grand affair. Slopes and turnings, turnings and tunnels, viaducts and sweeping descents, each down many hundreds of feet, that go as near to danger as practicable, and no further. All heads are looking out and downwards during these descents, and when it is over and done, all heads are turned upwards, and so remain for some time with the fixed stare of astonishment. This point was as far as the rail then reached. At the Bowenfells station we said to the porter,—

"The train starts at twelve punctually, does it not!" We don't know why we should have said so, for we had made quite sure about that at the beginning of the journey.

"No," he said; "no train to-night, and none back to Sydney until twelve to-morrow night!"

Open-mouthed dismay was all the answer we could show. Porter did not know nor care what had been said at the other end; he was right. We were in for it at Bowenfells for the rest of that day—that night—the next day and the next night—until that long twelve o'clock came.

72

HUME NISBET, *A COLONIAL TRAMP: TRAVELS AND ADVENTURES IN AUSTRALIA AND NEW ZEALAND*, 2 VOLS. (LONDON: WARD & DOWNEY, 1891), PP. 166–172, 233–234, 274–276

I had an adventure, as I was leaving Sandhurst Station for Echuca, which impressed that particular station upon my memory. My train left at eight o'clock, but finding time heavy on my hands, I went into the station about half an hour before the time of starting. As I had found out that the train was there waiting empty, I thought I would take my seat, and compose myself for the journey.

I found a porter at the gateway of the platform as I entered, who planted himself in front of me, saying, roughly: 'You can't get in here yet, mate.'

'I am going to Echuca, and have my ticket all right, and I believe that is my train,' I observed, pointing to the waiting train, and trying to get past him as I did so.

But the Sandhurst railway-porter had a high sense of his responsibility, and a forcible way of proving it, for without more words than 'Get back!' he brought his heavy fist down on my breastbone with a thud.

This was too much for me, so I returned the compliment, landing him on the flat of his back; after which I sought out a suitable carriage, and was just depositing my traps, when he came rushing up to me in a terribly excited manner, followed by a couple of his porter friends.

'Haven't you had enough of it?' I asked, as he made a wild clutch at me.

'No, you——; and I mean to have more before I leave you,' he roared, putting himself into position No. 1.

'All right,' I replied; 'hold on a minute.'

I hadn't any coat to take off, and it took only a second to fling my felt hat alongside my sketching-bag and turn up my sleeves.

'Now then, old man,' I said when I was ready; and we both set to for a warm five minutes of the manly exercise. He was a plucky fellow, but he didn't quite understand left-handed practice, so that at the end of the five minutes he threw up the sponge and declared that his outraged dignity was appeased, and himself quite satisfied, after which we shook hands, and as victor I had to stand drinks all round.

This ceremony over, he insisted on getting a more comfortable carriage for me, and then, time being up, we parted the best of friends.

I was talking to an American friend the other day about porters, hotel-boots, and gentlemen of the like professions. We agreed that there was not much difference between the American and the English waiters, excepting in the matter of 'tips.' There the marked difference showed up most strongly; for whereas the English waiter will thank you, and touch his forelock respectfully in exchange for a few coppers, the American professional will give you specimens of the 'spread eagle,' intermingled with the stars and stripes, if you attempt to put him off with a few cent pieces. He is a mighty independent citizen of the United States, and a free man and brother, upon anything under a dollar-piece; then the eagle may condescend to fold his wings and stoop his noble head, but for not one cent less.

The typical porter of Australia is a totally different specimen, particularly in side stations; in the larger towns, I am sorry to say that they are getting contaminated with the vices of civilisation. The typical porter will always find a real pleasure in carrying along a lady's baggage, nor will he object to lend a hand to a man who is over-heavily burdened. But you must be careful never to offer him a 'tip' for such a service—a drink is all very well, and 'chum-like'; but let it end there, and, unless you wish to be insulted, don't attempt to order him to carry a parcel for you that you can carry yourself. Remember that he has his feelings.

I had only one fellow-passenger to Echuca in the carriage which I had been escorted to—a very small young man, of the Sim Tappertit order of being, and supernaturally sharp, loquacious, and inquisitive. He was very youthful; indeed, he had not yet began to cultivate a moustache. But he was very old in experience and the ways of the world, and thoroughly self-possessed; a perfect representative of the colonial 'larrikin'—*i.e.*, the working, not the pickpocket, 'larrikin.'

He had been an appreciative spectator of my engagement with the Sandhurst porter, and introduced himself by remarking that it was a 'pretty mill'; after which he plied me with a most exhaustive number of personal questions as to my business, salary, name, address, destination, hopes, intentions, aspirations, and friends past and present. I used to fancy that the Scotch were very fair at this sort of thing, but they were not in the competition with this youthful Melbournite.

But if he was inquisitive, he was also equally confidential. He was much older than he looked—nearly twenty—and had been on the world and catering for himself since ever he could remember—before that period, most likely, which might account for his stunted growth.

A self-confident and patronising young man, he had tried art and literature, also acting, scene-painting, and the circus business, and pitied my position, for, as he remarked, they were the worst paying games he had ever been at. Indeed, I found out before we had got many miles upon our way that he had been everything that mortal man might aim at as a calling, except coach-painting; but he was now post-haste up to Echuca to add that to his general accomplishments.

454

'I saw an advertisement for a coach-painter wanted up here, and I thought that I'd give it a fair trial; so I wrote about the job, and got it,' he explained, composedly.

'As an apprentice, I suppose?'

'Apprentice be blowed! d'ye think I'd take an apprentice's job? Not for this child; an able-bodied coach-painter, that's what was wanted.'

'But you say that you haven't tried coach-painting?'

'Never saw it done in my life; but it might be useful, you know, mightn't it?'

'Oh yes, very; but how are you going to do the work expected of you?'

'This way. You see, the coachbuilder to whom I have engaged myself is likely to be a practical man, and well up to his business. I am also practical: I made him send me my railway-ticket, with a written promise of four weeks' constant work, or, at least, regular coach-painters' wages, and my fare back to Melbourne if I don't suit him. Now you see?'

'Not quite.'

'What slow duffers you English are, to be sure. Don't you see that I am on the job. My employer knows he has to pay me four weeks' wages, also that I don't understand the business; of course, he will swear a bit—that's quite natural in his case. But he won't lose his money more than he can help; therefore, to get something out of me, he will put me up to the way it is done; and as I always keep my optics skinned, before the month is up, and he kicks me out, I shall have learnt the whole trade. Don't you savay now, Boss?'

'Yes, I savay,' I replied, a little awed by his bravery. 'You're not afraid that your employer may ill-use you, or—or—even murder you, are you? He may be a hot-tempered fellow, you know.'

'Not a bit; none of them have hurt me much so far. And that's how I have learnt all my trades; a pity though, isn't it, that this is the last I have left to learn?'

There was a tone of real regret in this enterprising youth's voice, as he sighed, and looked for a moment out of the carriage-window. It was like young Alexander sighing for new worlds to conquer. I felt sincerely for him under the circumstances.

'And what will you do after you are kicked out from Echuca?'

'Go back to Melbourne, and apply at all the coach-builders there for a job,' replied this hero, promptly. 'I don't say that I may quite *please* the first or second job I get, but on the third or fourth I'll be all there.'

It was a noble idea, and one which could alone be generated in a fertile brain ripened by a generous, Southern sun. I looked over the weazened little impudent face, and the assertive but puny legs, now crossed in an easy fashion, with a dazed gaze of wonderment, as he produced his empty pipe and asked me for a fill; and then, yielding up my cake of Ruby Twist and my box of lights, I turned sadly to contemplate the passing landscape.

The moon had by this time risen, and was bathing the whole land with a warm glow—one of those moons which are never to be seen in the land of fogs, lustrous, mellow, and thrilling in its intensity. All objects could be seen almost as well as by daylight, only with softened edges and broader masses of light and shadow—a night and a land for Titania and her Court to come to and play. For such a rare delight as these moonlight nights give, one may well be scorched a little by day. We were flying over an enchanted land of filigree-work in pale gold.

Echuca, the half of which is claimed by New South Wales, lies on the River Murray. Like all border places, the party feelings of the two colonies become concentrated here; on this side of the bridge which crosses the Murray the Echucans are rabid Victorians, on the other side they are rabid Welshmen.

There are two big rivers at Echuca—the Goulburn and the Murray. There is also the Campaspe, which joins the Murray here, and forms a peninsula, upon which the town stands. It is flat ground all about here, and liable to winter floodings; but along the banks grow some very fine, heavy timber—the red gum, which is useful for building purposes, being easily cut and beautiful in colour. Barges and river-steamers ply constantly up and down the River Murray, carrying wood and other merchandise; there are also large sawmills on the banks, and a fine vineyard of over sixty acres of vine cultivation here.

I measured one of the red-gum trunks here on the banks of the Campaspe River, about four feet from where the roots began to spread out, and found it to be thirty-three feet in circumference.

I have seen all that I want to see for the present on the Southern Railway, and feel once more ready for work and braced up by the mountain air, so take the train back to sweet Sydney by the sea, the queen of ocean cities and home of luxurious palaces.

What an awful monster that is which comes roaring along the main street, vomiting out clouds of dirty smoke over this fair, sunlit city; a ruthless monster, which demands its weekly victims as sacrifice, either unwary man, woman, or child, who may trip and fall before its approach; as ugly and reasonless a malformation as ever Frankenstein raised up and let loose—the steam tramcar.

It is going out towards Woolloomooloo, so I jump on board, in spite of my hatred for it, and it goes on, snorting and defiling the air. I have a couple of days more on my hands before I can go to the Blue Mountains, therefore I mean to pass them amongst the many bays with which the harbour is scalloped out. I have already gone through the Domain, the Botanical Gardens, and Lady Macquarie's Chair and convict-carved walk; I want now to get the length of the South Heads.

I leave the car near Woolloomooloo, walk on through Paddington and Woolahra, and strike away from streets by Double Bay. What a delightful walk as one goes down the steep hill to the harbour—promontories, heads, islands, and sails of all sizes and shapes dotting the blue waters, while the fore part is filled in with the feathery tops of gardens!

Next I pass by Rose Bay, and get a delicious peep of it through a broken rail all covered with weeds and tendrils of honeysuckles and wild briar; ships, yachts, and buildings, peeping out of the richest of foliage, are everywhere to be seen, with rocky promontories and golden sands, and clusters of sea-birds waddling about.

Very different was my experience in one of the other hotels here, where I saw one of the most dastardly fights that I ever looked upon; fortunately neither of the combatants were colonials.

It was pay-night amongst the railway men, and they had gathered here to drink some of their wages. One of them, a tall ruddy-faced young Scotchman, who I discovered afterwards was a new chum, and therefore expected to fight his way into respect, had come in with a friend to have a drink, when a gang of his fellow-workmen entered, and straightway started to pitch offensive remarks at him. There had been a running-match that afternoon, in which he had been victor, which added to their malice and fury.

As I stood close by listening and waiting for the result, I noticed a very small ugly-looking man sidle sneakingly up to him with an empty quart pot in his hand, and address him in a strong Lancashire brogue, to which the young fellow replied in a laughing but broad Western accent. I could hear and see enough to understand that the little sneak wished to fasten a quarrel upon the stranger, sure of being backed up by the others, who were waiting as I was upon the result.

Then, all at once, as the Scotchman laughingly turned his face from his tormentors, I saw the quart pot hurled at his head, and him staggering backwards, with a great gash over his left eye, for a moment dazed and blinded.

I expected to see the other men cry 'shame,' and kick the little coward into the road, instead of which I was astonished to hear them shout out:

'Good, Bill; at him, now's your time; punish the—'

Like a tiger the little man sprang on to the still-dazed stranger, and bringing him to the floor, fastened his teeth in his cheek, and began to gnaw away like a savage dog.

I had often heard of these miners' and Black Country modes of fighting, where ears were eaten and eyes gouged out, but this was my first experience, and it filled me with rage and horror. Hastily looking round, and seeing no one attempt to separate this mongrel English-speaking cannibal from his victim, I ran forward, and, watching my chance, sat down with a sudden flop upon his beastly little stomach, knocking the wind out of him in an instant, and giving my countryman a chance for his life.

We had a stormy five minutes after this—pots flying about the bar, and things getting smashed up. However, the landlord came to my rescue, and helped me to clear the premises, and get the young Scotsman's face sponged, after which I offered to go with him and see the battle out in the moonlit streets.

'There is no use,' he said, despondently. 'They have all got a down on me, and will swear anything against me. They mean to drive me out.'

And, true enough, in a few moments some of the police broke in, and arrested the young man for breaking the peace and assaulting the little man. Fortunately for him I had a letter of introduction to one of the magistrates, so that I was able to give a fair account of the incident and get the ear of justice; otherwise he would have been fined, and disgraced, and deprived of all prospect of work.

73

MAY VIVIENNE, *SUNNY SOUTH AUSTRALIA* (ADELAIDE, AUSTRALIA: HUSSE & GILLINGHAM, 1908), PP. 299, 301, 303, 305–312, 314, 316–318

THE drive to Port Augusta was delightful. With fine weather, smiling country, and sleek horses, I started early one morning for that fine natural harbour which is the gateway to the interior of our Continent, and from whence goes the telegraph-line to Port Darwin, north, and another one, *via* Eucla, to Kalgoorlie, in Western Australia. It is also the starting-point of the Great Northern Railway, which leads to Quorn, thence to Hawker, Hergott Springs, and Oodnadatta, 688 miles from Adelaide, and the present end of the line which will some day—land-grant system or otherwise—be taken right on to Port Darwin at the extreme north of our great Australian continent. But to return to Port Augusta, named after the consort of King William IV. Steamers are in direct communication with Port Adelaide, call-ing at all the intermediate ports I have mentioned, and it must be a very pleasant and entertaining sea trip. The exports from the port are varied and rich: wool, wheat, flour, copper ore, copper, hides, skins, tallow, and ostrich feathers—for the splendid ostrich-farm is a feature of Port Augusta district, and no one should go there without seeing it.

From Port Augusta through the lovely and romantic Pichirichi Pass to Quorn is not quite 25 miles; but I was now 235 miles from Adelaide, and the weather, to say the least of it, was hot. The railway porters through the whole trip had been extremely kind and helpful to me, never looking for any reward for doing so. I often contrasted them with the porters in England and on the Continent; but they, of course, get such small pay that tips are really necessary for them to make up a good week's wages. A mean man who had travelled a good deal tipped with a penny a porter in England who was carrying his luggage, but discoursing freely about the beautiful scenery he had lately seen, and how the sun rose tipping the hills with gold, was suddenly interrupted by the porter remarking in a forlorn voice, "Them 'ills was luckier than us porters, wasn't they, Mister?"

Quorn is a nice little town, and the people are a friendly class. The night of my arrival a fancy-dress ball was on at the hall, which was very tastefully decorated with flowers, evergreens, and Chinese lanterns; the refreshment tables were really artistically set and decorated also, and the fancy dresses of the ladies were tasteful and pretty. Wanting, of course, to see everything on my travels, I had a good look at them, although but a stranger. The ladies were only too pleased to be admired by anyone from the City. The people in Quorn appear to thoroughly enjoy life, much jollity seems to go on in most parts of the little town, and they are so cordial in their ways and kind in their manner. This style is not confined to the towns-people only, but, as the following will show, kindness is a very strong point in the local police force. One morning a woman arrived by train with two children—a boy of 12 and a girl of 8—and having no money to continue by train, started to walk for Parachilna, *en route* for Blinman, where the poor woman had a lad of 18 years employed on the mine. The mounted constable at Quorn, knowing the terrible journey they would have to make, followed and overtook the travellers at Willochra cottages, some miles from Quorn. They were all tired and exhausted through their tramp in the heat, and on enquiry he found she had been turned out of her home in Port Augusta by the agent of the landlord, and that her husband had left some days previously carrying his swag to Blinman. The constable, by means of the telephone, obtained permission to send the travellers on by the North train, thereby probably saving their lives, as the heat was intense and there are neither houses nor water along the route; in fact, not even the slightest shelter for miles at a stretch.

As the train goes to Hawker only twice a week a railway motor-car has been arranged for every Wednesday from Quorn, to return there on the Thursday morning, and the people are all quite delighted at the Railways Commissioner arranging it so satisfactorily, as an agitation had been going on with regard to it for some time, and communication with the City only twice a week made them feel somewhat isolated. Quantities of wheat are sent to market from Hawker, and if labour were not so scarce a great deal more could be sent than the 20,000 bags which had just been dispatched by train, and which was only part of the harvest; magnificent yields are quite usual in this district, as the description of some heads of wheat lately sent down to the Rev. Henry Howard showed. Some of the heads were at least nine or ten inches in length, and 200 separate grains of wheat were counted on one of them. Agriculturally speaking, while at Hawker I was in what was called the doubtful wheat-region, but with much of that kind of grain there would, I think, be very little doubt about a rich harvest.

The stock for the western plains pass through Hawker, and it is a great sight to see hundreds of splendid cattle drinking at the watering-places there. There is no regular stock-road to the plains, and they have to travel for miles and miles over Crown lands. The names of the stations to which they travel are: Kalioota, South Gap, Arcoona, Pernatty, and others. It has lately been proposed to make a direct stock route to the stations, which would be of great convenience to stock-owners, and benefit to the town of Hawker.

In these far-off places one often sees splendid types of Australian manhood, and I have come across many a "white man," and woman also, in my travels, whom it has been a great pleasure to meet—but there, mostly all Australians, "men, women, or horses, are," to quote from A. B. Paterson, "white when they're wanted," and tales of bush heroism are of frequent occurrence. Where can braver men be found than our bush coachdrivers? I have travelled on many a bush track through our continent, and personally seen great acts of valour. A driver who will take a coach, and sometimes partly half-broken horses, over some of the bush roads on a dark night, sometimes on a waterless stage, other times through flooded creeks, and, worse still, through tracks where great bushfires are raging, calls for admiration; at those times passengers probably shirk the journey, and wait for a more propitious time; but the back blocks coachman goes on, for His Majesty's mails must be delivered in spite of drought, flood, or fire. And our bush women; often, with the exception of their little children, they are left alone for days in the lone bush, their husbands being, perhaps, employed miles away wood-splitting or in other occupations.

The next place of interest on the Great Northern Line is Parachilna, where, if one wishes to go to see the Blinman Mine, which is situated in the Flinders Range, about 2,000 ft. above the Parachilna plains, and distant 272 miles from Adelaide, and about 112 north-north-east from Port Augusta, they leave the train and travel by horse and buggy through the bush for several miles, and then a surprise awaits them. The smoke of the smelters has now arisen, and the hum of machinery now breaks the eternal stillness of the lonely bush, while the welcome sound of the clanging hammer or drill tells a tale of prosperity and gladness. The great Blinman copper-mine belongs to what is called the Tasmanian Copper Co., but it is known to be an English syndicate, the shareholders of which are some of the richest men in the world. There are no shares held in South Australia. Originally it started with the Rosebery Mine, in Tasmania, thence taking its name. The Company is very powerful, and a master-mind has worked out the scheme. The Company possesses 36 properties, including Blinman, Sliding Rock, Mountain of Light, Yudanamutana, Cutaway, Lady Falmer, Mount Borley, Four-mile, Jubilee, O'Loughlin's, Victory, Weedna, Nicholls Nob, Last Chance, Great Mount Lyndhurst, Warra Warra, and Warra Warra West.

Already this Company has spent about £500,000 in South Australia. It pays the railways from £13,000 to £14,000 in railway freight, employs over 400 men, besides 80 teams of 10 horses each, and from 350 to 500 camels, and has a wage-sheet of between £8,000 and £10,000 a month. In addition to that it spends thousands yearly in materials and supplies. On mines away from Blinman about 150 men are employed, and they purchase about 400 tons of ore a month from outside shows.

About 22 miles farther on comes Beltana, where there are more copper-mines; thence to Leigh Creek, through salt, cotton, and blue-bush country, growing on ironstone plains, and consequently a very nourishing food for stock. A change of scene is now opened up to the traveller's eye. Undulating plains bounded by ranges of splendid hills; great dry rocky water-courses, which plainly show where, at flood-time, immense bodies of water swept through them from the Alpine-looking hills; and in the ranges enormous gum-trees, stand their ground proudly, in company with flowering acacia, stately pines, and perfumed sandalwood, monarchs of all they survey in the great lone land, which is now fast changing to the busy hum of civilization.

The Leigh Creek Coal-mine is about five miles from the township, and is connected with the railway-line. It is the property of the Tasmanian Copper Co., and is in charge of a very smart manager. If Leigh Creek Mine in the future comes up to expectations, it will mean a lot to South Australia, for it is the only coal-mine of note in the State, and with so many copper-mines around the value of the large quantity of coal required for the engines can be understood, so that in the future Leigh Creek township may develop into a second Newcastle. At present it is not a great township; but there is a very comfortable hotel, and one must make the best of everything when travelling in the backblocks. One thing about these places is the energy that everyone seems to be possessed of in an almost inexhaustible supply. Their talk is on copper or coal. No doubt visions of huge fortunes have something to do with this; and then the air of the North is most invigorating, except in the real hot summer-time; then people subside a bit, no doubt. In a line, but a good many miles distant from Leigh Creek, is Lake Frome, with hundreds of little creeks running from it, enriching the country around. In this district there are many copper-mines, and little townships are springing up with amazing rapidity. Teamsters use donkeys chiefly for their waggons, and it is rather quaint to see about 40 of these patient and obstinate little animals dragging the heavy loads of ore to the railway station.

Farther away in the North comes Farina. Vans of fat cattle for the Adelaide markets are constantly arriving there from Stuart Creek, Hergott Springs, and numerous other places in the Central North and from far-away Innamincka. It would be impossible to even mention a quarter of the wonderful doings in this part of the State, but suffice it to say that sometimes 2,200 horses, 80,000 sheep, and from a Monday in one week to the following Wednesday week 2,000 head of cattle passed Farina, which I should say must then have been a pretty lively place. Camels are chiefly used in the North as beasts of burden, carrying large quantities of ore from the copper-mines to the railway, and immense caravans of these ungainly but useful animals frequently break up the monotony of the bush. Donkey teams are also much utilized, chiefly in bringing wool from the interior, vast quantities of which are sent from the outlying stations to Adelaide.

Hergott Springs, 231 miles from Quorn and 465 miles from Adelaide, is another place where enormous numbers of stock are transferred to the trucks at the railway station for Dry Creek and the metropolis. It is no unusual sight to see 11,000 sheep in one flock come into Hergott from the far-off stations in charge of a drover and assistants, who go through all kinds of troubles and trials to bring them safe to the trucks, especially when all the creeks are running—perhaps in flood—and they have to be swum across. A drover's life must indeed be a hard one, with so many sheep in his charge. Between Hergott Springs and Algebuckina lie the great Lakes Eyre, the smaller one not far from the railway-line, and the great north lake extending far away into unexplored country. The township of Hergott surprised me. Far away in the very back, one might call it, is to be found a large hotel, where as nice a meal and as comfortable accommodation can be got as at many a place in the city. Of course, the railway is at the door, so to say; although the train arrives only once a week, the people obtain the very best to be got from the market. The townsfolk of the Far North are no doubt a grand class of people. Living so far away from city life one would think they would be somewhat discontented; but no, these grand pioneers of the north country, and their brave little wives, have settled down in their far-away homes, and are living cheerful and contented lives; and when city people—visitors—grumble about the intense heat, 120 degrees sometimes, they merely smile, and say it is quite seasonable.

The natives of this part of Australia are mostly of a peaceable and nomadic class. Those who are not at the Mission Station travel about in tribes from one township to the other with great regularity, and beg for "tucker" from their white brother, frequently holding corroborees, which vary the monotony of township life. The fierce and bloodthirsty aborigine we hear about is not to be seen, unless one travels to the still very-much-farther-off Northern Territory, which is now the subject of so much discussion with the leading men of the State. The race of Australian aborigines is in fact fast disappearing. There are now only 150,000 natives on the whole of the continent of which they were once sole monarchs.

My travels did not extend beyond Hergott Springs, as the train went only once a fortnight to Oodnadatta, the end of the line—227 miles farther away—and the journey having been described to me I preferred to take hearsay evidence with regard to the remainder of the train route, and wait for the advent of the Transcontinental Railway, hoping then to (D.V.) reach Port Darwin. Between Hergott and Oodnadatta there are several important places—Alberrie Creek, Stuart Creek, Coward Springs, Anna Station, Peake Station, and Algebuckma. Peake Run or Station comprises 4,779 square miles of superior pastoral country, splendidly watered by permanent artesian wells and large waterholes, bounded on the east by Lake Eyre and on the west partly by the Great Northern Railway. Three thousand cattle, 400 horses, a large flock of Angora goats—which are very valuable animals, on account of their long silky hair—and the usual homestead, stores, and all appliances essential to a station, were put up for sale recently in Adelaide; but £8,000 was the highest bid, and the property was withdrawn from sale. At most of the places mentioned there are water-bores, which bring up a large supply of water; and also in the far-off places that one hears talked of lines of bores have been put down on the great stock routes, and the value of the artesian streams can be imagined in this great, wide waterless country.

The great mobs of cattle that come from the big runs and stations usually arrive in good condition, plenty of feed being available, the Mitchell grass and saltbush, which grows plentifully, being favourite feed with them. Near Coward Springs there is a strange phenomenon called Blanche Cup. Many other "cups" are to be seen in this vast land, but Blanche is the largest that has so far been discovered.

They are peculiar mounds like an inverted teacup without a handle, ranging in height from a few feet to scores. Many are seemingly solid; but others, of which Blanche Cup is the finest, are only a shell, and the inside cone filled with a very replenishing supply of water. The cups bubble and roar gently sometimes, and are a most remarkable sight. They are the result of natural artesian water depositing lime, which causes the formation.

Oodnadatta people have built their homes on high stony ground, like the man in the parable. The township and surroundings are very dry-looking; no trees or vegetation appear to thrive. A hotel, a church, three stores, the railway station, a few wooden and iron houses, and several native wurleys comprise the place. The dust and sand are stated to be almost intolerable, and yet people appear to live there in contentment, and say it is quite a health resort! A thriving business is done with the outback stations, and over a thousand camels carry supplies between Alice Springs—which may be described as almost the very heart of Australia— and Oodnadatta. High hopes were entertained by the inhabitants until lately that the line of railway would be continued from there to the Northern Territory, when it is built; but I fear that their hopes will be blighted, as it is very probable the line, when started, will go in a different direction.

It is wonderful what a number of different classes of people are to be met in these bush towns, and farther still away, in what is termed the Never Never Country, perhaps because they never return—prospectors, shearers, drovers, jackeroos (frequently the sons of old families who have come out to learn station life), sundowners, swagmen—all sorts and conditions of men are to be met on the saltbush plains.

463

74

MAY VIVIENNE, *TRAVELS IN WESTERN AUSTRALIA*, SECOND ED. (LONDON: W. HEINEMANN, 1902), PP. 325–326, 329–330

I REACHED the uninteresting township of Yalgoo at 2 o'clock, very cold, tired and hungry. I stepped from the train with my portmanteau and sallied out of the station to look for a vehicle to take me to the hotel to which I had been recommended; but, alas! there was no sign of a conveyance. A drearier-looking place I never saw. So disheartened did I feel that I returned and got back into the railway carriage again, intending to resume the journey and go on to Geraldton; but on looking out of the now open window I saw so many nice and jolly-faced people on the platform that I thought it might not be so bad a place after all, so I took a second thought and got out of the carriage once more. Approaching the gate I discovered a small boy in charge of a cart, on which I placed my belongings, and told him to take them to the Emerald Hotel, I walking behind. When we arrived there he put out my luggage and left me. Not a soul was about the hotel or the street. I felt like a sailor in a desert. I essayed to reconnoitre the place, and went in and out of several rooms, with no result. I then tried the kitchen, and found every one out there also, except the fire, which luckily was in, so I took possession and sat down on a box to warm myself. Looking out of the window, I saw two enormous emus stalking about and peering into everything. I was afterwards told that they are the most curious birds in existence, and their prying ways often cause them to be taken captive. Presently the cook turned up; strange to say, a woman cook, as most cooks in these parts are Japanese men. I asked her for some dinner; she said she had none in the hotel, it was all at the railway station. I may as well here explain that the proprietor of the hotel also caters for the railway station, and his staff goes down there to attend to the train passengers at the dinner-hour, everybody who requires dinner being supposed to get it there. The whole male population of Yalgoo goes to see the train come in; it is the event of the day. However, the cook made me a nice cup of tea and some hot toast, and boiled some fresh eggs, after partaking of which I felt myself again. Taking a look out of the front door I saw the street just as deserted as ever, so, going into a bedroom, I took a siesta until 4 o'clock, when sounds about the neighbourhood told me that the townsfolk had returned from the railway station. I accordingly went forth to make their acquaintance, and having done so I am able to speak of them in the warmest terms.

The township being such a barren-looking place I was surprised, on driving around, to find very beautiful environs. The rains had brought up millions of wild flowers of all colours, and the grass and trees were exceptionally green. There are a great many sheep stations in this district, and the mines are a considerable distance away, so I did not go to them. The exception was the Emerald Mine, which is almost in the township, and which has returned its owners a large fortune. Fifteen thousand pounds worth of gold was dollied out of it before it was sold to an English company, who then erected machinery and crushed large quantities of rich ore with big results. It was on this spot that Yalgoo's first find was made by a native shepherd and his lubra, who told some prospectors that they knew of a quartz-heap with bright stuff on it. You may be sure the prospectors lost no time in finding the heap; other finds followed, and the Yalgoo rush commenced. Aboriginal shepherds are almost the only ones to be had in the West, and they are not very reliable; yet if any animal is lost they can always find it; they are wonderful trackers, and can follow up the track of anything alive; this power has been cultivated in them by hunting for food from infancy.

The next day I left Yalgoo, longing ardently for a breath of sea air once more. After a journey of eight hours in the train I arrived at Geraldton, on the shores of Champion Bay; the town nearest the point at which the history of the colony really commences. It is a shipping port for a large agricultural and pastoral country, although as yet only 2000 acres are under cultivation. I went for many beautiful drives, and one night to a "social" given by the footballers, to which I was invited; but as I did not dance, and contented myself with being a "wallflower," my participation in the enjoyment was not very keen; I consequently returned early to my comfortable parlour at the Club Hotel. The new public buildings here are quite an ornament to the town, and the people may well be proud of them. There are also some other fine buildings and many nice shops. Altogether Geraldton is a very jolly place in which to spend a holiday. It can be reached from Perth by boat instead of the long train journey of 297 miles, for the steamers going to the far north of Western Australia and Singapore every fortnight always call; there are also several coasting-boats. The extensive and rich goldfields of the Murchison make Geraldton a very important place, and in course of time, when the North is more known and visited, it will, no doubt, become one of the most important towns in Western Australia.

Some beautiful pearls were shown me by a trader from Sharks Bay in the North-west district of Western Australia, and I wished I were a queen who could order a necklace of them. As it was I had to content myself with one for a ring. They were really exquisite gems, especially three pink ones. The trader also had two black ones, which are rare and very valuable, but I prefer those of delicate hue.

Pearls to the value of £285,000 and pearl shell valued at £1,000,000 have been raised from the North West Fisheries during the last ten years. Nearly two hundred luggers, with over a thousand Malay, Japanese, Chinese, and Manilla men, with whites for officers, are engaged in the pearl industry. For diving, natives are chiefly employed, they being such wonderful swimmers and divers. Occasionally dissensions take place between these mixed people and their masters. Not long ago a terrible tragedy occurred on a pearling vessel, the *Ethel*, and the captain, his son, and the first mate were cruelly murdered by some of the Manilla and Malay crew. The offenders escaped at the time, but were afterwards captured (chiefly by the instrumentality of a poor Chinese cook, who was loyal), and have since paid the penalty of their terrible crime.

75

ROBERT WATSON, *QUEENSLAND TRANSCONTINENTAL RAILWAY. FIELD NOTES AND REPORTS* (MELBOURNE: W. H. WILLIAMS, 1883), PP. 85–86

Transcontinental Railway

Brisbane, 15th June, 1881.

Sɪʀ,

You will have gathered from the progress reports which from time to time I have had the honour of submitting for your information, that the great difficulty attending the construction of a transcontinental railway from Roma to Point Parker is the almost entire absence of timber suitable for sleepers or bridges, culverts, &c.; in fact, it may be said that practically there is none all the way. It will have to be carried from the two ends, unless the railway be extended from Withersfield to a point at which it would cut the Transcontinental line probably somewhere near Barcaldine Station, in which case two fresh points would be available for carrying on the construction, viz., one in each direction.

The subject of sleepers, a heavy item, has received some consideration. I have been divided in opinion between the use of timber and iron. The cost of carriage must determine this.

The cost of iron delivered at Point Parker or at Roma would no doubt be greater per sleeper than the cost of timber, but the iron sleepers are very much lighter than timber, and there must be a certain mileage at which the first cost of the timber sleeper, with the cost of its carriage added, would equal the first cost of the iron sleeper with its carriage added, after which point it would clearly be more economical to use the iron sleeper. I am assuming so far that the two are equally durable. This is, of course, open to correction—there may be some advantages which one has over the other; no doubt the iron sleeper is proof against the ravages of the white ant, but it is said that certain colonial timbers are also free from the attacks of these pests. However, returning to the subject of the scarcity of suitable timber along the proposed route, I determined, as I had several days to spare, and

467

the Queensland Government schooner "Pearl" was, through the kindness of Captain Pennefather, placed at my disposal, to try if I could find any suitable timber on the Gulf of Carpentaria.

At the suggestion of Captain Pennefather, I determined to visit the Batavia River, which is within less than 100 (one hundred) miles of the northern extremity of the Peninsula, and I think about 300 (three hundred) miles from Point Parker; I was rewarded by finding, along the south bank of the river, a forest that I believe will supply all the timber that will be required for the line, or that it will be desirable to take from the Point Parker end. There is a variety of timber, but it is chiefly bloodwood, ironwood, and messmate or stringybark; it is all easily got at from the river, and I can see no reason why it should not be delivered at Point Parker at as low a rate as the average price of hardwood in any other parts of the colony. The cost of extra carriage on the railway is a matter for additional consideration. The river itself, as a means of bringing the timber away, demands some remarks; it is the finest I have seen in the colonies, but this is not saying much, because I have not seen many.

There is practically no bar. I had a favorable opportunity of seeing what the approach to the mouth of the river is like; the wind was dead against us, and we had to "beat" for several miles; the "lead" was kept going all the time, and I watched the soundings carefully. As soon as we reached three fathoms on one side of the channel, we turned and went in an almost opposite direction until we reached three fathoms on the other side. We continuously repeated this movement, and thus got a series of cross sections of the channel, and invariably in going from one three-fathoms point to the other the soundings in mid-channel showed five, six, seven fathoms, and, as we neared the mouth of the river, nine and ten fathoms.

Immediately inside the mouth of the river, which is nearly two miles wide, there is a large basin extending for several miles in each direction with a good depth of water; through this we passed and proceeded up the river to about 20 (twenty) miles from the entrance, where we anchored and went ashore in the ship's boat; it was here that I found the timber I have referred to.

The next day we proceeded in the ship's whaleboat about 35 or 40 (thirty-five or forty) miles up the river and camped for the night, returning the next day; from soundings we took on the way it was evident that the "Pearl" or a larger ship might have gone as far as we went.

The country appeared flat generally on both sides of the river, with one or two exceptions, and the soil rich—palms growing luxuriantly on either side; the water is perfectly fresh and sweet for miles before we turned back, but rising and falling several feet with the rise and fall of the tide.

We saw very few natives except at the mouth of the river; they appeared disposed to be friendly, and if kindly treated will probably make good allies; but those up the river are a strong muscular race, with finer limbs than any

I have before seen; they look self-reliant and as if they had "rights;" they would probably be troublesome if harshly treated.

Captain Pennefather some months ago prepared a rough chart of what he had then seen of the river, and wherever he has recorded actual measurements, soundings, &c., the utmost reliance may be placed upon their accuracy; where he has had to exercise his judgment in estimating distances, I am satisfied he has kept well and safely within the mark.

I think it very desirable that none of the land on this river should be alienated until it is ascertained what will be required for supplying the wants of the railway. A further survey of the river is desirable, although I am satisfied, from what I have seen, that there would be no difficulty in getting the timber away. There are many points where convenient wharves or staging could be erected at very trifling cost.

I have, &c.,

ROBT. WATSON, C.E., M. Inst. C.E.

The Honourable The Colonial Secretary.

76

MARK TWAIN, *MORE TRAMPS ABROAD*, THIRD ED. (LONDON: CHATTO & WINDUS, 1898), PP. 201–206

November 11. *On the Road.*—This train—express—goes twenty and a half miles an hour, schedule time; but it is fast enough, the outlook upon sea and land is so interesting, and the cars so comfortable. They are not English, and not American; they are the Swiss combination of the two. A narrow and railed porch along the side, where a person can walk up and down. A lavatory in each car. This is progress; this is nineteenth-century spirit. In New Zealand these fast expresses run twice a week. It is well to know this if you want to be a bird and fly through the country at a twenty-mile gait; otherwise you may start on one of the five wrong days, and then you will get a train that can't overtake its own shadow.

By contrast these pleasant cars call to mind the branch-road cars at Maryborough, Australia, and a passenger's talk about the branch road and the hotel.

Somewhere on the road to Maryborough I changed for a while to a smoking-carriage. There were two gentlemen there; both riding backward, one at each end of the compartment. They were acquaintances of each other. I sat down facing the one that sat at the starboard window. He had a good face and a friendly look, and I judged from his dress that he was a dissenting minister. He was along toward fifty. Of his own motion he struck a match, and shaded it with his hand for me to light my cigar. I take the rest from my diary:

In order to start conversation I asked him something about Maryborough. He said, in a most pleasant—even musical—voice, but with quiet and cultured decision:

'It's a charming town, with a hell of a hotel.'

I was astonished. It seemed so odd to hear a minister swear out loud. He went placidly on:

'It's the worst hotel in Australia. Well, one may go further, and say in Australasia.'

'Bad beds?'

'No—none at all. Just sand-bags.'

'The pillows too?'

'Yes, the pillows too. Just sand. And not a good quality of sand. It packs too hard, and has never been screened. There is too much gravel in it. It is like sleeping on nuts.'

'Isn't there any good sand?'

'Plenty of it. There is as good bed-sand in this region as the world can furnish. Aërated sand—and loose; but they won't buy it. They want something that will pack solid, and petrify.'

'How are the rooms?'

'Eight feet square; and a sheet of iced oil-cloth to step on in the morning when you get out of the sand-quarry.'

'As to lights?'

'Coal-oil lamp.'

'A good one?'

'No. It's the kind that sheds a gloom.'

'I like a lamp that burns all night.'

'This one won't. You must blow it out early.'

'That is bad. One might want it again in the night. Can't find it in the dark.'

'There's no trouble; you can find it by the stench.'

'Wardrobe?'

'Two nails on the door to hang seven suits of clothes on—if you've got them.'

'Bells?'

'There aren't any.'

'What do you do when you want service?'

'Shout. But it won't fetch anybody.'

'Suppose you want the chamber-maid to empty the slop-jar?'

'There isn't any slop-jar. The hotels don't keep them. That is, outside of Sydney and Melbourne.'

'Yes, I knew that. I was only talking. It's the oddest thing in Australia. Another thing: I've got to get up in the dark, in the morning, to take the 5 o'clock train. Now, if the boots——'

'There isn't any.'

'Well, the porter.'

'There isn't any.'

'But who will call me?'

'Nobody. You'll call yourself. And you'll light yourself, too. There'll not be a light burning in the halls or anywhere. And if you don't carry a light you'll break your neck.'

'But who will help me down with my baggage?'

'Nobody. However, I will tell you what to do. In Maryborough there's an American who has lived there half a lifetime; a fine man, and prosperous and popular. He will be on the lookout for you; you won't have any trouble. Sleep in peace; he will rout you out, and you will make your train. Where is your manager?'

'I left him in Ballarat, studying the language. And besides, he had to go to Melbourne and get us ready for New Zealand. I've not tried to pilot myself before, and it doesn't look easy.'

'Easy! You've selected the very most difficult piece of railroad in Australia for your experiment. There are twelve miles of this road which no man without good executive ability can ever hope——tell me, have you good executive ability?—— first-rate executive ability?'

'I——well, I think so, but——'

'That settles it. That tone of——oh, *you* wouldn't ever make it in the world. However, that American will point you right, and you'll go. You've got tickets?'

'Yes——round-trip; all the way to Sydney.'

'Ah, there it is, you see! You are going in the 5 o'clock by Castlemaine——twelve miles——instead of the 7.15 by Ballarat, in order to save two hours of fooling along the road. Now then, don't interrupt——let me have the floor. You're going to save the Government a deal of hauling, but that's nothing; your ticket is by Ballarat, and it isn't good over that twelve miles, and so——'

'But why should the Government care which way I go?'

'Goodness knows! "Ask of the winds that far away with fragments strewed the sea," as the boy that stood on the burning deck used to say. The Government chooses to do its railway business in its own way, and it doesn't know as much about it as the French. In the beginning they tried idiots; then they imported the French——which was going backwards, you see; now it runs the roads itself—— which is going backwards again, you see. Why, do you know, in order to curry favour with the voters, the Government puts down a road wherever anybody wants it——anybody that owns two sheep and a dog; and by consequence we've got, in the colony of Victoria, 800 railway stations, and the business done at eighty of them doesn't foot up twenty shillings a week.'

'Five dollars? Oh, come!'

'It's true. It's the absolute truth.'

Why, there are three or four men on wages at every station.'

'I know it. And the station business doesn't pay for the sheep-dip to sanctify their coffee with. It's just as I say. And accommodating? Why, if you shake a rag the train will stop in the midst of the wilderness to pick you up. All that kind of politics costs, you see. And then, besides, any town that has a good many votes and wants a fine station, gets it. Don't you overlook that Maryborough station, if you take an interest in governmental curiosities. Why, you can put the whole population of Maryborough into it, and give them a sofa apiece, and have room for more. You haven't fifteen stations in America that are as big, and you probably haven't five that are half as fine. Why, it's per-fectly elegant. And the clock! Everybody will show you the clock. There isn't a station in Europe that's got such a clock. It doesn't strike——and that's one mercy. It hasn't any bell; and, as you'll have cause to remember, if you keep your reason, all Australia is simply bedamned with bells. On every quarter-hour, night and day, they jingle a tiresome chime of half a dozen notes——all the clocks in town at once, all the clocks in

Australasia at once, and all the *very same* notes; first, downward scale: *mi, re, do, sol*—then upward scale: *sol, si, re, do*—down again: *mi, re, do, sol*—up again: *sol, si, re, do*—then the clock—say at midnight: *clang—clang—clang—clang—clang—clang—clang—clang—clang—clang—clang—clang*!—AND, by that time you're—hello, what's all *this* excitement about? Oh, I see—a runaway—scared by the train; why, you wouldn't think *this* train could scare anything. Well, of course, when they build and run 720 stations at a loss, and a lot of palace-stations and clocks like Maryborough's at another loss, the Government has got to economise somewhere, hasn't it? Very well—look at the rolling-stock! That's where they save the money. Why, that train from Maryborough will consist of eighteen freight-cars and two passenger-kennels; cheap, poor, shabby, slovenly; no drinking-water, no sanitary arrangements, every imaginable inconvenience; and slow?—oh, the gait of cold molasses; no air-brake, no springs, and they'll jolt your head off every time they start or stop. That's where they make their little economies, you see. They spend tons of money to house you palatially while you wait fifteen minutes for a train, then degrade you to six-hours' convict-transportation to get the foolish outlay back. What a rational man really needs is *dis*comfort while he's waiting, then his journey in a nice train would be a grateful change. But no, that would be common-sense—and out of place in a Government. And then, besides, they save in that other little detail, you know—repudiate their own tickets, and collect a poor little illegitimate extra shilling out of you for that twelve miles, and——'

'Well, in any case——'

'Wait—there's more. Leave that American out of the account and see what would happen. There's nobody on hand to examine your ticket when you arrive. But the conductor will come and examine it when the train is ready to start. It is too late to buy your extra ticket now; the train can't wait, and won't. You must climb out.'

'But can't I pay the conductor?'

'No; he is not authorised to receive the money, and he won't. You must climb out. There's no other way. I tell you, the railway management is about the only thoroughly European thing here—continentally European I mean, not English. It's the continental business in perfection; and down *fine*. Oh, yes, even to that peanut-commerce of weighing baggage.'

The train was slowing up at his place. As he stepped out he said:

'Yes, you'll like Maryborough. Plenty of intelligence there. It's a charming place—with a hell of a hotel.'

Then he was gone. I turned to the other gentleman:

'Is your friend in the ministry?'

'No—studying for it.'

IT was Junior England all the way to Christchurch—in fact, just a garden. And Christchurch is an English town, with an English park annex, and a winding English brook just like the Avon—and named the Avon; but from a man, not from Shakespeare's river. Its grassy banks are bordered by the stateliest and most

473

impressive weeping willows to be found in the world, I suppose. They continue the line of a great ancestor; they were grown from sprouts of the willow that sheltered Napoleon's grave in St. Helena. It is a settled old community, with all the serenities, the graces, the conveniences, and the comforts of the ideal home-life. If it had an Established Church and social inequality it would be England over again with hardly a lack.

ANNIE BRASSEY, *THE LAST VOYAGE:* *1887* (LONDON: LONGMANS, GREEN, 1889), PP. 233–239

Wednesday, May the 11*th.*—It had been settled that to-day should be devoted to an excursion to the forests which are now being opened up by the new line of railway in course of construction. The special train of ballast-trucks which had been provided for us was to have started at ten o'clock, soon after which hour we landed, some delay having been caused at the last moment by the receipt of a message requesting us to send ashore every rug we possessed, in order to make the truck in which we were to travel as comfortable as possible. The required wraps and furs had accordingly to be got up from the hold, where they had lain for months past. On landing we found a pleasant party assembled to receive us, including the engineer of the new line, Mr. Stewart, and his wife. In due course we were all seated on two long planks, back to back, in open trucks, behind an engine and tender. We commenced our journey by slowly passing the enclosures, gardens, and courts adjoining the houses of the town. About three-quarters of a mile out of Albany we stopped to water the engine at a primitive trough in a cutting about twelve feet deep—the deepest on the whole line, which in the main is laid over a surface as flat as a pancake.

About nine miles out we came to a broad stretch of water known by the very prosaic name of 'Nine-mile Lake.' It looked lovely this bright morning, with the opposite hills and a fine group of blue gum-trees sharply mirrored in its glassy surface. The train stopped for a few minutes to enable us to admire the view and to take some photographs. In the course of another mile or so we quitted the main line to Perth, and proceeded along a branch line leading into the heart of the forest. The undergrowth was nowhere very thick, and where it had been cleared by burning, fine grass had sprung up in its place. As we left the moorland and got into the real forest of grand gum-trees the scene became most striking. The massive stems of many of the eucalypti were between thirty and forty feet in circumference and over a hundred feet in height. The glimpses which we caught between these tall trees of Torbay, with the waves breaking in huge rollers on the shore or in angry surf against the steep cliffs of Eclipse Island, were quite fascinating.

We steamed slowly along the lightly ballasted line—only laid yesterday, and over which no engine has yet travelled—two men running on in front to tap the rails and joints. and to see that all was safe. About three-quarters of a mile of rail is laid each day. It is being built on what is called the land-grant system; that is to say, for every mile completed the Government give the railway company 6,000 square acres of land, to be chosen at the completion of the line by the company's agent, the Government reserving to themselves the right of alternate frontage to the railway. The distance from Albany to Beverly (a town standing about 120 miles equidistant from Perth and Fremantle, which will be the terminus of the line, at any rate for the present) is 220 miles. The line was commenced and should have been carried on from both ends, but the contractors find it much cheaper to work only from the Albany end. It ought to be a very cheap line, for it requires scarcely any earthworks and no rock-cuttings or bridges, the soil being loose and gravelly with a granite foundation. There are few rivers to cross; and timber for the sleepers is to be had in abundance, and of the best quality, from the trees which must necessarily be cut down to clear the forest for the passage of the line. The entire road was to have been completed in three years from the time of commencement; but it will probably be finished in about two, as a good deal of the work is already done.

We were taken by another branch line to some saw-mills, where the sleepers for the railway are prepared. Here some of us got into a light American buggy drawn by a fine strong pair of cart-horses, in which conveyance we took our first drive through the bush. To me it seemed rather rough work, for in many places there was no track at all, while in others the road was obstructed by 'black-boys' and by innumerable tree-stumps, which the horses avoided or stepped over most cleverly. Still the wheels could not be expected to show quite so much intelligence, and we consequently suffered frequent and violent jolts. From the driver—a pleasant, well-informed man—I learnt a good deal respecting the men employed on the line. There are about 130 hands, living up here in the forest, engaged in hewing down, sawing, and transporting trees. These, with the women and children accompanying them, form a population of 200 souls suddenly established in the depths of a virgin forest. They have a school, and a schoolmaster who charges two shillings a week per head for schooling, and has fourteen pupils. He was dressed like a gentleman, but earns less than the labourers, who get ten shillings a day, or 3l. a week, the best hands being paid regularly under all conditions of weather, and only the inferior labourers receiving their wages for the time during which they are actually at work.

There are four fine teams of Australian-bred horses, and a spare pair for road or bush work. Communication with Albany, the base of operations, is of course maintained by means of the line, some of the navvies even coming from and returning thither each day in the trucks. The married men who live in the forest have nice little three-roomed cottages, and those I went into were neatly papered and furnished, and looked delightfully clean and tidy. The single men generally live in a sort of tent with permanent walls of brick or wood, and mess at a boarding-house for eighteen shillings a week. This seems a good deal for a labourer to pay for food alone, but it really means five good meals a day. The little colony has a butcher attached to it, from whom meat of the finest quality may be purchased at sixpence per pound, all but the prime parts being thrown away.

The rest of the party having walked up the line, I waited for them at the house of the District Manager, who with his wife received me most hospitably. On the walls of the apartment I was interested to notice the portraits of some of those who had been connected with my father-in-law in business, and who are now in the employ of Messrs. Miller, the contractors for this line.

As soon as Mr. Stewart and the rest of the party had joined us, we proceeded to the saw-mills and watched some great logs of jarrah being cut into sleepers. There were no elephants to assist in the operation as in Burmah, so that all the work had to be done by steam, with a little help from men and horses. Quantities of fragrant rose-coloured sawdust, used for stable litter, were lying about. Tons of wood not large enough for sleepers were being burned in order to get rid of it. It seemed a terribly wasteful proceeding, but there was more material than was wanted, and space after all was the great thing needed.

From the saw-mills we penetrated further into the forest, in order to see more large trees cut down, hewn into logs, and dragged away. Some of the giants of the forest were really magnificent. We followed a double team of sixteen horses drawing a timber-cart composed of one long thick pole between two enormous wheels some seven or eight feet in diameter. Above these wheels a very strong iron arch is fastened, provided with heavy chains, by means of which and with the aid of an iron crowbar, used as a lever, almost any weight of timber can be raised from the ground. The apparatus is called a 'jinka.' The men engaged in the work sit upon the pole with the greatest *sangfroid* as it goes bumping and crashing through the forest, striking up against big trees, or knocking down small ones; sometimes one wheel and sometimes another high on the top of a stump, or sometimes both wheels firmly fixed in one of the numerous deep holes. The scene was altogether most picturesque, as well as interesting; and it must be remembered that the top of each stump was larger than the surface of a large dining-table. The trees were from eighty to one hundred feet in height, all their branches springing from near the summit, so that the shadows cast were quite different from those one is accustomed to see in an ordinary wood. The day was brilliant, the sun shining brightly, and the blue sky relieved by a few white fleecy clouds moving softly before a gentle air. The timber-cutters were of fine physique, with brawny limbs and sun-burnt faces.

We watched the adventures of one enormous log. A team of fourteen horses were yoked to a strong chain attached by large hooks to a trunk of such vast proportions that it seemed as if all the king's horses and all the king's men could never make it stir an inch. Twice the effort was made, and twice it failed. First, the hooks slipped off the end, and as the horses were pulling and tugging with all their might, directly the weight was removed away they went helter-skelter down the steep hill, up which they had just climbed with so much difficulty, being utterly unable to stop themselves on the steep slippery ground. Next time the chain broke as the horses were straining every muscle, and the same tantalising process was repeated with even more striking effect. The whole of the long team of the fifteen horses (for they had added another this time) became hopelessly entangled, two of the poor animals either falling or getting hampered and knocked down in their headlong gallop. The third time the log was got into position; the 'jinka,' with only one horse attached to it, was brought close, the pole was lowered, and the levers applied with such force that they not only raised the log but very nearly the unfortunate horse also into the air. When all was satisfactorily arranged, the other horses were attached to the jinka, and away they all went merrily down the hill, but only to come into collision with a big tree. The horses had again to be taken out, and harnessed this time to the other end of the jinka, so as to pull it in the opposite direction. At last the big log reached the saw-mills in safety, about the same time as we got there ourselves. We visited the village shop, which appeared to be well supplied with useful stores, and also the butcher's and carpenter's shops, and the smithy. They have never seen a clergyman or doctor up here, but by railway there is easy communication with the town if necessary. In the course of our rambles we heard the disheartening intelligence that, owing to some misunderstanding, our train had already gone back to Albany, taking with it not only our luncheon, but all the wraps. We proceeded, however, to the trysting-place, only to be greeted by blank looks of disappointment as each new arrival received the unpleasant news that the report of the train's erratic proceeding was only too well founded. Everybody was tired, cold, and hungry, and the conversation naturally languished.

78

JULIUS M. PRICE, *THE LAND OF GOLD* (LONDON: S. LOW, MARSTON & COMPANY, 1896), PP. 15–21, 23–24

The journey from Albany to Perth is not impressive, as far as speed is concerned, for in travelling a distance of 330 miles the train takes up about sixteen hours—which is not what may be considered dangerously rapid travelling. Still it must be remembered that high speed is never a feature of Colonial traffic.

Several prolonged stoppages in the case of the ordinary train have to be made *en route* for meals and other apparently important matters, which seem mostly to consist of experiments in shunting. So the average rate all through never amounts to more than twenty-three miles in an hour—which is nice quiet travelling, and gives one ample time to appreciate the scenery on either side. In my own case, however, I thoroughly enjoyed the novelty of being able to stop the train, which consisted of the saloon car and the luggage brake, at my own sweet will, and on several occasions I took advantage of my privilege either for the purpose of making a sketch or of taking a snapshot.

The line of the Great Southern Railway ends at a place called Beverley, some 242 miles from Albany, where it joins the Government railway from Freemantle to Perth. The rails are laid on a 3′ 6″ gauge, and the carriages and all the rolling-stock are on an equally small scale. Many of the carriages are built in America, although a good many of them are brought over in sections from England.

The country through which we passed was more than monotonous: dense flat wastes of forest and bush lay on either side, though the many miles of this dreary wilderness were occasionally lightened by extensive clearings or even by patches of cultivation, betokening the presence of the enterprising settler. When these oases were seen they made one recollect that the country was neglected not because it was deemed unworthy of cultivation, but simply because man has yet to learn its value.

"The great drawback here," said Mr. Wright, on my expatiating on the magnificent possibilities of the country as we sat smoking our cigars in the verandah of the car, "is that as soon as intending settlers from England arrive out here and see the enormous amount of work in the way of clearing they have before them, instead of finding farms ready made as they expected, they in many cases lose heart—get into debt with the store-keepers and end by flocking to the towns,

479

where in most cases they merge into the great army of loafers, living by hook or by crook. Of course, however, you will understand," he added, "this does not apply to men with a certain amount of capital, or to men with energy who have come out to the country with some experience at their back and the determination to make a home and a living—to such men the prospects which this country offers are unbounded. In my opinion," he continued, warming to a subject he evidently had at heart, "the great secret of successful colonisation would be solved by the selection of colonists before they left the mother country, though the difficulties of such a scheme are practically insurmountable."

Land, in this part of the colony, is absurdly cheap, and even along the line of railway there are still thousands and thousands of acres for sale, at the nominal figure of from 10s. to £1 per acre, according to the density of the timber and bush on them, that requiring least clearing fetching the higher figure.

The purchase money is payable in instalments covering a period of twenty years, subject to certain restrictions, such as compulsory living on the property, fencing it in, and generally improving it within certain fixed periods after possession is taken. The conditions did not, however, strike me as onerous.

The *modus operandi* of clearing the forest varies but seldom. "Ring-barking" is chiefly resorted to where the timber is very heavy and where time is no immediate object. This method of tree destruction is simple in the extreme. A ring of bark is cut away round the trunk some three feet from the ground. This effectually kills the sap, and within two seasons the entire tree is in a complete state of decay and ready for the big fire which is eventually kindled, and the effect of miles and miles of dead trees waving their gaunt leafless branches in the bright sunlight is indescribably weird and depressing, whilst the sight of

The great difficulty new settlers have to contend with out here is that of getting labour at anything like reasonable rates, the ordinary farm hand or common labourer having an exorbitant idea of his own value. The "working man" who, in England, would earn 18s. a week demands, the moment he sets foot in Western Australia, a weekly salary of three or four times the amount, and is indeed from all accounts the curse of the Colony.

On one or two stations we passed Chinese labour had been used, not only to great advantage, but with considerable gain on the score of economy, and, from what I gathered, the general idea of landowners out here is that the employment of a large number of the industrial Celestials would help considerably to open up and push forward the development of the Colony. Political motives, however, generally stand in the way of any employment of Chinese on a large scale—for many of the capitalist class of settlers have seats in the Parliament at Perth which they do not care to jeopardise. Meanwhile this magnificent country, with a line of railway to feed it, is lying idle in consequence, in most cases, of the dearth of cheap labour.

There are few stopping-places of any importance for some distance from Albany—most of the railway stations having sprung into existence since the Great Southern Railway was opened for traffic, and though many of them have high-sounding names, a few shanties and occasionally a "bush store" are what they generally consist of.

What chiefly strikes one in this solitude is the utter absence of human or animal life everywhere, not even so much as a bird is ever visible to break the eternal monotony. The aborigines themselves, to whom in the past these wilds were perhaps a happy hunting-ground, have long since departed, or are dying out so rapidly in obedience to some unaccountable law of nature, that in a couple of generations probably not one of them will remain. All, in fact, appears to point to a sort of intermediate or waiting stage. Nature is as though expecting the approach of the white man for the awakening from her long sleep.

With regard to the aborigines, Mr. Wright told me two amusing incidents of the effect the opening of the railway had on the natives. They assembled at many points in order to examine the new mystery, and all agreed that there was something very uncanny about the train because it left no sign of a track, and on seeing the telegraph wires on both sides of the line they expressed their opinion that it was a d—— bad fence, because anybody could get under it!

We stopped at a rising little place named Katanning for the night, our saloon carriage, in which we were to sleep, being shunted into a goods shed. A capital supper at the station "hotel" (which by the way was lighted by electricity) and a stroll through the village finished up an exceedingly pleasant and interesting day.

In the early hours of the morning we reached Beverley, the terminus of the Great Southern Railway, and I was awakened by a series of shunting, or rather bumping, manœuvres, through which our carriage particularly seemed to be undergoing. For fully half-an-hour this interesting operation lasted, though what the result of it was, except to effectually wake us up at five o'clock in the morning, could not be ascertained as we found ourselves when it was over within a few yards of our point of departure. The bumping was, I afterwards found, caused by the colonial system of loose coupling; the detrimental effect of such a method on rolling stock should be obvious, though the colonial mind has not yet grasped the fact. The Government line from Beverley to Perth, a distance of some hundred miles, is certainly the most curious specimen of railway engineering it has ever been my luck to travel over. Having been laid as cheaply as possible, from start to finish it is quite a series of surprises, which are more interesting to read about than to experience. To describe it as constructed on the "switchback" principle would be to put it mildly, for when laying it no attempt whatever was made to overcome any physical difficulties the country presented, with the result that the rail runs uphill and down dale without any attention to gradients and other such trifles. Cuttings are unknown quantities, and although a high range of hills, the "Darling" had to be crossed, there was no such a thing as a tunnel anywhere. Standing on the platform of the car looking back along the line, the effect is most extraordinary, and one wonders how any engine can be built to stand such terrific work; and as to the curves, well, I had never before believed the story of the new engine-driver, somewhere in South America, who pulled up in great alarm because he saw some lights in front of him which proved, however, to be the rear lights of his own train; but this bit of line could almost give that one points and win easily. Feeling oneself tearing at full speed down the steepest gradients (many of them I noticed were as much as one in thirty) was most exciting, and it was often a wonder to me that the train did not run away with the engine. That accidents have not been of frequent occurrence is more a matter of good luck than anything else.

79

ALBERT FREDERICK CALVERT, *MY FOURTH TOUR IN WESTERN AUSTRALIA* (LONDON: W. HEINEMANN, 1897), PP. 4, 6, 8

Then we stroll over to the railway station to arrange for a special train to convey us as far as Beverley, where we should catch up the mail train, that for some unexplained reason stops during the night at this wretched wayside village.

The visitor hastens to leave Albany behind him. He will live many years before he forgets his first taste of travelling in Western Australia. He flees to the trains to find surcease at Perth or Fremantle, and finds himself deeper in the toils. After a wild scramble for a seat, the train stops at the first refreshment station, of ignoble memory. A wretched hut, ten feet long and eight feet broad, that might be mistaken for the shabby shelter shed of a watchman, but for the array of cups on the counter, and the helter-skelter rush that is made for it by hordes of travellers, who see a forlorn hope in the crockery-ware. They jump out of the carriages at the risk of their limbs before the train stops, and gaspingly call for a chop or a steak. The girl in charge listens in cool disdain, and points to the cold, muddy tea which has long been waiting for the travellers, and to some ancient sandwiches as the sole resources of the menu, which is vanishing rapidly before clutchful fingers. It is whispered that the Katanning table is not worth waiting for.

So the tea and sandwiches are gulped; the coin rains like hail into the "cash box" saucer; the crush rocks and surges; the starting bell clangs brazenly; the travellers dash into their seats as the train moves. Many of them have failed to get a bite; those who have had a bite loathe it, and as the carriages recede into the distance, the damsel in the shed complacently counts and pockets her gains.

The packed passengers sit on each other's laps, or like trussed fowls, without room to move their elbows, and find a melancholy solace in thinking over the Pullman saloon and sleeping cars, and civilised cookery they have left behind—for a sleeping berth on a long night journey is unknown on the rails of the Golden West, where gate-keepers and interlocking signalling gear have yet to appear, either on the Government routes or this Great Southern Railway, which was made on the land grant system, by a private Company formed in England. The territory ceded to the Company has been so slowly settled, that the train passes over leagues of country upon which there is not a sign of stock, nor a single habitation.

At length the dreary stifling day, without rest or comfort, and the long evening without sleep, draws to a close, and Beverley comes in sight. The news stirs the most torpid to a keener sense of the pangs of hunger. The carriage windows are all thrown down; hands are on the knobs, and as the train is pulling up, the doors are flung open. It is now or never, and a peaked-capped army presses into a building about twice the size of the Mount Barker humpy. What is such a room among so many, what are tables set for forty among a hundred and fifty? A third of the den is taken up by a bar, the front of which is heavy with rows of flabby pies, which have never been in the same town with baking powder to stir them from the consistency of lead, and the inevitable plates of sandwiches, which are one of the most familiar things to be seen on a West Australian Railway. The chairs ought to be three-storied to seat all those who want them; the overflow, as "General" Booth would say, clamour in the bar for drinks, pies, and thin streaks of salt beef between hunks of bread. There is a Babel of shouting, for the situation is getting serious. The train will leave at five o'clock on the following morning, lodgings have to be found and sleep snatched, and, if possible, a wash. The overcrowded and far too "lively" hostelry cannot possibly give shelter to all, and while some secure a corner in the railway sheds, others crawl back into the stationary carriages, or camp out by the side of the line. The place seethes with excitement as the moments flit by. The women who serve out the plates of watery soup and hash alone are calm, while she who receives payment at the door might in imperturbable gravity sit as a study for a modern Sphinx. The outcry of complaint is loud, and yet the directors of the Railway are hardly to blame. While the Colony was in the egg there was so little traffic on the line that travellers might fairly expect to have to "rough it." The invasion of gold-seekers and those who come in their wake has been so sudden and overwhelming that there has not been time to provide any of the luxuries of old world travelling.

Five times before had I gone through the discomforts of this unlovely journey, but in the present case we are more fortunate in our mode of travelling. The train had left Albany at nine o'clock in the morning before we landed, but thanks to the peculiar arrangements already referred to, we are able to arrive in Perth next morning at the same time as the mail. An order for a "special" is something out of the common on the Great Southern Railway, and the station-master has his doubts as to the possibility of executing it. However, after much telegraphing, and the issuing of many orders, we are told that a train will be in readiness for us at five o'clock in the afternoon, and then everybody adjourns to the Freemason's Hotel for refreshments. In common with the rest of Albany's floating population, we are anxious to be on our way again, and the day would have been long indeed but for the hospitality of my good friend, Mr. Loftie. The train is ready at five o'clock according to promise; a little crowd of idlers are assembled to see it start, and at the last moment a thoughtful acquaintance arrives with a suspicious-looking wooden case, that had originally been intended for the storage of condensed milk. A sound of tinkling bottles that proceeds from it, as it is pushed under the seat, is an eloquent proof of its aptitude for carrying other commodities.

Our supper at Katanning is neither grateful nor comforting, for throughout Western Australia no regard is paid to comfort when travelling. Nobody seems to give it a thought. The travellers are too busy getting somewhere else, to worry about comforts by the way, and the natives are too busy getting money out of those who are going somewhere else to get more, to attend to these details. The night air is cool when we leave Katanning, and after having resource to the milk case and knocking out our pipes, we prepare to rest. There are only three of us in our compartment, so we retire luxuriously. Collars and boots are taken off, and coats are rolled up for pillows. The third man takes possession of the floor, and to the chirping music of the crickets and the rattle of the train, we fall asleep.

It is a rude awakening at Beverley, for a few of the passengers who arrived by the mail train overnight are up and waiting to continue their journey. They form an audience around our carriage, and study us without surprise or comment as we make our toilet. Every room at the hotel shows traces of having been used as a sleeping apartment. A few people are still wrapped in their blankets, others are waiting their turn at the wash bowl, and the bar is full. To call our efforts with the dirty water a wash is an impertinence, and the breakfast is a direct insult. We are glad enough to get back to the now overcrowded train, and be once more on our way towards the capital.

80

DAISY BATES, *THE PASSING OF THE ABORIGINES: A LIFETIME SPENT AMONG THE NATIVES OF AUSTRALIA* (LONDON: JOHN MURRAY, 1938), PP. 163–164, 168–171, 190–192, 194–195, 207–208

First days at Ooldea

The construction of the great Australian trans-continental railway line was the end of the native groups north, east and west for many hundreds of miles.

For some years, stray natives had been coming in to civilization, following the tracks of the explorers, Warburton, Giles, Forrest and Maurice. They had looked upon the white men with awe—bearded ghosts with a fire magic that could send little stones into their vitals. "Windinjirri! Run! Run! Run!" they shouted when they beheld those fearsome spirit monsters, the camels, and scattered to the four winds, dropping infants and food in their desperate fright. Windinjirri was the camel's name among them ever after. One woman gave birth to a baby while fleeing from the camels, and no harm resulting, the baby was given the camel as its totem.

At first they lived in abject fear of the "*waijela*" as they learned to call the white man, but after they had talked with him, touched him, and even eaten his food, the fear changed to anger. This *waijela* was killing their meat, leaving the bodies of the kangaroos to rot and taking only the skins. He was monopolizing the precious water-holes for the hated camel, forbidding the rightful owners to approach. Then, little by little, or rapidly, according to local circumstance, he assumed another, and though they did not know it, more terrifying aspect. He became a source of revenue to them, and he had come to stay. They were always familiar with the traffic in women. That the *waijela* knew the trade simplified matters.

So with the survey of the east-west railway began the extermination of the central native groups, not by the deliberate cruelty of the white man, but by the impossibility of amalgamating two such extreme races, Palæolithic and 20th Century, and through the natives' ready, and even eager, adoption of the white man's vices.

As the construction proceeded, with a great influx of railway workers of all classes and nationalities, along 1,000 miles of previously uninhabited country, they straggled in to the line in increasing numbers, drawn by the abundance of food-stuffs and the new fire-drink that made them "head no good." Each group through whose territory the line was passing saw its waters used up, the trees and bushes destroyed for firewood and fence-posts, and the whole country turned to strange uses. In their eagerness to "make the most of what they yet may spend," they did not know that they were bringing about their own annihilation. They thought that the train and its people would go away, and leave them the things to play with.

Bush rumours travelled far and rumours magnify. From over a thousand miles north and north-east and north-west the groups came, amalgamating with the tribes they met, or killing, on the way; smokes on the horizon telling of their coming as they skirted the Plain, still afraid to cross it for fear of the serpent devil. Eastward to Wynbring and Tarcoola, westward to Karonie and Kalgoorlie, they journeyed, but more frequently to the traditional camping-ground on the north-north-eastern rim of Nullarbor, known to the white man as the Ooldea Soak.

In the building of the trans-continental line, the water of Ooldea passed out of its own people's hand for ever. Pipelines and pumping plants reduced it at the rate of 10,000 gallons a day for locomotives. The natives were forbidden the soak, and permitted to obtain their water only from taps at the siding. In a few years the engineering plant apparently perforated the blue clay bed, twenty feet below surface. Ooldea, already an orphan water, was a thing of the past. Old blind Jinjabulla, the last of its emu men, whom I had tended at my Weerilya camp 100 miles south, was burned to death shortly after I left, in his shelter at Fowler's Bay.

When I came to Ooldea Siding in September, 1919, I found conditions difficult. Some hundreds of derelict natives had established their camps at the sidings, and travelled up and down the line, begging from the train at every stopping-place, a responsibility and a menace in that many of them were already ravaged by disease. There was no control of them. The few filthy rags they wore had been thrown to them in charity and decency. A policeman stationed at Tarcoola and another at Kalgoorlie dispensed rations, but Tarcoola and Kalgoorlie are nearly a thousand miles apart.

The newly formed railway settlements had not yet settled down after the chaos of the very recent construction. Aftermath of war was still in the air, and the unrest among the white communities was almost as distressing as the obvious degeneration of the black. I pitched my tent first on the south side of the line, where there was a small auxiliary railway for carting wood and a pipe-line, and a half-cast teamster camped with a motley crowd of natives. Such a diversity of creatures they were that, among remnants of all the south and central areas, and the east and west, I found an Arunta of the MacDonnell Ranges, a Dieri of Cooper's Creek, and even a Bibbulmun woman from Ravensthorpe in South-West Australia, the wife of this German half-cast, an unhappy creature, who had drifted with him through all the groups between.

Numbers of white derelicts and camp-followers were still on the line, strike-agitators, foreigners, pilgrims of one kind and another, "jumping the rattler" between the capitals, or recklessly walking the whole thousand miles, throwing themselves on the hospitality of each succeeding camp of fettlers. Some of them cut the telegraph wires in the throes of thirst, or held up the passing trains in starvation, and most of them stirred up trouble wherever they went. Prostitution of native women was rife, sought by the blacks and encouraged by the lowest whites, and many unfortunates had already reaped the wages of sin. When the first half-cast babies appeared, the wild mothers believed that they were the results of eating the white man's food, and rubbed them frantically with charcoal to restore their black health and colour, till often they died. Even when they had eaten the fruit of the White Man's Tree of Knowledge, they were not pleased, for they had seen piebald horses, and shared the primitive fear and distaste of the unusual.

News travels quickly by smoke signal, and soon my old Bight and Eucla and Fowler's Bay natives were arriving to sit down with me again. An epidemic of influenza broke out, and in tending and feeding the sick, making the acquaintance of strangers of the desert, clothing them for their first entry to civilization and smoothing out many a social problem, I was labouring every hour of the day when there came the disturbing news of an engine-drivers' strike. The six weekly expresses—three from the east and three from the west—were no longer to be expected, nor the weekly supply train. Moreover, there were rumours that the service would be discontinued for twelve months.

I had few stores in my modest larder for such an emergency, and no facility for obtaining them. Telegrams were useless. The strike was declared on October 30. The fettlers were paid off, and Port Augusta volunteers drove a train to take their women and children into Kalgoorlie. From these departing fettlers, I bought all the flour, tea and sugar available for my natives, and soon found myself the only white woman left on the line, alone at Ooldea save for the two pumpers at the Soak, three and a half miles north, the half-cast teamster and the various camps. Then I learned that a large gathering of natives had come in for an initiation ceremony at Tarcoola, and might be expected at any moment, but I had nothing to give them.

The next eight weeks were indeed difficult. I existed principally on porridge, and sometimes I would give that to my patients, and eke out the next day upon a meagre damper or a potato. Once I made a meal of an iguana that two friends, Nyirdain and Thangarri, caught and cooked for me. Worse than all, our water was limited. As it was no longer needed for the fettlers and the locomotives, the pumpers had ceased to work, and the daily supply had to be rationed scrupulously. I admit that I was on the verge of desperation, with no relief in sight, when there came the glad news that the strike was over. On December 3, by the first train through, I was able to purchase one loaf and a pound of butter. Never did I enjoy such a simple meal so heartily.

Following this harrowing experience, we were blessed for a time with the passing of six trains weekly, in an attempt to reduce the congestion in the railway sheds. The fettlers and their wives returned to their little homes so rudely deserted, and I was able to provide my natives with a Christmas dinner worthy of the name.

My own fare, day after day throughout the years, has always been so simple that to myself I am a miracle. I have consoled myself with the reflection that the simpler our needs, the nearer we are to the gods. A potato in the ashes, now and again a spoonful of rice that nine times out of ten was burned in my absence or absent-mindedness, occasionally the treat of a boiled egg, and always tea—my panacea for all ills—were the full extent of my culinary craft. Even so, after so many hardships, I determined that this Christmas should be a memorable one for us all, and passed the glad tidings of peace and goodwill and plenty *mai* along to the natives.

A big mob gathered about me in expectancy. Fires were quickly lighted and flour was given out for damper making.

"Who can make plum-pudding?"

"Injarradu pudding roongani." So Injarradu was given mutton fat and sugar, raisins and dates and prunes and figs, eggs and flour and carbonate of soda, and baking-powder, holus-bolus in a bath-tub, and duly produced a glutinous seething mass wrapped in one of Kabbarli's old night-dresses and boiled in a zinc bucket. After ten hours of cooking, the centre of the pudding was half-liquid, and its external appearance that of a diseased pancake, but it disappeared rapidly enough, with all the other good things. Each little family sat in such a position that it could not be overlooked by its neighbours while eating. It is an offence for a native to watch another eat, as evil magic might be conveyed to the food—which reminds one again of the old Irish saying, "I'd rather have six atin' wud me than wan lookin' at me." When the dinner had disappeared, they rubbed their stomachs and flicked their thumbs downward in satisfaction.

"*Jooni-bulga, Kabbarli*" (Full up, Grandmother!). They grinned and wended their way over the hill to the siding to beg for baccy on the Christmas trains.

Introduction to civilization

Ooldea Siding, in full view of the trains, with many passers-by, was scarcely the place to accomplish good work for the natives, and it was not long before I transferred my camp to a sandy gully a mile north, on the track that led to the Soak, with a convenient tap in the pipe-line for water supply. There I built an enclosing breakwind of mulga bushes, and set up the little household that was to be my domain for 16 years.

There was an 8×10 tent for my living and sleeping, an upturned tank which my natives and I rolled many miles across the plains where it had lain stranded for years, and which I utilized as library, storing there my manuscripts and my books; a bough shed "storehouse" that held everything from my daily provender and supplies for the natives to their most sacred totem boards and initiation properties, and a smaller bough shed on the crest of the hill, with a ladder leading to its leafy roof, that was my observatory. Here in the bright, still evenings,

I studied the skies, astronomy being an old love of mine, and compiled my aboriginal mythologies, many of them as poetic and beautiful as are the starry mythologies of the Greeks. A prickle-bush—"dead finish," as old white prospectors call it—was my barred gateway at night-time, a barrier for privacy passed by few in all my years of residence. Outside, the natives would come to await my attention, old friends sitting patiently beside the pipe-line, and naked newcomers shyly flitting about among the trees, sometimes two days before they summoned courage to approach this Kabbarli of whom they had heard so far away. Innocent as children, they would make their fires on the sand-hills and camp contentedly while I made or obtained from my store the clothing they needed before they approached the siding, too soon to learn the art of scavenging and selling all that was saleable.

They came to me from the Mann, the Gosse, the Everard, the Petermann and the Musgrave Ranges, occasionally from as far away as Tanami, from Kalgoorlie and Laverton in the West and Streaky Bay in the East, and from far across the north-western borders of the State. Sometimes two years on the journey, zigzagging in the desert for food and water, they followed the tracks of those who had come in before them, disintegrating, reuniting, mourning and rejoicing, and every moon fleeing farther from their hereditary waters. At last the remnants arrived on the rim of civilization outside my break-wind. As each little group appeared, I was made aware of its arrival by the wailing and shouting and spear-rattling of the groups already there. Every native who steps over his own boundary is in strange country and hostile. There are no groups in the lower centre now, only little mobs continually changing. The amalgamation of the totems is their frantic effort to coalesce. Each mob was more reckless and difficult to control than the preceding ones.

My duty, after the first friendly overtures of tea and damper, was to set them at ease, clothe them, and simply to explain the white man's ways and the white man's laws.

Sometimes a group of forty and more would arrive, families and vagrants following each other, finding their way across the desert, drinking water from the tree-roots, and setting fire to the bush as they came, hunting kangaroos and emus. They had fought and killed on the way south, and their only safety from each other now lay in their proximity to the white man. His novelties were also exciting. The first few weeks of their arrival were usually spent in ejaculating "Irr! Irr! Irr!" at the trains, the houses, the white women and babies, paper, pannikins, tea, sugar and all the mystifying belongings of the "waijela." Biscuits and cake and fruit were thrown to them from the train windows, while their boomerangs and native weapons, and their importance in the landscape as subjects for photography, brought many a shilling and sixpence for them to spend, which they promptly did, without any knowledge of its value, and sometimes were wickedly imposed upon. The train was their undoing. Amongst the hundreds that "sat down" with me at Ooldea, there was not one that ever returned to his own waters and the natural bush life.

The weekly stores obtained from the supply train consisted of two loaves of bread, toasted to the last stale fragment, one tin of powdered milk, a pound of rice or sago and a pound of butter when I could get it. A tin of jam lasted six weeks, and a pound of tea over two months. An occasional cabbage or lettuce was eaten leaf by leaf, day by day, and 12 lb. of dried potatoes lasted nearly four months. When friends sent me delicacies such as preserved fruits or tinned goods, gladly I exchanged them with the fettlers' wives for flour and tea and sugar. When times were lean, and the natives had only a small damper, they could be sure that I had an even smaller piece of toast. One day Gindigi misunderstood me, thought I was hungry, and brought me a billy-can of broken bread he had begged from the train-passengers.

I discouraged this begging to the best of my ability, but it was of no avail. Occasionally trouble came of it. One day a mean-spirited tourist, after some twenty minutes' haggling over the customary "tchillin" for a boomerang, kept possession of the curio till the moment of the train's departure when, with a wink at his fellow-passengers, he climbed on board and threw the puzzled native a penny. The enraged boy hurled a stone that broke the carriage window, and the natives were warned from the line for a period, but they were flies about a honey-pot and it was impossible to keep them away. It was old Kattigiri, climbing a moving van eager to be first for the sheep's head and other butcher's offal, who fell beneath the train and was cut to pieces. On another occasion, old blind Janjinga, something of a wit and always lucky, struck a group of particularly generous travellers, who loaded her with good things. As there were still more gifts and givers coming, Janjinga ripped off the travesty of a frock that was her only garment, spread it on the ground, and stood with arms outstretched, wearing nothing but her smiles of gratitude. She could never understand why all her benefactors suddenly disappeared, fleeing for the carriages to hide their blushes, while the siding rang with shouts of ribald laughter.

It was no unusual sight to see anything up to 100 of these cannibals, men, women and children, several of them but a week in civilization, climb aboard an empty truck and go off to an initiation ceremony farther up the line. I use the word cannibal advisedly. Every one of these central natives was a cannibal. Cannibalism had its local name from Kimberley to Eucla, and through all the unoccupied country east of it, and there were many grisly rites attached thereto. Human meat had always been their favourite food, and there were killing vendettas from time immemorial. In order that the killing should be safe, murderers' slippers or pads were made, emu-feathers twisted and twined together, bound to the foot with human hair, on which the natives walk and run as easily as a white man in running shoes, their feet leaving no track. Dusk and dawn were the customary hours for raiding a camp. Victims were shared according to the law. The older men ate the soft and virile parts, and the brain; swift runners were given the thighs; hands, arms or shoulders went to the best spear-throwers, and so on. Those who received skull, shoulder or arm kept the bones, which they polished and rounded, strung on hair, and kept on their person, either as pointing-bones or magic pendants.

In the grip of the drought

I could not keep them long enough with me to hope for the humblest results, for even when I had plenty of food for weeks, they would still go on, up and down the line, wandering for any reason or noreas on. "*Koorda kombinyi!*" (Heart getting hot!) they told me, and, clambering on the trains, would be off, in their nomad eagerness, to Tarcoola, to Kalgoorlie, to anywhere between.

Apart from the effects of malnutrition and epidemics and disease, death-magics and bone-pointing had always to be combated. When they believed that the bone of a dead man had been levelled at them by an enemy, they would lie down in their little beehive bough-shelters and refuse all food unless I took the magic out of their bodies. I was generally successful in my treatment of these purely psychological but often fatal illnesses, and would solemnly remove and burn and bury the offending magic, gaining a great reputation as *dhoogoor maamu ngangarli* (doctor of old-time witchcrafts).

Death quickly claimed the weakest of the new-comers. It is sad reading in my diary of the deaths of young people in those days at Ooldea. Some had been but a few months in touch with civilization when they turned aside from their groups to die, and those who had drifted away came back always with their numbers lessened.

There were a few who assimilated easily and survived amazingly. Nyan-ngauera, who came down with the first group in 1920, is still on the line, a case-hardened beggar. With another group from the border was one little girl, Nandari, about nine years old, of marked intelligence and spirit. After a few days she set off by herself on a goods train to Cook, where she changed for Kalgoorlie, and was so delighted with the adventure that she spent most of the next three years travelling up and down on every train that would give her a footing.

81

ANTHONY TROLLOPE, *AUSTRALIA AND NEW ZEALAND* (LEIPZIG: B. TAUCHNITZ, 1873), PP. 210–213, 222–224

Beginnings of railways, with railway rumours, railway prophecies, and railway fears, met us everywhere on our passage up the islands. It must always be remembered that these colonial railways are not private speculations as they are with us, but are constructed,—or to be constructed,—with money borrowed by the colony for the purpose. If it be calculated that the money can be borrowed at 5 per cent., and that the expected traffic will pay for the working of the railway,—two positions which the advocates for the New Zealand railway system take for granted,— then the question is this: will the value of railway communication to the colony be worth the interest which the colony must pay for the money borrowed? Any partisan could talk by the hour,—if given to talking, or write by the chapter,—if given to writing, either on one side or the other; or first on one and then on the other. Facts can prove nothing in the matter, and speculation must carry the day either on that side or on this. That a national debt is a grievous burden to a young community is of course not to be denied. That railways running through a country, at present deficient in roads, will increase trade, and add greatly to the value of the land and to the value of the produce of the land, is equally manifest. Such a question in a community governed by free institutions, representative parliaments, and responsible ministers, at last becomes simply one of partisan politics. There will be the borrowing and spending side of the House, the members of which will be great in their oratory on behalf of progress,—and there will be the cautious side of the House, which would fain be just before it is generous, whose oratory will be equally great in denouncing the reckless audacity of the spendthrifts. The borrowing and spending side will generally have some great prophet of its own who can look far into futurity, who can see ample returns to the community for any amount of expenditure, who is himself fond of political power, and who can see at any rate this,—that the great body of voters in the country, on whom he must depend for his power, are for the most part indifferent to future circumstances so long as money at the moment be spent in profusion. When I reached New Zealand Mr. Vogel was the great prophet of the hour,—and under his auspices money had been largely borrowed, and great contracts had been given for railways which are ultimately to run through the two islands from The Bluff up to Auckland and north of Auckland. Of Mr. Vogel and his fate, while I was in the colony, I shall have to say a few words when speaking of the parliament at Wellington; but I have found it impossible to touch the subject of railways in New Zealand without mentioning the name of a man who I was assured by one party will hereafter be regarded as the great promoter of the success of his adopted country,—or, as I was assured by another party, be denounced as her ruin.

At Selwyn we got upon one of these beginnings of railways, which took us into Christchurch, a distance of twenty-three miles, through one of the richest districts of the settlement. Christchurch as a town is certainly not magnificent, but it is comfortable and thoroughly English. The houses are chiefly of wood,—as are also the greater number of the churches. The banks here, as elsewhere, luxuriate in stone. Throughout all these colonies I have grudged the grandeur of the banks, being reminded by every fine façade of percentages, commission, and charges for exchange. I believe that in Australia and New Zealand a man might melt his money down to nothing quicker than anywhere else, simply by transferring it from one place to another. I feel myself to be ill-natured in saying this, as person-ally I received great courtesy from bankers;—but not the less did I find that the melting process was the practice.

Christchurch as a city is certainly much less imposing than Dunedin. The popu-lation of the city is about 8,000,—that of the electoral districts of Christchurch is something over 12,000. The special religious tenets of the founders of the colony may be gathered perhaps more clearly from the names of the streets than from any other characteristic which a stranger will observe. They are all named after some Church of England bishopric,—and in the choosing of the special dioceses which were to be so honoured, there has certainly been no mean time-serving, no special worship of the great ones of the Church. The Irish Church has been specially honoured, for there are Armagh Street, Tuam Street, and Cashel Street. There are also Gloucester Street, and Lichfield Street, and Hereford Street, and St. Asaph Street. But there is no York Street, or London Street, or Winchester Street. There is, however, an Antigua Street, a Barbadoes Street, and a Montreal Street; and the chief street of all is Columbo Street.

At Picton I found the son of an English friend, who himself had been among the earliest of the New Zealand settlers, superintending the creation of a railway from thence to Blenheim,—a railway with about 700 people at each end of it, and which may perhaps benefit in some remote way an entire population of 2,000 or 3,000! The financial ministers of New Zealand have certainly been very brave. Navvies I found had been brought out from England under contracts to work for a certain time at certain rates; but, of course, these contracts were ignored by the men when they found, or thought that they had found, that they could do better for themselves by ignoring them. It is absolutely useless for any employer of labour to take labour out to the colonies for his own use, paying the expense of the tran-sit. Unwilling services are of all services the dearest, and such services if they be kept at all are sure to be unwilling.

Picton itself is a pretty, straggling, picturesque little town, lying, as do all these New Zealand ports, pressed in between the mountains and the sea. It is a strangely isolated place, with no road anywhere but to its rival Blenheim. Once a week from Wellington, and once from Nelson, a steamer touches there, and thus it holds its communication with the world. How it lives I could not find out. The staple of the province is wool, and it owns over 600,000 sheep,—about as many as all Western Australia possesses,—but Nelson is not the port at which the wool is shipped. That goes down to another bay near to Blenheim. It is hard to discover how such towns do live, as 700 persons can hardly make their bread by trading on each other; and as they import their clothes, their brandy, their tobacco, and, I am sorry to say, their wheat also, they must produce something wherewith to purchase those good things. Whilst navvies are earning 6s. or 7s. a day by making a railway I can understand that trade should go on. The wages of the men fall into the little town like manna from heaven. But such a fall of manna as that is apt to come to a speedy end. As far as outward appearances go, Picton seemed to be doing very well. There were good shops, and tidy houses, and pretty gardens, and a general look of sleepy, well-fed prosperity. In all these places the people are well fed and well clothed, whatever may be the sources from whence the food and raiment come. I may say also that Picton enjoys a beautiful climate, produces all English fruits in rich abundance, is surrounded by fields deliciously green, and has for an immediate background some of the finest scenery in New Zealand.

The great sight of the province of Marlborough is a hill a few miles behind Picton, which was the scene of the so-called Wairau massacre. This was not exactly the beginning, but it was one of the beginnings of the rebellion of the Maoris against their English masters. The treaty of Waitangi, by which the Maoris professed subjection to the Crown of Great Britain and obedience to English laws, was made in 1840. In 1843 a party of English settlers, armed with proper magisterial authority, attempted to arrest two Maori chiefs, Rauparaha and Rangihaeta, who had interfered with the work of a surveyor who had been sent to survey the Wairau valley, on the plea that it had been purchased from the natives by the New Zealand Land Company. The two Maori chieftains denied the purchase, and resisted the arrest. A fight ensued, in which thirteen settlers were killed and five wounded, and after the fight Rauparaha murdered in cold blood nine other settlers whom he and his party had taken prisoners. But this was not all. After the massacre Rauparaha and Rangihaeta were not taken, and there arose a question, not only whether there was force enough in the country to apprehend them, but whether they were subject to English writs. It will easily be understood how such doings as this would shake the prestige of their British masters in the minds of these New Zealand savages. "The Wairau conflict," says Dr. Thompson, "attracted the attention of Europe, and created interest in the minds of men who never thought about colonies. It completely stopped emigration to New Zealand, called forth the sympathy of people in different parts of Great Britain; and at Paris,"—oh, unfortunate New Zealand!—"at Paris a proposition was made to commence a subscription to enable the unfortunate settlers to return home." What a bathos of misery into which to fall!